Reported Discourse

Typological Studies in Language (TSL)

A companion series to the journal *Studies in Language*

General Editor Michael Noonan

Assistant Editors Spike Gildea, Suzanne Kemmer

Editorial Board

Wallace Chafe (Santa Barbara)
Bernard Comrie (Leipzig)
R. M. W. Dixon (Melbourne)
Matthew Dryer (Buffalo)
John Haiman (St Paul)
Bernd Heine (Köln)
Paul Hopper (Pittsburgh)
Andrej Kibrik (Moscow)
Ronald Langacker (San Diego)

Charles Li (Santa Barbara)
Edith Moravcsik (Milwaukee)
Andrew Pawley (Canberra)
Doris Payne (Eugene, OR)
Frans Plank (Konstanz)
Jerrold Sadock (Chicago)
Dan Slobin (Berkeley)
Sandra Thompson (Santa Barbara)

Volumes in this series will be functionally and typologically oriented, covering specific topics in language by collecting together data from a wide variety of languages and language typologies. The orientation of the volumes will be substantive rather than formal, with the aim of investigating universals of human language via as broadly defined a data base as possible, leaning toward cross-linguistic, diachronic, developmental and live-discourse data.

Volume 52

Reported Discourse: A meeting ground for different linguistic domains
Edited by Tom Güldemann and Manfred von Roncador

Reported Discourse
A meeting ground for different linguistic domains

Edited by

Tom Güldemann
University of Leipzig / Max Planck Institute for Evolutionary Anthropology

Manfred von Roncador
University of Bayreuth

John Benjamins Publishing Company
Amsterdam / Philadelphia

∞ ™ The paper used in this publication meets the minimum requirements of American National Standard for Information Sciences – Permanence of Paper for Printed Library Materials, ANSI Z39.48-1984.

Library of Congress Cataloging-in-Publication Data

Reported Discourse : A meeting ground for different linguistic domains / edited by Tom Güldemann and Manfred von Roncador.
    p. cm. (Typological Studies in Language, ISSN 0167–7373 ; v. 52)
"The present collection of papers developed out of a workshop... hel at the 20th Annual Meeting of the German Linguistic Society. (Mar. 4-6, 1998 at Halle/Saale).
    Includes bibliographical references and indexes.
    1. Grammar, Comparative and general--Indirect discourse--Congresses. I. Güldemann, Tom. II. Roncador, Manfred von. III. Deutsche Gesellschaft für Sprachwissenschaft. Jahrestagung. Jahrestagung (20th: 1998: Halle an der Saale, Germany) IV. Series.

P301.5.I53 R45 2002
401'.41-dc21   2002023237
ISBN 90 272 2958 9 (Eur.) / 1 58811 227 6 (US) (Hb; alk. paper)

© 2002 – John Benjamins B.V.
No part of this book may be reproduced in any form, by print, photoprint, microfilm, or any other means, without written permission from the publisher.

John Benjamins Publishing Co. · P.O. Box 36224 · 1020 ME Amsterdam · The Netherlands
John Benjamins North America · P.O. Box 27519 · Philadelphia PA 19118-0519 · USA

Contents

Preface vii
Tom Güldemann and Manfred von Roncador

Abbreviations and symbols x

Part I. Categories of reported discourse and their use

1. Speech and thought representation in the Kartvelian
   (South Caucasian) languages 3
   Winfried Boeder

2. Self-quotation in German: Reporting on past decisions 49
   Andrea Golato

3. Direct and indirect speech in Cerma narrative 71
   Ivan Lowe and Ruth Hurlimann

4. Direct and indirect discourse in Tamil 91
   Sanford B. Steever

5. The acceptance of 'free indirect discourse':
   A change in the representation of thought in Japanese 109
   Yasushi Suzuki

6. Direct, indirect and other discourse in Bengali newspapers 121
   Wim van der Wurff

Part II. Tense-aspect and evidentiality

7. Evidentiality and reported speech in Romance languages 143
   Gerda Haßler

8. Discourse perspectives on tense choice in spoken-English
   reporting discourse 173
   Tomoko I. Sakita

Part III. Logophoricity

9. The logophoric hierarchy and variation in Dogon 201
   Christopher Culy

10. Logophoric marking in East Asian languages 211
    Yan Huang

Part IV. Form and history of quotative constructions

11. The grammaticalization of 'say' and 'do':
    An areal phenomenon in East Africa 227
    David Cohen, Marie-Claude Simeone-Senelle and Martine Vanhove

12. When 'say' is not *say*: The functional versatility of the Bantu
    quotative marker *ti* with special reference to Shona 253
    Tom Güldemann

13. Reported speech in Egyptian: Forms, types and history 289
    Frank Kammerzell and Carsten Peust

14. 'Report' constructions in Kambera (Austronesian) 323
    Marian A. F. Klamer

15. All the same? The emergence of complementizers in Bislama 341
    Miriam Meyerhoff

Part V. A comprehensive bibliography of reported discourse

16. A comprehensive bibliography of reported discourse 363
    Tom Güldemann, Manfred von Roncador and Wim van der Wurff

Index of names 417
Index of languages and language groups 422

Preface

Tom Güldemann and Manfred von Roncador
Universität Leipzig   Universität Bayreuth

The present collection of papers developed out of a workshop on *Function and form of reported speech* organized by the two editors and held at the 20th Annual Meeting of the German Linguistic Society (March 4–6, 1998 at Halle/Saale). In addition to selected papers presented there, further contributions from scholars involved in this research were invited for this publication in order to capture a wider genetic and geographical variety of languages and thus offer new insights in cross-linguistic similarities and differences within this linguistic domain.

For a long time, reported speech, or more generally *reported discourse*, has been a topic not only puzzling to linguists. It has also attracted philosophers interested in the distinction between *de dicto* and *de re*, in speech acts, and in the philosophy of mind, psycholinguists investigating the development of deixis, and literary critics studying the concepts of author, narrator and character (beginning with the Platonic *mimesis-diegesis* distinction). Although several contributions of this collection may well be relevant to these disciplines, they focus primarily on the narrow linguistic aspects of reported discourse in natural language.

The papers reflect the range of diverse problems which are currently under investigation in this area. A novelty of this collection compared to earlier ones is that it treats not only topics which are traditionally considered to be central problems in the study of reported discourse, but also focuses on questions which until recently played only a minor or peripheral role in the overall discussion. That is, scholars have increasingly shifted their interest toward the question of how grammatical, semantic, and pragmatic problems associated with functional and formal properties of reported discourse have repercussions in other linguistic domains of language. Several foci of interest can be identified and provide the basis for the structure of the book. Before these will be outlined, two other important aspects in this collection should be mentioned. First, almost all papers reflect a major shift away from analyzing reported discourse with the help of abstract transformational principles toward embedding it in *functional* and *pragmatic* aspects of language. The other central methodological approach pervading this collection and related to the former consists in the *discourse-oriented* examination of reported discourse based on large corpora of coherent spoken or written texts (cf. the contributions by Golato, Kammerzell and Peust, Meyerhoff, and Wurff). This is increasingly replacing analyses of constructed de-contextualized utterances which have been prevalent in many earlier treatments.

Part I: A traditional and still central topic is the conclusive classification of the different types of reported discourse. In a general sense, reported discourse can be taken as 'speaking about speaking' or 'text within text', that is, a secondary text is reproduced or mentioned within the primary, immediately produced text. Every text is associated with a particular deictic and interactional setting (predominantly encoded by so-called *shifters*). In the course of integrating two texts with *different* communicative perspectives/orientations in the relevant domain of reported discourse certain adjustments become necessary (the minimum being that the secondary, integrated text will no longer be a token, but rather a token-type). The problem becomes more complex by the fact that the *reporter* can be assumed to use and manipulate reported discourse for his purposes in the production of the immediate text. Thus, different degrees of speaker involvement in the reproduction of a non-immediate text also come into play. The major traditional classification of different types of reported discourse is achieved according to the relation between a reported, non-immediate text and its purported original utterance in terms of structure and contents. It is this paradigmatic aspect through which the basic traditional distinction between *direct* and *indirect speech* arose. Traditionally, direct discourse is associated with minimal syntactic (and semantic) adjustments, whereas indirect discourse tends syntactically to be a part of the surrounding structure. However, these two categories do not represent a clear-cut dichotomy, but are rather extreme poles along a scalar organizational space. The two traditional categories have been supplemented by different in-between categories. The existence of such intermediate forms as *semi-direct discourse, free indirect discourse* (alias *style indirect libre* or *erlebte Rede*), and different types of logophoric constructions (cf. part III) point to an analysis whereby the different forms of reported discourse are assigned a specific position on a continuum whose end points are characterized by a minimal or maximal shift of the deictic center, respectively (cf. *Roncador* 1988). The articles in the first part are primarily concerned with distinguishing and characterizing types of reported discourse on this dimension and — due to the still prevailing binary distinction between a direct and an indirect style — often focus on intermediate categories. Subsequent questions resulting from such a classification are how the determined types possibly correlate with different formal properties and how they are exploited in natural discourse.

Part II: Closely related to the above classification of types of reported discourse is a sub-domain of adjusting the orientation of the non-immediate text. As such verbal categories like tense, aspect and mode have shifter-properties they have been playing an important role in the study of reported discourse. The paper of Sakita contributes to this longstanding discussion in connection with the special use of certain verb forms in the domain of reported discourse. Another perspective is discussed by Haßler: She investigates reported discourse as a manifestation of one category of evidentiality (not in the sense of philosophical epistemology) and the evaluation of experience. The continuation of this discussion now prominent for some time (cf. *Hill and Irvine* (eds.) 1993) is important, because one of the major tasks in this area is to determine the place of reported discourse within the different functional domains of language (cf. also the papers by Golato and Huang).

Part III: An inherent characteristic of reported discourse is its close association with the expression and manipulation of interclausal relations in the syntagmatic organization of the immediate text. This relates in particular to the domain of reference tracking and the possible differentiation of pronominal categories. The papers in the third section by Culy and Huang investigate special pronoun marking within the reported text, so-called logophoric devices (cf. also Suzuki's contribution). The investigation of narrow logophoricity in reported discourse, and its comparison to mechanisms of marking *co-reference* and *switch-reference* in other domains leads to an interesting question: Which of the two alternatives, that is, continuity or discontinuity of the referent, is the marked one in a given context? In reported discourse the indication is that it is the co-reference of participants between the speech-introducing clause and the reported text that is more marked.

Part IV: The way reported discourse is integrated formally in its discourse environment is associated with another important area of discussion. Many languages employ specialized quotative constructions for signaling the presence of reported discourse and setting it off from the co-text. It has been observed again and again that these constructions as a whole or individual parts thereof are also employed in many other linguistic domains. The extreme functional versatility of relevant elements must be explained and plausible historical scenarios developed as to how a particular synchronic picture has emerged. The discussion on grammaticalization processes in this domain is thus another focus of the publication. The literature on this topic is already quite extensive, but has probably focused too much on the purported historical development of speech verbs, as some of the present contributions indicate. What can be stated so far is that the relation of quotative constructions to grammatical marking in other linguistic domains is to a large extent a function of the meaning of the elements that became a part of marking devices of reported discourse and these can be more diverse than has heretofore been expected (cf. also Boeder's contribution).

Part V: The book is closed by a comprehensive bibliography on reported discourse and related fields mentioned above. It is hoped to serve as a useful reference tool for future research in this area. It also contains all relevant references cited by contributors in their articles. Since these do not occur again in the bibliography following an individual article, they are marked in the text by italics.

Abbreviations and symbols

ACC	accusative	D	dual
ADDR	logophoric addressee pronoun	DAT	dative
		DEF	definite (article)
ADE	adessive	DEI	deictic
ADJR	adjectivizer	DEM	demonstrative
ADMIR	admirative	DEP	dependent verb form
ADV	adverbial (case)	DET	determiner
AGR	subject-verb agreement	DETER	determinative pronoun
ANA	anaphoric reference	DIM	diminutive
ANP	adnominal participle	DIR	directional
ANT	anterior taxis	DISP	displacement
AOR	aorist	DO	direct object
ART	article	E	exclusive
ASP	aspect	EMPH	emphasis
ASS	associative	ERG	ergative
ATTR	attributive linker	EVID	evidential
AUG	augmentative	EXAG	exaggeration
AUTOBEN	autobenefactive	EXCL	exclamation
AUX	auxiliary	EXP	experiential
BEN	benefactive	F	feminine (gender)
C	common (gender)	FACT	factitive
CAUS	causative	FOC	focus
CF	conjunctive form	FUT	future
CNJ	conjunction	GEN	genitive
COP	copula	HAB	habitual
COM	comitative	HORT	hortative
COMP	complementizer	HS	hearsay
COND	conditional	I	inclusive
CONS	consecutive	IA	inanimate
CONT	continuous	IAP	imperfective active participle
CONV	converb		
CPL	complement	IDEF	indefinite (article)
CTR	controlled complement clause	IDEO	ideophone
		IDEOR	ideophonizer

IMP	imperative		PQ	polar question
IND	indicative		PREP	preposition
INE	inessive		PRET	preterite
INF	infinitive		PREV	preverb
INIT	initiative		PRO	pronoun
INSTR	instrument		PROG	progressive
INTJ	interjection		PROH	prohibitive
IO	indirect object		PROP	proper name
IP	impersonal		PRS	present
IPERF	imperfect		PST	past
IPFV	imperfective		PTCL	particle
IPP	imperfective passive participle		Q	question
			QUAN	quantity
IRR	irrealis		QUOT	quotative
ITR	intransitive		RDP	reduplication
JUS	jussive		RECP	reciprocal
LOC	locative		REFL	reflexive
LOG	logophoric (pronoun)		REL	relative (clause)
M	masculine (gender)		REM	remote
MOD	modality		RV	resultative verb
N	neuter (gender)		S	singular
NEG	negation		SBJ	subject
NOM	nominative		SEQ	sequential taxis
NUM	numeral		SPEC	specificity
OBJ	object		SIM	simultaneous taxis
OBL	oblique		SIML	similative
ONOM	onomatopoeia		STAT	stative
P	plural		SUBJ	subjunctive
PAP	perfect(ive) active participle		TOP	topic
			TR	transitive
PART	participle		VN	verbal noun
PASS	passive		VOC	vocative
PERF	perfect		1, 2, 3	person categories
PFV	perfective		=	clitic boundary
POSS	possession/possessive			
POSTP	postposition			
POT	potential			
PPP	perfect(ive) passive participle			

Author citations in italics refer to the general bibliography

Part 1

Categories of reported discourse and their use

CHAPTER 1

Speech and thought representation in the Kartvelian (South Caucasian) languages*

Winfried Boeder
University of Oldenburg

The South Caucasian language family, also called "Kartvelian" after its dominant member (*kartvel-* 'Georgian'), comprises Svan, Georgian, Mingrelian and Laz. These languages are spoken in an area reaching from the Black Sea in the West to Turkic-speaking Azerbaijan and to Armenia in the Southeast. Both genetically and structurally, the Kartvelian languages are closely related to each other. Most speakers of Mingrelian and Svan can speak Georgian, the language of instruction in school, and use it as their literary language, while most Laz speakers live in Northeast Turkey and use Turkish as their official language.

The general characteristics of Kartvelian "speech-reporting" are more or less well described in the linguistic literature.[1] But there are a few details and problems that have been neglected or insufficiently understood so far, e.g. the variation between direct and indirect speech, complete and partial "indirectness", and use and absence of conjunction with direct speech; and in particular the history of quotatives and some aspects of Svan speech reporting. In the following survey, I will begin with some basic facts of Old Georgian, the language of a vast corpus of texts beginning with the 5th century AD (1.). A cursory assessment of the modern variants of Georgian (and of Mingrelian and Laz) leads to an overall picture of the historical development in this form of Kartvelian (2.). The Svan language spoken in the mountainous parts of the Western Caucasus is generally considered to be a very archaic form of Kartvelian. It is formally rather remote from its related languages; its various forms of reported speech deserve particular attention, and I will discuss at least some of its details (3.). In the last section (4.), some conclusions are drawn.

One of the main characteristics of reported speech is reference shift: in direct speech, the reference of person, time, etc is typically not orientated towards the speech situation of the reporting clause, and in this sense, it is not in the indirect speech that their reference "shifts", but rather in the direct speech, in which an "I" is not necessarily the reporter-speaker, a present is not the speech time etc.[2] However, I will follow the practice of school grammar and describe "indirect speech" as the result of a "shift" of person, time, etc. which adapts them to their reference in the matrix clause,[3] without, however, implying that indirect speech should be derived from direct speech in any theoretical framework. In particular, I use the term "shift" because Svan "semi-indirect" speech is easier to understand if we start from direct speech and describe the indirect variant as derivative.

Before entering into the details of Georgian, a simplified outline of some features of Kartvelian is in order that may help the reader to understand the data. The verbal system of both Georgian and Svan consists of at least three groups of tenses and moods, and these groups are characterised by specific alignments of relational coding: the subject of transitive verbs is in the nominative with the present-stem group (present, imperfect, imperfective subjunctive I and the corresponding perfective forms: future, conditional and perfective subjunctive I), in the ergative with aorist-stem verb forms (aorist and optative = subjunctive II), and in the dative with perfect-stem verbs (perfect, pluperfect and subjunctive III). The direct object is in the dative with present-stem verbs and in the nominative with aorist and perfect stem verbs. The indirect object is in the dative with present and aorist stem verbs, and is a demoted prepositional phrase ("for" + NP) with perfect stem verbs. Verbs of having, wanting, fearing, etc. have a dative subject (as with perfect-stem verb forms) and a nominative object.

In one of its meanings, the Georgian perfect is the evidential (indirective) counterpart of the aorist (or present in some contexts), indicating "hearsay" and "inference" or "surprise" (*Boeder* 2000). Mingrelian and Svan have a more elaborated system: in addition to the evidential perfect, they have for example evidential counterparts of the imperfect (suffix -(*i/u*)*na* and circumfix *lǝm-___-wn(e)/ne* in the Upper Bal dialect of Svan).[4] These evidential forms belong to the characteristics of Svan reported speech.

1. Old Georgian

1.1 Direct speech in Old Georgian

Old Georgian[5] is a highly standardised literary language which must have been under strong stylistic pressure from contemporary Byzantine Greek. Yet, there is no reason to believe that the forms of direct speech in the following passage from the first long non-translated text, the "Life of Grigol of Khanzta" by Giorgi Merchule (10th century), deviate from the "ordinary Georgian" of the time:[6]

(1) (a) mašin იkitxa neṭar-man Grigol, (b) vitarmed "sada ars q̇rma-j Basili."
     (c) da auc̣q̇es ʒma-ta sen-i mis-i. (d) da man brʒana c̣odeba-j: (e) xolo
     ma-t hrkues (f) "ver ʒaluc mislva-j." (g) mašin hrkua ma-t (h) "čem
     mier arkut, (i) vitarmed "giç̇ess šen mama-j Grigol" "(GrX LXI 4–8)

(a) then he.asked blessed-ERG Grigol, (b) CNJ "where he.is youth-NOM Basil". (c) and they.informed(AOR).him brother-P.OBL illness-NOM his-NOM. (d) and he.ERG he.commanded(AOR).it calling(VN)-NOM: (e) but he-P.OBL they.told(AOR).him (f) "IMPOSS force.he.has(PRS).it going-NOM." (g) then he.told(AOR).them he-P.OBL: (h) "me from tell(AOR.IMP).him, (i) CNJ "he.calls(PRS).you you father-NOM Grigol"."
'(a) Then the blessed Grigol asked: (b) Where is the young man Basil? (c) And the brethren informed him about his illness (= told him that he was ill). (d) And he told them to call him. (e) But they told him: (f) He is unable to go. (g) Then he said to them: (h) Tell him from me, (i) Father Grigol asks you to come.'

As in many other languages of the region (e.g. Greek and Armenian[7]), direct speech can, but need not, be introduced by a conjunction, *vitarmed*; compare (1b) and (1i) with (1f). Direct speech abounds in this text, while indirect speech is extremely rare.

The following passage from the oldest Georgian prose text (5th cent.) shows that the early authors were well familiar with the naturalistic "liveliness" of direct speech:

(2) da unda rajta-mca hrkua, tu "mṭḳice-d deg!" da tual-i hḳida (Piṭiaxš-man, sxua-j ver-ɣa ra-j scalda siṭqua-d, esten oden hrkua: "mṭḳi . . ." da dadumna xolo (Šušaniḳis çameba IX 2–5) and he.wanted.it CNJ-OPT he.said.to.her, CNJ "fast-ADV stand!" and eye-NOM he.fixed.it.on.him Pitiashkh-ERG, other-NOM IMPOSS-PTCL something-NOM he.had.the.time.for.it saying(VN)-ADV, so only he.said.to.her: "sta . . ." and he.became.silent only.
'[St. Shushanik was taken from her palace to prison, her husband came behind her, cursing; her deacon stood near her way] and wanted to say: "Stand fast!", when the Pitiashkh cast his eye on him. So he could say nothing but "sta . . .", and became just silent.'

1.2 The syntactic status of reported speech in Old Georgian

But what is the syntactic status of direct speech in Old Georgian? There is no doubt that "to say" is a morphologically transitive verb in Georgian. It is true that direct speech is not normally marked for case, although it can be, if it is conceptualised as a repeatable entity:[8]

(3) cisḳr-ad *"neṭar arian"-n-i* da galoba-n-i çartkunian (GrX XVII 42) dawn-ADV *"Blessed they.are"*-P-NOM and song-P-NOM they.said(AOR.habitual).them
'At dawn, they used to recite the psalm "Blessed are" and songs.'

But direct object pronouns also refer to reported speech and behave like nominal direct objects (in the nominative):

(4) ʒma-ta hrkues: ". . . ." *esē* raj tkues . . . . (GrX LXXII 51)
brother-P.OBL they.said.to.him: ". . . ." *this*.NOM when they.said . . . .
'The brethren said to him: ". . . ." When they said *this*, . . .'

In this, reference to direct speech is not different from pronouns referring to embedded complement clauses:

(5) *esē* aɣmitkwit, *romel* čemda siḳudidmdē ara ganhmravldet adgil-sa ama-s šina (GrX VI 95)
this.NOM promise(AOR.IMP).me, CNJ my.ADV death.until not that.you.multiply(SUBJ.II) place-DAT this-DAT in
'This I ask you to promise me: that you do not let your community become larger in this place until I die.'

However, it is much less clear if for instance (1f) is a direct object constituent clause of the reporting clause (1e). Notice that direct speech is normally referred to by modal pronominals like *ešrēt* 'thus' (like ancient Greek *hōs*), *vitar-ca* 'as' or even *ešrēt saxe-d* 'thus shape-ADV' (= 'in the following manner' = 'as follows'):

(6) tkua *esrēt* "upal-o, [. . .]" (GrX XLVII 15)
he.said.it *thus* "Lord-VOC, [. . .]"
'He spoke *thus*: O Lord [. . .].'

(7) *vitarca* iṭqwis mocikul-i "mouḳlebel-ad ilocvedit-o" (GrX I 14)
as he.says(PRS).it apostle-NOM "incessant-ADV pray-QUOT"
'*As* the apostle says: Pray without ceasing.'

where the pronoun is cataphoric and refers to the subsequent direct speech, or rather: to one of its aspects that has still to be determined (- is it its propositional content or rather its locutionary aspect, "how s/he put it"?). Notice that although "to say" is "intransitive" or "semi-transitive" in many languages (*Munro* 1982), the use of "so" cannot be taken as a criterion of intransitivity (*Roeck* 1994:336) in the case of Georgian: a Georgian verb form is either transitive or intransitive, and I think that (6) can only be interpreted as "he said *something (specific)* thus" — whatever the meaning of "thus" is.

The use of "thus" must be old. It is in accordance with the origin of the conjunction *vitar-med* in (1b) and (1i), which is an enlarged form of *vitar* 'how?'. As so many wh-words in the Indoeuropean languages, *vitarmed* became a conjunction by its coalescence with the subsequent "answer"-sentence it asks for (Boeder 1993/94: 36): besides (a) "X said (it) thus (*ešrēt*): "Y" ", we may posit (b) "X said (it) how (*vitar(med)*) ? "Y" ". As a result of reanalysis we get: (c) "X said *vitar(med)* "Y" ", where *vitar(med)* marks the dependence of the direct speech sentence. It is less clear, however, if *vitarmed* is a constituent of the direct speech sentence or rather of the preceding reporting clause (see below 2.2 and 3.2).

After *vitar(med)* had become a conjunction, *esrēt* 'thus', which had been in complementary distribution with *vitar* 'how?' at stage (a)–(b), may co-occur with the latter:

(8) da uḳuetu vinme gḳitxvides: "rajsa-twis ayhqsnit?" *esrē* (E esre, C esret) arkut, *vitarmed*: "upal-sa uqms ege" (Luke 19,31)
and if somebody he.may.ask.you: "what-for you.loosed.it?" *thus* say.to.him: CNJ "Lord-DAT him.needs.it this.NOM"
'And if any man ask you, Why do ye loose him? *thus* shall ye say unto him, *(that)* The Lord hath need of him.'

Finally, the *vitarmed*-sentence could be reanalysed as a clausal constituent of the preceding sentence, i.e. embedded:[9]

(9) (a) vitar cna, (b) *vitarmed* ma-s dye-sa saerto-d igi saçmel-i ara qopil ars, (c) mašin romel-i igi mimeyo, (d) špot-it dastxia [...] (GrX LXXXVI 8)
as he.understood(AOR).it, CNJ that-DAT day-DAT common-ADV that.NOM meal-NOM not been it.is,[10] then which-NOM PTCL I.had.taken.it, fury-INSTR he.poured.it.out
'When he understood: *(that)* "This has not been the common meal", he then in agitation poured out what I had taken (to him).'

The internal position of (b) suggests its status as an embedded constituent. But most direct speech occurs on the periphery of the sentence, in particular in final position. In these cases, there is no reason to believe that the direct speech is embedded in the reporting clause. While anaphoric pronouns referring to an independent direct speech antecedent are direct objects, it is not at all sure if *everything* "which was said represented the complement of the clause of saying" (Harris and Campbell 1995: 69), if complement clauses are understood as embedded. Similarly, it is rather doubtful if direct speech after cataphoric *esrēt* etc. is a complement, because, as far as I can see, complements cannot be referred to by "so", and there is no indication that sentences like (1f) are complements in Old Georgian; rather, they could be thought of as "adjoined" (in the sense introduced by Hale 1975).

1.3 Indirect speech in Old Georgian

It is generally believed that indirect speech is embedded. "Indirect speech" *in a broad sense* does occur in Old Georgian side by side with "direct speech", and some authors (e.g. ȝiȝiguri 1965) insist on its "naturalness" and its occurrence in the oldest texts. Indeed the following passage shows person shift (*Hewitt and Crisp* 1986: 126):

(10) (a) movides da tkues, (b) vitarmed [vitar E] gamočineba-j-ca angeloz-ta-j *ixiles*, (c) romel-ta hrkues ma-t, (d) vitarmed: "cxovel ars igi"
(a) they.came(AOR) and they.said, (b) CNJ appearance-NOM-too angel-P.OBL-NOM *they.saw(AOR).it*, (c) who-P.OBL they.told.them she-P.OBL, (d) CNJ: "alive he.is(PRS) he.NOM"
'(a) they came, saying, (b) that *they had* also *seen* a vision of angels, (c) who told them (d) that he was alive.'

where another manuscript has direct speech throughout:

(11) (a) movides da iṭqodes, (b) vitarmed "xilva-j angeloz-ta-j *vixilet*, romel-ni iṭqodes, (c) vitarmed: "cxovel ars"" (Luke 24,23 C)
(a) they.came(AOR) and they.said(IPERF).it, (b) CNJ "sight-NOM angel-P.OBL-NOM *we.saw(AOR).it*, (c) who-P-NOM they.said(IPERF).it, (d) CNJ: "alive he.is(PRS)".".

Notice, however, the contrast between the Georgian version of (10d) and its English counterpart: the Georgian version has no tense shift. I do not know since when the first examples of tense shift are attested as it is optionally used in Modern Georgian (see below 2.2). But indirect speech *in the narrow sense* seems to be very rare in non-translated, original Old Georgian texts.[11] Languages that have "indirect speech" in complement clauses (as in (9b), need not have the type of "indirect quotation sentence whose matrix is a verb of saying" (*Li* 1986:39).

1.4 The transitivity of "to say" in Old Georgian

Nominalised reported speech does not seem to occur after the simple verb "to say", but it is attested with verbs of command (see (1d)) and information (see (1c)), and in an idiom:

(12) ma-s žam-sa neṭar-sa Grigol-s *gul-man utkua* qseneba-j Saban Išxnel-isa-j (GrX XXVI 1)
that-DAT time-DAT Grigol-DAT *heart-ERG it.told.him* memory(VN)-NOM Saba Ishkhnel-GEN-NOM
'At that time it occurred to the blessed Grigol to recall to mind Saba of Ishkhan.'

1.5 The position of the quotative particle in Old Georgian

Some authors feel that the most natural form of direct speech in Georgian is the one with quotative particles,[12] and that the literary language tends to oust quotatives: the older the folklore texts and the less literate their speakers are, the more quotatives occur (Γlonṭi 1975:42–3). Only a few examples of the quotative particle -*o* occur in the oldest texts, e.g. in the Khanmeti version of the Gospels (7th cent.?):

(13) man mactur-man tkua [. . .] *vitarmed* "šemdgomad sam-isa dɣ-isa aɣvdge-*o*" (Matthew 27,63)
that.ERG deceiver-ERG he.said.it [. . .] CNJ "after three-GEN day-GEN I.will.rise-QUOT"
'That deceiver said, [. . .] (that) After three days I will rise again.'

We do not know what the reason for the rareness of the quotative particle in classical Old Georgian is, but the absence of an equivalent in the prestigious Greek model language might have contributed to it (*Hewitt* 1984a:555). The "Life of Grigol of Khandzta" (see (1)) has a few examples (see (7)), but the Sinaitic Polykephalion manuscript of 864 offers more. -*o* occurs in clause-final position:

(14) (a) romel-n-i iṭqwian, (b) vitarmed "qorc-n-i ara šeisxna upal-man ḳac-ta-gan-*o*, (c) aramed zec-it hkondes-*o*" (Sinuri Mravaltavi ed. A. Šaniʒe 48,2–3)
who-P-NOM they.say(PRS), (b) CNJ "flesh-P-NOM not he.put(AOR).them.on lord-ERG man-P.OBL-QUOT, but heaven-INSTR he.will.have.them-QUOT"
'Who say: (that) Our Lord did not put on flesh from man, but he will have it from heaven.'

I. Imnaišvili (1975:99–100; cp. ʒiʒiguri 1973:204) speaks of a postverbal position, which — with a few exceptions as in (14b) — very often coincides with the clause-final position in an essentially verb-final language. Indeed, the postverbal (not necessarily clause-final) position was predominant in medieval Georgian, e.g. in Rustaveli's poem (*c*.1200):

(15) mepe-man brʒana: "vnaxe-*o* mizez-i lxin-ta lev-isa" (97[98],4)
king-ERG he.commanded: "I.saw(AOR).it-QUOT cause-NOM joy-P.OBL waning-GEN"
'The king said: I have seen cause for loss of joy.' (transl. M. Wardrop).

It also occurs in the 19th century classics.

-*o* is similar to the Old Georgian interrogative particle -*a* in that it is a clitic and occurs in the same, postverbal position; compare:

(16) hxedav-*a* ama-s dedaḳac-sa (Luke 7,44)
thou.seest(PRS)-Q this-DAT woman-DAT
'Seest thou this woman?'

2. Modern Georgian

2.1 The transitivity of "to say" in Modern Georgian

As in Old Georgian, "to say" is a transitive verb. Conceptualised direct speech is again case-marked.[13] Occasionally, a concept may be formed on the basis of "who says "X" habitually":

(17) *"ar vici"-s* deda icinis, *"vici"-sa* deda t̟iris-o (proverb)
 "not I.know.it"-GEN mother(NOM) she.laughs, *"I.know.it"*-GEN mother(NOM) she.weeps-QUOT
 'The mother *of "I don't know it"* laughs, the mother *of "I know it"* weeps.'[14]

2.2 Indirect speech in Modern Georgian

Modern Georgian has both direct and "indirect" speech. Consider the following counterpart sentences (Žikia 1972: 62):

(18) a. P̟ep̟ia-m tkva: "sacodav-o P̟ep̟ia-v! čem-i Tamro aba exla k̟i cocxal-i damarxul-i ik̟neba"
 Pepia-ERG he.said: "poor-VOC Pepia-VOC! *my*-NOM Tamro.NOM PTCL now but alive-NOM buried-NOM *she will be(FUT)*"
 'Pepia said [to himself]: Poor Pepia! My Tamro *will be* buried alive by now.'
 b. sacodav-ma P̟ep̟ia-m tkva, rom *mis-i* Tamro exla k̟i cocxal-i damarxul-i ik̟neba
 poor-ERG Pepia-ERG he.said, CNJ *his*-NOM Tamro.NOM now but alive-NOM buried-NOM *she.will.be(FUT)*

While person shift (*my* > *his*) is an unambiguous indicator of indirect speech in b), vocatives and some particles (here: *aba* 'well then') resist systematic transposition, as usual. But what is more important is the lack of tense shift in b), which is rather the norm, although shift also does occur:

(19) a. vtkvit: "c̟ign-s vk̟itxulobt-o" (*Hewitt and Crisp* 1986: 123)
 we.said: "book-DAT we.are.reading(PRS).it-QUOT"
 'We said: We are reading a book.'
 b. vtkvit, rom c̟ign-s vk̟itxulobdit (ib.)
 we.said, CNJ book-DAT we.were.reading(IPERF).it
 (with a shift from present tense to imperfect)

Notice that the modern translation of (10) has an evidential perfect in (b) and (c) on the basis of its hearsay meaning (see *Boeder* 2000):

(20) (a) da movidnen da gvitxres, rom (b) *uxilavt* angeloz-eb-i, (c) roml-eb-sa-c *utkvamt*, (d) "cocxal-i-a-o" (Biblia. Sakartvelos Saṗaṭriarko gamocema 1989)
(a) and they.came(AOR) and they.said(AOR).to.us, CNJ (b) *they.have.seen* (PERF).*them* angel-P-NOM, (c) who-P-DAT-REL.PTCL *they.have.said* (PERF).*it*, (d) "alive-NOM-he.is-QUOT".

In this example, then, "indirect speech" also comprises a shift in evidentiality that we will find in Svan, too (3.4.2). — The details of variation between shifted and non-shifted tense, time and local deixis in indirect speech cannot be discussed here;[15] suffice it to say that the shift is "optional", as in some other languages (*Plank* 1986):

(21) gušin xom gitxari, rom *xval/dyes movlen/movidodnen* (*Hewitt and Crisp* 1986:128)
yesterday PTCL I.said.to.you, CNJ tomorrow/today
they.will.come(FUT)/they.would.come(COND)

where all combinations can mean: 'I told you, didn't I, yesterday that they would come *today* [and — look! — here they come] (ib.)', although the variant: *gušin gitxari, rom xval movlen/movidodnen* can also mean: 'I told you yesterday that they would come *tomorrow*'. The factors that favour the choice of "shifted" and "non-shifted" forms are unknown so far. Similarly, as with Old Georgian *vitarmed* (see 1.1), we do not know under what conditions the use of the conjunction *rom* is preferred. An examples with *rom* is:

(22) aste egonat, *rom* siʒe aris-o (Bl 110)
so they.thought(AOR), CNJ son.in.law(NOM) he.is-QUOT
'They thought: (that) He is their son-in-law/that he was their son-in-law.'

The absence of *rom* seems to be preferred in the literary language,[16] but *rom* is particularly common in folklore texts (Γlonṭi 1975: 30–6).[17]

From a phonetic point of view, *rom*, like other conjunctions, normally belongs to the preceding reporting clause: a pause, if it is heard at all, comes after, not before, *rom* (see Boeder 1982; 2001), which does not speak for an embedded status of direct speech.

2.3 The position of quotative particles in Modern Georgian

In the modern literary language the repetition of quotative particles is avoided, and a speech-final position is preferred,[18] but in colloquial Georgian, quotative *-o* occurs after (almost) every (phonological) phrase; in fact, *-o* "punctuates" the text (*Wigger* 1998:970) and can be used to determine phrase boundaries (Boeder 1982:384; 1983a:99). It seems to conform to the predominantly left-branching structure of

Georgian that direct speech units are marked as such at their closure: the "object", the reported speech, follows its verb of saying (*tkva, utxra* etc.), but a final verb-like quotative particle (see 2.9 below) "recovers" the left-branching structure:[19] Consider the following passages from a Georgian dialect (Kartlian) text:

(23) ert-ma ḳac-ma tkva: çavedit-o Leḳ-ši-o ḳamečebi unda viqidot-o (I 41)
one-ERG man-ERG he.said: we.went.off-QUOT Daghestan-in-QUOT, buffaloes it.is.necessary that.we.buy.them-QUOT
'One man said: We went off into Daghestan in order to buy buffaloes.'

A possible line of development is from postverbal[20] to clause-final position (-positions which very often coincide, see 1.5), then from clause-final position to phrase-final position (which again very often coincide), on the one hand, and — according to the literary norm — to exclusively sentence-final or speech-final position, on the other.

2.4 The speaker-reporter in Modern Georgian direct speech

The speaker of "direct speech" can be definite or indefinite (see *Hewitt* 1984a: 356):

(24) maga-s es codv-at açevs, ert-i vir-i ucvalebia-o (Bl 84)
she-DAT this sin-ADV it lies on.her: one NOM ass NOM
she.has.tormented(PERF.EVID).it-QUOT
'This sin weighs on her: she has tormented an ass, *they* say.'

In this indefinite sense ("they say, people say"), the quotative is the rule with proverbs and with all types of aphorisms and "commonly known" truths;[21] see (17) above. But this rule is not just triggered by proverbs but by their use in everyday argumentation: proverbs are used as a backing of conclusions, where the speakers represent a social group and need not be specified more than other details of reported speech that are deemed irrelevant by the speaker (*Mochet* 1996; see 3.5.2).

2.5 Distribution of Modern Georgian quotative particles

In archaic Georgian dialects like Khevsur, and optionally in some other dialects (e.g. Kakhian), *-o* (or its allomorph *-v*) is used for *all* reported speech (Ḳačarava 1950:254):

(25) (a) [sc. Abas] utkom, šinš-isa-d, (b) ro "šen daibrale-v, (c) ro Aba-isgan [sc. bič-i] ḳi ar as-a-v, (d) čem-gan as-a-v" (Doliʒe 1975:61,15)
(a) [sc. Aba.DAT] he.has.said(PERF.EVID), cousin-GEN-ADV, (b) CNJ

"you take(AOR.IMP).the.blame.on.you-QUOT, (c) CNJ Aba-GEN-from [sc. illegitimate child-NOM] but not he.is-PTCL-QUOT, (d) me-from he.is-PTCL-QUOT"
'(a) Aba, they say, said to him, to his cousin (b) (that): Take the blame on you, say: (c) He [sc. the illegitimate child] is not Aba's, (d) he is mine.'

Rustaveli has the Khevsurian use of -*o*, e.g. with 1st-person singular and plural reported speech (in (26d) and (27)):

(26) (a) "mona-a-*o* Asmat-is-i", (b) šemoqvana utxar šina. / (c) gul-sa šina *dauzraxe*: (d) "ra mpova-*o*, anu vina?" (361[363],3-4)
(a) "slave.NOM-he.is-QUOT Asmat-GEN-NOM", (b) leading.in(NOM) I.told.him inside. / (c) heart-DAT in I.reproved.her: (d) "what.NOM she.found(AOR).me-QUOT, or who(NOM)"
'(a) It is Asmath's slave, he said. (b) I told him to bring him in. / (c) I thought in my heart: (d) What has she found in me, or who is she?' (transl. M. Wardrop)

(27) *vtkvit*, tu: "mze-a-*o* kveqan-ad [...]!" (202[205],2)
we.said: tu "sun(NOM)-he.is-QUOT earth-ADV"
'*We said*: (that?) He is a sun on the Earth [...].' (transl. M. Wardrop)

In addition, however, he uses -*tko*, a particle used when the speaker is instructing the addressee to transmit the quote to somebody (Topuria and Gigineišvili 1970: 161); compare *tko* in (28) with -*o* in (25c) in the same context:

(28) miḳitxos, hḳadre: "iqo-*tko* aka ert-ita çam-ita" (102[103],4) should.he.ask.for.me, dare(AOR.IMP).to.say.to.him: "she.was-QUOT here one-INSTR moment-INSTR"
'When he asks for me, say, She was here but now.' (transl. M. Wardrop)

The particle -*metki* is used with reported 1st-person singular speech in modern literary Georgian and some of its dialects:[22]

(29) "xom iloce-o?" — "rogor ara-metki" (A. Çereteli apud 3i3iguri 1973: 202)
"PTCL you.prayed(AOR)-QUOT?" — "how not-QUOT"
'You prayed, didn't you? — Of course, I said.'

tko < *tkv-a* in (28) is the 2nd-person singular subjunctive of *tkv*- 'say' ('thou shall say'; see Hewitt 1984a). *metki* is obviously a simplified form of *me v-tkv-i* 'I 1SBJ-say-AOR.Suffix' (= I said), but the form lost its past time reference and became a particle: it can refer to the future and to the present:[23]

(30) "momšordi-metki", — veubnebi (Q̇azbegi apud Ɨlonṭi 1996)
"go(AOR.IMP).away.from.me-QUOT", — I.say.to.him
'Go away from me, I tell him [. . . I have no time for you].'

The co-occurrence of *metki* with a finite verb of saying in the last example shows that *metki* counts as a particle and not as a verb (or a clause).[24] But as we will see below (2.9), this does not necessarily preclude it from having verbal properties. Notice that *metki* and *tko* occur in the same, preferably postverbal, position as -*o*.

The quotative particles *metki/tko*, then, are etymologically transparent.[25] But why did they develop in the first place? On the one hand, we may speculate about their "expressive" origin: *tko* is a kind of command that could underline the imperative form of the verb of saying, and *metki* contains an "emphatic",[26] possibly contrastive, pronoun *me* 'I' (- the verb form *vtkvi* 'I.said.it' is a self-contained sentence without *me*!). As usual, the expressive character got lost and present-day *metki/tko* have become grammaticalised particles. — On the other hand, the introduction of -*metki*/-*tko* marks a difference in epistemic status: -*o*, but not -*metki* and -*tko*, gives the reported speech a hearsay meaning that is closely related to evidentiality (see (20b, c) and 3.4.2).

2.6 The instructional quotative in Modern Georgian

The description of -*tko* given above is incomplete: according to the modern literary norm, -*o* is used with reported first person plural speech as in Medieval Georgian (see (27)), but -*tko* also occurs:[27]

(31) rogorc vutxarit — "mepestan unda çamoxvide-*tko*", imav çams dagvetanxma (N. Lortkipaniʒe)
as we.told.him — "to.the.king it.is.necessary that.you.come.away-QUOT", that.very moment he.agreed.with.us
'As soon as we said to him: You must come away to the king, at that very moment he agreed with us.'

In addition, some western dialects of Georgian, in particular Imeretian, Lechkhumian and Rachian, and even some writers from this area, use -*tko* with reported first person singular speech where the standard language has -*metki*.[28]

(32) ḳac-ma utxra: me ase mivçere čem ded-mama-s, čem mosvl-amdin šeinaxet čemi col-švil-i, ranairic unda iqos-*tko* (ʒiʒiguri 1956: 302,11, Imeretian)
man-ERG he.told.her: I so I.wrote.it.to.them my mother-father-DAT, my coming-till take.care.of.them (IMP) wife-child-NOM, whatever.kind.NOM it.is.necessary that.it.be-QUOT
'The man told her: I wrote thus to my parents: Until I return, take care of my wife and my children, no matter how.'

This shows that *-metki* and *-tko* are in a disjunctively ordered rule relation: *-tko* occurs with first person speakers where *-metki* does not — either because the reported speaker is non-singular or because *metki* is simply unavailable in the dialect.

But what do this use of *-tko* and the "instructional" use have in common? Notice that the rule for *-tko* is not: "occuring after a reporting clause with 2nd-person subject + verb of saying + 3rd-person indirect object", or the like; the rule is not of a morpho-syntactic nature, but is based on speech act meaning. The wording of what counts as an instruction directed at the addressee may vary (*Hewitt* 1984a:359), as for instance in: *I should have been commanded by you:* "..." or: *you might simply have said to me:* "..." (ib.). In other words, the verb form *tkva* 'you shall say' lost its syntactic 2nd-person subject constraint and became a particle controlled by *pragmatic* conditions (see *Hewitt* 1984a:360). A link between the two stages is offered by a semantic peculiarity: Starting from the latter use ("(you shall) tell him/her"), we should bear in mind that imperatives (and other speech acts[29]) in some respects behave as if their subject were the speaker, not the performer of the act itself. Consider purpose clauses like (a) *They left the door open for him to hear the baby* vs (b) *Leave the door open for him to hear the baby*. While it is the subject person of the matrix clause in (a) who has the intention expressed by the subordinate clause, it is the speaker's intention in (b). Similarly, *-tko* marks the speech of first person matrix clause subjects *and* the speech ordered by the first person speaker of the sentence. Pronominalization in reported speech, on the other hand, crucially depends on the notion of underlying *syntactic* matrix clause subject: as *Hewitt* (1984a:356) rightly points out, a first person pronoun in the following example is normally understood as being identical with the (implicit) matrix subject ("the husband"), and not with the speaker of the sentence:

(33)   utxari šens cols, "me ver moval-tko" (ib.)
       say.to.her your.DAT wife.DAT, "I IMPOSS I.will.come-QUOT"
       'Tell your wife: I cannot come.'[30]

2.7 The development of quotative particles in Georgian

The history of Georgian quotative particles might be reconstructed as follows: at an initial stage, postverbal *-o*, comparable in its clitic position to interrogative *-a*, was used with all reported speech (Kačarava 1950:254); this stage is preserved in some dialects (e.g. in Khevsur). Then two "expressive" verb forms of "to say" developed into the grammaticised particles *-metki* and *-tko*, and *-o* became the residual, default marker with a hearsay meaning. However, *-tko* developed beyond its original, instructional use: it became a marker of reported 1st-person speech wherever the 1st singular marker -*metki* could not be used, that is, in the plural, and also in the singular in the western dialects that lack -*metki*.

2.8 The scope of quotative particles in Modern Georgian

So far, reported speech has been presented as the integral block of a "direct speech sentence". However, clauses with an operator (interrogative or relative pronoun) are more complex — at least in colloquial Georgian. Consider:

(34) "vina-a?" — "ra vici me." — "vin *var*-o ar tkva?" — vḳitxe (N. Dumbaʒe)
"who(NOM)-he.is?" — "what I.know.it I." — "who(NOM) *I.am*-QUOT not he.said?" — I.asked(AOR).him
'Who is he? — No idea. — Didn't he say who *he is*?, I asked.'

(35) "Ali Xorava čem-tana-c iqo!" — tkva Periʒe-m. — "Ra *minda*-o, Ali Xorava-m"? — vḳitxe me (N. Dumbaʒe)
"Ali Khorava(NOM) me-at-too he.was!" — he.said Periʒe-ERG. — "what(NOM) *I.want(PRS).it*-QUOT, Ali Khorava-ERG?" — I.asked(AOR).him I
'Ali Khorava came to see me, too!, said Periʒe. — What did he say *he wanted*, Ali Khorava?, I asked.'

In these examples, the operator behaves as in English, but the rest of the clause is direct speech, without the shift phenomena characteristic of English dependent interrogative clauses. This phenomenon remains to be explored. In particular, it would be interesting to know if the behaviour of the operator is somehow related to the fact that conjunctions sometimes occur with direct speech (see above 1.1; 2.2). Consider:

(36) čad-ze tit-eb-i daaḳaḳuna, *tu* gamocxva-o (N. Dumbaʒe)
maize.bread-on finger-P-NOM he.tapped(AOR).on.them, CNJ it.was.baked(AOR)-QUOT
'He tapped with his fingers on the maize-bread, [to see] *if* it was ready-baked.'

where the conjunction *tu* 'if' marks a matrix clause-orientated "indirect question", whereas -*o* marks *gamocxva* as direct speech.

2.9 The verb-like properties of quotatives in Modern Georgian

In the older texts, direct speech is normally introduced by a reporting clause. In the modern Kartvelian languages, however, the absence of a verb of saying is quite common.[31] Georgian grammarians assume ellipsis here,[32] but while this is an intuitively plausible description of the historical origin, it might not capture the synchronic reality of (35): supplying *tkva* 'he said' would probably change the scope of the question: "Did Ali Khorava say what he wanted?, I asked". I think that "free direct speech" marked by quotative particles is autonomous in the sense that there is no need to posit an underlying verb of saying. The speaker is determined by the pragmatic rules of story-telling: it is for instance the protagonist or his or her interlocutor.

On the other hand, the ergative of the "speaker" Ali Khorava in (35) presupposes a transitive verb of saying. If we dismiss "ellipsis" as a synchronic description, this suggests an intermediate position of Kartvelian quotative particles: they are not verbs in the sense that their position is different (they are never clause-initial), they are not "tensed", and they co-occur with finite verbs of saying (see above 2.5); but they are like verbs in their autonomy (their capability to mark reported speech of 1st-, 2nd- and 3rd-person reporter-speakers[33]), and in their transitive verblike behaviour, i.e., their occurrence with an optional speaker-argument.[34] However, the restrictions on constructions like (35) have still to be determined.

2.10   Quotatives in Mingrelian and Laz

Mingrelian and Laz cannot be studied here. As described by Kipšidze (1914: 142–3) and others, the distribution of quotative particles in these languages is the same as in literary Georgian.[35] Surprisingly, the distribution thus differs from that of the western Georgian dialects mentioned above (2.6), and of Svan (see below 3.3). Laz also uses Turkish verb forms as quotative particles: *dei* < Standard Turkish *diye* 'saying' (Čikobava 1936:136; Kutscher *et al.* 1995:110, note 2), *dedum* 'I said' (Kutscher *et al.* 1995:110).[36]

3.   Svan

Svan is a neighbour of both Mingrelian and Georgian. A schematic map may help to understand the situation (settlements in italics; see Figure 1). Upper Bal is the dialect that most materials in this chapter come from; it is considered to have undergone less influence from Georgian than Lower Svan. Svan is not used as a literary language. Our main sources are field work notes taken in Mestia, the administrative center of Upper Svanetia, which belongs to the Upper Bal region; and in particular the volumes of texts from all dialects written down in the 1920s and 1930s.[37]

Svan reported speech is a very manifold phenomenon: it occurs with or without a verb of saying (3.1); with or without a conjunction, both as direct or as some form of indirect speech (3.2); with or without quotative particles (3.3); in

	CAUCASUS MAIN RIDGE
	Upper Svanetia (in the north, along the Engur River):
Mingrelian	Lower Bal dialects: Upper Bal dialects:
	Becho *Mestia* *Mulakh*
	Etser *Ipar*
	SVANETIAN MOUNTAIN RIDGE *Ushguli*
Mingrelian	Lower Svanetia (in the south, "Svanetia of the Dadians"):
	Lower Svan dialects:
	Lentekh *Lashkh(et)*
Mingrelian	Georgian dialects:
	Lechkhumian Imeretian

Figure 1.

more or less "indirect speech" characterised by a shift of person and epistemic status (3.4), but otherwise with all kinds of direct speech properties (3.5).

Svan reported speech deserves particular interest: while Georgian has the more or less European type of distinction between direct speech on the one hand, and indirect speech as complement clauses with a main clause orientation on the other, Svan has three forms: complement clauses with a main clause orientation (see (69a) below), direct speech and non-direct speech with a partial shift of person and epistemic category, called "semi-indirect speech" by *Hewitt* (1982). Of these three forms I will concentrate on the last one. But it should be noted that reported direct speech does exist. It can, but must not, occur in the absence of a *preceding* reporting clause (see (37) and (38) below, with and without a subsequent reporting clause). On the other hand, there are only a few examples of direct speech after an introductory reporting clause (see (53b) below), although I suspect it occurs more often in contemporary Svan. But semi-indirect speech is certainly the preferred variant, and, as one of my Svan informants put it, it is "more Svan" than direct speech.

3.1 Free direct speech in Svan

In the texts, most reported speech is introduced by a reporting clause, but it need not be:

(37) [...] i ču ibzi. "ā, näṭlav si, mäjḳäpd xizbi?" (242,23)
    and PREV he.eats.it. "O, would.that you, what.kind.ADV you.eat?"
    'And he eats it: O, how on earth can you eat this?'

Long dialogues are often free direct speech not introduced by any reporting clause (or a quotative particle, for that matter).[38] The same is true of semi-indirect speech (see e.g. (47) and (60) below). In other words, Svan reported speech is "autonomous" (see 2.9). Verbs of saying are rarely postposed to direct speech (38) or semi-indirect speech (39) or both preposed and postposed to reported speech (40):

(38) "atxe dēmad žahvdi", *dǟvd xǟkv*. ečka miča apxnegd xǟkv [...] (243,11–12)
"now not.yet I.give(PRS).it.to.you", *dev.ERG he.said.to.him*. then his fellow.ERG he.said.to.him
'I will not give it to you now, *the dev said*. Then his fellow said to him [...].'

(39) "ala eser xoča gämäš xāra!", *päršmägd rǟkv* (247,36–7)
"this.NOM QUOT good taste.GEN it.has.had.it(PERF)", *parshmag.ERG he.said*
'This tasted good !(lit.: I had it of good taste!), *the parshmag said.*'

(40) *yertem xǟkv*: "ešdjori lavǟš-u eser annaqe [...] i ečk' ēser ž' äxqočvi gezal." — *xǟkv yertem* (234,11–14)
God.ERG he.told.him: "twelve lavash-OPT QUOT he.baked(AOR).them [...] and then QUOT PREV he.will.recover(FUT).to.him son.NOM." — *he.said.to.him God.ERG*
'*God said to him*: Bake twelve lavash-breads [...] and then your son will recover, *God said to him.*'

3.2 Conjunctions with reported speech in Svan

Similar to Georgian (see 1.2 and (22)), Svan also has cataphoric "so" referring to subsequent direct speech:

(41) (a) ečk' ēser eža läxčvedn', (b) ere "mäj eser xār xoča?" (c) ečkas eser mižnēm *amžī*-v xǟkv-á: (d) "läčvä ləžatān eser dēsamagveš xār". (250,18–19)
(a) then QUOT that.NOM he.will.ask(FUT).her, (b) CNJ "what.NOM QUOT she.has.it good?" (c) then QUOT she.ERG *so*-OPT she.said.to.him-PTCL: (d) "chamois.GEN milk.like nothing she.has(PRS).it"
'[A wife and her lover dev converse about the means of getting rid of the wife's husband. The lover's advice is to feign illness, and:] (a) Then he [sc. your husband] will ask you: (b) "What will help you?" (c) Then you should speak to him thus: (d) "There is nothing better for me than the milk of a chamois."'

And as with Georgian *rom* (see 2.2), the conjunction *ere* belongs to the preceding reporting clause: in (a)–(b) . . . *läxc̣vedn' ere* . . ., its initial vowel elides the final vowel of the preceding verb. Again, this casts some doubt on its embedded status in the reporting clause.

But while the syntactic status of reported speech is sometimes debatable, there are cases where it is not: direct speech can be case-marked (Boeder 1985b: 69):

(42) bäč či ladeɣ ingriv i "Kəntəziš dašniš näqir mak̇u"-s išk̇adal (Davitiani et al. 1957: 169,34–5, Lower Bal dialect)
stone.NOM all day.NOM it.grew(IPERF).bigger and "Kentez.GEN sword.GEN hit(PPP).NOM I.want(PRS).it"-DAT it.shouted(IPERF).it
'The stone [being a transformed woman] grew bigger every day and used to shout: "I want to be hit by Kentezi's sword."'

In this example, direct speech seems to refer to repeated tokens of a type established before in the text ("it shouted its "I want . . ."""). More often, this occurs with single words:

(43) dede-š mūkvīsg mi dor miri (Šaniʒe et al. 1939b: 268, no. 91a,25)
mother.GEN saying(PRS.PART).NOM I not I.have(PRS).him
'I have nobody who would say "Mother!" to me.'[39]

As in the case of Old Georgian *vitạrmed* (1.1) and Modern Georgian *rom* (2.2), the conjunction *ere* 'that' can introduce reported speech with a quotative particle (44) or without (45):

(44) xăkv Q̇alačūqlāns, *ere* "mäj eser xek̇vdeni, ečis eser xäčo" (247,23)
he.said.to.him Qalachuqlan.DAT, CNJ "what.NOM QUOT he.will.want(FUT).it, that.DAT QUOT he.will.do(FUT).it.for.him
'[sc. the Parshmag] said to Qalachuqlan: (*that*) Whatever you want, I will do it for you.'

(45) miča xexvd xăkv, *ere* "mäj li imɣa xäri xolām gu-ži?" (242,13–14)
his wife.ERG she.said.to.him, CNJ "what.NOM it.is why you.are(PRS) bad heart-in"
'His wife said to him: (*that*) Why are you in a bad mood?'

But direct speech may occur without *ere* or a quotative:

(46) Q̇alačūqlānd xăkv: amnoš nabord mād mak̇u (246,30)
Qalachuqlan.ERG he.said.to.her: this.INSTR stirred(PPP) not I.want(PRS).it
'He said to her: I do not want bread prepared with this [sc. urine].'

It is unknown so far which contexts favour the use of *ere*.[40] Where the quotative comes with a delay (see 3.3.6), introductory *ere* seems to ensure that reported speech stands out against its non-reported context.

3.3 The distribution of quotative particles in Svan

Svan has three quotative particles: *-əž, eser*[41] and *rok*.[42] These entail semi-indirect reported speech (or rather: the application of the corresponding rules), and most semi-indirect speech is marked by quotative particles (see however 3.4.1.1).

3.3.1 -əž

-əž corresponds to Georgian *-tko* in its "Imeretian" distribution (2.6). That is, it is used with 1st-person singular and plural speakers[43] (see (47b–c) and (48)) and with an instructional meaning with its "hidden" 1st-person speaker (2.6) (see (49)):[44]

(47) (a) "im rokv xvičod, Švanär?" — (b) "im-əž i am lüntv jeru tve ameču eķälisga nimšia (c) i tetrs-əž dem nahvdix (d) i atxe Gagräšte ɣuri (e) i ka xoščivle." (39,3–8 Ipar)
(a) "what.DAT QUOT we.do(PRS).it, Svans?" — (b) "what-QUOT and this winter two month here thorn.in we.have.worked(PERF) (c) and money.DAT-QUOT not they.give(PRS).it.to.us (d) and now Gagra.to I.go(PRS) (e) and PREV I.will.sue(FUT).him."
'(a) What do you do, Svans? — (b) What? During this winter, we worked in the thorns here for two months, (c) but they do not pay us. (d) And now I will go to Gagra [a city in Abkhazia] (e) and will sue him.

(48) amčūn ätvzelǟl: "hēsā-ž ime īra nāzv Bečvitēsga" (41,11–12 Mestia) here I.went.by: "if-QUOT where he.will.be(FUT) going(PART) Becho.to.in"
'I went by: In case there is somebody going to Becho [, I thought].'

(49) a. (si) xēka (ere) "mī-ž məxar qvedni" (Inf)
(you) you.tell.him(AOR.IMP) (CNJ) "I-QUOT tomorrow I.will.come"
'Tell him: (that) I [the speaker] will come tomorrow.'
b. mi maķu xãkva (ere) "məxar-əž qvedni" (Inf)
I I.want.it that.you.tell.him (CNJ) "Tomorrow-QUOT I.will.come"
'I want you to tell him that I will come tomorrow.'

Notice that the use of *-əž* does not require a 1st-person singular matrix clause subject in variant (49b) (cp. 2.6). Also, *-əž* crucially refers to the speech of the *actual* 1st-person speaker. "Underlying" 1st-person speakers, when shifted, do not trigger 1st-person quotatives (see (58c–e) below). The same is true for instructions, not to reported 1st-person speaker instructions; for instance, although (41d) is an instruction to a 2nd person, it is marked by *eser*, not by *-əž* (cp. (87b)). In this, Svan seems to differ from Georgian, which allows *-tko* to be triggered by a *reported* 1st-person reporting clause (see (32)).

3.3.2 eser

Eser is the "elsewhere" form of the quotative particle paradigm: it occurs with reported 3rd-person speakers (see (39), (40), (44)), and with 2nd-person speakers:

(50) (si) (ka) mēka: "məxar eser (ka) qvedni" (Inf)
 (you) (PREV) you.said.to.me: "tomorrow QUOT (PTCL)
 I.will.come(FUT)"
 'You told me: I [= addressee] will come tomorrow.'

but not with the instructional meaning:

(51) *(si) xēka (ere): "məxar eser qvedni/qedni" (Inf)
 (you) you.tell(AOR.IMP) (CNJ): "tomorrow QUOT
 I.will.come/he.will.come"
 (in the sense of: 'Tell him: I [speaker or addressee] will come tomorrow.')

We can tabulate now the distribution of quotative particles in Georgian and Upper Svan:

	Instructional	1st Sg	1st P	Elsewhere
Khevsurian ...	o	o	o	o
Rustaveli	tko	o	o	o
Literary Georgian	tko	metki	o/tko	o
Imeretian	tko	tko	tko	o
Svan	əǯ	əǯ	əǯ/rok(v)	eser/rok(v)

3.3.3 The interchangeability of Svan eser and rok(v)

In most contexts, *eser* and *rok(v)* are interchangeable, and all authors so far (e.g. Gudjedjiani and Palmaitis 1986:35–6; Tuite 1997:40–1) seem to consider them as free variants. Indeed, *eser* and *rok(v)* occur close to each other within the same text:

(52) (a) xäkv, (b) ere "bāzi *eser* jervǟj mǟnḳvi anqes mineštēsga, (c) eǯa *rokv* šišd ču̅-v adgärx!" (333,35–6)
 (a) he.said.to.him, (b) CNJ "this.evening QUOT who.NOM first.NOM he.may.come(SUBJ.II) to.them, (c) that.NOM QUOT immediately PREV-OPT they.killed(AOR).him"
 '(a) He said to him: (b) Whoever comes first to you (plural) this evening, (c) you shall kill him.'

(53) (a) miča dis xäkv: (b) "mišgu di, lädi zugv-ži mǟkvx, (c) ere "Sulasaxel *eser* xajšxa." (d) eǯa xexvd vode *rok* do onqude, (e) ečkad lišvem *rok* nōma-v mār!" (100,7–9 Ipar)
 (a) his mother.DAT he.said.to.her: (b) "my mother, today hill-on

they.said.to.me, (c) CNJ "Sulasakhel.NOM QUOT she.is.called(PRS)." (d) that.NOM wife.ADV as.long.as QUOT not I.should.lead(SUBJ.II).her.home, (e) so.long rest.NOM QUOT not-OPT I.have(PRS).it"
'(a) He told his mother, (b) Mother, today they told me on the hill, (c) that her name is Sulasakhel/"Her name is Sulasakhel." (d) As long as I do not marry her, (e) I shall have no rest.'

As in so many fairy tales, there are often three people saying or promising one thing after the other: in a Lower Bal text, there are three brothers saying one after the other: "I will keep watch over him". Inspite of their parallelism, the speeches of the eldest and of the intermediate brother have *eser* (Davitiani *et al.* 1957:167,3; 8); the speech of the youngest brother has *rok* (ib. 167,13).[45]

3.3.4 The difference between Svan eser and rok(v)

However, *eser* and *rok(v)* have a different distribution. Firstly, *rok(v)*, but not *eser* can replace *əǯ* with reported 1st-person plural speakers (see Hewitt 1982:208):

(54) ečas läxvçveddad: "ame-isga rokv im nahvdid kiräjs?" (38,20–2 Ipar; cp. 38,27)
that.DAT we.asked(AOR).him: "this-in QUOT what you.give(PRS).us hire.DAT"
'Him we asked: How much hire will you give us for this?'

(55) äxvmäzred ɣērbet: "ɣērbet rokv, si lanešd [...]" (36,4 Mestia) we.prayed(AOR).(to.)him God.NOM: "God QUOT, you you.help(AOR.IMP).us"
'We prayed to God: God, you help us!'

Second, even a cursory look at the texts shows that both their syntactic behaviour and their distribution in the dialects differ: the Lower Svan dialects (Lashkh and Lentekh) have *lok* < *rok(v)*, and not *eser* (Topuria 1985:143; Čanṭlaʒe 1998:227). *eser* dominates in most dialects of Upper Svanetia, with the notable exception of Ushgul, which has *rok(v)* because of its connections to Lower Svanetia and to Georgian Imeretia.[46] A careful analysis of all the texts may modify this picture, but it seems reasonable to assume that *rok* spread from the south.

3.3.5 Svan quotatives as clitics

As we saw above, Georgian quotative particles are enclitics that attach to the verb, the clause or the sentence they belongs to; in addition they may attach to any phonological phrase in Modern Georgian. The Svan quotative particles are different: as so many other Svan particles, they are clitics that attach to their preceding host and occur before the verb or after the first (phonological) phrase of the clause (Wackernagel's position[47]): these positions often coincide with each other in a spoken language. While the latter position seems to dominate in the Upper Bal prose texts, the preverbal position is more frequent e.g. in the Lower Bal proverb collection of Davitiani (1974). It should be noted here that *eser* can occur more than once in a clause:

> (56) mič eser imnär xaq̇lūni? mine mənçir eser māma eser äri. (255,32)
> he.DAT QUOT how he.is.afraid(PRS).of.it? their subduer.NOM QUOT not QUOT is
> '[The dev says to his horse:] Why are you afraid? There is nobody who can overpower us.'

The second clause probably consists of two phonological phrases, and the multiple occurrence of *eser* would be similar to that of Georgian -*o* (2.3).

3.3.6 Use and non-use of the Svan quotative
From a processing point of view, it is interesting that quotatives may come with a "delay", e.g. after an address without quotative (see (57)) or after an initial part identified by other means, e.g. the conjunction *ere* (see (58)):

> (57) haṭ xolāl, kvitrārs eser čāžar otxvjax i ime jär ärix? (53,26 Lendjer)
> go.ahead bads, thieves.DAT QUOT horses they.have.led(PERF).them.away and where who they.are?
> 'Hurry up, you lazybones, the thieves have stolen our horses, and where are you ?' (lit.: 'where is who of you?')

> (58) (a) zurāld xākv, (b) *ere* "miča lažmila mič otdagra. (c) mič eser nākvīsgv eser xāra: (d) ervāj eser miča lažmilas čvadgrina, (e) eža eser čäsd xaḳu" (256,35)
> (a) woman.ERG she.said.to.him, (b)CNJ "her brothers.NOM he.DAT he.has.killed(PERF).them, (c) she.DAT QUOT something.that.was.said.NOM QUOT she.has.had(PERF).it: (d) whoever.NOM QUOT her brothers.DAT he.would.kill(PFV.COND).them, (e) that.NOM QUOT husband.ADV she.wants.him"
> '(a) The woman told him: (b) You have killed my brothers. (c) I had vowed: (d) Whoever would kill my brothers, (e) him I want for my husband.'

On the other hand, the quotative particle can be omitted after its occurrence in the initial clause(s):

> (59) ečka dävä xexvd xākv, *ere* "lemesgs eser, mäj mizez īra, dōm laxhödne, mare [. . .]" (379,38–380,1 Mestia)
> then dev.GEN wife.ERG she.said.to.her, CNJ "fire.DAT QUOT, what.NOM reason.NOM it.will(FUT).be, not she.will.give(FUT).it.to.her, but [. . .]"
> 'Then the dev's wife said to her: As for the fire, there is no reason why I should not give it to you, but [. . .].'

3.4 Shift phenomena in Svan semi-indirect speech

It is time now to characterise "indirectness" of reported speech in Svan which consists of a shift in person and epistemic category ("evidentiality"). In the following, I will give a rule that possibly allows a deeper understanding of its functional basis. Its tentative character should, however, be underlined. In particular, examples involving speech act participants are extremely scarce and inconclusive in the published materials, and it is my impression that contemporary Svan shows some variation which may be due to Svan-Georgian bilingualism and which I have not yet been able to capture.

3.4.1 Svan person shift
The rule for person shift seems to be:

> In semi-indirect speech, person is orientated towards the (actual) speech-act, to the extent that its reporting clause is orientated towards the actual speech act, except in reported 1st-person speech.
> This rule is optional with present and future tense clauses.

In other words, 1st and 2nd person refer to the actual speaker and addressee, respectively, if they do in the reporting clause, and 3rd person is used elsewhere; in 1st-person reported speech, on the other hand, we have the usual speaker-addressee reversal of reported direct speech.

To make clear the impact of this rule, I will consider two examples illustrating its first half (3.4.1.1), before I discuss the impact of its restriction and optionality condition (3.4.1.2).

3.4.1.1 Examples of person-shift in Svan
Person shift is particularly frequent in narrative texts. Consider the following example:

(60) "(a) mädil-u eser xēra (b) i alamäg märe no-v eser anxviṭ, (c) ka-v eser apišvd. (d) mäj eser xaḳu, (e) ečas eser xäčo." — "(f) mič eser xaḳuč miča mahvrēne gezal, (g) učīžad mäj äǯsäd, eǯa." (242,1–4)
"(a) grace.NOM-OPT QUOT he.will.have(FUT).it (b) and so.many man.NOM not-OPT QUOT he.slew(AOR).them, (c) PREV-OPT QUOT he.released(AOR).them. (d) what.NOM QUOT he.wants(PRS).it, (e) that.DAT he.will.do(FUT).it.for.him." — "(f) he.DAT QUOT he.wants(PRS).it his youngest child.NOM, (g) wifeless.ADV who.NOM he.remained(AOR).to.you, that"
'[A man meets a dev who does not let him pass by. He says:] (a) I beseech you, (b) do not slay so many men, (c) allow us to go. (d) Whatever you want (e) I will do it. — (f) I want your youngest son, (g) the one who is left to you unmarried, that one.'

(a) The 1st person (Svan *mi*) is shifted to 3rd-person *mič* 'he.DAT'. The nominative of *mič* is *ža* 'he' (see (76), (80), (90c), (91) below). *ža/mič* is a 3rd-person pronoun; it is the short form of the demonstrative pronoun *eža* 'that', and has a contrastive or intensifier meaning ("s/hé (him/herself"[48]) in subject and object positions, as in:

(61) anqäd atxe ägi-te, dīna larda-te adgene; *ža* sga ačäd kor-te i laxvbas ägis esxīd (253,2–4)
he.came(AOR) now home-to, girl.NOM abode-to he.put(AOR).her, he.NOM PREV he.went(AOR) house-to and brothers.DAT home.DAT he.met(AOR).them
'[The hero] came home now [with the king's daughter], the girl he accommodated in a room; *he himself* went into the house and met his brothers at home.'

This meaning of *ža/mič* is a corollary of its contrast with zero anaphora[49] ("pro drop"); notice that subject and object arguments are marked in the verb.

In semi-indirect speech, *ža/mič* is the 3rd-person counterpart of explicit 1st/2nd-person pronouns; it replaces them where they would occur in direct speech. As a non-shifted 3rd-person pronoun it has the meaning illustrated in (60f). In positions where *ža/mič-* does not contrast with zero anaphora (i.e. where verb-internal marking is excluded), it is a normal 3rd-person pronoun, for instance in expressions like *miča xexv* 'his wife.NOM' or *mičeš-te* (382,24) 's/he.GEN-to' ('to her/him').[50] Since *ža/mič* neutralises an underlying opposition of person (Deeters 1930:184), it is of some functional relevance that my informants sometimes had to look at the later context before they could decide "who did what to whom".

(b) As a corollary of person shift, 2nd-person imperatives, i.e. 2nd-person aorist indicatives, have to be shifted into 3rd-person optative (subjunctive II) forms (Deeters 1930:185 § 345): "let us go (allow us to go)" must become optative "he is to let them go" in (c). However, the optative is (almost?) always replaced in this context by an alternative, synonymous form, namely an optative particle (-*u*) plus the 3rd-person indicative counterpart of the optative, which is the aorist ("he let us go"). Similarly, 2nd-person present tense prohibitions appear as a 3rd-person present tense plus optative particle:

(62) amɣ' ēser numa-v li luçxvave (291,29 apud Šaraʒeniʒe 1946:305)
for.this QUOT not-OPT s/he.is(PRS) worried(PPP)
'Don't be worried about this.'

(c) Persons occurring in idiomatic expressions are not exempt from shifting: the unshifted form in (60a) would be: *mädil-u žēra* 'grace-OPT you.will.have(FUT).it' in the sense of "I implore you".

My data seem to suggest that Svan semi-indirect speech is normally restricted to quotative-marked speech. However, the following example shows semi-indirect speech without a quotative particle:

(63) zurāld laxṭvīl: "mädil-u xēra, miča semi šaur mičnēm-u adje i heb nomā-v oxḳərcxe." (56,12–13 Lendjer)
woman.ERG she.called(AOR).to.him: "grace.NOM-OPT he.will.have(FUT).it, his three shaur.NOM he.ERG-OPT he.took(AOR).them.away and cherry.NOM not-OPT he.hewed(trimmed)(AOR).it.to.her"
'The woman called to him: I implore you, take your three shaurs [= coins], and don't cut off the branches of my cherry!'

3.4.1.2 *Examples of speech act participant orientation in Svan*
The non-shift condition with 1st-person speech captures e.g. the fact that no person shift occurs with *əǯ* (3.3.1) in (47)–(49) (but see 3.6) and in reported speech with *rok(v)* and 1st-person plural speakers (see (54)–(55) above). Now consider:

(64) (a) rãkvx, (b) ere "aljär eser otqidx-u mine xošām i xãkvx-u, (c) ere "eǯ zurāl rokv čvädsōq̇ān i gezlīr rokv čväʒih i cxvad-isga rokv ž' anǯäb""
(371,13–15 Mulakh)
(a) they.said, (b) CNJ "these.NOM QUOT they.brought.them.to.him-OPT their senior.DAT and they.said.to.him-OPT, (c)CNJ "that woman.NOM QUOT she.went.mad(AOR) and children.NOM QUOT she.killed(AOR).them and boiling.water-in QUOT PREV she.boiled(AOR).them"."
'(a) They said: (b) (that) Let us take these to our senior and let us say: (c) (that) That woman went mad and she killed her children and boiled them in boiling water.'

As the reported 1st-person speaker in (64c) is himself shifted to a 3rd-person form according to the usual rule ("let us say" → "let them say"), it does not prevent person shift.[51] In other words, the rule works from top downwards. As pointed out by Čanṭlaʒe (1998:226), the rule does *not* require a general shift to 3rd-person (Šaraʒeniʒe 1946:290). Indeed, we get examples like:

(65) mišgu apxnegd mäkwe: emoš eser *m*ämeda *nišge* nazimži zagärteži čkärd lizi, ečkas išgen bargär mič-oɣ *loxo* (Davitiani *et al.* 1957:85,26–7, Lower Bal)
my fellow.ERG he.said.to.me: if QUOT it.is.possible.*for.me* our opposite.on mountain.to.on quick.ADV going(VN).NOM, then other piece.of.luggage.P.NOM him.OPT I.gave.them.to.him
'My fellow said to me: If you can climb the mountain in front of us quickly, then you should give me the other luggage.'

where the 2nd person of the "underlying" direct speech is shifted to 1st person because it refers to the (actual) speaker of the sentence (cp. (47a): "you Svans" > "we Svans"), and the 1st-person exclusive possessive correctly codes the 1st-person + 3rd-person combination (where 3rd person refers to the "you" of the addressee in the underlying direct speech).[52] Similarly, the following example offers a shift of 1st person to 3rd person ("me" > "him"), whereas the 2nd person is shifted to 1st person because it refers to the speaker:

(66) eǯnem mäkv: (ere) "al läir eser oxqida mišgovd i mičašd māma" (ČG)
s/he.ERG s/he.said.to.me: (CNJ) "that book.NOM QUOT
s/he.has.bought(PERF.EVID).it me.for and him/her.for not"
'S/he said to me: I bought the book for you and not for me.'[53]

As for the tense condition, person shift with present and future reference seems to be the preferred variant in the texts; cp. (44), (47a), (56), (58)–(60), (90). But there are occasional cases of non-shift (431,24; 433,10–11 apud Čanṭlaʒe 1998 230), and my informants offered both alternatives:

(67) eǯnem xäkv: "ḳanpeṭs eser laxvedne, hēma eser xoča čqinṭ īra / ḳanpeṭs eser laʒhvedne, hēma eser xoča čqinṭ xira" (ČG)
s/he.ERG s/he.said.to.him/her: "sweets.DAT QUOT s/he.will.give(FUT).it.to.him/her, if QUOT good child.NOM s/he.will.be(FUT) / sweets.DAT QUOT I.will.give(FUT).it.to.you, if QUOT good child.NOM you.will.be(FUT)"
'He said: I will give you sweets, if you are a good child.'

3.4.1.3 Quotative particles in Svan proverbs

As we saw above (2.4), Georgian proverbs are represented as direct speech plus quotative particle. In Svan, proverbs are semi-indirect speech with a regular person shift: even generalizing "you" becomes "s/he" etc.:

(68) mä či xocxa, mič-ov-i eži xocxon (Davitiani 1973:83 no. 245, Lower Bal)
what.NOM everybody.DAT s/he.prefers(PRS).it, s/he.DAT-OPT-and that.NOM s/he.preferred(IPERF).it
'What everybody prefers, that you should prefer too.'

3.4.2 Svan "tense shift"

As Deeters (1930:184–5) observes, person shift is somehow related to "tense shift".[54] This is true in the sense that if one of the rules applies, the other must apply, too (be it vacuously), and that the optionality of person shift depends on tense. However, "tense" should not be understood in the sense of "sequence of tenses". In Svan complement clauses, backshift of tenses does occur (69a), although not in the speaker-indexical time adverbials (69b) (see 3.5.3):

(69) a. läšqäd ečka Ämirans eǯ' ē, mič er xangär xā̈bəda (95,28 apud Abesaʒe 1978:8)
he.remembered(AOR).it then Amiran.DAT that PTCL, his CNJ dagger.NOM it.hang(IPERF).on.him
'Then Amiran remembered that he had his dagger hanging [on his side].'

b. zurāl ačḳuarda, he anqedni miča muxvbe məxar ägite (C. Margiani apud Abesaʒe 1978:8)
woman.NOM she.worried, if he.will.come(FUT) her brother.NOM tomorrow home
'The woman worried if her brother would come home the day after.'

But instead of backshift, semi-indirect speech shows a shift of epistemic category from non-evidential to evidential ("indirective", "inferential"). The following rule seems to hold:

In semi-indirect speech, indicative tenses with past time reference shift to their evidential counterparts, except in reported 1st-person speech.

The exception repeats the condition on person shift (see 3.4.1). Notice that this shift occurs where person shift is not optional (as in present and future tense clauses). Examples for non-shift with non-past tenses are found in (47a-c) and (60a-f). The indicative aorist, which otherwise is a narrative tense with past time reference, counts as non-past with the optative particle in (60c). Similarly, present (56), future (70), conditional (71) and subjunctive (72) are not shifted:

(70) amī lāšis eser eǯgvärs oxqide, ere ɣo ivaladäɣ mič ämzərdēdx (54,14–15 Lendjer)
this.GEN.too seed.DAT QUOT such.DAT he.will.bring(FUT).it.to.him, that PTCL ever.day he.DAT they.shall.bless(SUBJ.I).him
'I also will find you such a seed of this that you will be grateful for ever.'

(71) ka-j atəmbažənx: "jär eser anʒēlvălīs i jed sädils jär anmărīs?"
(379,13–14 Mestia)
PREV-too they.wondered: "who.NOM QUOT
s/he.will.have.swept(PFV.COND) and or meal.DAT who.NOM
s/he.will.have.prepared(PFV.COND).it"
'They also wondered: Who will have swept and who have prepared a meal?'

(72) šomvăj eser xäidəndēds, ečka ašxv čū-v izobda (287,5)
when QUOT he.should.be.hungry(SUBJ.I), then one.DAT PREV-OPT
he.ate(IPERF).it
'Whenever you will be hungry, eat one.'

Consider now the shift of past time verbs to their evidential counterparts. The evidential counterpart of the narrative aorist tense is the perfect (see introductory section):[55]

(73) xäʒi Dautd xăkv miča gezals, ere "mäj eser xočvmina, otʒih' ēser mă?"
(369,26–7)
Hadji Daud.ERG he.said.to.him his son.DAT, CNJ "what QUOT
he.has.done(PERF).it, he.has.killed(PERF).her QUOT Q"
'Hadji Daud said to his son: What did you do, have you killed her?'

(cp. the contrast between direct and semi indirect speech in (90b) vs. (90c) below). Imperfect forms of stative verbs like "to stand" and "to know" (see (90f)) count as aorists and are shifted to the perfect:

(74) letnapd eser mäj *xägnēna* amzav? (51,18 Lendjer)
letnap[cattle fed for the Easter-meal].ADV QUOT what
it.has.stood(PERF).for.them this.year
'What *did you have* for slaughter-cattle on Easter this year?'

Unlike Georgian, Svan has special evidential forms for the imperfect:

(75) xola kvin eser imži xeqni, čigar eser ləmsqävin lezöbs i ala eser dēsa moš xōkva miča baba Xäʒi Dauts! (368,25–7)
bad breath.NOM QUOT how it.will.smell(IPFV.FUT), always QUOT
she.used.to.make(IPERF.EVID).it meal.DAT and this.NOM QUOT not PTCL
he.has.said(PERF).it her father Hadji Daut.DAT
'How can a bad odour come from it [sc. the meal], I always used to prepare the meal, and hardly has my father Hadji Daud said this.'

In a sense, sequence of tenses and shift of epistemic category are complementary: the controlling property is the past vs. non-past distinction in the reporting clause in the one case and in the reported clause in the other; in both cases the target is the dependent clause. But the controlled properties are different: tense vs. epistemic status, and this explains the difference between the exceptions: 1st-person reporting, which guarantees continuing reliability, with semi-indirect speech vs. "continuing applicability" with indirect speech (*Comrie* 1986:284–5). But why should evidentials be used in reported speech in the first place, and why is the shift to evidential forms restricted to past time reference forms, and excluded from reported 1st-person speech? The domain of evidentiality and reported speech overlap: one meaning of evidential forms is "hearsay", and the Georgian evidential perfect can be used in complement clauses to code this epistemic meaning (*Boeder* 2000:292–4): in sentences like: *I have heard/I know that she wrote the letter*, the verb *wrote* can be either in the aorist (neutral meaning) or in the perfect ("somebody told me that she wrote it"; cp. (20b, d)). — As for time reference, we may speculate that the most frequent domain of hearsay information is the past and conclusions from accessible evidence most often refer to the past. In fact, most evidential forms in the languages of the world refer to the past.[56] — Notice that future and conditional tenses (as in (71)) have an inherent relation to epistemic status (*Boeder* 2000: 280–1). — The absence of tense shift from 1st-person speech is to be expected, too. While 2nd and 3rd-person reporter speech is "hearsay" per se,[57] this is not necessarily true for 1st-person reporter speech. It is true that a sentence like: *I told him that she wrote the letter* can have *she wrote* in the evidential perfect form if I want to give the complement clause a hearsay meaning ("I told him that, apparently, she wrote the letter"),[58] but this use does not result from the application of the tense shift rule for semi-indirect speech.[59] Notice that the perfect in (73) occurs in a question, although the opposition between evidential and non-evidential forms is normally restricted to non-modal assertions (*Boeder* 2000:291–2). In other words, the tense shift as described above, although originally motivated by "evidentiality", has become a grammaticised, automatic rule of semi-indirect speech, and (73) in all probability has no "inferential" meaning: neither the story-teller nor Hadji Daud give their question an "evidential" epistemic status.

3.4.3 *Distributional differences between Svan* eser *and* rok(v)

In general, *rok(v)* (or its variant *lok*) follows the rules given above:

(76) xekv [sic] miča xaxvem: "ǯa rokv xola māre, leɣv čotcvīra i šdəmrär sgōxqīda" (378,8–9 Mestia)
she.said his wife.ERG: "he.NOM QUOT bad man.NOM, meat.NOM he.has.left(PERF).it and ears.NOM he.has.brought(PERF).them.in"
'His wife said to him: You bad man, you left the meat and brought the ears home.'

But there are instances of *rok(v)* with direct speech where person shift would be expected with *eser*:

(77) läxvčvedda: šuḳvži rok ǯäxviēnax jär? (103,6–7 apud Čanṭlaʒe 1998:229)
he.asked.them: way.on QUOT they.met(PERF).you who.NOM?
'He asked them: Who met you on your way?'

As with *eser*, the person-shift role does not (necessarily) apply to clauses with non-past tenses, even if the embedding clause has tense and person shift:

(78) (a) ečkas eser eži ḳils iḳed (b) i mič *eser aq̇alve*, (c) mare vodo-do miča vidläš kvin ädẏvenas, (d) ere demgvaš *rokv ǯeco*, (e) ečkad nomeg-u apišvd (Davitiani *et al.* 1957:34,27–9 apud *Hewitt* 1982:209)
(a) then QUOT that.NOM shrieking.DAT she.leads(PRS).it (b) and he.DAT QUOT *she.frightens(PRS).him*, (c) but until-not her sister.GEN soul.DAT she.may.swear(SUBJ.II).on.it (d) CNJ nothing QUOT *I/she.do/es(PRS). it.to.you* (e) till.then not-OPT he.let(AOR).her go
'(a) Then she will begin to shriek, (b) and *she will frighten you*. (e) But do not let her go (c) until she swears on her sister's soul (d) that *she will do you no harm*.' (transl. Hewitt) or: '. . . (d) I will do you no harm . . .'

I feel unable to give a reliable rule for *rok*. Hewitt (1982:211–12) suggests that one factor determining the form of reported speech in Svan is co-referentiality of referents in the reporting and dependent clauses.[60] But while person shift seems to be optional, tense shift, as far as I can see, is not: the simple aorist *adgarx* is unacceptable even with *rok(v)/lok* in:

(79) eǯnēm lekv, ere "lāt lok *adgarx/otdagrax" (*Hewitt* 1982:212)
s/he s/he.said, CNJ "yesterday QUOT
*they.killed(AOR).her/they.killed(PERF.EVID).her"
'S/He said: They killed him/her yesterday.'

because the references of "s/he" and of "they"/"him/her" are diverse. However, more data are needed to substantiate the rule.

3.4.4 The development of quotatives in Svan

The historical development may be reconstructed as follows: originally, *rok(v)* was simply "s/he said", used with direct speech. It has a transparent etymology like Georgian *metki* and *tko*, in that it has developed from *răkv* 's/he said it' (Topuria 1967:248 note 2). In the southern dialects, which have contact with the "Imeretian" type of Georgian dialects, *rok(v)* replaced *eser* in the neutral contexts where no shift is required (non-past tenses, 1st-person reporter speech). As a concomitant result, *răkv* became a clitic quotative particle and was phonetically reduced to *rok*. On the basis of partial equivalence, *rok* could extend into other areas of *eser*: on the one hand, it replaced it in semi-indirect speech, thus preserving the typical Svan form (as in (76)). On the other hand, in many contexts, it was used without shift, as it had before, with the result that *rok(v)* occurs in more instances of non-shifted direct speech.[61] This latter development could have two models, one internal and the other "external". Firstly, there is the 1st-person reporter speech with *-əž*, which never occurs with semi-indirect speech. Second, the development could be reinforced by the Georgian type of speech reporting. This latter model has the "advantage" of avoiding the neutralization of person with its specific difficulties (see 3.4.1.1). In Kartvelian, then, we have a combined geographical expansion of two types. (1) Verb forms of "to say" like Georgian *metki* and *tko* and Svan *rok(v)*, that are still etymologically transparent, replace non-transparent particles like Georgian *-o* and Svan *eser*. (2) Svan semi-indirect speech is more and more replaced by non-shifted variants that have the form of direct speech. If this is a general trend, there is no basis for the assumption that semi-indirect speech developed from direct speech without completely reaching the level of indirect speech (*Hewitt* 1982). Rather, the stricter rules of *eser* could be an archaism, while the intrusion of *rok* entails a "bleeding" of the person-shift rule.[62]

3.5 Direct speech properties in Svan semi-indirect speech

Svan semi-indirect speech has many properties that are considered typical of direct speech in languages like English.

3.5.1 Main clause privileges in Svan semi-indirect speech

Firstly, main clause privileges like vocatives, expressive elements, formulas (see (60a), (63), (76), (86a)) and the like are preserved, but their pronouns are shifted:

(80)   Sosruqvd xǎkv: "txēre, miča-v mäzig laxqeda, laīš-u eser zisx!" "Ah, γertem-u eser xakdis, ž'ēser dēm itre miča zisxs" (394,19–22)
Sosruq.ERG he.said.to.him: "wolf.NOM(= VOC), his-OPT pain.NOM it.has.come(PERF).to.him, he.drank(AOR).it-OPT QUOT blood.NOM!" — "Ah, God.ERG-OPT QUOT he.may.avert.it.(from)him(SUBJ.II), he.NOM-QUOT IMPOSS he.drinks(PRS).it his blood.DAT"
'Sosruq said to him: Wolf, my dear, please drink my blood! — O, God forbid, I cannot drink your blood.'

(81)   ōō, atx' ēser deš xārx xočēmiš (Chr 162,29 Mestia)
o, now QUOT IMPOSS they.have.it good.GEN
'O, now our matters are not in a fair way.'

This combination of speaker-indexical elements with person-shift is the real "anomaly" (*Hewitt* 1982) in Svan speech reporting: on the basis of the shift phenomena of more or less indirect speech, speaker-indexicality normally implies non-shift in other respects; in particular, no person shift would be expected in languages such as German (*Plank* 1986:296). However, it is not obvious that Svan "semi-indirect" speech is to be located somewhere on the direct-indirect speech-scale — no more so than free indirect ("experienced") speech, to which it bears some resemblance.

3.5.2 Non-verbatim reported speech in Svan

Some direct speech expressions testify to the fact that "direct speech" is not always to be understood as a realistic reproduction of reported utterances:[63] see Modern Georgian *ese da es* 'this and this' and *ama da am dros* 'at that and that time' and its Svan equivalent in:

(82) aš-i-aš eser xora (260,32)
so-and-so QUOT he.has.done(PERF).it
'He has treated me in such and such a fashion.'[64]

In examples of this type, direct speech is simply reduced to those aspects of its "original" that are intersubjectively relevant where details of place, time and action can be omitted (*Mochet* 1996:73).

3.5.3 Non-shift of deictic categories in Svan semi-indirect speech

Last but not least, deictic expressions of time and space (like "now" in (81), (90d), "today" in (91) and "tomorrow" in (69b)) are preserved, which demonstrates their difference from "person":

(83) imnär eser i däv axšgebax *lädi* (245,31 = 246,4)
why QUOT and dev.NOM he.has.assaulted(PERF).them *today*
'Why? The dev assaulted us *today* [and ate all our bread].'

Deixis includes directional semantics (as in "come" vs. "go", "bring" vs. "take"): *otqid* 's/he took it (there)' contrasts with: *oxqid* 's/he brought it' as in:

(84) šiär labar-ú eser oxqid! (244,11)
hands(GEN?) washwater.NOM-OPT QUOT he.brought(AOR).it
'Bring me water to wash my hands!'

3.6 Embedding in Svan semi-indirect speech

Most clauses and reported speech embedded in reported speech do not differ from their matrix clauses: conditional clauses (85a), complement clauses (86b) and embedded reported speech (41b) (if we take the conjunction *ere* as an indicator of embedding) are marked as semi-indirect:

(85) (a) lax ätu xăc, (b) ečka eser ibda-v lics (256,8–9)
(a) if hot he.should.have(SUBJ.I).it (b) then QUOT
he.poured(IPERF).it.on.himself-OPT water.DAT
'When you feel hot, pour the water on you.'

(86) (a) á, xiadūl eser Xvtisavar, (b) mič eser mäj xaḳu, (c) aš eser xoxal (d) i žī-v anqäd i [. . .](251,24–5)
(a) a, pleasure.diminutive QUOT Khvtisavar, (b) he.DAT QUOT what.NOM he.wants(PRS).it, (c) so QUOT he.knows(PRS).it (d) and PREV-OPT he.came(AOR) and [. . .]
'O well, Khvtisavar, you know well what I want anyway. Come on and [. . .].'

Repeated embedding poses an interesting question: how do the quotatives conditioned by the different layers of clauses interfere? Gudjedjiani and Palmaitis (1986:35) give an example:

(87) (a) mi xvēka Siḳos: (b) babas-əǯ xēka, (c) čūǯ [= ču+u+əǯ] eser atčem, (d) mič-əǯ māma xožib
(a) I I.said.to.him Siko.DAT: (b) dad.DAT-QUOT say(AOR.IMP).to.him, (c) PREV.OPT.QUOT QUOT he.mowed(AOR), (d) he.DAT-QUOT not he.can
'(a) I told Siko: (b) Tell thy dad: (c) Do mow, (d) he cannot.'

əǯ is used in (b)–(d) because the whole sentence is reported 1st-person speech. In other words, as in the examples given above, the quotative marking "percolates" into the lowest clause of the sentence. *eser* in (c), on the other hand, seems to be triggered by the second person of the imperative "(you) tell him" in (b), because it is a reported instruction (see 3.3.1). The result is double quotative marking in one and the same clause. "You" (subject of imperative) in (b) is not shifted because (a) is reported 1st-person speech; whereas "he" in (d), although it is co-referential with "I" in (a), has no 1st-person counterpart in (b) and therefore cannot appear as a 1st person. As we saw above (3.4.1.2), the rule works from the top downwards, and the resulting orientation of the lower reporting clause overrules the orientation of the higher clause.[65] Notice, however, that my own informant found a non-shifted variant of (87) (without quotative particles) more natural:

(87′) (a) mi xvēka Siḳos: "(b) babas xēka, (c) ere čvādčemas, mi mām mižib" (CG)
(a) I I.said.to.him Siko.DAT: "(b) father.DAT tell.him, (c) that he.shoud.mow(SUBJ.II), I not I.can".[66]

As *Ebert* (1986:151,156) points out, pragmatic speech-act orientation of its participants (i.e., avoidance of 3rd person for the actual speaker and hearer) is natural in even in those languages where indirect speech does not exist. (87′) is an attempt to remedy "unnaturalness" against the workings of the general rule.[67]

3.7 Svan embedded clauses without shift

Yet there seem to be exceptions: for instance the relative clause in (60g) in a final (afterthought) position has a non-shifted form without quotative. Indeed, semi-indirect speech can "fade away" in long passages of reported speech. Such a transition from semi-indirect to a long direct speech without quotative we find in:

(88) jaɣv atxʼ ēser lax čvädɣanvēns, ečkʼ ēser ɣo ka čq̇inṭ xetni i ečas Zurabū atžäx. mi eʒcvire lalsgura čǟžs, [. . .] (232,15–17)
PTCL now QUOT if she.should.become.pregnant(SUBJ.II), then QUOT PTCL PREV boy.NOM he.will.be.borne(FUT).to.her and that.DAT Zurab.NOM.OPT she.called(AOR).him. I I.will.leave(FUT).you to.sit.on(PART) horse.DAT [. . .]
'Now, if you should become pregnant, then you will give birth to a boy, and call him Zurab. I will leave you a riding horse.' [four more lines in direct speech]

But the opposite case, a transition from direct speech to indirect speech, also seems to occur: Deeters (1930:184) offers examples from the Lashkh dialect where indirect speech forms begin in the second clause of the sentence and even inside the clause. These cases still await a careful study.

3.8 The devs' speech in Svan

The devs, bad, clumsy giants in Caucasian fairy tales, have their own "language", characterised by the special particle *unq̇vs*. This particle seems to occur with direct speech only, and in the same clitic position as the quotative particles. As far as I can see, *unq̇vs* and the "normal" quotative particles are in complementary distribution:

(89) xočā-v unq̇vs ladäɣ ʒārx! (Chr 155,20–1)
good-OPT unq̇vs day.NOM you.have.it
'May you unq̇vs have a good day!' (German Guten Tag!)

(90) (a) ečka dǟv läxčvedda: (b) "jär-unq̇vs läsv ala?" — (c) "ʒʼ ēser ləmār Rosṭom." — (d) "Rosṭom eser mič atxe mād otḳvaraja ʒuɣva-te?" — (e) "mičäš-šāl xolʼ ēser mād li: (f) corev eser xaxlēna i kǟmṭexli." (235,31–5)
(a) then dev.NOM he.asked.him: (b) "who.NOM-unq̇vs he.was this.NOM?" — (c) "he.NOM QUOT he.has.been(PERF.EVID) Rostom.NOM" — (d) "Rostom.NOM QUOT he.DAT now not he.has.thrown(PERF).him sea-into?" — (e) "his-like bad.NOM QUOT not he.is: (f) swimming.NOM QUOT he.has.known(PERF).it and he.has.returned(PERF).out"
'(a) Then the dev asked him: (b) Who unq̇vs was this? (c) — I was it, Rostom. — (d) Didn't I throw Rostom into the sea now? — (e) I am not so bad as you: (f) I knew swimming and came back out of it.'[68]

(91) mäj eser xak̲u? — mäj eser i lädi moxärǯ eser ǯa li (Chr 162,20 Ipar)
what.NOM QUOT he.wants(PRS).it? — what QUOT and today
bearer.of.tribute.NOM QUOT he.NOM QUOT he.is
'[Sosruq says:] What do you want? — [The dev answers:] What else
than that you must bear me the tribute today.'

As we see in (90d) and (91), the devs otherwise use "normal Svan", including Svan semi-indirect speech in clauses without *unq̇vs* (see (90b) vs. (90c)). — Both *unq̇vs* and the quotatives signal different "voices" in speech. We may say that *unq̇vs* offers an example of overlap between the marking of speech reporting and the function of characterizing individuals or "species" — similar to the distinct language characteristics of different animals found e.g. in San ("Bushman") fairy tales (Westermann 1940:7). In a sense, speaker-indexicality is one of the functions of reported speech.

4. Conclusion

1. Georgian and Svan share some formal features of speech reporting that are quite common in the languages of the Near East and of Europe: reported speech tends to be preceded by a conjunction both with indirect and direct speech; local and temporal indexical expressions tend to be preserved in all types of reported speech; tense shift (consecutio temporum) tends to be avoided; and both languages use quotative particles that differentiate between 1st-person and non-1st-person speech reporting — a distinction that recurs in other languages of the Near East like Late Akkadian (Soden 1952 § 121b) and Elamite (Khačikjan 1998:61–2) and fits well into the picture of languages that differentiate between the epistemic status of direct experience and that of indirect experience (evidentiality). The rules for the quotative particles are based on speech act meaning, not on the morphosyntactic form of a reporting clause.

2. In spite of genetic relationship and long-lasting contact, the two languages differ in some respects: while Georgian has indirect and direct speech, with a definite preference for the latter, Svan has (free) direct speech, semi-indirect speech and indirect speech, the latter being restricted to "real" complement clauses. Svan semi-indirect speech is characterised by a shift of epistemic status category (use of evidential forms) and by a person shift. This latter shift also affects expressions known for their main clause privilege (for instance vocatives). However, semi-indirect speech is restricted to non-1st-person speech and — largely — to past tense clauses, restrictions that are related to the epistemic status of reported speech (see 3.4).

3. Person shift in Svan works from the top downwards. It is orientated

towards the actual speech act to the extent that its reporting clause is orientated towards the actual speech act. The orientation of a lower reporting clause overrules the orientation of the higher clauses.

4. Quotative particles tend to develop from verb forms of "to say" and to replace non-transparent particles. Svan semi-indirect speech tends to be replaced by the Georgian type of direct speech; it is an open question whether direct speech is more easily processed than semi-indirect speech in a face-to-face language such as Svan, but by partly neutralising the opposition of 1st, 2nd and 3rd person, it can obscure personal reference.

5. The function of the different types of speech reporting has not been studied here. But there is good reason to say that direct or semi-indirect speech is the preferred variant in the Kartvelian. This preference is no less a characteristic feature of these languages than their categorical rules, and it is a task of future research to look for other linguistic features that co-vary with this preference.

Notes

* My thanks go to the Deutsche Forschungsgemeinschaft, which supported work on part of the Svan materials on which the present study is based. I wish to express my gratitude to Ciuri Gabliani (Mestia) and Aleksandre Oniani (Georgian Academy of Sciences, Tbilisi) for their most generous and patient help over the years: they translated large portions of the Upper Bal text collections for me into Georgian. A. Oniani also kindly checked the interpretation of many Svan verb forms. However, they should not be held responsible for any misunderstandings contained in this article. I also thank Chato Gudjedjiani (Mestia) for providing me with Svan translations of some test sentences. — I am indebted to Kevin Tuite (University of Montreal) and in particular to George Hewitt (School of Oriental and African Studies, London: letter of Nov. 11th, 2000, hereafter: p.c.) for extremely valuable critical comments and corrections; to Gernot Wilhelm (University of Würzburg) for information on Akkadian and Elamite; to Robert McLaughlin (University of Oldenburg) for correcting the English of an early version of this chapter; and to Manfred von Roncador for his unending patience as an editor and, last not least, for encouraging me to write a contribution to this volume in the first place.

1. See e.g. Deeters (1930); for a recent survey see *Hewitt and Crisp* (1986).

2. See *Roncador* (1988) for a profound analysis of reference shift.

3. See e.g. *Li* (1986) for an elaboration of co-reference rules ("pronominalisation strategies").

4. See Topuria (1967:130–6; 191–3); Tuite (1997:31); Oniani (1998:205–7). For some discussion of Svan evidentials see Sumbatova (1999).

5. The most complete historical survey of Georgian direct and indirect speech is ʒiʒiguri (1973:177–207).

6. The Kartvelian languages have **polypersonal verb** forms that can be used as self-contained sentences ("pro-drop", verb-external "zero anaphora"). In the following, the glosses do not mirror the polysynthetic structure of the verb forms; for the sake of simplicity, they give a paraphrase rather than an analysis. Also, the very frequent sequence: "... said(AOR).it ..." will be simplified as: "... said ..." in the glosses.

The following abbreviations are used: Bl = Bleichsteiner 1931; CG = Ciuri Gabliani; ČG = Čato Gudjedjiani; Chr = Šaniʒe — Kaldani (edd.) 1978; Γ = Γlonṭi 1974; GrX = Marr 1911; I = G. Imnaišvili 1974; Inf = informants from Mestia; other abbreviations refer to private letter writers.

7. See the extensive study by *Kieckers* (1915–16: 14–34) with data from Armenian, Ancient and Modern Greek (in particular in the former Greek dialects of Turkey), Modern Persian, Turkish (*ki*), Lithuanian, Coptic, and many other languages. Kieckers also discusses the possibility of calquing (e.g. of a grecism in Romance languages, Old Church Slavonic and Gothic).

8. Cp. *Our Father* as a noun and Latin *tum vero suo more victoriam conclamant* (Caesar, *Bellum Gallicum* 5,37,3) 'Then they shouted "Victory!", as they were used to'. For more details see *Hahn* (1929); Boeder (1985b).

9. This history of *vitar(med)* parallels that of the Old Greek conjunction *hōs* 'how, so > that'.

10. *Qopil ars* is an analytic perfect form. It is also probable that (b) has an inferential meaning ("*from what I understand I conclude that* this has not been the common meal").

11. The Old Georgian examples of "indirect speech" cited by ʒiʒiguri (1965:97) are not particularly convincing. Complement clauses like the following involve more than simple person shift: *ubrʒane, romel ertxel cixe-d movides* (GrX LXVIII 70) command.him, CNJ once fortress-Adv he.should.come 'Tell him that he should come once to the fortress.'; *utxra Rut dedamtil-sa twis-sa, sada-igi ḳriba* (Ruth 2,19) she.told.her Ruth mother.in.law-DAT her.own-DAT, where-PTCLR she.collected 'Ruth told her mother-in-law where she had gleaned.'.

12. Xundaʒe (1901:126–30 cp. ʒiʒiguri 1965). — Schuchardt (1902:369–70) in his interesting review of this pedagogic grammar rightly stresses the natural preference for direct speech in Georgian, but he seems to have misunderstood Xundaʒe's terminology: "Es verhält sich also gerade umgekehrt wie der Verfasser meint: die direkte Rede stehe dem Georgischen nicht an; durch die angegebenen Anhängsel wird ja die Rede nicht zur indirekten." Xundaʒe distinguishes between "direct speech" (*p̣irdap̣iri mimartva*) and speech "with particles" (*naçilaḳebit*), which is *not* "indirect speech".

13. Cp. the proverb: *vai-s gaveq̇are da ui-s ševeq̇are-o* woe-DAT I.moved.away.from.it and dear.me-DAT I.met.with.it-QUOT 'I left a "Woe!", and I met with a "Dear me!"'.

14. Cp. word formations like: *zarmac-* 'lazy' < *zar-mac-* fear-it.is.laid.on.me 'I fear/hesitate to do something'); *dačemeba* 'to usurp' < *da-čem-eba* PREV-my-Suffix 'to say "it's mine"'.

15. See, however, *Hewitt and Crisp* (1986:123–8). As far as I can see, the problem of shift in reported speech is not discussed in native Georgian grammars.

16. The following example was deemed "old-fashioned" by one informant: *utxari, rom coṭa*

damagviandeba-tko (Šaniʒe 1955:106) tell.him/her, CNJ little I.will.be(FUT).late-QUOT 'Tell him/her I will be a bit late!'. See also note 30 below.

17. See ʒiʒiguri (1973:192); ǯikia (1972:192).

18. Compare the European literary tradition that shuns the constant repetition of "s/he said".

19. In this regard, the quotative particle is similar to a resumptive pronoun after postposed relative clauses of the type (60f–g) below, which is very common in the Kartvelian languages, in particular in Mingrelian.

20. In the collection of Γlonṭi (1996:256–61), only 8 out of 37 examples with -*o* are clause-final, but not postverbal; the numbers for -*tko* (see below 2.5) are: 4 out of 31, and for -*metki* : 2 out of 36.

21. ʒiʒiguri (1973:202); Boeder (1985a). — Šaniʒe (1973:610 § 650) explains this usage by invoking explicit or implicit expressions introducing the proverb: *natkvamia* and *tkmula* 'it is said', *amboben* and *iṭqvian* 'they say' (cp. Quintilianus IX 2,37 *incertae personae fictae oratio*). However, direct speech is autonomous (see 2.9).

22. The first examples of *metki* and *tko* are found in a 10th-11th cent. manuscript: *Marxvata saḵitxavebi* (ed. I. Abulaʒe apud Erteliśvili 1962:184, note 1); see also Harris and Campbell (1995:410 with note 25). — Činč̣arauli (1960:114) points out that speakers are well aware of the difference between dialects with regard to quotative particles: in one poem, a Khevsurian says: *me ḵi čamave Ḵaxeta, ḵldet magiera xenia* [. . .] "*xolme*" da "*metki*" siṭqvani satkmelad saḵvirelnia. 'But I came to Kakhetia, where there are trees instead of rocks [. . .] The use of the words *xolme* ['use to'] and *metki* is remarkable [in Kakhetia]'.

23. ʒiʒiguri (1973:446); Harris and Campbell (1995:170).

24. See ʒiʒiguri (1973:446), who interprets this as a sign of becoming "functionally opaque". — On the development of the particles *metki/tko* see Harris and Campbell (1995:168–70).

25. Quotative -*o* is not. A development *tkua* 's/he said' > *tko* > *o* (Topuria 1985:143), although it conforms to a frequent source of quotative particles (see 3.4.4), is phonetically arbitrary and in no way necessary.

26. Harris and Campbell (1995:410–11, note 30).

27. Ḵačarava (1950:256); Topuria — Gigineišvili (1970:166); ʒiʒiguri (1973:198–9), Hewitt (1984a:358).

28. Topuria and Gigineišvili (1970:165); ʒiʒiguri (1973:195; 198).

29. See Ebert (1986:155) for a Newari parallel with switch reference in clauses embedded in questions.

30. If it is the speaker of the sentence who cannot come, a different construction is preferred: *čem-ze utxari šen-s col-s, ver mova-tko* (Inf) me-on tell(AOR.IMP).it.to.her your-DAT wife-DAT, IMPOSS he.will.come-QUOT 'Tell your wife that I, the speaker, will be unable to come'. I have the impression that the use of the conjunction *rom* in (33) (see note 16 above) would suggest the reading where the "I" refers to the speaker of the sentence (*utxari*

šen-s col-s, rom ver moval-tko). If this is correct, the use of a conjunction makes reported speech more "indirect".

31. For a collection of examples, see Ḳvanṭaliani (1990:17–18); Suxišvili (1999).

32. Žikia (1972:61) assumes a zero introducer (*nulovani čamrtveli* 'null inserter') in reported dialogues without verbs of saying; for "ellipsis" see Quintilianus IX 2,37 *detractum est enim qui diceret*.

33. The deficiency of person-marking in quotative particles does not in itself contradict their verblikeness, because it occurs in many finite verb forms of languages like English, too. (For a different view, see Harris and Campbell 1995:410 note 26.)

34. A somewhat similar idea with regard to *metki/tko* is found in Harris's comment on Ȝiȝiguri's example of Kakhian: *metki gaetrie akedan* (Ȝiȝiguri 1973:446) 'I.said drag.yourself. away from.here' with *metki* in initial position, which behaves like a finite verb: "in this dialect the change is incomplete" (Harris and Campbell 1995:410 note 27). — There is not the slightest evidence, however, that (35) is the survival of an older construction (in fact, it is rather doubtful if -*o* was a "real" verb in prehistoric times). Rather, the intermediate position of the quotatives may receive several different historical interpretations. For instance, the construction in (35) could be the result of a secondary analogy between quotatives and verbs of saying.

35. It is interesting that Ḳačarava (1950:252) considers the co-occurrence of Mingrelian *mak ptkvi* = Georgian *metki vtkvi* 'QUOT I.said.it' a case of Georgian influence. *mak(i/ə)* < *ma ptkvii* corresponds exactly to *metki* < *me vtkvi* (Kipšidze 1914:142). However, Ḳačarava (1950:249) considers -*k* an "addition" (*dartuli*). The Mingrelian-Laz equivalent of -*tko* is -*šo*, which has no convincing etymology so far (but see Ḳačarava 1950:252). Only -*a* with its variants unambiguously corresponds to Georgian -*o*. Notice that -*a* occurs before clause-final conjunctions: *dovyuri-a-v-a-da, do mingaria-a* I.will.die-linking.element-QUOT-linking.element-when, and weep.for.me-QUOT 'If I die, mourn for me' (Ḳačarava 1950:255).

36. Čikobava (1936:136) also gives *deri*, which seems to be *dedi* 's/he said'. Bernt Brendemoen (University of Oslo, letter of Febr. 18th, 2000) informs me that *deri* does not occur in his Turkish dialect materials from the Atina/Pazar region.

37. For the rest of this chapter, simple numbers in the brackets refer to the volume of Upper Svan texts edited by A. Šaniȝe and V. Topuria (1939a), specifically to texts from the village of Mulakh, if not stated otherwise.

38. See e.g. Šaniȝe and Topuria (1939:267–9).

39. Cp. "*žekar*"-"*mekar*"-*šv gveš dem eser isketi* (Davitiani 1974:198,11) "I.told.you"-"you. told.me"-INSTR matter not QUOT it.will.be.done 'By saying: "I told you" and: "You told me" there is nothing done.'; *medukän xeqvămiēl i* "*dabȝandi, dabȝandi*"-*s xaǫle* (52,15–16) shopkeeper.NOM he.is(PRS).grateful.to.them and "take.a.seat, take.a.seat"-DAT he.says(PRS). to.them 'The shopkeeper was very grateful to them and said: Sit down! Sit down!', where *dab(r)ȝandi* is a Georgian polite form: as *Wigger* observes for Irish (1998:981), the foreign language of the "original speech" very strongly tends to be preserved.

40. For some attempts to describe an interaction between *ere*, quotative, and person identity relations between main and dependent clauses, see Hewitt (1982).

41. The etymology of *-əǯ* and *eser* is unknown. Topuria (1985:143) reports a proposal to connect *eser* with Armenian *aser* 's/he said', but this would not explain the syntax and position of *eser*, and I see no reason for a borrowing from this language.

42. Γlonṭi (1975:41–2), relying on information given by A. Davitiani (probably a speaker of Lower Bal), has a fourth quotative particle *oyv*, without however offering an example. According to him, *rokv* is more used with the future (*momavlis gagebis natkvami*), while *oyv* refers to past speech. This must be a misunderstanding: *oyv* is a variant of the optative particle *-u*, and if there is any time reference in these particles, *-oyv* refers to the future. On the other hand, it remains to be explained why my informants, too, sometimes mistook *-u* for a quotative particle (Georgian *-o*).

43. According to Topuria (1985:143), *-əǯ* is also used with 2nd-person speaker reporters. I could not confirm this use, but maybe it is the instructional meaning that he had in mind.

44. According to Šaraʒeniʒe (1958:248), the Lower Bal dialect of Tskhumar has *-id* instead of *-əǯ*.

45. Similarly in a text from Becho (Davitiani *et al.* 1957:54,28–30). — However, the speeches of the *kadj* (sorcerers) in an Upper Bal text from Ushguli (61,26–32) have *rok*. The speeches of three wives in a text from Mestia (Chr 168,9–10), on the other hand, all have *eser*.

46. Ivane Nižaraʒe, the author of a Russian-Svan dictionary from 1910 and originating from Ushgul, offers only *rok* as a translation of Russian *mol*! — Among the Lower Bal dialects of Upper Svanetia (see "map" at the beginning of Section 3.), most have *eser* and a few occurrences of *rok* in the texts, in particular in Etser (with old connections to the south?), while Becho (a village somewhat remote from the main valley) has almost no occurrence of *rok*. Similarly, the Upper Bal dialect texts have almost exclusively *eser* (with an average of 10 instances per page!), in particular in Mulakh (which is again "communicatively" more remote from the southern regions). — In addition to possible pragmatic and processing factors, a variational study would have to consider sociolinguistic factors as well: in the Upper Bal village of Ipar, halfway between Mulakh and Ushgul, *eser* predominates in the texts, but the members of two families seem to prefer *rok* or its preferred Lower Svan variant *lok*!

47. This is also the position of the Hittite quotative particle, see Friedrich (1960:148–9); for Kartvelian clisis, see Boeder (1994).

48. My informants tend to translate it by Georgian *tviton* 'her/himself'.

49. See Tuite (1997:43); Boeder, forthcoming.

50. There seems to be no reason, then, why *ǯa/mič-* should be "a special pronoun" (Tuite 1997:40). Its remote similarity to "long distance reflexives" and logophoric anaphora remains to be determined.

51. Cp. Gudjedjiani and Palmaitis (1986:36): "If the speaker refers to himself but is not the 1st person, forms of the 1st person cannot be used."

52. Under my interpretation, then, this example is not due to an "influence of narration on the psychic disposition of the speaker himself" (Čantlaʒe 1998:233), but a perfectly normal person shift: It is also not true that in Svan speech reporting "if the verb is 3rd person, then a pronoun must also be 3rd person, and there is no mixing" (Čantlaʒe ib. 229). — In a poetic text, a 1st-person speaker tells about his encounter with another Svan who threatens him; inspite of the 1st-person speaker's pacifying speech, the other Svan levels his gun at him and says: *dēm rokv igni ǯ' ečkad, vode / mišgva zisxs rokv do läjtəre!* (Šaniʒe et al. 1939b:66, no. 21, 21–3) not QUOT he.will.stand.there he.NOM so.long, as /*my* blood.DAT QUOT not he.will.drink. it 'I will stay here until/I drink *your* blood!'. Čantlaʒe (1998:229) finds fault with the Georgian translation, which has "*your* blood", as in English, whereas Svan has "*my* blood". But this is exactly what we expect: the Svan pronoun is orientated towards the understood reporting clause: "he said to *me*", whereas the Georgian and English translations have the pronouns of direct speech. The 1st-person of direct speech ("*I* will stay"), on the other hand, is shifted, because its counterpart is 3rd person in the understood reporting clause ("*He* said...").

53. Still, there may be examples that do not fit into the picture. For example, one informant offered me: *lāt eʒnem mākvin: "məxär eser qedni mišgva-te"* (Inf) yesterday s/he.ERG s/he.said.to.me: "tomorrow QUOT s/he.comes(PRS) me.to" 'Yesterday, s/he said to me: I will come to you tomorrow', where the 2nd person ("to you") of the reported clause is correctly shifted to 1st person because it refers to the (actual) speaker ("to me"), whereas the 1st-person subject of the underlying reported clause is shifted to 3rd person because it refers to a non-participant of the speech act ("s/he said"). Afterwards, however, my informant corrected *mišgvate* into *isgvate* 'to.you', with the speaker-addressee reversal typical of direct speech. But the reported clause refers to the future, where the "underlying" direct speech variant *qvedni isgvate* 'I.come to.you' is an option according to the rule. So the correction could be a contamination of the two admissible versions (semi-indirect speech with *qedni mišgvate* and non-shifted direct speech with *qedni isgvate*.

54. "Hand in Hand mit der Personenverschiebung geht eine Tempusverschiebung."

55. See *Boeder* (2000).

56. It is a common feature of evidentiality that it is optional with non-past tenses (Kozinceva 1994:100) and that "it is not marked in future, and there is typically no secondhand specification in present tense" (Aikhenvald and Dixon 1998:247).

57. A sentence like: *si ḁele, ere emčedēlxi* you you.say(PRS), CNJ you.went(PERF.EVID) 'you say that you went' (*Hewitt* 1982:212) is unacceptable and must be marked by *lok*. On the other hand, speakers do not give their assertions about themselves a "hearsay" or inferential status (except in rare cases where they were unconscious of what they did). For similar reasons, an evidential form would be strange in: *mi ʒaḁle (ere) c̣igns-iʒ xvič̣vdānis* I I.say(PRS).it.to.you (CNJ) book.DAT-QUOT I.was.reading(IPERF).it 'I tell you that I was reading the book' (ib. p. 211).

58. Compare the following examples elicited by *Hewitt* (1982:211): *mi ʒaḁle (ere) lāt-iʒ adgarx / otdagrax* I I.say(PRS).to.you (CNJ) yesterday-QUOT they.killed(AOR).her/they.apparently.killed(PERF.EVID).her 'I tell you that they killed her yesterday/that they apparently killed her yesterday'.

59. This is perhaps what *Hewitt* (1982:211) had in mind: "Where the main verb's subject

is 1st person, the inferentials will not be used if that same 1st person functions in any way within the dependent clause, otherwise the inferential necessarily indicates that the information is hearsay or inferred in some way".

60. *Hewitt*'s comment on (79) is: "if the main verb's subject is not a participant in the dependent clause, then not only may the speech-particle be omitted, but it is no longer obligatory to substitute the inferential for the indicative" (1982:212).

61. Čanṭlaʒe (1998:233–4) gives some examples where the Lashkh text of Arsena Oniani has *lok* with direct speech, whereas its Upper Bal translation, again with *lok*, has person shift. However, as the contexts are unavailable to me, I am unable to check their relevance here.

62. G. Hewitt (p.c.) rightly points out to me that the two possibilities are not necessarily mutually exclusive: "failure to develop fully *oratio obliqua and* contamination from (say) Georgian, with its preference for *oratio recta*". But disregarding glottogonic speculation, I do not see any indication of an earlier stage when Svan had no (or less) "indirectness" in reported speech.

63. For a detailed study of direct speech elements that cannot reproduce an "original" speech "realistically", see *Roncador* (1988:88–126).

64. Cp. *ečīš-i-ečī* 'so (and so) much' (332,20); *ependis eser miča bedži amži-amži läir oxzɔza* [...] (369,18) efendi.DAT QUOT her concerning so-so letter.NOM he.has.written(PERF).it 'The efendi wrote *such and such a letter* about you [...]' (cp. 52,26 Lendjer).

65. The rule given by Gudjedjiani and Palmaitis (1986:35–6) reads as follows: "If the speaker mentions himself in the 3rd person [aз iu (d)], -ǯ and *eser* are to be used together, -ǯ relating to the 1st and *eser*–to the 2nd or to the 3rd person. [...] As can be seen, direct speech is used in Svan when it is double, i.e. when one quotation is subordinated to another." The term "direct speech" seems to be applied here in the sense of "non-shift of person", but I do not see how this applies to (c) and (d).

66. For G. Hewitt (p.c.), "this looks suspiciously like a "foreign" influence in order to avoid the complexities discussed earlier [in this article]. One could well imagine a Georgian saying: *me vutxari Siḳos: mamas utxari, rom momḳas — me ar šemiʒlia(-metki)* 'I I.told.him Siko.DAT: father.DAT tell.him, that he.shall.mow(SUBJ.II) — I not I.am.able.to(-QUOT)' in order to avoid having to sort out to logically anticipated, but actually impermissible: * ... *mamas utxari-metki, momḳi-tko-metki — me ar šemiʒlia-metki* ... father.DAT tell.him-QUOT, mow(IMP)-QUOT-QUOT I not I.am.able.to-QUOT".

67. For some discussion, see *Roncador* (1988:122).

68. Other examples: 162,23; 240,27; 243,34; 245,13; 16; 390,25sqq.; Chr 154,1; 10; 12; 18–20.

References

Abesaʒe, Nia. 1978. "Grʒnobis da tkma-brʒanebis gamomxaṭvel zmnata šemcveli kvecqobili çinadadebebi Svanurši". *Tbilisis Universiṭeṭis Šromebi* 200: 5–20.

Aikhenvald, Alexandra Y. and R. W. W. Dixon 1998: "Evidentials and areal typology: a case study from Amazonia". *Language Studies* 20: 241–57.
Bleichsteiner, Robert. 1919. *Kaukasische Forschungen. Erster Teil: Georgische und mingrelische Texte* (Osten und Orient. Erste Reihe: Forschungen 1). Wien: Verlag des Forschungsinstituts für Osten und Orient.
Boeder, Winfried. 1982. Review of I. Tevdoraʒe: *Kartuli prozodiis saḳitxebi* 1978. *Bedi Kartlisa* 40: 384–6.
Boeder, Winfried. 1985a. "La structure du proverbe géorgien". *Revue des Etudes Géorgiennes et Caucasiennes* 1: 97–115.
Boeder, Winfried. 1985b. "Zur Grammatik des Vokativs in den Kartwelsprachen", In Ursula Pieper and Gerhard Stickel (eds.): *Studia Linguistica Diachronica et Synchronica. Werner Winter Sexagenario Anno MCMLXXXIII gratis animis ab eius collegis, amicis discipulisque oblata*. Berlin, New York and Amsterdam: Mouton de Gruyter, 55–80.
Boeder, Winfried. 1993–94. "Semantisch-pragmatische Tendenzen in der Entwicklung der altgeorgischen Satzgefüge". *Iberiul-Ḳavḳasiuri Enatmecnierebis Ċeliċdeuli/Annual of Ibero-Caucasian Linguistics* 20/21: 24–46.
Boeder, Winfried. 1994. "Kartvelische und indogermanische Syntax: Die altgeorgischen Klitika". In Roland Bielmeier and Reinhard Stempel unter Mitarbeit von René Lanzweert (eds.): *Indogermanica et Caucasica. Festschrift für Karl Horst Schmidt zum 65. Geburtstag* (Untersuchungen zur indogermanischen Sprach- und Kulturwissenschaft 6). Berlin and New York: de Gruyter, 447–71.
Boeder, Winfried. 2001. "Protasis und Apodosis in den Kartvelsprachen". In *Varlam Topuriu 100*. Tbilisi: Tbilisis Universiṭeṭis gamomcemloba, 31–45
Boeder, Winfried, forthcoming. "Anapher im Swanischen".
Čanṭlaʒe, Iza. 1998. *Kartvelologiuri ʒiebani* I. Tbilisi: Kartuli Ena.
Čikobava, Arnold. 1936: *Čanuris gramaṭiḳuli analizi ṭeksṭebiturt/Analyse grammaticale du dialecte tchane (laze) avec les textes*. Ṭpilisi: SSRḲ Mecnierebata Aḳademiis Sakartvelos Pilialis gamocema.
Činčarauli, Aleksi. 1960. *Xevsurulis taviseburebani. Ṭeksṭita da indeksit*. Tbilisi: Sakartvelos SSR Mecnierebata Aḳademiis gamocemloba.
Davitiani, Aleksi. 1974. *Svanuri andazebi*. Aḳaḳi Saniʒisa da Maksime Kaldanis redakciit (Masalebi Kartvelur enata šesċavlisatvis V). Tbilisi: Mecniereba.
Davitiani, Aleksi, Varlam Topuria and Maksime Kaldani. 1957. *Svanuri prozauli ṭeksṭebi* II. *Balskvemouri ḳilo/Svanskie prozaičeskie teksty II. Nižnebal'skoe narečie* (Masalebi Kartvelur enata šesċavlisatvis III). Tbilisi: Mecniereba.
Deeters, Gerhard. 1930. *Das kharthwelische Verbum. Vergleichende Darstellung des Verbalbaus der südkaukasischen Sprachen* (Sächsische Forschungsinstitute in Leipzig. Forschungsinstitut für Indogermanistik, Sprachwissenschaftliche Abteilung. Band 1). Leipzig: Markert & Petters.
Doliʒe, Givi. 1975. *Xevsuruli ṭeksṭebi (leksiḳoniturt)/Chevsurskie teksty*. Tbilisi: Tbilisis Universiṭeṭis gamomcemloba.
Ʒiʒiguri, Šota. 1956. *Kartuli dialekṭebis kresṭomatia leksiḳoniturt*. Tbilisi: Samecnierometoduri Ḳabineṭis gamomcemloba
Ʒiʒiguri, Šota. 1965. "'Iribi meṭqvelebis' dasacavad". *Cisḳari* 1965,7: 94–101.

ʒiʒiguri, Šota. 1973. *Ḳavširebi Ḳartul enaši/Conjunctions in the Georgian Language.* Tbilisi: Tbilisis universiṭeṭis gamomcemloba.
Ǯikia, Neli. 1972. "Sxvata siṭq̇va Ḳartulši"/Čužaja reč' v gruzinskom jazyke. *Ḳartuli Ena da Liṭeraṭura Sḳolaši* 1972,2: 59–63.
Ǯikia, Neli. 1976. "Naçilaḳiani p̣irdap̣iri natkvamis sçavleba VIII ḳlasši"/Izučenie prjamoj reči s časticej v VIII klasse. *Ḳartuli Ena da Liṭeraṭura Sḳolaši* 1976,4: 23–6.
Ertelišvili, Parnaoz. 1962 [1963]. *Rtuli çinadadebis isṭoriisatvis Ḳartulši I: Hip̣oṭaksis saḳitxebi* (Axali Ḳartuli Enis Ḳatedris Šromebi 4). Tbilisi: Tbilisis Universiṭeṭis gamomcemloba.
Friedrich, Johannes. 1960. *Hethitisches Elementarbuch. 1. Teil: Kurzgefaßte Grammatik.* Zweite, verbesserte und erweiterte Auflage. Heidelberg: Winter.
Γlonṭi, Aleksandre. 1974. *Ḳartuli zyap̣rebi. Šeadgina, šesavali da šenišvnebi daurto A. Glonṭma.* Tbilisi: Ganatleba.
Γlonṭi, Aleksandre. 1975. "Sxvata siṭq̇vis o dialogši". In *Xalxuri p̣rozis enisa da sṭilis saḳitxebi/Voprosy jazyka i stilja narodnoj prozy.* Tbilisi: Tbilisis Universiṭeṭis gamomcemloba, 39–43.
Γlonṭi, Aleksandre. 1996. *Ḳartuli çinadadeba. Savaržiso masala sinṭaksši.* Meotxe ševsebuli gamocema. Tbilisi: Ganatleba.
Gudjedjiani, Chato and Mykolas L. Palmaitis. 1986. *Upper Svan: Grammar and texts*/Čato Gudžedžiani and Mykolas L. Palmaitis: *Aukštutinių Svanų kalbos gramatika su tekstų pavydžiais* (Kalbotyra XXXVII (4) Kalbų aprašai: Svanų kalba). Vilnius: Mokslas.
Hale, Kenneth. 1975. "Gaps in grammar and culture". In M. Dale Kinkade, Kenneth L. Hale and Oswald Werner (eds.): *Linguistics and Anthropology. In Honor of C.F. Voegelin.* Lisse: Peter de Ridder Press, 295–315.
Harris, Alice C. and Lyle Campbell. 1995. *Historical Syntax in Cross-Linguistic Perspective* (Cambridge Studies in Linguistics 74). Cambridge: Cambridge University Press.
Imnaišvili, Grigol. 1974. *Ḳartluri dialekṭi II: Ṭeksṭebi.* Tbilisi: Mecniereba.
Imnaišvili, Ivane. 1975. *Sinuri mravaltavi. Gamoḳvleva da leksiḳoni/Sinajskij mnogoglav (pervaja gruzinskaja datirovannaja rukopis' 864 goda. Issledovanie i slovar')* (3veli Ḳartuli Enis Ḳatedris Šromebi 17). Tbilisi: Tbilisis Universiṭeṭis gamomcemloba.
Ḳaçarava, Giorgi. 1950. "Sxvata siṭq̇vis naçilaḳebi Ḳartulsa da Zanurši (Megrul-Zanurši)" /Časticy kosvennoj reči v gruzinskom i zanskom (megrel'sko-čanskom) jazykach. *Sṭudenṭta samecniero šromebis ḳrebuli* 5: 242–57.
Khačikjan, Margaret. 1998. *The Elamite Language* (Documenta Asiana 4). Roma: Consiglio Nazionale delle Richerche, Istituto per gli Studi Micenei ed Egeo-Anatolici.
Kipšidze, I. 1914. *Grammatika mingrel'skago (iverskago) jazyka s" chrestomatieju i slovarem"* (Materialy po jafetičeskomu jazykoznaniju VII). S.-Peterburg": Tipografija Imperatorskoj akademii nauk".
Kozinceva, Natalija A.. 1994. "Kategorija évidential'nosti (problemy tipologičeskogo analiza)", *Voprosy Jazykoznanija* 1994,3: 92–104.
Kutscher, Silvia, Johanna Mattissen and Anke Wodarg. 1995. *Das Mutʿafi-Lazische* (Arbeitspapier Nr. 24 (Neue Folge)). Köln: Institut für Sprachwissenschaft, Universität Köln.
Ḳvanṭaliani, Leila. 1990. *Ḳartuli zep̣iri meṭq̇velebis sinṭaksis saḳitxebi.* Tbilisi: Mecniereba.

Marr, Nikolaj Ja. 1911. *Georgij Merčul*": *Žitie sv. Grigorija Chandzt'ijskago*. Gruzinskij tekst". Vvedenie, izdanie, perevod" N. Marra [. . .]. S.-Peterburg".
Oniani, Aleksandre. 1998. *Svanuri ena (ponologiisa da morpologiis saḳitxebi)* (Kartvelologiuri biblioteḳa 2). Tbilisi: Sulxan-Saba Orbelianis saxelobis Tbilisis Saxelmçipo P̣edagogiuri Universiṭeṭis gamomcemloba.
Šaniʒe, Aḳaḳi. 1955. *Kartuli enis gramaṭiḳa*. Naçili II: *Sinṭaksi martlçeris saḳitxebiturt* (VII– VIII ḳlasis saxelmʒɣvanelo). Tbilisi: Saxelgami.
Šaniʒe, Aḳaḳi. 1973. *Kartuli enis gramaṭiḳis sapuʒvlebi* I. *Morpologia*. Meore gamocema. Tbilisi: Tbilisis Universiṭeṭis gamomcemloba.
Šaniʒe, Aḳaḳi and Maksime Kaldani (eds.). 1978. *Svanuri kresṭomatia*. *Ṭeksṭebi šeḳribes A. Šaniʒem, M. Kaldanma da Z. Ĉumburiʒem* (3veli Kartuli Enis Ḳatedris Šromebi 21). Tbilisi: Tbilisis Universiṭeṭis gamocemloba.
Šaniʒe, Aḳaḳi and Varlam Topuria (eds.). 1939a. *Svanuri prozauli ṭeksṭebi* I. *Balszemouri ḳilo*. *Ṭeksṭebi šeḳribes A. Šaniʒem da V. Topuriam* (Masalebi Kartvelur enata šesçavlisatvis I). Tbilisi: SSRḲ Mecnierebata Aḳademiis Sakartvelos Pilialis gamomcemloba.
Šaniʒe, A., V. Topuria and M. Gužežiani (eds.). 1939b. *Svanuri poezia* I: *Simɣerebi*. *Ṭeksṭebi šeḳribes da Kartulad targmnes Aḳaḳi Šaniʒem, Varlam Topuriam, Meri Gužežianma/ Poésie svane I: Chansons recueillies et traduites en géorgien par A. Chanidzé, V. Topouria et M. Goudjedjiani* (Masalebi Kartvelur enata šesçavlisatvis II). Tbilisi: SSRḲ Mecnierebata Aḳademiis Sakartvelos Pilialis gamomcemloba.
Šaraʒeniʒe, Tinatin. 1946. "Uarqopiti naçilaḳebi Svanurši"/ Otricatel'nye časticy v svanskom jazyke. *Iberiul-Ḳavḳasiuri Enatmecniereba* 1: 289–328.
Šaraʒeniʒc, Tinatin. 1958. "Svanuri enis Cxumaruli ḳiloḳavis ʒiritadi taviseburebani"/ Osobennosti cchumarskogo podgovora svanskogo jazyka. *Iberiul-ḳavḳasiuri Enatmecniereba* 9–10: 221–50.
Schuchardt, Hugo. 1902. Review of Xundaʒe 1901. *Wiener Zeitschrift für die Kunde des Morgenlandes* 16: 362–79.
Soden, Wofram von. 1952. *Grundriß der Akkadischen Grammatik*. Roma: Pontificium Institutum Biblicum.
Suxišvili, Murman. 1999. "Meṭqvelebis semanṭiḳis gardamaval zmnata sinṭaksisatvis". *Enatmecnierebis Saḳitxebi* 1: 73–9.
Sumbatova, Nina. 1999. "Evidentiality, transitivity and split ergativity. Evidence from Svan". In Werner Abraham and Leonid Kulikov (eds.): *Tense–aspect, Transitivity and Causativity. Essays in honour of Vladimir Nedjalkov*. Edited by (Studies in Language Companion Series 50). Amsterdam/Philadelphia: Benjamins, 63–95.
Topuria, Varlam. 1967. *Svanuri ena* I. *Zmna/Svanskij jazyk I. Glagol* (Varlam Topuria: *Šromebi* I /*Trudy I*). Tbilisi: Mecniereba.
Topuria, Varlam. 1985. "Svanskij jazyk", *Iberiul-Ḳavḳasiuri Enatmecnierebis Ĉeliçdeuli/ Annual of Ibero-Caucasian Linguistics* 12:100–148
Topuria, Varlam and Ivane Gigineišvili. 1970. "Sxvata siṭqvis martlçeris saḳitxebi". In *Tanamedrove Kartuli saliṭeraṭuro enis normebi*. P̣irveli ḳrebuli. Tbilisi: Mecniereba, 161–7.
Tuite, Kevin. 1997. *Svan* (Languages of the World. Materials 139). München — Newcastle: LINCOM EUROPA

Westermann, Diedrich. 1940. *Afrikanische Tabusitten in ihrer Einwirkung auf die Sprachgestaltung* (Abhandlungen der Preußischen Akademie der Wissenschaften 1939. Phil.-hist. Klasse Nr. 12). Berlin: Verlag der Akademie der Wissenschaften.

Xundaʒe, Silovan. 1901. *Saliṭeraṭuro Kartuli*. Silov. Xundaʒis gamoḳvleva. Kutaisi: Ḳilaʒisa da Xelaʒis sṭamba.

CHAPTER 2

Self-quotation in German
Reporting on past decisions[*]

Andrea Golato
University of Illinois at Urbana-Champaign

1. Introduction

Using conversation analysis as methodology, this chapter studies some aspects of the phenomenon of reported discourse in everyday spoken German. It has been observed that reported discourse is such a widespread phenomenon, in German and in other languages, probably because so much of our talk consists of relating to coparticipants what others have said before (*Bakhtin* 1981, *Parmentier* 1993). Goffman notes that it is part of our social life and society in general: "This embedding capacity is part of something more general: our linguistic ability to speak of events at any remove in time and space from the situated present" (Goffman 1981:3). Based upon an analysis of German conversational data, this study defines reported discourse in a much broader sense than many other studies, in that here it refers to introducing both talk and body behavior of other speakers or of oneself into a current conversation. It shows that reported discourse is more than just a grammatical topic: I will demonstrate that it is an interactional and social phenomenon and that particular grammatical forms are used by speakers for particular interactional functions. Specifically, I will show that according to the given interactional activity (in this instance troubles-tellings) speakers systematically use specific quotatives and quotes. Likewise, I will show evidence that the coparticipants in the aforementioned interactional activity will respond in an equally systematic fashion. I will argue that the overall context of reported discourse and reported discourse itself are collaboratively constructed by speaker and listener.

Reported discourse is often defined as a report of something someone else has said before, and it can also be extended in its definition to include internal discourse. This chapter, however, will focus on the aspect of self-quotation or self-reporting and examine particular instances in which speakers are quoting themselves. One such everyday speech situation in which self-quotation is abundant is that of reporting on decisions within troubles-tellings. I will present typical data segments in which a speaker reports on a decision. It will become apparent that the quotative is always given in the present perfect tense (the German conversational past tense, equivalent to the English simple past) while the quote itself is given in the form of direct discourse in the present tense. I will argue that in reporting a past decision, the speaker takes a past event (as indicated by the context and the quotative in the German conversational past tense) and makes it more immediate for the coparticipants (by using present tense direct discourse along with deictic markers). In so doing, the speaker casts the coparticipant as a witness of the decision and thus allows him or her to give an assessment of the decision. In connection with this interpretation, I will discuss the sequence, turn shape, and interactional achievement associated with reporting on decisions. In a last step I will show that this phenomenon not only exists in German but also in English and Modern Greek.

2. Data collection and transcription

For the present study, I analyzed 17 hours of unsolicited spontaneous video-taped face-to-face interaction, and 9 hours of audio-taped telephone conversation.[1] Altogether, 58 different speakers were recorded from various regions in Germany (Brandenburg, Hamburg, Mannheim, Würzburg, Köln, Pirmasens, and Konstanz). Most speakers are from either middle class or upper middle class. For analysis, the data were transcribed according to the transcription method developed by Jefferson (1983, 1985). See also Sacks, Schegloff, and Jefferson (1974: appendix) for an early description of the transcription notation and Atkinson and Heritage (1984:ix–xvi) for a more detailed version. For the sake of accessibility and readability, the transcripts were simplified in that a more standard orthography was used in the present chapter.[2] Each line of the transcript consists of two lines: the top one, in italics, shows the original German utterance, while the bottom line gives an idiomatic English translation. The following transcription notations were used: materials within slashes were uttered in overlap; an "h" in parentheses indicates a laugh token within a word; a period within parentheses shows a micropause; material between pointed brackets indicates speech spoken at a faster rate; underlining indicates special emphasis or stress; and finally, brackets above the speech line indicate nonverbal behavior.

3. Reporting on decisions, sequence, relevant next turn

As is apparent from the literature on decision-making in general (Bargiela-Chiappini and Harris 1995; Chappell 1995; Condon 1986; Henderson and Jurma

1981; *Lancy* 1980; Liberman 1990; Manzo 1996; Mehan 1990; Ravnholt 1995) and on decisions, solutions, and advice-giving in troubles-telling (Jefferson 1984b, 1984c; Jefferson and Lee 1992; Heritage and Sefi 1992), the research focuses primarily on the *process* of advice-giving and advice-receiving in troubles-tellings and on the *process* of decision-making. To my knowledge there is currently no research on retrospective talk on decision-making. In other words, it has yet to be studied how speakers refer back to decisions and solutions negotiated in previous conversations. In my data, I have so far found only one way of referring back to decisions reached in earlier conversations, and this was through the use of reported discourse.[3] This study will show that reported discourse is used for referring back to former decisions and that there is a particular sequence associated with reporting on past decisions:

(a) troubles-telling on part of the speaker,
(b) troubles-recipiency (Jefferson 1984c: 351), that is, acknowledgment or assessment of the trouble by the recipient,
(c) reporting on a decision on the part of the speaker, and
(d) evaluation of the decision by the recipient.

These sequential components are indicated by an arrow and a corresponding letter (a–d) in the left margin of the decision-reporting data segment below.[4] After the presentation of the segment, I discuss each of the components in a separate section. In my analysis, I refer back to this segment but I also introduce very brief outtakes of other data segments in order to support my line of analysis.

Kirsten and her sister-in-law have been talking about financial matters, first about Rita's recent moving expenses and now, in this segment, Kirsten tells her sister-in-law Rita about her dilapidated fence and the action she and her husband decided to take. Kent, the person mentioned in line 2, is Kirsten's husband.

(1) Kirsten [B2: 145–50]
⇒ a 1 K: Aber bei uns kommt auch wieder wat. Unser *Zaun* fällt
But with us something is coming up, too. Our *fence*
⇒ a 2 K: draußen zusa(h)mmen. He. Kent hat so ne olle Hecke
outside is colla(h)psing. He. Kent yanked out an old hedge
⇒ a 3 K: rausjerissen am Wochene(h)nde. Und //jetz//
last weeke(h)nd. And //now//
4 Ri: //°Ja°//
//°Yes°//
smile voice
_____|_____
⇒ a 5 K: stellte sich raus, daß dahinter der ja(h)nze Zaun
it turns out that behind it the who(h)le fence

```
                         smile voice
                         ┌─────┴─────┐
⇒  a  6  K:  von Termiten total zerfressen wird. > Der war ja
             is eaten up entirely by termites. It was anyway
⇒  a  7  K:  sowieso schon schief und< krumm, aber jetzt fällt er
             already leaning and< crooked but now it is
⇒  a  8  K:  so richtich in sich zusammen. Jedes Wochenende repariert
             really collapsing. Each weekend he repairs
⇒  a  9  K:  er ein Zaunfeld und dann fällt's nächste wieder ei(h)n,
             one area of the fence and then the next colla(h)pses,
⇒  a 10  K:  weeßte.
             you know.
⇒  b 11  Ri: //A:ch Gott! hhhe//
             //O:h God! hhhe//
⇒  c 12  K:  //hhhhe Ham wir// jesacht,
             //hhhhe We// said
⇒  c 13  K:  müssen wir im Herbst mal sehn,
             we have to see in the fall that we
                         smile voice
                         ┌─────┴─────┐
⇒  c 14  K:  daß wir dat Ding ersetzen.
             exchange that thing.
     15      (.)
     16  K:  //Is im//mer sowas Blödes, weil, dat
             //It's //always something stupid because it
     17  Ri: //mhm//
             //uhum//
     18  K:  interessiert mich überhaupt nich, nen Zaun zu ersetzen!
             does not interest me at all to exchange a fence!
     19  K:  Da würd ich lieber irgendwie wat anderet damit
             I would rather somehow do something different with it
     20  K:  machen mit dem Geld ja. he he he
             with the money, right. he he he
⇒  d 21  Ri: Ja gut, //aber muß denn wahr//scheinlich
             Alright,//but this probably// has to
⇒  d 22  K:  //Aber mußte machen//
             //But you have to do it//
⇒  d 23  Ri: doch sein //da, oder?
             be done //right?
     24  K:  //Mußte, sonst kriegste auch Ärger.
             //You must, otherwise you are in trouble.
```

3.1 The troubles-telling

As mentioned above, the first component (a) of the sequence is that of the troubles-telling, i.e., the recounting of some problem, trouble, or annoyance which occurred in the speaker's past. In this data segment, the troubles-telling occurs in lines 1–10, in which Kirsten defines a financial problem (a collapsing fence) that she and her husband face. Immediately before the segment described above, Kirsten and Rita had been talking about the expenses involved in Rita's recent move, thus Kirsten's talk in line 1 *Aber bei uns kommt auch wieder wat* 'But with us something is coming up, too' refers back to the topical talk of money and expenses. Kirsten describes to Rita how her husband discovered that the fence was rotting (lines 2–8) and was beyond repair (lines 8–10). Note that her description of the trouble contains laugh tokens and that part of her description is given in smile voice. In doing so she is signaling that she is coping with the problem.

It appears that in troubles-talk, laughing troubles-tellers are doing a recognizable sort of job. They are exhibiting that, although there is this trouble, it is not getting the better of them; they are managing; they are in good spirits and in a position to take the trouble lightly (Jefferson 1984c: 351).

3.2 Troubles-recipiency

The sequentially relevant next (and preferred) action after a speaker has completed a troubles-telling is for the interlocutor to express "troubles-recipiency" (Jefferson 1984c: 351). In other words, the preferred next action for the recipient is to acknowledge the trouble, to take it seriously and to address his or her talk to it. This means that when a recipient laughs during a telling (as described above) the respondent usually declines to laugh and instead gives a serious response (Jefferson 1984c: 350). If he or she does join in the laughter it is because a "buffer-topic" (Jefferson 1984c: 351) was introduced into the conversation as a "time out for pleasantries" (Jefferson 1984c: 351). We can see that in line 11 (arrow b) of the above data segment, Rita first gives a serious response to the problem *A:ch Gott!* 'Oh God!' in overlap with Kirsten's talk. Rita is thereby producing the second component (b) of the sequence, acknowledging the existence of the trouble and thereby expressing troubles-receptiveness. Moreover, by uttering *A:ch Gott!* 'Oh God!' in line 11 Rita is also expressing pity or empathy. Interestingly, this is followed by a short laugh token, which is contrary to what one would expect since no buffer-topic has been introduced by the troubles-teller. Note, however, that Kirsten set up the troubles-telling like a scene from a slap-stick movie: Her husband is repairing one part of the fence while the next part of the fence is collapsing. In doing so she is inviting laughter from her coparticipant. In general, recipients of the troubles-telling express their troubles-recipiency by acknowledging the trouble, addressing serious talk to the trouble or, in some instances, by uttering an assessment of the trouble (Auer and Uhmann 1982:25, Pomerantz 1984:63, and *Vlatten* 1997:125).

3.3 Reporting the decision

The next component of the overall sequence is the report on the decision itself (element c). Going back to data segment (1), we can see that the reported decision can be found in lines 12–14 (arrow c). In overlap with Rita's acknowledgment of the problem, Kirsten here produces a decision or solution to the problem: *Ham wir jesacht, müssen wir im Herbst mal sehn, daß wir dat Ding ersetzen* 'We said we have to see in the fall that we exchange that thing'. Note that the decision is cast in the form of reported discourse. Tannen (1983:364) observes that decisions can be presented in this format, and *Firle* (1988:179) points out that reported discourse or experienced discourse occurs in written texts when the characters in a story face difficulties and have to work out unpleasant experiences. In the segment above, the quotative itself is in present perfect, which is the conversational past tense of German, and the quote is rendered in direct discourse. In the study of literary texts, the use of *historical present*, i.e. a present tense verb when logically a past tense verb would be expected, is linked with making a story more dramatic (Fleischman 1990; Schiffrin 1981:59), similarly, *Johnstone* (1987:35) and Wolfson (1978:19) observe that a quotative can be used in conversational English in the present tense in order to give the impression that the quoting person is reliving the event he or she is talking about. Moreover, it is the switch of tenses that seems to separate important events from each other (Wolfson 1978:220). Note that in this study the quotative is in the past tense and only the quoted material is rendered in present tense. By rendering the decision in this way, one can argue that the speaker is making the past situation more immediate and is making it available for judgment or assessment. Put differently, while the situation is clearly marked as an event in the past, the decision (the quote itself) is delivered in present tense direct discourse as an on-line decision, as if it were a decision made at the moment of speaking. *Scheidweiler* (1991:341) also observes this switching of tenses, albeit in written German texts, especially those in which internal mental processes are described. He likewise notes:

> Vergangene Ereignisse werden so intensiv nachvollzogen, daß sie sprachlich vergegenwärtigt werden. Hierzu muß der lebendigere, ausdruckskräftigere Ind. Präs. eingesetzt werden. Konjunktive wirken abstrakter und haben einen literarischen Beigeschmack [Past experiences are relived so intensely that they are made present in the language. In order to do so the more lively and more expressive present indicative has to be used. Subjunctive forms have a far more abstract effect and taste of literary language; translation mine].

A noteworthy aspect of the production of the decision is the form of the quotative itself. In data segment 1, the verb of saying in the quotative is given in the first person plural, and in fact Kirsten is reporting on a situation both she and her husband had to face. It is relatively safe to assume that the couple did not suddenly and in unison utter the sentence *Ham wir jesacht, müssen wir im Herbst mal sehn, daß wir dat Ding ersetzen* 'We said we have to see in the fall that we exchange that thing'; it is far more likely that there was first a process of discussion concerning what decision to make. However, in the segment above it is not the *decision-making process* that is reported on (such a process might include listing several arguments in favor or against a possible decision, and weighing options). Rather, it is the *decision itself* that gets reported and subsequently commented on by the interlocutor. Thus *Ham wir jesacht, müssen wir im Herbst mal sehn, daß wir dat Ding ersetzen* 'We said we have to see in the fall that we exchange that thing' (lines 13–14) expresses the consensus Kirsten and her husband Kent reached when talking about the dilapidated fence, and not the decision-making process which led to that consensus. My data show that different speakers have different styles of reporting on couple-decisions; some use the first person plural while others use the first person singular in the quotative, as is the case in the following data segment. Here, Rita is telling her sister-in-law Kirsten about the troubles she and her husband Udo faced when they wanted to organize their move to a city approximately 250 miles away. Rita and Udo were quoted a price of 2000 marks (approximately $1200) for renting the equivalent of a U-haul — a price that seems extraordinarily high. The following segment shows the couple's decision which she reports using the first person singular (*ich* 'I'):

(2)   Kirsten [B2 020–3]
⇒ 1 Ri: Da hab ich gesacht, das mach ich
            there I said I won't do that!
    2 Ri: //>nich! Seh ich nich ein!<//
            //>I don't see the point! <//
    3 K: //.hhhhh hhhhh//
            //.hhhhh hhhhh//
    4 Ri: Soviel ham wer- also, soviel wertvolle
            We don't have that much- well, we don't
    5 Ri: Sachen ham wir nich.
            have that many valuables.

Again, this decision is one that clearly affected both husband and wife (incidentally, they are both packing up boxes at the moment Kirsten and Rita are talking) yet the decision is reported as one made by Rita herself. The choice of either pronoun does not seem to be linked to the gender of the speaker since both men and women use both persons (*ich* 'I' and *wir* 'we') in my data. I do not wish to give the impression that only decisions made by couples are referred back to, as speakers also refer back to their own personal decisions which did not involve their significant other. In the following data segment, for instance, Heiner describes a trip to the movies with friends and children who cannot seem to agree on a movie they want to see. He reports on his decision to this "trouble" by using a quotative in the first person singular:

(3) Kirsten 2 [A 021]
1 H: Und da hab ich gesacht: >Na gut, o.k., is ja kein Problem!<
And there I said: >Well, okay, it's no Problem!<
2 H: Treffen wir uns alle wieder am Eingang.
Let's all meet each other again at the entrance.

On some occasions, when problems of a third party are discussed, decisions of this party or the advice of the speaker are presented with reported discourse as well. In the following data segment, for example, Annette (A) is talking about a computer problem a friend of hers (David, *er* 'he' in the transcript) has. His computer was not able to handle certain programs and he wanted to upgrade the computer but was worried about the cost factor involved. Annette reports on the decision David made when faced with a relatively inexpensive upgrade:

(4) GIS 1 [A: 102, simplified]
→ 1 A: Meint er: Ach das geht ja. Achtundachtzig Dollar.
he says: Oh, that's okay. Eighty eight dollars.

Although it is possible to refer back to the decision of another speaker with reported discourse as is demonstrated in data segment (4), referring back to one's own decisions in the form of self-quotations seems to be more frequent in my data. Further analysis of a larger corpus might indicate if this is a typical finding or merely something idiosyncratic about this particular corpus.

3.4 Evaluation of the decision

After the decision has been presented in the form of reported discourse, the next sequentially relevant action is for the coparticipant to give an assessment of the decision (d). Unlike in storytellings which are performative in character, it is not the performance of the quote that is to be evaluated; rather, it is the decision itself which is evaluated. Pomerantz (1984: 57–8) observes that in order to make an assessment, speakers need to have access to it; likewise, by giving an assessment a speaker claims to have access and knowledge of the event that is assessed. Looking back at data segment (1), we can observe that it is the coparticipant Rita who makes the assessment (line 21–3, arrow d) although she herself did not experience the trouble or reach the decision concerning the fence. Rita's knowledge and thus access of the event needed for making an evaluation stems from a different resource, namely from Kirsten's telling of the event. In other words, since the speaker provides the decision in direct discourse, he or she makes it accessible to the coparticipant. Here one could argue that the coparticipant is cast as a witness of the decision.

Whereas in data segment (1) the coparticipant's reaction was not the preferred action since it was minimally delayed,[5] all other data segments show an agreement with the reported decision in one of two ways: i) First, the coparticipant can address talk directly to the reported decision. In this form of alignment, the coparticipant produces adverbs such as *natürlich* 'of course', *klar* 'clearly' or alternatively is giving advice that basically restates what the troublesteller said before. (For a detailed discussion see *Vlatten* 1997:136–8). ii) Secondly, the alignment can take the form of a collaborative completion (Lerner 1987:82, 1993:173) of the quote. This form of alignment is of particular interest for the present discussion.

In the following segment a decision is conveyed for a particular situation which could potentially have been problematic but which turned out to be non-problematic: the coparticipants are talking about coexisting in peace with one's neighbors. Tobias (T) and Ricki (R) had recently bought one half of a duplex house and certain decisions needed to be made concerning the yard, the color of the house, etc. The neighbors in the other half of the duplex could have potentially made these personal choices difficult for Tobias and Ricki. In the interest of brevity, only the decision (marked with arrow c) and the following agreement with the decision (marked with arrow d) are shown in the transcript.

(5) GIS B [147]
    c ⇒ 1 R: Und dann ham wir irgendwann gesacht, also, wir
                   And then we said at some point, well, we
    c ⇒ 2 R: zahlen jeder so viel *Geld* für das Haus,
                   all pay so much *money* for the house,
        3 S: Ja
               Yea
        4 R: //das is-
               //that is-
    d ⇒ 5 B: //dann möcht ich's auch//so haben wie's ( )
                   //then I want to have// it like ( )
    c ⇒ 6 R: //dann soll'n wir auch
                   //then we should not
    c ⇒ 7 R: keine faulen Komp*romis*se eingehn.
                   make any cheesy compromises.

d ⇒ 8 S: Nee:, dann macht man das so, wie man's haben will
No::, people do like they want to have it
9 R: Eben, genau!
Right, exactly!
10 S: °Ja°
°Yes°
11 A: //°Stimmt°
//°True°
12 B: //Is ja immer so, dann ( ) die Nachbarschaft . . .
//It is always like this, then ( ) the neighbors . . .

Right before this segment, Ricki and her husband had co-told the trouble (potential problems with neighbors) and the other participants in the conversation (Sybille, Bernhard, and Annette) had aligned themselves with the tellers by expressing their agreement with the tellers. As can be seen in this segment, Ricki then proceeds to present her and her husband's decision with reported discourse (lines 1–2), explaining that they spent so much money on their house that they did not want to make compromises on their decisions concerning the house. In other words, they literally feel *entitled* to make the changes they want to. Note that the quotative is again given in the first person plural when referring back to a decision that she and her husband had previously reached. As pointed out earlier, Ricki is reporting on the decision and not on the decision-making process that took place between her and her husband Tobias. In latched position, Sybille produces *Ja* 'Yes' (line 3) and Ricki starts to continue her talk in overlap with Bernhard. Ricki drops out momentarily (line 4) and Bernhard produces *dann möcht ich's auch so haben wie's* ( ) 'then I want to have it like ( )'. Bernhard is *not* Ricki's husband, thus the first person pronoun *ich* is a bit surprising at this point. It can only be explained if one regards Bernhard's talk as a continuation of Ricki's talk in lines 1–2. By finishing the sentence for her, Bernhard is not only a witness to a decision, he actually takes on Ricki's perspective. He is taking over Ricki's role and in order to do so he must be in full alignment with her decision. Ricki comes in in overlap again in line 6, finishing her own sentence. She does not repeat Bernhard's words but instead uses her own which state the same thing. Having already received Bernhard's approval of the decision, Ricki is still missing two other positive evaluations from the other two coparticipants Annette and Sybille. These positive evaluations are forthcoming in lines 9 and 11. The talk then continues about neighbors and the relationship with neighbors in general.

Ochs *et al.* (1992) treat storytelling and especially troubles-tellings among familiars (i.e. family and good friends) as collective "theory building activity" (p. 37). Members of these tellings "jointly construct, deconstruct, and reconstruct the theories of everyday events" (p. 37). That is, they present, negotiate and/or challenge (a) what actually happened to them and others, (b) how others behaved in certain situations, and (c) what makes the focal point of a story. Ochs *et al.* argue that participants in storytellings and particularly in troubles-tellings practice critical thinking and perspective-taking in a non-institutional and non-academic setting.

Applying Ochs *et al.*'s findings to my data, it becomes clear that troubles-tellers certainly tell their troubles from their own perspectives; as such, these tellings are replayings (Goffman 1974:504–6). In my data, the coparticipants are also invited by the teller to take on the perspective of the speaker and to support the decision the teller has made concerning the trouble. It is noteworthy that in *all* 37 data segments of this category the recipient of the troubles-telling does the preferred action: he or she supports the decision of the teller, i.e. takes on the teller's perspective of the event itself. In none of the segments does the recipient "challenge" the perspective of the teller or take on a different perspective. It would be interesting to see if further research on a larger data-base would yield similar findings.

In this section, I showed that a past decision can be in the form of reported discourse and that there is a particular sequence associated with such reporting: First, there is typically a presentation of the trouble at hand for which a decision is required. Next, the coparticipant(s) acknowledge the existence of the trouble and generally show their alignment with the speaker. Then the speaker presents his or her decision in the form of reported discourse. That is, the decision is cast in the form of direct discourse, thus making it more immediate. The last element in the sequence is the alignment or approval of the decision. Since the entire telling of the decision itself is set up to imply that the speaker had to make this decision, the coparticipant's evaluation follows this same line of thinking. The evaluation presents the general opinion that a reasonable and sensible person had no other choice but to make that decision.

3.5 Format of the quote

As mentioned above, there seem to be some features that are always associated with the turn in which a past decision is conveyed. First of all, in all analyzed data segments the quotative is presented in the conversational past tense, and the quote itself is always given in the present tense. In addition, self-quotation seems to be favored over other-quotation.

The concept of multivoicedness or polyphonic speech as described by *Bakhtin* (1981, 1986) is commonly applied to other-quotation but it is also very applicable to self-quotation. When a speaker quotes himself or herself, the reporter and the reported speaker are actually the same physical person. However, they represent different characters in the quoting event, that is, "they are not identical in terms of the characters represented in discourse" (*Maynard* 1996:208). In self-quoting, speakers dramatize the event talked about and distance themselves from it at the same time (*Maynard* 1996:208). A similar description is given by *Macaulay* (1987) who notes that, in self-quotation, the speaker can be thought of "as an actor in a scene" (p.22). The same observations are also made by Goffman (1974:517–23) who points out that the speaking character can be split up in different parts (i.e. animator, author, and principal). In addition, he notes that the "I" used in the quotation does not necessarily have to correspond to the speaking "I". The speaker might have changed or developed somehow in the time between the original event and its telling, possibly permitting him or her to thus look at the event itself from a different perspective.

I pointed out elsewhere (*Vlatten* 1997:14) that any reported discourse event consists of several parts, namely the quotative, the quote itself and the unquote. The unquote indicates the end of the reported talk and consists either of a verbal element (e.g. a response solicitation marker and exit device *ne?* (Jefferson 1980)) or a non-verbal element (e.g., a gesture or a gap). A close analysis of the quotes contained in the category of reporting on past decisions shows that the quotative and the beginning of the quote can be easily identified. However, the boundary between reported discourse and other talk following the quote is a fuzzy one. In segment 6 below I illustrate the indistinct nature of this boundary. The arrow marks the beginning of quoted discourse (i.e. as marked by the quotative), yet it is quite difficult (if not impossible) to locate the end of the quote:

(6)   Kirsten 1 [B2 065–74]
⇒   c 1   Ri: Ich hab auch zum >Udo< gesacht: >Ich laß mir das nich
                 I also said to >Udo<: >I won't let them
⇒   c 2   Ri: bieten! Ich hab laut< Notarvertrag einunddreißigster *Mai*
                 do this! According to the < contract I have thirtyfirst of *may*
      3   K: mhm
                 uhu
⇒   c?4   Ri: Und es sind jetz sechs Wochen im Prinzip- >ach, das
                 and now it is six weeks in principle- >oh, it
      5   Ri: wärn ja fast sieben Wochen< später, ne? Und da muß
                 would almost be seven weeks< later, right? And something
⇒   c?6   Ri: irgendwas passiern! Also, da müssen se schon auf Kulanz
                 has to happen! Well, they must already out of fairness
⇒   c?7   Ri: irgendwas machen, //und das is// scheißegal,
                 do something,//and I don't// give a shit,
      8   K: //natürlich//
                 //of course//
⇒   c?9   Ri: wer das da dran //Schuld is ( )//
                 whose fault it //is ( )//

10   K: //*Ihr* müßt euch da// melden! Die werdn freiwillich ja nischt
              //*You* have to// tell them! They won't give anything out
11   K: rausrücken . . .
              willingly . . .

In segment (6), the quotative can be found in line 1 *Ich hab auch zum >Udo<
gesacht* 'I also said to >Udo<'. The material following the quote is uttered with
varying tempo and in a slightly agitated voice; both of these phenomena can be
considered indications of direct discourse (*Coulmas* 1986c). Using grammatical
units or intonation patterns, it is not possible to decide exactly where the quote
ends. The first turn constructional unit (TCU) in the quote itself is *Ich laß mir das
nich bieten!* 'I won't let them do this!' but Rita produces a second TCU *Ich hab
laut< Notarvertrag einunddreißigster Mai* 'According to the< contract, I have
thirty-first of may' in continued fast discourse. It is simply not clear whether this
part still belongs to the decision, i.e. if it is a reported explanation, or if it is an
explanation that is not reproduced but newly produced for her coparticipant's
benefit. Kirsten produces a continuation marker and Rita continues to talk. The
response solicitation marker *ne?* 'right?' and the self-repair on the deictic marker
(*sechs Wochen* 'six weeks' gets changed to *ach, das wärn ja fast sieben Wochen* 'oh,
it would almost be seven weeks') indicate that line 5 seems to be an interjection
which is not reported but is instead directly constructed at the moment with
reference to Kirsten. The talk in line 6 following the response solicitation marker
ne? could be interpreted either as direct discourse (i.e., as still belonging to the
quote), as a description or restatement of the decision, or as a current response
solicitation. The coparticipant Kirsten produces *natürlich* 'of course' in line 8,
thereby giving an assessment of Rita's talk and aligning with her. Since evaluations
of decisions follow immediately after the decision is presented, Kirsten is here
orienting to Rita's talk up to this point as reported decision. Yet Rita goes on (line
7 and 9) and again it is not clear if this is part of the reported decision or part of
a telling. In sum, this segment shows that in reporting decisions the end of a
decision does not seem to get marked.

In the following segment the end of the direct quote is again not apparent.
Rita is talking about her upcoming move and the fact that she wants her son to
stay in touch with his friends.

(7)   Kirsten [A2: 590–617, simplified]
⇒   1   Ri: Und ich hab auch gesacht, ich möchte o:ch, daß der den
                      and then I also said that I also want
⇒   2   Ri: Kontakt aufrecht erhält,
                      him to keep in touch
⇒   ? 3   Ri: >weil, wir ham auch noch nen Steuerberater hier
                      >because we have also an accountant here

⇒ ? 4 Ri: und ich werd ab und zu noch mal rüber fahrn, dann
         and I will drive over every now and then, then
    5 K: ja:a
         ye:es
⇒ ? 6 Ri: nehm ich ihn mit,< ne?
         I take him along,< right?

It seems that the quote itself only contains *ich möchte o:ch, daß der den Kontakt aufrecht erhält* 'I also want him to keep in touch' but as Rita causally links additional material to this TCU, the following material could still belong to the direct quote. Thus, after a TCU in the quote is completed the coparticipant has to interpret whether the quote has been completed and thus needs to be assessed, or if further TCUs belonging to the reported decision are forthcoming. If there are no apparent indications in the talk that a reported decision is completed and thus is to be evaluated or assessed by the coparticipant, problems in turn-taking might follow. Indeed, the following segment shows that assessments are not always immediately forthcoming and that a gap occurs in the conversation (marked with arrow 1), and only after a response pursuit marker (Jefferson 1980; marked with arrow 2), does the coparticipant produce a minimal response. In this segment, Heiner is telling his sister about a court proceeding in which he and his wife are suing somebody else for a considerable amount of money.

(8) Kirsten [A1: 139–43]
    1 H: Wir ham inzwischen den >Punkt, daß wir da ganz locker
         by now we have reached the >point that we approach it
    2 H: rangehen. Wir sagen (wir) det Geld, das is sowieso schon
         rather coolly. We say (we) the money, that is already
    3 H: verplant. Also, det kriegen wir sowieso nich mehr.
         alloted. Well, that we don't get back.
    4 H: Dat is abjehakt<
         that is over<
⇒ 1 5   (0.2)
⇒ 2 6 H: ne?
         right?
    7 K: joa
         yeah

Heiner produces the quotative in line 2; note the very unusual present tense Heiner is using (this is in fact the only segment in my data where present tense is used for the quotative). A possible explanation is that the lawsuit is not yet over at the time of speaking). Notice too that Heiner is speaking particularly fast and is rushing through turn-transitional relevance spaces (lines 3 and 4), and that thus it is difficult for Kirsten to gain access to the floor. However, as there is no preturn in-breath and no overlap in this segment at all, Kirsten in fact makes no noticeable attempt to get a turn. In Heiner's turn at talk, it is again not clear which TCUs actually belong to the decision reported in direct discourse. As noted earlier, since there are no markers signaling the end of the quote, the coparticipant has no way of knowing whether additional quoted material might follow. This seems to be the case in the segment above: Heiner speaks very quickly and his turn consists of several TCUs. After his turn comes to completion, a gap emerges in line 5 since Kirsten is not immediately forthcoming with her reaction to the talk and because Heiner is not continuing to talk. Heiner then indicates more strongly that a response by the coparticipant is the next relevant action by producing the response-pursuit marker and exit-device *ne?* in post-gap position (Jefferson 1980), whereupon Kirsten finally produces an agreement token and the participants produce further talk concerning the lawsuit (not shown in transcript).

In this section we have seen that the quotation format in decision reporting does not have a precise sequential demarcation (cf. the quotation format in storytelling and in the use of *und ich so* 'and I'm like' (*Vlatten* 1997, *Golato* 2000)). Rather, the transition from quote to regular talk is fluid and stretches over one or more TCUs. This feature of these types of quotes can result in problems in turn-taking as segment 10 displayed.

The following generalizations can be drawn for the quotation format in reporting on past decisions: (a) decisions can be presented with direct quotation, (b) the quotative usually consists of a first person pronoun and a verb in the present perfect tense, although sometimes additional material (adverbs, a person reference, etc.) can be included,[6] (c) the quote itself is given in the present tense in direct discourse, and (d) there does not seem to be an unquote that clearly marks the end of the direct discourse, which can lead to problems in turn-taking.

This type of quotative is typical of the interactional activity of troubles-tellings when a decision or solution is rendered to a problem; other interactional activities show other very specific quotation formats: I argued elsewhere (*Vlatten* 1997, *Golato* 2000) that the German quotative *und ich so/ und er so* 'and I'm like/ and he's like' is used to introduce both discourse and gestures as quotables, particularly in storytellings when materials contributing to the climax of the story were quoted. This type of quotative turns the telling of a story into a performance that involves the audience. Similarly, the interactional activities of claimbacking or explaining come with a particular quotation format (*Vlatten* 1997). Thus, it becomes obvious that grammar (here reported discourse) cannot be treated as an autonomous phenomenon but has to be seen as one element of a broad range of resources (Schegloff, Ochs, and Thompson 1996:2). In other words, grammar is viewed here as an interactional phenomenon: quotatives and quotes are designed to the current actions (either storytelling, troubles-telling, explaining etc.) as indicated by the different formats of the quote. Thus when a speaker designs a quote it is the local context[7] that is relevant to the speaker who is quoting, not the distant context in which the original discourse occurred.

4. Interpretation and cross-cultural comparison

Self-quotations are particularly interesting since they have been much neglected in the study of reported discourse (*Maynard* 1996:211). Research on reported discourse has been defined mostly as reporting something that somebody else has said or thought before, and this definition is already an indication that most research has focused on other-quotation and not on self-quotation. There are, however, a few exceptions to this. *Ely and McCabe* (1993) find that self-quotation in combination with direct discourse is particularly prevalent in the speech of young children (ages 1 year, 2 months to 9 years). In their speech samples, directives were the most common speech act. An analysis of self-quoting in adult speech shows that in self-quoting, speakers adapt the original speech to give a depiction of a previous speech situation (*Falk* 1991) with this use of self-quotation lending more expressiveness to the talk (*Maynard* 1996:208).

Looking at the corpora of other researchers one can easily find many instances of self-quotation. Of particular interest, however, is one study of reported discourse in Greek (Tannen 1983), because, similar to the present study, all data segments stem from troubles-tellings. In the following example, Marika tells about her decision to call a friend of a friend:

(9) [adapted from Tannen 1983:364]
1 Tis leo tis xadelfis mou,
   I say to my cousin,
2 "Kaiti, den pame kai ston sistimeno ton
   "Katie, shouldn't we go see the fellow we were told to
3 anthropo na mi fygoume apo tin Rodo
   look up so as not to leave Rhodes
4 kai den echoume patisi to podaraki mas?"
   without having set foot [on his doorstep]?"

Unfortunately, the chapter does not include the entire troubles-telling sequence, so it is impossible to see if the sequential organization and orientation of the participants that we observed for the German data holds in Greek as well. One difference that is apparent though, is that the quotative in this Greek example is given in the historical present tense whereas the German quotative has always been given in the present perfect. Again, one would have to analyze more than one example in order to see (a) if the historical present is the common tense of the quotative, and (b) which interactional achievement might be associated with this function. However, it is clear that the reported discourse is used in other languages as well in order to relate a personal decision. One only has to turn on daytime television in the US with its many talk shows to find the relevant data. In the following segment, a woman is telling the audience of the William Montel talk show about her decision to get in touch with the mother of her husband's alleged illegitimate child:

(10) [William Montel Show, Dec. 22, 1998)
1 W: ... I said if that child is his we have to
2   communicate for the child's sake.

The troubles-telling preceding segment (10) was too lengthy to be included here. The main point to be argued, however, is that the decision is introduced with a quotative in the past tense, followed by the quote in direct reported discourse. In other words, the decision is rendered in the same way as were the decisions in the German data seen earlier in this chapter. The sequence of turns (not shown), however, seems to be a slightly different one, which I at this point attribute to the different setting (i.e. television talk show vs. face-to-face interaction). The sequential differences and their interactional achievements need to be addressed in additional research.

It is interesting to see that at least three different languages, German, English and Greek, use the grammatical phenomenon of reported discourse for a particular interactional achievement: reporting on a decision and rendering it in a fashion as to get support from their interlocutors. Obviously, one can imagine other procedures a speaker could use to refer back to decisions reached in earlier conversations. For example, if one partner in a relationship discusses the plans of the couple and uses the modal verb in the first person plural as in *wir wollen* 'we want', then this implies a decision for the wish to be expressed in this form. Although segments of this kind were not analyzed in detail in the present study, let us consider the following example in which Kirsten is telling her sister-in-law about vacation plans which both she and her husband have made. The arrow indicates the use of a modal verb which implies a decision:

(11)   Kirsten [A2: 241]
⇒ 1 K: Und //dann// wolln wir
           and //then// we want to
   2 Ri: //mhm//
          //mhm//
   3 K: nach Deutschland fahrn und ich bleib dann
          go to Germany and I might possibly stay then
   4 K: vielleicht selbst noch länger in Deutschland
          a bit longer by myself in Germany

Another possibility that one could imagine using to refer back to a past decision would be to label a statement directly as a decision, as in *wir haben uns entschieden* ... 'we decided' — interestingly, though, I did not find any such statements in my data. These forms of reporting on past decisions are very much different from the use of reported discourse: The distinction that exists between reported discourse and other forms of summarizing talk has been referred to as the distinction between "demonstrations" and "descriptions" by *Clark and Gerrig* (1980:765). With respect to the phenomenon discussed in this study, the distinction can be summarized as follows: Reported discourse in the form of direct discourse is a *demonstration* of a decision; it is not the actual decision itself, but it is presented as such; it is made immediate for the coparticipants. This decision is presented by the teller for evaluation by the cotellers. Presenting a decision with a modal verb or a labeling statement is not a demonstration of a decision, but rather a *description* of a decision; the coparticipant does not become a witness to the decision and does not have immediate access to the decision and thus cannot readily evaluate the described event. In positively evaluating or at least addressing the decision a speaker made when facing a troublesome situation, the coparticipants build closeness and intimacy in the relationship between them and the speaker and thereby take part in "theory-building activity" (Ochs *et al.* 1992). That is, they show their ability to weigh a story told from a different perspective and help co-construct and make sense of ideas and recast facts as interpretations.

In all the segments belonging to the category of reporting on decisions, the decisions which were presented all dealt with issues of fairness and responsibility, or of being good citizens (e.g. fixing a fence as a responsibility toward the community and a home owner's association; fighting for fair treatment by money lenders or unpleasant business people; fairness among neighbors concerning everybody's entitlement to make decisions concerning their own homes; fairness and responsibility towards a son to allow him to stay in touch with very good friends even if the family has to move; fair treatment in a court of law). Goffman (1974) points out that much of our talk actually revolves around issues of fairness and responsibility: "... what the individual spends most of his spoken moments doing is *providing evidence for the fairness or unfairness of his current situation* and other grounds for sympathy, approval, exoneration, understanding, or amusement" (p.503, italics added). Goffman then remarks that even if speakers present the facts of an event, they present their version of the event in question, and this version "may be intrinsically theatrical" (Goffman 1974:504). This is exactly the case in the decision-reporting situations discussed in this study. Speakers present their decisions as revolving around issues of fairness in their specific situations. The theatrical nature of the telling is highlighted by the use of direct discourse. The quotative in the conversational past indicates a past event but the direct discourse of the quoted material brings the decision into the present and stages it;

the decision is in effect replayed. As Goffman notes, the listeners are easily able to emphatically insert themselves into this replaying. They are thus very likely to evaluate the decision the way the reporter of the decision intended. The decision is constructed and evaluated as one that "had to be made" by any fair and responsible person.

Notes

* I would like to thank Maria Egbert and Jürgen Streeck for their extensive comments on earlier drafts of this chapter. My thanks also go to Tom Güldemann and Manfred von Roncador, the editors of this volume. All remaining errors are mine.

1. Three hours of the video-taped conversation and 6 hours of the telephone interaction were kindly made available by Maria Egbert.

2. The original, more detailed transcripts can be obtained from the author.

3. One other way of referring back to a decision would be to present the decision with a labeling statement, as for example *da haben wir uns entschieden* 'then we decided', however, such verb forms were not found in the present corpus. However, speakers make extensive use of modal verbs and those imply a decision, see Section 3.5 for a discussion.

4. In this segment, the sequential component (d) is produced with some delay which is somewhat unusual. However, I still opted to use this data segment as an example for the basic sequence structure since the other segments in my collection either are very long (spanning several pages of transcript) or have a rather involved troubles-telling.

5. Indicators that the response is indeed delayed are the minimal gap in line 18, Kirsten's in-breath (not displayed in data), and Rita's minimal response in the form of the continuer *mhm* (Goodwin 1986, Schegloff 1982, Jefferson 1984a, Gardner 1995). Only after Kirsten has produced more talk does Rita actually give an assessment of the decision.

6. When adverbs such as the deictic marker *da* 'there, then' are included, they are usually placed sentence initially, requiring the use of a VS-construction instead of the standard SV word order in German main clauses. This particular word order in quotatives has also been found in Hungarian (Sasse 1995a:175, 1995b:30), Italian (Bernini 1995:46, Sornicola 1995:75), Modern Greek (Sasse 1995a:150, 1995b:30), Russian (Miller 1995:129) and Spanish (Sornicola 1995:75) and thetic structures in general also in some African languages (Güldemann, p.c.). While it has tentatively been suggested that VS order in quotatives may possibly be connected with theticity, I do not believe the same can be said of the German data in the present study. In German, theticity is usually expressed via stress or with impersonal *es* 'it' constructions and not via VS word order (in contrast to Romance languages; Sasse 1987:527–31; Lambrecht 1994). Consider the following representative example which includes a deictic adverb:

9 *Und da hab ich gesacht: Das mach ich nich!* . . .
And there I said: I won't do that! . . . .

Note that in this quotative (as in the others of my data set) the stress is on the auxiliary verb *hab.* In this sentence, the focus is on the predicate. That is, it is a sentence "about me" in which the speaker is a topic. This excludes a thetic structure (Lambrecht, p.c.).

7. See Duranti and Goodwin (1992) for a detailed discussion of the concept of context, see Egbert (1996) for a discussion of context-sensitivity with regard to repair and turn-taking.

References

Atkinson, J. Maxwell and John Heritage (eds.). 1984. *Structures of social action.* Cambridge: Cambridge University Press.
Auer, Peter and S. Uhmann. 1982. "Aspekte der konversationellen Organisation von Bewertungen". *Deutsche Sprache* 10: 1–32.
Bakhtin, Mikhail M. 1986 [1952/3]. "The problem of speech genres". In Bakhtin, Mikhail M. (ed. and translated by Emerson, Caryl and Michael Holquist), *Speech genres and other late essays.* Austin: University of Texas Press, 60–102.
Bargiela-Chiappini, Francesca and Sandra J. Harris. 1995. "Towards the generic structure of meetings in British and Italian managements". *Text* 15: 531–60.
Bernini, Giuliano. 1995. "Verb-subject order in Italian: an investigation of short announcements and telecast news". *Sprachtypologie und Universalienforschung* 48,1/2: 44–71.
Chappell, Virginia A. 1995. "Expert testimony, 'regular people,' and public values: arguing common sense at a death penalty trial". *Rhetoric Review* 13,2: 391–408.
Condon, Sherri L. 1986. "The discourse functions of 'ok'". *Semiotica* 60,1/2: 73–101.
Drew, P. and John Heritage (eds.), *Talk at work: interaction in institutional settings.* Cambridge: Cambridge University Press.
Duranti, Alessandro and Charles Goodwin (eds.). 1992. *Rethinking context: language as an interactive phenomenon.* Cambridge: Cambridge University Press.
Egbert, Maria. 1996. "Context-sensitivity in conversation analysis: eye gaze and the German repair initiator *bitte?*". *Language in Society* 25: 587–612.
Fleischman, Suzanne. 1990. *Tense and narrativity: from medieval performance to modern fiction.* Austin: University of Texas Press.
Gardner, R.J. 1995. *On some uses of the conversational token mh.* Ph.D. thesis: University of Melbourne.
Goffman, Erving. 1974. *Frame analysis.* New York: Harper.
Goffman, Erving. 1981. *Forms of talk.* Philadelphia: University of Pennsylvania Press.
Goodwin, Charles. 1986. "Between and within: alternative sequential treatments of continuers and assessments". *Human Studies* 9,2/3: 205–18.
Henderson, Linda S. and William E. Jurma. 1981. "Distributional and sequential communication structure: a case study in organizational decision-making". *Psychological Reports* 48: 279–84.
Heritage, John and Sue Sefi. 1992. "Dilemmas of advice: aspects of the delivery and reception of advice in interactions between health visitors and first-time mothers". In Drew and Heritage (eds.), 359–417.
Jefferson, Gail. 1980. "The abominable 'ne?': an exploration of post-response-inititiation response-solicitation". In Schröder, P. and H. Steger (eds.), *Dialogforschung.* Düssel-

dorf: Pädagogischer Verlag Schwann, 53–88.
Jefferson, Gail. 1983. *Two explorations of the organization of overlapping talk in conversation* (=Tilburg Papers in Language and Literature 28). Tilburg: Tilburg University.
Jefferson, Gail. 1984a. "Notes on a systematic deployment of the acknowledgement tokens 'yeah' and 'Mm hm'". *Papers in Linguistics* 17: 197–216.
Jefferson, Gail. 1984b. "On stepwise transition from talk about a trouble to inappropriately next-positioned matters". In Atkinson and Heritage (eds.), 191–222.
Jefferson, Gail. 1984c. "On the organization of laughter in talk about troubles". In Atkinson and Heritage (eds.), 346–69.
Jefferson, Gail. 1985. "An exercise in the transcription and analysis of laughter". In Dijk, T. van (ed.), *Handbook of Discourse Analysis*. London: Academic Press, 25–34.
Jefferson, Gail and J.R.E. Lee. 1992. "The rejection of advice: managing the problematic convergence of a 'troubles-telling' and a 'service encounter'". In Drew and Heritage, 521–48.
Lambrecht, Knud. 1994. *Information structure and sentence form: topic, focus, and the mental representations of discourse referents* (=Cambridge Studies in Linguistics 71). Cambridge: Cambridge University Press.
Lerner, Gene H. 1987. *Collaborative turn sequences: sentence construction and social action*. Ph.D. thesis: The University of California at Irvine.
Lerner, Gene H. 1993. "Collectivities in action: establishing the relevance of conjoined participation in conversation". *Text* 13: 213–45.
Liberman, Kenneth. 1990. "The collective character of disputes in aboriginal communities". *Sociolinguistics* 19,1/2: 89–98.
Manzo, John F. 1996. "Taking turns and taking sides: opening scenes from two jury deliberations". *Social Psychology Quarterly* 59,2: 107–25.
Mehan, Hugh. 1990. "Oracular reasoning in a psychiatric exam: the resolution of conflict in language". In Grimshaw, A.D. (ed.), *Conflict talk: sociolinguistic investigations of arguments in conversations*. Cambridge: Cambridge University Press, 160–77.
Miller, Jim. 1995. "VS clauses in Russian: contrast, new episodes and theticity". *Sprachtypologie und Universalienforschung* 48,1/2: 125–41.
Ochs, Eleanor, Carolyn Taylor, Dina Rudolph and Ruth Smith. 1992. "Storytelling as a theory-building activity". *Discourse Processes* 15: 37–72.
Pomerantz, Anita. 1984. "Agreeing and disagreeing with assessments: some features of preferred/dispreferred turn shapes". In Atkinson and Heritage (eds.), 57–101.
Ravnholt, Ole. 1995. "The role of communicative goals in the structuring of conversation". *Gothenburg Papers in Theoretical Linguistics* 73: 75–91.
Sacks, Harvey, Emmanuel A. Schegloff and Gail Jefferson. 1974. "A simplest systematics for the organization of turn-taking for conversation". *Language* 50: 696–735.
Sasse, Hans-Jürgen. 1987. "The thetic/categorical distinction revisited". *Linguistics* 25,3: 511–80.
Sasse, Hans-Jürgen. 1995a. "A contrastive study of VS clauses in Modern Greek and Hungarian". *Sprachtypologie und Universalienforschung* 48,1/2: 142–88.
Sasse, Hans-Jürgen. 1995b. "'Theticity' and VS order: a case study". *Sprachtypologie und Universalienforschung* 48,1/2: 3–31.

Schegloff, Emmanuel A. 1982. "Discourse as an interactional achievement: some uses of 'uh huh' and other things that come between sentences". In Tannen, Deborah (ed.), *Georgetown University Roundtable on Languages and Linguistics.* Washington, DC: Georgetown University Press, 71–93.

Schegloff, Emmanuel A., Eleanor Ochs and Sandra A. Thompson. 1996. "Introduction". In Ochs, Eleanor, Emmanuel A. Schegloff and Thompson, Sandra A. (eds.), *Interaction and Grammar.* Cambridge: Cambridge University Press, 1–51.

Schiffrin, Deborah. 1981. "Tense variation in narrative". *Language* 57: 45–62.

Sornicola, Rosanna. 1995. "Theticity, VS order and the interplay of syntax, semantics and pragmatics". *Sprachtypologie und Universalienforschung* 48,1/2: 72–83.

Tannen, Deborah. 1983. "'I take out the rock-dock!': how Greek women tell about being molested and create involvement". *Anthropological Linguistics* 25,3: 359–74.

Wolfson, Nessa. 1978. "A feature of performed narrative: The conversational historical present". *Language in Society* 7: 215–37.

CHAPTER 3

Direct and indirect speech in Cerma narrative

Ivan Lowe and Ruth Hurlimann
Summer Institute of Linguistics

1. Introduction

This chapter deals with the discourse function of direct and indirect speech in Cerma[1,2] narrative discourse. Several authors, notably *Aaron* (1992), *Chia* (1986), and *Hedinger* (1984) have described the surface forms for direct and indirect speech in different West African languages. However, none have, to the knowledge of the authors of this chapter, done a data based analysis of the discourse function of direct and indirect speech. We will begin our treatment with a short introductory section on the surface forms of direct and indirect speech in that language. The main body of the chapter, dealing with their discourse function then follows. To recognise and understand direct and indirect speech forms, we need first to be clear about the relationships between coreferential nominals. Here we state the rules which apply. The rules themselves have been established in *Pike and Lowe* (1969), and *Lowe* (1969).

In a speech situation, there is always a speaker, whose role we will designate as S, the subject of the 'say' verb, and always an addressee whose role we will designate as O (for object of the 'say' verb), and there can also be a third participant with role X in the situation, who may be a bystander or the participant who is the third person topic of the conversation.

Then the rules are:

For direct speech
Subject (S) of 'say' verb (speaker) is coreferential with first person pronoun in QC.
Object (O) of 'say' verb (hearer) is coreferential with second person pronoun in QC.
Third role (X) of 'say' verb (bystander) is coreferential with third person pronoun in QC.

For indirect speech
First person of 'say' verb is coreferential with first person pronoun in QC.
Second person of 'say' verb is coreferential with second person pronoun in QC.
Third person of 'say' verb *may be* coreferential with third person pronoun in QC.

The 'may be coreferential' part of the statement for third person is needed because the same surface third person pronoun may occur more than once in the same sentence and may refer to different participants on its two occurences.

Here are some typical examples of surface forms of Cerma direct and indirect speech at the first and second degrees of embedding.

(1) First degree embedding, direct speech
QM   QC
wúɔ   dá mì hán-nì   bùɔnŋ dá'ákù-í
cat$_C$ say (to hyena$_H$) if I$_C$ give-you$_H$ leg   this-DEF
                  mí tá   mì wúɔ nìɛ̀
                  I$_C$ PRS.CONT I$_C$ walk how
'The cat$_C$ said (to the hyena$_H$) "If I$_C$ give you$_H$ this leg, how am I$_C$ going to walk?"'

It will be seen that the first person pronouns *mì* 'I' within the quotation content are coreferential with the speaker (i.e. the cat$_C$) of the embedding 'say' verb *wúɔ* and that the second person pronoun within the quotation content is coreferential with the hearer or indirect object (i.e. the hyena$_H$) of the 'say' verb. Thus the requirements for direct speech are satisfied

(2) First degree embedding, indirect speech
QM   QC
wúɔ   bísínúɔ ú ká jó   jì   bíɛ̀ tètèrìeŋó
he$_A$ say (to fish$_B$) tomorrow he$_A$ FUT come DISPL take fish$_B$
'He$_A$ (the partridge$_A$) said to the fish$_B$ that he$_A$ would come and take the fish$_B$ the next day.'

In the above example, the third person pronoun *ú* 'he' within the quotation content is coreferential with the third person subject (the partridge$_A$) of the embedding 'say' verb *wúɔ* in the quotation margin. This satisfies the criterion for indirect speech. If the quotation content had been direct speech, the pronoun referring to the partridge$_A$ within the quotation content would have been *mì* 'I', and the noun *tètèrìeŋó* 'fish' would have been replaced by the pronoun *ni* 'you'

(3) Second degree embedding, direct speech within direct speech
    QM1   QM2   QC2
    cat_C said to míɛ̀   dá mì gbár bùɔnŋ   dá'ákù-í hán
    rabbit_R   I_C say (to   if I_C cut shoulder this-DEF give
                  hyena_H)   nú'ɔ́ŋo-i   múɔ̀   mì
                                   you_H-EMPH I_C-EMPH I_C
                                   tìɛn   híe   túgú
                                   be-left where after.that

                  DIRECT   DIRECT
                  S → 1st (C)   S → 1st (C)
                  O → 2nd (R)   O → 2nd (H)

'The cat_C said to the rabbit_R "I_C said (to the hyena_H) "If I_C cut this shoulder to give to you_H what will be left of me_C.""'

The pronoun coreferentiality relationships across the various quote stretches of the above report are shown by the formulas written underneath the boundaries in the above display. (here the arrows simply mean 'coreferential with'.)

Here the middle stretch QM2 consists solely of the speech verb *míɛ̀* 'I_C say (to the hyena_H)' in which the addressee has been inferred from the context.

If we check across the boundary between QM2 and QC2, we see that the subject (or speaker of QM2) 'I' in *míɛ̀* 'I say' is coreferential with the first person pronouns *mì* 'I', and *múɔ̀* 'I.EMPII' of QC2, while the understood indirect object (addressee) of QM2 is the hyena and is coreferential with the second person pronoun *nú'ɔ́ŋo-i* 'you.EMPH' of QC2. Hence there is a direct quote relationship between QM2 and QC2. By a similar check across the boundary between QM1 and QM2 we see that 'cat_C', the subject of QM1, is coreferential with the first person in *míɛ̀* 'I say' of QM2. Hence there is also a direct quote relationship between QM1 and QM2. Thus we can say that QC2 is a direct quote within a direct quote.

(4) Second degree embedding, indirect speech within direct speech
    QM1   QC1
    cat_C said to rabbit_R   mí ŋyúgúnŋ hīiŋ-u-rá
    about hyena_H   I_C climb.up take-him_H-down
                  QM2   QC2
                  ú bír   'wúɔ mí hán-yò   mì cór'réī
                  he_H reply that I_C give-him_H my_C shoulder
                  DIRECT   INDIRECT
                  S → 1st (C)   1st → 1st (C)
                  X → 3rd (H)   3rd → 3rd (H)

'The cat_C said to the rabbit_R about the hyena_H "I_C climbed up and took him_H down. He_H replied that I_C should give him_H my_C shoulder".'

The pronoun coreferentiality relationships across the various quote stretches of the above report are shown by the formulas written underneath the boundaries in the above display (here, the arrows simply mean 'coreferential with').

It is necessary to look at the middle stretch in some detail. This consists of two parts. First 'I climbed up and took him down' is the cat's description of what he did for the hyena — this is QC1, shown in the upper part of the display above. Second, "He replied that I should give him my shoulder" is the cat's description of what the hyena said to him (cat) in response to his kindness. This second part of the cat's speech has its own QM2 which has a 'say' verb (reply) and its own QC2 which is the cat's quote of what the hyena said to him on a previous occasion. This is shown in the lower part of the display above.

Looking at the first boundary, between the QM1 and the combined QC1/QM2 stretch, 'cat$_C$', the subject of the 'say' verb of QM1 is coreferential with the first person pronoun *mí* 'I' of QC1, and the third role X of QM1 'about the hyena$_H$' of the QM1 is coreferential with the third person pronoun *ú* 'he$_H$' of QM2. Hence there is a direct quote relationship between QM1 and the complex QC1/QM2.

However, at the second boundary, that between the complex QC1/QM2 and the final stretch QC2, we see that the first person pronoun *mí* in QC1 is coreferential with the two first person pronouns in QC2, while the third person subject pronoun *ú* in QM2 is coreferential with the third person (indirect object) pronoun yó in QC2. Hence there is an indirect quote relationship between the middle stretch QC1/QM2 and the final stretch QC2.
So what we have in this example is an indirect quote within a direct quote.

In the data that we have studied, there is quite a sprinkling of examples of second degree quotes, both direct within direct, and indirect within direct. However, what has never been found to occur are examples of either direct within indirect, or indirect within indirect. That is to say, the penultimate quote must always be direct.

Why must we always go to the trouble of checking coreferentiality relationships in studying direct and indirect speech forms? Because there is no other reliable way of determining which form we have, whether direct or indirect.

In English, we have the relative luxury of a complementiser 'that' which clearly marks indirect speech reports; thus: 'He said that I had seen you' is unambiguously an indirect speech report. However, even this criterion is not completely reliable for English, because the complementiser is optional; thus, for instance 'He said I had seen you' is ambiguous between a direct or an indirect speech quote. In West African languages, such a complementiser-like particle marking indirect speech reports is very rarely found, and even in languages that do have it, it is optional.

In Cerma, in particular, it is optional and very rare. So we have to resort to some other criterion. The one that is always reliable is the criterion of pronominal reference.

2. The function of direct and indirect speech in discourse

The function of direct versus indirect speech in Cerma discourse can be explained according to the following principle:

Direct speech is a foregrounding device.
Indirect speech is a backgrounding device.

What remains, then, is to describe the use of foregrounding and backgrounding in Cerma discourse. We start by setting out some general principles and then we will illustrate these by examples.

Consider a narrative to be made up of a *main body* and a *remainder*.
The main body of the narrative starts with the report of the first realised event and finishes with the report of the last realised event of the story. In between will be found:

(i)   the material events that move the story forward;
(ii) the speech events that move the story forward; these include arguments, assertions, premises, commands etc. The content of such speech events will at times include quotes from previous speech events performed by participants;
(iii) the mental processes in the minds of the participants that accompany (i) and (ii); these include wants, desires, purposes, etc.;
(iv) included also within the main body will also be flashbacks, background and collateral information.

In short, everything that is 'current', everything that moves the story forward will be found in the main body.
The remainder will, by contrast, consist of everything that comes before or after the main body. Thus both the setting (usually at the beginning) and the moral will be parts of the remainder.

Reverting back to reported speech information, all the speech information in the remainder will be backgrounded, and therefore in the indirect speech form. This is true in all the data we have examined.

In the main body, on the other hand, there are some stretches where there is an option for either foregrounding (direct) or backgrounding (indirect.) (see Section 2.1) There are also other stretches in the main body where backgrounding is the only possible option for speech information (Section 2.2).

The strategy of this chapter will be to deal first with the cases where there is an option for either foregrounding or backgrounding, and then only second with those cases where backgrounding is the only option. From the point of view of discourse function, this seems to the authors to be by far the simpler and more insightful strategy.

2.1 Stretches where there is an option for either foregrounding or backgrounding

There are three kinds of such cases, which we have classified in terms of criteria of choice for foregrounding-backgrounding

(i) cases where the foregrounding criteria are in terms of the relative salience between speech events and material events. (treated in Section 2.1.1)
(ii) cases where the foregrounding backgrounding criteria are in terms of *participant* salience (treated in Section 2.1.2)
(iii) cases of choice of direct or indirect forms in multiply embedded speech (Section 2.1.3)

2.1.1 *Foregrounding according to relative salience between speech events and material events*

This is often a narrator choice. There are stretches on the main story line where there are speech act—speech act interactions between two equally salient participants, and the content of the speech information moves the story forward.[3] Thus the speech events are highly interactive, and are therefore foregrounded and reported in the direct speech form. (cf example 5) (for situations where the interacting participants are not equally salient, see the next Section 2.1.2)

There is also one rather special case in this same category, viz.

> *Special preclimactic salience report in direct speech form*
> An important usage of direct speech quote is to report a speech act that is immediately followed by a climactic material event, (including a material event that resolves a problem.) This is a case of event salience par excellence (see example 6).

There may also be stretches where the story line consists of a sequence of events, some speech events and some material events, but where it is the material events that advance the story line forward. There are indeed also speech events in the sequence, but their content is almost completely predictable so one might say that their content is subsidiary rather than new and highly interactive. In such a situation, the narrator backgrounds the speech events by reporting them with the indirect form, so that the material events alone are foregrounded. (see example 6) In fact, the narrator can always choose to foreground the material events by backgrounding the speech events in the sequence.

2.1.2 *Foregrounding according to relative participant salience*

There are situations in which the narrator wants to present one participant as being more salient, more important, than another. Two kinds of such situations have been found in the data:

(i)   first, when one participant is dominant over the other (for example, having authority over the other.)
(ii) second, when one participant is approved of and the other disapproved of by the narrator. (so this is a case where the narrator imposes his evaluation on the participants.)

The narrator can express either kind of participant salience by reporting speech act—speech act interactions in such a way that the more salient (i.e. dominant or approved) participant's speech is reported in the direct speech form, while the less salient (i.e. dominated or disapproved) one's speech is reported with the indirect speech form.

Table 1 below summarises the discussion of the preceding two subsections. Salient items are shown in bold type.

2.1.3 Choice of direct or indirect forms in multiply embedded speech forms

In the course of a speech act—speech act (or occasionally also in a speech act—material act) interaction, the participant-speaker may quote a speech act made on another (usually anterior) occasion, and usually by another speaker, but sometimes by himself. He does this either to support an argument he is presenting or to justify a course of action he is about to take. Such a quote will clearly have to be a second degree quote, or at times even a third degree quote.

The content of such a second or third degree quote is always in the indirect form, with one exception to be dealt with later. When indirect speech is used, the deictic anchorage is oriented to the current story situation. If the direct speech form were used, the deictic anchorage would be oriented to the anterior situation when the quote was originally uttered, and thus the audience attention would be directed away from the current situation on the story line.

The one exception to the use of indirect speech for the content of second and third degree quotes is when the speaker-participant quotes what he himself said on the anterior situation. In this case, what was said is reported using direct speech because the speaker wants to draw attention to himself and to foreground the content of what he said.

Table 1.

	Equally salient participants	Unequally salient participants
Marking salient participants	**direct speech** –direct speech	**direct speech** –indirect speech
Marking unequally salient events	**indirect speech** –material event	
Marking equally salient events	**direct speech** –material event	

2.2 Information in the main body which must be backgrounded

Such information falls into one category: mental processes. Mental processes, i.e. wants, desires, purposes do not, of themselves, move a story forward. Rather they are the motivation for the associated material events which do move the story forward. As such they are one step removed from the main line of interaction and story advance, so we would expect them to be backgrounded. In fact, mental processes are always described using indirect speech forms in Cerma.

3. Presentation of illustrative data

We now present Cerma data to illustrate and clarify the points which hitherto have been made only in the abstract. The following order of presentation has been adopted.

First are presented data for all the cases where options are possible and there can be a choice between direct and indirect speech forms. Specifically these are

- contrasts in terms of relative event salience
- contrasts in terms of relative participant salience
- second and third degree speech quotes.

Second, are presented data for all the cases where only indirect speech can be used. Specifically these cases are:

- speech in settings
- mental processes in the main body of the narrative.

This order of presentation has been chosen because the functions of direct and indirect speech in Cerma discourse are best understood in terms of the foreground–background contrast. To present first all the functions of direct speech and then separately all the functions of indirect speech would result in a much less insightful description because at no point in such a presentation would it be possible to contrast the uses of direct versus indirect speech.

3.1 Foreground–background contrasts in terms of relative event salience

Here is an example of use of direct speech for salient speech acts that move the story forward.

(5) Context: The hyena had weeded his fonio (cereal) plot and had said that the animals would not eat his fonio. But the geese had decided to outwit him and eat it, so they invented a story to entice the hyena to

leave his field. They went to the hyena and told him that they had found some dead cows and were looking for someone to go with them to eat the cows. The events then run as follows:

1. The hyena said, "*I can't fly*".
2. The geese said, "You are going to fly today".
3. The hyena said, "Take this part of the field, divide it and go on eating until you get to this point".
4. They (the geese) took that part of the field, divided it and ate the cereal and returned,
5. saying, "We have finished eating".
6. He (hyena) said, "*How is it?*"
7. She (geese's spokesperson) said "We will pierce you with a nail, and give you feathers to fly with".
8. He (hyena) took the nail and gave it to them (geese)
9. They (geese) pierced the hyena and stuck feathers in him.
10. The hyena flew with them (geese.)

The information in the ten clauses of this excerpt is all on the main story line. All the quotes (1 to 3, and 5 to 7) are in the direct form. There are speech act—speech act interactions in the pairs 1–2, 2–3, 5–6, 6–7. There are material act—material act interactions in the pairs 8–9 and 9–10. And there is a speech act—material act interaction in the pair 3–4.

The material events are important in pushing the story forward. The content of each of the speech acts is also important in pushing the story forward, and none of the speech acts have predictable contents. Thus the speech act contents are interactive and so are reported in the direct speech form.

Here is an example of the use of indirect speech for non salient speech events in an event sequence where salience is given to the material events.

(6) Context. The father had found a fish in the field who could sing. He brought it home and put it in a flask. One morning the children took the fish out so that it would sing for them. He sang once and then told them he could not sing again. The following events then ensue:

Fish
1. he **said** he would not sing again (indirect)

3. he **said** that he was hungry (indirect)

6. he **said** he was thirsty (indirect)

Children
2. They **asked** him to sing (indirect)

4. they **brought** him food (responding material event)
5. and **told** him to sing (indirect)
7. they **brought** him water (material)

8. he **said** he would not drink well water but water from the pool

13. he **said**
You hold me round my stomach. The water cannot get through. I cannot drink. Let me go so that I can drink, and then I will come and sing for you so you can dance (direct)
15. he **disappeared** (material)

9. they **took** him (material)
10. and **went** with him to the pool (material)
11. they **held** him (material)
12. and **told** him to drink (indirect)
14. they **let** him *go* (material)

In the above presentation, the bold verbs express the interactions between the protagonists, i.e. the children and the fish. There are material actions in clauses 4, 7, 9, 10, 11, 14 and 15, and speech acts in clauses 1, 2, 3, 5, 6, 8, 12, and 13.

Before the climax, every speech act by the fish, triggers off a responding material act by the children:

Fish (speech act)	Children (material act)
said hungry	brought food (and asked him to sing)
said thirsty	brought water
said wanted water from pool	took him to pool (and told him to drink)

All the indirect speech forms are terse, without detail, and the rhetorical effect conveyed is one of a rapid flow of events.

By contrast the climax of the story is told in the last three 'turns' 13, 14, 15. Turn 13 is the fish's final speech contribution; it is preclimactic and is reported with direct speech. This has a great deal of detailed, elaborating content within it, and has the rhetorical effect of slowing down the flow of events, and adding to the tension just before the actual climax. Turn 14 describes the children's response to that, and turn 15 is the resolution to the whole story, the fish's successful escape for which it had been striving all along.

Note that turns 1 to 12 (inclusive) consist of interactions initiated by speech acts and responded to by material acts. The speech acts are reported using indirect speech and each one is a terse statement making just one point. The content of the speech acts is never elaborated by adding any detail; there is just enough information given for the addressee to respond to with the next turn and no more. In this way the story line moves ahead rapidly towards the climax.

Here is another example:

(7) When the white men *came* Yuohie and his people *fled* and they *entered* a big clump of bushes in order to *hide* themselves. The white men then *reached* the bushes and *started to fire* bullets at them. Yuohie *made* his people *lie down* and *said* to the mothers that they should get hold of their children, and that they should not let them cry.

This is a report of a sequence of material events, happening rapidly one after another. The narrator renders the speech information in the indirect speech form, and so backgrounds it. This has the net effect of foregrounding the material events and so preserving the rhetorical effect.

3.2 Foreground–background contrasts in terms of relative participant salience

Participant salience can be in terms of dominance, i.e. whether one participant is more powerful or has more authority or more status than the other. It can also be in terms of narrator approval, i.e. a participant whose values or viewpoint the narrator approves of will be more salient than another that the narrator disapproves of.

3.2.1 *Participant salience in terms of dominance*
Verbal interactions between two equally dominant participants are reported by direct speech for both participants.
But when the dominance is unequal, the more dominant participant will be reported with direct speech and the less dominant with indirect speech.

(8) Context: There was a quarrel between the sun and the moon because of a woman. The village chief invited all the animals to decide who should get the woman as wife. As they were discussing, the bat stood up and said:
The bat (dominant) said (to the people)
Do YOU *not know that it is not good to give the woman to the sun? The sun will kill* US *with* HIS *heat when* HE *comes to fetch the woman.* (direct speech)
The people (dominated) said
that the bat had told the truth. THEY would not give the woman to the sun; THEY would give the woman to the moon. (indirect speech.)

Here the bat who initiated the proposal that was immediately accepted is dominant in authority, and therefore his speech is reported with direct speech forms. (see the italicised pronouns in small caps.)
On the other hand, the people did not initiate anything but merely gave passive

assent to the bat's proposal. They are non dominant and so are reported with indirect forms (see pronouns in ordinary small caps.)

3.2.2 Participant salience in terms of narrator approval

In reporting a conversation, a narrator can show his approval of one participant by quoting him/her with direct speech forms, and his disapproval of the other by quoting that one with indirect speech forms.

(9) Context: Abi, a child with a bad toe, had come to Laura and Ruth every day for treatment. One day the child came with black powder on her wound. Laura and Ruth refused to clean it, and told Abi to get her mother.

In the speech interaction which follows, Laura and Ruth are quoted in direct speech (italics) while Abi's mother is quoted in indirect (roman).

Laura and Ruth said (to Abi's mother)
Why, when Abi already comes here for US to treat HER wound, do YOU put this black powder on. (direct)

Abi's mother said that
SHE had not put the other medicine on. It was HER cowife who had put it on. (indirect)

Laura and Ruth said
If YOU want US to deal with the wound then do not interfere with what WE do. If YOU want to put YOUR black powder on, then the child must stay at home, and YOU must clean the wound YOURSELVES. (direct)

Abi's mother said that
THEY would not put medicine on Abi's wound again, that SHE (Abi) would continue to come in order for THEM to treat HER wound. (indirect)

Then Laura and Ruth gave Abi's mother advice on how to clean the wound at home, all using direct speech. Subsequently, the mother was reported as saying that 'she had understood' (again using indirect speech.)

In this example, the narrator shows his approval of Laura and Ruth by quoting them with direct speech, and his disapproval of Abi's mother who had not taken enough care of her child by quoting her with indirect speech.

It is probable that the mother also felt threatened and inferior, that is to say, she was dominated in this situation.

3.3 Direct or indirect speech in the final quotation content when there are two or three degrees of embedding

Second degree quotes are more common than might be first supposed. They are used in a speech interaction whenever one of the interlocutors quotes what was said on another occasion in order to support a point s/he is currently making. The speaker of that other quote can be either the interlocutor himself or someone else. Here is a very simple example from English. In that example, the second part of Mary's response contains a second degree quote. The first alternative shows a second degree quote content using indirect speech (shown in roman), while the second alternative shows a second degree quote using direct speech (in italics).

(10) First alternative
A: I was listening yesterday to what John and Mary were saying about their finances.
John said that he was worried about paying for their new house.
Mary said 'Don't worry'
Mother said to me that she would pay all the bills. (indirect second degree quote alternative)'

Second alternative
A: I was listening yesterday to what John and Mary were saying about their finances.
John said that he was worried about paying for their new house.
Mary said 'Don't worry'
Mother said to me yesterday '*I'll pay all the bills*'. (direct alternative)

Turning now to Cerma, when there are two or three degrees of embedding, the final quotation content is always in the indirect speech form unless the speaker of the underlying performative is quoting himself. Then it is direct speech. (see example 13). All the intervening quotation margins, however, are in the direct speech form.

Why is the final quotation content given so often in the indirect form? The indirect speech form orients the quotation content to the current situation in the story, that is to say, its deictic anchorage is the situation in which the quoter quotes it, and in which s/he is currently involved. On the other hand, the original speaker of the quote first said that quote at a different (anterior) time and place and with a different set of interlocutors. In fact, looking at the two alternatives of the English example above, the first alternative with the indirect second degree quote does feel a bit more natural than the other, simply because the reader does not have to reset his deictic anchorage.

3.3.1 Example of a second degree embedded indirect speech

(11) Context: The geese wanted to eat the hyena's fonio (cereal). To get him away from his field where the cereal was, they flattered him, saying they needed his help. They even gave him feathers so that he could fly. So the geese and the hyena all flew together and finally they all landed on a tree. Whereupon the geese took their feathers back and left the hyena stranded in the tree.

At this point, the geese (reported with direct speech) tell the helpless hyena that they are about to eat his fonio. Then in order to justify their action, they quote (reported in indirect speech) what God had said to them at an anterior time when he had created them, viz. '*We* (the geese) should eat between *your* (hyena's) claws' By putting this in the form of indirect speech, the geese are invoking what God had said long ago to justify what they are about to do in their current situation. Note that with the indirect quote form the pronouns 'we' and 'your' give a much more confrontational flavour to that quote content than the corresponding direct quote ones ('you' and 'his', respectively) would have done.

Here is the information concerning that quote in tabular display (direct speech quotes are shown in italics, indirect in roman).

Said by narrator at narration time QM1	Said by geese at time t_1 (current story time) QM2	said by God at time t_2 (anterior time) QC2
geese$_G$ said to hyena$_H$	*we$_G$ will eat your$_H$ fonio. God said to us$_G$ when he created us$_G$*	we$_G$ should eat between your$_H$ claws.

3.3.2 Example of a third degree embedded indirect speech quote

(12) Context: Sungalo's pigs had been poisoned by some unknown person. Sungalo's uncle suggested using a fetish to punish whoever had been responsible. But Sungalo himself argues against this idea. The conversation is shown in the accompanying table.

The quotation margin, QM1 is direct, and introduces Sungalo talking at time t_0. The first degree quote is direct, and reports what was said by Sungalo to his uncle at the current point in the story (time t_1 which is before t_0).

The second degree quote is also direct and reports what people will say at some time (time t_2) which is subsequent to current discourse time t_0. The third degree quote reports what had been said at some time t_3 which was anterior to the current discourse time t_0. It is the last stretch in the string of embedded speech, and the most remote from the initial quotation margin QM1 in terms of stretches of embedding and therefore the indirect speech form is used. The following table sets out the various stretches schematically and gives the speech styles used in each stretch.

Sungalo the narrator says to his audience at time t_0 (current discourse time t_0)	Sungalo said to uncle at time t_1 (t_1 before t_0)	People will say at time t_2 (t_2 after t_1)	Sungalo said at time t_3 (t_3 before t_0)
I_S replied to my uncle$_U$	No, but I_S do think that if we do what you$_U$ suggest, it would not be good. It would spoil my$_S$ testimony.		
QM1	QM2 and QC1 *They will say about me$_S$*	QM3 and QC2 *This Sungalo$_S$, he$_S$ says* *He$_S$ and his fellow Christians$_C$, did they$_{SC}$ not say* *But now that his$_S$ pigs have died, he$_S$ uses a fetish (to harm people)*	QC3 **he$_S$ believes in God** **they$_{SC}$ do not do harm to anybody**
	first degree-direct	second degree-direct	third degree: indirect

In the part of the data which is shown bold, the speaker (Sungalo) quotes what he expects people will comment concerning what he (Sungalo) had previously said. This is all reported in indirect form. During the course of their comment, he expects them to actually quote what he (Sungalo) had previously said.

Sungalo here applies to his current situation what he expects people to say about Christians in another (projected, future) situation. That is his argument to his uncle which explains why he does not want to use a fetish.

3.3.3 Example of a second degree embedded direct speech

In a reported argumentation, whenever someone other than the quoter is quoted, the second degree embedded quote is in the indirect speech form (as shown in example 12). However, when the quoter *quotes himself,* the second degree embedded quote is in the direct speech form. So, in the context of a reported argumentation, if a quoter quotes someone else and then later himself, he can foreground his own quote (using direct form) and background his quote of someone else (using indirect form) in order to shade the argument for his own benefit.

(13) Context: The geese had left the hyena stranded up in a tree, and gone off to eat his fonio grain. The cat came, saw the hyena and took him down. But as soon as the hyena was safely on the ground, he treacherously wanted a part of the cat's body to eat. But the cat refused and the two began to argue. The rabbit then comes and wants to know what all the argument was about. Whereupon the cat reports to the rabbit what had happened.

Quote margin	First degree	Second degree
Cat said to rabbit	*It was I who came out to play with my children. I came and found the hyena up there. I climbed up to get him*	
	he said that (cat quotes hyena)	I should give **him my** thigh to eat (indirect)
	I said (cat quotes self)	*If **you** (hyena) eat this thigh, what will be left of **me** after that.* (direct)
	he said that (cat quotes hyena)	in that case I should give **him my** shoulder (indirect)
	I said (cat quotes self)	*If cut **my** shoulder and give it to **you**, what will be left of **me** after that.* (direct)

Direct speech is shown in italics, indirect speech is shown in ordinary Roman type. Note the forms of the pronouns (shown bold) in all the quotes. It is seen that the first degree quote is always direct, but the second degree quotes of the cat are indirect when she quotes the hyena, and direct when she quotes herself. By this means the cat is foregrounding her own speech content, and backgrounding and distancing herself from the hyena's speech, showing her disapproval.

3.4 Stretches where backgrounding (indirect speech) is the only option

There are some parts of a Cerma narrative where indirect speech is the only possible option. These are found both outside the main body of a narrative and also within it.

Outside the main body of a narrative, settings are where speech quotes must be in the indirect form. The setting does not contain any current events of the story, but can report both events anterior to the events of the story or a repetitive event pattern which occurred before the events of the story proper began.

Within the main body of the narrative, mental processes are normally backgrounded. Mental processes include wants, desires and purposes. For the purposes of this chapter, we are considering speech events separately from mental processes which are not speech events.

3.4.1 Reported speech within the setting of a narrative

(14) Here is the very first sentence of a story. The events of the story proper have not yet started, What is being reported here is an anterior situation which poses a problem for the protagonists.
The hyena had weeded his fonio (cereal) field and had said
that the animals would not eat it,
that the birds would not eat his funio at all.

This reports a situation obtaining anterior to the beginning of the story. By making the assertion reported above, the hyena had thrown down a challenge, and it was therefore up to him to defend his fonio, and for the other animals to overcome his challenge. The story proper tells how the geese did so.

The reported speech here is in the indirect form; it is backgrounded because it is in the setting.

(15) Here again are the first sentences in the setting of another story. The same principles as above apply, and reported speech is in the indirect form.
The sun and the moon had a dispute because of a woman.
The sun said that the woman was for him.
The moon said that the woman was for him.

3.4.2 Mental world of a participant within the main body of a narrative

Thoughts, desires, wants, and purposes belong to the mental world of the participant concerned and are not directly in the real world of the story. Of course such information usually relates indirectly to the main events (and thus to the real world) of the story.

Desires

(16) Context: The father had found a fish in the field, and he had brought it home in a gourd. His children took it out and let it go. When the father came back home he wanted to look inside the gourd in order to have the fish sing.
bà tó wúɔ ù né kòlúoŋū-ná
their father he:want he look gourd-LOC
'Their father wanted to look inside the gourd'.

Here the father's desire is part of his own private mental world, and has not been verbally expressed by him. So the above report is not the report of a speech event in the real world. The indirect speech form (shown by the pronoun *ù* 'he') has backgrounded the content of his desire (want), and we know that what is reported is a mental event and not a speech event. The form of the verb *wúɔ*, here glossed as 'he.want' is in fact identical to the form of the 'say' verb.

Purposes

Purposes are rather more complex than wants and desires in that more than one participant can be involved. In Cerma constructions expressing purpose, there is a matrix clause whose verb describes a material process, and an embedded verb in indirect speech form which describes the purpose of the matrix verb process.

The agent of the matrix verb performs the action of the matrix verb so that either he himself or another participant can perform the action expressed by the purpose verb. Who then might this other participant be? The options open depend on the transitivity of the matrix verb. The data examined shows that

- If the matrix verb is an intransitive verb, the agent of the embedded purpose verb is usually coreferential with the agent of the matrix verb. (no data found to the contrary)
- If the matrix verb is a transitive verb with an animate theme (and direct object), then the agent of the embedded purpose verb can be either the agent of the matrix verb or the (animate) theme of the matrix verb.
- If the matrix verb is a ditransitive verb involving transfer of some entity (e.g. give) and has an animate recipient (as indirect object), then the agent of the purpose verb can be either the agent of the matrix verb or the recipient of the matrix verb.

It is clear from the above that the agent of the purpose verb can, but need not be coreferential with the agent of the matrix verb. To distinguish the two cases, Cerma marks with a low tone those agents of the purpose verb that are coreferential with the agent of the matrix verb, and with a high tone those agents that are not. Illustrative data now follows.

With an intransitive matrix verb and a coreferential agent in the purpose verb.

(17) váà kàn wùɔ́   ù kà   cór gbòŋhàllé ˈnáŋdéná
     dog go SO.THAT he DISPL pass houses   other.LOC
     'The dog_D went so that he_D passed between the houses'.

Here the verb *kàn* 'go' in the matrix clause is intransitive, and the subject (agent) pronoun *ù* 'he_H' of the purpose verb is coreferential with *váà* 'dog_D', the subject (agent) of the matrix verb. Thus the embedded subject pronoun has low tone to mark the coreferentiality.

With a transitive matrix verb, and a non coreferential agent in the purpose verb

(18) ú híèl   tètèrìeŋó wùɔ   ú hánl
     he take.out fish   SO.THAT he sing
     'He_A took the fish_B SO.THAT he_B would sing'.

Here the matrix verb *híèl* 'take out' is transitive, with *tètèrìeŋó* 'fish_B' as direct object and animate theme. The subject pronoun in the purpose clause is *ú* 'he_B', and is coreferential with this theme, and thus not with the agent of the matrix verb. Thus the embedded subject pronoun has high tone to mark the *non* coreferentiality of the two agents.

With a ditransitive verb involving transfer as a matrix verb and a non coreferential agent in the purpose verb

(19) bá   hán ˈkáagbúɔ̀ŋò wùɔ   ú cál
     they give ram   SO.THAT he divide
     'They_A gave (the fish) to the ram_B so that he_B would divide it'.

Here the matrix verb *hán* 'give' is ditransitive involving transfer (of the fish) and the recipient of this verb is *ˈkáagbúɔ̀ŋò* 'ram_B'. The agent (and subject) *ú* 'he_B' is coreferential with this recipient, and therefore non-coreferential with the agent of the matrix verb (they_A). Thus the embedded agent pronoun *ú* carries a high tone to mark the noncoreferentiality of the two agents.

Notes

1. Cerma is spoken by some 50,000 people in the south western region of Burkina Faso and in the neighbouring region in northern Côte d'Ivoire. Westerman and Bryan (1970: 55-75) places Gouin (his term for Cerma) within both the Lobi and the Senufo dialect clusters of the Gur languages of West Africa. More recently there has been some doubt cast on the accuracy of this classification, and Manessy (1975) places both Kirma (his term for Cerma) and Tyurama within the Gur (Voltaic) group but definitely outside the Lobi and Senufo

dialect clusters. Mensah and Tchagbalé (1983) agree with this classification. Naden (1989) classifies Cerma (his Cerman, or Kirma or Gouin) as a Gur language belonging to Southern branch of Central Gur, and located on his dialect map (1989: 140) as spoken in the region near Banfora, just north of the border between Burkina Faso and Côte d'Ivoire, West Africa.

There are mainly three different but mutually intelligible dialects spoken around Niangoloko, Banfora and Soubaka. The dialect studied in this chapter is that of Niangoloko.

The language data on which this study is based consists of eight narrative texts, totalling some 110 pages. Hurlimann commenced field work in the language in July 1981, and this continues till the present. She wishes to thank the members of the Cerma community of Niangoloko for teaching her the language, and more especially she conveys her thanks to Soulama Emile, Hema Pierre and Soma Etienne who not only provided most of the eight texts, but also did the transcription, and patiently answered many questions during the course of the analysis.

2. The transcription used in the data of this chapter is based on a phonological analysis carried by Edward and Dayle Lauber of SIL in 1978-80.

The phonemes of Cerma are: voiceless stops *p, t, k*; voiced stops *b, d, g*; voiceless and voiced affricates, *tʃ, dʒ*; double stops, *kp, gb*; nasals *m, n, ŋ*; voiceless and voiced fricatives, *f, s, h, v*; semivowels *w, y*; lateral *l*, and vibrant *r*. Nasal consonants assimilate to the place of articulation of a contiguous following consonant.

The oral vowels are *i, e, ɛ, a, o, ɔ, u*, the nasal vowels are *ĩ, ẽ, ã, õ, ũ*.

In the practical orthography, the symbols used are the same as above except that /tʃ/ is written as *c*, and /dʒ/ as *j*. Nasalisation on vowels is represented by the consonant *n* after the corresponding oral vowel, e.g. (*an*), and lengthened vowels by the double vowel, e.g. (*oo*).

There are four contrastive tones, represented as follows: high level by the acute accent, e.g. (*ó*), low level by the grave accent, e.g. (*ò*), downglide by the circumflex, e.g. (*ô*), and upglide by the inverted circumflex, e.g. (*ǒ*). Downstep is represented by an exclamation point before the vowel carrying the downstepped tone.

3. In the formula here, the elongated hyphen between 'act' and 'speech' simply means sequence in surface form.

References

Manessy, Gabriel. 1975. *Les langues Oti-Volta*. Paris: Société d'Études Linguistiques et Anthropologiques de France.

Mensah, Emmanuel N. A. and Zakari Tchagbalé. 1983. *Atlas des langues gur de Côte d'Ivoire*. Abidjan: Institut de Linguistique Appliquée; Paris: Agence de Coopération Culturelle et Technique.

Naden, Tony. 1989. "Gur". In Bendor-Samuel, John (ed.), *The Niger-Congo languages*. Lanham: University Press of America, 140–68.

Westermann, Diedrich and Margaret A. Bryan. 1970. *The languages of West Africa* (=Handbook of African Languages, part II). 2nd ed. with a supplementary bibliography by D.W. Arnott. London: International African Institute.

CHAPTER 4

Direct and indirect discourse in Tamil

Sanford B. Steever
New Canaan, Connecticut

1. Introduction

The grammar of reported speech in Modern Tamil,[1] embracing direct and indirect discourse, stands firmly grounded in the grammar of complex sentences, and must from one point of view be viewed as an instance of the grammar of complementation. Reported speech, as analyzed in the structuralist framework formulated in Jakobson (1971),[2] embeds one speech event within another. While we may readily list and catalogue the characteristics that distinguish reported speech from other forms of complex syntactic structures, treating it as a phenomenon in and of itself, the fact that reported speech syntactically embeds one structure within another in Tamil is sufficient to place its analysis firmly within the analysis of complementation.

The following sketch presents an outline of certain salient features of the grammar of complementation in Tamil; a fuller treatment is to be found in Steever (1988). A complex sentence in Tamil straightforwardly consists of two or more simple sentences joined together through a variety of syntactic devices. A simple sentence in Tamil, in turn, consists of a subject and a predicate. While the subject is generally a noun phrase in the nominative case (1a, b), the language also possesses a dative-subject construction in which the notional subject of a verb of emotion, sensation, cognition or possession appears in the dative case (1c, d). Unlike datives with a purposive or an allative meaning, dative-subjects have certain subject-coding properties that the other datives lack, such as the ability to serve as the antecedent of a reflexive pronoun. The predicate of a simple sentence may be either a finite verb (1b, d) or a predicate nominal (1a, c). Note that, as is common for many other Dravidian languages, sentences with predicate nominals are well-formed without the presence of any copula.[3] By combining the two kinds of subject with the two kinds of predicate, four basic patterns of simple sentence may be generated.

(1) a. avaL   en manaivi.
       she-NOM my wife-NOM
       'she (is) my wife'
    b. avaL   anta kaTitattai eZut-in-āL.
       she-NOM that letter-ACC write-PST-3SF
       'she wrote that letter'
    c. avar-ukku oru makan.
       he-DAT   one son-NOM
       'he (has) a son,' lit., 'to him (is) one son.'
    d. en makan-ukku.k kōpam   va-nt-atu.
       my son-DAT   anger-NOM come-PST-3SN
       'my son got angry'

In Modern Tamil, simple sentences generally show agreement between subject and predicate when the predicate is a finite verb, as in example (1b).[4] The basic agreement pattern is nominative-accusative: a verb, transitive or intransitive, necessarily agrees in person, number and gender with its subject. All such verb forms are treated as finite verbs.[5] In the minor sentence pattern, the dative-subject construction, the verb generally agrees with the nominative case noun phrase.

We may begin to extrapolate certain syntactic generalizations from the four examples given above. As exemplified in (1b), the basic word order of Tamil is SOV, or subject, object and verb. Despite the morphological marking of grammatical relations through case marking, the verb remains in sentence-final position and is removed from there only under marked circumstances. We may predict that, in keeping with the general head-final character of Tamil morphosyntax and consistent with well-known word-order typology, genitives precede the nouns they modify, main verbs precede their auxiliaries, postpositions are used instead of prepositions and, importantly for the purposes of this chapter, subordinate clauses precede main clauses.[6]

Complex sentences, as already noted, consist of two or more clauses: in keeping with the dominant SOV word order, dependent clauses precede main clauses. It should be pointed out that the distinction between subordination and coordination seems not to be well defined in Tamil. While some evidence is available to distinguish between subordinate and coordinate structures, such as the possibility of backward pronominalization into subordinate but not coordinate clauses, Tamil morphosyntax appears not to make much of this distinction, often using the same set of morphsyntactic devices in both structures.

Two sets of devices that are not readily available for the formation of complex sentences in Tamil are a formally independent word-class of conjunctions and a formally independent word-class of adverbs.[7] Although Tamil does possess certain clitic particles that may function as quantifiers and conjunctions, their use is marked relative to the use of free words; with one exception noted below, they are not relevant to the grammar of reported speech. The absence of conjunctions as a separate part of speech in Tamil thus shifts the burden of coordination and subordination to the two basic parts of speech in the language, nouns and verbs, but particularly to verbs.

Tamil morphology, as is common for Dravidian languages, encodes a fair amount of information that would in other languages be handled through syntax. Just as the case-marking of nouns signals much of the internal syntax of the clause, verb morphology generally bears the burden of specifying the syntactic relations that may hold between two or more clauses. Dependent clauses in both subordinate and coordinate constructions are generally signaled by a nonfinite verb form whose morphology requires it to combine with some element of the following clause. The following clause may be a conjunct of a larger coordinate structure or the main clause in a subordinate-matrix construction. Nonfinite verbs fall into one of two sets: those verb forms that combine with a verb form in the following clause and those that combine with a nominal expression in the following clause. It is the first set that primarily concerns us here: it contains such forms as the conjunctive form (cf), the infinitive (inf) and the conditional (cond), as illustrated below. The second set contains adnominal verb forms (anp), often called relative or adjectival participles in the literature: they help to form relative clauses, complex NPs and other structures. The following set of sentences illustrate the use of nonfinite verb forms that combine with a following verb.

(2) a. maZai   pey-tu   veyil   aTi-ttu   vānavil
       rain-NOM rain-CF sunshine-NOM beat-CF rainbow-NOM
       tōnr-i.y-atu.
       appear-PST-3SN
       'It rained, the sunshine beat down and a rainbow appeared'
    b. avan   pōk-a ivan   van-t-ān.
       that.man-NOM go-INF this.man-NOM come-PST-3SM
       'As that man went, this man came.'
    c. makan pāttirattai uTai-ttāl   ammā   avan-ai cummāka
       son-NOM pots-ACC break-COND mother-NOM him-ACC alone
       viTamāTTāL.
       leave-FUT-NEG-3SF
       'If the son breaks the pots, (his) mother will not let him alone.'

The conjunctive form, often labeled the adverbial or conjunctive participle in the literature on Tamil, joins two or more clauses in (2a). While the finite verb at the end of the sentence (*tōnriyatu* 'it appeared') varies in person, number and gender with its subject, the conjunctive forms (*peytu* 'raining', *aTittu* 'striking') remain invariant no matter what the subject is. The infinitive, the most unmarked nonfinite form in Tamil, also joins two clauses in (2b): the infinitive *pōka* 'go' joins the first clause to the second clause, which contains the finite verb *vantān* 'he came'. Its uses are wide, ranging from marking clauses of circumstance as in (2b) to marking clauses of purpose. The conditional, illustrated by *uTaittāl* 'if (one) break' in (2c), most commonly marks the protasis, or 'if-clause', of a conditional proposition.

A close examination of these and many other Tamil sentences reveals that the distribution of finite predicates within complex sentences is severely restricted. We may stipulate as a first approximation that no sentence of Modern Tamil can have more than one finite predicate: that predicate occurs highest in the sentence's tree structure and c-commands all others (see McCawley 1988:340 for a definition of c-command). Given the head-final characteristics of Tamil syntax, this means that the unmarked position for the lone finite predicate in a Tamil sentence falls at the end of the sentence; all remaining verbs within the complex sentence structure must assume nonfinite verb morphology. The three sentences presented in example (2) illustrate this restriction.

This preliminary observation on the distribution of finite and nonfinite verbs in the Tamil sentence has numerous structural implications, some of which bear directly on the analysis of reported speech. It must be noted for the topic of this chapter that the restriction against multiple finite predicates in a complex syntactic structure implies the lack of direct discourse in Tamil language (this assumes — perhaps counterfactually across languages — that all reported discourse is a construction of syntactic embedding). Why should this be so? The clause that represents the reported speech would in its original, unreported form have had a finite predicate to satisfy the rule requiring one finite predicate per sentence. However, once that clause comes to be syntactically embedded within the clause that represents the reporting speech, it would not be able to preserve the finite predicate it originally had, but would have to substitute it with some nonfinite counterpart in accordance with the rule against multiple finite predicates. This means when sentences (1b) or (1d) are embedded under a verb of reporting, their finite verb forms should assume some nonfinite form. The restriction against more than one finite verb per sentence also suggests that sentences with predicate nominals, such as (1a) and (1c), could never appear in any kind of reported speech; as nouns, predicate nominals lack the nonfinite verb morphology — indeed, they lack all verb morphology — needed to be embedded within complex sentences. The morphosyntactic inability to form direct discourse is perhaps unexpected on typological grounds: across languages, direct discourse appears to be far more common than indirect discourse. In fact, in language after language, the existence of indirect discourse generally implies the existence of direct discourse.[8] The converse does not often hold in that there are many examples of languages with direct discourse that lack indirect discourse.

A more exhaustive study of Tamil grammar reveals the presence of certain morphosyntactic devices that do permit syntactic structures with multiple finite predicates in the language; hence, permit the formation of direct discourse. Investigation of Tamil syntactic structures reveals a number of principled exceptions to the constraint against multiple finite verbs in a complex sentence. First, two verbs *ena* 'say' and *āka* 'become', in all their various forms, may function as predicates in a matrix sentence which embeds subordinate clauses with finite predicates without imposing any morphological change on the verb morphology of the subordinate clause. These same predicates may also embed in a subordinate clause sentences that have predicate nominals. Consider the following set of sentences.

(3) a. _{S0}[nān _{S1}[kaNNan nallavan]_{S1} enru ninaikkirēn]_{S0}.
I-NOM Kannan-NOM good.man-NOM say-CF think-PRS-1s
'I think that Kannan is a good man'.

b. _{S0}[_{S1}[avan iŋkē vantān]_{S1} enpatu uNmai.t=tān]_{S0}
he-NOM here come-PST-3SM say-VN truth-NOM=indeed
'It (is) the truth that he came here'.

(4) a. _{S0}[_{S1}[avan vantān]_{S1} ānāl nān avanai.p pārkka.v illai]_{S0}
he-NOM come-PST-3SM become-COND I-NOM he-ACC see-INF be-NEG
'Though he came, I didn't see him.'

b. _{S0}[_{S1}[_{S2}[cāmān (unakku) vāŋka vēNTum]_{S2} ānāl vāŋku]_{S1} allatu kaTaiyai viTTu iraŋku]_{S0}
goods-NOM you-DAT buy-INF want-FUT-3SN become-COND buy-IMP become-NEG-VN store-ACC leave-CF get.down-IMP
'Unless you are going to buy something you want, step out of the store.'

The two verbs *ena* 'say' and *āka* 'become' play a crucial role in the formation of complex sentences: they may take as their "direct objects" linguistic expressions of any category and internal complexity without imposing any morphological change on those "objects." In example (3a), the predicate nominal *nallavan* 'good man' of the subordinate clause is embedded under *enru*, which is the conjunctive form of the verb *ena* 'say'; in (3b), the finite verb *vantān* 'he came' is similarly embedded by *enpatu*, a verbal noun of *ena* 'say'. In (4a), the finite predicate *vantān* 'he came' is embedded under the form *ānāl*, the conditional form of *āka* 'become'. In example (4b), there are two instances in which a form of the verb *āka* 'become' embeds a finite predicate in a subordinate clause. The conditional verb form *ānāl* 'if becomes' embeds the finite verb form *vēNTum* 'want(s)'[9] in S₂ while the negative verbal noun *allatu* 'unless become(s)' embeds the finite imperative verb form *vāṇku* 'buy!' in S₁. Although the presence of two finite predicates in examples (3a) and (4a) might suggest that direct discourse is formed by stringing together two independent sentences, there is evidence that the reported speech is embedded in the reporting speech: in example (3a), the reported speech in S₁ appears between the subject of the reporting speech, *nān* 'I' and the finite verb *niṉaikkirēṉ* 'I think' in exactly the position where one might expect a direct object. The counterproposal that direct discourse consists of two independent sentence strung together would then be forced to treat the reporting sentence in (3a) as a discontinuous structure into which the reported speech has been parenthetically inserted, itself a species of embedding. The simpler analysis would treat (3a) as an instance of canonical SOV word order in Tamil. In the sentences above, *eṉa* 'say' is used when the verb of the matrix clause is a verb of propositional attitude, cognition and perception; below we see that it may also be used when the verb in the matrix sentence is a *verbum dicendi*.¹⁰ This permits it, among other things, to form direct discourse.

2. Reported speech in Tamil

Up until this point, we have concentrated on the syntactic dimension of reported speech, treating direct and indirect discourse both as specific instances of more general patterns of complement structures in Tamil. Now in order to distinguish between direct and indirect discourse, we must address the semantics of the two kinds of reported speech. The discussion of semantics that follows relies on the structuralist program of analysis of grammatical categories to illuminate the differences between direct and indirect discourse and what binds them together as instances of reported speech. Jakobson (1971:130) characterizes reported speech as "a speech within speech, a message within a message ...". Reported speech may therefore be thought of as a speech event whose narrated event is itself another speech event, one that has been displaced from its original context. Reported speech is commonly divided into direct and indirect discourse. Jespersen (1965:292) adroitly characterizes indirect discourse by a shifting of person, tense and mood away from the forms it would have had in direct discourse. In this shifting, the deictic center of the reporting speech captures and assimilates the deictic center of the original, reported speech event. For example, a noun phrase in indirect discourse is assigned first person if it refers to the speaker of the reporting speech event, second person if it refers to the addressee and third person in other cases. Any grammatical form that makes reference to the speech events or its participants, such as person P^s/P^n, tense E^s/E^n, attitude P^s/E^n (see below), is affected by the deictic shift from direct to indirect discourse. Such a shift is illustrated in the English example of indirect discourse *he said that he would come home*: in the interpretation where the subject of the main clause is coreferential with the subject of the subordinate clause, the pronoun in the original speech would have been *I* and the verb phrase would have been *will come home*, as are preserved in the direct discourse counterpart *he said, "I will come home."*

Such changes do not occur in direct discourse. The original speech in (5a) is reported in both (5b and c). Example (5b) illustrates direct discourse: the original speech is embedded by the so-called complementizer *enru* 'that': it is actually the conjunctive form of the verb *ena* 'say', which, as we have seen above, does not alter the morphological features of the forms it embeds. The verb in the subordinate clause continues to bear the inflections of the imperative singular and the subject appears in the nominative case, the forms they would respectively have had in the original speech now being reported. But a marked shift takes place in the indirect discourse counterpart in example (5c): the finite imperative form is replaced by the nonfinite infinitive and the nominative case second person singular pronoun (*nī* 'thou') of the original speech is replaced by the accusative case first person singular pronoun (*ennai* 'me'). Further, the accusative pronoun is now grammatically construed as the object of the verb of reporting *colla* 'tell, say' in the matrix clause. In (5d), the underlying second person subject pronoun has been shifted to a first person accusative pronoun, as in (5c). Furthermore, the finite verb *vantān* 'he came' has been replaced by the composite form *varum paTi* 'manner of coming', which consists of the future adnominal form *varum* 'which will come', a nonfinite verb form, and the head noun *paTi* 'manner'. The shift from finite to nonfinite form in both examples, as well as the change in the case and person of the pronoun, indicates that clause union has taken place to some extent, partially obscuring the fact that the reported speech originally consisted of two separate sentences which, on certain analyses, may derive from an underlying biclausal structure. It also obscures which noun phrases and which verbs originally appeared in the original speech being reported and which should be attributed to the speech reporting the original.

(5) a. $_{S1}$[nī vā!]$_{S1}$
you-NOM come-IMP
'You come!'

b. $_{S0}$[$_{S1}$[nī vā]$_{S1}$ enru connān]]$_{S0}$.
you-NOM come-IMP that say-PST-3SM
'He said, "You come!"'

c. $_{S0}$[ennai vara.c connān]$_{S0}$.
I-ACC come-INF say-PST-3SM
'He told me/said to me to come.'

d. $_{S0}$[ennai varum paTi connān]$_{S0}$
I-ACC come-FUT-ANP manner say-PST-3SM
'He told me to come'

Subsequent research, e.g., *Roncador* (1988), has come to treat the dichotomy between direct and indirect speech as a scalar opposition, not a polar one. The phenomenon of semi-direct discourse, well known from Romance linguistics, exemplifies a kind of speech that falls between the two poles of direct and indirect speech. One instance of semi-direct discourse in Tamil is given below in example (16). For the time being, however, we will concentrate on bringing the grammatical contrasts between direct and indirect discourse as it occurs in Tamil into sharper focus, something which has not been reported hitherto in the literature.

Figure 1 lists some of the major differences between direct and indirect discourse that occur in the language.

Direct Discourse	Indirect Discourse
[[Reported Speech] Reporting Speech] ↳ No Assimilation ⟶	[[Reported Speech] Reporting Speech] ↳ Assimilation ⟶
1. Two Deictic Centers	1'. One Deictic Center
2. Finite Embedded Verbs	2'. Nonfinite Embedded Verbs
3. Quotative Complementizer *enru*	3'. Infinitival Complementizer Adnominal Form + *paTi* 'as'
4. Imperative and Optative Forms	4'. Infinitival Forms
5. Affective Lengthening and Lexis	5'. No Affective Lengthening or Lexis
6. Non-shifted Deixis	6'. Shifted Deixis
7. Vocatives and Exclamations	7'. No Vocatives or Exclamations
8. Interrogative Forms	8'. No Interrogative Forms
9. Attitudinal Auxiliary Verbs	9'. No Attitudinal Auxiliary Verbs

Figure 1. Differences between direct and indirect discourse in Tamil

The alternation of person and finiteness are not the only changes that accompany the alternation between direct and indirect discourse. In indirect discourse, any linguistic form that conventionally encodes the (original) speaker's sentiments, opinions or the like is systematically excluded from the reported speech represented in the embedded clause, as the following examples demonstrate. Example (6a) includes the curse *nācamāy pō* 'go to hell'; (7a), the idiomatic exclamation *tīyai vai* 'holy smokes, no kidding' (lit. 'place the fire'). As examples (6b) and (7b) show, both occur in direct discourse but, as their counterparts in (6c) and (7c) show, neither may occur in indirect discourse.[11] Both expressions are highly affective utterances with relatively little propositional or denotational content; they are expressive of the (original) speaker's emotive state. When the shift from direct to indirect discourse takes place and the original deictic center is eliminated, these forms lose the frame of reference they once had to the original speaker and are accordingly eliminated in the reported speech. According to the rules of etiquette that govern the use of Tamil, they cannot be properly attributed to the speaker of the reporting speech in which the original speech is embedded.

(6) a. nācamāy pō!
    hell-ADV go-IMP
    'Go to hell.'
  b. $_{SO}[_{S1}$[nācamāy pō]$_{S1}$ enru connān]$_{SO}$.
    hell-ADV   go-IMP say-CF tell-PST-3SM
    'He said, "Go to hell."'
  c. *nācamāy pōka.c connān.
    hell-ADV go-INF tell-PST-3SM
    ?'He said that go to hell.'

(7) a. tīyai   vai!
    fire-ACC place-IMP
    'Holy smokes.'
  b. $_{SO}[_{S1}$[tīyai vai]$_{S1}$ enru connān]$_{SO}$
    fire-ACC place-IMP say-CF tell-PST-3SM
    'He said, "Holy smokes!"'
  c. *tīyai   vaikka.c connān.
    fire-ACC place-INF tell-PST-3SM
    ?'He said to holy smokes.'

Other conventional expressions of the speaker's emotional state are eliminated in the shift from direct to indirect discourse. In (8c) and (9c), both instances of indirect discourse, the finite verb form of the original speech is syntactically replaced by a combination of the future verbal noun and *āka* (the infinitive of *āka* 'become'). It contrasts with the form *enru*, which signals direct discourse in (8b). In (8a), the modifier *periya* 'big' is intensified and exaggerated by lengthening its second vowel to four times its original length to *perīiiya* 'reeeally big'.[12] Such lengthening is a conventional stylistic figure that expresses the speaker's feeling — surprise, astonishment, shock — that the subject of the conversation is extraordinarily important, abnormal, noteworthy, strange, etc. It is permissible in direct discourse (8b), but not in indirect discourse (8c), as the unacceptability judgments of that sentence shows. Affective lengthening also occurs in the expression in (9a), *ittanūNTu* 'itsy-bitsy, teensy-weensy' (*tammatūNTu* 'id.' in and around the state capital of Chennai). As before, it is permitted in direct discourse (9b), but excluded from indirect discourse (9c). Here it is not merely the affective lengthening that disqualifies this word from appearing in indirect discourse; the word itself, with or without affective lengthening, belongs to the vocabulary of affective speech, much like baby-talk. These and similar elements of affective lexis cannot occur in indirect discourse because they conventionally encode the speaker's attitudes or emotions, all reference to which is eradicated once the original speech is embedded in indirect discourse and the original deictic center and, consequently, the original speaker's authority are suppressed.

(8) a. perīiya ma<u>nuSan</u> varuvā<u>n</u>.
big-EXAG man-NOM come-FUT-3SM
'A reeeally big man is coming/will come.'

b. _{S0}[ava<u>n</u> _{S1}[perīiya ma<u>nuSan</u> varuvā<u>n</u>]_{S1} enru connā<u>n</u>]_{S0}.
he-NOM big-EXAG man-NOM come-FUT-3SM say-CF say-PST-3SM
'He said, "A reeeally big man is coming/will come."'

c. *perīiya ma<u>nuSan</u> varuvatu āka.c connā<u>n</u>.
big-EXAG man-NOM come-FUT-VN become-INF tell-PST-3SM
'He said that a reeeally big man would come.'

(9) a. miTTāy ittanūuuNTu koTu!
sweets itsy-bitsy-EXAG give-IMP
'Give me just an itsy-bitsy piece of candy.'

b. _{S0}[_{S1}[miTTāy ittanūuuNTu koTu]_{S1} enru connāL]_{S0}.
sweets itsy-bitsy-EXAG give-IMP say-CF say-PST-3SF
'She said, "Give me just an itsy-bitsy piece of candy."'

c. *miTTāy ittanūuuNTu koTuppatu āka.c connāL.
sweets itsy-bitsy-EXAG give-FUT-VN become-INF tell-PST-3SF
'She told me to give her just an itsy-bitsy piece of candy.'

Similarly, vocative phrases and exclamations that appear in the original speech that is being reported are also absent from indirect discourse. The exclamation *aTa* 'alas' and the vocative phrase *kaTavuLē* 'O God' occur in direct discourse, as in (10b), but not in indirect discourse, as in (10c). Other exclamations, such as *bēS* 'wow' or *cī* 'gee, sheesh', and other vocative phrases follow the same pattern. As indices of the original speaker's emotional state, they are removed when indirect discourse erases the original speech's frame of reference.[13] Restrictions such as these have been extensively studied and reported in *Banfield* (1982).

(10) a. aTa kaTavuLē! avaL ōTippōy viTTāL.
alas god-VOC she-NOM run.away-CF leave-PST-3SF
'O God, she's run away (from home).'

b. _{S0}[_{S1}[aTa kaTavuLē! avaL ōTippōy viTTāL]_{S1} enru connā<u>n</u>]_{S0}
alas god-VOC she-NOM run.away-CF leave-PST-3SF say-CF
tell-PST-3SM
'He said, "O God, she's run away (from home)."'

c. _{S0}[_{S1}[(*aTa kaTavuLē) avaL ōTippōy viTTatu]_{S1}
alas god-VOC she run.away-CF leave-PST-VN

āka.c   connān]_SO.
become-INF tell-PST-3SM
'He said that O God, she ran away from home.'

In much the same vein, the grammar of direct and indirect discourse influences the Tamil auxiliary verb system.[14] Approximately 24 auxiliary verbs may combine with a main verb in its conjunctive form to create an auxiliary compound verb, or AVC. The AVCs so formed convey verbal categories that are not encoded in the basic verbal morphology of the language; for example, the auxiliary *koTukka* 'give' is used to signal benefactive voice, a category that is not conveyed by primitive personal endings or other verbal suffixes. As many as half of these auxiliaries are marked for a category called attitude, one which conveys the speaker's subjective evaluation of the narrated event, or P^s/E^n in a Jakobsonian formula. Examples of such auxiliaries are given in several examples below. Auxiliaries that do not mark attitude occur freely in both direct and indirect discourse; for example, both auxiliary *viTa* 'leave', which marks disjunctive taxis and *vaikka* 'place', which marks future utility, are equally at home in both contexts (see Steever 1983).

(11) a. pōy   viTu!
         go-CF leave-IMP
         'Go away.'
    b. _SO[_S1[pōy viTu]_S1 enru connān]_SO.
         go-CF leave-IMP say-CF tell-PST-3SM
         'He said, "Go away."'
    c. pōy   viTa.c   connān.
         go-CF leave-INF tell-PST-3SM
         'He said to go away.'

(12) a. oru kaTitam eZuti   vaippān.
         one letter write-CF place-FUT-3SM
         'He will write a letter for subsequent use.'
    b. _SO[_S1[oru kaTitam eZuti   vaippān]_S1   enru   connān]_SO.
         one letter   write-CF place-FUT-3SM say-CF tell-PST-3SF
         'She said, "He will write a letter for subsequent use."'
    c. oru kaTitam eZuti   vaippatu   āka.c   connāL.
         one letter write-CF place-FUT-VN become-INF tell-PST-3SF
         'She said that he would write a letter for subsequent use.'

This pattern does not apply equally to all 24 indicative auxiliaries: speakers of conservative dialects do not permit attitudinal auxiliary verbs to appear in representations of indirect discourse. They replace them instead either with a simple form of the main verb or with an AVC that uses the auxiliary *viTa* 'leave'(cf. 15d), which marks disjunctive taxis (see Steever 1983). The attitudinal auxiliary phrase *pōy tolaiya* 'go, damn it' appears in (13a),[15] *colli oZintān* 'he went and said (it)' in (14a),[16] and *aZintu pōkum* 'it will get destroyed' in (15a).[17] In conservative dialects, none of these auxiliaries may occur in indirect discourse, as the unacceptability of the corresponding c-versions of these sentences reveals.

(13) a. pōy tolai!
go-CF lose-IMP
'Go away, damn it!'
b. ₍ₛₒ₎[ₛ₁[pōy tolai]₍ₛ₁₎ enru connān]₍ₛₒ₎.
go-CF lose-IMP say-CF tell-PST-3SM
'He said, "Go away, damn it."'
c. *pōy tolaiya.c connān.
go-CF lose-INF tell-PST-3SM
'He said to go damn it.'

(14) a. colli oZintān.
say-CF purge-PST-3SM
'He went and said it.'
b. ₍ₛₒ₎[ₛ₁[colli aZintān]₍ₛ₁₎ enru connāL]₍ₛₒ₎.
tell-CF purge-PST-3SM say-CF tell-PST-3SM
'She said, "He went and said it."'
c. *colli oZintatu āka.c connāL.
tell-CF purge-PST-3SM become-INF tell-PST-3SM
'She said that he went and said it.'

(15) a. payiru aZintu pōkum.
crops destroy-CF go-FUT-3N
'The crops will get destroyed.'
b. ₍ₛₒ₎[ₛ₁[payiru aZintu pōkum]₍ₛ₁₎ enru connān]₍ₛₒ₎.
crops-NOM destroy-CF go-FUT-3N say-CF tell-PST-3SM
'He said, "The crops will get destroyed."'
c. *payiru aZintu pōvatu āka.c connān.
crops-NOM destroy-CF go-FUT-VN become-INF tell-PST-3SM
'He said that the crops would get destroyed.'
d. payiru aZintu viTuvatu āka.c connān.
crops-NOM destroy-CF leave-FUT-VN become-INF tell-PST-3SM
'He said that the crops would get destroyed.'

As defined here, the verbal category of attitude, symbolized as P^s/E^n, characterizes the speaker's subjective evaluation of the narrated event (see Steever 1983, Chapter 8). However, in the shift from direct to indirect discourse, the original deictic center to which P^s (the participants in the speech event) refers is eliminated, neutralizing the category of attitude in favor of mood, the least marked verbal category, defined as the qualifier of the other remaining element, viz. the narrated event, E^n. So in general, the attitudinal auxiliary compound verb (AVC) is replaced by a simple, nonauxiliated form of the main verb (or by an AVC with auxiliary *viTa* 'leave', which marks disjunctive taxis, as in (15d)). The speaker who makes a report with indirect discourse does not take responsibility for the opinions and feelings of the person whose speech is being reported.

Direct discourse, on the other hand, preserves the deictic center of the original speech within quotation marks, as it were. As a consequence, attitudinal auxiliaries may be retained in the representation of the original speech. It is thus the loss of the original deictic center in indirect discourse that catalyzes the loss of attitudinal auxiliary verbs, along with the other grammatical devices that convey the speaker's attitude, e.g. affective vowel lengthening, exclamations, vocative phrases, etc. This behavior can therefore be referred to the pragmatic distinction between direct and indirect discourse, rather than inscribing it directly in the syntax of AVCs.

As suggested earlier, the distinction between direct and indirect discourse is not absolutely drawn in Modern Tamil; there are examples which exhibit a mixing of these two primary ways of presenting a report. Consider the following set of sentences.

(16) a. nān varuvēn.
I-NOM come-FUT-1s
'I will come'.
b. $_{S0}$[avan $_{S1}$[nān varuvēn]$_{S1}$ enru connān]$_{S0}$
he-NOM I-NOM come-FUT-1s say-CF tell-PST-3SM
'He said, "I will come."'
c. $_{S0}$[avan$_i$ $_{S1}$[tān$_i$ varuvēn]$_{S1}$ enru connān]$_{S0}$
he-NOM self-NOM come-FUT-1s say-CF tell-PST-3SM
'He said he will come'.

The original speech in (16a) is reported in direct discourse in (16b). On the reading where the subject of the subordinate clause is coreferential with a third-person subject of the main clause, the first person pronoun *nān* 'I' of the original speech may be replaced with the so-called reflexive pronoun *tān* 'self', as in (16c). Unlike English reflexive pronouns, Tamil reflexive pronouns need not occur in the same clause as their antecedents, but may occur in indefinitely many embedded clauses (also see Huang in this volume). Example (16c) may be considered an example of 'semi-direct discourse' in Tamil, one in which the change in the form of the original speech is induced, not by a shift in the deictic center of the original speech presented in the subordinate clause, but by the application of a general syntactic rule into the subordinate clause. It seems most probable that further gradations may be found between the two poles of direct and indirect discourse in Tamil as has been amply documented in the literature and in other contributions to this volume.

3. Additional ways to present a report

A further grammatical device in Modern Tamil appears to share certain features of indirect discourse, viz., the hearsay-evidential clitic. In pragmatic terms, a speaker uses the hearsay clitic to report an event or situation whose content he is unable or unwilling to affirm. Such a device differs from indirect discourse in that the event being reported is not necessarily represented as a speech event. While the hearsay-evidential clitic might conceivably be used to represent a speech event, the prior existence of forms of direct and indirect discourse, embedded in the grammar of the language, make such a use nugatory. Use of the hearsay-evidential clitic does not commit the speaker to the belief that there was an original speaker who authentically uttered the words now appearing in his utterance; they could easily paraphrase what was originally said. As Jespersen (1965:294) notes, shifting of responsibility away from the speaker of the reported speech is a marked characteristic of indirect discourse. But this hearsay-evidential grammatical device is even more indirect than indirect discourse itself inasmuch as the use of indirect discourse implies an original speech event even though it may have undergone certain grammatical modifications.

Such a sentence is formed by cliticizing the hearsay particle =ām 'it is said that' to the sentence itself or to any major category within the sentence.[18] In (17b) the hearsay particle attaches to the finite verb *vantān* 'he came' and in (17c) to the subject NP *avan* 'he'.

(17) a. avan vantān.
he-NOM come-PST-3SM
'He came.'
b. avan vantān=-ām.
he-NOM come-PST-3SM-HS
'It is said that he came.'
c. avan=ām vantān.
he-NOM-HS come-PST-3SM
'It is said that it was he who came.'

Like indirect discourse in Tamil, the hearsay particle -ām 'it is said that' embeds nonattitudinal auxiliary verbs, but not — in conservative dialects — attitudinal auxiliary verbs. The hearsay particle readily embeds a nonattitudinal auxiliary such as *viTa* 'leave' in (18b), but not an attitudinal auxiliary, as examples (19b) and (20b) show. Since by use of the hearsay particle the speaker disavows responsibility for the content of his report, he cannot fairly ascribe to the subject information or attitudes for which the speaker would have had to be present.

(18) a. nī   pōy   viTuvāy.
        you-NOM go-CF leave-FUT-2S
        'You'll go away.'
    b. nī   pōy   viTuvāy=ām.
        you-NOM go-CF leave-FUT-2S-HS
        'Word has it you're going away.'

(19) a. nī   pōy   tolaivāy.
        you-NOM go-CF lose-FUT-2S
        'You're going away, damn it.'
    b. *?nī   pōy   tolaivāy=ām.
        you-NOM go-CF lose-FUT-2S-HS
        'Word has it you're going away, damn it.

(20) a. avan   oru nāvalai   eZuti.t taLLinān.
        he-NOM one novel-ACC write-CF push-PST-3SM
        'He dashed off a novel in no time at all.'
    b. *avan   oru nāvalai   eZuti.t taLLinān=ām.
        he-NOM one novel-ACC write-CF push-PST-3SM-HS
        'It is said he dashed off a novel in no time at all.'

I note in passing that the clitic particle -*ām* 'it seems that' historically descends from a contracted form of the third person neuter singular verb *ākum* 'it will become', a finite form of the verb *āka* 'become', discussed above. Even though it inherits from the verb *āka* 'become' the ability to combine with a wide variety of constituents without imposing any morphological change on them, the hearsay particle creates a grammatical context that does not permit the expression of the affective and emotive states of the original speaker.

While the use of the hearsay-evidential clitic shares with indirect discourse the idea that the speaker has distanced himself from the content of what is being said, unlike indirect discourse, its use does not purport to represent a speech event of any sort.

At this point, it should be stressed that speakers of Tamil have means to report speech that involve neither the syntactic frames used for direct and indirect discourse nor the morphological means used for the hearsay-evidential clitic. The analysis of any moderately long corpus of spoken Tamil would reveal that a speaker can present another's speech event through extra-grammatical, dramatic means. He may report a speech event simply by enacting a scene in which he assumes the role of the original speaker whose speech he wishes to represent. In presenting such a scene, our actor might imitate characteristics of the original speaker's bearing and mannerisms, going so far as to mimic his voice quality and pitch. To frame what is presented as the original speech in such a case, the speaker draws essentially, not on the specific morphosyntactic devices of the language, but on the conventions of dramatic performance. While an expanded study of how speakers of Tamil use language this way to report a speech event is clearly relevant to the study of reported speech, a detailed analysis must await systematic study of large corpora of the language. Such an analysis might attempt to determine, among other things, whether these "dramatic" forms of reported speech can be assimilated to Jakobson's program of analysis as a neutralization between the speech event and the narrated event.

4. Conclusion

The evidence above suggests that Tamil makes a clear distinction between the grammar of direct and indirect discourse, even though this distinction is susceptible to gradation. Once we are within the domain of reported speech, we find that semantic parameters govern the disposition of the syntactic structures. A variety of expressions ranging from lexical items to vocatives, from expressive lengthening of vowels to attitudinal auxiliary verbs, all respect the distinction between direct and indirect discourse. Conservative dialects of Tamil prohibit the occurrence in indirect discourse of any sort of expression that conventionally marks the beliefs, opinions, feelings or judgements of the speaker of the original discourse being reported. The presence or absence of these conventional ways of expressing the (original) speaker's affective and emotive state varies as the original deictic center of the speech being reported is preserved or is assimilated to the deictic center of the reporting speech.

Direct and indirect discourse in Tamil, as illustrated above, both make extensive use of the general structures of sentence complementation. For example, the reported speech appears as a complement of a verb of reporting within a larger sentence in exactly the position where a direct object or another kind of sentential complement would independently occur. Tamil has therefore embedded these two basic forms of reported speech in the grammar of the language where they are readily amenable to syntactic and morphological analysis. Even so, the possibility exists of reporting another's speech through nongrammatical, dramatic devices whose systematic study remains to be undertaken. Only once such a study appears will we be able to assess whether and to what extent Jakobson's model of grammatical analysis can embrace and explain all the various ways in which speakers of Tamil report what other people say.

Notes

1. For a description of Modern Tamil, see Lehmann (1989) and Annamalai and Steever (1998). The transcription of Tamil used here is broadly phonemic, and closely approximates a transliteration of the literary variety of the language. This chapter follows the transcription system used in Annamalai and Steever except that capitals letters are used to represent a retroflex manner of articulation.
2. I use Jakobson's model here because it provides a common, elemental vocabulary of concepts to speak about both grammatical categories and varieties of reported speech. For the admittedly descriptive goals of this chapter, Jakobson's model, while lacking some of the sophistication and concentration of purpose found in more recent models, utilizes concepts that most schools of linguistic thought will readily recognize.
3. See Steever (1988) and Steever (1998: Chapter 1) for a discussion of the components of simple and complex sentences in the full range of Dravidian languages.
4. In fact, in Old Tamil and several modern Dravidian languages, predicate nominals also show agreement with their subject NPs through the use of desinences that mark the person, number and gender of the subject.
5. In point of fact, predicate nominals may also be analyzed as finite predicates. They appear in the same set of contexts as finite verbs. For a review of the arguments treating finite verb forms and predicate nominals as two instances of finite predicates, see Steever (1988).
6. Or, as subsequent examples show, are embedded within them. More precisely, the subordinate clause precedes the expression which is its head in the main clause regardless of whether that head is a noun, as in a relative clause or a verb, as in an adverbial clause (see Steever 1988).
7. While there are certain words that appear to have the function of conjunctions or adverbs, they have the form of nouns and verbs, the two basic parts of speech in Tamil.
8. However, see Boeder (this volume) who shows that the Kartvelian language Svan has no "embedded" direct discourse, but only a free discourse not introduced by a verb of speech or thought. In narratives, where direct speech may be represented, direct speech appears in a "theatrical" form, e.g., as a dialogue; once there is an appropriate introductory verb embedding takes place
9. Please note that the verb *vēNTum* 'wants' is a dative-subject verb, as illustrated above in example (1d). Dative-subject verbs do not agree in person, number or gender with these subjects, but instead assume the least marked cell of the paradigm, the third person singular neuter form.
10. See Steever (1988) for a more detailed discussion of the various types of predicates that these two verbs may embed.
11. An alternative explanation is available for the inability of the phrase *tīyai vai* to appear in the context of indirect discourse. It is an idiom, and may well lack, as many other idioms and cliches do, the flexibility to change shape or undergo transformations, such as Relativization.

12. The overlong vowel is approximately twice as long as ordinary long vowels in Tamil. The graphic convention used here to represent it mimics the traditional Tamil orthographic convention.

13. One reason for choosing direct discourse over indirect in a given situation may be to preserve the indications of the original speaker's emotional or affective state. It appears to be contrary to the pragmatic rules that govern orderly discourse in Tamil (and many other languages) to represent any conventional expressions of the original speaker's emotive state in indirect discourse.

14. The auxiliary verb system is intensively analyzed in Steever (1983).

15. The use of auxiliary *tolaiya* 'lose' in (13) signals the speaker's antipathy toward the content of the narrated event, as signaled by the epithet 'damn it', tagged onto the sentence in the English translation.

16. The use of *oZiya* 'be purged' in (14) is a conventional means of marking the speaker's relief that the event named by the main verb has ended.

17. The use of *pōka* 'go' in (15) is a conventional means of signaling the speaker's belief that the event named by the main verb has resulted in an undesirable state.

18. It does not, however, combine with imperative verb forms.

References

Annamalai, E. and Sanford Steever. 1998. "Modern Tamil". In Steever, Sanford (ed), *The Dravidian languages*. London: Routledge, 100–28

Jakobson, Roman. 1971. "Shifters, verbal categories and the Russian verb". In Jakobson, Roman, *Selected writings II: word and language*. The Hague: Mouton, 130–47.

Jesperson, Otto. 1965. *The philosophy of grammar*. New York: Norton and Company.

Lehmann, Thomas. 1989. *A grammar of Modern Tamil*. Pondicherry: Pondicherry Institute of Linguistics and Culture.

Lehmann, Thomas. 1994. *Grammatik des Alttamil*. Stuttgart: Steiner.

McCawley, James D. 1988. *The syntactic phenomena of English*. Chicago and London: University of Chicago.

Steever, Sanford. 1983. *A study in auxiliation: the grammar of the indicative auxiliary verb system of Tamil*. Ph.D., Department of Linguistics, University of Chicago.

Steever, Sanford. 1988. *The serial verb formation in the Dravidian languages*. Delhi: Motilal Banarsidass.

CHAPTER 5

The acceptance of "free indirect discourse"
A change in the representation of thought in Japanese

Yasushi Suzuki
Nagoya Institute of Technology

1. Introduction

Free Indirect Discourse (FID) makes its first appearance as early as the medieval epic. In the 16th–17th century, it was already used as a stylistic device by writers such as La Fontaine. It is since the second half of the 19th century that FID has been consciously used as a typical narrative style with great frequency (see Steinberg 1971:55f., Roncador 1988:134f.). The following tendencies which appeared from the 19th century possibly contributed to making FID a general stylistic phenomenon in narrative literature in Europe: 1) Claims for objective description; 2) Preference for "the figural narrative situation" over "the authorial narrative situation"; 3) The interest in the description of the (un)consciousness of a character; 4) The tendency to use spoken language in the literature and so on (see Stanzel 1981:39f.). Another major reason for the spread of FID is the influence of authors such as Flaubert, who used FID extensively, on other writers.

From the 19th century, European literature had a major influence on modern Japanese writers. Did the Japanese writers wrestle with the narrative style of FID in European literature and accept it? In contrast with the acceptance of FID in various European languages it was not easy for Japanese writers. Let us observe FID in Buddenbrooks and its English and Japanese translations in order to examine this point.[1]

(1) "Aber ich beleidige Sie nicht, Herr Grünlich", sagte Tony, denn sie bereute, so heftig gewesen zu sein. *Mein Gott, mußte gerade ihr dies begegnen!* Sie hatte sich so eine Werbung nicht vorgestellt.
(Th. Mann: Buddenbrooks)

(2) "But I am not insulting you, Herr Grünlich," said Tony, repenting her brusqueness. *Oh dear, oh dear, why did all this have to happen to her?* Such a wooing as this she had never imagined. (English Translation)

(3) "Watashi, bujoku nado shimasen wa, Grünlich-san." to Tony-wa, kotoba-ga sugita koto-o kôkai-shite itta. *Aa, konna koto-ga, watashi ni (me) [zibun ni/ø] okorô (does) towa!* Tony-wa, kyûkon-o konna yô ni sôzô shita koto-ga nakatta. (Japanese Translation)

The italic passage is the FID which represents the thought of Tony. This is signaled through the expression *mein Gott* (*oh dear*) and the exclamatory (the interrogative) sentence. While these emotional elements of the character are repeated in Japanese (*Aa, towa*), the tense (*mußte* (*did*)) and the person (*ihr* (*her*)) of FID cannot be directly rendered as in the English translation. In contrast to European languages, the representation of the speech and thought of the characters in a novel through the narrative tense (*-ta* = the morphophonemic form of the perfect) in Japanese is exceptional, because tenses in Japanese are not shifted. Thus, the narrative tense (*okotta* (*did*)) is reduced by the translation to the present tense (*okoru* (*does*)) of direct speech, *Tony dachte, "Mein Gott, muss gerade mir dies begegnen." (Tony thought, "Oh dear, why does all this have to happen to me.")*. Usually, the category person is also reduced to the first person (*watashi ni* (*me*)) of direct speech or is substituted for by a reflexive pronoun (*zibun* 'self'). When the person agrees with the subject of the preceding or following sentence, it is often omitted as zero-morph (ø).[2]

In short, Japanese has a problem that impeded the acceptance of FID in European languages: no shift of tenses and persons.[3] Did Japanese writers have no interest in the acceptance of the FID in European literature for this reason? Or did they accept this style in their works by overcoming this difficulty? At present, the situation concerning the category person has changed. In literary works of modern Japanese writers who are under the influence of European literatures passages appear in which the person is often shifted into the third person (*kare* (*he*)) as in FID in European languages or represented by use of the proper noun, though this is unusual in Japanese.

2. A change in the representation of thought in Japanese

2.1 The shift into the proper noun (Bunzô, Shigematsu)

The pioneer work at this point is *Ukigumo* ("A Floating Cloud") (1887) by Shimei Futabatei (1864–1909). Let us observe the famous sentences which have been the subject of critical debate in Japanese literature.[4]

(4) Oyoso sôai-suru futatsu no kokoro-wa, ittai bunshin de koritsu-suru mono demo naku, mata shiyô tote dekiru mono demo nai yue ni, katakata no kokoro-ga yorokobu toki niwa katakata no kokoro mo

tomoni yorokobi,katakata no kokoro-ga kanashimu toki niwa katakata no kokoro mo tomoni kanashimi, [. . .] kesshite sogo-shi kankaku-suru mono de nai to kyô ga hi made Bunzô-wa omotte ita ni, *ima Bunzô-no* (usual: *ore-no* (my)) *tsûyô-o Osei no kanzenu-wa dôshita mono darô.*
Dômo ki-ga shirenu, Bunzô (usual: *ore* (I)) *niwa heiki de sumashite iru Osei no kokoroiki-ga nomikomenu.*

(5) Bunzô had always believed that two people in love were bound together and could not act separately. When one of them was happy, the other was happy too, and the sadness of one was shared by the other [. . .] They could never disagree, never be out of harmony. Believing this, *how could Bunzô explain the fact that Osei did not sympathize with him in his present ordeal?*
He (Bunzô) could not understand it. He could not comprehend why Osei was indifferent to him.

About the italic passages the Japanologist Noguchi wrote in his book *Japanese in the novel*: "Who says this sentence? Bunzô? No, it is inconceivable that Bunzô calls himself "Bunzô" like a little child. Well then, the narrator? But this sentence includes too many expressions characteristic of Bunzô. In short, it is the middle style of "Bunzô could not comprehend why Osei was . . ." and "I can not comprehend why Osei is . . .". A European literary critic would call this style "Free indirect speech (erlebte Rede)"" (Noguchi 1980:129f.). Noguchi thinks that this sentence corresponds to the FID in European languages because the first person (*ore*) is shifted into the proper noun (*Bunzô*), though the thought of the figure is being represented here.

In *Ukigumo* one can find many passages like this. From the studies of the Japanologist Komori or of the Japanese Slavist Kinoshita it can be proved that Futabatei was reading and translating Russian novels with FID when he was writing the novel *Ukigumo*. Therefore it is easy to imagine that these passages are under the influence of Russian literature with many FID passages such as in the work of Dostoevsky.

Let us now turn to passages from *Kuroi Ame* ("Black Rain") (1966) by Masuji Ibuse (1898–1993). Shigematsu, the hero of this novel, is thinking about the marriage of his niece Yasuko, who was exposed to black rain, radioactive rain which fell after the explosion of the atomic bomb in Hiroshima.[5]

(6) Kore de Yasuko-no ichinichi bun no kiroku-ga owari ni natte iru. Kanai-no iu tôri, kuroi ame ni utareta kijutsu-no bubun-wa shôryaku-suru ni koshita koto wa nai. Shikashi shôryaku shite seisho shita nikki-o kekkon-no sewanin ni watashite kara, moshi Yasuko-no nikki-no

genbutsu-o misete kure to iidasareru to sureba donna koto ni naru darô
. . . .
Bakudan no ochita 8 gatsu 6 ka no gozen 8 ji sugi, Yasuko-wa bakushin-chi kara 10 kiro ijô mo hanareta tokoro ni ita hazu da.
Shigematsu-wa (usual: *ore-wa* (I)) *anotoki bakushinchi kara 2 kiro gurai no Yokogawa-chô de hoho-o yakedoshita-ga, sore demo mada kôshite ikite iru* . . .
(7) Yasuko's diary for August 9 ended here.
Ideally, he (Shigemastu) realized, it would be better to cut out the account of the black rain as his wife had suggested. But what would happen if, when they sent a copy of the diary to the go-between, she asked to see the original? . . .
And yet, he told himself, at sometime after eight on August 6, when the bomb fell, Yasuko must have been more than ten kilometers from the center of the blast. *He (Shigematsu) himself had been at Yokogawa, only two kilometers from the center, and his cheek had been burned, but even so he was alive, wasn't he?*

The irritation of Shigematsu is represented here. The proper noun *Shigematsu* is also used instead of the first person (*ore*) which would be suitable here in Japanese. Thus, this passage also has a similar form to FID. Ibuse is one of the writers who uses this style frequently. One can find many passages like this not only in *Black Rain*, but also in other works of Ibuse (see Hosaka 1981, Fludernik 1993: 102f.). Ibuse was a translator of *Der Katzensteg* by Hermann Sudermann in which many passages of FID appear. According to the Japanologist Wakuta *Der Katzensteg* had a big influence on Ibuse concerning motifs and themes. He is also generally admitted to have been a devoted reader of Chekhov who uses FID as much as Dostoevsky. There is no room for doubt that Ibuse was under the influence of Euopean literature with FID. One can hypothesize that this influence is not only reflected in his motifs, but also in his style as shown above.

Incidentally, in the English translations the third person (*he*) is used instead of the proper nouns *Bunzô* and *Shigematsu*. A reason for this is that the proper noun is used in European languages only in the narrative part.[6] On the contrary, the proper noun is often used in Japanese in the representation of thought. It is related to the fact that the concept of the third person (*kare* as translation of *he*) was not established in Japanese until encounters with European languages. It seems to me that the proper noun in Japanese is often closer to the figure than the third person. Therefore the representation of thought with the proper noun is often successful in the function of "Dual Voice". And in translations from Japanese, the past or past perfect are used, though the original is in the present or perfect (*-ta*), because tenses aren't shifted in Japanese. In other words, the

Japanese counterpart of FID is possible without the mediation of a narrator with regard to the use of appropriate tenses. In this sense, these passages can (should) be translated using the present or the perfect. The choice between mediated and non-mediated tenses shows the difficulty of translating these passages into European language.

2.2 The shift into the third person (*kare*)

To use the third person (kare) in representation of thought in Japanese is more unusual. But in literary works of modern Japanese writers, passages appear in which the person is often shifted into the third person as in FID in European languages. We find it in *Jibun-no ana-no nakade* ("In one's own hole") by Tatsuzô Ishikawa (1905–1981) which has often been cited as a typical example of Japanese FID.[7]

(8) Sakki, kare-wa wakareta tsuma kara hisashiburi ni tegami-o uketotta tokoro datta. . . . (Itsumo aijô ni michita otegami-o itadaite, kansha shite orimasu) to kaite atta. *Wakarikitta uso da.* **Kare-o** (usual: *ore-o* (me)) *okorasenai yô ni, sotto nadame satoshite iru no da.* (Iro-iro na jijô ga gozaimashite, kongo-wa otegami-o gojitai mousaneba narimasen . . .) *Sore ga wakaranai no da. Iro-iro na jijô to wa donna jijô de aru no ka. Haibyô-kanja kara tegami-ga kuru urusasa ni taerarenaku natta no kamo shirenai.* (Dôzo ichinichi mo hayaku kenkô ni nararemasu yô ni, kagenagara inotte orimasu.) *Hayaku shinde kure to iu imida.* . . .

(9) He (Junjirô) just received a letter from his ex-wife after a long time. . . . (I have always been grateful for your affectionate letters) said the letter. *That is an obvious lie. She calms **him** down so that (**he**) won't get angry.* (For various reasons I must refuse your letters from now on.) (*He*) *can not understand it. What are these various reasons, then? What kind of reasons are there? Perhaps she can't bear to receive letters from a tubercular patient any more.* (I hope you will get well as soon as possible. I will be secretly praying for you.) *It means that she will be happy if (he) dies soon.* . . .

In this passage the thought of Junjiriô is represented. Though *ore-o* (*me*) or *zibun-o* (*himself*) is usually suitable in Japanese, *kare-o* (*him*) is used here as in FID in European literature.

Interestingly enough, the Anglicist Yamada interviewed the writer Ishikawa about this sentence: "Did you learn this style from foreign literature or from the translation of foreign literature or from Japanese writers? Or have you created this style by yourself?" Although the answer of Ishikawa does not confirm that this passage is under the influence of foreign literature, he referred to the transposion of the third person (*kare-o*): "I still remember that I wrote this sentence very consciously. I stopped for several minutes after using *kare-o*, which you pointed out, and also remember I thought about it again when I reread the manuscript. If one substitutes *ore-o* for *kare-o*, the sentence would sound too "close" to this character and would not fit in the narrative part. As *kare* is used here subjectivity and objectivity overlap in the following sentences, which creates a complex projection for the reader" (Yamada 1957). It is very important that the writer Ishikawa used such a style consciously in which the thought of character overlaps with the part of narrator, although this isn't usual in Japanese. As Ishikawa himself wrote, it becomes a curious sentence because Junjirô calls himself *kare*. This is a typical example of Japanese writers accepting FID in their works by overcoming the problem of Japanese morphology.

Let us observe two other examples from *Nire-ke no hitobito* ("The House of Nire"), 1971, by Morio Kita (1927–) in (10) and (11)[8] and *Sukyandaru* ("A Scandal"), 1980, by Shûsaku Endô (1923–1996) in (12) and (13), which Mikame (1996:628f.) took up in his article.[9]

(10) [. . .] ima aratamete tsuisô suruto, dôshiyô mo nai kûkyosa-ga mune-o shitashita. *Byôin-wa itsu no hi ka saiken sareru kamo shirenai. Shikashi ano bunken-o futatabi atsumenaosu koto-wa muzukashii. Iya,* **kare-wa** *(usual: zibun-wa) byôin no saiken no tame mi-o kona ni shite hataraka nebanaranu darô. Shite miru to, muni kishita byôin to shomotsu to wa kare no shôgai-o kettei zuketa koto ni naru.* ***Kare-wa, Tetsukichi-wa,*** *(usual: zibun-wa) tsumaru tokoro kenkyû to iu michi niwa en-ga naku, ichi rinshôi toshite shôgai-o oeru koto ni naru no darô.*

(11) [. . .] Thinking about it again now, he (Tetsukichi) was possessed with the numbing futility. *The hospital may be rebuilt some day, but it is difficult to collect those books again. No,* **he** *will have to work very hard to rebuild the hospital.* This means the fact that the hospital and books burnt down to nothing will determine the rest of his life. *He, Tetsukichi, will never be a scholar, but will end his life as just another practitioner.*

Tetsukichis resignation to not being a scholar is represented here. In representations of thought of the protagonist in the "The House of Nire" *zibun* (*himself*) is mostly used, but sometimes *kare* is also used, as in the passage above.

(12) Kare-wa Thomas Mann no "Benisu ni shisu" no rôjin-ga hitori no bishônen ni deatta tame, jinsei no subete-o ushinatta hanashi-o omoidashita. *Ano rôjin-wa ikutsu dattarô ka.* **Kare-to** (usual: *ore-to* or *zibun-to*) *onaji yô ni 65-sai-o koeta nenrei dattarô ka.*

(13) He (Suguro) thought of the old man from "Death in Venice" by Thomas Mann, who had lost all of his life after an encounter with a beautiful boy. *How old was the old man? (Was the man) over 65 years as old as he?*

The novelist Suguro, the hero of this novel, is thrown into confusion after an encounter with his Doppelgaenger. His situation overlaps in his mind with that of the old man (Aschenbach) in "Death in Venice". The third person (*kare*) is used here, though the first person (*ore*) or *zibun* were used in other passages. Both examples are not, it seems to me, so unusual in Japanese, probably because the thought of the character here partly overlaps with that of the narrator. Here one can hear not only the voice of the figure, but also that of the narrator, in a sort of dual voice. Actually one can substitute *kare* for *ore* or *zibun*. This means that the third person (*kare*) in Japanese has the function of a "dual voice" in this special context.

3. Why is the shift of the category person regarded as the Japanese counterpart of FID?

In contrast with European languages, it is exceptional in Japanese that both tenses and persons are shifted in the representation of thought. As we have seen in our examples, tenses are not shifted (cf. ex. (4), (5): *Bunzô niwa . . . nomikomenu–Bunzô cannot comprehend . . .* and (8), (9): *kare-o . . . satoshite iru no da–She calms him . . .*). Why is the shift of persons more noticeable than that of tenses in the representation of thought in Japanese? Narrative texts show another temporal peculiarity in contrast to ordinary communication texts: The interchangeability of the "preterite tense (-*ta*)" and the "non-preterite tense (-[*r*]*u*)" in the same text. This commutation is possible in the passages of the thought-representation of a character. Let us take another look at example (8):

(14) Sakki, kare-wa wakareta tsuma kara . . . tegami-o uketotta tokoro datta . . . .(Itsumo aijô ni michita otegami-o itadaite, kansha shite orimasu) to kaite atta.
(a) *Wakarikitta uso da.*
(b) **Kare-o** *okorasenai yô ni, sotto nadame satoshite iru no da.*
(Iro-iro na jijô ga gazaimashite, kongo-wa otegami-o gojitai mousaneba narimasen . . .) . . .
(c) *Iro-iro na jijô to wa donna jijô de aru no ka.* . . .

We can replace every non-preterite tense in this italicized part (a), (b) and (c) by the preterite tense without any contextual contradictions.

(a′) **Wakarikitta** uso **datta**.
'That **was** an obvious lie.'
(b′) **Kare-o** okorasenai yô ni sotto nadame satoshite iru no datta. . . .
'She **calmed him** down so that he would not get angry'
(c′) Iro-iro na jijô to wa donna jijô de **atta** no ka . . . .
'What **were** these various resons, then?'

If the non-preterite tense is replaced by the preterite as in sentences (a') and (c') above, the direct interior monologic expression becomes weak. The sentence sounds close to the narrative part, but is not the complete narrative part. It keeps a trace of the character voice because of the support of literary context [no person]. In this sense, a shifting of the tense is also possible in Japanese, but it is then hard to say that this sentence represents the thought of the character as clearly as FID in European languages. If not only the tense but also the person are shifted as in sentence (b'), it is difficult to regard this sentence as a thought-representation, even in this context. On the other hand, if the preterite tense is replaced by the non-preterite, the direct voice of the character is clearly inferred. If the sentence is supported by the direct representation of the non-preterite tense and the particles *no da*, even the sentence with the third person as in example (14b) can be regarded as the representation of thought, because the subjectivity of the non-preterite tense and *no da* is stronger than the objectivity of the third person. When using Japanese FID with the mediation of a narrator, it is most suitable to use the non-preterite tense and a person which is close to the narrator.

A scale representing the degree of distance to the figure or to the narrator in the representation of thought can be established having the first person as closest to the figure at one pole and the third person closest to the narrator at the other:

first person (*watashi/ore*) > omission of the subject (ø) > *zibun* ('self') > proper noun (*Bunzô, Shigematsu*) > third person (*kare*).

As we have seen from the translations of *Buddenbrooks* (cf. note 2), the third person and the proper noun are not usually used. They belong to the narrative domain in written Japanese. In short, if one seeks the Japanese counterpart of FID in European languages, it is most suitable to use the non-preterite tense + the third person (*kare*) (or a proper noun or *zibun*). Japanese writers have used these forms (un)consciously. In contrast to the combination of non-preterite tense plus a person close to the narrator the form of the preterite tense plus the person close to the character (no person or *zibun*) can also be regarded as the Japanese counterpart of FID, as Kudo (1995:193f., 204f.) has indicated. But in this case the borderline between FID and the narrative part becomes blurred. These possibilities can be summed up in Figure 1.

The acceptance of "free indirect discourse" 117

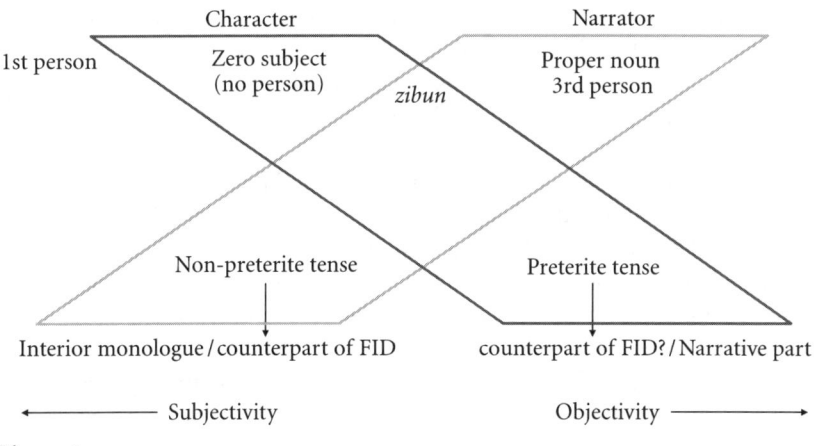

```
           Character                        Narrator
1st person    Zero subject                   Proper noun
              (no person)    zibun           3rd person



          Non-preterite tense            Preterite tense
                  |                             |
     Interior monologue / counterpart of FID    counterpart of FID? / Narrative part
     ←————— Subjectivity                        Objectivity —————→
```
Figure 1.

4. Application of the shift of persons in translation

What is the situation in the area of the translation? Such changes as those mentioned above appear also in the translation of European literature, mostly not in translation by scholars, but in those by novelists. We will take the example of the translation of *Der Katzensteg* written by Hermann Sudermann which was translated by the novelist Shungetsu Ikuta.[10]

(15) Regine — wahrhaftig — Regine.
      "Was tust du hier? Steh auf!"
      Kein Laut — keine Regung.
      *Wo war **er** ihr doch zuletzt begegnet? Richtig — dort unten vor der Kirchhofspforte, als die Mündung des Gewehrs — und plötzlich stand das Bild des fürchterlichen Augenblicks in Tagesklarheit vor seiner Seele.*
      *Für **ihn** hatte sie sich dem Mörder entgegengeworfen . . .*
(16) Regine-da — tashika ni — Regine-da.
      "Konna tokoro de, dô-shitan da, tatanai ka"
      Nanno koe mo nai miugoki hitotsu shinai.
      *Ittai, dokode **kare-wa** saigo ni kono onna ni atta no darô. Sôda ano mura no hakaba no iriguchi de datta. Teppô no tsutsuguchi-ga — suruto tachimachi, ano osorubeki shunkan no kôkei-ga hakkiri to kare no kokoro ni ukabiagatta.*
      ***Kare** no tame ni, onna-wa kano hitogoroshi ni tobi kakatte itta no da.*

Many instances of FID appear in *Der Katzensteg*. Ikuta translated almost all of them (the thought of the hero Boleslav) using the third person *kare*. It seems to me that Ikuta used the third person *kare* with great difficulty. Perhaps he thought that he could not express the dual voice of FID in German with the Japanese first person *ore*.

It has been the subject of much critical debate in Japan how to translate the FID in European literature into Japanese. It has been asserted that it must be reduced to the first person (*watashi*, *ore*) of direct speech (or to *zibun*) because that would be suitable in Japanese. Another opinion says (e.g., Nakagawa 1983) that one should use the numerous possibilities of Japanese, and she showed many passages in Japanese literature in which the third person is used. But it was this very procedure which had had been attempted before by the Japanese novelist Ikuta. Perhaps he was thinking seriously of how to represent the "dual voice" of FID in European literature. In other words, he sensed the stylistic value in FID which would be lost if one reduced the third person into the Japanese first person.

5. Conclusion

Japanese has a problem that impeded the acceptance of FID of European languages: no shift of tenses and persons. As we have seen, modern Japanese writers have overcome this difficulty and uniquely incorporated this style into their works. They preferred then to mark the representation of thought by the combination of the non-preterite tense and the third person (or the proper noun), because the subjectivity of the non-preterite tense and the objectivity of the third person overlap in the Japanese sentence. This creates a complex projection very much like FID in European languages. Thus it constitutes a change in the representation of thought in Japanese through the acceptance of FID in European languages. This tendency spread gradually in Japanese. Actually, it is already applied in translation. It is supposed that the shift into the third person *kare* will be even more widely accepted in the near future in Japanese. However, for general research on FID in Japanese, it is important to collect more examples and to compare them with FID in European languages.

Notes

1. Thomas Mann: *Buddenbrooks. Verfall einer Familie*. Frankfurt am Main: Fischer Taschenbuch Verlag, 1989, 108–9; English: translated by H.T. Lowe-Porter, Penguin Books, 1957, p.86; Japanese: translated by I. Mochizuki, Tokyo: Iwanami bunko, 1988, p.155.

2. For instance, taking seven Japanese translations of *Buddenbrooks*, two translators

(Mochizuki, Morikawa) use *watashi*, two (Naruse, Saneyoshi) use *zibun*, and in the other three translations (Kawamura, Matsuura and Maruko) the person is omitted.

3. From the opposite point of view, the Japanese counterpart of FID is possible without the mediation of a narrator. This is, as *Hirose* (2000) has stated, because Japanese has a special word for private self (*zibun*) and the use of tense in private expression is associated with the private self in Japanese. In this chapter I take up the passages in which the person is shifted as in FID in European languages.

4. Futabatei, Shimei, 1991 (1st ed. 1887). *Ukigumo*, Tokyo: Iwanami bunko, p.99. English translation by M.G. Ryan, 1971, Columbia University Press, p.273.

5. Ibuse, Masuji, 1992 (1st ed. 1966). *Kuroi Ame*, Tokyo: Shincho bunko, 32–3. English translation by John Bester, 1979, Tokyo: Kodansha International, p.35; translation slightly changed.

6. Needless to say there are exceptions. See *Steinberg* (1972:284f.)

7. Ishikawa,Tatsuzô, 1958. *Zibun no ana no nakade*, Tokyo: Shincho-bunko, p.179. See Yamada (1957), Tokuzawa (1965) etc. The English translation is mine; I wish to thank Michiyo Yamaguchi for helping me to translate the passages from Japanese literature.

8. Kita, Morio, 1992 (1st 1962). *Nire-ke no hitobito*. Tokyo: Shincho bunko, p.257. English translation is mine.

9. Endô, Shûsaku, 1996 (1st 1986). *Sukyandaru*. Tokyo: Shincho bunko, p.243. English translation is mine.

10. Hermann Sudermann, 1905. *Der Katzensteg*, Stuttgart und Berlin, p.131. translated by Ikuta Shungetsu, Tokyo: Shincho-sha, 1930, p.78. "Regine | indeed | Regine/ "What are you doing here? Stand up!"/*No sound | no movement./ Where had he met her last? Right | down there in front of the gate of the churchyard, when the muzzle /*And suddenly the sight of the dreadful moment appeared in his mind clearly./ *For him she had thrown herself on the killer . . .*" (my translation)

References

Hatano, Kanji. 1965. "Taiken wahô no shinrigaku (1), (2)" [The psychology of the "erlebte Rede"]. *Eigo kyôiku* 11: 6–9; 12: 18–21.

Hosaka, Muneshige. 1977. "Nihongo no taiken wahô ni tsuite" [The "erlebte Rede" in Japanese]. In Nobayashi and Nomoto (eds.), *Japanese and Culture*. Tokyo: Sanseido, 161–96.

Hosaka, Muneshige. 1981. "Nihongo ni okeru taiken wahô — Seiyô-go no taiken wahô to no hikaku ni oite" [The "erlebte Rede" in Japanese in comparison with the European languages]. *Ibaraki Daigaku Kyôyôbu Kiyô* 13: 95–109.

Kudo, Mayumi. 1995. *Asupekuto tensu taikei to tekusuto -gendai nihongo no jikan no hyougen* [A system of aspect/tense and texts — the temporal expresssion in modern Japanese] Tokyo: Hitsuji-shobo.

Mikame, Hirofumi. 1996. "Nihongo to Doitsugo no taiken wahô ni tsuite" [On FID in

Japanese and German]. *Hitotsubashi ronso* 115.3: 616–36.

Nakagawa, Yukiko. 1983. "Jiyû kansetsu wahô no nihongo yaku ni tsuite" [On Japanese translation of FID]. In Y. Nakagawa (ed.), *Free indirect speech.* Kyoto: Aporon-sha, 201–37.

Noguchi, Takehiko. 1980. *Shôsetsu no Nihongo.* [Japanese in the novel] Tokyo: Chûou kôron.

Nomura, Makio. 2000. *Nihongo no tekusuto* [Texts in Japanese]. Tokyo: Hitsuji-shobo.

Shibata, Tetsuo. 1995. "Wahô to Shiten — Saikô". [Speech and the point of view -reconsideration] *Eigo shousetsu kenkyu,* Eichosha: 1–52.

Stanzel, Franz K. 1981. *Typische Formen des Romans.* Göttingen: Vandenhoeck & Ruprecht.

Terakura, Hiroko. 1995. "'Byôshitsu wahô' towa nani ka?" [What is the 'represented speech'?] *Nihon gogaku* 14.11: 80–90.

Tokuzawa, Tokuji. 1965. "Taiken wahô-ga motarasu mono" [What FID brings]. *Bungei kenkyû* (Meiji Daigaku bungaku-bu kiyô) 14: 32–65.

Yamada, Yoshiharu. 1957. "Gendai sakka to daiko byôsha" [Representation of the agent in modern Japanese writers]. *Gengo-seikatsu* 9: 57–64.

Chapter 6

Direct, indirect and other discourse in Bengali newspapers*

Wim van der Wurff
Universiteit Leiden

1. Introduction

This chapter investigates the occurrence of reported discourse in Bengali newspapers, taking data from a recent study of English newspapers as a baseline for comparison. Specifically, the frequencies of different modes of reporting in news articles in (Eastern) Bengali newspapers will be compared with those found by Short, Semino and Culpeper (1996) in (British) English newspapers. The aim is to establish to what extent the distribution of modes of reported discourse in the register of news articles is similar in the two languages and to determine what factors are responsible for the similarities or differences. It will be argued that the factors involved are register-specific, i.e. they crucially relate to the nature of the text-type investigated. In other text-types, there may be other factors at work, yielding a different distribution of modes of reporting. Data such as these cast doubt on global approaches to the choice between reporting modes, as found for example in *Uchida* (1997), and provide support for approaches which allow the choice to be viewed within the context of the specific text-type involved. A promising approach of this type can be found in *Clark and Gerrig* (1990), which relates the difference between direct and indirect discourse to that between depiction and description.

In general, work on reported discourse has tended to concentrate either on the grammatical characteristics of reporting in one or more languages or on the occurrence and function of speech reports in specific texts or registers in one language (see the Bibliography at the end of this volume for numerous examples of these two types of approach). However, it is also interesting to study the occurrence of speech reports from a cross-linguistic point of view, in order to establish the types and amount of variation that exists in this area. Although the scope of the present study is limited to a single register (news reports in national daily newspapers, with some comparative data coming from prose fiction and retold narratives) in no more than two languages (Bangladeshi Bengali and British

English), it is hoped that the comparison presented may contribute to the development of a typology of reported discourse in actual use.

The empirical part of this study is primarily based on an investigation of a (small) corpus of Bengali newspaper reports, consisting of current news articles in two national dailies published in Bangladesh. The type of language represented in this material is therefore standard Eastern or Bangladeshi Bengali. It is true that Bengali has sometimes been claimed to have only one standard, based in the city of Calcutta in West Bengal (see for example Saha 1984:115, Klaiman 1987:512). However, there are today some 120 million speakers of Bengali in Bangladesh, who broadly agree on what is good Bengali and that is certainly not Western Bengali for them. In fact, in terms of attitudes held, Eastern speakers tend to regard spoken Western Bengali as a quaint and somewhat laughable type of language. In terms of linguistic properties, it is well-known that there are many differences between the two varieties in pronunciation, lexis, and morphology and some in syntax, but little is known about possible differences in the use to which linguistic options are put in the two varieties. The main reason for this is no doubt that there is very little descriptive material in this area for either variety. In what follows, a beginning will be made in filling this lacuna, as far as speech reporting in the specific register of news articles in Eastern Bengali is concerned.

Details of the sources of the Bengali material examined are given in (1).[1]

(1) Bengali material examined
bhorer kagoj (quality newspaper; issue of 3/7/97)
doinik jOnokOnTho (popular newspaper; issue of 3/7/97)

The two newspapers in question, *bhorer kagoj* 'Paper of Dawn' and *doinik jOnokOnTho* 'Daily Voice of the People', are generally regarded as being quality and popular respectively. For example, the paper *doinik jOnokOnTho* has colour photographs, larger headlines and shorter articles than *bhorer kagoj*. From an impressionistic point of view, however, the two papers are somewhat closer to each other stylistically than are quality papers and tabloids in Britain, which are well-known to differ sharply in tone, perspective, and also grammar and lexis (see the sample analyses in Freeborn 1993:164–95, Thorne 1997:229–56, Reah 1998, and references given there). But of course, this impression of relative stylistic uniformity of the two Bengali papers needs to be tested by actual analysis, as will be done here with respect to discourse reporting.

In both newspapers, articles have been analyzed dealing with the following topics: Prime Minister Sheikh Hasina's visit to Japan; the strike called for 3 July 1997 by the main opposition party; the disruption of train services in the north of Bangladesh due to continued gas leaks at a drilling site close to a major rail-line; the discovery by police of a rocket launcher in a house in the capital Dhaka. These were all current news events of national interest, and both papers reported on them. The total number of words analyzed was roughly 7,000 (3,500 words for each newspaper).

The structure of the rest of this chapter is as follows. Section 2 contains a brief outline of the various modes of speech reporting distinguished in *Short et al.* (1996), illustrating them where possible with examples from the Bengali corpus analyzed. In Section 3, some comment will be provided on orthographic and grammatical features of the speech reports in the Bengali material, mainly in so far as they differ from what is found in English. Section 4 presents data on the frequency of each of the modes of reporting in the Bengali corpus, and compares these findings with newspaper data for English, as given by *Short et al.* (1996). This is followed in Section 5 by discussion of possible factors determining the choice between modes of reporting, in particular direct and indirect speech, which are the main modes of reporting found in the Bengali data. Two specific proposals whose applicability to the data will be investigated are that of *Uchida* (1997) and that of *Clark and Gerrig* (1990). *Uchida* (1997) argues that factors related to the notion of Relevance play a crucial role in the choice between direct and indirect speech, while the account of *Clark and Gerrig* (1990), who view direct speech as a type of demonstration or depiction, would imply that the choice is determined by the different effects of demonstration and description. A brief summary of the main findings will be presented in Section 6.

2. Modes of discourse reporting

From among the many proposals for distinguishing modes of reported discourse, the classification of Leech and Short (1981) will be adopted here. This classification, which has been used in various other studies (see, e.g., *McKenzie* 1987, *Short* 1988, *Roeh and Nir* 1990, Simpson 1993, and *Semino, Short and Culpeper* 1997), includes the major intuitively distinct modes of reporting in English, and all of these modes can also be recognized more or less clearly in Bengali. It is also the classification used by *Short et al.* (1996) for their empirical study of reporting in British newspapers, and adoption in the present study thus ensures comparability of the findings for Bengali with the findings for English. In (2), the categories distinguished are given, as described and explained in *Short et al.* (1996).[2]

(2) Narrator's Report of Voice (NV)
Narrator's Representation of Speech Act (NRSA)
Indirect Speech (IS)
Free Indirect Speech (FIS)
Direct Speech (DS)
Free Direct Speech (FDS)

The category 'Narrator's Report of Voice' refers to an indication that a speech event occurred, without any further information being given as to what was said or what type of speech act was carried out. An example from the Bengali corpus can be found in (3), where talk is stated to have taken place, but its nature is left completely unspecified.

(3) e   SomOy taNra eSe   dirgho SomOy niye
    this time they come.PAP long   time   for
    elakaTi porikkha   kOren eboN dhakay
    the.area examination do   and   Dacca.LOC
    tader lokjOner   Sathe kOtha bOlen.
    their people.GEN with words say
    'At this point they come and examine the area for a long time and they talk with their people in Dacca.' (doinik jOnokOnTho 3/7/97, p. 19)

The category 'Narrator's Representation of Speech Act' also lacks information about the words used, but it does include a representation of the speech act value of the speech event.[3] In (4), an example from the Bengali corpus is given; the speech act verb *kamona koren* explicitly indicates that a request was made.

(4) prodhanmontri Sekh   haSina rupSa   nodir   upOr
    prime.minister Sheikh Hasina Rupsha river.GEN over
    rupSa Setu o   SORok nirmane   japaner
    Rupsha bridge and road construction.LOC Japan.GEN
    SOhojogita kamona kOren.
    cooperation request does
    'Prime Minister Sheikh Hasina requests Japan's cooperation in building the Rupsha bridge and road across the river Rupsha.' (bhorer kagoj 3/7/97, p. 1)

The category of 'Indirect Speech' in the model of (2) has its traditional meaning. In this type of report, information is given about the propositional content that was expressed (or at least, the content that the reader is asked to imagine was expressed), but deictic elements need to be interpreted from the perspective of the reporter, not the original speaker. An example from the Bengali corpus is (5).

(5) prodhanmontri bOlen, tar SOrkar   japani
    prime.minister says   her government Japanese
    biniyogkarider baNladeSe   biniyoge   akrisTo
    investors.GEN Bangladesh.LOC investment.LOC attracted
    kOrar   cesTa   korche, kEnona japan edeSer
    doing.GEN attempt is.doing because Japan this.country.GEN

unnOyoner SObceye guruttopurno SOhojogi.
development.GEN most important partner

'The Prime Minister says her government is trying to attract Japanese investors to invest in Bangladesh, because Japan is the most important partner in this country's development.' (bhorer kagoj 3/7/97, p. 12)

In this sentence, the intention is clearly to report the Prime Minister's words, but the reporter's deictic perspective is evident in the use of the third person pronoun *tar* 'her' and of *edeSer* 'of this country' (which the Prime Minister is not likely to have uttered, since (5) is part of a speech that she gave in Japan).

The category 'Free Indirect Speech' is defined by *Short et al.* (1996: 119–20) as involving a mixture of direct and indirect speech. This can take the form of a report with conflicting markers (as in *Was it his fault if I didn't listen to him?*, where the interrogative nature of the clause suggests that it is direct speech, but the deictic elements suggest that it is an indirect report corresponding to *Is it my fault if you don't listen to me?*) but also the form of a report showing ambiguity or indeterminacy (i.e. vocabulary and deixis are appropriate to either mode and there are no clear markers to force a particular interpretation). An ambiguous or indeterminate example of this sort in the Bengali corpus can be seen in (6).

(6) arambag theke uddhar kOra rOketlONcarTi biddhONSi.
Arambag from recovery done the.rocket.launcher destructive
dhONSoSadhone uccu khOmotaSOmpOnno. projuktite
destruction.LOC highly powerful technique.LOC
ottadhunik. uddharkale eTa chilo karjokOr.
very.modern recovery.time.LOC this was active
SOrkarer tinTi goyenda SONSthar toiri kOra
government.GEN three detective agency.GEN ready made
riporTe rOketlONcarTi SOmpOrke e kOtha bOla hoyeche.
report.LOC the.rocket.launcher about this word said was

'The rocket launcher recovered from Arambag is destructive. Its destructive capacity is very powerful. Technically, it is state-of-the art. At the time of recovery it was ready for use. In a report prepared by three governmental detective agencies this was stated about the rocket launcher.' (doinik jOnokOnTho 3/7/97, p. 1)

The example in (6), which is the opening paragraph of an article, starts with four sentences that have no quotation marks or any other kind of indication that they represent reported discourse. Only after these four sentences does a reporting clause follow (with *e kOtha bOla hoyeche* 'this was said'), making the reader realize that the preceding passage is to be interpreted as reported discourse. Hannay

(1981:787) comments on the absence of this strategy for opening news reports in English-language newspapers, and notes its frequent use in Dutch-language newspapers.[4] The example in (6) shows that it is also found in Bengali. Since the words used allow an interpretation as either direct or indirect speech, (6) is a plausible example of the category of free indirect speech.

The category of 'Direct Speech' in (2) has its conventional meaning. The words supposedly uttered are given, and the deictic center is that of the speaker. An example from the Bengali corpus is given in (7).

(7) Ek adday   lalu-i dOmbher Sathe boleche,
    a chat.LOC Lalu boast.GEN with said
    amader kache Emon jiniS ache amra SOb kichu
    us.GEN by   such thing is   we   every thing
    uRiye   dite pari
    fly.CAUS.PAP give can
    'While chatting, Lalu said boastfully, "We have such a gadget, we can blow up everything"'. (doinik jOnokOnTho 3/7/97, p.19)

The category of 'Free Direct Speech', finally, refers to direct speech that lacks an accompanying reporting clause (or quotation marks). In the Bengali newspapers examined, this category does not really occur. The closest approximation is found in headlines, where the speaker is sometimes identified by merely giving his/her name; (8) is an example.

(8) Sehk   haSinar   SONge boiThOke   haSimoto. gONga
    Sheikh Hasina.GEN with   meeting.LOC Hasimoto Ganges
    bEraj   nirmane   aNcolik SOhojogita dOrkar.
    barrage building.LOC regional cooperation necessary
    SOmbhabotta Somikkhay tOhObiler bEboStha   hobe.
    feasibility   testing.LOC budget.GEN arrangement will.be
    'Hasimoto in meeting with Sheikh Hasina. For building the Ganges dam, regional cooperation is necessary. Money for testing the feasibility will be found.' (doinik jOnokOnTho 3/7/97, p. 1, headline)

That the second and third sentences consist of reported discourse is clear from the body of the article concerned: there the same words are explicitly presented as having been uttered by Hasimoto. In the headline, it is the bare mention of his name (in the nominative) that serves as a signal for the intended interpretation. This is a convention that also exists in English-language newspapers (in both headlines and captions; see *Short* 1988 and Koderitsch 1998).

Examples of free direct speech without any reporting element at all can readily be found in Bengali fiction, especially in representations of dialogue, where indentation or the use of a dash often serves as the only sign of a change of turns.

But examples sometimes also occur inside narrative passages, as in (9), taken from a children's book.

(9) khObor Sune to SObai Stombhito.
news hear.PAP of.course everyone astonished
tahole ghOrer bhitor oTa ki? pinTur mone
then room.GEN inside that what Pintu.GEN mind
kemon jEno SOndeho holo.
how as.if doubt was
'Of course everyone is astonished to hear the news. Then what is that in the room? Pintu started to have some doubts.' (mamar biyer bOrjatri, Khan Mohammod Farabi, 1976, Dhaka, p.65)

The change of perspective implied by the fact that a question is asked (*tahole ghOrer bhitor oTa ki?* 'Then what is that in the room?') flags this sentence as representing direct discourse, but this is not marked by a reporting clause or any typographical device.

3. Some typographical and grammatical features of reported discourse in Bengali

From what has been said so far, it may appear as if reporting in Bengali works in exactly the same way as in English, since the same categories of reported discourse are found. However, there are differences in the typographical and grammatical properties of some of the categories; the most important ones of them will be briefly mentioned here. A first difference is typographical. In English newspapers, direct speech is usually flagged by the use of quotation marks, but in the Bengali material examined the use of quotation marks is quite variable. The example of direct speech in (7) does not have them, but other examples do. The two newspapers examined are not consistent in this respect, not even in one and the same article.

There are a few examples of directly quoted elements forming not an entire clause but only part of a clause, and for them the quotation marks are the only signal to the intended status of the words concerned. An example is (10).

(10) colti OrthobOchorer bajete kOr o bhEter
current financial.year.GEN budget.LOC tax and VAT.GEN
auta briddhi, SOrbograSi Sarcarj arop,
scope increase all.devouring surcharge imposition
Sarer mullo briddhi, kagojSOho nittoproyojoniyo
fertiliser.GEN price increase with.paper daily.necessary

drobbadi, Silper kaNcamal o meSinarijer
goods industry.GEN raw.material and machinery.GEN
opOr bordhito o notun kOr aroper maddhome
on increased and new tax imposition.GEN through
'jatiyo Orthoniti o silpo protiSThan dhONSo
national economy and industrial organisations destruction
kore amdaninirbhOr o pOronirbhOrSil kOrar
do.PAP import.dependent and foreign.dependent making.GEN
cOkranter' obhijog ene bi-en-pi ajker
conspiracy accusation bring.PAP BNP today.GEN
hOrtaler Dak diyeche.
strike.GEN call has.given

'The BNP [Bangladesh National Party] has called today's strike, bringing forward the accusation of "a conspiracy to destroy the national economy and industry and make them dependent on imports and dependent on another nation" through an increase in the budget of the current financial year of tax and the scope of VAT, through the imposition of an all-devouring surcharge, through an increase in the price of fertilizer, and through the imposition of increased and new taxes on paper and daily necessities, and on industry's raw materials and machinery.' (bhorer kagoj 3/7/97, p.1)

The quotation marks around the sequence *jatiyo Orthoniti ... pOronirbhOrSil kOrar cOkranter* 'a conspiracy to make the national economy ... dependent on another nation' signal that this is to be taken as a literal quotation of BNP's statement about the strike. Note that the element preceding this sequence, i.e. the very long phrase *colti OrthobOchorer bajete ... notun kOr aroper maddhome* 'through the imposition of a new tax ... in the budget of the current financial year', is itself an instance of indirect discourse. This is clear from the presence in it of the phrase *SOrbograSi Sarcharj* 'all-devouring surcharge', which must be assumed to represent the BNP's evaluation rather than the reporter's, and also from the value-judgement implicit in the listing of the budget measures.

Grammatically, Bengali is unlike English in not having tense-shift in indirect discourse embedded under a reporting verb in a past tense (see *Dutta Baruah* 1994 and *van der Wurff* 1996). In (11) for example, the reporting verb *janalo* 'told/said' is simply followed by the present tense *nOy* 'are-not' that we might expect in a direct rendering.

(11) bholar puliS porikkha kore janalo,
Bhola.GEN police examination having.done said
ogulo rOkeT lONcar nOy.
those rocket launcher are.not

'Having examined them, the Bhola police said that they were not rocket launchers.' (bhorer kagoj 3/7/97, p.1)

Another phenomenon involving tense in the Bengali data is as follows: many of the verbs referring to speech activity are in the present tense, even if it is clearly a speaking event in the past that is being reported, as in (3), (4), (5) and many other examples in the Bengali data. Usually in such cases, an earlier sentence has a verb in the past tense, which serves to locate the whole scene in the past. Various events — and not only speech events — within that scene are then signaled by verbs in the present tense. An example of this can be seen in (12), which is the opening of the article of which example (5) forms the second paragraph.

(12) prodhanmontri Sekh   haSina baNladeSe   eSe
      prime.minister Sheikh Hasina Bangladesh.LOC come.PAP
      bOstroSilpo   o   onnanno SromoghOno   Silpe
      garments.industry and other   labour.intensive industry.LOC
      biniyog   korte   eboN edeSe   tader nijOSSO
      investment to.make and   this.country.LOC their own
      ekTi rOptani prokriyajatkOron ONcol goRe   tulte
      an   export processing   area   establish.PAP to.raise
      japani   uddoktader   ahban janiyechen. [...] baNladeSe
      Japanese entreprencurs call   has.made.known Bangladesh.LOC
      biniyog   SONkranto Ek SOmmElone boktritay e   ahban
      investment about   a   meeting.LOC speech.LOC this call
      janan.   SOmmEloner ayojon   kOre   japan cembar,
      makes.known meeting.LOC arrangement makes Japan chamber
      bissObENk eboN japane   baNladeS miSon.
      world.bank and Japan.LOC Bangladesh mission
      'Prime Minister Sheikh Hasina has called on Japanese entrepreneurs to come to Bangladesh and make investments in the garments industry and other labor-intensive industry and to establish an export-processing zone of their own in this country. [...] She made this call in a speech at a meeting on investments in Bangladesh. The meeting was organized by the Chamber of Commerce of Japan, the World Bank, and the Bangladeshi mission in Japan.' (bhorer kagoj 3/7/97, p.12)

The opening sentence of the article has a reporting verb in the perfect (*janiyechen* 'has said/made known') but the second sentence, in which the same verb is used to report some further discourse uttered on the same occasion, has a present tense (*janan* 'says/makes known'). In the third sentence, a non-reporting verb in the present tense (*kOre* 'makes') is used, which shows that this use of the present tense is not limited to reporting verbs. The effect in (12) is therefore not the same as in

English examples like (13), where the present tense of the reporting verb conveys that, although the act of telling took place in the past, it could be repeated now or in the future (see Denison 1992 on this English usage and its origins).

(13) John tells me you want to resign.

The reported clause in Bengali need not always be finite; it can also have a non-finite verb, as in the first sentence of (12), in which the use of the forms *korte* 'to do' and *tulte* 'to raise' signals directive force, in the same way as does the infinitive in the English translation. Directive force can also be expressed by a verbal noun in the genitive, as in example (14), where the verbal noun *calanor* 'running.GEN' is a dependent of the (reporting) noun *pOramOrSo* 'advice'.

(14) kintu agun na dhOray tara biSOytite
 but fire not burning.LOC they the.matter.LOC
 gurutto na diye cole jan eboN
 importance not give.PAP go.PAP go and
 tren calanor pOramOrSo den
 train running.GEN advice they.give
 'But attaching no importance to the matter because the fire does not burn, they leave and give the advice to start the train.' (doinik jOnokOnTho 3/7/97, p.19)

In the corpus examined, there are no examples of a finite form of the reporting verb *bOla* 'say' following the reported clause, i.e. no examples corresponding to English '*That is right,*' *he said* (except in cases like (6), which has free indirect speech). Instead, the order is REPORTING CLAUSE–REPORTED CLAUSE, as in (5) and (7). In these cases, the reporting verb is regularly separated from the report by a comma. The corpus contains no examples of *bOla* 'say' followed by the complementizer *je* 'that', although this option exists in Bengali, both in direct and indirect speech. (15) and (16) are examples, taken from spoken interaction and a children's book respectively:

(15) bolben je apnar bon phon korchen
 say.IMP that your sister phone has.done
 'Say, "Your sister has called"'

(16) rikSawala bolche je ekTi chele (titumir)
 rickshaw.driver says that a boy Titumir
 naki take baRi theke bhaRa ene dichche
 then him house from fare get.PAP gives
 bole cole gElo
 say.PAP go.PAP went
 'The rickshaw driver says that a boy (Titumir) had gone away, saying

that he was going to get the fare for him from his home.' (mamar biyer bOrjatri, Khan Mohammod Farabi, 1976, Dhaka, p.53)

Reporting verbs in Bengali can also take another complementizer, which happens to be the word *bole*. In such cases, the order of the elements is REPORTING CLAUSE–*bole*–REPORTED CLAUSE, as in the following example from the corpus:

(17) e duTi prokOlper SOmbhabbota Somikkhar jonno
these two project.GEN possibility test.GEN for
tOhobil SONgroho kOra jabe bole tini janan
money collection do goes that he makes.known
'He states that the money can be raised for testing the feasibility of these two projects.' (doinik jOnokOnTho 3/7/97, p.19)

The complementizer *bole* can also head not a full clause but a so-called small clause, similar to the sequence *the prince a traitor* in the English sentence (18).

(18) He called the prince a traitor.

Although cases like this are not usually discussed in studies of reported discourse, they are in fact explicit examples of reporting. In comparable cases in Bengali, the complementizer *bole* is found marking this 'reportive' character:

(19) prodhanmontrir mukkhoSocib dO eS e Samad
prime.minister.GEN chief.secretary D. S. A. Samad
SaNbadikder kache brifiNer SomOy aloconake
journalists.GEN to briefing.GEN time discussion
'ottOnto bondhuttopurno o fOloproSu' bole obhihito kOren.
extremely friendly and fruiful that declared does
'At a briefing for journalists, the Prime Minister's chief secretary, D. S. A. Samad, called the talks "extremely friendly and fruitful"' (bhorer kagoj 3/7/97, p.1)

Again, the word *bole* follows the reported (small) clause. Note that the sentence in (19) features another instance of the device also used in (10): the quotation marks surrounding the phrase *ottOnto bondhuttopurno o fOloproSu* 'extremely friendly and fruitful' mark it as being a direct report.

4. Frequency of modes of reporting

Short et al. (1996) present data on the frequency of modes of reporting in a corpus of British tabloids and broadsheets published in 1994, using the categories given in (2).[5] Analysis of the Bengali newspaper data using the same procedure makes it possible to compare the frequencies for the two languages. The combined results are given in (20). The figures represent the number of words in each speech presentation category as a percentage of the total number of words for each text type.

(20) Frequency of reporting modes in British newspapers (data from *Short et al.* 1996:128) and Bangladeshi newspapers

	British broadsheets	British tabloids	*bhorer kagoj*	*doinik jOnokOnTho*
FDS	1%	2	0	0
DS	12	24	11	19
FIS	3	1	1	4
IS	14	7	19	13
NRSA	13	9	8	4
NV	1	1	10	6
Total	43	44	50	46

A first point to note about the figures in (20) is the similarity of all the newspapers with respect to the total amount of reporting, which is around 45%. In concrete terms, this means that nearly half of the news articles examined is given over to representing what people have said. As *Short et al.* (1996:128) point out, "the representation of speech is crucial in newsreports"; the large amount of reporting in the British and Bengali newspapers therefore appears to have a shared functional motivation, which has to do with the nature of the text-type in question and is relatively independent of audience aimed at (as in quality versus popular newspapers) or language used (English or Bengali). *Short et al.* (1996:128) give the corresponding figures for 'high' literature and popular fiction in English, and these are some 15% lower (roughly 30% of all words are represented speech).

The English and Bengali data in (20) show some further broad agreement. In neither language is there much free direct speech or free indirect speech in news articles, while there is a modest amount of narrator's report of a speech act (ranging from 4 to 13%). The category narrator's report of voice, in which only the bare occurrence of a speech situation is mentioned, is rare in the British newspapers (1%), but there is somewhat more of it in the Bengali newspapers (some 8%). In terms of frequency, the most prominent modes of reporting in all the newspapers are the prototypical categories of direct and indirect speech: together they make up about 30% of the news articles.

As (20) shows, *Short et al.* (1996) found one clear difference between British quality and popular papers: the popular papers strongly favor direct speech, while in the quality papers the category of indirect speech (and also 'Narrator's Representation of Speech Act') is more frequent. Interestingly, a difference of the same type is found in the Bengali data examined: the popular Bengali paper has some 50% more direct speech than indirect speech, while the categories are reversed in the quality paper (which also has some more 'Narrator's Representation of Speech Act' and 'Narrator's Report of Voice' than the popular paper). The preference for direct speech in popular newspapers is somewhat less pronounced in the Bengali material than in English, which may be one of the causes of the impressionistic judgement, mentioned in Section 1, that the Bengali newspapers examined are less conspicuously different from each other than British broadsheets and tabloids. Nevertheless, it is clearly the case that in both languages the popular papers favor direct speech, while the quality papers favor indirect reporting. What could be the reason for this?

5. The difference between direct and indirect discourse

To answer this question, it is necessary to address the issue of what is the essential difference between the prototypical categories of direct and indirect discourse. In a recent article, *Uchida* (1997) proposes a Relevance-based account of this difference (building on Sperber and Wilson 1995), in which a crucial role is played by the amount of cognitive effort required for successful processing of deictic elements. Since this cognitive effort is presumably not affected by the specific language used, *Uchida*'s proposal might yield an explanation for the cross-linguistic pattern in the use of direct and indirect discourse uncovered above. However, it turns out this hope is somewhat too optimistic: application of *Uchida*'s (1997) ideas to the newspaper data brings to light some serious limitations in the proposal.

Uchida (1997: 153–4) starts his analysis of reported discourse by distinguishing an utterance's Primary Immediate Context (PIC) from its Secondary Immediate Context (SIC), which correspond to the reporter's here-and-now and the speaker's here-and-now respectively. For example, in sentence (21), which consists of the relevant elements of (7), there is a reporter who refers to the quoted speaker in the third person (*Lalu*) and to his speech act by means of a verb in the past tense (*said*). This is because the sentence has a PIC deictically anchored in the reporter and in the time and place that this reporter utters (or writes down) the sentence. However, the sentence also contains a SIC, which is subordinate to the PIC. The SIC is deictically anchored in the quoted speaker Lalu, and in the time and place that Lalu carried out his speech act. Within the SIC, Lalu refers to himself (and several others) by means of a first person pronoun (*we*) and he uses a present tense (*can*) to describe his abilities.

(21)   Lalu said, "We can blow up everything".

In sentence (22), which contains the relevant elements of (5), there are two elements instantiating deixis of person, i.e. *the Prime Minister* and *her*. Unlike in (21), both elements can be interpreted within the PIC.

(22) The Prime Minister says her government is trying to attract Japanese investors.

Uchida's approach to the choice between direct and indirect reports is to say that a direct report, as in (21), demands more processing effort, since it requires a shift in deictic interpretation, i.e. a shift from PIC to SIC. An indirect report, as in (22), can be interpreted entirely within the PIC and is therefore easier to process. *Uchida* (1997) then proposes the following principle:

(23) Elements interpretable within PIC will be favored.

The effect is that direct speech will be disfavored, because it requires more effort in processing. In any specific case, this extra effort will need to be compensated for in the form of added relevance. As *Uchida* (1997: 157) puts it, "if extra processing effort is demanded of the hearer, compensating contextual effects should result".

This seems clear enough. Direct speech will need to bring with it a special bonus, to justify the hard processing work that it involves. Cases lacking such a compensatory bonus will tend to take the form of indirect discourse. Unfortunately, *Uchida* (1997) does not make clear what kinds of compensating contextual effects he has in mind, since his rhetorical strategy is to cite (invented) examples of indirect speech and point out that they agree with the principle given in (23).[6]

One possible type of compensating effect caused by the use of direct speech could concern the well-known absence from indirect speech of certain interactional features. Elements such as address forms, exclamations, tags, imperatives, and incomplete sentences cannot be reported indirectly, and direct speech could therefore be said to compensate for the added processing cost by its ability to include such elements. However, among the instances of direct discourse in the Bengali newspapers, there are none that have interactional features of exactly this type, so this explanation does not seem to be applicable. The problem for *Uchida*'s (1997) account is that the utterances reported directly and those reported indirectly do not appear to show any systematic differences that could explain their different forms. There is only one phenomenon, found in (24) and a few more sentences in the Bengali articles examined, that could be said to promote the use of direct reporting because the (deictic) reference in the indirect version might be difficult to work out.

(24) prodhanmontri Sekh haSina bOlen, 'baNladeS
 prime.minister Sheikh Hasina says Bangladesh
 poribOrtoner jonno prostut eboN ami apnader
 change.GEN for ready and I you.P

aSSOSto korte pari Ekbar amader deS
assured make I.can once our   country
ghure   ele   baNladeS SOmpOrke
turn.PAP coming Bangladesh about
apnader driStibhoNgi bodle   jabe.'
your.P   view   change.PAP will.go
'Prime Minister Sheikh Hasina says, "Bangladesh is ready for change and I can assure you that, once you visit our country, your view of Bangladesh will change."' (bhorer kagoj 3/7/97, p.12)

The Prime Minister was here addressing a public of potential Japanese investors in Bangladesh, and the choice for direct reporting allows the reporter to use the pronoun *apnader* 'you(r).P', to be interpreted within the SIC. Since the participants in the SIC are described in the first paragraph of the news article that (24) comes from (it is given in (12)), the reference of *apnader* is unambiguous: the initial reporting clause with the verb *bOlen* 'says' is a signal to the reader that the SIC may have to be activated again at this point. In an indirect report, the deictically appropriate pronoun would be the third person (*tader* 'them/their'), to be interpreted within the PIC. However, since there is a vast number of potential third person referents within the PIC, the indirect version of (24) would be somewhat harder to work out than the direct version. Further guidance might need to be provided to facilitate reference-tracking, i.e. to make clear that the intended reference is to the Japanese investors or entrepreneurs mentioned in the article's first paragraph. Such guidance might take the form of full repetition of the relevant noun phrase in either the reporting clause or the reported clause, leading to undesirable and avoidable wordiness.

In this way, *Uchida*'s (1997) proposals concerning the processing of deictic elements could be applied to some of the sentences in the Bengali data. Note, however, that there are only a handful of such sentences, and that they occur in both the quality and popular papers. While *Uchida* (1997) identifies a factor that may play a role in the choice between direct and indirect reporting for specific sentences, it does not seem to be the case that this factor can be used to distinguish popular from quality newspapers. Yet the data in (24) show that there is a clear difference in preferred reporting strategies between the two types of newspaper, in both English and Bengali. Further data could be cited to reinforce the point that the choice of reporting strategies may differ from one type of text to another. For example, *Short et al.* (1996: 128) give figures for the frequency of reporting modes in English prose fiction which show that nearly all reporting there takes the form of (free) direct discourse, making it quite different from both quality and popular newspapers. Another example comes from the register of retold narratives in Bengali: there, indirect reporting has been found to be virtually absent (see *van der Wurff* 1999).

The conclusion must be that global approaches to the choice between direct and indirect discourse need to allow for the importance of register-specific factors if they are to account for the frequencies of reporting modes in actual texts. As shown above, *Uchida*'s (1997) approach does not easily allow such further factors to be incorporated in it. It raises the question whether and why certain deictic phenomena are more frequent in certain (sub)registers than others, and suggests no plausible line of answer to this. As Tom Güldemann points out to me, this register-related difference is not explained by the proposals referred to in note 6 either, since these also predict that the choice in reporting modes depends only on processing cost, irrespective of other factors. The most we can say, therefore, is that *Uchida*'s model provides a precise and systematic account of one of the factors playing a role in speech reporting, making it attractive to explore the limits to which it can be taken. However, it turns out that the data in (20) lie well beyond these limits.

Short et al. (1996:219) themselves explain the difference between the British quality and popular newspapers as follows: "Th[e] predominance of D(irect) S(peech) in the tabloids is presumably the result of a wish to present news stories in a vivid, dramatic and striking manner." The idea that direct speech has a certain dramatic quality is of course not a new one. An account of direct speech which proposes a specific modern version of the idea can be found in *Clark and Gerrig* (1990), who suggest that direct quotation involves demonstration or depiction, i.e. it involves showing what someone did in saying something. Just like one can demonstrate what a tennis player did, which would entail a demonstration of (selected) aspects of the relevant movements, one can also demonstrate what a speaker did, which entails demonstration of (selected) aspects of the relevant speech act.

Clark and Gerrig (1990) provide various types of supportive evidence for their views, including the divergence of the functions that have been attributed to the use of direct quotation. As they point out (792–4), direct speech can be used by a reporter to dissociate himself from responsibility for the content that is being quoted, but it can also create an effect of vivid re-enactment or re-experience. The first function follows from the fact that someone demonstrating a speech act need not agree with all aspects of what he is demonstrating (in particular, with its propositional content), just like someone can demonstrate a serving technique even if s/he thinks it is actually no good. The second and very different function follows from the fact that demonstration of a speech act makes it come to life (again), so that the addressee may become engrossed in it.[7] The function that a particular instance of direct discourse has (and several more functions beyond the two mentioned here are distinguished by *Clark and Gerrig* 1990:792–5) will depend on the nature of the utterance quoted and the situation in which the act of demonstration takes place.

In allowing direct discourse to have a variety of functions, depending on the situation, *Clark and Gerrig*'s (1990) account seems well-placed to explain the differences in frequency of direct reports in different registers or text-types. Specifically, it provides a handle on the data on reporting modes in newspapers given in (20). In the register of news articles in popular newspapers, there is a relatively large amount of demonstration or depiction of speech acts, enabling the readers to experience these acts from as close by as is possible in the context of a written register. Quality newspapers, on the other hand, describe rather than depict, resulting in less use of direct speech and more use of indirect speech and narrator's report of a speech act (and, in Bengali, narrator's report of voice, the least engrossing of the reporting modes in (2)). This explanation receives support from some of the other differences between popular and quality newspapers mentioned in Section 1. All of these show that popular newspapers in English and Bengali employ various strategies to engross their readers' attention.

Clark and Gerrig's (1990) account thus provides a fairly articulated background to the suggestion by *Short et al.* (1996:219) that direct discourse is favored in popular newspapers because of its vivid and dramatic qualities. The articulated background, however, makes it possible to recognize that these characteristics are not necessary attributes of direct quotation, but depend on the context of the situation. As discussed above, the use of direct discourse can also serve to express impartial detachment, as in example (10), and the conventions for normal or permissible methods of verbal demonstration may differ from register to register, and language to language (though this is not the case for newspaper reports in English and Bengali). For example, *Clark and Gerrig* (1990:792) point out that quotation in newspapers, law courts and literary essays is conventionally implied to be verbatim (see also *Waugh* 1995; but compare *Short* 1988 and *Caldas-Coulthard* 1994), but that this convention does not exist in everyday conversation. In *van der Wurff* (1999), the near-categorical use of direct quotation in retold narratives in Bengali is also argued to be due to a specific convention for verbal demonstration in this register in Bengali (though not in English).

6. Conclusion

In this chapter, data have been presented on the frequency of modes of reporting in two Bengali newspapers, and they have been compared with those in British newspapers (as given by *Short et al.* 1996). Newspapers in the two languages were shown to be quite similar in their choice of reporting modes. Strikingly, the preference for the mode of direct discourse in British popular newspapers turned out to exist in the Bengali popular newspaper as well. A recent proposal concerning the choice between direct and indirect discourse (*Uchida* 1997) was shown not to have sufficient generality to shed much light on the reasons for this preference. A proposal that fares better is the one of *Clark and Gerrig* (1990), who regard direct quotation as a type of demonstration: the vividness of direct discourse, which derives from one of the characteristic effects of demonstration, provides a natural explanation for its high frequency in popular newspapers. Apart from their intrinsic interest, these findings suggest that cross-linguistic study of patterns in the use of discourse reporting modes is a viable undertaking. As shown above, the framework of *Clark and Gerrig* (1990) may be a useful one for such study.

Notes

* I would like to thank Badruza Nasrin and the editors of this volume for helpful suggestions. The research reported on here was made possible by a grant, gratefully acknowledged, from the Netherlands Foundation for the Advancement of Tropical Research (WOTRO).

1. In transliterating Bengali words and sentences, the system of Ray, Hai and Ray (1966) will be adopted. This means that the symbols E and O stand for (half-)open vowels, the symbols T, D, and R stand for retroflex sounds, S is a prepalatal sibilant, and N stands for a velar nasal (and for nasalization of a preceding vowel).

2. *Short et al.* (1996) add one category to those of Leech and Short (1981). For some discussion of how the classification has evolved, see *Short, Semino and Wynne* (1997).

3. The categories of 'Narrator's Report of Voice' and 'Narrator's Representation of Speech Act' together correspond to what *Baynham* (1991) calls 'lexicalisation'.

4. This strategy is also common in Dutch television news broadcasts.

5. In fact, they also provide figures for prose fiction, both popular and literary, and they deal with thought presentation as well as speech presentation. Below, some of these further findings will be referred to for comparative purposes.

6. Besides evading in this way the crucial question raised so clearly by his own proposal, some even more startling things happen in his article. Thus, on p.162, Uchida suddenly suggests that items interpretable within SIC may not be replaced by PIC-interpretable ones unless there is a danger of confusion. This amounts to saying that, in principle, direct reports are favored, a complete reversal of what he argues for in the first half of the article. On p.164, this reversal receives the following motivation: "Generally speaking, indirect speech is more complex in structure than direct speech, since deictic changes are required, so the effort required to process indirect speech will be greater than for direct speech. We can therefore expect compensating contextual effects." It is difficult to escape the conclusion that Uchida seems bent here on arguing that direct and indirect discourse both require more processing effort than each other (and themselves).

7. Due to this capacity to engage the addressee's full attention, direct quotation fits in naturally in some contexts that at first sight may seem to be alien territory to speech reporting, as for example a mathematics class. See *Baynham* (1996) for an analysis along these lines of the communicative function of reported discourse in an English adult

numeracy classroom. As Golato (this volume) shows, direct reporting serves a similar function in reports of past decisions in spoken German.

References

Freeborn, Dennis. 1993. *Varieties of English.* London: Macmillan.
Hannay, Mike. 1981. "Het T1-T2 vertalen en syntactische idiomaciteit". *Levende Talen* 365: 782–8.
Klaiman, Miriam H. 1987. "Bengali". In Comrie, Bernard (ed.), *The world's major languages.* London: Croom Helm, 490–513.
Koderitsch, Ed. 1998. *Captionese: the language of captions in English and Dutch.* M.A. thesis: University of Leiden.
Leech, Geoffrey N. and Michael H. Short 1981. *Style in fiction: a linguistic introduction to English fictional prose.* London: Longman.
Ray, Puna S., Muhammad A. Hai and Lila Ray. 1966. *Bengali language handbook.* Washington, D.C.: Center for Applied Linguistics.
Reah, Danuta. 1998. *The language of newspapers.* London: Routledge.
Saha, P.K. 1984. "Bengali". In Chisholm, William S. Jr. (ed.), *Interrogativity: a colloquium on the grammar, typology and pragmatics of questions in seven diverse languages, Cleveland, Ohio, October 5th 1981-May 3rd 1982* (=Typological Studies in Language 4). Amsterdam: John Benjamins, 113–43.
Simpson, Paul. 1993. *Language, ideology and point of view.* London: Routledge.
Sperber, Dan and Deirdre Wilson. 1995. *Relevance: communication and cognition.* Oxford: Blackwell.
Thorne, S. 1997. *Mastering advanced English language.* London: Macmillan.

PART 2

Tense–aspect and evidentiality

CHAPTER 7

Evidentiality and reported speech in Romance languages

Gerda Haßler
Universität Potsdam

1. Introduction

In this chapter, I will discuss different theoretical approaches to reported speech which have been applied to the Romance languages: Bally (*figure de pensée*), Benveniste (*discours/récit*), Weinrich (*erlebte Welt/erzählte Welt*), the discussion on polyphony, and attempts to solve the problem in the framework of generative grammar. Even if these approaches are very different in detail, they explain reported speeches as a dichotomic phenomenon, affirming that with direct reported speeches the perspective of the original speaker is maintained and that with indirect reported speeches the perspective shifts towards that of the reporting speaker. Most of the approaches to the Romance languages regard reported speeches as embedded and classify them as complement clauses which function as subjects or objects of the main predicates.

I will go on to examine some borderline cases in language use that show that these solutions cannot explain the relation between reported speech and epistemic modality in the Romance languages. It will be shown that there are syntactic and pragmatic deviations from the rules of direct and indirect speech, and that, as well, speakers can even delegate the responsibility for an utterance to other sources without indicating clearly whether it is reported speech or not.

Finally I introduce the notion of evidentiality currently used in the description of some Slavic and American languages which will be helpful in the conceptualization of phenomena which are situated between reported speech and modality in the Romance languages. I will give a functional definition of evidentiality which avoids limiting this category to grammaticalized evidentials which indicate only something about the source of the information of the preposition. It will then be argued that there is an intersection between evidentiality and reported speech that cannot be limited to quotatives as a lower part of the evidential hierarchy.

2. Grammatical and pragmatic approaches to reported speech in Romance languages

The study of reported speech has a long tradition in the Romance languages. One might therefore ask why a functional typological approach would be useful in the case of languages which have extended descriptions of reported speech phenomena even in the 'transition area' between direct and indirect speech. As early as 1886 *Tobler* wrote on phenomena of reported speech which are neither direct nor indirect speech. *Bally* (1914:468) characterizes this transition as a *procédé de pensée*, a cognitive procedure which is probably not language specific and which might be found in any language marked by the same mentality and related to a similar way of thinking.

If the Romance languages were an early experimental area for the study of less specific phenomena of reported speech, it is nevertheless striking that the round table on grammar at the Palermo Congress of the "Société de Linguistique et Philologie Romanes" in 1995 stressed the necessity of the view from 'outside'. This view may help us study not only grammaticalized features, but also phenomena which can only be described using scalar and prototypical properties. In the case of reported speech, this means that the old dichotomy of direct and indirect speech will no longer work and that we will even have to search for functions and their realizations in the Romance languages, taking into account categories given in non-Indo-European languages, but not in the Romance languages themselves.

2.1 Normative and descriptive grammars

The description of the parts of speech in the Latin tradition did not generally deal with reported speech as such. Nevertheless we do find statements concerning this problem, for example in Sanctius Brocensis' *Minerva* (1587:156) in the chapter on the conjunction *quod*. The complementizer being the head word of the introduction of reported speech seems to determine its further explanation as a complement. The same tradition is responsible for discussing indirect speech in terms of sequence of tenses.

Traditionally in the grammars of Romance languages, direct speech is described as the starting point from which indirect speech is derived by definable rules. The following examples may illustrate this for French grammar:

> Il y a plusieurs façons de rapporter les paroles ou les pensées (ou un texte écrit) de quelqu'un.
> a) Le narrateur les rapporte censément telles quelles, sans les modifier. C'est le **discours** (ou **style**) direct: *Paul a dit: «Je suis content.»* — *«Je suis content», a dit Paul.*
> b) Le narrateur rapporte les paroles selon son point de vue: dès lors, *je*, c'est le narrateur; *tu*, la personne à qui il s'adresse; *ici*, le lieu où il se trouve ; *maintenant*,

le moment où il parle ou écrit. C'est le **discours** (ou **style**) **indirect**. [...]: *Paul a dit qu'il est content.* — *Paul a dit être content.* (Grevisse/Goosse 1993:674)

Le discours direct constitue apparemment la forme la plus littérale de la reproduction du discours d'autrui. Celui-ci est attribué explicitement à un locuteur généralement distinct du locuteur de base, et il est rapporté tel quel, comme une citation. [...] Le discours direct est inséré dans un autre discours, avec des marques explicites du décalage énonciatif produit: il est encadré par des guillemets ou dans le cas d'un dialogue, inséré dans un récit. [...]

Le discours rapporté au style indirect perd son indépendance syntaxique et énonciative. Il se construit comme une proposition subordonnée, qui est complément d'un verbe principal signifiant «dire» ou «penser». Il est davantage intégré au discours premier que le discours direct; la démarcation est indiquée par la conjonction *que* (ou un équivalent), et non plus par la ponctuation (guillemets ou tirets). L'énonciateur est généralement le sujet du verbe introducteur: *Robespierre a dit que Danton était un traitre.* (Riegel, Pellat and Rioul 1994:597/598)

It is typical in these examples that direct and indirect speech are defined in terms of a mutual relationship. There is no formal or functional description of the nature of the analyzed phenomenon. The criterion for the bipartition of reported speech is the speaker's perspective: in direct speech the perspective of the speaker is maintained, in indirect speech, perspective and deixis switch to the position of the reporter. That is why direct speech maintains the most important features of the original utterance, while indirect speech changes pronouns, tenses, deictic elements, intonation and even referential words. In this context, neither the existence of the original utterance nor the reliability of its report (the latter is the case in direct speech) are questioned. Direct and indirect speech are described in normative grammars in terms of a transformation or derivation of indirect speech from direct speech.

Since Brunot (1922), it is not unusual for a grammar to discuss borderline cases, just after the statement of these rules of transposition. But these problems are discussed in very different ways in recent grammars of Romance languages. Grevisse/Goosse (1993:675) assume that there are two kinds of *discours indirect*, one called *discours indirect lié* and another called *discours indirect libre*. It is remarkable that the latter is not held to be limited to narrative discourse in literature. The idea of free indirect speech as a stylistic device for describing interior monologues beginning with 19th century literature which should then not be the subject of descriptive grammar, is no longer sustainable in grammars of Romance languages. There are actually occurrences of free indirect speech in Romance languages beginning with medieval texts, even if the number of these forms increases considerably in the nineteenth century. Of course, grammars which regard the sentence as the limit of their object of description will have difficulties in describing the problems of reported speech in their complexity.

2.2 The 'discours indirect libre'

The term *discours indirect libre* was proposed by *Bally* (1912 and 1914). The usual expressions in the Romance languages (*discours indirect libre, estilo indirecto libre* etc.) are perhaps less misleading than *erlebte Rede* or *interior monologue* with respect to the mental reality, but they presuppose a relationship to indirect speech which has to be questioned as well. The dualism we have seen in the Latin grammar tradition is preserved by subordinating transitional phenomena under indirect speech. The opposite procedure, which consists in explaining such transitional phenomena as derived direct reported speech (Rauh 1978, *Steinberg* 1971, *Wierzbicka* 1974) is obviously more coherent, if the complement character is stressed as the distinctive criterion; but it maintains the same dichotomy and is not very frequent in Romance grammar.

2.3 Solutions in generative grammar

The interpretation as a complement is the central point of analysis of reported speech in generative grammar. In this context, direct reported speech becomes more problematic than indirect reported speech because its complement character is not at all obvious and has to be reconstructed by transformational rules. In Ross' (1970) performative analysis, it is the indirect discourse structure which models every declarative sentence. Following this assumption, every declarative sentence is supposed to have a deep structure in which it appears as an NP-complement of a performative sentence. This performative sentence has a subject representing the speaker, an indirect object representing the person to whom the message is addressed, and a declarative verb representing the assertional character of the speech act. Following the logic of this analysis, even direct speech should be derived from a structure corresponding to the indirect one. This is contradicted in other proposals of a 'pragmatic' or 'quotative' analysis (*Roncador* 1988:45), which explain reported speech segments as independent, following metalinguistic characterizations of direct reported speech. On the other hand, *Wierzbicka* (1974) emphasizes the assumption of deep structure paraphrases, holding that direct speech is the basis of indirect speech, but in contrast to the latter, it not only expresses but also shows. In this explanation, indirect speech has one semantic-pragmatic dimension less than direct speech.

The assumption that reported speech has a complement character is also the reason for its implicit introduction in Spanish functionalism. In Alarcos Llorach (1994:325), the form amenable to syntactic description is indirect speech, which is declared to be a nominal transformation inside the complex sentence. The relation between direct speech and the introductory sentence is described as juxtaposition and set aside for further description: In generative grammar, as well as in Spanish functionalism, reported speech segments are considered to be arguments of performative verbs denoting speech acts. This point of view contains two implicit presuppositions which are not necessarily related to the nature of the reported speech: the introductory verb (actually existing in the utterance or supposed in deep structure) has to be transitive, and the reported segment has to be embedded into the sentence.

The most developed generative approach to reported speech is *Banfield's* (1995) attempt to take into account the relation between the introductory clause and direct speech. The central idea of this approach is the introduction of an element E ('Expression') as a non-recursive initial symbol which dominates structures such as interjections, exclamations, epithets, verbal forms, pronouns and other deictic forms. Indirect speech, however, would never have this kind of E-dominance, which explains why it does not contain vocatives, incomplete sentences and expressive elements. Banfield's evidence comes exclusively from English and French, which is held to be sufficient for universal statements.

What is interesting in Banfield's work is the discussion of free indirect speech as a discrete category and a potentially universal phenomenon which can be observed in its historical development in different languages. In the categorial distinction between S and E Banfield classifies free indirect speech as a class of E-dominated expressions. Consequently, it allows incomplete sentences, interjections, exclamations etc. The hypothesis that free indirect speech is E-dependent excludes an analysis of it as a type of indirect speech which is obviously S-dominated. This may create a terminological problem in Romance linguistics which have opted for *indirect speech* as the hyperonym.

In Banfield's theory, the possibility of 'transitional phenomena' in reported speech is explained on the basis of a distinction between the expressive and the communicative functions of language. But this universal possibility can only develop with the emergence of writing cultures. There are reported speech phenomena in narrative texts which cannot be explained by the supposition of a transmitter and a recipient.

3. Approaches to reported speech in the context of the dichotomies *discours/récit* and *Besprechen/Erzählen*

Another explanatory framework distinguishes between the use of language in relation to the current situation and the narration of events, facts and procedures. In the case of *discours* or *Besprechen* the speaker refers to the given situation. Therefore he can use verbal forms in their referential function and deictic elements. There is no distance marking or modalization of the utterance which is given in its primary form. In the case of *récit* or *Erzählen* the perspective of a narrator becomes dominant. Deictics have to be subordinated to this perspective which also constraints the shift of verbal forms. From this point of view, it is possible to develop an hypothesis that meets postmodern literary theories: the narrator is considered to be superfluous in impersonal narration. This hypothesis has been especially fruitful in the explanation of verbal tenses. Weinrich (1982:161) distinguishes two 'registers of tenses' (*Tempusregister*), one of them being related to the immediately discussed world (*besprechende Tempora*) and the other to narration (*erzählende Tempora*). Following this opposition in the case of French, he distinguishes present tense, *passé composé* and future tense from the narrative tenses (imperfect, *passé simple*, past perfect, *passé antérieur*, conditional). This bipartite system largely coincides with the transformation rules described for direct and indirect speech, and it reappears in a more realistic form in Maingueneau (1993:37) who follows Benveniste and assigns to the imperfect a place in both systems:

Discours	Récit
Passé composé/Imparfait	Passé simple/Imparfait
Présent	
Futur simple/Futur périphrastique	(Prospectif)

The distinction between *discours* and *récit* or *Besprechen* and *Erzählen* has attributed a central role to context in the recognition of transitional reported speech phenomena. It has been possible to state, for instance, that in free indirect speech, adverbial elements are constrained by the perspective of the acting figure, but verbs by the narration perspective.

3.1 The impact of the discussion of polyphony in literary studies

In literary studies, the notion of polyphony, which developed out of some suggestive ideas of Bakhtine (1970 and 1978), drew attention to the linguistic expression of different voices in a text. In Ducrot's (1972) theory the concept of polyphony is related to a pragmatic linguistic perspective. Ducrot has developed a notional device that allows application to the utterance level, following especially speech act theory. He distinguishes between the *locuteur*, the EGO of the reported utterance, and another speaker (*énonciateur*) who is responsible of the illocution. This theoretical frame stresses the necessity of giving up the dominant principle of the speaker's unity.

The extensive literature on these subjects has brought forth very few grammatical conceptualizations. An exception is Reyes (1990a) and Reyes (1994) on Spanish verbs, another is Wilmet's (1997:447) introduction of a *discours absorbé*. This *discours absorbé* may appear as a quoted component inside a sentence marked by elements such as 'so-called' or italics.

The impact of discourse analysis and pragmatics has been more important in explaining the status of the lexeme in the text. Following Kristeva (1978), there are three dimensions of the textual space: subject, addressee and the already existing text corpus. With the notion of intertextuality, she introduced an historical dimension into the structural description of texts. There is a double reading of the text and of its relation to reality; one is related to the historical stage attained in the development of a language, including the texts produced in this language, the other is related to the social process in which the text acts as discourse (Kristeva 1978:11/12).

The approaches mentioned above have contributed to questioning the complement character of reported speech and to opening the view to pragmatic criteria.

4. Language use and "unwelcome" transitional phenomena

If we examine the capacity of the different approaches to describe certain cases of presumed reported speech which appear in language use, some questions discussed above become irrelevant. The problem whether direct or indirect speech are to be considered transformationally related, and to which category free indirect speech should be related is important for a coherent theoretical explanation. In a conclusive description of utterances it will be more important, however, to examine how the existing approaches are able to recognize instances of linguistic forms of reported speech and to determine transition areas.

4.1 Reported speech in oral language use

It is especially difficult to explain reported speech phenomena in oral language use, where breaks in intonation and imitation of different kinds may be more important than syntactic and discourse markers. The dominance of that direct speech called "theatrical impact of DSRs" by *Wierzbicka* (1974:272) allows for different degrees of analyzability. Even the report of utterances or parts of utterances in another language is possible, as can be demonstrated by the following examples from a Franco-Canadian corpus of interviews:[1]

(1) Ah oui, comme si j'les vois, j'les dit eh . . . bonjour, "hello" . . . "whatever". Pis eh j'joue au "bromball" ici pis on joue contre les professeurs. (01810)
'Oh yes, when I see them, I say eh . . . bonjour, "hello" . . . "whatever". Then eh I play "broomball" . . . here they used to play against the teachers.'

(2) L'autre jour hein, pas mal excité, elle dit . . . avait un problème en français et puis . . . heu . . . un moment donné elle dit: "you're a frog", elle dit: "you tell me the answer" en voulant dire: t'es t'un "French man" dis-moi donc la réponse. (14720)
'The other day, pretty excited, she says . . . had a problem with French and then . . . in a later moment she says: "you're a frog", she says: "you tell me the answer" meaning: you are a "French man", so tell me the answer.'

Imitation may be limited to intonation and rhythm. So the reported element in the following sentence is pronounced very quickly and the tonal sequence goes from high to low:

(3) Il dit: «Ris pas». (CM, 131/761)[2]
'He says: "Don't laugh".'

The changes which are observable in oral language use concern the context of reported speech as well. An example is the French form *il dit*, more precisely [idi:], which would be described in grammars as the less specific form of an introductory clause of direct or indirect speech. Using this form should mean delegating the responsibility of the content of the message to a third (male) person, the speech act is not specifically determined. But there are occurrences of [idi:] even when the speaker does not know the source of the information or when he wants to avoid mentioning this source. It may even be situationally or textually related to females, groups of persons or invented sources. In the latter case, the speaker just delegates responsibility, because he is not sure or because he does not want to be identified with the message.

This generalized function of [idi:] as a marker of reported speech seems to depend upon its neutral character. This can be demonstrated by the following examples:

(4) Puis il lui (y) a dit, parce qu'il marchait vite, il dit «Pourquoi tu marchais vite?» Il dit «Tu avais tu peur de nous-autres?» (CM 131, 766).
'And then he says to him, because he was walking very quickly, he says "Why are you walking so quickly?" He says "Were you afraid of us?"'

The tensed introductory clause at the beginning, which is even followed by explicitly marked background information about causal relations, is interrupted, and the speaker continues using the neutral and less complicated [idi:].
In the following utterance the non specific [idi:] is used as the characterization of the kind of speaking (whispering), which is regarded as important and described by imitation.

(5) Lui était là il dit [en chuchotant] arrête (CM, 131, 761).
'He was there and says [whispering] stop.'

The common feature of such occurrences of [idi:] is the introduction of a textual break. This break may be limited to personal deixis. There are self-corrections in the use of pronouns just after [idi:]. The speaker in (6) starts as if he wanted to follow the regular use of pronouns deictically, using the object pronoun *me* for himself. He corrects himself after a moment and takes up the utterance again, this time with the pronouns following direct speech. This example is particularly interesting because it is not the report of a real speech act but a hypothetical one which is deduced from typical reactions of a certain person:

(6) [...] il [mon père] me laisse choisir toujours tu-sais. Mais quand qu'il a quelque chose à dire i: il va le dire tu-sais là c'est tout tu sais, il dit ... il dit «ça m'empê: ça t'empêchera pas de faire qu'est-ce que tu as à faire là, c'est juste qu'est-ce-' ja: qu'est-ce-que j'avais à dire». (CM 127, 72 ff.)
'he (my father) always lets me decide. But if he has something to say he: he will say it you know that's all you know, he says ... he says "this will not stop me, this will not stop you doing what you have to do, that's all what, I, what I had to say".'

For the recipient of the message the function of [idi:] is reduced to a disclaimer not to consider the producer of the utterance as responsible for the truth of its contents. Intonation contributes to the recognition of reported speech as an entity, in addition, pronouns create another deictic system.

There is another psychological factor which is typical in oral speech. The speaker wants to delegate the responsibility unequivocally (it is the father who says this and not the speaker himself), maybe because he is not sure or he does not consent to the message. The element [idi:] amply repeated becomes in this sentence nearly asemantic. Its function is close to a filler acting as a hesitation phenomenon.

In another example, [idi:] is even used in relation to a woman-teacher, a tendency which clearly contradicts the coherent use of feminine forms in Canadian French:

(7) Ben, comme le premier jour qu'on vient à l'école, on ... la maîtresse donne des livres, i'dit «OK».
'Well, the first day you're going to school, they ... the teacher distributes the books, he [she] says "OK".'

4.2 The relation between reported speech and modality

There are some other transitional phenomena involving the relations between reported speech and modality. The relation between reported discourse and modal verb has been studied in Bybee/Fleischmann (1995) and there are several recent studies dedicated to special aspects of the problem in Romance languages (e.g. Dendale 1994, *Reyes* 1994, Vet 1994, Haßler 1996). If grammarians accept a functionally and semantically determined category of modality, it ought to be easy to recognize a relation between (8) and (9), but not necessarily between these two and (10):

(8) Je crois qu'il viendra.
'I think he will come.'
(9) Il viendra probablement.
'Probably he will come.'
(10) Il dit qu'il viendra.
'He said he would come.'

On the other hand, the conventional form of indirect speech (10) is related to other forms of reported speech, such as direct reported speech (11) and free indirect speech (12):

(11) Il dit: «Je viendrai.»
'He said: "I will come".'
(12) Elle dit qu'avant de se mettre à table, elle serait bien gentille de lui ouvrir la porte. Il venait ce soir!
'She said that before going to dinner she would be nice enough to open the door to him. He would come this evening.'

There is a pragmatically determinable function common to the different phenomena of reported speech and modality which can be called provisionally 'the marking of the source of information'. Looking at this marking from a pragmatic point of view will not exclude a consideration of its grammatical consequences. Cases in which the sources of information are different from the evidence the actual speaker has may be:

1. the information is generally known or part of some tradition,
2. the speaker has indirectly learned the fact he communicates from a third person or by hearsay,
3. the content of the message has been deduced,
4. the content of the message is the result of reflection.

According to this division, which is founded on cognitive criteria deduced from the kind of the source of knowledge the speaker has, reported speech is just one discrete part of this field. But this discrete classification is not matched in the grammatical coding in the Romance languages. French, for instance, does not allow one in every case to distinguish between these different kinds of sources. Guentchéva (1994: 17, 18) points out that the *conditionnel* is ambiguous in this respect in the following example:

(13)　Les résultats des examens réalisés, notamment à l'hôpital neuro-cardiologique de Lyon, par le docteur T., neuro-cardiologue, et par le professeur V., toxicologue, font état de la présence dans le sang, où le taux d'alcoolémie atteignait 1,8 gramme, d'opiacés, de la morphine en particulier. La cause de la mort *serait* ainsi une crise cardiaque déclenchée dans un contexte de prise d'opiacés par voie buccale qui ne semble pas devoir être assimilé à une «surdose». Ces constatations des experts donnent lieu à l'ouverture d'une instruction pour infraction à la législation sur les stupéfiants qui va tenter de retrouver le fournisseur d'éventuels produits prohibés. (Le Monde, 17 juin 1993)
'The results of the examinations that have been done, especially at the neuro-cardiological hospital of Lyon, by Dr. T., neuro-cardiologist, and by Professor V., toxicologist, have found in the blood, where the alcohol level was up to 1,8, the presence of narcotics, of morphine in particular. The cause of death may be attributed to cardiac arrest due to the ingestion of narcotics unrelated to an "overdose". This expert diagnosis opens the way for an investigation of infraction of laws regulating narcotics, which will try to find the dealer of possibly prohibited products.'

In this case it is impossible to determine definitely whether the assessment of the cause of death had been deduced from the diagnosis given before or from a reported speech quoting what the doctor had said. It is only possible to establish without any doubt that this sequence is not an account of the speaker's own empirical experience and insight into the matter. The speaker has no 'evidence' of the case and cannot be made responsible for its truth or reliability. The example suggests a research perspective which asks where the content of the message comes from, whether the speaker has his own evidence of the facts, whether there is second-hand information, or whether the facts and relations ascertained are concluded from others or presumed.

It is possible to add similar remarks concerning the following Spanish passage:

(14)　Me dijeron que a medianoche el mismo avión en el que había venido regresaba a Milan. Consideré con pesadumbre que no podría tomarlo y que esa inmotivada postergación deshacía todos mis cálculos sobre la duración del viaje y volvía inútiles los pasajes de ida y vuelta y las reservas de hotel. Quise pensar que aún era posible que el enlace llegara, porque su retraso quizás obedecía a una norma suplementaria de cautela. «Un joven alto y con barba», me habían explicado, «que llevará bajo el brazo una revista española». Alguién en París había concebido mi llegada y el reconocimiento como un juego de simetrías y signos: *también yo, al bajarme del avión, llevaba bien visible un ejemplar de la misma revista*, y el otro, en correspondencia, debía dejar a mis pies en la

cantina una maleta idéntica a la mía. (Antonio Muñoz Molinas, Beltenebros, Barcelona 1989)
'They told me that at midnight the same aircraft in which I had come would go back to Milan. I considered with sadness that I would not be able to take it and that this unmotivated delay would destroy all my calculations on the duration of the journey and make useless the return ticket and the hotel reservations. I tried to think that it was still possible that the contact person would arrive, because his delay perhaps depended on a supplementary security norm. "A tall young man with a beard", they had explained to me, "who will be carrying a Spanish journal under his arm". Somebody in Paris had decided my arrival and the identification as a game of symmetries and signs: leaving the aircraft I would be carrying as well a copy of the same journal, easy to see, and the other, on his side, had to put down in the cafeteria a suitcase similar to mine.'

This passage contains several reported speeches, including the canonical forms of direct and indirect speech: «*Un joven alto y con barba*», *me habían explicado*, «*que llevará bajo el brazo una revista española*». — *Me dijeron que a medianoche el mismo avión en el que había venido regresaba a Milan.* If the emphasized sentence (*también yo* . . .) appeared as an isolated utterance it would be regarded as an assessment of a repeated or habitual action. The imperfect is currently used with this function in the description of background in literary texts, as has been described by Benveniste and Weinrich in the theoretical framework mentioned above (1.4). In the example given, which already contains marked reported speech, the obvious thing to do would be to consider this utterance as reported speech as well. It could be expressed in canonical forms of reported speech In (a) and (b) of (15) the voice reported would be that of a particular person (x), in (c) responsibility is just delegated to a source which is not mentioned:

(15) a. El jefe dijo: «Usted llevará un ejemplar de la misma revista.» v = x
'The boss said: "You will carry a copy of the same journal."'
b. El jefe dijo que también yo llevaría un ejemplar de la misma revista. v = x
'The boss said that I would carry a copy of the same journal as well.'
c. también yo, al bajarme del avión, llevaba bien visible un ejemplar de la misma revista, y el otro, en correspondencia, debía dejar a mis pies en la cantina una maleta idéntica a la mía.v → i'
'Leaving the aircraft I would be carrying as well a copy of the same journal, easy to see, and the other, on his side, had to put down in the cafeteria a suitcase similar to mine.'

In the passage actually chosen by the author (15c), the precision, which specific canonical forms of reported speech would demand is avoided.

The following sentence refers to a moment after the reported speech moment as well, but first of all it expresses uncertainty with respect of the proposition:

(16) El tren llegaba (IPERF) a las ocho.
'The train will arrive at eight, won't it.'

The Spanish verbal form *llegaba* is used in this example in a non-prototypical sense, not expressing either past tense or functions related to its aspectual value, such as duration or iteration. It marks merely an 'inactual' process or action which allows further modal and evidential uses, such as in the case of the Italian *andava* in (17), where information received from or a conclusion from facts is reported:

(17) A: —Sai dovè Franco?
B: —Andava a casa.

Utterances of this kind have to be analysed in more detail if we want to understand how verb tenses in combination with marked forms allow the expression of the source of knowledge. The emphasized sentence in (18) cannot be clearly determined as reported:

(18) «Je ne quitterai jamais l'Iran», nous confiait M. Bani Sadr peu avant son entrée dans la clandestinité, le 12 juin. Deux jours auparavant il avait été démis de ses fonctions de commandant en chef des forces armées, et il s'attendait à être destitué de la présidence. (Le Monde, quoted in *Cunha* 1992:28)

It is possible to regard the highlighted text as reported speech because there is a marked segment of reported speech at the beginning of the passage. In addition to this, the following "il s'attendait" would indicate that the middle segment would also be a reported speech. Formally, however, it is not decidable whether it is part of the reported speech or part of the narration. Did the dismissal two days before really cause a public declaration or any other kind of really produced source text? We face here the unsolvable dilemma of narrative texts that reported speech may become a simple description of actions. There is no way to decide between the alternative analyses.

As we have seen, the recognition of reported speech in its non-canonical forms cannot be regarded as a trivial problem in language processing. The material presented suggests that *Roncador*'s (1988:14) approach, which consists in considering the canonical forms of direct and indirect speech as the extreme points on a scale of possible realizations of reported speech, may be applied successfully to Romance languages. Roncador invites us to study whether any language with a literary tradition is able to develop *erlebte Rede* and he suggests that languages which have no tense difference between direct speech and *erlebte Rede* might use this device in literary works in other contexts than languages which have different tenses in the two cases. On the other hand, in languages with obligatory markers of the person whose consciousness is expressed by *erlebte Rede* (for example languages with logophoric pronouns), this device might lose some degree of the indistinctness between the author's and the person's speech (*Roncador* 1988:301).

In regard to the Romance languages it seems legitimate to turn the question around. Does the existence of narrative literacy with developed forms of free indirect speech (cf. 1.1, 1.4 and 1.5) produce special devices of reported speech? If we can answer this question in an affirmative way we should not exclude an influence of these devices on other uses of language and we might suppose cases in which reported speech is not clearly distinguished from marking of other sources of evidence to arise.

5. The explanatory power of 'evidentiality' as a function

5.1 'Evidentiality' as a function and its foundation

It is important for the speaker to mark or even to screen the source of his or her information. Consequently we will have to take into account the degree of responsibility of the speaker for the content of the utterance. Authors like Jakobson (1971), Chafe/Nichols (1986), Nølke (1994), and Tasmowski (1994) introduced the term 'evidentiality' in order to designate the linguistic function indicating the source of the speaker's knowledge.[3] Bybee's (1985:184) definition for evidentiality states that "Evidentials may be generally defined as markers that indicate something about the source of the information of the proposition."

The concept of evidentiality comes from research on Native American languages and it can easily be related to cognitive categories. According to Willett (1988:57) languages tend to distinguish three kinds of evidentiality (see Figure 1).

Evidentiality does not, however, appear as a specialized grammatical category in most languages. Where such special *evidentials* have developed, they have often emerged from expressions of perception ('see', 'hear', 'feel') which lose their lexical meaning and get grammaticalized as evidentials. On assuming their new function, they do not play a great role in predication, but they are not reduced to pragmatic relations either, because their evidential meaning is based on semantic properties.

For the Tuyuca language which belongs to the Eastern Tucanoan language family and is spoken in the border region of Colombia and Brazil, Barnes (1984)[4] has described different forms of evidentiality added to the verbal forms (see (19)).

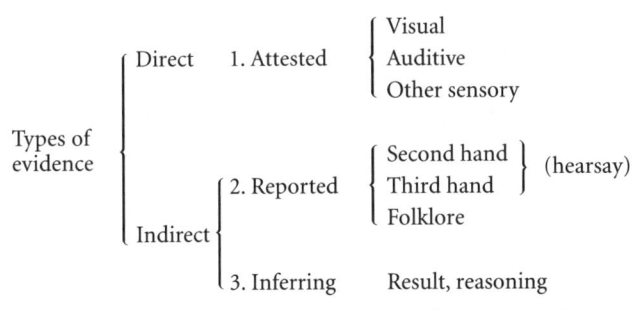

```
                          ┌ Visual
              ┌ Direct   1. Attested  ┤ Auditive
              │                        └ Other sensory
  Types of  ┤
  evidence    │                        ┌ Second hand ┐
              │           ┌ 2. Reported ┤ Third hand   ├ (hearsay)
              │           │              └ Folklore    ┘
              └ Indirect ┤
                          │
                          └ 3. Inferring    Result, reasoning
```

Figure 1. Three kinds of evidentiality (Willett 1988: 57)

(19) a. díiga apé-*wi* (I have seen him playing soccer.)
 b. díiga apé-*ti* (I have heard him playing, but I did not see him.)
 c. díiga apé-*yi* (I have had some hints that he was playing, for example traces of his shoes on the playground, but I did not see him)
 d. díiga apé-*yigi* (I have got the information that he was playing)
 e. díiga apé-*hiyi* (It is reasonable to think that he was playing)

The examples in (19) illustrates the three most frequent sources of information a speaker can refer to: his own perception, which can be visual (a) or auditive (b), inference (c) or supposition (e), finally, receiving and transmitting information from a third party (d).

Evidentials indicate the reliability of the evidence of the statement in which they are used (Hoff 1986:49). Languages may use special kinds of suffixes or prefixes for the expression of evidentiality (Willett 1988:64).[5] In other cases, we can find special pronouns referring to the person whose speech is reported. The development of quotatives from 'say'-verbs has been discussed by Harris and Campbell (1995). The development of resultatives or anteriors into evidentials of indirect evidence is known in Turkish, Bulgarian, Macedonian, and Georgian, and Bybee/Perkins/Pagliuca (1994:95) have studied it for Udmurt (west-central Russia), Inuit (Greenland) and Tucano (Colombia). Such sources suggest that the resultative indicates a state which exists due to a past action. This meaning is very close to the evidential meaning of an inference from results, which indicates that a past action is known or inferred on the basis of the current state.

Anderson (1986:274–7) proposes a number of criteria for classifying evidentials. They show the kind of justification for a factual claim which is available to the person making the claim. They are not themselves the main predication of the clause, but are rather a specification added to a factual claim about something else. They express evidence as their primary meaning, not just on the result of a pragmatic inference. Morphologically, evidentials are inflections, clitics, or other free syntactic elements. In addition to these semantic, syntactic and morphological features, Anderson suggests three criteria for the use of evidentials: (a) They are normally used in assertions, not in irrealis clauses, or in suppositions. (b) They are rarely used when the claimed fact is directly observable by both speaker and hearer. (c) They are often omitted when the speaker was a knowing participant in some event, since the knowledge of that event is normally direct. As can been seen from the formulation of the criteria, they must be seen as tendencies, rather than as absolute universals.

The hierarchy which categorizes degrees of evidence and sources of information is especially rich in Tuyuca. Evidentiality is even an obligatory and overt category in sentences referring to real events. In Tuyuca the verb consists minimally of the stem and an evidential suffix. In example (19) (a), the verb consists of the stem *apé-* 'play' and the visual evidential suffix *-wi* which is used for 3rd-person masculine singular past tense. The evidential system of Tuyuca comprises two sensory-based categories (visual and non-visual), and three non-sensory categories (apparent, secondhand, and assumed). Within each category, different morphemes are used depending on tense (past-present distinction) and person/gender (3rd person — other). Evidentials do not occur with the future tense since it is not possible in Tuyuca to possess evidence of future events. The full system is shown in Barnes (1984:258).

The visual evidential is used when the speaker has seen or is seeing the action (19) (a). But it is also used to denote timeless expressions for permanent states of which the speaker has experience:

(20) ana waweköti-yo
  Ana is.named-VISUAL.3S.F.PRS
  'She is named Ana.'

Even if the speaker cannot possibly have direct visual evidence for the statement (20), the visual evidential is used. This shows that the visual evidential is the preferred one in the sentence. The nonvisual evidential is used when the speaker wishes to convey the fact that the information in the sentence was obtained by means of a sense other than sight:

(21) mutúru bösö-tö.
  motor roar-NONVISUAL.3S.M.PST
  'The motor roared.' (Barnes 1984:260)

For evidence not directly witnessed by the speaker Tuyuca has a secondhand category available which has no present tense evidentials because the fact must have taken place before the reception of the secondhand evidence:

(22) weérige boá-yigö.
       fishhooks want-Quot
       'He wanted some fishhooks (he said).' (Barnes 1984:260)

In a language with a developed evidential hierarchy the Quotative represents the most important intersection of evidentiality and reported speech. But Quotative includes all forms of secondhand information, from reports of witnesses to the use of markers of myth.

In Tuyuca, there is a still lower step on the evidential hierarchy, which is called Assumed. It is used when the speaker has no evidence for his or her statement. Tuyuca requires the presence of an evidential morpheme even in realis clauses. Therefore reference must have access to a level that can be used if all other levels are inappropriate:

(23) Bogotápö nii-ko.
     Bogotá.in be-ASS.3S.F.PRS
     'She is in Bogotá.' (Barnes 1984:262)

Resuming Barnes (1984) the evidential hierarchy in Tuyuca can be represented as follows:

   visual > nonvisual > apparent > secondhand > assumed
      (direct)   >   (indirect)   (absent)

The highly developed evidential hierarchy of Tuyuca may serve as a model for understanding the intersection of evidentiality and reported speech in languages which have no specialized evidentials. In these languages it may be possible to suppose a reduced evidential hierarchy as a scale of functions which are secondarily expressed by other devices, such as modal verbs, past tenses, adverbs or reported speeches. Building up their evidential hierarchy from the bottom, languages will start with a quotative category, then develop an inferential category and then they may acquire some kind of sensory evidential as well.

The basic distinction among evidentials is between those that indicate that the speaker has the information via direct evidence, which may be further divided into reported evidence or inferred evidence. Evidentiality is a heterogeneous category, of which the only general criterion is the fact that certain elements mark the source of evidence. If we view the evidential system of a language as a hierarchical system we can assume that a speaker will always choose the highest level on the hierarchy for which he/she has evidence. This follows the Gricean maxims of quality: "Try to make your contribution one that is true" and "Do not say what you believe to be false". Following these maxims, the speaker will use the highest level available, namely that of direct evidence.

Once we can find grammaticalized distinctions of different evidential meanings, it becomes possible to search for the expression of this function in other languages. While reported speech in languages with a developed evidential hierarchy is clearly a part of 'secondhand evidentiality' and might even be defined more precisely as an intentional Quotative, the indistinctness of evidentiality in such languages as the Romance enlarges the borderline zone of reported speech (for oral language use, see the examples (4), (5), (6), (7) given in 2.1, and for written texts (13), (14, (16), (18) in 2.2.).

From a functional perspective, there exist roughly two conceptions of evidentiality: a broad one which includes epistemic modality, and a narrow one which contrasts evidentiality and the marking of the speaker's attitude (modality). Even in this narrow understanding of evidentiality, it would have in common with modality the epistemic marking of a proposition.

Even if we look upon reported speech as one of the aspects of evidentiality, there are more precise formal markers than those we can find in the Romance languages. While the sentence (10) *Il dit qu'il viendra* allows two different interpretations depending on the reference of the pronoun in the complement clause (*Il$_i$ dit qu'il$_i$ viendra* → co-reference between the source and the subject of the reported speech; *Il$_i$ dit qu'il$_j$ viendra*→ disjoint reference), languages with logophoric pronouns would disambiguate the reading of such sentences by the obligatory use of logophoric or simple referential pronouns; see the articles on logophoricity in this volume. The use of logophoric pronouns is related moreover to a more general problem which has been discussed in heterogeneous and contradictory ways with regard to Romance languages, namely the role of the context in the recognition of a sequence as reported speech.

5.2 'Logocentric situations'

The conditions of grammaticalization in languages like Tuyuca may be very useful to understand the pragmatic concept of a 'logocentric situation' and to define, with regard to Romance languages, the functional category of evidentiality. It seems to be the semantics of the verb of communication which is responsible for creating a logocentric context which constrains the use of a grammaticalized form which marks coreference of the subject in the reported speech sequence with the NP of the matrix clause. But since not only verbs of communication in the strict sense can create such contexts, we can suppose a logocentric verb hierarchy which ranks verbs of communication, verbs of thought, psychological state, and perception (Stirling 1993:259).

An utterance in which the speaker is forced by grammaticalized language rules to distinguish between the logophoric and the simple third person pronoun is produced in a logocentric situation, one where a noun phrase with a logophoric pronoun indicates coreference with the noun phrase of the matrix clause. The main clause NP co-occurs with a verb of communication, which Stirling (1993:51) calls a *logocentric NP*.

A logocentric context may be responsible not only for the use of certain pronouns and verbal affixes, but also for the selection of mood or tense. If languages allow a choice between logophoric and personal pronouns, the choice permits a semantic difference which expresses the speaker's attitude to the truth of what is reported. Stirling (1993:266/7) argues:

> [. . .] if the ordinary pronoun is used, it indicates that the speaker has assimilated the proposition being reported into her own scheme of things, and accepts its truth and/or approves of its content. If the logophoric pronoun is chosen, it indicates that the speaker has not assimilated the proposition into her knowledge base, and does not necessarily accept its truth or approve of its content: in some sense, responsibility for its truth, content or linguistic characterization is distanced, and left to the referent of the logophoric pronoun. That is, the optionality of logophoric reference allows the speaker to express her attitude to the truth of what she reports — and logophoricity must thus be seen as part of the evidential system of the language.

5.3 Means of expressing evidentiality in the Romance languages

It can be taken as certain that for speakers of Romance languages there are situations in which the way the speaker's knowledge was obtained has to be marked and such markers are recognized by the receiver of a message. Speakers have at their disposition lexical, morphological and syntactic, intonational and typographical means which can thus mark differences in evidentiality.

In French, for instance, certain phrasal adverbs or impersonal constructions can mark doubts about the truth and the source of the speaker's knowledge:

> *apparemment; visiblement* (affirmation after own perception)
> *certainement; sûrement* (inference, supposition)
> *Il semble que; il paraît que* (hearsay)

The field of the expressions of evidentiality contains as well modal verbs in their epistemic meaning (*devoir, pouvoir*), verbs of perception (*voir, entendre, sentir*), verbs of communication (*dire, annoncer, affirmer*), prepositions (*d'après, selon, pour*), future tense and conditional for the expression of hearsay (*il viendra, il viendrait*), epistemic particles (*donc*), quotation marks, and intonation.

This list, which cannot be presented in detail within the limits of this contribution, should be sufficient to show that the expression of the function of evidentiality includes means of different complexity and level of language. In the case of the Romance languages we do not have to take into account specialized morphological means, which does not exclude that existing grammatical forms which may have become redundant in their original meaning (cf. 3.5.), can be used secondarily with evidential function. In the following we will discuss some borderline cases between reported speech and conjecture.

5.4 Modality and evidentiality as epistemic marking

One might ask why it should not be sufficient, in the case of verbs like epistemic *devoir* or *pouvoir*, to describe them just as modal verbs. As an important reason to introduce evidentiality as an independent category, Dendale (1994) assumes a wide range of modal meanings of *devoir*. So an utterance like (24) would allow several conclusions, among others (25) and (26):

(24) Caroline a mauvaise mine.
    'Caroline looks bad.'

(25) Caroline doit être malade.
    'Caroline seems to be sick.'

(26) Elle doit avoir mal dormi.
    'It seems she did not sleep well.'

The distinctive property of *devoir* is now to select only one of these conclusions and to declare it as probable. In the case given above the following conclusions would be considered:

(27) Caroline n'est pas au travail.
    'Caroline is not at work'.
    Si quelqu'un n'est pas au travail, il est malade.
    If somebody is not at work, he must be sick.

(28) Caroline a mangé des conserves contaminées hier.
    'Caroline has eaten bad tinned food yesterday'.
    Si quelqu'un mange des conserves contaminées, il tombe malade.
    If somebody eats bad tinned food, he falls ill.

(29) C'est le lendemain du Réveillon.
    'It is the day after Christmas Eve'.
    Le lendemain du Réveillon tout le monde est malade.
    The day after Christmas Eve everybody is ill.

Following Dendale's hypothesis *devoir* does not primarily mark the epistemic quality of a message, but it relates it to the epistemic operation of creating information. As a marker of evidentiality it is first of all opposed to the absence of such markers:

(30) Caroline n'est pas au travail aujourd'hui. Elle est malade.
'Caroline is not at work today. She is sick.'
Caroline n'est pas au travail aujourd'hui. Elle *doit être* malade.
'Caroline is not at work today. She must be sick.'

As a marker related to the creation of information *devoir* has to be seen in opposition to other markers of evidentiality, such as the epistemic conditional or a conditional clause:

(31) Tiens on sonne à la porte. Ça doit être le facteur.
'Someone is ringing at the door. This must be the postman.'
Tiens on sonne à la porte. Ce serait le facteur.
'Someone is ringing at the door. This would be the postman.'
Si on sonne à la porte à midi, c'est le facteur.
'If somebody is ringing at the door, it is the postman.'

The following examples can be analyzed in a similar way. While future tense because of its 'non-actual' meaning allows one to understand the utterance as a conjecture, the use of *devoir* in the verbal periphrasis emphasizes the creation of information. Out of the possibilities which could explain a certain kind of action, one is chosen; the others are presupposed to have been considered.

(32) Il l'aura fait par pitié.
'He will have done it by compassion.'

(33) Il doit l'avoir fait par pitié.
'He must have done it by compassion.'

Finally *devoir* is used in opposition to expressions of perception by the speaker, which make superfluous the relation to conclusions or other sources of knowledge. That is the reason why a combination of the following sentences sounds strange or even unacceptable:

(34) Ça doit être ma mère. ?* Je l'avais immédiatement vue et reconnue.
'This must be my mother. I saw her and recognized her immediately.'

The fact that the modal values of *devoir* are very unstable and cover a wide range of meanings from necessity to insecurity, leads Dendale (1994:37) to the conclusion that it must be primarily a marker of evidentiality. As we have seen in the examples, *devoir* always shows that a proposition has been derived from premises and then evaluated, while the modal value of this verb cannot be determined with the same clarity. Therefore, the starting point for introducing the concept of evidentiality is economy of grammatical description, which allows one to reduce a diversity of meanings to a unitary function.

The structural argument for the distinction of evidentiality and modality is convincing, but there is an even more striking pragmatic fact which leads to the same conclusion, namely the indication of a source of knowledge by opening a logocentric situation. In such contexts, evidentiality can neutralize assumptions on modal values which in isolation may be correct. The combination of adverbs which describe the speaker's attitude (*unfortunately, correctly, prudently*) with adverbs which question the truth of the proposition (*possibly, certainly, perhaps*), is usually disapproved of in grammars. The complexity of references created by the marking of the origin of the speaker's knowledge may allow the interpretation of utterances of this type. The unusual combination of modal adverbs may even indicate the existence of a logocentric situation in which the reference switches to another speaker:

(35) Hélas, hélas, sans doute n'a-t-il pas eu le temps, cette fois encore.
'Unfortunately, without doubt, he has had no time, this time again.'

(36) Sans doute, hélas (malheureusement), n'a-t-il pas eu le temps, une fois de plus.
'Without doubt, unfortunately, he has had no time, one time more.'

(37) Une fois de plus, hélas/malheureusement, il n'a sans doute pas eu le temps.
'One time more, unfortunately, he has without doubt not had the time.'

The background for the understanding of these utterances is the following. A person is always late in finishing his or her work and begs to be excused saying 'Sorry, I had no time to do it'. Reference to this usual speech act supposed to be produced again induces a change in personal deixis, but the adverb which presupposes the factual value of the proposition (*hélas, malheureusement*) is maintained.

Reference to non-actual utterances seems to make it possible to remove restrictions in the use of opaque and transparent marker's of attitude. Consequently it is useful to distinguish between evidentiality and modality, even if both have points of contact. Both can be regarded as subcategories of an epistemic marking of utterances.

5.5 Evidentiality and conventional or unconventional forms of reported speech

If we regard reported speech as a part of evidentiality, more precisely of marking an indirect or even secondhand source of knowledge, we can follow *Reyes* (1994) who uses the example of a weather forecast reported the next day. The speaker on television had used the form (38), and the reported speech may use different means to emphasize the evidential character of the utterance (which in this case even increases reliability):

(38) Para mañana por la mañana se pronostican lluvias intensas.
'Heavy rain is predicted for tomorrow morning'
> a. Dijeron: «Mañana por la mañana va a llover.»
'They said: "Tomorrow morning it is going to rain."'
> b. Dijeron: «Se pronostican lluvias fuertes para la mañana.»
'They said: "Heavy rain will fall in the morning".
> c. Dijeron que a la mañana iba a llover a cántaros.
'They said that in the morning it would rain cats and dogs.'
> d. Dijeron que a esta hora se iba a largar una buena.
'They said that at this time there would be a downpour.'
> e. Dijeron que hoy va a llover mucho.
'They said that it will rain a lot today.'

With the utterance (39), however, the speaker takes the responsibility for the message. This sentence is evidentially unmarked, that means there is no indication whether the knowledge of the speaker comes from his own perception (approaching clouds, for example), whether it is surmised or just reported from another source (the weather forecast).

(39) Va a llover
'It is going to rain.'

Reyes even goes as far as regarding the ironical presupposition of a previously pronounced utterance as a type of quotation. People who are just having breakfast in the sun could pronounce (40) "quoting" the weather forecast which was not right:

(40) Qué mal día para un picnic ¿eh?
'What a bad day for a picnic, isn't it?'

This way of thinking could lead to a very broad concept of evidentiality which would include presuppositional and intertextual relations which have no related theoretical explanation. It seems more possible to ask whether the function of marking reported speech can be taken up by grammatical elements. In certain contexts it might even become their main function. Such consequences can be seen in the case of verbal forms in Romance languages.

In the case of the intertextual function of the Spanish *imperfecto*, Reyes (1990b), Reyes (1994) has used the term *valor citativo*. It might be useful, however, to avoid this very general attribution of a function and to remove it from the very confused discussion on intertextuality (cf. Haßler 1997). Nevertheless Reyes' (1990a: 99–112 and 1990b) approach to a secondary evidential function of a verbal form is remarkable. She argues that the sentence (41) could be reformulated as (42), using the evidential function of the *imperfecto*:

(41) Juan viene mañana, según me anunciaron.
'John will come tomorrow, I have been told.'

(42) Juan venía mañana.
'John would come tomorrow.'

In (42) it is not possible to understand *venía* as a reference to the past, the use of the temporal adverb *mañana* is restrictive with regard to this simple time dimension. The imperfect *venía* refers to an utterance which was produced before and which has announced Juan's arrival. The imperfect has partially lost its prototypical reference with respect to time and aspect, namely the expression of an action in the past which is regarded in its duration. Instead of this function it has acquired, in some contexts, an epistemic signification.

For Spanish, it is possible to affirm that this evidential function of the *imperfecto* works in colloquial use even without further markers. The utterances (43), (44) and (45) will be understood as information about facts supposed to become reality in the future, but facts which the speaker has learned from other sources:

(43) a. El tren llegaba (IPERF) [mañana] a las ocho, ¿verdad?
'The train will arrive at eight, won't it?'

(44) a. No voy [a buscar al niño a la escuela] porque hoy iba (IPERF) su padre a buscarlo.
'I am not going [to take the child home after school] because his father will do it.'

(45) a. ¿Viste al novio? Venía (IPERF) ayer... a ver a Lita.
'Did you see the bridegroom? He came yesterday... to see Lita.'

These utterances could be reformulated with lexical or syntactic markers of evidentiality which would explicitly delegate responsibility to the sources of information:

(43) b. Anunciaron que el tren llegaba (IPERF) a las ocho, ¿verdad?
'It was announced that the train would arrive at eight, wasn't it?'

(44) b. No voy a buscar al niño porque hoy su padre, según está programado, iba (IPERF) a buscarlo.
'I am not going to take home the child because his father will do it, as has been arranged.'
Or: Su padre dijo que lo iba (IPERF) a buscar hoy.
'His father said he would take it today.'

(45) b. ¿Viste al novio? Me dijeron que venía ayer... a ver a Lita.
'Did you see the bridegroom? I was told he had came yesterday... to see Lita.'

The relation between the utterances (43b)–(45b) and (43a)–(45a) can be interpreted as the omission of explicit lexical and syntactic markers of reported speech. The function of delegating responsibility assumed by these elements is taken up by the verbal form which appears regularly together with these markers. Because it habitually appears in such contexts, the Spanish *imperfecto*, which has become unstable and redundant in its original temporal meaning, is refunctionalized. Taking up the evidential function by the verbal form makes it possible that specific lexical and syntactic support of this function is lost. Instead of (46) (a) it is possible to use (46) (b) in order to remember a source utterance in which the proposition has been communicated:

(46) a. Hoy daba una conferencia Maria, según anunciaron.
 'Today Maria gave a paper, as has been announced.'
 b. Hoy daba una conferencia Maria.
 'Today it is said that Maria will give a paper.'

Finally even the deictic markers may be omitted which exclude any clue about explaining the meaning of the verbal form as metaphorical and only related to a specific context:

(46) c. Daba una conferencia Maria.
 'It is said that Maria will give a paper.'

The plain German sentences (47) (a) or even (47) (b), on the contrary, would be understood as assessments of a fact without any evidential meaning:

(47) a. Heute hielt Maria eine Vorlesung.
 'Today Maria gave a paper.'
 b. Heute hat Maria eine Vorlesung gehalten.
 'Today Maria has given a paper.'

Epistemic particles such as *doch*[6] allow an evidential interpretation as a possible reading of the sentence (47a), while the perfect form keeps its factual meaning even with the epistemic particle (47d):

(47) c. Heute hielt doch Maria eine Vorlesung.
 'Today it is said that Maria will give a paper.'
 d. Heute hat Maria doch eine Vorlesung gehalten.
 'But today Maria has given a paper.'

Epistemic readings of past tense sentences would also be possible if the contrast between the non-actuality expressed by the verbal form and the actuality of the object argument is made explicit by the definite article. In addition, an adverb denoting future (*morgen*) would make an evidential reading more plausible (48). But such sentences seem to be restricted to narrative texts, especially to literature.

(48) Morgen hielt Maria die Vorlesung.
'Tomorrow Maria might give the paper.'

As we have seen, formally identical sentences in German and in Spanish give different instruction for understanding. The key to explaining this has to be seen in the complexity of functional features related to the verbal form. The possibility of interpreting utterances like (43) (a) or (46) (c) as propositions related to an earlier produced utterance or a conclusion from other facts, is given by the aspectual meaning of this verbal form which becomes redundant as such. There is no aspectual feature in German past tenses, consequently a verbal form *hielt* or *hat gehalten* cannot represent a process in its duration and therefore allow one to question its factual validity, which is possible in the respective Spanish utterances.

The possibility in Spanish of using the imperfect to express evidential meanings can be compared to similar phenomena in other Romance languages with a similar past tense system. It can be regarded as common place in French grammar that the *valeurs modales de l'imparfait* are dependent on aspect (cf. Riegel, Pellat and Rioul 1994: 309). But if we translate literally into French the Spanish sentence (49), it will be understood prototypically as the affirmation of an habitual action in the past, not as an expression of insecurity of the speaker with regard to the question whether a certain train will really arrive at a certain time, related to the attempt of the speaker to ask for confirmation of this previously received or induced information.

(49) El tren llegaba a las ocho.
'The train will arrive at eight, won't it?'

(50) Le train arrivait à huit heures.
'The train (usually) arrived at eight.'

In French evidential meanings of the imperfect would have to be supported by lexical items (*Dis donc, le train arrivait à huit heures*; *Voyons, le train arrivait à huit heures.*).

To what degree is the evidential meaning a function the aspectual value permits, or can it even be sufficient itself to indicate evidentiality? This question can only be answered if we look at the contextual and situative markers indicating what we have called a 'logocentric situation'. It can be affirmed for Romance languages that the possibility of using aspectual features for the expression of modal and evidential values is dependent on textual traditions, especially on the impact of narrative texts on oral language. While we can find this use of the *imperfecto* in spoken and even colloquial Spanish, there are contextual restrictions in Portuguese and Italian, and especially in French. In written narrative discourse, the use of the imperfect as a marker of reported speech in logocentric contexts, is common to all Romance languages in the so-called 'free indirect speech'.

6. Conclusions

We have seen that the transition area between reported speech and conclusion is well represented in Romance languages. Not only is there an intersection between the devices of evidentiality and reported speech, but in many cases the linguistic forms just mark indirect evidence which can be either reported speech or conclusion. The possibilities of this transition area can even be used intentionally to be less explicit in mentioning the source of the information. Using the concept of evidentiality in the description of Romance languages, we try to look from the outside, because the functional and pragmatical category of evidentiality is borrowed from the description of non-Indo-European languages. The pragmatic reality of marking the source of the speaker's knowledge, however, can be regarded as general. In the Romance languages, it leads to special uses of linguistic means and even to the refunctionalization of grammatical forms, which may cause difficulties in grammatical descriptions.

Looking at reported speech as a part of the evidential devices in Romance languages and studying its borderline cases with regard to other forms of evidentiality can help us to see functional analogies between phenomena which would not be related in a description limited to a single language. 'Transitional' phenomena which are difficult to describe within the canonical description of reported speech can be explained conclusively in the context of the more general category of evidentiality. We have discussed this with regard to the Spanish *imperfecto*, and we have mentioned that the French *conditionnel* or the modal verb *devoir* can be explained coherently in spite of their modal polysemy.

In addition to these functional considerations, the concept of a 'logophoric situation' may invite study of the grammatical consequences of pragmatic conditions. In this context, it is even necessary to take into account different text traditions and expressions of narrativity.

Languages express attitudes toward knowledge in quite different ways. From the kind of devices Romance languages make available to their speakers, we can learn a great deal about an important ingredient of language itself, especially the distinction between evidentiality and modality. Evidentiality is a linguistic category which applies to predications that the speaker assumes have a reasonable likelihood of being true, but which he cannot vouch for out from direct observation or experience. This is distinct from mood, in which the speaker disavows the factual truth of a predication.

Notes

1. The examples (1), (2) and (7) come from a corpus of interviews with young persons

from Hawkesbury, Ontario (cf. Mougeon/Beniak 1991) which the authors have kindly allowed us to use.

2. The letters behind this and the following examples mean: CM = Corpus Montréal (Université de Montréal, Laboratoire Ethnolinguistique), the first number = number of the speaker, the second number = line of transcript. Cf. Thibault/Vincent (1990).

3. This term has been criticized by Guentchéva (1994:8) who calls the same category *médiatif*, pointing out that it consists in keeping one's distance because there is only mediated knowledge of some facts. The term *evidentiality* would suggest just the contrary, that is to say the existence of evidence. Guentchéva (1996:14/15) discusses other fundamental research on evidentiality in Maya languages, Albanian and Bulgarian. Finally *Haarmann* (1970) and *Willett* (1988) are especially important in the development of evidentiality as a category in language description.

4. See also Dendale/Tasmowski (1994:4); Guentchéva (1996:13).

5. With regard to logophoric forms, see *Roncador* (1988).

6. Or other elements such as *wohl, wie ich hörte, wie X sagte*.

References

Alarcos Llorach, Emilio. 1994. *Gramática de la lengua española*. Madrid: Espasa Calpe.
Anderson, Lloyd B. 1986. "Evidentials, paths of change, and mental maps: typologically regular asymmetries". In Chafe and Nichols (eds.), 274–312.
Bakhtine, Michael. 1970. *La poétique de Dostoïevski*. Paris: Seuil.
Bakhtine, Michael. 1978. *Esthétique et théorie du roman*. Paris: Gallimard.
Barnes, Janet 1984. "Evidentials in the Tuyuca verb". *International Journal of American Linguistics* 50: 255–71.
Benveniste, Émile. 1966. *Problèmes de linguistique générale*. Paris: Gallimard.
Brunot, Ferdinand. 1922. *La pensée et la langue*. Paris: Masson.
Bybee, Joan and Suzanne Fleischmann (eds.). 1995. *Modality in grammar and discourse* (=Typological Studies in Language 32). Amsterdam: Benjamins.
Bybee, Joan, Revere Perkins and William Pagliuca (eds.). 1994. *The evolution of grammar: tense, aspect and modality in the languages of the world*. Chicago: University of Chicago Press.
Chafe, Wallace and Johanna Nichols (eds.). 1986. *Evidentiality: the linguistic coding of epistemology in language*. Norwood, N.J.: Ablex.
Comrie, Bernard. 1983. "Switch-reference in Huichol: a typological study". In Haiman, John and Pamela Munro (eds.), *Switch-reference and universal grammar: Proceedings of a Symposium on Switch Reference and Universal Grammar, Winnipeg, May 1981* (=Typological Studies in Language 2). Amsterdam: Benjamins, 17–37.
Dendale, Patrick. 1994. "*Devoir* épistémique, marqueur modal ou évidentiel?". In Dendale and Tasmowski (eds.), 24–40.
Dendale, Patrick and Liliane Tasmowski (eds.). 1994. *Les sources du savoir et leurs marques linguistiques* (= *Langue Française* 102). Paris: Larousse.

Dendale, Patrick and Liliane Tasmowski (eds.). 2001. *Evidentiality* (= *Journal of Pragmatics* 33). Amsterdam etc.: Elsevier.
Ducrot, Oswald. 1972. *Dire et ne pas dire*. Paris: Hermann.
Fleischmann, Suzanne. 1990. *Tense and narrativity: from medieval performance to modern fiction*. London: Routledge.
Grevisse, Maurice and André Goosse. 1993. *Le bon usage: grammaire française*. Paris: Duculot.
Guentchéva, Zlatka. 1994. "Manifestations de la catégorie du médiatif dans les temps du français". In Dendale and Tasmowski (eds.), 8–23.
Guentchéva, Zlatka. (ed.). 1996. *L'énonciation médiatisée*. Louvain/Paris: Peeters.
Harris, Alice C and Lyle Campbell. 1995. *Historical syntax in cross-linguistic perspective*. Cambridge: Cambridge University Press.
Haßler, Gerda. 1996. "Intertextualität und Modalität in einer verstehensorientierten Textgrammatik". In Gil, Alberto and Christian Schmitt (eds.), *Kohäsion, Kohärenz, Modalität in Texten romanischer Sprachen: Akten der Sektion "Grundlagen für eine Textgrammatik der romanischen Sprachen" des XXIV. Deutschen Romanistentages. Münster 25.-28.9.1995*. Bonn: Romanistischer Verlag, 310–38.
Haßler, Gerda (ed.). 1997. *Texte im Text: Untersuchungen zur Intertextualität und ihren sprachlichen Formen*. Münster: Nodus.
Hoff, Berend Jacob 1986. "Evidentiality in the Carib: particles, affixes and a variant of Wackernagel's Law". *Lingua* 69: 49–103.
Jakobson, Roman. 1971. "Shifters, verbal categories, and the Russian verb". Jakobson, Roman, *Selected writings*, Vol. II, The Hague: Mouton, 130–47.
Kristeva, Julia. 1978. *Recherches pour une sémanalyse*. Paris: Seuil.
Maingueneau, Dominique. 1993. *Eléments de linguistique pour le texte littéraire*. Paris: Dunod.
Mougeon, Raymond and Beniak, Edouard. 1991. *Linguistic consequences of language contact and restriction: the case of French in Ontario, Canada*. Oxford: Clarendon Press.
Nølke, Henning. 1994. "La dilution linguistique des responsabilités: essai de description polyphonique des marqueurs évidentiels *il semble* que et *il paraît que*". In Dendale and Tasmowski (eds.), 84–94.
Rauh, Gisa. 1978. *Linguistische Beschreibung deiktischer Komplexität in narrativen Texten*. Tübingen: Narr.
Reyes, Graciela. 1990a. *La pragmática lingüística. El estudio del uso del lenguaje*. Barcelona: Montesinos.
Reyes, Graciela. 1990b. "Tiempo, modo, aspecto e intertextualidad". *Revista Española de Lingüística* 20: 17–53.
Riegel, Martin, Pellat, Jean- Christophe and Rioul, René. 1994. *Grammaire méthodique du français*. Paris: Presses Universitaires de France.
Ross, John Robert. 1970. "On declarative sentences". In Jacobs, Roderick A. and Peter S. Rosenbaum (eds.), *Readings in English transformational grammar*. Washington, D.C.: Georgetown University, 222–72.
Sanctius Brocensis, Franciscus. 1986. *Minerva seu de causis linguae Latinae*. Reprint of the edition Salamanca 1587 with an introduction by Manuel Breva Claramonte.

Stuttgart/Bad Cannstatt: frommann-holzboog.
Stirling, Lesley. 1993. *Switch-Reference and discourse representation*. Cambridge: University Press.
Tasmowski, Liliane. 1994. "POUVOIR$_E$: Un marqueur d'évidentialité". In Dendale and Tasmowski (eds.), 41–55.
Thibault, Pierrette and Diane Vincent. 1990. *Un corpus de français parlé Montréal 1984: historique, méthodes et perspectives de recherche* (=Recherches sociolinguistiques 1). Québec: Université Laval.
Vet, Co. 1994. "Savoir et croire". In Dendale and Tasmowski (eds.), 56–68.
Weinrich, Harald. 1982. *Textgrammatik der französischen Sprache*. Stuttgart: Klett.
Willett, Thomas. 1988. "A cross-linguistic survey of the grammaticalization of evidentiality". *Studies in Language* 12,1: 51–97.
Wilmet, Marc. 1997. *Grammaire critique du français*. Louvain-la-Neuve: Duculot.

CHAPTER 8

Discourse perspectives on tense choice in spoken-English reporting discourse[*]

Tomoko I. Sakita
Doshisha University

1. Introduction

Reporting discourse in English has been traditionally viewed in a dichotomy of direct and indirect styles:

(1) a. Sarah said, "my sister will buy this house tomorrow."
 b. Sarah said that her sister would buy that house on the following day.

(1a) as a direct discourse retains the verb and its tense of the reported speaker's discourse. (1b) as an indirect discourse, however, is not a direct adoption of the original discourse, and hence there must be some rules to determine the tense in its complement clause. The most widespread principle for such rules is the sequence of tenses (SoT) that Comrie (1986) formalized. Comrie considered the principles only within the scope of a single sentence. He treated tense in reporting discourse as a purely syntactic phenomenon. However, his treatment of tense is too mechanical, and does not cover the whole range of reporting behaviors in language performances. Declerck (1990) has incorporated semantic and pragmatic information into the SoT rule, in an attempt to account for wider sets of examples. This study will examine tense in reporting discourse within the scope of actual language performances and introduce discourse perspectives in which tense in indirect reporting discourse is viewed as a discourse functional phenomenon.

The main argument of this article will be that speakers often choose to maintain discourse coherence by reporting from their own perspectives rather than to maintain syntactic integrity. In spoken English, tense in the complement clause is often determined not by its relation to the head clause, but rather by its direct relationship to the moment of speaking. I will show that in many cases in spoken English, tenses of reported verbs are naturally determined by the reporter's perspective. I will cite three points of evidence to support my view. First, speakers often avoid the past perfect tense in spoken English. Even when they use it, they use it as the absolute tense for a discourse functional necessity, rather than as the backshifted or the relative tense. Second, indirect reporting discourse has tense-alternation phenomena, which have long been considered a feature in direct reporting discourse. Third, reporting clauses behave flexibly as dialogue markers. In these three cases, it is significant to keep reporters' perspectives in terms of discourse coherence.

In Section 2 below, I will outline how traditional English grammar has treated tense in reporting discourse by briefly introducing Comrie's formal rule. I will point out that the formal tense rule has overlooked pragmatic information, which is important for successful communication. In Section 3, I will outline Declerck's hypothesis which incorporated pragmatic and semantic information in the tense theory. In Section 4, I will present my own view that tense in indirect reporting discourse in natural spoken English does not behave as rigidly as standard theories have considered. From naturally occurring language data, I will raise examples in which standard theories do not work. I will present discourse perspectives which will supplement Declerck's theory. Finally, I will suggest that in spoken discourse, the reporting clause and the reported clause do not have a subordinate relationship as has long been assumed.

2. Formal rule of tense

Traditional English grammar (e.g., Leech and Svartvik 1975; Thomson and Martinet 1980; Quirk *et al.* 1985) has presented tense in indirect reporting discourse with a very formal sequence of tenses (SoT) rule. Jespersen (1924) made it popular, and its recent proponents are *Comrie* (1986) and Hornstein (1990). They treat it as a purely syntactic operation, which is applied mechanically without semantic motivation. *Comrie* (1986) formalized the rule as follows:

> If the tense of the verb of reporting is non-past, then the tense of the original utterance is retained; if the tense of the verb of reporting is past, then the tense of the original utterance is backshifted into the past, except that if the content of the indirect speech has continuing applicability, the backshifting is optional. (*Comrie* 1986:284)

Comrie's formal SoT rule describes tense in indirect reporting discourse by reference to the relationship between a subordinate clause and its main clause counterpart. The rule predicts how the direct reporting discourse is switched into indirect style, and how tense in the complement clause is realized in indirect discourse. Comrie tested the mechanical operation of his rule in single sentences, and provided English grammar with a formal rule at the sentential level.[1] To illustrate the operation of the formal SoT rule, traditional grammarians often list the mechanical changes: e.g., present to past; present continuous to past continuous; present perfect to past perfect; past to past perfect; past continuous to past perfect continuous; future to conditional; future perfect to conditional perfect. They provide examples in pairs of direct and indirect discourse such as the following to demonstrate the above rule:

(2) a. Mary said, "My mother is on the phone."
    b. Mary said that her mother was on the phone.

(3) a. Jane said, "I saw him the other day."
    b. Jane said that she had seen him the other day.

(4) a. Eric said, "I have been waiting over an hour for her."
    b. Eric said that he had been waiting over an hour for her.

However, there are some cases that the formal SoT rule cannot account for. In the following examples, the formal SoT rule fails to predict indirect reporting discourse:

(5) a. Walter regrets saying to Joy, "I love you."
    b. *Walter regrets telling Joy that he loves her.
    c. Walter regrets telling Joy that he loved her.

(6) a. This is John's wife. — Yes, I THOUGHT he was married.
    b. *This is John's wife. — Yes, I THOUGHT he is married.

(Declerck 1991: 185)

For the direct reporting discourse (5a), the formal SoT rule predicts (5b) as an indirect version, simply because there is no past-tense reporting verb to trigger backshifting in the head clause. But normal speakers use (5c) for indirect discourse. In (6), John continues to be married. The formal SoT rule predicts (6b) instead of (6a). (Recall that if the content of the indirect discourse has continuing applicability, the backshifting is optional.) However, (6b) is a wrong prediction. These cases demonstrate that if we mechanically apply the formal SoT rule in some cases, we will form unacceptable sentences. Indeed, such a mechanical way of viewing reporting discourse is what Voloshinov (1986:128) pointed out as "a typical grammarian's error." He claimed that the "mechanical, purely grammatical mode of translating reported speech from one pattern into another, without the appropriate stylistic reshaping" is a highly objectionable way of manufacturing classroom exercises in grammar. As he emphasized, "This sort of implementation of the patterns of speech reporting has nothing even remotely to do with their real existence in a language."

From a typological point of view, it is becoming more obvious that sequence of tenses is not a universal requirement for tense systems or for linguistic systems. Growing numbers of studies have supported that there is considerable cross-linguistic variation in tense determination systems. Languages like German and

English have long been considered to have a rigid sequence of tenses. On the other hand, languages such as Hungarian (*Kiefer* 1986), Russian (*Comrie* 1986; *Barentsen* 1996), and Japanese have no rules for backshifting of tense. There are even languages like Yoruba that have no tense system at all (*Bamgboṣe* 1986). As *Coulmas* (1986: 15), one of the followers of SoT admits, shifting of tenses is "by no means logically necessary or implied by the presence of a tense system." The sequence of tenses is therefore not a prerequisite for human communication systems or for human cognitive operations.

Even in English, which has been viewed as having a rigid SoT system, there is doubt at a practical level whether the formal rule is actually operative in communication settings. Goodell (1987) raised some cases where the formal rules could fail to form utterances suitable to the situations. For instance, suppose that a mother has made the utterance (7). (8) is a case in which Mary reported it immediately after her mother's utterance. (9) is a case in which Mary reported it after a distinct period of time:

(7) Mother: Girls, I want you to clean up the kitchen.
(8) Debbie: What did Mom say? I couldn't hear her.
    Mary: She said she *wants* us to clean up the kitchen.
(9) Debbie: What did Mom say before she left yesterday? I couldn't hear her.
    Mary: She said she *wanted* us to clean up the kitchen
                                                    (*Goodell* 1987: 309)

The appropriate tense forms in the complement clauses are the present in (8) and the past in (9). If we mechanically apply the formal SoT rule, we cannot distinguish such context-sensitive differences. The example suggests that we need to know the semantic and pragmatic concerns to determine the tenses in some indirect reporting discourses. The formal theories have long set aside such cases as exceptions to their rules.

3. Declerck's tense theory

Declerck (1990) proposed the incorporation of pragmatic and semantic information into the tense theory. He proposed a new hypothesis by combining the relative time hypothesis and the absolute deixis hypothesis.[2] I will call it "the combination of relative and absolute tense (CoRA) hypothesis" in this study. According to this new hypothesis, tense in an indirect discourse complement clause is usually the relative tense, relative to tense in a head clause. The hypothesis also includes the absolute tense which can appear, subject to certain conditions. Table 1 summarizes his explanation of relative tense.

Table 1. Relative tense in complement clause by its temporal relation with head clause

	Simultaneity	Anteriority	Posteriority
Head clause: past	preterite	past perfect	conditional
Head clause: non-past	present	preterite; present perfect	future

For instance, in (2a), tense in the head clause is the past and the temporal relation between the head clause and the complement clause is simultaneity. Therefore, the reported verb is realized as preterite in (2b). In (3a) and (4a), the head clauses are both in the past, and the information in the complement clauses is anterior to the head clauses. So, the reported verbs are both in the past perfect in (3b) and (4b). The following is a case in which the head clause is in the non-past:

(10) a. Thomas will say, "We are playing chess."
      b. Thomas will say that they are playing chess.

Here, the head clause is in the non-past, and the content of the complement clause is simultaneous with the head clause. So the reported clause has the present verb in (10b).

In addition to the use of the relative tense as the unmarked choice, Declerck includes the absolute tense in his hypothesis, by allowing it in marked, restricted cases. In some restricted cases, tense in the reported clause may be directly related to the moment of speaking, having the speaker's deictic center as the reference point. Declerck raised the following example:

(11) John said that Bill was in London the day before.   (Declerck 1990: 519)

In this sentence, neither the formal SoT rule nor Declerck's relative tense explanation work. They both predict the reported verb in the complement clause to be *had been* instead of *was*. Declerck solves this problem by saying that in such sentences the complement clause shifts the domain instead of incorporating its situation into the head clause domain.[3] That is, the situation is reported from the speaker's deictic center, not from the reportee's. He explains that the absolute tense is allowed only if the temporal order of the situations is clear from a temporal adverb, the context, or from the hearer's pragmatic knowledge of the world.[4] Since (11) contains the time adverbial *the day before*, it is clear that Bill's being in London is anterior to John's report of it.

In this way, Declerck introduced a possibility that the tense used in a complement clause in indirect speech may be either a relative tense or an absolute tense.[5] The complement clause situation can either (1) be incorporated into the domain referred to in the head clause and express a domain internal relation, or (2) shift the domain (i.e., create a new domain). The speaker's choice of relative or absolute tense forms is governed by the following principle:

If both clauses refer to the same time-sphere, the use of relative tense in the complement clause is the unmarked choice. This means that, in such sentences, relative tense is always possible, whereas there are restrictions on the absolute tense form. For example, absolute tense is allowed only if the temporal order of the situations is clear from a temporal adverb, the context or from the hearer's pragmatic knowledge of the world. (Declerck 1990:519)

Declerck raised two main reasons for using the absolute tense: (1) the tendency towards tense simplification; (2) the speaker sometimes wishes to represent a past situation as still relevant at the speaker's deictic center (1991:183).

4. Tense in discourse

4.1 Prevalence of speaker's viewpoint

In the following, I will investigate reporting discourse in natural language situations to show that tense in indirect reporting discourse in spoken English does not behave as rigidly as standard theories have considered. I generally agree with Declerck's CoRA as it has included semantic and pragmatic concerns into the tense theory. He has shown examples in a scope of sentences. I will apply discourse perspectives to his hypothesis, and show that the absolute tense is common in spoken discourse. In spoken discourse, it is not only contextual clarity that allows the absolute tense. Speakers often prefer the absolute tense to the relative tense to preserve the coherence of the discourse. In addition, the type of verb introduces linguistic restrictions that affect the choice of tense. The following discussion will show uses of tense within a wider scope of discourse with contextual variations. Examples will include naturally occurring language data in such settings as casual talks, telephone conversations, elicited narratives in semi-formal settings, movies, news-reports, etc.

The first examples show verbs that obviously do not behave as Comrie's SoT and Declerck's relative tense rule in CoRA predict. The first two examples are from a telephone conversation. In (12), M is referring to their previous conversation about his class:[6]

(12) M: ahh I wrote one thing about .hh remember I told you the first couple days a cl:ass
W: un hum
M: *was* kind of ah .hh a weird game situation
W: uhyeah
M: ynah I sit down I sat down 'n en wrote that   (JR)[7]

In the reporting discourse which starts with *I told you*, M used the past-tense verb *was* in the complement clause. Here the formal SoT and the relative tense rule both predict *had been*, since the original discourse for this utterance is assumed to be:

(13) The first couple of days a class *was* kind of a weird game situation.

Here, contrary to what the formal SoT and the relative tense rule predict, tense of the original discourse is retained in the indirect discourse. The next example is a similar case. M asks W if she has seen her mother:

(14) M: Have you seen her yet
W: Yeah we saw her tonight=
M: =What was the reaction (0.2)
W: Uhhum (0.3) good you know after I kn- I knock on the doo:r (0.8) Who's there Jean no she starts laughing wow y'know, heh (0.2) en y'know sorta like waited a while en then told her we *had* hitchhike cause she didn't know y'know an then   (JR)

In answering M, W mentions that she told her mother about a hitchhike. Here, W uses the simple past form *had* rather than the past perfect form *had had*, which the formal SoT and the relative tense rule predict from the original discourse that W uttered to her mother:

(15) We *had* a hitchhike.

Only the absolute tense explanation works for (12) and (14). The following example is from a news-report:

(16) Tokyo Governor Yukio Aoshima announced that he *decided* to cancel the World City Expo which was scheduled for next year. The writer-turned governor made the decision although the Tokyo Metropolitan Assembly overwhelmingly adopted a resolution demanding the Expo proceed. (CE 1995. 8: 92)[8]

In (16), since the verb in the head clause *announced* is in the past tense, and the assumed original discourse by Yukio Aoshima is (17), both the formal SoT and the relative tense rule predict the past perfect form *had decided* in the complement clause. However, the verb in the complement clause keeps the past tense from the assumed original discourse:

(17) I *decided* to cancel the World City Expo which was scheduled for next year.

It does not follow either the formal SoT or the relative tense rule.

In the above three cases, we can observe the use of the absolute tense, i.e., the reporter's deictic center is the reference point. Tense in the complement clause is not backshifted as the formal SoT predicts, nor is it determined relative to tense in the head clause. The reporter uses the past tense simply because the reported event happened in the past from her or his standpoint. Declerck allowed the absolute tense in his hypothesis as a marked restricted case only when there is contextual clarity of temporal orders. (12) exactly fits in this idea. What M is reporting is the repetition of his former conversation with W, thus the temporal order of M's reporting and the event in the complement clause is a shared knowledge between the speakers. In natural language use, speakers and hearers generally share some pragmatic knowledge or, at least, some common knowledge of the world. Or the speakers contextualize their stories beforehand. It is natural that speakers use the absolute tense more often in spoken English discourse.

With respect to (14) and (16), the temporal order is supported by the common linguistic information. That is, because of the characteristics of the reported verbs in (14) and (16), the temporal orders are clear between the reporting clauses and the reported clauses. It is clear that the verbs in the original discourses of (14) and (16) are not in the present tense, because the verbs *have* and *decide* generally do not appear in the present tense:

(18) a. We had a hitchhike.
 b. ??We have a hitchhike.
 c. We are having a hitchhike.

(19) a. I decided to cancel the World City Expo which was scheduled for next year.
 b. ??I decide to cancel the World City Expo which was scheduled for next year.
 c. I will decide to cancel the World City Expo which was scheduled for next year.

In these cases, *have* and *decide* are used as event verbs, thus they will not appear in the present tense unless the event occurs habitually, e.g., "I walk to school." According to Leech (1987), there are state verbs and event verbs that are used to refer to states or events. For instance:

> state verbs: *be, live, belong, last, like, stand, know, have, contain, seem, owe.*
> event verbs: *jump, nod, get, put, land, begin, find, hit, fall, go, become, take.*
> (Leech 1987:9)

'State' and 'event' are semantic rather than grammatical terms. *Decide* belongs to event verbs. Although *have* generally belongs to state verbs in the above list, when it appears in '*have a* verb' construction (Dixon 1991:346) with an emphasis on the activity, it is used as an event verb. In terms of event verbs, the instantaneous use of the present tense that signifies an event simultaneous with the present moment as in (18b) and (19b), is generally the marked or abnormal alternative to the progressive present tense, "because there are few circumstances in which it is reasonable to regard an action as begun and completed at the very moment of speech" (Leech 1987:7).[9] So, Leech's findings suggest that event verbs are generally used in the past tense. When there is an indirect reporting discourse (20a) which contains event verbs (*jumped; got*), it is generally assumed that (20c) is the direct discourse version instead of (20b), except in contextually restricted cases:

(20) a. He said that he jumped and got hurt.
 b. ??He said, "I jump and get hurt."
 c. He said, "I jumped and got hurt."

There is no ambiguity in temporal relations between the content of the reporting clause and the content of the reported clause in (20a). Therefore, even without any contextual information to clarify the temporal order, there is no ambiguity in (14) and (16). Therefore, these sentences may keep the absolute tense.

Let me cite a few more examples which contain the absolute tense:

(21) The study showed that under normal circumstances, high quantities of allergen *were* needed to cause an asthma attack, but when other pollutants *were* also introduced, the amount of allergen needed *decreased* significantly. (EJ 1995. 7: 21)[10]

(22) Ann Stone, leader of Republicans For Choice, says 50,000 people have joined to seek pro-choice language in the platform. She complained that Republican convention planners *allotted* her only a few moments to discuss the question of abortion. (ABC News 1992. 10)

(21) is from an interview on scientific research. (22) is from a news-report. At first glance, if we do not examine the contents with their contexts, we may think that the formal SoT is working in these examples. Since the head clauses and the complement clauses are both in the past tense, the two tenses seem to be in sequence. For instance, in (22), *she complained* and *allotted* are both in the past. But the formal SoT works only if we assume Ann Stone's complaint to be (23). (The same is said to the relative tense rule.) But according to the context, it is natural to assume that her complaint was not (23) but (24):

(23) *Republican convention planners *allot* me only a few moments to discuss the question of abortion.

(24) Republican convention planners *allotted* me only a few moments to discuss the question of abortion.

(22) retains the past tense from its original discourse (24), since it is the past event also from the present speaker's viewpoint. That is why it is the absolute tense. In

(22), the reporting verb *says* in the first sentence is in the present, and the reporting verb *complained* in the second sentence is in the past. This is a case of tense-alternation in which tense in the head clause is not fixed but rather freely switches between the present and the past (e.g., Schiffrin 1981; Wolfson 1982; Johnstone 1987; Sakita 1998).[11] If the reported verbs switch their tenses along with the freely switching tenses of reporting verbs, it breaks the discourse coherence. In such cases, the speaker keeps her or his point of view to maintain coherence.

The formal SoT and the relative tense rule are based on the assumption that tense in the complement clause is determined by relation to its head clause. However, by contemplating the above discourse examples, we can see that this is not the case. The complement clause is uttered from the speaker's (reporter's) viewpoint. The head clause does not have such a strong influence on the complement clause as was supposed in previous theories. This is partly supported by the free indirect discourse in which the reporter does not use the reporting clause.[12] It is also supported by the tense-alternation shown in (22), where the tense in the head clause freely switches between the present and the past.

4.2 Avoidance of the past perfect tense

In spoken discourse, people often avoid using the past perfect when it is not necessary (and even sometimes when it is). The examples shown above had the past tense where the formal SoT and the relative tense rule would predict the past perfect. The following is another example:

(25) V: But still it covers eighty percent.
C: Yeah
V: hh Anyways hh so the next day your Mom told me that she *talked* to my Mom 'n that it *was* a:ll confusing 'n that she *didn't*- my mother *sounded* real upset that she she *didn't* know what was going on about why they didn't change the knee.   (F)

This is a conversation between female friends. V says that C's mother told V that V's mother had been upset about V's father's operation. The formal SoT and the relative tense rule predict all the reported verbs in this example to be in the past perfect. But the simple past tense was used throughout the report. The following is a similar case from a casual talk between two men:

(26) G: Well 'e took Bill, a good friend a' mine, he weighs about two hundred'n s:;
B: rrrraaaaaah
(0.5)
B: hh AAW YAWWWW!

G: two hundred's five pounds I think 'e weighs. Took 'im for a ride on that'n Bill said that he *was* at least goin' eighty miles'n hour. With the two of 'em on it.= (AD)

Here, G tells B an episode in which one man took his friend Bill for a ride on a snowmobile. In his last remark, Bill's speech is reported with the past-tense verb *was* rather than with the past-perfect-tense verb. There are many such cases in which the past tense is used instead of the past perfect tense.

The phenomenon of avoiding the past perfect tense has been largely absent from the frameworks of SoT and CoRA. Previous studies describe the tense by reference to the relation between a subordinate clause and its main clause counterpart, rather than by the relation between indirect reporting discourse and the actual speech utterance being reported (Huddleston 1984). Such a rigid mode of analysis commits serious errors in discourse interpretation. Previous studies often present pairs of indirect and direct reporting discourse such as the following:

(27) a. The guy in the visitor's chair responded that he *wasn't* feeling well either.
 b. The guy in the visitor's chair said, "I'*m not* feeling well either."

When they face an indirect reporting discourse (27a), SoT and CoRA are most likely to predict that its direct speech counterpart is (27b) with its verb in the complement clause having the present tense. However, it could be a wrong interpretation of the utterance (27a). The sentence (27a) is indeed a report that was uttered in elicited narratives that I collected (*Sakita* 1996). I asked 19 native speakers of English to describe a film that contained short conversations, and the outcome contained varieties of ways of reporting. (27a) is one of the typical ways of reporting the original utterance (28) in the film:

(28) I *wasn't* feeling well, but I got the muffin because I thought it would help my stomach.   [original discourse](*Sakita* 1996)

It is clear that, in reality, the speaker who produced (27a) has not chosen the tense in the complement clause in its relation to the verb tense in the main clause. The speaker simply conveyed the fact that the man was not feeling well from her own viewpoint. The speaker's use of the simple past rather than the past perfect in (27a) does not mean that the situation in the complement clause (the man's not feeling well) is happening simultaneously with the man's utterance. Such an interpretation distorts the fact. The original speaker's point is that he was not feeling well, but that he feels better now because of the muffin. The speaker who produced (27a) simply used the past tense from her own viewpoint, and not the past perfect. Following SoT and CoRA, one would have reported the original utterance (28) by using the past perfect as in (29):

(29) The guy said that he *had* not *been* feeling well, but he *had gotten* the muffin because he *had thought* it would help his stomach. [predicted direct discourse]

But many people actually reported (28) using the simple past tense as in the following ways:

(30) The guy in the visitor's chair responded that he *wasn't* feeling well either, but he *got* a muffin because he *thought* it would settle his stomach . . .
(31) The other guy, Kevin, said he *wasn't* really feeling well either, but he *got* a muffin because he *thought* it would make him feel better . . .
(32) Kevin said that he *didn't* feel well also, and ah once he *had* the muffin, he *was* feeling better . . .
(33) Kevin said that he *got* the muffin because he *thought* it would make him feel better . . . (*Ibid.*)

4.3 Discourse functional use of the past perfect tense

There still are some cases, however, in which the past perfect is used. In such cases, the past perfect is used not as a result of the formal SoT nor the relative tense rule. It is rather used as an absolute tense simply because of a discourse functional necessity.[13] Consider the following example. It is an extract from the elicited narratives mentioned above:

(34) The man on the right said that he *had not been* feeling well, but he *got* his muffin so he now *feels* better. (*Ibid.*)

In this sentence it is odd to say that the past perfect form *had not been* is determined relative to the reporting verb *said*, since we cannot explain the other verbs *got* and *feels* in this way. Rather, the reported clause is seen from the reporter's viewpoint and organized in a sequence of events. The tenses in the reported clause are realized as the absolute ones with the function of clarifying the causality of the three events: the man's not feeling well; his getting a muffin; his feeling better. The speaker used the past perfect and showed that the man's feeling unwell was a continuous state until he got a muffin. It may be argued that the latter half of this sentence is not a reporting discourse, thus the reporting verb *said* influences the tense only in the reported part, *he had not been feeling well*. But we can see in (35) that the absence of the reporting phrase from (34) does not affect the coherence of this sentence:

(35) He *had not been* feeling well, but he *got* his muffin so he now *feels* better.

The whole reported clause in (34) keeps its coherence, independent of the reporting clause.

The following example shows how reporters attempt to maintain the causal relationship or order of reported events:

(36) The man on the right <u>talks</u> about, ah excuse me, the man on the left <u>mentions</u> that he *had* ah *contemplated* buying a muffin but he <u>said</u> he *didn't feel* well, and the man on the right <u>says</u> he also *did not feel* well but *decided* to buy the muffin anyways. (*Ibid.*)

Tenses of reporting verbs (which are underlined) alternate between present and past in this example. Here, tenses of reported verbs are determined not in relation to the switching tenses of reporting verbs. The reported discourse rather keeps its own coherence. The speaker reports the events about the man on the left in their orders: the man had considered buying a muffin, then he gave it up since he did not feel well. So the past perfect tense comes first and the past tense comes next.

The following example also involves the use of the past perfect tense as a reporter's attempt to clarify the order of reported events:

(37) Bill said that something to the effect of he *thought* of getting a muffin but *didn't* feel well, . . . and Kevin, Kevin said that ah earlier he *hadn't been* feeling well either, and they seemed little bit more happy and I think I saw Kevin smiling at the very beginning, they were both seated at a desk, in about the same position except that Kevin was leaning over and eating, and I believe that Bill said that the problem *was* with his stomach, an that's why he *didn't* want to have a muffin, because he *was* having some kind of stomach problem. (*Ibid.*)

Here, the formal SoT and the relative tense rule may conclude that the use of *hadn't been* in lines 2–3 is determined relative to the past-tense verb in the head clause *Kevin said*. But I would argue rather that this past perfect is triggered by *earlier* immediately before *he hadn't been*. This speaker keeps the absolute tense throughout his discourse. It is natural that he consistently used the absolute tense, and only once did he use the past perfect in combination with *earlier* to clarify the temporal relation of his speech events.

Let us look at another example in which we can see the discourse functional use of the past perfect:

(38) U.S. Secretary of State Warren Christopher announced that Israel and Syria *had agreed* on a framework clearing the way for detailed negotiations on security agreements. Christopher said that top military officials from Israel and Syria *agreed* to meet in Washington by the end of June to

resume their stalled peace talks mainly concerning conditions of Israeli withdrawal from the Golan Heights. Peace talks between the two countries had been frozen since last December. (CE 1995. 8: 89)

The formal SoT and the relative tense rule fit the first sentence, but they cannot explain the second sentence. If we consider that both verbs *had agreed* and *agreed* are in the absolute tense, we can give a consistent explanation for the whole discourse. The two tenses italicized are in a chronological order and in a causal relationship. Thus, it is common in spoken discourse that the simple past tense is used where the past perfect is expected by the formal SoT and the relative tense rules. The past perfect tense is rarely used unless the need to report a sequence of events creates a discourse functional necessity.

4.4 Reporting clause as dialogue marker

In examining (22) and (36), I pointed out that tense-alternation may occur in indirect reporting discourse. Previous theories assumed that the tense of the reporting verb is faithful to the event time, and that the tense in the complement clause is determined by its relation to the reporting verb tense. But in spoken discourse, the tense in the head clause may remain in the present or past, or more flexibly switch between the present and the past, regardless of the actual speech settings. It seems that reporting clauses in such cases do not function to indicate temporal settings nor as a reference point for reported clauses.

In narratives, narrators often keep whole discourse coherence, rather than keep sentential coherence by relating reporting clauses and reported clauses. In such cases, a reporting clause simply functions as a marker to introduce dialogue. Consider the following narrative excerpt, where a woman narrates a story of an emergency that she heard from her friend who fell on the floor and could not get out of her house. People lifted a little girl through the kitchen window to help the woman. After reporting detailed exchanges with direct reporting style, the narrator switches to indirect style:

(39) So that's what they did. So she goes through and she says she *landed* in the sink . . . well, naturally, it's like our kitchen. So she had taken her shoes off, right? She had heels on and she took them off when they hoisted her. She was on a little step ladder but then they still had to give her a little push, right? So she got in, she said she *sat* right in the sink. So she had to work her way out of that and she got in and here she opened up the front door and it took the four of them to get her up and she was screamin' when they got her up, she was in such pain.

(Wolfson 1982: 94–5)

There are two indirect reporting parts in this excerpt (reporting clauses are underlined). In line 1, the narrator states the fact that the little girl entered the house and landed in the sink by saying, "So she goes through and she says she landed in the sink." Here she adds detailed explanations for how she went into the house (". . . well, naturally, it's like our kitchen. . . . they still had to give her a little push, right?"). In line 5, the narrator resumes describing the little girl's entering the house, saying, "So she got in, she said she sat right in the sink," and continues the story. Although these repeated reporting parts are about the one event of the little girl's landing in the sink, they have different tenses. In line 1, the reporting clause (*she says*) is in the present tense,[14] while in line 5, the reporting clause (*she said*) is in the past tense. We see that the tense variation of these reporting clauses has not affected the past tense forms in the reported clauses. It indicates that the reporting clauses in these cases are not temporal reference points for the reported clauses. The reporting clauses are more like dialogue introducing markers, while the reported event of the girl's landing in the sink is in the discourse flow over the event line. Even without reporting clauses, the reported event that the girl landed in the sink fits in the narrative line and does not cause any confusion to the story:

(40) a. So she goes through and she landed in the sink . . .
 b. So she got in, she sat right in the sink.

In these cases, the reported clauses belong to the main event line. The reporting clauses are markers that indicate the source of the reported information, and their tense variations may have some discourse functions, just as dialogue-introducer[15] tense-shift in direct reporting discourse has significant discourse functions.[16]

The same is true in the post-posed reporting clauses. In the following excerpt which occurs before (39) in the same narrative, the reporting clause in line 2 is post-posed:

(41) So then after a while, she thought one of them'll have enough sense to come to the door, ring the bell, right? So she couldn't get up <u>she said</u>, she, it was a- — so she crawled to the door and then finally one of the women came and rang the bell and she said to 'em, "I'm on the floor, I fell and I can't get up." So Nancy said, "Well, open the door," (*Ibid.*)

In this case, the reporting clause *she said* could be pre-posed (42a) or could even be omitted (42b) without changing the tense in the reported clause:

(42) a. So she said she couldn't get up, she, it was a- — so she crawled. . .
 b. So she couldn't get up, she, it was a- — so she crawled . . .

Since it is contextualized that the whole story that the narrator is telling is based on her friend's report, the inclusion of the reporting clause is not obligatory as an indication of its being reported by her friend.

When we look at the flexibility of these reporting clauses, we notice that they behave more like comment clauses which are characteristic of spoken English. "Comment clauses are either content disjuncts that express the speakers' comments on the content of the matrix clause, or style disjuncts that convey the speakers' views on the way they are speaking" (Quirk *et al.* 1985:1112). Comment clauses are parenthetical disjuncts, and they may occur initially, finally, or medially, and generally have a separate tone unit. They are generally marked prosodically by increased speed and lowered volume. Some reporting clauses in spoken English, as we saw above, share these characteristics with comment clauses. From among six types of comment clauses that Quirk *et al.* distinguish,[17] I assume that reporting clauses are related to the type (i) of comment clauses that are "like the matrix clause of a main clause." As in (43a), such type of comment clause generally contains a transitive verb or adjective which elsewhere requires a nominal *that*-clause as object (43b):

(43) a. There were no other applicants, I believe, for that job.
 b. I believe that there were no other applicants for that job.
(Quirk *et al.* 1985:1113)

In (43), the sentence (a) and (b) are not exact paraphrases, but have different meanings. The verb in the comment clause in (43a) may have only one of the meanings possible for the verb in the matrix clause. Especially, verbs like *believe* and *think* in comment clauses may have merely a hedging meaning.[18] Although the verbs in most of the comment clauses of this type (i) are in the simple present, Quirk *et al.* (*ibid.*: 1114) admit that, in some cases, clauses can be fairly freely constructed, permitting variations of subject, tense, and aspect, or additions of adjuncts, etc.:

(44) The Indian railways (my uncle was telling me some time ago) have always made a profit. (*Ibid.*: 1114)

Some reporting clauses in indirect reporting discourse seems to function as comment clauses in this category. They are constructed like the matrix clause of a main clause, but are more freely constructed with variations of tense and aspect. What is significant is that the reporting clauses that have been considered definitely as main clauses in the previous frameworks may also function as comment clauses in spoken English. In such cases, they do not function to indicate temporal reference points for reported clauses in tense determination. The use of reporting clauses as comment clauses is often seen in narratives, as in (39) and (41). It also appears in casual conversations:

(45) Yihknow she really eh — so she said you know, theh-ih- she's had experience. hh with handicap' people she said but hh ih-yihknow ih-theh- in the fie:ld. — thet they're i:n::.= (TG)

Here reporting clauses are posed before and after a reported clause, "she's had experience with handicap' people." The tense in the reported clause is not backshifted. Quirk *et al.* (*ibid.*: 1115) note that reporting clauses for direct reporting discourse are related to the semantic roles of type (i) comment clauses, and may be considered an additional semantic category within type (i):

(46) "It's time we went," I said. (*Ibid.*: 1115)

Reporting clauses in indirect reporting discourse that I characterized as comment clauses function similarly to such dialogue-introducers in direct reporting discourse in (46). In both indirect reporting (45) and direct reporting (46), the speaker comments, by using the reporting clause, that the content of the matrix clause is not the present speaker's immediate utterance but is a report.

The use of reporting clauses as comment clauses in indirect reporting discourse seems to be related to 'syntactic dependency' that *Declerck and Tanaka* (1996:293) claim in discussion of the factors that prevent the use of the present tense in reported clauses. They point out that the degree of syntactic dependency of the reported clause on the reporting verb is one of the factors that restrict the tense in reported clauses.[19] In the case of basic comment clauses that Quirk *et al.* (1985) raise, they are surely syntactically independent of main clauses since they are parenthetical disjuncts. In such terms, some reporting clauses fit in the frame of comment clauses. The reporting clauses are independent of reported clauses and may be easily omitted or moved to other positions.

However, the dependency between reporting clauses and reported clauses should be defined in a more flexible way rather than in terms of syntax, when we view spoken English discourse. If what a speaker does with a reporting clause is to comment on, or to add information to, or even to contextualize the reported event, then the reporting clause behaves as a comment clause and does not necessarily function as a temporal reference point. It depends on how the reporter cognizes the relation between the information in the reporting clause with the information in the reported clause. In the following excerpt, the speaker P introduces a new topic in a form of report. At the beginning, he provides an information source Mike in reporting clause:

(47) P: Mike says there was a big fight down there las'night,
     C: Oh really?
         (0.5)
     P: with Keegan en, what. Paul de Wa::ld?]
     M: Paul de Wal] d. Guy out of,=
     C: =De Wa:ld yeah I know 'm.   (AD)

The speaker's focus is on the reported event that there was a fight, and the hearer's response "Oh really?" is a reaction to the content of the reported event ("there was a big fight down there last night") and not to the report itself ("Mike says . . ."). Although the reporting clause provides the source information, the speaker does not relate the reported event as dependent on the source information. So it could be more directly presented as source information as follows:

(48) a. According to Mike, there was a big fight down there last night,
b. You know what I heard from Mike? There was a big fight down there last night,

In (48a), the reporting clause from (47) behaves more as a comment clause, and in (48b), it even becomes a totally independent sentence. Again, in the following:

(49) he said he *was* standing there and he *was* just out dancing around on the edge of the dance floor and Don who looks real Butch but is this major Nillie Queen comes running up to him and goes: "now just nod your head — nod your head" and Bob was standing over there watching with this horrified — Alan said he *had* this totally horrified look on his face-- and eh — Don goes: "nod your head — nod your head" and so Alan's like: "oh okay" . . .   (Yule and Mathis 1992:208)

In both occurrences of indirect reporting discourse in this excerpt, tenses in the reported clauses are not backshifted in their relations to the reporting verbs. The second occurrence is excerpted in (50a) below:

(50) a. and Bob was standing over there watching with this horrified — Alan said he *had* this totally horrified look on his face.
b. and Bob was standing over there watching with this horrified look on his face.
c. and Bob was standing over there watching with this horrified look on his face, which Alan told me.

In (50a), the speaker describes how Bob looked when Don came up to Alan (the first *he* in [49]) and gave him a strange order. Here, the speaker makes a repair. At first, the speaker is about to describe Bob as shown in (50b). But since the description "horrified look" is a subjective assessment, the speaker repairs himself and makes clear the source of the subjectivity which is Alan, to support his point. Such source information could also be post-posed as in (50c). There is no indispensable dependency or subordinate relationship between the source and the reported event. Obviously, the inclusion of the reporting clause *Alan said* has not caused backshifting of the past tense verb *had* to the past perfect tense. The event line has its own discourse coherence, and the source information is added as a comment to supplement the event line. In this way, the speaker's consciousness smoothly flows over the narrative line.

In spoken English, people do not always set temporal reference points in reporting clauses in either indirect or direct reporting discourse. Reporting clauses function more often as hedges, evidential markers, source markers, or personal deictic markers, rather than as reference points for temporal relationships with reported clauses. The reporting clauses commonly seen in news-reports may also be considered as comment clauses. The following excerpt contains an indirect reporting discourse:

(51) A U.S. F-16 fighter on a NATO mission over northern Bosnia-Herzegovina was shot down by a surface-to-air missile launched by Bosnian Serb forces. <u>NATO and the U.S. defense Department said</u> the plane *was downed* over Bosnian Serb-occupied territory near the northern town of Banja Luka while enforcing the no-fly zone over the nation. It was the second time that an aircraft on a NATO mission had been shot down in Bosnia. (CE 1995. 8: 90)

In the indirect reporting discourse in this report, the reported verb phrase *was downed* is not backshifted. Reporting clauses in this type of news-report function as evidential markers and as source markers, but do not set temporal reference points, since it is commonly assumed that news-reports are based on past events. Even if we totally omit reporting clauses, there is often no confusion to the information structure of the whole discourse, nor to the temporal relationship between the events, as we can see in the following excerpt which is presented without the original reporting clause from (51):

(52) A U.S. F-16 fighter on a NATO mission over northern Bosnia-Herzegovina was shot down by a surface-to-air missile launched by Bosnian Serb forces. The plane *was downed* over Bosnian Serb-occupied territory near the northern town of Banja Luka while enforcing the no-fly zone over the nation. It was the second time that an aircraft on a NATO mission had been shot down in Bosnia.

Here, the whole sentences have a discourse flow with the constant use of the absolute tense, having the reporter's deictic center as a reference point. What the reporting clause does in (51) then is to indicate that the report is not based on the reporter's subjective opinion and to provide source information that adds credibility to the detailed information concerning the place of the shooting. It does not function to set a temporal reference point. Therefore, it is not a surprise that news-reports often have tense-alternation in reporting clauses without confusing the temporal relations between events as in (22) and (53), or they may use the present tense in reporting clauses as in (54):

(53) <u>The government says</u> a law permitting soldiers to serve in foreign countries will take effect August 10th. <u>Officials said</u> the Japanese cabinet also

decided to permit some troops and civilians serving in foreign countries to carry guns. But they will be able to use them only in self-defense. Troops will not be permitted to fight. Japan plans to send troops to Cambodia to join other United Nations forces to help secure the peace between the country's opposing groups. A law permitting Japanese soldiers to operate as U.N. peacekeepers was passed by parliament in June after a major debate. (VOA News 1992. 8. 4)

(54) Japan says it will send another fact-finding team to Cambodia next week to prepare for Japan's first involvement in a United Nations peacekeeping force. The team will seek to learn how a Japanese peacekeeping group can help repair roads and bridges. Team members also want to learn more about the Cambodian peace agreement. (*Ibid.* 8. 6)

In these two cases, the reporting clauses function as source markers, marking where the information came from, and as evidential markers to support the credibility of the information. They do not carry any temporal information.

In summary, in natural spoken discourse, tense in reporting discourse is more flexible than previous studies have assumed. In this section, I mainly discussed the flexible behavior of reporting clauses. Some may have tense-alternation, which shows that tense forms of reporting verbs do not directly reflect their tenses. Some may even function as comment clauses. In such cases, reported events themselves are cohesively constructed in whole discourse, and reported verb tenses are determined according to how the present speakers view the reported events. This does not mean, however, that the reported verb tense has no relationship to the reporting verb tense. If the speakers consider that the temporal relationship between the time of reported speakers' speaking and the spoken events is significant, they may clarify the relationship by what appears to be backshifting, as has been argued in the past. However, when speakers focus more on their reported events and construct discourse cohesively around the reported events, the events are more likely to have their own coherence independently from reporting verbs. In spoken discourse, there are many cases in which it is more significant to keep the discourse coherence of the reported events themselves, and the reporting clauses simply function as speech introducing markers.

5. Conclusion

In natural spoken English, tense in indirect reporting discourse does not behave as has been supposed in traditional grammar. Comrie's formal SoT rule and the relative tense rule of Declerck's CoRA are based on the assumption that tense in the complement clause is determined by its relation to the head clause. But the absolute tense rule in Declerck's CoRA is common in spoken discourse. Tense is determined often by the reporter's here-and-now, relating directly to the moment of speaking. The prevalence of the absolute tense in spoken discourse is due in part to the fact that the temporal order of the events is often clear from the context. In natural language use, for the most part, speakers and hearers share some common knowledge of the world or speakers contextualize their stories beforehand. In addition to Declerck's account of the absolute tense, linguistic restrictions and discourse coherence are keys to the use of the absolute tense in spoken English.

Backshifting of tenses once seemed to fulfill the logical requirement with aesthetic synthesis within grammatical sentences. But in natural discourse, speakers prefer to maintain discourse coherence that fits in the communicative framework at the expense of syntactic integrity. The sequence of tenses is, as numbers of typological studies have also demonstrated, by no means logically necessary for human communication systems or for human cognitive operations.

In spoken discourse, the relationship between the reporting clause and the reported clause is more flexible than has previously been considered. The previous theories viewed the relationship as a subordination of a head (or main) clause and a subordinate (or complement) clause. However, in spoken discourse, a reporting clause often appears as extra information which the reporter can choose to include or not. In spoken discourse, the main information is the content in the reported clause and the reporting clause often behaves as if it were a comment clause. For discourse coherence, it is more natural to base tense determination consistently on the reporter's viewpoint rather than on extra information. Some reporting clauses behave flexibly as dialogue markers that function not as temporal reference points, but rather as hedges, evidential markers, source markers, and personal deictic markers. This study demonstrates the prevalence of the speaker's viewpoint by the fact that indirect reporting discourse exhibits tense-alternation. Reporting clauses that have tense-alternation cannot serve as temporal reference points, thus speakers are reporting from their own perspectives.

The choice between the relative and the absolute tenses seems more of a matter of different uses of reporting discourse for different genres, such as spoken and written discourse, formal and informal language. In written discourse, temporal order and pragmatic knowledge of the reported events may not be shared as much as in spoken discourse. Therefore, writers more carefully monitor the choice, sequence and relationship of tenses. In spoken discourse, backshifting tenses may obstruct the flow of conversation. Speakers will ignore details of tense to maintain discourse flow and coherence. For successful conversations, the important thing is to maintain the discourse flow and coherence. We further need to elucidate how tense in indirect reporting discourse behaves in actual language performance.

Notes

* I would like to express my deep appreciation to Carl Becker, Wallace Chafe, Shinobu Kitayama, Mitsuru Ohki, and Masa-aki Yamanashi for their invaluable comments on the earlier versions of this article. I wish to thank Kevin Lesher and William Crawford for help in collecting elicited-narrative data. I especially wish to express my gratitude to David W. Drummond for giving me encouragement and editorial support. Naturally, all shortcomings are solely my own.

1. Comrie's analytical framework is based on traditional theories of reporting discourse: a dichotomic approach (e.g., Celce-Murcia and Larsen-Freeman 1983; *Comrie* 1986); derivational relationships (e.g., Jespersen 1964; Jackson 1990); verbatim assumption (e.g., *Coulmas* 1985; *Li* 1986). In such framework, analysts examine pairs of constructions of direct and indirect reporting styles. *Comrie* (1986:267–8) defines the set of pairs of constructions in the following way:

> An indirect speech construction will be said to correspond to a direct speech construction if the former carries the same message as the latter and if there is no other direct speech construction carrying the same message to which the given indirect speech construction is closer.

In contrast, I assume that direct discourse and indirect discourse constructions are independent (e.g., *Banfield* 1982; *Clark and Gerrig* 1990; *Mayes* 1990).

2. The 'relative time hypothesis' supposes that the tense form in the complement clause depends on the tense of the head clause, and on the temporal relation that is expressed between the complement clause and the head clause. Some (e.g., Allen 1966; Huddleston 1984) supported this hypothesis. *Comrie* (1986) denied the possibility of this hypothesis operating in English, but admitted that it works in some other languages, for instance Russian.

The 'absolute deixis hypothesis' treats tense as relating directly to the moment of speaking, i.e., the reporter's deictic center is the reference point, not that of the original speaker. This hypothesis was propounded by Brecht (1974), Riddle (1978), and Heny (1982). *Comrie* (1986) claimed that the absolute deixis hypothesis cannot account for the use of tenses in English indirect discourse. It predicts that the indirect discourse version of (ia) is (ib), not (ic), because Jim's baking cookies is in the future. But it is not a correct prediction.

  (i) a. Jim will say, "I am baking cookies."
      b. *Jim will say that he will be baking cookies.
      c. Jim will say that he is baking cookies.

3. A (temporal) domain is a time interval taken up either by one situation or by a number of situations that are temporally related to each other by means of special tense forms (Declerck 1990:515).

4. Declerck bases his idea of the choice of the absolute tense on Grice's (1975) maxims of conversation.

5. There still are some cases in which Declerck's hypothesis does not work. *Huddleston*

(1989) raised the following examples:
 (i) a. It is time you said to her, "I am married.".
     b. It is time you told her you were married. (*Huddleston* 1989:335)
 (ii) a. I wish I knew the answer to the question, "Where is she?"'
      b. I wish I knew where she was. (*Ibid.*: 336)

The past tense in the head clauses in these sentences has modals rather than past-time meaning. The past-tense forms *were* in (ib) and *was* in (iib) do not express simultaneity in a past time sphere with their head clauses, because the time of saying and knowing in the head clauses is non-past. In such cases, the past tenses must be accounted for by reference to the syntactic fact that they occur in the complements of the past-tense reporting verbs, not in terms of the relative time of the situations.

6. The following notational conventions are used in the transcripts of the conversational examples:

(0.0) Length of silence
: Lengthened syllable
- Sound cut off in a delivery
= Two utterances are latched without a usual beat of silence
] Offset of simultaneous talk
hh Audible breath or laughter (hh shows exhalation; .hh shows inhalation)
? Rising intonation

Italics are used to draw attention to the tense of reported verbs. Their original verb forms are italicized as well, in examples of their original discourse versions.

7. Conversational data referenced as (JR), (F), (TG), and (AD) originate from the 1984–6 class packets collected by John Reeves, Cecilia Ford, Emmanuel Schegloff, and Charles Goodwin respectively. They are analyzed with transcriptions and audiotapes.

8. CE: *The Study of Current English*. Tokyo: Kenkyusha.

9. The instantaneous use of the simple present tense occurs with verbs expressing events, in contrast to the unrestrictive use that occurs with verbs expressing states. The instantaneous use of event verbs normally occurs only in certain easily definable contexts as in sports commentaries and in the patter or commentary of conjurors and demonstrators. It may also occur as a dramatic use in the following example (i) that insists on the total enactment of the event as it is reported, in contrast to (ii) that contains a progressive verb form and is a neutral description in answer to the question "What are you doing?":

 (i) I *open* the cage.
 (ii) I *am opening* the cage. (Leech 1987:7)

It also occurs in asseverations with performative verbs:

 (iii) I *beg* your pardon.
 (iv) We *accept* your offer.
 (v) I *deny* your charge. (*Ibid.*)

10. EJ: *English Journal*. Tokyo: ALC Press.

11. Tense-alternation is more commonly seen in direct reporting discourse.

12. Free indirect discourse is common in literature. The second sentence in the following is a free indirect discourse:

(i) He begged her to believe him when he said he could not earn. *Had* he not already *sunk* a small fortune in attempts to do so? He begged her to believe that he was a chronic emeritus. But it was not altogether a question of economy.

(Samuel Beckett, *Murphy*: 18)

It is a problem for the formal SoT what determines tense of *had sunk* since this sentence lacks a reporting clause which, it claims, determines tense in reported clause. It attempts to solve this problem by considering free indirect discourse to be derived from indirect reporting discourse by deleting the head clause. CoRA claims that in this case the speaker simply relates the situations to a particular past time rather than to his own here-and-now (Declerck 1991:176).

13. 'Absolute tense' generally refers to the present perfect, the present tense, the future tense, and the past tense. They are directly defined in relation to the moment of speech (Declerck 1990:514). Since the past perfect is located relative to a certain point in the past, it is generally treated as a relative tense. Here I claim that speakers use the past perfect tense in an analogous way to the absolute tense. They use the past perfect from their own standpoints, not relative to the tenses in the head clauses. Speakers do not shift their deictic centers to the reportees' deictic centers as their temporal reference points.

14. Quirk *et al.* (1985:1026) point out that the reporting verb may be in the present tense for communications in recent past time (i), for reports attributed to famous works or authors which have present validity (ii), or for verbs of cognition (iii):

(i) Joan tells me she's going to the airport in an hour's time.
(ii) Chaucer somewhere writes that love is blind.
(iii) Sylvia thinks Paul went to Lancaster last night.

But the present tense in (39) does not belong to any of such cases.

15. The term 'dialogue-introducer' is currently used interchangeably with 'reporting phrase' of direct reporting discourse.

16. Since such reporting clauses behave similarly to dialogue-introducers of direct reporting discourse, they may have the analogous discourse functions. Sakita (1998) discusses various discourse functions of dialogue-introducer tense-alternation, for example, as 'attitudinal contrasting devices' or as 'consciousness flow markers.' See also Sakita (1997, 1999).

17. The six types of comment clauses that Quirk *et al.* (1985:1112) distinguish are the following:

(i) like the matrix clause of a main clause:
There were no other applicants, *I believe*, for that job.
(ii) like an adverbial finite clause (introduced by *as*):
I'm working the night shift, *as you know*.
(iii) like a nominal relative clause:
What was more upsetting, we lost all our luggage.
(iv) *to*-infinitive clause as style disjunct:
I'm not sure what to do, *to be honest*.

(v) -*ing* clause as style disjunct:
I doubt, *speaking as a layman*, whether television is the right medium for that story.
(vi) -*ed* clause as style disjunct:
Stated bluntly, he had no chance of winning.

18. 'Hedge' is any linguistic device by which a speaker avoids being compromised by a statement that turns out to be wrong, a request that is not acceptable, and so on. Thus, instead of saying, "This argument is convincing," one might use a hedge and say, "As far as I can see this argument is convincing" (Matthews 1997:160).

19. They raise the following examples:

(i) a. John imagined that his wife was/?*is pregnant.
b. What John imagined was that his wife was/?is pregnant.
c. That John's wife was/is pregnant was said by Bill, not by John.

(*Declerck and Tanaka* 1996:293)

According to their claim, in (ia), the present tense is virtually impossible because of the strong intentional verb *imagine* and the highly private contents of the *that*-clause. However, in (ib), the present tense looks slightly better, because the *that*-clause is no longer syntactically dependent on *imagined*. Its syntactic form is '*wh*-clause + *be* + *that*-clause,' and "the *that*-clause is on a par with the *wh*-clause, and this looser syntactic relation renders it better possible to locate the *that*-clause situation in a world that is different from the strong intentional world created by *imagined*" (*Declerck and Tanaka* 1996:293). In (ic), "since the *that*-clause is used as subject rather than as a constituent of the VP," "a subject does not syntactically depend on the verb the way an object does. (A subject is an 'external argument' of the predicate; it does not belong to the VP.)" The present tense is perfectly all right in this case. The case as (ib) with the present tense in the reported clause certainly often appears:

(ii) Well, I can see that's what people think, but <u>what we were saying was</u>, Japan *has* always *been* very slow. (AE 1992. 9: 95)

References

Allen, Robert L. 1966. *The verb system of present-day American English*. The Hague: Mouton.
Brecht, Richard D. 1974. "Deixis in embedded structures." *Foundations of Language* 11: 489–518.
Celce-Murcia, Marianne and Diane Larsen-Freeman. 1983. *The grammar book*. Cambridge, MA: Newbury House.
Declerck, Renaat. 1990. "Sequence of tenses in English." *Folia Linguistica: Acta Societatis Linguisticae Europaeae* 24: 513–44.
Declerck, Renaat. 1991. *Tense in English: its structure and use in discourse*. London: Routledge.
Dixon, Robert M.W. 1991. *A new approach to English grammar, on semantic principles*. Oxford: Oxford University Press.

Grice, H. Paul. 1975. "Logic and conversation." In Cole, Peter and Jerry L. Morgan (eds.), *Speech acts* (Syntax and Semantics 3). New York: Academic Press, 41–58.
Heny, Frank. 1982. "Tense, aspect and time adverbials: Part 2." *Linguistics and Philosophy* 5: 109–54.
Hornstein, Norbert. 1990. *As time goes by: tense and universal grammar.* Cambridge: MIT Press.
Huddleston, Rodney. 1984. *Introduction to the grammar of English.* Cambridge: Cambridge University Press.
Jackson, Howard. 1990. *Grammar and meaning: a semantic approach to English grammar.* New York: Longman.
Jespersen, Otto. 1924. *The philosophy of grammar.* London: Allen & Unwin.
Jespersen, Otto. 1964. *Essentials of English grammar.* Alabama: University of Alabama Press.
Leech, Geoffrey N. 1987. *Meaning and the English verb.* 2nd ed. London: Longman.
Leech, Geoffrey N. and Jan Svartvik. 1975. *A communicative grammar of English.* London: Longman.
Matthews, Peter H. 1997. *The concise Oxford dictionary of linguistics.* Oxford: Oxford University Press.
Quirk, Randolph, et al. 1985. *A comprehensive grammar of the English language.* London: Longman.
Riddle, Elizabeth M. 1978. *Sequence of tenses in English.* Ph.D. dissertation, University of Illinois at Urbana-Champaign.
Sakita, Tomoko I. 1997. "Tense alternation in English conversational narratives." *Annual Review of English Learning and Teaching* 2: 1–14.
Sakita, Tomoko I. 1999. "Manifestations of speaker attitudes in conflict stories." *Studies in Pragmatics* 1: 74–88.
Schiffrin, Deborah. 1981. "Tense variation in narrative." *Language* 57, 1: 45–62.
Thomson, Audrey J. and Agnes V. Martinet. 1980. *A practical English grammar.* London: Oxford University Press.
Voloshinov, Valentin N. 1986. *Marxism and the philosophy of language.* Trans. L. Matejka and I.R. Titunik. Cambridge: Harvard University Press. (=Vološinov, Valentin N. 1929. *Marksizm i filosofija jazyka: osnovnye problemy sociologičeskogo metoda v nauke o jazyke.* Leningrad.)
Wolfson, Nessa. 1982. *CHP: The conversational historical present in American English narrative* (Topics in Sociolinguistics 1). Dordrecht: Foris.
Yamanashi, Masa-aki. 1986. *Hatsuwa Koui [Speech acts].* Tokyo: Taishukan.
Yamanashi, Masa-aki. 1991. "Hatsuwa no chikara no kanten kara mita in'you no mekanizumu [The mechanism of quotation: from the standpoint of illocutionary forces]." In Ukaji, M. and S. Chiba (eds), *Gendai Eigogaku no Shosou [Aspects of present-day English linguistics].* Tokyo: Kaitakusha, 501–13.
Yule, George and Terry Mathis. 1992. "The role of staging and constructed dialogue in establishing speaker's topic." *Linguistics* 30: 199–215.

PART 3

Logophoricity

CHAPTER 9

The logophoric hierarchy and variation in Dogon*

Christopher Culy
The University of Iowa

1. Introduction

An implicational hierarchy of predicates licensing logophoric pronouns has been shown to exist both typologically (*Culy* 1994b) and within a single system in Dogon (Culy et al. 1994). This chapter will show how the logophoric hierarchy is manifested across the speech of several speakers of Donno Sɔ, a Dogon language.

Logophoric pronouns are pronouns used in indirect discourse to refer to the person whose discourse is being reported (*Hagège* 1974, *Clements* 1975, *Roncador* 1992, *Culy* 1997). In general, the use of a logophoric pronoun is obligatory in indirect discourse when reference to the person whose discourse is being reported is intended. Otherwise, a personal pronoun is used. Examples from Donno Sɔ (DS), a Dogon language, of a logophoric pronoun contrasting with a personal pronoun are given in (1).

(1) Logophoric pronoun in DS (*Culy* 1994b: 1080)
    a. Logophoric pronoun in a logophoric domain
        Oumar$_i$ Anta *inyemɛñ*$_i$ waa be gi
        Oumar Anta LOG-ACC seen AUX said
        'Oumar$_i$ said that Anta had seen him$_i$.'
    b. Personal pronoun in a logophoric domain
        Oumar$_i$ Anta$_j$ *woñ*$_k$ waa be gi
        Oumar Anta 3S-ACC seen AUX said
        'Oumar$_i$ said that Anta$_j$ had seen him$_k$.'

Culy (1994b) showed that there is a cross-linguistic implicational hierarchy of predicates which license logophoric pronouns. This hierarchy is given in (2). Speech predicates are the canonical logophoric licensors (as illustrated in (1)), followed by thought predicates, knowledge predicates and finally direct perception predicates which never license logophoric pronouns.

(2) Logophoric licensor hierarchy (*Culy* 1994b:1062)
Speech > Thought > Knowledge > Direct perception

In a comparative study of three Dogon languages, Culy *et al.* (1994) found evidence from one language, Togo Kā (TK), for a level on the hierarchy intermediate between thought and knowledge predicates, filled by non-factive perception predicates (e.g. 'hear that'). The extended logophoric hierarchy is given in (3).

(3) Extended logophoric hierarchy[1]
Speech > Thought > Non-factive Perception > Knowledge > Direct perception

The evidence from TK for the logophoric hierarchy comes primarily from the variable distribution of logophoric pronouns and personal pronouns.[2] Each type treats different segments of the logophoric hierarchy as creating a logophoric domain.

Let's compare speech predicates with non-factive perception predicates. Since speech predicates are the highest part of the logophoric hierarchy, they should always create a logophoric domain. In other words, logophoric pronouns should be possible in their complements with the person whose discourse is being reported (the logophoric trigger) as the antecedent, while personal pronouns should not. This is true in TK, as illustrated in (4).

(4) Speech predicates create logophoric domain in TK.
    a. Logophoric pronoun with logophoric trigger antecedent (Culy *et al.* 1994:339)
        Madu$_i$ [Omar$_j$ wa [Ali$_k$ ɛnɛ$_{i/*j/*k}$ laran ɔɛ] ĩ wɔ] gi
        Madu Omar SBJ Ali LOG sister saw know AUX said
        'Madu$_i$ said that Omar$_j$ knows that Ali$_k$ saw his$_{i/*j/*k}$ sister'
    b. Personal pronoun disjoint from logophoric trigger[3]
        Madu$_i$ [Omar$_j$ wa [Ali$_k$ wo.$_{*i/j/*k/l}$ laran ɔɛ] ĩ wɔ] gi
        Madu Omar SBJ Ali 3s sister saw know AUX said
        'Madu$_i$ said that Omar$_j$ knows that Ali$_k$ saw his*$_{i/j/*k/l}$ sister'

However, when we look at non-factive perception predicates, we find that while logophoric pronouns can still occur in the complement with the logophoric trigger as the antecedent, personal pronouns do *not* have to be disjoint from the logophoric trigger, and can also have it as the antecedent. These facts are illustrated in (5):

(5) Thought predicates create differing logophoric domains in TK
    a. Logophoric pronoun with logophoric trigger antecedent (Culy *et al.* 1994:339)
        Anta$_i$ [Mariam$_j$ wa [Hawa$_k$ ɛnɛ$_{i/*j/*k/l}$ ĩ wo lagaju] ɔɛ] ɛgɛ
        Anta Mariam SBJ Hawa LOG child 3s hit saw heard
        'Anta$_i$ heard that Mariam$_j$ saw Hawa$_k$ hit her$_{i/*j/*k/l}$ child'

b. Personal pronoun may also have logophoric trigger antecedent
Anta$_i$ [Mariam$_j$ wa [Hawa$_k$ wo$_{i/j/*k/l}$ í   wo lagaju] ɔɛ] ɛgɛ
Anta Mariam sbj Hawa   3s   child 3s hit   saw heard
'Anta$_i$ heard that Mariam$_j$ saw Hawa$_k$ hit her$_{i/j/*k/l}$ child'

Another twist on the variability of logophoric domains in TK is that different grammatical positions in the complements of the reported discourse predicates have different domains. For example, logophoric pronouns can be used as the complement subject with speech, thought, and non-factive perception predicate predicates, but as the complement object they can only occur with speech and thought predicates, not non-factive perception predicates. These facts are suggested by the examples in (6):

(6) Logophoric domain varying by position in TK (Culy *et al.* 1994:331)
   a. Subject in complement of non-factive perception is logophoric
      Anta$_i$ [ɛnɛ$_i$ farāsi yaju] ɛgɛ
      Anta log France go   heard
      'Anta$_i$ heard that she$_i$ will go to France.'
   b. Non-subject in complement of non-factive perception is not logophoric
      Omar$_i$ Anda ɛnɛ$_i$ ɔɛ ɛgɛ
      Omar Anda log saw heard
      ('Omar$_i$ heard that Anda saw him$_i$.')

We can denote speech predicates by L1, thought predicates by L2, non-factive perception predicates by L3, and knowledge predicates by L4.[4] Now we can summarize the behavior of the TK logophoric and personal pronouns as in (7):

(7) The logophoric hierarchy in TK (cf. Culy *et al.* 1994:338–9)[5]

	Logophoric pronoun			Personal pronoun		
	S	Poss of S	Non S	S	Poss of S	Non S
L1	√	√	√	√	√	√
L2	√(-)		√			√
L3	√(-)		(√)			
L4						

In this chapter, we will see that the logophoric hierarchy is reflected in another one of the Dogon languages from Culy *et al.* (1994), namely DS. As with TK, we will see variation across position. However, we will also see variation across speakers for a given position. In all cases, the variation seems to be constrained by the logophoric hierarchy, thus providing it further support.

2. Logophoric domains in varieties of DS

2.1 DS as primary language

The DS speech reported in *Culy* (1994a) and Culy *et al.* (1994) is that of people whose first language is DS, and who are from the area southwest of Bandiagara, the principal town in the DS speaking area. For the sake of ease of reference, we will refer to this speech as DS-1. In this speech there is no variation across position, and only L1 and L2 create logophoric domains:[6] logophoric pronouns can occur with the logophoric trigger as their antecedent, while personal pronouns cannot have the logophoric trigger as their antecedent. Some representative examples are given in (8). The logophoric domains can be summed up as in (9).

(8) Logophoric domains in DS-1
   a. L1 subject
      Anta$_i$ {inyemɛ$_i$/ wo$_j$} faransi {bojɛm/ bojɛ} gi
      Anta LOG   3s   France go-1s   go-3s said
      'Anta$_i$ said that {she$_i$/she$_j$} is going to France'
   b. L2 object
      Anta$_i$ Oumar {inyemeñ)$_i$/ woñ)$_j$} wɛ ma mari
      Anta Oumar LOG-ACC   3s-ACC saw Q thinks
      'Anta$_i$ thinks that Oumar saw {her$_i$/her$_j$}'
   c. L3 possessor of subject
      Anta$_i$ anige {*inyem'$_i$/ wo$_{i/j}$} mɔ̃) boli ɛgɛ
      Anta friend LOG   3s   POSS left heard
      'Anta$_i$ heard that {her$_i$/ her$_{i/j}$} friend left'
   d. L4 possessor of object
      Anda$_i$ Oumar$_j$ anige {*inyem'$_i$/ wo$_{i/j/k}$} mɔ̃) wɛ igi wɔ
      Anda Oumar friend LOG   3s   POSS saw know AUX
      'Anda$_i$ knows that Oumar$_j$ saw {his$_i$/(her$_i$) his$_{j/k}$} friend'

(9) Summary of logophoric domains in DS-1
    All positions: L1, L2 only

2.2 DS as second language

In this section we will discuss the speech of two people from villages northeast of Bandiagara. Their first language is a different Dogon language, Mombo Sɔ, but they also speak DS.[7] We will refer to this speech as DS-2.

The first thing that distinguishes DS-2 from DS-1 is that it not only uses L1 and L2 for logophoric domains, as DS-1 does, but it also uses L3 and L4 when the position is the possessor of an object. Thus, it uses more of the logophoric hierarchy than both DS-1 and TK. Some examples are in (10):

(10) DS-2 logophoric domains for possessor of object
  a. L1
     Anta$_i$ Oumar$_j$ anige {inyem'$_i$/ wo$_{j/k}$} mɔ̃ wɛ gi
     Anta Oumar friend LOG   3s POSS saw said
     'Anta$_i$ said that Oumar$_j$ saw {her$_i$/his$_{j/k}$} friend'
  b. L2
     Anta$_i$ Oumar$_j$ anige {inyem'$_i$/ wo$_{j/k}$} mɔ̃ wɛ ma mari
     Anta Oumar friend LOG   3s POSS saw Q think
     'Anta$_i$ thinks that Oumar$_j$ saw {her$_i$/his$_{j/k}$} friend'
  c. L3
     Anta$_i$ Oumar$_j$ anige {inyem'$_i$/ wo$_{j/k}$} mɔ̃ wɛ ɛgɛ
     Anta Oumar friend LOG   3s POSS saw heard
     'Anta$_i$ heard that Oumar$_j$ saw {her$_i$/his$_{j/k}$} friend'
  d. L4
     Anta$_i$ Oumar$_j$ anige {inyem'$_i$/ wo$_{j/k}$} mɔ̃ wɛ igi wɔ
     Anta Oumar friend LOG   3s POSS saw know AUX
     'Anta$_i$ knows that Oumar$_j$ saw {her$_i$/his$_{j/k}$} friend'

Unlike DS-1, DS-2 has variation across positions. So if we consider possessors of subjects, we find that L1–L3 are clearly logophoric domains, but in L4, both the logophoric pronoun and the personal pronoun can refer back to the logophoric trigger. Examples are in (11). This behavior is unexpected, since personal pronouns and logophoric pronouns are usually in complementary distribution in indirect discourse environments with the logophoric trigger as the antecedent (*Culy* 1994b, *Culy* 1997). It perhaps indicates a weakening of the logophoric domain, as suggested for TK in Culy *et al.* (1994).[8]

(11) DS-2 logophoric domains for possessor of subject
  a. L1
     Anta$_i$ anige {inyem'$_i$/ wo$_j$} mɔ̃ boli gi
     Anta friend LOG   3s POSS left said
     'Anta$_i$ said that {her$_i$/ her$_j$} friend left'
  b. L2
     Anta$_i$ anige {inyem'$_i$/ wo$_j$} mɔ̃ boli ma mari
     Anta friend LOG   3s POSS left Q thinks
     'Anta$_i$ thinks that {her$_i$/her$_j$} friend left'
  c. L3
     Anta$_i$ anige {inyem'$_i$/ wo$_j$} mɔ̃ boli ɛgɛ
     Anta friend LOG   3s POSS left heard
     'Anta$_i$ heard that {her$_i$/her$_j$} friend left'

d. L4
Anta$_i$ anige {inyem'$_i$/ wo$_{i/j}$} mɔ̃) boli igi   wɔ
Anta friend LOG   3s POSS left knows AUX
'Anta$_i$ knows that {her$_i$/ her$_{i/j}$} friend left'

The object position also has a weakened logophoric domain, but this time it is L3. L4 is clearly not a logophoric domain for objects, while L1-L2 clearly are. Logophoric pronouns are not allowed as objects in L4, while in L1 and L2, logophoric pronouns and personal pronouns are in complementary distribution as objects, as expected. In L3, the weakened logophoric domain, both the logophoric pronoun and the personal pronoun can refer back to the logophoric trigger. Examples are in (12):

(12) DS-2 logophoric domains for object
   a. L1
      Anta$_i$ Oumar {inyemɛñ$_i$/ woñ$_j$} wɛ gi
      Anta Oumar LOG-ACC   3s-ACC saw said
      'Anta$_i$ said that Oumar saw {her$_i$/ her$_j$}'
   b. L2
      Anta$_i$ Oumar {inyemɛñ$_i$/ woñ$_j$} wɛ ma mari
      Anta Oumar LOG-ACC   3s-ACC saw Q thinks
      'Anta$_i$ thinks that Oumar saw {her$_i$/ her$_j$}'
   c. L3
      Anta$_i$ Oumar {inyemɛñ$_i$/ woñ$_{i/j}$} wɛ ɛgɛ
      Anta Oumar LOG-ACC   3s-ACC saw heard
      'Anta$_i$ heard that Oumar saw {her$_i$/ her$_{i/j}$}'
   d. L4
      Anta$_i$ Oumar {*inyemɛñ$_i$/ woñ$_{i/j}$} wɛ igi   wɔ
      Anta Oumar LOG-ACC   3s-ACC saw know AUX
      'Anta$_i$ knows that Oumar saw {*her$_i$/ her$_{i/j}$}'

Finally, the position of subject has the most restricted possibilities for logophoric domains, using only L1-L2, which have the familiar pattern of logophoric pronouns and personal pronouns in complementary distribution. L3 and L4 do not allow logophoric pronouns at all. Examples are given in (13):

(13) DS-2 logophoric domains for subject
   a. L1
      Anta$_i$ {inyemɛ$_i$/ wo$_j$} faransi {bojɛm/ bojɛ} gi
      Anta LOG   3s   France go-1s   go-3s said
      'Anta$_i$ said that {she$_i$/ she$_j$} is going to France'

b. L2
Anta$_i$ {inyemɛ$_i$/ wo$_j$} faransi {bojɛm/ bojɛ} ma mari
Anta LOG   3s   France go-1s   go-3s Q   thinks
'Anta$_i$ thinks that {she$_i$/ she$_j$} is going to France'

c. L3
Anta$_i$ {*inyemɛ$_i$/ wo$_{i/j}$} faransi bojɛ ɛgɛ
Anta LOG   3s   France go-3s heard
'Anta$_i$ heard that {*she$_i$/ she$_{i/j}$} is going to France'

d. L4
Anta$_i$ {*inyemɛ$_i$/ wo$_{i/j}$} faransi bojɛ igi wɔ
Anta LOG   3s   France go-3s know AUX
'Anta$_i$ knows that {*she$_i$/ she$_{i/j}$} is going to France'

We can summarize the variation in logophoric domains in DS-2 as in (14):

(14) Summary of logophoric domains in DS-2

	Poss of O	Poss of S	O	S
L1	+	+	+	+
L2	+	+	+	+
L3	+	+	±	−
L4	+	±	−	−

There are several things to notice about DS–2. First, the logophoric hierarchy is very strongly attested. All of the positions use a contiguous section of the hierarchy, starting with L1, as is expected of a true hierarchy. Second, we can see that the positions themselves form a hierarchy, from possessor of object to subject.

Third, we can see that possessors use more domains than non-possessors, and that the object position (both simple and possessor) uses more domains than the subject position (both simple and possessor). In other words, the possessor of object position uses more domains than the possessor of subject position, and the object position uses more domains than the subject position. This striking contrast between the subjects and objects is one for which I have no explanation at this point.

Finally, if we take the information about logophoric and personal pronouns in TK and represent it in the same way (15) as we did for DS-2, we find that the "logophoric strength" of the different positions is essentially the same as that of the positions in DS-2, though the possessor of Subject is a weaker logophoric position in TK than it is in DS-2 .

(15) Recapitulation of TK logophoric domains

	O/Poss of O	S	Poss of S
L1	+	+	+
L2	+	±	−
L3	±	±	−
L4	−	−	−

2.3 Passive DS

The third speech that we will examine is that of a person who has only a passive knowledge of DS. His parents are fluent speakers of DS (one from southwest of Bandiagara, one from Bandiagara itself), but he grew up outside of the DS speaking zone, speaking only Bambara and French, neither of which have logophoric pronouns. We will call his speech DS-p.

The data is given in (16), though unfortunately it is limited to the object position. We can see that in DS-p object position, only L1 is a clear logophoric domain. L2 is a weakened logophoric domain, while L3-L4 are not logophoric domains at all. This is summarized in (17):

(16) DS-p logophoric domains for object
  a. L1
     Anta$_i$ Oumar {inyemɛñ$_i$/ woñ$_j$} wɛ gI
     Anta Oumar LOG-ACC 3S-ACC saw said
     'Anta$_i$ said that Oumar saw {her$_i$/ her$_j$}'
  b. L2
     Anta$_i$ Oumar {inyemɛñ$_i$/ woñ$_{i/j}$} wɛ ma mari
     Anta Oumar LOG-ACC 3S-ACC saw Q thinks
     'Anta$_i$ thinks that Oumar saw {her$_i$/ her$_{i/j}$}'
  c. L3
     Anta$_i$ Oumar {*inyemɛñ$_i$/ woñ$_{i/j}$} wɛ ɛgɛ
     Anta Oumar LOG-ACC 3S-ACC saw heard
     'Anta$_i$ heard that Oumar saw {*her$_i$/ her$_{i/j}$}'
  d. L4
     Anta$_i$ Oumar {*inyemɛñ$_i$/ woñ$_{i/j}$} wɛ igi wɔ
     Anta Oumar LOG-ACC 3S-ACC saw know AUX
     'Anta$_i$ knows that Oumar saw {*her$_i$/ her$_{i/j}$}'

(17) Summary of DS-p logophoric domains

	O
L1	+
L2	±
L3	−
L4	−

While DS-p alone still supports the logophoric hierarchy, we can find even stronger evidence for the logophoric hierarchy by comparing the object position across the three varieties of DS that we have seen, as in (18). This chart clearly shows the effect of the logophoric hierarchy across the varieties of DS: DS-2 uses L1-L3, while DS-1 and DS-p use L1-L2, with DS-p having a weakened L2.

(18) Comparison of object position logophoric domains

	DS-2 (=TK)	DS-1	DS-p
L1	+	+	+
L2	+	+	±
L3	±	−	−
L4	−	−	−

3. Conclusion

Aside from the clear supporting evidence for the logophoric hierarchy, several questions remain. One question is why there should be such a strong subject/non-subject asymmetry, not only in DS-2 but in TK. This asymmetry is particularly striking since the object position favors logophoricity more than the subject position does, which goes against the general tendency for the subject position to be more logophoric than the object position (Wiesemann 1986).

Another question is what possible influences there are on the speakers.[9] For example, the first language of the DS-2 speakers, Mombo Sɔ, does not have a non-possessor logophoric pronoun at all. Is this what is influencing their DS patterns? These speakers also spend 9 months or so of the year outside of the DS speaking zone. Does that influence their DS patterns?

Finally, all of the speakers whose speech is reported here are men in their 30s. Is there also variation according to age and/ or gender?

The data in this chapter provides evidence for the strong effect of the logophoric hierarchy in DS, both within varieties (DS-2, DS-p) and across varieties (in the object position). There is no *a priori* reason why the facts in DS should turn out the way they do. The logophoric hierarchy is not a logical necessity, but a contingent fact about human language. However, many questions still remain about the extent of the variation to be found.

Notes

* I would like to thank Bazili Banou, Ibrahima Djiguiba, Daouda Kassogué, Douro Etienne Kassogué, Abdou Maïga, Linda L. McIntyre, Issiaka Tembiné, Patrice Togo, and Ibrahima Boncana Touré for help with this chapter. I remain responsible for any errors, of course. Acknowledgement is gratefully made for funding from The University of Iowa's Arts and Humanities Initiative.

1. Cf. Culy et al. (1994:337), Culy (1994b:1067).
2. Reflexive pronouns have split properties. In non-Subject positions, they show no logophoric properties at all, while in Subject positions, they behave as personal pronouns would in the same domains that the logophoric pronoun can occur in. See below for more on Subject vs. non-Subject.
3. Examples are from my own fieldwork unless otherwise indicated.
4. Even though TK doesn't allow logophoric pronouns with knowledge predicates, other languages do, so it will be useful to extend the terminology.
5. The √(-) indicates that L2 and L3 are logophoric domains for subjects only at one level of embedding. Similarly, the (√) indicates that L3 is a logophoric domain for non-subjects only at more than one level of embedding. See Culy et al. (1994) for more discussion of the differences according to level of embedding. It will not play a role in the discussion here.
6. L3 is marginally possible when the antecedent is the source: "hear from" (*Culy* 1994a: 119).
7. Multilingualism is the norm among Dogon speakers. Most Dogon speak more than one Dogon language, as well as Bambara, Fula, and/ or French (Plungian and Tembiné 1994).
8. No assumption about direction of language change is intended here, merely a comparison between L4 and the other domains.
9. Thanks to Issiaka Tembiné for stressing this point.

References

Culy, Christopher, Koungarma Kodio and Patrice Togo. 1994. "Dogon pronominal systems: their nature and evolution". *Studies in African Linguistics* 23,3: 315–44.

Plungian, Vladimir A. and Issiaka Tembiné. 1994. "Vers une description sociolinguistique du pays Dogon: attitudes linguistiques et problèmes de standardisation". In Dumestre, Gérard (ed.), *Stratégies communicatives au Mali: langues régionales, bambara, français*. Paris: Didier, 163–95

Wiesemann, Ursula. 1986. "Grammaticalized coreference". In Wiesemann, Ursula (ed.), *Pronominal systems*. Tübingen: Narr, 437–64.

CHAPTER 10

Logophoric marking in East Asian languages*

Yan Huang
University of Reading

1. Introduction

This chapter has two goals: (i) to provide a straightforward description of logophoric marking in Chinese, Japanese and Korean, and (ii) to present a neo-Gricean pragmatic analysis of logophoricity and related phenomena in these East Asian languages. In what follows, I shall first give background information about logophoricity in Section 2. Next, in Section 3, I shall discuss logophoric marking in Chinese, Japanese and Korean. Finally, I shall provide a neo-Gricean pragmatic account, one couched in a general neo-Gricean pragmatic theory of anaphora (Huang 1991, 1992, 1994, 1995a, b, 2000a, b, Levinson 1991), in Section 4.

2. Background

Logophoricity refers to the phenomenon whereby the 'perspective' of an internal protagonist of a sentence or discourse, as opposed to that of the current, external speaker, is being reported by some morphological and/or syntactic means (e.g. Huang 1994, 1995b, 2000a). The term 'perspective' is used here in a technical sense and is intended to encompass words, thoughts, knowledge, emotion, perception and space-location. The concept of logophoricity was introduced in the analysis of African languages like Aghem, Efik and Tuburi, where there is a separate paradigm of logophoric pronouns, which is employed for such a purpose.

Cross-linguistically, logophoricity may be morphologically and/or syntactically expressed by one or more of the following mechanisms: (i) logophoric pronouns, as in (1); (ii) logophoric addressee pronouns, as in (2); (iii) logophoric verbal affixes, as in (3); and (iv) long-distance reflexives, as in (4).

(1) *Logophoric pronouns* (Yoruba, Armstrong 1963)
ó ní wón pè òun.
3s:SBJ say 3P:SBJ call LOG
'He₁ said that they called him₁.'

(2) *Logophoric addressee pronouns* (Mapun, *Frajzyngier* 1985)
n-sat n-wur taji gwar dim n Kaano.
I-say BEN-3s PROH ADDR go PREP Kano
'I told him₁ that he₁ may not go to Kano.'

(3) *Logophoric verbal affixes* (Gokana, *Hyman and Comrie* 1981)
à nyímá kɔ aè dɔ-ɛ̀.
he knows that he fell-LOG
'He₁ knows that he₁ fell.'

(4) *Long-distance reflexives* (Icelandic, Sigurðsson 1990)
Jón segir að María elski sig.
John says:IND that Mary loves:SUBJ self
'John₁ says that Mary loves self₁.'

Generally speaking, these logophoric marking devices can be ranked according to the following hierarchy.

(5) Hierarchy of grammatical mechanisms for logophoric marking
 a. Logophoric pronouns/addressee pronouns/verbal affixes
  [+logophoric, +coreference]
 b. Long-distance reflexives [±logophoric, +coreference]

What (5) basically says is this: for logophoric marking, a logophoric pronoun/addressee pronoun/verbal affix will be used if there is one; otherwise, a long-distance reflexive will be used. A second point to be borne in mind is that logophoricity and coreference are two distinct, though closely related notions; logophoricity entails coreference, but not vice versa (see Huang 1995b, 2000a for further argumentation).

Next, a number of implicational universals relating to logophoric marking can be set up.

(6) Person hierarchy for logophoric pronouns
 3 > 2 > 1
 First-person logophoric pronouns imply second-person logophoric pronouns, and second-person logophoric pronouns imply third-person logophoric pronouns.[1]

Given (6), it is predicted that in all languages with logophoric pronouns, logophoric pronouns can be third person; in some, they can also be identified as second person; in a few, they can be distinguished on first person as well (cf. *Hyman and Comrie* 1981, Wiesemann 1986, see also *Roncador* 1992 for a two way marking system based on the argument that some languages such as Ewe exhibits syncretism for second and third person with regard to logophoric pronouns). For example, the logophoric pronoun *ni* in Sango can be third person only (Zribi-Hertz p.c.). By contrast, in Mundani, the logophoric pronoun *ye* is used for third- and second-, but not for first person (Parker 1986). Finally, in languages like Lele, logophoric marking can be done in all three persons (Wiesemann 1986).

Clearly, there is a functional/pragmatic explanation for (6); for referential disambiguity, the third-person distinction is the most, and the first-person distinction, the least useful, with the second-person distinction in between, for third person is closer to nonperson than either first- or second person. It follows therefore that the fact that first-person logophoric pronouns are very rare, if not nonexistent, in natural languages, is hardly surprising, given that logophoric pronouns are one of the (most common) devices the current, external speaker (which is encoded usually in terms of a first-person pronoun) utilises in reflecting the perspective of anyone else (usually an internal protagonist) but him- or herself.

(7) Number hierarchy for logophoric pronouns
 Singulars > plurals
 Plural logophoric pronouns imply singular logophoric pronouns.

The implicational universal in (7) summarizes the general pattern of number specification for logophoric pronouns. While all languages with logophoric pronouns allow singular logophoric pronouns, only some permit plural logophoric pronouns as well (cf. *Hyman and Comrie* 1981, Wiesemann 1986). Mundang, for instance, is a language which has only singular logophoric pronouns (*Hagège* 1974). But Ewe has both singular and plural forms (*Clements* 1975).

At this point, mention should be made of logocentric triggers, namely those NPs that can act as an antecedent for a logophoric pronoun. First, logocentric triggers are generally constrained to be a core-argument of the logocentric predicate (to be elucidated later) of the matrix clause. Secondly, they are typically subjects.

But logocentric triggers can also be some other, nonsubject argument, provided that this argument represents the 'source' of the proposition or the 'experience' of the mental state that is being reported. Two types of construction are particularly common in African languages. The first involves the predicate 'hear from', as in the Ewe sentence (8):

(8) (Ewe, *Clements* 1975)
 Ama se tso Kofi gbɔ be yè-xɔ nunana.
 Ama hear from Kofi side COMP LOG-receive gift
 'Ama$_1$ heard from Kofi$_2$ that she$_1$/he$_2$ had received a gift.'

The second involves 'psychological' predicates expressing emotional states and attitudes, of which the 'experiencer' frequently acts as direct object or object of preposition. This is illustrated by the Gokana sentence (9).

(9) (Gokana, *Hyman and Comrie* 1981)
à kyé lébàrè kɔ aè dO-è.
it angers Lébàrè that he fell-LOG
'It angers Lébàrè₁ that he₁ fell.'

In fact, there seems to be an implicational universal for logocentric triggers.

(10) Hierarchy for logocentric triggers
Surface structure: subject > object > others
Semantic role: agent > experiencer/benefactive > others[2]

The higher an NP is on the hierarchy, the more likely it will function as an antecedent for a logophoric pronoun. Given that the subject of the matrix clause is typically the NP that is highest on the hierarchy (and incidentally most animate), it is hardly surprising that it is the typical antecedent for a logophoric pronoun.

Taken together, the above three hierarchies predict that the most basic, unmarked pattern of logophoric marking is one which encodes logophoricity by the use of a third-person, singular, logophoric pronoun which refers to a human subject.

Finally, it should be pointed out that logophoric pronouns usually occur in a logophoric domain, that is, a stretch of discourse in which the internal protagonist's perspective is being represented. The logophoric domain is commonly created by a logocentric licenser, which consists mainly of a logocentric predicate. Logocentric predicates can be distinguished largely on a semantic basis. The most common types of logocentric predicates are predicates of speech and thought. But other types of predicates such as those of mental state, knowledge and direct perception can also trigger a logophoric domain. While languages differ in allowing precisely which type of predicate to function as a logocentric licenser, cross-linguistically there does appear to exist an implicational universal for logophoric predicates (Stirling 1993, *Culy* 1994b[3], Huang 1994, 1995b, 2000a).

(11) An implicational universal for logocentric predicates
Speech predicates > epistemic predicates > psychological predicates > knowledge predicates > perceptive predicates

What (11) basically states is this: if a language allows (some) predicates of one class to establish a logophoric domain, then it will also allow (some) predicates of every class higher on the hierarchy to do the same. Thus, if a language has logophoric marking with predicates of, say, psychological state, then it will necessarily have it with predicates of thought and communication.

Another point to note is that logophoric domains in African languages can be extended to syntactic constructions other than those which are directly related to the reporting of an internal protagonist's perspective. This is particularly common with regard to purpose and relative clauses. Furthermore, 'binding' of logophoric pronouns across sentences into discourse is also commonly observed in African languages.

3. Logophoric marking in East Asian languages

With the above background information in place, we now move to logophoric marking in Chinese, Japanese and Korean. To begin with, given hierarchy (5), a long-distance reflexive is predicted to be selected if logophoric marking is intended, for there is no logophoric pronoun/addressee pronoun/verbal affix in these languages. This prediction is indeed borne out: marking of logophoricity in Chinese, Japanese and Korean is mainly encoded syntactically in terms of a long-distance reflexive.

3.1 Logophoric long-distance reflexives and logocentric triggers

The Chinese long-distance reflexive *ziji*, the Japanese long-distance reflexive *zibun*, and the Korean long-distance reflexive *caki* are not specified for person, number or gender, hence are devoid of φ-features.[4] But what is of relevance to us here is that this pattern of person and number distinctions does not run counter to the person and number hierarchies in (6) and (7) set up for logophoric pronouns in African languages.

Next, antecedents for logophoric long-distance reflexives in Chinese, Japanese and Korean also run parallel to those for logophoric pronouns in African languages. In the first place, they are normally limited to be a core-argument of the predicate of the matrix clause. Secondly, they are typically subjects, as the Chinese example (12) shows.

(12) (Chinese)
Xiaoming gaosu Xiaohua Xiaolan bu   xihuan ziji.
Xiaoming tell   Xiaohua Xaiolan NEG like   self
'Xiaoming₁ tells Xiaohua₂ that Xiaolan₃ does not like self$_{1/*2/3}$.'

Again, as in the case of logocentric triggers for logophoric pronouns in African languages, antecedents for long-distance reflexives in the East Asian languages can also be some nonsubject argument, provided that this argument represents the 'source' of the proposition or the 'experience' of the mental states that is being described. Once more, the two most common types of construction are (i) those involving the predicate 'hear from', as in the Korean example (13), and (ii) those involving psychological predicates, as in the Japanese example (14).

(13) (Korean, Kim 1993)
John-un Bill-loputhe caki-ka tayhak iphaksihem-ey
John-TOP Bill-from self-NOM college entrance:examination-at
hapkyekhayssta-nun iyaki-lul tulessta.
passed-that story-ACC heard
'John$_1$ heard from Bill$_2$ that self$_{1/2}$ passed the college entrance examination.'

(14) (Japanese, Sells 1987)
Yosiko ga zibun o nikundeiru koto ga Mitiko o
Yosiko SBJ self OBJ be:hating COMP SBJ Mitiko OBJ
zetuboo e oiyatta.
desperation to drive
'That Yosiko$_1$ hated self$_2$ drove Mitiko$_2$ to desperation.'

3.2 Logophoric domains and logocentric licensers

Turning next to the syntactic and discourse environments in which a long-distance reflexive in Chinese, Japanese and Korean is used, we can see that they typically constitute a logophoric domain. The 'binding' domain for long-distance reflexives in these East Asian languages is usually triggered by a logocentric predicate. All the five types of predicates listed on hierarchy (11) are allowed in these languages to act as a logocentric licenser. This explains why long-distance reflexivisation occurs predominantly within the sentential complements of predicates of speech, thought, mental state, knowledge and perception in the East Asian languages. The Korean example (15) below shows that even perceptive predicates can be used as logocentric licensers.

(15) (Korean)
Kim-nun Inho-ka caki-ul chingchahanun-kes-ul tulessta.
Kim-TOP Inho-NOM self-ACC praise-fact-ACC heard
'Kim$_1$ heard Inho praising self$_1$.'

Furthermore, as with logophoric domains in African languages, long-distance reflexive binding domains in Chinese, Japanese and Korean are not restricted to clausal complements of a logocentric predicate, either. First, they can be extended to other types of syntactic construction such as the topic construction, as in (16); and the relative construction, as in (17).

(16) (Chinese)
Xiaoming zuiba guan bu zhu ziji.
Xiaoming mouth control NEG RV self
'Xiaoming$_1$, mouth$_2$ cannot control self$_1$.'

(17) (Japanese, Kuno 1973)
John-wa zibun-o nikunde-iru onna to kekkon-sita.
John-TOP self-DO hate woman with married
'John$_1$ married a woman who hated self$_1$.'

Secondly, they can also operate across sentence boundaries, extending over an arbitrarily long stretch of discourse, provided that this portion of discourse falls under the scope of the logocentric NP which antecedes the long-distance reflexive.

(18) (Korean, Kim 1993)
Kokayt malu-ey olla-se-ni kuliwun caki cip tungpul-i
hill slope-at rise-stand-as lovely self house lamplight-NOM
poinita. Sekpong-i-nun ... transwum-e kokay-lul ttwie naylye
visible Sekpong-TOP ... in one breath hill-ACC run down
kassupnita.
went.
'Upon standing on the slope, the lamplight from self's$_1$ lovely home is visible. Sekpong$_1$ ... ran down the hill in one breath.'

In the Korean passage above, which is written in the so-called style indirect libre, the use of the connective ending -*uni* 'as' is of some significance. (Note that -*uni* becomes -*ni* when preceded by a vowel-ending verb.) According to Kim (1993), -*uni* is usually employed by the first-person, current, external speaker. Its use by the narrator of the passage here enables him or her to adopt the point of view of the central character of the story, thus creating a logophoric context.

So far I have been showing that there are strong parallels in the use of logophoric pronouns in African languages and in that of long-distance reflexives in Chinese, Japanese and Korean. But there is one pattern of long-distance reflexivisation in the East Asian languages which has not been attested for logophoric pronouns in African languages. This concerns the use of deictically-oriented directional predicates such as 'come/go' and 'bring/take'. As can be shown by the Chinese example (19) below, while the use of 'come' in (19a) allows long-distance reflexivisation, the use of 'go' in (19b) does not. Furthermore, note that this contrast is independent of whether or not a logocentric predicate occurs in the matrix clause.

(19) (Chinese)
    a. Yinwei tongxue lai kan guo ziji le, suoyi Xiaohua
       because classmate come see EXP self PFV so Xiaohua
       hen gaoxing.
       very happy
       'Xiaohua$_1$ was very happy because his classmates have come to see self$_1$.'
    b. ?Yinwei tongxue qu kan guo ziji le, suoyi Xiaohua
       because classmate go see EXP self PFV so Xiaohua
       hen gaoxing.
       very happy
       'Xiaohua$_1$ was very happy because his classmates have gone to see self$_1$.'

This contrast seems to be attributed to the fact that the use of 'come' in (19a) makes clear what is reported is from the space-location of the matrix subject, therefore the matrix subject is the pivot, or the relativised 'centre of deixis' in the logophoric domain. Hence the possibility of long-distance reflexivisation. In other words, 'come' must be interpreted as describing movement towards the matrix subject. On the other hand, the use of 'go' in (19b) is an indication that what is described is not from the 'camera angle' of the matrix subject, rather it indicates movement away from the matrix subject, therefore the matrix subject cannot be the pivot or the logocentric trigger. Hence long-distance reflexivisation is bad. How, then, can examples like (19) be accounted for? One simple solution might be to incorporate deictically-oriented directional predicates into hierarchy (11), namely:

(20) A revised implicational universal for logocentric predicates
     Speech predicates > epistemic predicates > knowledge predicates > psychological predicates > unmarked directional predicates

4. A neo-Gricean pragmatic account

In the last section, I have given a description of logophoric marking by long-distance reflexives in Chinese, Japanese and Korean. In this section, I shall provide a neo-Gricean pragmatic analysis of logophoricity and related phenomena in these East Asian languages.

    Let me start with the three neo-Gricean pragmatic principles proposed by Levinson (1991).

(21) Levinson's (1991) Q-, I-, and M-principles (simpified)
   a. *The Q-principle*
      Do not say less than is required (given I).
   b. *The I-principle*
      Do not say more than is required (given Q)
   c. *The M-principle*
      Do not use a marked expression without reason.

The basic idea of the Q-principle is that the use of an expression (especially a semantically weaker one) in a set of contrastive semantic alternates Q-implicates the negation of the interpretation associated with the use of another expression (especially a semantically stronger one) in the same set. In other words, the effect of this inferential strategy is to give rise to an upper-bounding conversational implicature: from the absence of an informationally stronger expression, we infer that the interpretation associated with the use of that expression does not hold. Schematically (I use the symbol +> to indicate 'conversationally implicate'):

(22) Q-scale: <x,y>
     y +> Q ~ x

(23) a. Q-scalar: <all, some>
        Some of his friends like linguistics.
        +> Not all of his friends like linguistics
     b. Q-clausal: <know, believe>
        I believe that John likes linguistics.
        +> John may or may not like linguistics — I don't know which

Next, the basic idea of the I-principle is that the use of a semantically general linguistic expression I-implicates a semantically specific interpretation. In other words, the operation of the I-principle induces an inference to a proposition that is best in keeping with the most stereotypical and explanatory expectation given world knowledge. Schematically:

(24) I-scale: [x,y]
     y +>I x

(25) (Conjunction buttressing)
     p and q +> p and then q
     +> p therefore q
     +> p in order to cause q
     John turned the key and the drawer opened.
     +> John first turned the key and then the drawer opened
     +> John turned the key and therefore the drawer opened
     +> John turned the key in order to cause the drawer to open

Finally, the basic idea of the M-principle is that the use of a marked expression M-implicates the negation of the interpretation associated with the use of an alternative, unmarked expression in the same set. In other words, from the use of a marked expression, we infer that the stereotypical interpretation associated with the use of an alternative, unmarked expression does not hold. Schematically:

(26) M-scale: {x,y}
 y +>M ~x

(27) a. The train comes frequently
 +> The train comes, say, every ten minutes
 b. The train comes not infrequently
 +> The train comes not as frequently as the uttering of (a) suggests, say, every half an hour

Taken together, the I-, and M-principles give rise to complementary interpretations: the use of an unmarked expression tends to convey an unmarked message, whereas the use of a marked expression, a marked message. Furthermore, inconsistencies arising from the Q-, I-, and M-principles are resolved by an ordered set of precedence.

(28) Levinson's resolution schema
 a. Level of genus: Q > M > I
 b. Level of species: e.g. $Q_{-clausal} > Q_{-scalar}$

This amounts to saying that genuine Q-implicatures tend to precede I-implicatures, but otherwise I-implicatures take precedence until the use of a marked expression triggers a complementary M-implicature to the negation of the applicability of the pertinent I-implicature (see e.g. Huang 1991, 1994 for further discussion).

We move next to a neo-Gricean pragmatic theory of anaphora. The underlying idea is that the interpretation of certain patterns of anaphora can be made using pragmatic inference, parasitic on the language user's knowledge of the range of options available in the grammar, and of the systematic use or avoidance of particular linguistic expressions or structures on particular occasions (see Huang 1991, 1992, 1995a, b, 1996, 2000a, b for detailed discussion).

Coming back to logophoric, long-distance reflexives in Chinese, Japanese and Korean, the interpretation of them and their associated regular pronouns can be determined by the systematic interaction of the three neo-Gricean pragmatic principles mentioned above. Needless to say, any interpretation generated by these pragmatic principles is subject to the general consistency constraints applicable to Gricean conversational implicatures. These constraints include world knowledge, contextual information, and semantic entailments.

Notice that in Chinese, Japanese and Korean, logophoric, long-distance reflexives are normally not in complementary distribution with regular pronouns, as the Korean example (29) indicates.

(29) (Korean, Kim 1993)
   a. John-un caki-ka   salang-ey ppacyessta-ko malhayssta.
      John-TOP self-NOM love-in   fell-COMP   said
      'John₁ said tht self₁ was in love.'
   b. John-un ku-ka   salang-ey ppacyessta-ko malhayssta.
      John-TOP 3s-NOM   love-in   fell-COMP   said
      'John₁ said that he₁/₂ was in love.'

Now, by the hierarchy in (5), a long-distance reflexive will be selected if logophoric marking is intended, for there is no logophoric pronoun/addressee pronoun/verbal affix in these languages. However, for coreference, a regular pronoun can also be employed. In other words, while the use of a long-distance reflexive encodes both logophoricity and coreference, the use of a regular pronoun may or may not encode coreference, but definitely not logophoricity. This is sufficient enough to form a Q-scale <long-distance reflexive, regular pronoun>, to the effect that the unavailability of the semantically stronger long-distance reflexive will Q-implicate the speaker's intention to avoid at least one of the features associated with its use, namely logophoricity (see also Levinson 1991, O'Connor 1992). Long-distance reflexives are semantically stronger than regular pronouns in that (i) syntactically they usually require to be somewhat bound, and (ii) semantically they typically have to be referentially dependent. Schematically for (29):

(30) <caki [±logophoric, +coreference], ku [−logophoric, ±coreference]>
      ku +> Q ~ caki

Alternatively, (29) can also be accounted for in terms of the systematic interaction between the I- and M-principles. Since the grammar allows the unmarked regular pronoun to be used to encode coreference, the speaker will use it if such an interpretation is intended. On the other hand, if the unmarked pronoun is not used, but the marked (morphologically more prolix) long-distance reflexive is employed instead, then an M-implicature is created, namely not only coreference but logophoricity as well is intended. Schematically:

(31) {ku [−logophoric, ±coreference], caki [±logophoric, +coreference]}
      caki +> M ~ ku

How, then, are logophoric long-distance reflexives themselves interpreted under our account? Within the proposed system, the interpretation of them is subject to the I-principle. What the I-principle does here is to invite a local coreferential interpretation for logophoric long-distance reflexives, provided that such an interpretation does not run contrary to the general consistency constraints on conversational implicatures. In fact, there appears to be a rather rigid I-heuristic here: a root clause antecedent is in general preferred to a nonroot one; a subject, to a nonsubject; a nonsplit antecedent, to a split one; and a c-commanding NP, to a nonc-commanding one. Failure to find an intrasentential antecedent will lead to the search for a previous discourse antecedent, preferably a topic. As is easy to verify by the reader, this interpretation mechanism can be successfully applied to the examples discussed so far to locate the correct, preferred antecedent for the logophoric long-distance reflexive.

One principal advantage of advocating a neo-Gricean pragmatic approach to the interpretation of logophoric long-distance reflexives, as to that of anaphora in general, is that conversational implicatures being defeasible, we can always arrive at an interpretation that is best in accord with world knowledge. One or two examples may suffice to illustrate this point. Consider first (32).

(32) (Japanese, Kato 1994)
Takasi-ga Yamada sensei-ni zibun-ga siken-ni goukaku-sita
Takasi-SBJ Yamada teacher-IO self-SBJ examination passed
koto-o kiita.
COMP-DO heard
'Takasi$_1$ heard from Professor Yamada$_2$ that self$_{1>2}$ passed the examination.'

Note that (32) has the logocentric predicate 'hear from'. Intuitively, it is two way ambiguous, the preferred antecedent being *Takasi*. Now, the I-principle articulates that the preferred antecedent of *zibun* is the subject of the matrix clause. This I-implicature is further reinforced by the background assumption that it is stereotypically a student rather than a professor who would sit for an examination. Next, essentially the same world knowledge constraint can be shown to hold for the interpretation of a so-called psych-sentence (33).

(33) (Chinese)
Tongxuemen laoshi caonong ziji shi Xiaoming he kunao.
classmates always laugh:at self make Xiaoming very worry
'That (his) classmates$_1$ always luagh at self$_2$/selves$_1$ worries Xiaoming$_2$.'

Given the syntax and semantics of (33), the set of possible antecedents for *ziji* would be delimited to *tongxuemen* 'classmates' and *Xiaoming*. Now, by the I-heuristic, *tongxuemen* would be I-implicated to be the preferred antecedent. However, given background assumption, it is more likely that Xiaoming's worries are caused by his classmates's constant laughing at him rather than themselves. Consequently, the original I-induced preferred interpretation evaporates, and *ziji* would then be correctly I-implicated to be preferably bound to *Xiaoming*. From all this follows the conclusion that it is pragmatics that is responsible for determining the actual, preferred antecedent where there is more than one structurally possible antecedent for logophoric long-distance reflexives.

5. Conclusion

In this chapter, I have described logophoric marking by means of a long-distance reflexive in Chinese, Japanese and Korean. I have also provided a formal analysis of logophoricity and related phenomena in these East Asian languages within a general neo-Gricean pragmatic theory of anaphora.

Notes

* This chapter is one of a series of works reporting on my research on logophoricity and related topics. Parts of the material contained here were presented to various audiences at the universities of Cambridge, Cornell, EHESS-CNRS (Paris), Essex, Groningen, Leiden, MIT, Massachusetts (Amherst), Oxford, Reading, Saarlandes, UCL, and Utrecht. I am particularly grateful to Bruce Connell, Chris Culy, Steve Levinson, Peter Sells, Nigel Vincent, Manfred von Roncador, and Anne Zribi-Hertz for helpful comments. Thanks also to Gerry Latawiec for putting the manuscript into John Benjamins format. The research reported on here was in part supported by a Research Leave Award from the Humanities Research Board of the British Academy and by grants from the Travel and General Fund of the Reseach Board of the University of Reading.

1. Cf. the similar implicational universal for the person distinction of reflexives (e.g. Comrie 1989).

   (i) An implicational universal for the person distinction of reflexives
       First-person reflexives imply second-person reflexives, and second-person reflexives imply third-person reflexives.

2. See also *Hyman and Comrie* (1981).
3. For predicates licencing logophoric marking see also Culy (this volume).
4. Chinese also has a morphologically complex reflexive 'pronoun *ziji*', Japanese, two morphologically complex reflexives 'pronoun *zisin*' and '*zibun zisin*, and Korean, two morpologically complex reflexives 'pronoun *casin*' and '*caki casin*'. Given that their basic distributions are a matter of controversy, I shall not discuss them here. For some discussion, see e.g. Huang (1994, 2000a).

References

Armstrong, Robert G. 1963. "The Kwa working-group at Dakar". *Actes du Second Colloque International de Linguistique Négro-Africaine, Dakar 12.-16. 4. 1962*. Dakar: Université de Dakar and West African Linguistic Society, 213–14.
Comrie, Bernard. 1989. *Language universals and linguistic typology*. Oxford: Blackwell.
Huang, Yan. 1991. "A neo-Gricean pragmatic theory of anaphora". *Journal of Linguistics* 27: 301–35.
Huang, Yan. 1992. "Against Chomsky's typology of empty categories". *Journal of Pragmatics* 17: 1–29.
Huang, Yan. 1994. *The syntax and pragmatics of anaphora: a study with special reference to Chinese* (=Cambridge Studies in Linguistics 70). Cambridge: Cambridge University Press.
Huang, Yan. 1995a. "On null subjects and null objects in generative grammar". *Linguistics* 33: 1081–123.
Huang, Yan. 1995b. "Logophoricity: logophoric pronouns in African languages and long-distance reflexives in East Asian languages". Unpublished manuscript.
Huang, Yan. 1996. "A note on the head-movement analysis of long-distance reflexives". *Linguistics* 34: 833–40.
Huang, Yan. 2000a. *Anaphora: a cross-linguistic study*. Oxford: Oxford University Press.
Huang, Yan. 2000b. "Discourse anaphora: four theoretical models". *Journal of Pragmatics* 32: 151–76.
Kato, Kumiko. 1994. *On reflexives in Japanese: some syntactic and pragmatic approaches*. MA dissertation, University of Reading.
Kim, Sun-Hee. 1993. *Division of labour between grammar and pragmatics: the distribution and interpretation of anaphora*. Ph.D. thesis, Yale University.
Kuno, Susumu. 1973. *The structure of the Japanese language*. Cambridge, Mass.: MIT Press.
Levinson, Stephen C. 1991. "Pragmatic reduction of the Binding Conditions revisited". *Journal of Linguistics* 27: 107–61.
O'Connor, Mary Catherine. 1992. *Topics in Northen Pomo grammar*. New York: Garland.
Parker, Elizabeth. 1986. "Mundani pronouns". In Wiesemann, Ursula (ed.), 131–66.
Sigurðsson, Halldór Armann. 1990. "Long-distance reflexives and moods in Icelandic". In Maling, Joan and Annie Zaenen (eds.), *Modern Icelandic syntax*. New York: Academic Press, 309–46.
Stirling, Lesley. 1993. *Switch-reference and discourse representation*. Cambridge: Cambridge University Press.
Wiesemann, Ursula. 1986. "Grammaticalized coreference". Wiesemann, Ursula (ed.), 437–64.
Wiesemann, Ursula (ed.). 1986. *Pronominal systems* (=Continuum 5). Tübingen: Narr.

PART 4

Form and history of quotative constructions

CHAPTER 11

The grammaticalization of 'say' and 'do'
An areal phenomenon in East Africa*

David Cohen, Marie-Claude Simeone-Senelle
and Martine Vanhove
Professeur Emérite, CNRS-LLACAN, CNRS-LLACAN

1. Introduction

In this volume devoted to reported discourse and quotatives, we would like to deal with a very particular development of the use of main verbs meaning 'say'. Our purpose is to show how, in some languages, the quotative 'say' has come to be used both as an auxiliary verb and as a formative of verbs derived from various word categories, leading ultimately to a reorganization of the verb system. We had to include the verb 'do' as well, given its similarity and complementarity of its behavior in the languages studied.

In several language families, Egyptian, Cushitic, Omotic, Semitic, and Nilo-Saharan, spoken in Eastern Africa (i.e. Egypt, Sudan, Ethiopia, Eritrea, Somalia, Djibouti, Northern Kenya and Northern Tanzania), full verbs meaning 'say' and 'do' (and a few others with related meanings such as 'think, have in mind, intend, consider, shout' and 'put, place') are frequently found to have uses as auxiliary verbs and as formatives for new verbs. M. Cohen (1970), following Junod (1933), called the resulting forms 'descriptive compounds'. This has become the conventional designation in Hamito-Semitic studies and will be used in this chapter. The base of the new verbs may be nouns, adjectives, adverbs, onomatopoetic/ideophonic forms, verbs or even phrases. Descriptive composition thus involves both transcategorial and intracategorial processes. The antiquity of this process of verb creation is attested by its presence in Old Egyptian.

As auxiliaries, 'say' and 'do' may have other modal values such as 'future', 'injunctive', 'inchoative', 'volitive', 'assertive', 'authenticative'. They may also be used as focalizers. These values are usually linked to different syntactic constructions.

In this chapter, we will focus on the process of verb creation and its morphological consequence, the renewal of verb inflection. Indeed, in some languages, such as most Cushitic languages, in Egyptian, and, to some extent, in Dongolese Nubian, auxiliary verbs have been reduced to the status of verb morphology.

The role of 'say' and 'do' as auxiliaries and in the creation of new verb inflection has been recognized for more than a century (see Isenberg 1842, Praetorius 1879, Afevork 1905, 1911, Armbruster 1908–20, Walker 1928, and Baeteman 1929 for Amharic; Reinisch 1878 for Cushitic; and Praetorius 1894 for Hamito-Semitic). The work of these scholars was elaborated in France by M. Cohen (1939, 1970).

As far as we know, there are no comparative linguistic studies describing this areal phenomenon in detail.[1] We therefore provide below a comparative and typological survey. We will see that, in some languages, verbs meaning 'say' and 'do' work in this way, while in others, only one of these verbs may be used.

Illustrations will be provided from a variety of languages in different families, and we will give particular attention to Afar, a Cushitic language for which we can use data from our own fieldwork. We will also show that the East African data can be related to similar phenomena, hitherto unrecognized as such, in Aiki, a Nilo-Saharan language spoken further west in the Central African Republic. Kanuri, another Nilo-Saharan language, and Hausa, a Chadic language, also show the same tendency. We will also take into account languages where the process of grammaticalization has gone to completion, i.e. Old Egyptian and Cushitic for 'say', and Coptic for 'do'.

Within the framework of D. Cohen's general theory of verb auxiliarization (see D. Cohen 1983–5; Vanhove 1993: 101–5; Simeone-Senelle and Vanhove 1997; and D. Cohen, Simeone-Senelle and Vanhove in prep.), proposals will be made to explain how 'say' and 'do' become auxiliaries and to define which semantic features of these two verbs account for their comparable behavior, setting them apart from other categories of verbs.

2. The function of 'say' and 'do' in East Africa

2.1 Cushitic

2.1.1 *The case of Afar*
The following study is based on data collected by Simeone-Senelle and Vanhove in Eritrea in 1996, and in Paris between 1996 and 1998 (Djibouti dialect). We have also consulted Parker and Hayward (1985), Morin (1995), and Hayward (1996). We will first review the morphology of descriptive compounds and then discuss their syntactic and semantic features.

The descriptive compounds of Afar are formed with one of two auxiliaries, *edḥe* 'say', an irregular verb based on two different roots, and *hee* 'put, place', which is regularly inflected with suffixes. The periphrastic word order is always *base verb–auxiliary verb*. Compounds may coexist with a corresponding 'ordinary' verb, or be created from any other word class.

Semantically, *eḍḥe* forms intransitive or middle verbs, while *hee* is used to construct transitive ones, but a few onomatopoeic bases may use either auxiliary (though *eḍḥe* is by far more frequent).

(1) a. danán haahíssi-hee
       donkey bray-put:3M.S.PERF
    b. haahíssi-iyye
       bray-say:3M.S.PERF
       'the donkey brayed' (cf. haahisé 'it brayed')

Outside certain specific contexts such as negative or coordinated sentences, the compound constitutes a prosodic unit with main stress on the penultimate syllable of the stem. Moreover, the auxiliary may undergo phonetic reduction.

The morphology of the stems varies. The most common ones in our data have a geminated final consonant, followed by a vowel harmonizing with the preceding one. Some dialectal differences in vowel quality exist: the data in Parker and Hayward (1985) and Bliese (1981: 146) show no vowel harmony, the final vowel is always *a*. With this pattern, the stem is most often derived from a verb (in base or derived form).

The two examples below illustrate intransitive compounds with *eḍḥe*:

(2) kobóḍḍu-iyyaanah
    gather-3P.IPERF:say
    'They gather themselves' (cf. koboḍán 'they gather themselves')

(3) *way-tímmi*-itte   awká baḍa
    lack-PASS-3F.S.PERF:say girl   daughter
    'The little girl *could not be found*' (cf. way-timté 'she was not found')

The following are examples of transitive compounds with *hee*:

(4) wáyya-heeni
    lack-put:3P.PERF
    'They did not find' (waytén 'they lacked, did not find')

(5) ḥulú-ssu-hee
    enter-CAUS-put:3M.S.PERF
    'He made enter' (ḥulu-sé 'he made enter')

The same pattern may sometimes be used with nouns as in (6) or ideophones which cannot be used in isolation as in (7) and (8):

(6) tíbbi-iyye
silence-3M.S.PERF:say
'He fell silent' (cf. tibba 'silence')

(7) kábba-iddeḥ
IDEO-say:IMP.S
'come near!'

(8) bir dongoló sugtéh óh yí
yesterday.evening noise stay:3F.S.PERF this.is mine
ḥuggaane-ey dúbbu itta haak sugté
neighbors-REL IDEO RECP put:PART stay:3F.S.PERF
'Yesterday evening there was a dull thudding sound, my neighbors were fighting'

Monosyllabic CVC ideophones may also be made into verbs by a derivational morpheme *-y*. The stem is then lengthened to CVVC: *duubuyé* 'he beat'. The origin of this *-y* could have been a verb meaning 'say'. This possibility of verb derivation varies with the dialect.

In the data we elicited from our Tadjoura (Djibouti) informant, and in Parker and Hayward (1985), we find other patterns for the base of descriptive compounds. Monosyllabic ideophones (CVC) may keep their stem unchanged:

(9) dub má-dḥ-in
IDEO NEG-say:IMP.S-NEG
'Do not kick up a row!'

They also may have it expanded by full or partial reduplication ($C_1V(C_2)C_1VC_2$), or by vowel lengthening which conveys different meanings. Thus, *dubdúb-edḥe* and *dudúb-edḥe* are variants of

(10) a. dúbba-edḥe
IDEO-1S.PERF:say
'I made a dull thudding sound' (Parker and Hayward)

Opposed to these are:

(10) b. dúub-edḥe 'I collapsed slowly to the ground'
c. dúub-hee
IDEO-put:3M.S.PERF
'he dropped (a heavy load)'

Vowel lengthening also applies to verb stems:

(11) dáaf-iyye
sit.down-3M.S.PERF:say
'he hardly sat down' (cf. dáffa-iyye 'he sat down')

(12) ḥulúu-s-hee
    enter-CAUS-put:3M.S.PERF
    'he hardly made (someone) enter' (cf. ḥulússu-hee in (5))

The lengthening of the final stem vowel of verbs and ideophones thus conveys an 'attenuative' sense. According to our Tadjoura informant, this device is used only in literary language. His observation seems to be corroborated by the fact that these forms are unattested in our spontaneous data.

When the base is an adverb or a noun that can be used in an adverbial function, the form of the compound is stem + -*h* 'towards' + 'say' or 'put':

(13) bisó-h   iddeḥ
    far/forward-DIR say:IMP.S
    'Step back; go ahead; push; progress!'

(14) ínni   addá-h   hee   *or* addá-h ínni hee
    myself depth-DIR put:1S.PERF
    'As for myself, I humiliated myself'

(15) addá-h   edḥe
    depth-DIR 1S.PERF:say
    'I was humble'

As stated above, descriptive compounds can undergo morphological derivation, like any other verb in the language. In addition to the process found in our spontaneous data, i.e. derived stem + 'say' or 'put' (see (3), (5), and (12)), the auxiliary may bear the derivational morpheme and the stem be in base form:

(16) galbó kaa-k   kálla-*hay-sitéeh*
    skin him-from take.off-put-AUTOBEN.3M.S.PERF
    'He skinned for his own benefit' (cf. kalsítti-hee) (Morin 1995:100)

(17) tíbbi-yeddeḥe
    silence-3M.S.PERF:say:AUTOBEN
    'He held his tongue for his own benefit'

Another process involves the derivation of both the base and the auxiliary:

(18) ḥulú-ssu   hay-site
    enter-FACT put-AUTOBEN.3M.S.PERF
    'He caused (someone) to enter for his own benefit' (cf. ḥulsité)

Syntactically, the stem and the auxiliary of descriptive compounds may be separated by two word classes: the adverbial particles *eddé* and *ellé*, and the personal pronouns (with or without a postposition). Their prosodic unity is then broken:

(19) aká   akat aḍúyyu-haynah   giitná   waʕdiina úsuk
     other rope fasten-put:1P.IPERF pull:1P.IPERF when   he
     tíbbi   edde iyya   awki baḍí tíbbi   edde iyya
     silence in 3M.S.IPERF:say boy son silence in 3M.S.IPERF:say
     'We fasten another rope (to the cradle) and when we pull it, he quiets
     down, the small boy becomes quiet'

(20) ibbíḍḍi kaa hee
     catch   him put:3M.S.PERF
     'He caught him'

(21) dúb ko-t   hée-yyo
     IDEO you-on put-1S.FUT
     'I'll beat you'

Another important syntactic feature is that, in a series of coordinated stems, a single auxiliary, the last one, may apply to all of them:

(22) ḥangoyséena baaḍó-l háyya-ay, gíli   baaḍó-l háyya-ay,
     forefinger floor-on put-and thumb floor-on put-and
     ánnah booha baḍá   takké-m   gidaháa,
     little hole daughter 3F.S.IPERF:become-REL so.that
     wóo guri gabatáa ḥangoyséena kee gíli   baaḍó-l háyya han
     this left hand   forefinger and thumb floor-on put-put:3P.IPERF
     'They put the forefinger on the floor, they put the thumb on the floor
     so that it will form a small hole, they put the forefinger and the thumb
     of the left hand that way on the floor'

If the verb stems do not take the same auxiliary, the one that applies to the last verb predominates:

(23) ḍini-k   ugú-ttu-y,   fóoḥa kaʃl-íssi-y,   af   ʃadássa-y,
     sleep-from wake-PASS-and face wash-FACT-and mouth brush-and
     duuli ḥúllu-y, šanta akúʃʃu-y, afá-k   ewéʃʃi-iyye
     toilets go.to-and bag carry-and door-through go.out-3M.S.PERF:say
     'He got up, washed his face, brushed his teeth, went to the toilets, took
     his bag, and went out through the door'

Descriptive compounding of verbs is very productive in Afar. Longacre (1990: 18–19), following Bliese, considers such verbs as marking "pivotal storyline action/events". Indeed, they are often used in narratives where they may alternate with their corresponding uncompounded verbs. They are also frequent in discourse. Their use depends on the speaker's intention and expresses his attitude towards the predicate. The reported facts and processes are not indifferent to the speaker; rather, the compound verbs are used to convey his emotions such as astonishment, admiration, disapproval, etc. In the following example, indignation is perceptible in the answer (where use of the simple form *yo-l usuuléh* would be a simple statement of fact):

(24) ka-t daawitéh – háyyee? – *usúullu* yo-l *hee*
him-at scold:1s.PERF – so.what? – laugh me-at put:3M.S.PERF
'I scolded him — So what? — (Well) he had laughed at me!'

The aim is to narrow down the range of possible interpretations of the utterance by the other discourse participant. In the following example, the old woman leaving the recording session early lets us know that she has a good reason for going:

(25) anú dóhri abítti-hee
I noon.prayer make:AUTOBEN-put:1s.PERF
'As for me, I am going to pray'

The speaker's involvement also accounts for the use of descriptive compounds when giving orders or instructions:

(26) ifissírri kaa hays
translate him put:IMP.S
'Translate for him!'

To some extent, then, the use of descriptive compounds falls within the domain of discourse-participant interplay. This is confirmed by the fact that these compounds can be used with any verb inflection (simple or compound tenses) conveying values of tense, aspect, or epistemic or deontic modal categories.

2.1.2 *Other modern Cushitic languages*

Other modern Cushitic languages use descriptive compounds. Below are a few examples from languages which, unlike Afar, only use the verb 'say' as auxiliary.

In Oromo, a Lowland East Cushitic language, the use of the verb 'say' appears in two examples in Stroomer (1987). 'Say' is *yed'a, jed'a* or *yaa*-.[2] It would seem that 'do' is not used to create verbs (Stroomer p.c.). The base can be either a noun or a verb with slightly modified stem (reduction of final long vowel or vowel harmony):

(27) c'alla yed'a
only say
'to be silent, remain silent'

(Three derived verb forms of the above base may also be used: *c'alleed'd'a* 'be silent, remain silent', *c'alleesa* 'be quiet, silent', and *c'allised'd'a* 'be silent'.)

(28) odoo innii mina śeene yed'u
    when he house enter say:3s.PERF
    'When he entered the house'

To judge from the few examples given by Roper (1929:84), Beja, a Northern Cushitic language, also uses only *di* 'say'. The base component may be from any word class.

(29) miči di
    ONOM say
    'to make the click meaning "no"'

(30) fídig índi
    depart 3s.IPERF:say
    'He is going'

(31) jar di
    shoo! say
    'to shoo (hens) away'

2.1.3 *Early Cushitic*

From a diachronic viewpoint, it is important to note that most Cushitic languages have suffixal conjugations for both perfect and imperfect. It is generally believed that these conjugations are recent and developed from the prefixal conjugation of variable stems. It has been recognized since Praetorius (1894) that the suffixes go back etymologically to a very short auxiliary verb conjugated with prefixes. Reconstruction based on comparative studies has shown that this auxiliary is a verb meaning 'say, be', *Vn, *a, *y, etc. (see for instance Zaborski 1975, D. Cohen 1984, 1988). Moreover this reconstruction is supported by the fact that some Cushitic languages (Beja, Afar, Somali, South-Agaw) have remnants of earlier prefixal inflection, which is still used for a limited number of verbs (the proportion varies from 60% of all verbs to five verbs only).

The following is the conjugation of a Somali verb (Digil variety) *rog* 'stay' in the imperfect (see D. Cohen 1984:89). The stem *rog* is thus inflected with the auxiliary *a, conjugated with the Hamito-Semitic personal prefixes.

	Singular		Plural
1.	*rog-ä*	1.	*rog-n-ā*
2.	*rog-t-ä*	2.	*rog-t-ān(a)*
3. M	*rog-ä*	3.	*rog-ān(a)*
3. F	*rog-t-ä*		

2.2 Ethio-Semitic

Modern Ethio-Semitic languages make widespread and colorful use of descriptive compounds. Typologically, they can be distributed into five groups:

1. languages using only a verb meaning 'say' in base form
2. languages using only 'say' in base and derived form
3. languages using both 'say' and 'do' in complementary distribution
4. languages using both 'say' and 'do' in free variation
5. languages using both 'say' and 'do' with their derived forms.

2.2.1 *Languages using only a verb meaning 'say' in base form*

From the examples given by Leslau (1956:145–6) for Ethio-Semitic, it seems that only Zway, out of a list of 15 languages, has a system with only one auxiliary, *balo* 'say' (e.g., *sam balo* 'be quiet').

2.2.2 *Languages using 'say' and a derived form of 'say'*

Leslau (1956:145–6) mentions the use of *balä* 'say' and its causative derived form *a-balä* 'make say' to create verbs in Gafat. The invariable stem used with *balä* expresses mainly intransitive action; transitive action is expressed by *a-balä*. To judge from the examples provided, the stems of descriptive compounds are restricted to this particular usage. This is why no word-for-word translation is given. Leslau recorded only bi-consonantal stems: *qaṭ balä* 'be straight', *ənga balä* 'disobey'; as a causative form, he gives *käf a-balä* 'raise, make higher'.

Leslau also mentions Tigrinya, Gogot, and Aymellel with the same pattern of verb creation, the only differences being a larger syllabic range of bases and the fact that the compounds may alternate with an uncompounded verb.

2.2.3 *Languages using both 'say' and 'do' in free variation*

Some languages can use both 'say' and 'do' in free variation with no difference in meaning. This usage is only marginal in Amharic (32) and in Tigre (33) where it is limited to ideophones. Leslau also provides one example from Harari (34).

(32) tuss ālä *or* tuss adərrəgə
 IDEO say   IDEO do
 'to pour' (M. Cohen 1970:265)

(33) koy bela *or* koy wada
 IDEO say   IDEO do
 'to hurry' (Raz 1983:67)

(34) čäf bāya *or* čäf äša
 IDEO say   IDEO make
 'to jump' (Leslau 1956:145)

2.2.4 Languages using both 'say' and 'do' in complementary distribution

In many of the languages using both 'say' and 'do', their syntactic roles generally turn out to be complementary: 'say' forms intransitive verbs while 'do' forms transitive ones, whatever class the base belongs to.

The Gunnän-Gurage languages belong to this typological category. Verbs can be formed from interjections and onomatopoeias or derived from verbs. 'Say' is *balä/barä* and 'do' is *amännä*. Here are some examples provided by Hetzron (1977: 109–10) in various dialects:

(35) bäy balä
all.right say
'to agree'

(36) žaa amännä
IDEO do
'to drop'

(37) daqq barä
laugh say
'to laugh'

Leslau (1956: 145) attributes the same pattern to Argobba.

2.2.5 Languages using both 'say' and 'do' with their derived forms

This typological category shows several patterns of distribution of the base and derived forms.

According to M. Cohen (1970: 262–75), Amharic makes considerable use of descriptive compounds with expressive value. They are formed from an uninflected base (final consonants are most often geminated) derived from any word class, and an auxiliary verb. *ālǝ* 'say' forms verbs with a "neutral meaning" (i.e. middle verbs), and is the most frequent auxiliary. The less frequent *adǝrrǝgǝ* 'do' forms active verbs. In addition, derived forms of 'do' (*asdǝrrǝgǝ* 'make do') and 'say' (*tǝbālǝ* 'be said') may also be used:

(38) yǝqǝr tǝ-bālǝ
stay:3M.S.JUS PASS-say:3S.PERF
'He was forgiven'

(39) yǝhǝn nǝgǝr lǝbb asdǝrrǝgǝ-ñ
DEM thing intelligence FACT:do:3S.PERF-1S.OBJ
'He pointed this thing out to me'

Onomatopoeic stems, occasionally used as interjections, can only appear in the form of descriptive compounds; no regular verb exists alongside the compound:

(40) da   āla *or* dada   āla
     ONOM say   RDP.ONOM say
     'to be slow to speak, walk'

(41) šagg *or* šəgg *or* šagagg   adarraga
     ONOM   ONOM   RDP.ONOM   do
     'to cool down'

Verbs can also be converted into descriptive compounds by special stems. The result is considered to be more expressive. Compounds have intensive or attenuative value,[3] according to stem morphology. We thus have an intracategorial process of verbal creation giving rise to semantic derivation:

(42) sabarr   āla   sabarbarr   āla
     be.broken say   be.smashed say
     'to be somewhat broken'   'to be somewhat smashed'

(43) səbbərr   āla   səbərbərr   āla
     be.broken say   be.smashed say
     'to be totally broken'   'to be totally smashed'
     (ta-sabābbara 'to be somewhat broken, smashed')

(44) sakakk adarraga   səkəkk   adarraga
     put.on.partially do   put.on.in.large.quantities do
     'to put on partially'   'to put on in large quantities'

A transcategorial process allows a few descriptive compounds with idiomatic structure to be formed from nominal bases and short expressions:

(45) ṭalātən dəl   adarraga
     enemy victory make:3s.PERF
     'He beat the enemy'

(46) hullun əmbi āla-ñ
     all   no   say:3S.PERF-1S.OBJ
     'He refused everything to me'

In Southern Ethio-Semitic, the examples provided by Leslau (1956: 145–6) show that some languages such as Ennemor use 'say', 'do', and derived forms of 'do': the causative of *ṭis barä* (lit. 'say ṭis') 'drip' is formed with *epa* 'make', and the factitive, with the derived factitive form of *epa*, *atepä*. Leslau gives other examples from Selti and Wolan. In Čaha and Muher, the passive derived form of 'do' is semantically equivalent to 'say': *ṭis baräm* (lit. 'say ṭis') 'drip' is equivalent to *ṭis mänäm* (lit. 'be made ṭis'), and their causative form is formed with the derived causative form of 'be made', *amänäm*.

Tigre uses still another pattern: *bela* 'say', its derived causative form *ʔabala*, and *wada* 'do', are in complementary distribution. Raz (1983:66) specifies that most *bela* compounds happen to be intransitive. They may be rendered transitive or become causative of the intransitive by the use of the verb *ʔabala* 'be said': *kaf bela* 'sit' vs. *kaf ʔabala* 'make sit', *bah bela* 'rejoice' (intransitive) vs. *bah ʔabala* 'rejoice' (transitive).

As in Amharic, the stem may be limited to its use in the compound:

(47)   qaʕ   bela
       IDEO:sharp.noise say
       'to make a sharp noise'

or may be used along with a regular verb:

(48)   bəḥəl   bela
       pardon   say
       'to pardon, excuse' (baḥala 'to pardon')

Example (48) shows no semantic difference between the regular and the compound verb. The example below, however, shows semantic derivation:

(49)   waswas   bela
       move   say
       'to move fast/to and fro' (waswasa 'move')

Similarly to Amharic, the compound form may convey according to Raz (1983:67):

> further information concerning the aspect of action or state of happening — as compared with the semantic content of a coexisting verb of the same origin as the first element of the compound. The addition in meaning can be specified in terms of intensity or manner of the activity, such as: augmentative, attenuative or iterative.

Some stems may only be used with *wada* 'do', and not with *bela*, to form intransitive verb compounds (e.g., *yak wada* 'hurry', *ʕaqəl wada* 'be patient').

2.3 Egyptian

2.3.1 *Old/Middle Egyptian*

In Old Egyptian, the verb system was based on several patterns involving a stem + inflection whose origin is, in some cases, auxiliary + subject pronoun.

One such inflection, the so-called pseudo-participial, stem-*j/w*, was probably a vestigial form lying outside the regular verb system. One also finds the basic patterns of suffixal conjugation, stem-SBJ (*sǧm.f* = hear-SBJ) and stem-*n*-SBJ (*sǧm.n.f* = hear-*n*-SBJ), together with three other conjugations stem-*k3*-SBJ, stem-*ḫr*-SBJ, stem-*j.n*-SBJ which later superseded the basic ones in Middle Egyptian, thereby renewing the tense–aspect system.

The most ancient evidence of grammaticalization of a verb 'say' as a verb inflection is provided by the pseudo-participial inflection whose final morpheme *j* has been suggested to come from a verb *j* 'say' conjugated with prefixes (perhaps related to Cushitic *y 'say', see above 2.1.3.) (see M. Cohen 1922, Lefebvre 1955, Diakonoff 1965, Gardiner 1969, and D. Cohen 1984: 117, 123).

The three conjugations, stem-*k3*-SBJ, stem-*ḫr*-SBJ, and stem-*j.n*-SBJ, have been diachronically analyzed as: stem+auxiliary+subject pronoun (D. Cohen 1984: 130–6, Vernus 1988: 172). -*j*- 'say' (giving -*j.n*- when conjugated according to the stem-*n*-SBJ pattern) has been thought a possible source for the stem-*j.n*-SBJ conjugation. The other two conjugations, stem-*k3*-SBJ and stem-*ḫr*-SBJ, are also formed with auxiliaries (also used as main verbs in Middle Egyptian) with meanings akin to 'say': *k3* 'think, have in mind, intend' and *ḫr* 'shout'.[4] All three auxiliaries became grammaticalized as conjugational elements. They were first suffixed to the verb stem before subject pronoun. Two of them, *k3* and *ḫr*, even gained enough autonomy to precede the verb stem, with or without the subject attached to them. They became so-called "enunciative auxiliaries" (Vernus 1988: 172, 180), indicating the speaker's attitude towards the sentence, in the following forms: *k3*-SBJ-stem-SBJ or *k3*-stem-SBJ, *ḫr*-SBJ-stem-SBJ or *ḫr*-stem-SBJ.

The 3000-year history of Egyptian provides the best available evidence of all the steps to full grammaticalization by a transcategorial process, starting from a free syntactic construction (stem+auxiliary), through morphologization (verbal inflection), and on to the ultimate formation of a grammatical morpheme with a new semantic value (modal particle).

These etymological hypotheses, while highly probable, are as yet unproven. They are nevertheless significant in view of the parallels between Egyptian and the Cushitic verb system, where verbs meaning 'say' have also renewed the conjugation (see 2.1.3.).

2.3.2 *Later Egyptian/Coptic*

The constructions which gave rise to the Coptic verb system are attested in earlier stages of Egyptian. One of the most productive is etymologically a conjugated auxiliary 'do' plus an infinitive (see D. Cohen 1984: 126 ff.).

Already in Later Egyptian, the stem-SBJ and stem-*n*-SBJ conjugations mentioned above were vestigial, and when the verb root had more than three consonants, the stem-SBJ form was no longer used; it was replaced by a periphrasis formed with the auxiliary *irj* 'do':

(50) irj-i   smtj
do-1s.PERF examine
'I examined (the documents)'

This construction was generalized in later stages. By the end of a process which began as early as the Middle Empire, the structure of the verb system in Coptic, the latest attested stage of Egyptian, was radically changed. But by a process reminiscent of Cushitic, the conjugation of some kinds of the so-called 'form I' are historically based on an older verb conjugated in the original way, i.e. by suffixing possessive personal pronouns. The affixes of the new Coptic conjugation are *a* which comes from *i.irj.f*, the emphatic form of *irj* 'do', and *re* from *irj.f*, the subjunctive of the same verb. The tenses involved are exemplified with the verb *sōtm* 'hear':

Perfect I	*a-f-sōtm*
Perfect II	*nt-a-f-sōtm*
Habitual	*š-a-f-sōtm*
Optative	*ma-re-f-sōtm*
Final	*ta-re-f-sōtm*

The structural evolution here shows the same kind of renewal as in Egyptian and Cushitic, except that the verb 'do' is used instead of 'say'. The descriptions that follow show that the same process involving both 'say' and 'do' is at work today in a large variety of modern languages and language families in Africa. The semantic developments are also the same.

2.4 Other language groups

2.4.1 *Dongolese (Nubian)*

In Dongolese Nubian, a Nilo-Saharan language spoken in the Sudan, there is a compound conjugational form: invariable stem + conjugated verb 'say' (= -ε/-έ/ -ḗ). The stems can be interjections, onomatopoeias, or any word of Nubian or Arabic origin. Their stem is specific to the construction, and cannot be used independently (Armbruster 1960: 192). Armbruster (p. 32) notes that a "large [...] number of verbs in -ḗ should have been formed in the last 1000 years", since Old Nubian times.

The verb 'say' is clitic to the stem, but the stress is placed differently depending on the linguistic origin of the stem: 99% of Nubian bases are stressed, and -ε 'say' is unstressed, while the opposite occurs with Arabic bases. This could be indicative of differing degrees of grammaticalization, Arabic bases being less well integrated into the verb system, so that the compound form keeps the stress on the verb 'say' and its long vowel as when used as a main verb.[5] This is supported by the fact that almost all Arabic loanwords (99%) are conjugated in this way. Here are some examples of borrowings (Armbruster 1960: 246):

(51) ǧámm-ε
assembly-say
'to come together (one to another)'

(52) íngu fadl-ếran
these stay-say:3P.IPERF
'These are staying'

Armbruster classifies other stems into two different categories, which may also reflect differences in the degree of grammaticalization. (1) Nubian onomatopoeic stems with (C)VCC pattern, which he says are mostly intransitive (Armbruster 1960:192), cannot be used outside this construction; there are, however, a few transitive verbs: *kítt-ε* 'be silent', *gúrr-ε* 'rejoice', *úff-ε* 'blow' (intransitive and transitive). (2) Other transitive or intransitive bases (whose meanings outside this construction are not provided) have diverse morphological patterns: *bagáš-ε* 'step over' (transitive), *ǧíll-ε* 'think, remember' (transitive), *nếw-ε* 'breathe' (intransitive).

Dongolese uses another verb *an* 'say' to create compound conjugational forms. It "appears much less often than -ε" according to Armbruster (1960:271). Contrary to -ε, *an* is subject to combinative and semantic restrictions. It can only be suffixed to some word classes: adverbs, adjectives, participles, cardinal numerals, nouns indicating condition, and can only create verbs of "becoming":

(53) dúl-an
great/aged-say
'to become great, increase, grow old'

(54) mıssı-wέr-an
eye-one-say
'to become of fixed opinion' (lit. 'become one-eyed')

2.4.2 Omotic

In Kafa, an Omotic language, Cerulli (1951) mentions the use of a verb *y* 'say' to derive verbs from nouns or verbs, for example, *qaǧǧō y* 'refuse' (=*qaǧ*) and *čufačufā y* 'fumigate' (*čufō* 'smoke').

3. Languages outside East Africa

The use of 'say' and 'do' as auxiliary verbs for verb creation is not limited to East Africa. Discussions with our colleagues at the unit 'Langage, Langues et Cultures d'Afrique Noire' (LLACAN) have led us to conclude that other language families, spoken further west, are affected by this process.

Although the present distribution of the use of the descriptive compounds with 'say' and 'do' and their tendency to develop into verb inflection is without doubt largely due to areal diffusion, the extent of the phenomenon outside East Africa and the languages mentioned above is remarkable. Before concluding, we would like to cite three other languages: Kanuri (a Nilo-Saharan language spoken in Northern Nigeria), Aiki (a Nilo-Saharan language spoken in the south of Chad and north of the Central African Republic), and Hausa (a Chadic language spoken in northern Nigeria and southeastern Niger).

3.1 Kanuri (Saharan)

In Kanuri, where there are two verb classes, verb class 2 is inflected by a morpheme which is reconstructed as a verb 'say' (*ngin*), still in use as a main verb today. According to Hutchison (1981:225), "verb class 2 is virtually unlimited in size since any lexical item of Kanuri or of a contact language can today be inflected [in such a way]". Cyffer (1997:34) states that "more than 95% of verbs belong to this group. It is highly productive and all verbs introduced through innovation or borrowing belong to class 2."

Moreover, ideophones can be inflected in class 2 or be introduced by the full form of the verb *ngin* 'say' (Hutchison, p.229), a process clearly parallel to the one found in Afar and Amharic for instance:

(55) kàrə́gè-nzə́ (bàdàk) bádákcìn
heart-POSS.3S   is.beating
'His heart is beating (loudly)'

(56) kàrə́gè-nzə́   bádák (bádák) shìn
heart-POSS.3S   IDEO   say:3M.S.IPERF
'His heart is going badak badak'

Hutchison assumes that the class of ideophones was the first to be inflected in verb class 2.

3.2 Aiki (Maban)

In Aiki, Nougayrol (1989:141) mentions the existence of verbal periphrases formed with a stem and a verb *ir*. He translates this verb as '*do*', where the asterisk indicates that this sense cannot be found outside this particular context ('do' is otherwise εεs). The data presented here have led him to revise his translation, particularly in view of the fact that the paradigm of *ir* is, with the exception of the imperative singular form, strictly identical to that of a verb meaning 'say' (Nougayrol p.c.). His choice to translate *ir* as 'do' was dictated only by the irregularity of the imperative singular form and by the existence of a French equivalent using *faire* 'do' (e.g., *faire vite, faire risette*, etc.).

The stems used with *ir* may be Aiki bases, but unlike the situation in Afar or Amharic, no Aiki verb can be used as the base of a compound form. This also constitutes the only way to integrate loanwords into the verb system. Overall, 30% of the verbs recorded in the lexicon are formed solely by this procedure. Compound verbs can be both transitive and intransitive.

(57) lèèmbá dáráp ir
fabric dáráp say
'to weave' (< Chad Arabic *ḍarab čāqa* 'weave')

Compare also *jàr ir* 'breathe one's last (human being or animal)' and *ájép ir* 'astonish' (< Arabic). Furthermore, the verb *ir* can itself be in a derived form, namely in the reciprocal/reflexive form with a suffix *-o* only used in such compounds (e.g., *tə̀rìk ir-o* 'collide', cf. *tə̀rìk ir* 'knock, run against, into'), the factitive form with a prefix *nind-* (e.g., *bàŋ nind-ir* 'warm up', cf. *bàŋ ir* 'be warm'), and a rare derived form with a suffix *-ε* having no definable meaning (e.g., *jím ir-ε* 'rot, decay, turn septic').

Although rarely used, the verb *εεs* 'do' may also form compound verbs like *kòní εεs* 'be ashamed'. Like *ir*, *εεs* is used for both transitive and intransitive verbs. There is only one example of a doublet with 'say' and 'do', *gánás ir* and *gènísí εεs* 'hunt', where, however, the Arabic stems are different — in the former the verb *ganaṣ* 'hunt' and in the latter the verbal noun *ganīṣ* 'hunting'.

3.3 Hausa (Chadic)

In Hausa, the situation is similar, though compounding is less widespread and limited in the verb system to some conjugations where the verb *yi* 'do' is used as an auxiliary or a copula with nominals (Abraham 1962 and Caron p.c.).

In the perfect form, the stem, which is a *nomen actionis*, can only be introduced by the verb *yi*:

(58) sun yi kuukàa
they:PERF do crying
'They cried'

In the continuous, one finds the regularly formed inflection with the verbal noun

(59) yanàa shàafa-n bangòo
he:CONT rubbing-of wall
'He is whitewashing the wall'

or its counterpart in which the verbal noun of the verb *yi* is added

(60) yanàa   yî-n   shàafa-n   bangòo
    he:CONT doing-of rubbing-of wall
    'He is whitewashing the wall'

According to Caron (p.c.), the latter construction with *yi* is very productive as the marked emphatic counterpart of the former and can be used freely.

This is similar to the case cited above, where a regularly inflected verb has a counterpart formed with a stem and 'say' or 'do' (cf. Afar and Ethio-Semitic).

In addition, *yi* is a copula in predicative sentences:

(61) yā   yi tsàadā
    he:PERF do expensiveness
    'It is (too) expensive'

4. Discussion and conclusion

This typological study has linked geographically distant and genetically unrelated African languages having three common features: the use of 'say' and/or 'do' as a means of verb creation, the ability to grammaticalize the resulting compounds into verb inflection, and the absence of restrictions on the choice of the base component.

The involvement of verbs 'say' and 'do' in the process of renewal of the verb system has been remarked at various synchronic stages. This is an areal linguistic feature as the process is unknown in Semitic languages other than those spoken today in East Africa, namely Ethio-Semitic. This feature may thus be attributed to Cushitic influence.

The auxiliary verbs 'say' and 'do' used to create new verbs are integrated into various typological systems which vary with the language. We have thus far identified six such systems. We must, of course, recall that our tentative classification depends mainly on second-hand data not expressly collected to match our framework. While some languages may have to be reclassified after further research, the six-fold classification below should not be affected, though:

- the only auxiliary is a verb meaning 'say', never 'do' (Cushitic: Oromo, Beja; Ethio-Semitic: Zway; Omotic: Kafa; Old and Middle Egyptian; Nubian: Dongolese; Saharan: Kanuri);
- the only auxiliary is a verb meaning 'do', never 'say' (Later Egyptian, Coptic; Chadic: Hausa);
- the verbs 'say' and 'do' are in complementary distribution (Cushitic: Afar; Ethio-Semitic: Gunnän-Gurage, Argobba, Amharic, Ennemor, Selti, Wolan, Čaha, Muher, Tigre);

- the verbs 'say' and 'do' vary freely (Cushitic: Afar; Ethio-Semitic: Amharic, Tigre, Harari; Maban: Aiki);
- verb compounds with 'say' and 'do' may alternate with their simple equivalent (Cushitic: Afar, Oromo, Beja; Ethio-Semitic: Amharic, Gunnän-Gurage, Argobba, Tigre; Omotic: Kafa; Chadic: Hausa);
- 'say' and/or 'do' undergo morphological derivation (Cushitic: Afar; Ethio-Semitic: Gafat, Tigrinya, Gogot, Aymellel, Amharic, Ennemor, Selti, Wolan, Čaha, Muher, Tigre; Maban: Aiki).

The languages of East Africa bear witness to a recurrent process of grammaticalization, i.e. the use of quotative verbs meaning 'say' and active verbs meaning 'do' as auxiliaries in order to create new verbs of which they may ultimately become inflectional markers. This phenomenon has been recurring cyclically over more than 5000 years in Hamito-Semitic languages. It is also attested in varying stages of advancement in languages from other areas of Africa. Furthermore, the process exists elsewhere in the world, for instance in Chinese (*Waley and Armbruster* 1934), in Kambera (Klamer, this volume) for 'say', and in pidgins for 'do' (Mühlhäusler 1986:173).

Such an extension in space and time forces the linguist to consider the problem in terms of general linguistics, and not only in terms of areal diffusion, as for Ethio-Semitic and Cushitic. What is at stake here is the morphogenesis of the verb systems insofar as it can be envisaged from the standpoint of a general theory of the syntax and semantics of auxiliarization.

We will now consider how verb periphrases develop and change, then look at their values and functions. We will conclude with a tentative analysis of what makes 'say', 'do', and verbs of related meanings suitable for verb creation.

Our survey has shown an absence of restrictions on the terms used with the auxiliaries 'say' and/or 'do'. This differs from languages such as those of the Bantu family (Samarin 1971; Creissels 1997; Güldemann, this volume) or Cushitic Iraqw (Mous 1993:227–8, p.c.) where the periphrastic construction is limited to a specific lexical class, viz. ideophones. In the languages considered here, the stem may belong to a range of grammatical classes: bases may be verbs, nouns, adjectives, adverbs, phrases, ideophones, onomatopoeias. These differences reflect semantic restrictions on this periphrasis, or equivalently, restrictions on the ability of the two verbs to act as auxiliaries.

Languages which make use of both auxiliaries may also impose syntactic restrictions whereby the distribution of 'say' and 'do' may be free or complementary, according to whether intransitive or transitive verbs are to be formed. The data here suggest that only ideophones can be auxiliarized by either 'say' or 'do' without distinction. Further research is nevertheless needed to confirm this observation and clarify its semantic entailments.

Be that as it may, it would seem that the construction may originate not only with ideophones, as prior literature has remarked, but also with elements such as loanwords which initially have a peculiar status in the language (cf. Aiki and Dongolese Nubian).

Any item, whether its choice be categorially restricted or not, can be constructed with 'say' or 'do'. But when the base component is not morphologically modified, sometimes only the context or the intonation may clarify whether 'say' is used as a main quotative verb or as an auxiliary. In Tigre for instance, *baḥal bela* as in (48) may either mean 'to pardon, to excuse' or 'he said: 'pardon!''. In both cases, the syntactic construction is asyndetic, but both elements keep their own meaning in the latter. The difference between a solely asyndetic structure and an auxiliary structure is semantic, not formal: asyndeton involves the sum of two meanings, while the components of an auxiliary structure form a semantic unit.

Such constructions may also lead to the emergence of special verb paradigms where the two components of the periphrasis can still be identified. This is the case in all the contemporary languages studied here. In some of these, some verb inflections could themselves be derived from similar structures whose constituents can only be identified through reconstruction (cf. Egyptian, early Cushitic, Kanuri). The range of languages considered thus enables us to envisage the grammaticalization process diachronically at various stages, the last of which is full morphologization.

Synchronic degrees of auxiliarity correspond to diachronic stages of auxiliarization. By degrees of auxiliarity, we mean the semanto-syntactic constraints that govern the distribution of the auxiliary (restrictions on the class of the base constituent, or on the subject and/or object of the periphrasis). Stages of auxiliarization are the steps leading from main to auxiliary verb status, and perhaps ultimately to full morphologization. Note that this process does not prevent a verb from continuing to function as a main verb. Within our framework, one may consider that the synchronic restriction of the periphrasis to ideophones represents a first stage in the auxiliarization process. A given language may not go beyond this first stage, or any subsequent stage prior to full morphologization.

Thus, starting from what we may call a free creation, insofar as it depends on the speaker's personal strategy, the scope of auxiliarization may widen progressively until the construction becomes automatic or generalized and enters the language as an idiomatic construction.

Once integrated into the verb system, the periphrasis will be subjected to the internal pressure of this system, and to processes such as derivation, inflection, etc., like any other verb. Likewise, contextual phonetic attrition may affect the auxiliary structure as its frequency of use progresses, opening the way to full morphologization. Thus, in Afar, the juncture between the two components of the periphrasis is rarely audible and it is the unstressed clitic auxiliary that undergoes various assimilatory processes: shortening of geminated consonants, loss of vowels. Only under unusual speech conditions (emphasis, deliberate speech, stopping to look for the next word, etc.) or syntactic constraints (insertion of pronouns and adverbs) will the two components recover clearly separate identities. Yet, the transition to inflectional status is never inevitable and can be thwarted by various factors which modify the organization of the emerging system.

Thus, auxiliarity should not be dealt with as an invariant phenomenon, but from a dynamic perspective, i.e. as the result of a process that can be captured at different stages at different moments in the history of a language. 'Say' and 'do' are not alone in this.

The use of descriptive compounds has a very peculiar and characteristic function in the verb systems of the languages under consideration here. It is well known that tense, aspect, voice, mood, and modal notions in general are values conveyed by auxiliaries (cf. Guillaume 1964, Tesnière 1939, Benveniste 1974, and Heine 1993), but the specific values of 'say' and 'do' have received little attention in the literature. These are directly linked to a need for expressivity, often a driving force of change affecting forms with a high frequency of use. It is not by chance that 'say' and 'do' can be used with all verb inflections in languages of East Africa and elsewhere, and that they have a tendency to be used with all kinds of base constituents, resulting in a doubling of the whole conjugation, or even its replacement. Independently of any specific epistemic modal sense linked to particular patterns of auxiliaries or base constituents (cf., e.g., the attenuative and intensive values in Amharic), descriptive compounds are created to express the relationship between the discourse participants, as we saw in Afar.

The question thus arises why this particular intersubjective modal function happens to be expressed by structures using precisely 'say', 'do', and verbs of related meanings (including 'be' as in Saho where 'say' and 'be' are the same term, cf. Reinisch (1878); 'be' is, of course, the basis of historical change in the verb systems of many of the world's languages).

From a communication viewpoint, the expressive nature of an ideophone or a loanword may help to explain why a speaker selects a construction with 'say': the item is, as it were, "quoted", hence actualized in the language. Quoting is equivalent to posing an item as existing in the language. To say something is to make it be, to make it exist. A construction with 'say' reproduces an external sign standing for an event, be it phonic (as in the case of ideophones) or expressed by any item of the language (for instance a verb). This is parallel to the role of 'say' in reported discourse (see Klamer, this volume). Moreover, uttering a process may be equivalent to achieving it. Like any performative verb, 'saying' can therefore be 'doing' an action. At a certain level of abstraction, the three notions of 'be', 'say', and 'do' are identical. This semantic continuum is, as a matter of fact, also found when 'be', 'say', and 'do' are used as main verbs in certain languages. Apart from Saho mentioned above for 'be' and 'say', other languages may use either 'say' or 'do' to express either notion. In colloquial French both *faire* 'do' and *dire* 'say' can introduce direct speech. Such is also the case for Maltese *għamel* 'do'. On the other hand, in Yemeni dialectal Arabic, it is the verb *qāl* 'say' which may be used in the sense of 'do, make'. In Soqotri (a modern South Arabian language), the same verb *fɔ́mɔr* expresses both 'say' and 'do'. As far as periphrases with 'say' and 'do' are concerned, the possibility of using one or both verbs within a single language is syntactically motivated: in some languages, the valence of the base component is the determining criterion for the distribution of the auxiliaries; in others, this criterion plays no part, and only one of them, most often 'say', is used.

Understanding how descriptive compounds are formed not only leads to a better understanding of morphogenesis in a language or group of languages, but also to a more general awareness of how human language works. These features, which are common to languages with no genetic connection or areal contact, seem to derive from a process inherent in human language in general.

Notes

* We are indebted to Raymond Boyd, Bernard Caron and Pierre Nougayrol for fruitful discussions, and to Manfred von Roncador and Tom Güldemann for providing us with a rich bibliography and for valuable comments on this chapter. Last but not least, we would like to take this opportunity to thank the Eritrean authorities for facilitating our fieldwork, and all our language assistants, particularly Makki Houmedgaba, Kadiga Abdallah and Addaawa Hasan Ali.

1. Except Palmer's (1974) short study.
2. The authors' transcriptions have been retained throughout this chapter, except for Egyptian which has been harmonized with Vernus (1988).
3. Compare the examples (10b), (10c), (11), and (12) of Afar which do not have the intensive meaning.
4. Vernus (1988:172) gives them as all meaning 'say'.
5. Some Dongolese compounds also attest this process of grammaticalization in that they may have alternative stress on either the base or the verb 'say', for example, *wɛlés-ɛ* or *wɛlēs-ɛ́* 'leave, let be, abandon' (Armbruster 1960:192).

References

Abraham, Roy C. 1962 [1946]. *Dictionary of the Hausa language*. London: Hodder and Stoughton.

Afevork, Ghevre Jesus. 1905. *Grammatica delle lingua amarica: metodo pratico per l'ensegnamenta.* Roma: Tipografia dela R. Academia dei Lincei.
Afevork, Ghevre Jesus. 1911. *Il verbo amarico.* Roma: Tipografia Poliglotta Vaticana.
Armbruster, Charles H. 1908–20. *Initia amharica: an introduction to spoken Amharic.* Cambridge: Cambridge University Press.
Armbruster, Charles H. 1960. *Dongolese Nubian: a grammar.* Cambridge: Cambridge University Press.
Baeteman, Joseph. 1929. *Dictionnaire amarigna-français, suivi d'un vocabulaire français-amarigna.* Dire Daoua: Imprimerie St Lazare des rr. pp. Capucins.
Benveniste, Emile. 1974 [1965]. "Structures des relations d'auxiliarité". In *Problèmes de Linguistique générale II.* Paris: Gallimard, 177–93.
Bliese, Loren F. 1981. *A generative grammar of Afar* (=Summer Institute of Linguistics Publications in Linguistics 65). Arlington: University of Texas at Arlington.
Cerulli, Enrico. 1951. *Studi Etiopici IV: La lingua caffina.* Roma: Istituto per l'Oriente.
Cohen, David. 1983–5. "Rapports". In *Annuaires de l'Ecole Pratique des Hautes Etudes, IVe section.* Paris: Université de la Sorbonne.
Cohen, David. 1984. *La phrase nominale et l'évolution du système verbal en sémitique, étude de syntaxe historique.* Leuven: Peeters.
Cohen, David. 1988. "Couchitique — Omotique". In Perrot (ed.), 243–95.
Cohen, David, Marie-Claude Simeone-Senelle and Martine Vanhove. in prep. *Evolution des langues et morphogenèse I, Le cas des auxiliaires.*
Cohen, Marcel. 1922. "Sur la forme verbale égyptienne dite 'pseudo-participe'". *Mémoires de la Société de Linguistique de.* Paris 22: 242–56.
Cohen, Marcel. 1939. *Nouvelles études d'éthiopien méridional.* Paris: Champion.
Cohen, Marcel. 1970 [1936]. *Traité de langue amharique (Abyssinie).* Paris: Institut d'Ethnologie.
Cyffer, Norbert. 1997. "A survey of the Kanuri language". In Geider, Thomas (ed.), *Advances in Kanuri scholarship.* Köln: Rüdiger Köppe, 17–66.
Diakonoff, Igor M. 1965. *Semito-Hamitic.* Moscow: Nauka.
Gardiner, Alan H. 1969. *Egyptian Grammar.* Oxford: Oxford University Press.
Guillaume, Gustave. 1964 [1938]. "Théorie des auxiliaires et examen de faits connexes". In *Langage et Science du Langage.* Paris/ Quebec: Nizet/ Presses Universitaires de Laval, 73–86.
Hayward, Richard J. 1996. "Compounding in Qafar". *Bulletin of the School of Oriental and African Studies* 59,3: 525–45.
Heine, Bernd. 1993. *Auxiliaries: cognitive forces and grammaticalization.* Oxford: Oxford University Press.
Hetzron, Robert. 1977. *The Gunnän-Gurage languages.* Napoli: Istituto Orientale di Napoli.
Hutchison, John P. 1981. "Kanuri word formation and the structure of the lexicon". In Bender, M. Lionel and Thilo Schadeberg (eds.), *Proceedings of the 1st Nilosaharan Colloquium.* Dordrecht: Foris, 217–37.
Isenberg, Charles W. 1842. *Grammar of the Amharic language.* London: Christian Mission Society.

Junod, Henri A. 1933. "Le parler descriptif des Bantous". In *Comptes Rendus du Congrès de l'Institut International des Langues et des Civilisations Africaines*. Paris, 76–81.
Lefebvre, Gustave. 1955. *Grammaire de l'égyptien classique*. Le Caire: Institut Français d'Archéologie Orientale.
Leslau, Wolf. 1941. *Documents tigrigna (éthiopien septentrional): grammaire et textes*. Paris: Klincksieck.
Leslau, Wolf. 1956. *Etude descriptive et comparative du gafat (éthiopien méridional)*. Paris: Klincksieck.
Leslau, Wolf. 1959. *A dictionary of Moča (Southwestern Ethiopia)*. Berkeley and Los Angeles: University of California Press.
Longacre, Robert E. 1990. *Storyline concerns and word order typology in East and West Africa* (=Studies in African Linguistics. Supplement 10). Los Angeles: Department of Linguistics, University of California.
Morin, Didier. 1995. *"Des paroles douces comme la soie", introduction aux contes dans l'aire couchitique (bedja, afar, saho, somali)*. Leuven: Peeters.
Mous, Maarten. 1993. *A grammar of Iraqw*. Hamburg: Helmut Buske.
Mühlhäusler, Peter. 1986. *Pidgin and creole linguistics*. Oxford: Basil Blackwell.
Nougayrol, Pierre. 1989. *La langue des Aiki dits Rounga (Tchad — République Centrafricaine): esquisse descriptive et lexique*. Paris: Geuthner.
Palmer, Frank R. 1974. "Some remarks on the grammar and phonology of the 'compound verbs' in Cushitic and Ethiopian Semitic". In *IV Congresso Internazionale di studi Etiopici (Roma 10–15 aprile 1972), Tomo II (Sezione Linguistica)*. Roma: Academia Nazionale dei Lincei, 71–7.
Parker, Enid M. and Richard E. Hayward. 1985. *An Afar-English-French dictionary (with grammatical notes in English)*. London: School of Oriental and African Studies.
Perrot, Jean (ed.). 1988. *Les langues dans le monde ancien et moderne, langues chamitosémitiques*. Paris: Centre National de la Recherche Scientifique.
Praetorius, Franz. 1879. *Die amharische Sprache*. Halle: Buchhandlung des Waisenhauses.
Praetorius, Franz. 1894. "Über die hamitischen Sprachen Ostafrika's". *Beiträge zur Assyriologie und vergleichenden semitischen Sprachwissenschaft* 2: 312–41.
Raz, Shlomo. 1983. *Tigre grammar and texts*. Malibu: Undena.
Reinisch, Leo. 1878. *Die Sprache der Irob-Saho in Abessinien*. Wien: Karl Gerolds Sohn.
Roper, E.M. 1929. *Tu Beḍawiɛ: an elementary handbook for the use of Sudan government officials*. Hertford: Stephen Austin and Sons.
Samarin, William J. 1971. "Survey of Bantu ideophones". *African Language Studies* 12: 130–68.
Simeone-Senelle, Marie-Claude and Martine Vanhove. 1997. "La formation et l'évolution d'auxiliaires et particules verbales dans les langues sémitiques: les langues sudarabiques modernes et le maltais". In *Mémoires de la Société de Linguistique de Paris. Grammaticalisation et Reconstruction* (n.s.) 5: 85–102.
Stroomer, Harry. 1987. *A comparative study of three southern Oromo dialects in Kenya*. Hamburg: Helmut Buske.
Tesnière, Lucien. 1939. "Théorie structurale des temps composés". In *Mélanges de Linguistique offerts à Charles Bally*. Genève: Georg et Cie, 153–83.

Vanhove, Martine. 1993. *La langue maltaise, études syntaxiques d'un dialecte arabe "périphérique"*. Wiesbaden: Otto Harrassowitz.
Vernus, Pascal. 1988. "L'égypto-copte". In Perrot J. (ed.), 161–206.
Walker, C.H. 1928. *English-Amharic Dictionary*. London: The Sheldon Press.
Zaborski, Andrzej. 1975. *The verb in Cushitic*. Krakow: Nakladem Uniwersytetu Jagiellonskiego.

CHAPTER 12

When 'say' is not *say*
The functional versatility of the Bantu quotative marker *ti* with special reference to Shona*

Tom Güldemann
Universität Leipzig/Max-Planck-Institut für Evolutionäre Anthropologie

1. Introduction

Bantu possesses a verbal lexeme with a wide distribution in the family whose sound shape is reconstructed by Guthrie (1967–71) as *-ti*. In many languages it plays a prominent role in the domain of reported discourse, but it is also used in a great variety of other, frequently highly grammaticalized contexts. The treatment of this element in grammatical descriptions and dictionaries of various languages reveals its astonishing semantic and functional versatility and at the same time the enormous problems encountered by many scholars in assigning a consistent meaning to it.

This chapter attempts to bring order to the multitude of idiomatic uses and grammatical functions of *ti*. It is based predominantly on data from Shona, the major language of Zimbabwe, showing a particularly high functional load and discourse frequency of *ti*, but data from other genetically related languages are also incorporated. The findings of this analysis allow a semantic interpretation of *ti*, which is different from most of the meaning accounts of this element presently available in individual languages. My claim is that *ti* is not a canonical speech verb 'say' but was originally a lexical stem meaning 'be/do thus' with a strong performative and deictic connotation.

The implications of this lexical characterization in turn have an important bearing on theoretical approaches to grammaticalization processes observed cross-linguistically at the intersection of reported discourse and other functional domains. The data show in particular that the prevailing reconstruction of quotative markers and complementizers as earlier speech verbs cannot be taken as a kind of default account.

2. The traditional treatment of *ti* in Shona

2.1 Semantic characteristics

A summary of the previous lexical treatments of *ti* in Shona philology will serve as a useful starting point of the discussion. The principal entry for *ti* in the *Standard Shona Dictionary* by Hannan (1984:646) is as follows:

> -ti ... defective v[erb] Say. Think. Do. 2. ... Address a person with a term expressing relationship.

The four meanings given above are then illustrated by the author with the following examples:[1]

(1) nda-*ti* uya neni
    1s:PERF-X come:IMP COM:1s
    'I said: "Come with me!"'

(2) nda-*ti* zvimwe chi-poko
    1s:PERF-X perhaps COP:7-ghost
    'I thought that perhaps it was a ghost.'

(3) tai-*ti* mu-rume ku-tsvaga namo
    1P:HAB.PST-X 1-man INF-search beeswax
    mu-dzimai ku-onga ndarama
    1-wife INF-extract.gold gold
    'What we used to do was this: the man went in search of beeswax, his wife panned gold.'

(4) u-no-mu-*ti*-i
    2s.SBJ-PRS-1OBJ-X-what
    'What [presumably: kin] relationship has he to you?'

The main body of the entry, however, consists of a long list of uses and illustrating examples which reveals that *ti* is a functionally versatile element of great grammatical importance.

A similar approach is taken in another extensive characterization of this element by Dale (1972:122ff.). He states that 'the verb -TI (say, think or name) has a wide range of uses in Shona ...' and lists twenty 'common applications' of this lexical item.

That the meaning of *ti* cannot easily be accounted for by an obvious monosemic analysis becomes also evident in Fortune (1955: §§774–83, 780–3, 785–8, 814–5). This reference grammar also gives great attention to the verb demonstrating again that its description is not an exclusively lexical problem. Fortune's short definition of *ti* is as follows:

-*ti* is a fully conjugated verb with a large variety of uses and meanings. Its primary significance seems to be 'act' or 'do'. This covers activity which is mental (to think), and verbal (to say), as well as other more complex forms of activity. (Fortune 1955:346)

Given that all the above translation equivalents of *ti* are semantically very general and that it has in addition a wide range of clearly idiomatic and grammatical functions, it cannot surprise that Shona scholars fell back upon a descriptive approach by listing its many different uses rather than providing a unitary meaning account.

2.2 Grammatical characteristics

The stem *ti* is not only complicated in semantic terms; it also displays marked grammatical properties. As stated by Fortune, *ti* inflects via prefixing for subject cross-reference and tense–aspect categories like any other Shona verb. Nevertheless, it is far from being a canonical verb stem. While normal verbs possess an inflectionally changing final vowel and can be extended by derivational suffixes, the stem form of *ti* is invariable. This unusual morphological behavior motivates its characterization as a conjugationally 'deficient'/'defective' verb.

The stem *ti* also has another peculiar property in one of its central uses, namely when it introduces reported discourse and occurs in its assumed core meaning 'say'. In this context to be called here 'quotative construction', it has a marked valence behavior: only the addressee of the speech act can be its second participant. Accordingly, it is only this syntactic argument that can be cross-referenced in the inflected verb form by a prefixed object concord.

(5) raka-mu-*ti* ...
5SBJ:REM.PST-1OBJ-X
'It said to him, "..."' (Chifamba 1982:11–5)

A nominal constituent potentially referring to speech or content of speech is not a complement of this verb so that it cannot be pronominalized in a *ti*-clause. Compare in this respect the following examples:

(6) *ndi-cha-chi-*ti*
1S.SBJ-FUT-7IA.OBJ-X
'I will say it.'

(7) *waka-a-*ti*   ma-zita aya
2S.SBJ:REM.PST-6OBJ-X 6-name 6:DEM
'You said those names.'

(8) a-no-*ti* chi-Shona
    3S-PRS-X 7-PROP
    'He says, "Chishona."' (*He speaks in Shona/the Shona language.)

In fact, any following word referring to something other than an addressee is consistently outside the direct extension of *ti* and outside the syntactic frame of such a quotative construction. This even applies to a potentially adverbial expression:

(9) aka-*ti*   zvikuru
    3S:REM.PST-X much/extensively
    'He said, "Zvikuru."' (*He said/spoke a lot.)

Such a syntactic behavior — not really uncommon for verbs used with reported discourse (see *Munro* 1982) — shows that one is not confronted with a canonical speech verb like, for example, the English lexeme *say*.

3. The functions of *ti* in Shona

3.1 The verb *ti* in predicative and related contexts

Although irregular, the stem *ti* has the basic properties of a verb. Accordingly, it is primarily used as a finite predicate nucleus of a verbal clause. These uses will be discussed subsequently. While the contexts involving *ti* are presented in traditional treatments in fairly unstructured lists of often more than a dozen different uses, I have grouped them according to a smaller number of functional domains. These are first of all defined by the type of constituent that follows *ti*. It serves to:

1. introduce reported discourse,
2. mark sentential complementation and related clause linkage,
3. introduce ideophones and related expressions,
4. identify an entity by name and introduce nominal lists,
5. introduce expressions of quality and manner,
6. foreground states of affairs on the level of discourse in general and adverbial clause linkage in particular.

3.1.1 *Reported discourse*

The use of *ti* in reported discourse will be examined at the beginning of the presentation as it is one of its most salient functions often inducing scholars to view this lexeme primarily as a speech verb (compare in this respect Hannan's and Dale's short definitions). The examples (1), (5), (8), and (9) demonstrate that *ti* is used as the predicative nucleus of a quotative construction where it can be viewed as the default marker.

In Shona, this construction type does not need to be subject to formal changes when the reported speech is rendered in indirect style. That is, it does not necessarily covary with different categories of reported discourse. Indirect style is discernible first of all by quote-internal adjustments affecting such deictic shifters as pronouns and tense–aspect markers. The following examples demonstrate this:

(10) ri-ka-*ti* rai-da ku-mbo-tsvaga mu-nhurume
      5-SEQ-X 5:HAB.PST-want INF-at.first-search 1-man
      'And it said that it wanted to look first for the man.' (Chifamba 1982:10–15)

(11) va-chi-*ti* va-ri.ku-ndo-guta
      2-SIM-X 2-PROG-go.and-become.satisfied
      'Thinking that they would become satiated.' (Chifamba 1982:5–10)

A variety of construction types employing *ti* are highly conventionalized, idiomatic expressions. Some of them are structurally and semantically so close to reported discourse, however, that they can safely be viewed as specialized uses of the above quotative construction together with a specific type of quote.

One such idiom is called by Dale (1972:134) 'action that is attempted but thwarted'. Here, the *ti*-clause is followed by a subjunctive verb form expressing direct or indirect speech. This structure is an instance of the widespread expression of *intention* by means of reported discourse. The special 'frustrative' connotation is conveyed by an additional clause expressing the ultimate failure of the attempted action.

(12) ma-kudo aka-*ti* ti-dye ma-barwe ndoku-furwa
      6-baboon 6:REM.PST-X 1P-eat:SUBJ 6-maize CONS-be.shot
      'The baboons tried to eat the maize but they were shot' [lit.: '... said, "Let's eat the maize!" and were shot.'] (Hannan 1984:646)

When internal conflict or hesitation is to be expressed, the capacity of reported discourse to render mental awareness is again employed in a fixed correlative expression using the noun *mwoyo* 'heart' as the subject of *ti*:

(13) mw-oyo waka-*ti* chi-enda ku-basa
      3-heart 3:REM.PST-X POL-go:IMP LOC-work
      mu-mwe u-ka-*ti* chi-vata
      3-other 3-SEQ-X POL-sleep:IMP
      'He was torn between going to work and sleeping.' [lit.: 'One heart said, "Go to work!" and the other said, "Sleep!"'] (Dale 1972:132)

Another use of *ti* clearly pertaining to the domain of reported discourse is characterized by Dale (1972:127) as follows:

Shona has a great capacity for dramatizing speech. It frequently puts words into the mouth of the agent, in the manner of reported speech, which were never in fact enunciated. An obvious example is that where the agent is not human yet the emotion expressed is rendered in indirect [or direct] speech.

(14) aka-tarisa   mu-hari ru-te   ru-ka-*ti* uya
     1:REM.PST-look   INE-POT 13-saliva 13-SEQ-X   come:IMP
     ti-ende
     1P-go:SUBJ
     'He looked into the pot and saliva started to form.' [lit.: 'He looked into the pot and the saliva said/thought, "Off we go!"'] (Dale 1972: 127)

As name and description suggest, 'dramatizing speech' serves to express story line events in vivid parts of narratives and is especially salient in story peaks.

The use of *ti* 'address a person with a term expressing relationship' mentioned by Hannan and exemplified in (4) above is also proposed to belong here. Although more conclusive information is needed, the phrase appears to be a specialized naming construction by means of reported discourse. The relationship term is not the mere complement of *ti*, but rather instantiates the quotation of a conventionalized label for a certain entity, here a kin-related human being. The answer to example (4) above would be literally something like 'I say to/call him "Father"'.

Another conventionalized structure involving reported discourse serves to describe a quality. The tense–aspect and person category of the *ti*-form and the copulative in the following quote are necessary ingredients to render this idiom:

(15) ma-zino ku-sviba   wai-*ti*   i-tsito
     6-tooth INF-be.black   2s:HAB.PST-X COP-charcoal
     'His teeth were as black as charcoal', i.e. you would say/[think] it is charcoal. (Dale 1972: 130)

3.1.2 *Sentential complementation and related clause linkage*

Simple quotative constructions as given above can be paraphrased by an expression in which the semantic aspect of the matrix verb and the syntactic orientation toward the following quote are structurally bisected. That is, a specialized speech or cognition verb is followed by some form of the semantically generic quotative verb *ti*. Especially with indirect reported discourse, the form of *ti* is the verbal noun *kuti* consisting of the noun prefix of class 15 and the plain verb stem. Compare the following versions of the examples (10) and (11) with quotative constructions for indirect discourse:

(10') ri-ka-*ti* > °ri-ka-taura ku-*ti*
      5-SEQ-X   5-SEQ-say INF-X
      'and said that'

(11')   va-chi-*ti* > °va-chi-funga ku-*ti*
        2-SIM-X   2-SIM-think INF-X
        'thinking that'

This construction is not only prominent in indirect reported discourse but is also essential for the domain of sentential complementation (Fortune 1955:406f., 416; Dale 1972:126). It is used with a wide range of verbs of speech, cognition, perception, and obligation. Mostly depending on the meaning of the matrix verb, the sentences introduced by *kuti* can be of variable illocutionary type, that is, realis and irrealis clauses, imperatives, or polar and constituent questions. Their structure is largely as if they were uttered independently. Clause complexes expressing result and purpose are also rendered by this construction. Below are various examples for these functions:

(16)   ha-ndi-zivi   ku-*ti* a-kura   zvaka-dii
       NEG-1s-know:PRS INF-X 1:PERF-grow 8MA:STAT-be.how
       'I don't know how big he is.' (Dale 1972:126)

(17)   i-one   ku-*ti* chi-i   chai-itika
       9-see:SUBJ INF-X COP:7IA-Q 7:REL:HAB.PST-happen
       'So she may see what was happening...' (Chifamba 1982:11–33)

(18)   va-chi-da   ku-*ti* va-go-shaya   nzira
       2-SIM-want INF-X 2-possibly-loose way
       'Intending that they possibly would go astray.' (Chifamba 1982:5–19)

(19)   va-rase   v-ana   ku-*ti* va-zo-rega   ku-tambudzika
       2-leave:SUBJ 2-child INF-X 2-FUT-leave INF-be.afflicted
       'They would leave the children so that they would no longer be in pain.' (Chifamba 1982:5–7)

A comparison of these data with the treatments of lexical items used as quotative markers in other languages such as Lord (1976), Frajzyngier (1984), Heine and Reh (1984:276), Saxena (1988), Crowley (1989), Ebert (1991), Heine, Claudi and Hünnemeyer (1991:216, 246–7), Plag (1992), Lord (1993:151–213), Heine *et al.* (1993:190ff), Saxena (1995), Frajzyngier (1996:146–57), and various contributions in this volume makes it clear that *ti* shares many functional properties with comparable elements. The wide cross-linguistic evidence suggests that there exists a universal grammaticalization complex of *quotation* in the sense that a quotative construction is a frequent source of more grammaticalized strategies of sentential complementation and other related types of clause linkage. Shona is certainly another exemplary case.

However, the majority of the above works go further in their analysis and give for many quotative elements an ultimate origin in a speech verb. The universal grammaticalization chain is presented most frequently as follows:

> verb 'say' > quotative marker > complementizer > result/purpose clause marker

Does the fact that the situation encountered in Shona regarding the quotation complex is identical to previous findings mean that it is also an instance of the so often assumed grammaticalization chain that starts with a speech verb source? Before this question can be answered, the many additional functions of *ti* must be considered. These were, after all, responsible for the vague lexical characterization of *ti* by previous Shona scholars; they never viewed *ti* as having the exclusive meaning 'say'.

3.1.3 *Ideophones and ideophonic expressions*

Shona is like many other Bantu languages rich in ideophones. This separate lexical category is extensively discussed in Fortune (1962, 1971). Suffice it to say here that these largely uninflected words are used to invoke the mental image of a state of affairs, possibly including even the type of participant, in contexts of vivid and expressive language. They are functionally close to verbs in predicative use and, unsurprisingly, can be derived from them (see (21) below). In order to embed such a word into discourse and give it predicative force, different strategies are available. The most important one is a *ti*-clause (see Fortune 1955:421f., Dale 1972:128f.) illustrated in the examples below:

(20)　mu-komana aka-*ti*　　zii　　　　a-chi-funga
　　　1-boy　　1:REM.PST-X IDEO:be.quiet 1-SIM-think
　　　'The boy lapsed into silence while he thought.' (Dale 1972:128)

(21)　va-*ti*　　　　fambei　　　mu-sango-mo　　　　raka-mu-ti
　　　2:DEP:ANT-X walk:IDEOR INE-woodland-INE:ANA 5SBJ:REM.PST-1OBJ-X
　　　'After having walked a bit further into the forest it said to him.'
　　　(Chifamba 1982:11–5)

A *ti*-clause introducing an ideophone is another rare context where an object concord can appear on this verb. Here, it always refers to the patient or experiencer of the encoded event.

(22)　imbwá yáka-í-*ti*　　　　nyama mu-mbá　pikú
　　　9.dog　9SBJ:REM.PST-9OBJ-X 9.meat INE-house IDEO:take.up
　　　'The dog took the meat from the house.' (Fortune 1971:254)

The idiom labeled by Dale (1972:129) 'sudden physical contact with a thing, e.g. grabbing or greedily consuming' is not yet completely understood. Following a proposal by N.C. Dembetembe (p.c.), it is presented here in a preliminary fashion as an ideophonic construction. A pronoun preceded by the comitative marker *na* follows the *ti*-clause. It is possible that the affected object is in addition referred to by a noun as is the case in the example below:

(23) mu-kadzi aka-*ti* na-hwo hwahwa
   1-woman 1:REM.PST-X COM-14:ANA 14.beer
   'The woman set about drinking the beer.' (Dale 1972:129)

3.1.4 *Identification and nominal lists*

Another domain of *ti* is to identify an entity by its name and to introduce a list of nominal entities (Dale 1972:133). The following examples exemplify this:

(24) va-nhu vaka-enda ku-musha va-*ti*
   2-person 2:REL:REM.PST-go LOC-home.village 2:PERF-X
   baba mwanakomana wake no-muroora
   father son   his COM-daughter.in.law
   'The people who had gone home were [as follows:] the father, his son and the bride.' (Dale 1972)

(25) pa-va-sikana ava vaka-uya pai-*ti*
   16ADE-2-girl 2:DEM 2:REL:REM.PST-come 16:HAB.PST-X
   va-refu va-pfupi ...
   2-tall 2-short
   'Among the girls who came were the following, tall ones, short ones ...' (Dale 1972:133)

3.1.5 *Expressions of quality and manner*

A *ti*-clause can also be followed by an expression describing or specifying the quantity, quality, or manner of the referent encoded in the *ti*-form as subject. The descriptive constituent can be of variable length and structural complexity. Often it consists of more than one clause. Compare the following example:

(25) motokari iyi i-no-*ti* u-ka-famba na-yo
   9.car 9:DEM 9-PRS-X 2S-COND-go COM-9:ANA
   no-ku-svika mu-matope ha-u-nyuri
   COM-INF-arrive INE-mud NEG-2S-sink:PRS
   'What this motor-car does is this, if you travel in it and reach a boggy spot you will not sink.' (Hannan 1984:646)

In Manyika dialects, *ti* replaces *va* 'be(come)' in expressing the frequency of events:

(26) ka-*ti*   ka-tatu
   11QUAN:PERF-X 11-three
   'That makes it three times.' (Hannan 1984:646)

3.1.6 *Emphasized states of affairs and marked adverbial clause linkage*

The domain treated in this section is very extensive and complex. Its common denominator is that *ti* serves to foreground and emphasize the state of affairs it introduces. Thus, it conveys a contrast to other information of the discourse. This is closely connected with the general cataphoric introductory function shown in 3.1.1+3+4+5 and a treatment of a particular use to follow separate from one exemplified previously will sometimes appear arbitrary. However, the bias of *ti*-uses discussed here towards operating more frequently on a higher level of discourse and clause linkage is unmistakable. Again, the constituent being under the scope of *ti*, that is, the emphasized and foregrounded information, can be a simple clause or a sequence of several clauses.

Hannan's (1984:646) information that *ti* 'emphasizes events or facts through idiomatic use of *oti*, *kwoti*' would be an instance where a state of affairs is contrasted against some information available in the pragmatic context. The fixed *ti*-clause is the 3rd-person singular or impersonal form of a verbal category called *exclusive* in Shona grammars. It is called here *initiative* as it usually expresses the exact commencement of an event — often translatable as 'now'. In a *ti*-clause, it serves presumably as a pragmatic hedge vis-à-vis the emphasized statement. Compare the following example where the addressee of the utterance is apparently reminded of his responsibilities presumably because he somehow negates or neglects them:

(27) kwo-*ti* v-ana ndo-va-ko
 IP:INIT-X 2-child COP-2:ASS-2S/POSS
 'The point [now] is, the children are yours.' (Hannan 1984:646)

The following example is a construction where *ti* enhances the expression of restrictive focus which is translated as 'just, only'.

(28) va-mwe va-no-*ti* ku-ngo-dzvuta vo-dhakwa
 2-some 2-PRS-X INF-just-sip 2:INIT-get.drunk
 'Some people just take a sip and at once get drunk.' (Hannan 1984: 646)

The emphasizing character of *ti* also has led to a process of auxiliarization in the expression of marked verbal categories. Hyman and Watters (1984) observed that certain categories are inherently focussed and pragmatically sensitive in their use. Among them are the *perfect* with the meaning 'already'/'not yet' and the *experiential* conveying 'ever'/'never'. In Shona, these two functions can only be expressed with the help of quite complex periphrastic constructions. The most important one is a sequence of a perfect form of *ti* and a dependent verb form encoding the communicated state of affairs (see Fortune 1955:353, Dale 1972:131). Two dependent taxis forms after *ti* are possible: *anterior* (the semantic and formal counterpart of a main clause perfect) and *coincidence* (the counterpart of a main clause initiative, see above). The following examples have anterior forms:

(29) wa-*ti* wa-mbo-enda ku-Ingirandi here
2S:PERF-X 2S:DEP:ANT-at.first-go LOC-PROP PQ
'Have you ever (yet) been to England?' (Dale 1972:77)

(30) ha-va-sa-*ti* va-ya kubva
NEG-2:PERF-NEG-X 2:DEP:ANT-come from
ku-ndo-tsvaga ma-roro
INF-go.and-search 6-PLANT
'They haven't returned yet from looking for maroro.' (Chifamba 1982:5–24)

To facilitate a better understanding of the above and following examples, the notion *dependent verb form* must be explained (see Güldemann (1997a, b) for a more extensive discussion of this problem): Clause linkage does not need to be expressed in Shona syndetically or even segmentally. Especially the expression of adverbial hypotaxis (and relative clauses) can be achieved through changes in the verb form only and is to a large extent a conjugational phenomenon. A dependent form can be distinguished from a main clause form in the majority of inflectional categories through a distinctive suprasegmental pattern (glossed in examples by DEP or REL behind the subject cross-reference). Only with the categories of *sequential* and *simultaneous* taxis (glossed as SEQ and SIM, respectively) the marking device is a special segmental verb prefix.

The above periphrastic construction has an additional function. It can itself be subject to the strategy of asyndetic hypotaxis in that the *ti*-clause is also suprasegmentally subordinated. Such a structure with stacked dependent verb forms is the only possibility to express 'before'-clauses in Shona:

(31) va-sa-*ti* va-svika ku-tsime mu-komana
2:DEP:ANT-NEG-X 2:DEP:ANT-arrive LOC-well 1-boy
aka-taurira hanzvadzi ya-ke
1:REM.PST-speak.to 9.sibling 9:ASS-1/POSS
'Before they had arrived [lit.: not yet having arrived] at the well, the boy spoke to his sister.' (Chifamba 1982:9–13)

While the above uses demonstrate the foregrounding function of *ti* against a wider communicative context, the following constructions can be analyzed as cases where a state of affairs is contrasted against some information in another adjacent clause. Here, *ti* becomes important for Shona clause linkage. One such case has already been discussed in 3.1.1 above as *frustrated intention*. This expression has regularly a reading of adversative linkage. This is triggered by the contrast holding between the emphasized intention clause involving *ti* and the following sequential having vis-à-vis this intention a connotation of counterexpectation. Such a construction can be conveniently paraphrased by something like 'x did want to/tried hard to/almost . . . , but . . .' and acquires even a concessive connotation like 'Although x did . . . , . . .'. Another representative example follows:

(32) aka-do-*ti*   a-teme   gomana
      1:REM.PST-almost-x 1-strike:SUBJ 5.big.lad
      ri-ka-bva   ra-nzvenga
      5-SEQ-turn.out 5:DEP:ANT-dodge
      'He tried hard to strike the big lad, but he dodged.' (Dale 1972:134)

A similar contrast between two events is achieved when a sequential *ti*-clause accompanied by a main clause verb form follows a preceding clause encoding some event on the story line (see Fortune 1955:348, Dale 1972:133). Again, an adversative relation between the two encoded events emerges. Here, it is the clause introduced by *ti* that conveys the unexpected state of affairs.

(33) mu-komana uya   ndoku-tsvaga no-ku-tsvaga   basa
      1-boy   1:DEM CONS-search COM-INF-search 5.work
      a-ka-*ti* a-ri-shaya
      1-SEQ-x 1SBJ:PERF-5OBJ-lack
      'That boy looked and looked for work and did not find it [*but did not find it*].' (Hannan 1984:646)

(34) a-chango-tanga ku-tema huni   ri-ka-*ti* ra-uya
      1-just-start   INF-cut firewood 5-SEQ-x 5:PERF-come
      zi-nyoka
      5AUG-snake
      'He had just started cutting wood, when along came a huge snake.' (Dale 1972:133)

According to Hannan (1984:646), there is a form *kukati* with an impersonal subject concord *ku-* of class 17 no longer having subject agreement with the following clause. Such a generalized form similar to a conjunction indicates an ongoing process of grammaticalization of this clause linkage type.

Another instance where *ti* serves to emphasize a state of affairs vis-à-vis another is when a coordinate clause type 'both . . . and . . .' is to be expressed (see Fortune 1955:349f., Dale 1972:132). The only way to convey this in Shona is a construction of two *ti*-clauses the second being in the sequential form. This correlative structure is motivated by the fact that here both conjuncts have to be highlighted. A comparison with (13) in 3.1.1 above reveals that this expression is structurally identical with that used for internal conflict.

(35) tsika   iyi   yaka-*ti*   ku-naka   i-ka-*ti*   ku-ipa
9.custom 9:DEM 9:STAT-X INF-be.good 9-SEQ-X INF-be.bad
'This custom is both good and bad.' (Fortune 1955:349)

The elements *kutoti*, *kusati* or *kusatoti* being morphologically complex verbal nouns of *ti* are followed by a dependent form and serve to mark clause linkage relations like 'only after', 'until', and 'unless' (Fortune 1955:411). There is a close semantic link to the marked verbal categories of perfect and experiential which is also expressed by *ti*-constructions: The clause following *ti* always focuses on the final achievement of some state of affairs and there is a frequent interaction with irrealis contexts such as negation or question:

(36) ha-u-mbo-pfeka   ma-bhurukwa ma-refu
NEG-2S-at.first-wear:PRS 6-trousers   6-long
ku-sa-to-*ti*   wa-pedza   giredhi re-chi-nomwe
INF-NEG-already-X 2S:DEP:ANT-finish 5.grade 5:ASS-7IA-seven
'You will wear long trousers only after you have passed grade seven.' [You do not wear long trousers, before/as long as you have not yet passed grade seven.] (Hannan 1984:294)

(37) ha-ti-nga-endi   asi   ku-to-*ti*   a-svika
NEG-1P-POT-go:PRS except INF-already-X 1:DEP:ANT-arrive
'We may not go unless he comes.' [We may not go except he has already arrived.] (Hannan 1984:295)

The clause preceded by the latter *ti*-conjunctives can be pre- or postposed to the main clause. All the following *ti*-constructions have a fixed order configuration. The underlying structure is as follows: One constituent is a complex sentence consisting of an initial dependent and a final main clause (the boundary between these two clauses will be marked in the following schemas and examples by #). This phrase, which is itself a complete utterance, is in turn introduced by a *ti*-clause. The following schema and example illustrate this:

[ti-clause] [(dependent clause) # (main clause)]

(38) ai-*ti*   kana a-chi-taura #
1:HAB.PST-X if 1-SIM-speak
wai-ngo-nzwa   tsamwa
2S:HAB.PST-just-perceive sound.of.displeasure
'Whenever he spoke, you would hear expressions of annoyance.' [It used to be like this: when he spoke, ...] (Dale 1972:130)

The *ti*-clause has a syntactic scope over the entire complex sentence — the latter as a whole being the information to which the hearer's attention is drawn. This analysis explains why the order of clauses cannot be reversed — for example, placing the main clause before the sequence *ti*-clause + dependent clause as in (36) and (37) — and why the medial clause can in spite of the occurrence of the initial *ti*-clause have a conjunction on its own — as in (38) with *kana* 'if'.

That being said regarding the original syntactic structure, the configuration within this complex of three clauses is more intricate. This is first of all due to an intimate interlacing of semantic features between *ti*-clause and following dependent clause in that there often exist subject coreference and a unitary tense–aspect orientation. The result is the more or less clear impression of a closer bond between these two initial clauses against the final main clause. This semantic constellation also has syntactic consequences in that an incipient boundary shift among the three constituents can be observed vis-à-vis the above structure schema:

[(ti-clause) (dependent clause)] # [main clause]

In fact, the prevailing analysis of this construction type in previous Shona studies is that the medial dependent clause is subordinated directly by the *ti*-clause — an analysis fostered by the observation that *ti* is capable of controlling a dependent verb form (see above). As a result, the *ti*-clause is more and more perceived as a conjunctive element serving exclusively the subordination of the medial background clause. This impression is increased by the recurrent phenomenon of reducing the paradigmaticity of the *ti*-clause toward an inflectionally more general phrase: either its subject concord becomes the impersonal *ku* or its verbal noun form *kuti* is employed. Both cases lead to the loss of subject agreement between *ti*-clause and medial dependent clause.

The introductory and emphasizing function of *ti* still transpires in that the construction always has a connotation of focus on some piece of information in the specific adverbial relation vis-à-vis less marked clause-linkage devices. The type of relation mostly depends on the tense–aspect feature of the *ti*-clause.

For example, when the *ti*-clause is used in the past habitual (as in (38) above, compare also Dale 1972: 130) or in the present (as in (39) below), it is not just a simple temporal relation that is expressed. Instead, there is a clear focus on the *regular coincidence of two events* and the appropriate translation of the adverbial relation is 'whenever':

(39) ku-no-*ti* va-ka-svika   # ku-no-bva
      IP-PRS-X 2-COND-arrive   IP-PRS-turn.out
      kwa-tanga   ku-naya
      IP:DEP:ant-start INF-rain
      'Whenever they come, it starts raining.'

The inseparable connection between the use of *ti* as an introductory device and certain uses as a quasi-conjunction, is evident from a comparison between (39) and (25) in 3.1.5 serving the expression of quality: the two are structurally and semantically identical.

If the *ti*-clause has the auxiliary prefix *zo*, the focus in the clause relation is on a *specific time point* (see Fortune 1955:411, Dale 1972:79,124). This is translated conveniently by 'when eventually', 'when finally', 'and then when':

(40) ku-zo-*ti*   mu-sikana a-uya   #
INF-come.and-x 1-girl   1:DEP:ANT-return
aka-shamiswa
1:REM.PST-be.astonished
'When the girl eventually returned, she became astonished.' (Chifamba 1982:8–5)

The plain verbal noun *kuti* can also be preposed to such a complex sentence whereby a very general temporal or conditional relation is expressed.

(41) ku-*ti* u-ci-manya # rega   ku-ceuka
INF-X 2S-SIM-run   leave:IMP INF-turn.around
'When you run, don't look around.' (Fortune 1955:411)

As the *ti*-form is here morphologically less marked than in all the previous contexts it is not surprising that the semantic relation in the clause complex is the least specific. Recall that (41) without *kuti* is also a complete utterance with no difference in meaning. Only the discourse context could reveal why *kuti* with its function of emphasis would be used.

A clear discourse function can be identified for the following structure. When the *ti*-clause occurs in the remote past form which marks story line events it introduces a complex sentence whose final main clause is also in the remote past. A grammatically more general *ti*-clause with the impersonal subject concord of class 17 is also possible. Compare the following examples:

(42) vaka-*ti*   va-famba   chi-nhambwe chi-kuru # aka-ti
2:REM.PST-X 2:DEP:ANT-walk 7-distance   7-big   1:REM.PST-X
'What happened to them was this: having walked a long distance she said.' (Chifamba 1982:6–10)

(43) kwaka-*ti*   mi-edzi mi-tatu ya-pfuura   #
IP:REM.PST-X 4-month 4-three 4:DEP:ANT-pass
vaka-mu-tandanisa   pa-chikoro
2SBJ:REM.PST-1OBJ-expel ADE-school
'What happened was this, after three months there, he was expelled from the school.' (Hannan 1984:646)

The narrow syntactic scope of *ti* again reaches only over the two following clauses. However, if the occurrence of this construction is analyzed in texts, it can be observed that it tends to mark the boundary between larger thematic units of a narrative (cf. Güldemann 1997a: 47 ff., 57 ff.). It can therefore be said from a text-thematic viewpoint that the *ti*-clause acquires a scope over an entire paragraph. Significantly, when trying to elicitate a translation for the *ti*-clause alone, native speakers came up with something like 'some time elapsed' indicating that the hearer is orientated toward a different scene of the story by foregrounding a new subsequent event against the previous text. The whole construction is a kind of internally complex pivot between narrative paragraphs: the *ti*-clause serves to highlight the existence of a paragraph boundary, the medial dependent clause creates coherence between previous information and the initial event in the new paragraph, and the final main clause encoding this event sets the scene for what will happen next.

These are the most frequently described *ti*-constructions in the domain of adverbial clause-linkage. Note that *ti* in those cases where it is used in its verbal noun form is very close to its occurrence in sentential complementation discussed in 3.1.2 above. The major difference is that it is associated with a distinct order of the linked clauses. This is motivated by the fact that the subordinate clause in adverbial clause linkage does not depend on the verb in the main clause. Nevertheless, the isomorphism of the conjunctive element *kuti* in so many different contexts may well have had a cumulative effect in the development of *ti* toward a multi-purpose subordinator in Shona.

3.2 The verb *ti* in attributive and related contexts

The discussion has heretofore considered exclusively those constructions where *ti* is used predicatively. However, it can and frequently does occur also as an attribute of a nominal nucleus. As such, it can be either the predicative basis of a relative clause or, in the form of a verbal noun, the satellite of an associative construction. In the former structure, a finite form of *ti* is only marked by suprasegmental features as the predicate of a subject-relative clause. In the latter, the verbal noun *kuti* is treated like a nominal constituent by virtue of its morphological form. As a third structural possibility, the verbal noun of *ti* can be inflected by nominal prefixes. As a nominal modifier *ti* serves to:

1. introduce reported discourse,
2. mark sentential complementation and related clause linkage,
3. introduce ideophones and related expressions,
4. identify an entity by name and introduce nominal lists,
5. introduce expressions of quality and manner,
6. denote a specific quality or amount without a following constituent.

This list of domains of uses reveals when compared to that in 3.1 that most of the uses of *ti* in predicative contexts are also available when it is a nominal modifier.

The only differences are the occurrence of one new function under 6. and the lack of the foregrounding domain. Most functions have already been treated so that few remarks will be made to the examples below.

3.2.1 *Reported discourse*
Beside the possibility to use *ti* as a nominal modifier there is another structure worth mentioning in reported discourse. The following example shows that *kuti* can have the agentive prefix *nya* and then means 'the one/someone saying':

(44) nya-ku-*ti* ndi-ri mu-ngwaru aka-birwa
      AG-INF-X 1s-COP 1-clever   1:REM.PST-be.stolen
      'The one/someone who said/thought "I am clever!" was stolen sth.'

3.2.2 *Sentential complementation and related clause linkage*
Sentential complementation is achieved when the head noun denotes an abstract concept to which the verbal noun *kuti* can attribute a proposition. Compare the two examples below:

(45) zano   ro-ku-*ti*   va-zo-enda ku-sango
      5.idea 5:ASS-INF-X 2-FUT-go   LOC-woodland
      'The idea that they would go into the forest.' (Chifamba 1982:10–28)

(46) pfungwa yai-va   yo-ku-*ti*   v-ana
      9.thought 9:HAB.PST-be 9:ASS-INF-X 2-child
      vai-zo-dyiwa   ne-garwe
      2:HAB.PST-come.and.be.eaten AGV-crocodile
      'The intention was that the children would finally be eaten by the crocodile.' (Chifamba 1982:5–21)

With other head nouns, a reading of purpose can be found:

(47) ndi-no-ku-pa   mari   yo-ku-*ti*
      1s.SBJ-PRS-2s.OBJ-give 9.money 9:ASS-INF-X
      u-tenge   hembe
      2s-buy:SUBJ shirt
      'I give you money so that you may buy a shirt/... money for you to buy a shirt/... money you can buy a shirt with.'

Various conventionalized conjunctions have developed from this use, too (Fortune 1955:408f., Dale 1972:135–7). Compare the following items:

(48) so-ku-*ti*
      SIML-INF-X
      'as if'

(49) no-ku-*ti*   OR ne-zvo-ku-*ti*
 COM-INF-X   COM-8MA:ASS-INF-X
 'because'

(50) zvo-ku-*ti*
 8MA:ASS-INF-X
 'in such a way that, with the result that, so that'

(51) ne-mhaka yo-ku-*ti*   OR pa-musana po-ku-*ti*
 COM-9.guilt 9:ASS-INF-X   16ADE-back 16:ASS-INF-X
 'for the reason that'

(52) ne-nzira   yo-ku-*ti*
 COM-9.path 9:ASS-INF-X
 'by means of, on account of'

(53) no-ku-da   kwo-ku-*ti*
 COM-15INF-want 15:ASS-INF-X
 'on account of'

3.2.3 *Ideophones*

The following example shows that ideophones which are usually predicative can also be attributed to a noun when the *ti*-clause is in the relative form:

(54) dziva dema raka-*ti*   svii
 5.hole 5:dark 5:REL:STAT-X IDEO:grow.dark
 'a very dark hole' (Chifamba 1982: 5–13)

3.2.4 *Identification and nominal lists*

The following examples illustrate the function of *ti* in identifying and listing nominal entities. It can often be translated as 'namely' or 'that is'.

(55) izwi   iro   ro-ku-*ti*   maDzviti
 5.word 5:DEM 5:ASS-INF-X PROP
 'That word, namely Matabele.' (Dale 1972: 136)

(56) ndaka-ona   shiri   zhinji   dzi-no-*ti*
 1S:REM.PST-see 10.bird 10:many 10:REL-PRS-X
 hanga   makwari   njiva ...
 guinea.fowl frankolins doves
 'I saw many birds namely, guinea fowl, frankolins, doves ...' (Dale 1972: 133)

3.2.5 *Expressions of quality and manner*

The use of an attributive *kuti* to introduce descriptions is in form and function very close to its use in sentential complementation and related contexts. Already a purpose clause reading as in (47) above can hardly be distinguished from a *relative* modifier of instrument. Sometimes, such a clause clearly gives information about the substantial quality of the nominal head and a kind of quasi-relative clause emerges. Compare in this respect:

(57) pai-ve   no-moto   wa-pachokwadi wo-ku-*ti*
    ADE:HAB.PST-be COM-3:fire 3:ASS-truth   3:ASS-INF-X
    dai   maka-kandwa   zana   ra-va-nhu
    IRR.COND INE:DEP:STAT-be.thrown 5.hundred 5:ASS-2-person
    vai-dai   vaka-bvira   sa-ma-shiza
    2:HAB.PST-IRR.COND 2:DEP:STAT-burn SIML-6-leaf
    'There was an immense fire of such a kind that if a hundred men were cast into it they would have been burnt up like leaves.' (Dale 1972:136)

3.2.6 *Specific quality or amount*

The presentation of the functions of *ti* will be closed with a use that has not yet been discussed. It has a structurally aberrant behavior compared to all previous cases. So far, *ti* was always followed by some constituent. Here, however, it occurs on its own as a postnominal modifier in the relative stative form and means 'such and such', 'certain', or 'particular' (Dale 1972:134). As the use will be discussed further below, two illustrating examples will suffice here:

(58) ndi-no-da   n'ombe dzaka-*ti*
    1S-PRS-want 10.cattle 10:REL:STAT-X
    ndi-go-ku-pa   mari   yaka-*ti*
    1S.SBJ-CONS-2S.OBJ-give 9.money 9:REL:STAT-X
    'I want such and such cattle and I will give you so much money.'
    (Hannan 1984:646)

(59) mu-fambo   waka-*ti*
    3-walking.distance 3:REL:STAT-X
    'some/a certain walking distance'

4. Another lexical account of *ti*

4.1 The reconstructed monosemous sense of *ti* 'thus'

Section 3 is a fairly exhaustive presentation of the many diverse idiomatic and grammatical uses of *ti*. It will have shown that it defies a coherent semantic analysis at first glance. I will try to show, however, that such is possible.

In principle, there are two approaches available in order to account for the multiplicity of functions of one linguistic sign. A kind of agnostic approach would be to assume that different lexical items are involved in the different uses. This does not have any research tradition in Shona studies: in spite of the difficulties encountered by previous scholars they never doubted that *ti* in its many functions is one and the same verb stem.[2] This approach will also be employed here. It implies, however, that all the uses of *ti* should be accounted for by a network of relations, whereby an individual meaning or function is linked to at least one other meaning or function via a plausible relationship of family resemblance. Various solutions are possible in such a theoretical framework.

It can be assumed, for example, that one lexical meaning in the previously available accounts is basic. That is, it is either original from a diachronic viewpoint or conceptually central from a synchronic viewpoint. From this basic meaning, all the remaining uses must be derived in a plausible scenario. As far as I can see, there are two candidates that have been implicitly entertained previously in this sense.

Inter alia Hannan and Dale tend to focus on a primary meaning 'say' and — by extension to internal speech — 'think'. This also seems to be the most widely assumed position in Bantu studies in general, although there are rarely any explicit statements to this effect. This approach has its parallel in the treatment of comparable cases in more theoretically oriented grammaticalization research. Again, there is hardly any account available, where the derivation of the multiplicity of non-utterance uses of a similarly versatile element from a verb 'say/think' is explicitly spelled out. For non-utterance uses, scholars have repeatedly made reference to a fairly diffuse notion of a development starting with some more grammaticalized function in the quotation complex where the original meaning is said to have been bleached out. In my view, many functions of *ti* in Shona cannot be related plausibly to the meaning components of a speech or cognition verb, be it within a diachronic or a synchronic approach. Accordingly, this solution is not entertained here.

A second proposal for a basic meaning of *ti* was given above by Fortune with 'do/act'. This is a very general semantic core capable of capturing a very wide range of different event types. Such a kind of verb covering meanings like 'be', 'do', 'say', 'think' is reported to exist in various languages. Compare in this respect Foley (1986:119ff.) for Papuan languages or Cohen, Simeone-Senelle and Vanhove (this volume) for Northeast African languages. Note, however, that the existence of such a linguistic item in the respective languages tends to be accompanied by typical phenomena in the general structure of their lexicon — these are lacking in Shona. Another problem of this approach is that such a stem would be lexically almost vacuous coming close to a kind of dummy verb. The explanatory task with respect to the emergence of the functional polysemy of *ti* would merely be moved into the realm of the lexicon. However, the new question as to how such a semantically vacuous lexeme developed in the first place would not be less serious. Nevertheless, the idea of some original meaning of *ti* like 'do/act' will not be discarded here on these grounds. It will not be entertained because there exists a better explanation.

For a large part of the attested functions of *ti*, another abstract common denominator can be identified. Fortune (1955:347), for example, writes: 'One of the most widely met functions of *-ti* is the introductory function.' This aspect is emphasized by all Shona scholars and also evident in the above presentation (compare especially 3.1/2.1+3+4+5). It is accompanied in some uses by the reference to the quality or manner of the constituent identified by *ti* (compare 3.1/2.5 and 3.2.6). These two aspects offer the possibility of establishing a monosemically oriented definition of *ti* that differs from previous approaches:

> The verb stem *ti* provides a cataphoric orientation for the hearer towards some subsequently identified information about the entity cross-referenced in its subject concord.

Note that a cataphoric orientation entails some deictic meaning component. In the search for an English equivalent, a demonstrative stem comes to mind that largely conforms to such a definition, namely 'thus'.

I leave the exercise to the reader to substitute this word for the gloss x in the above examples. In fact, many translations contain already expressions of identification and discourse deixis such as 'namely', 'as follows', '(like) this', 'that', etc. In my view, they are adequate renderings of *ti* despite the fact that the information following it is so diverse. This can be a referential entity, a quality, a state of affairs, or an expression with a different pragmatic anchoring such as enacted speech and thought or events evoked by the symbolic means of ideophones. It is this diversity which gives the impression that *ti* is a highly polysemous element.

The above meaning 'thus' is also capable of explaining the syntactic behavior of *ti* as a verb. Recall that the constituent following it is outside its syntactic frame. This is due to the fact that *ti* is first of all an introduction device on the level of discourse and the constituent introduced by it is simply not its syntactic argument. The *ti*-clause can only have a non-subject participant if the whole construction consisting of *ti*-clause and a following constituent is a representation of an event. These are *ti*-constructions used to introduce reported discourse and ideophones. Here, the only possible role of the second participant is the patient or experiencer of the event encoded by the complex structure. With reported speech, this is the addressee of the utterance.

I should point out that I view 'thus' as the *original* monosemous meaning of *ti*. An adequate *synchronic* analysis of its semantics in Shona must be based on a statistically representative study on native speaker judgements. But trying to evaluate the competence and intuition of speakers requires a kind of research very different from that pursued here. The results of such a study could yield a far less straightforward picture than a monosemous account would suggest. One might instead come up with a complex network of related senses, probably even with a marked salience of the quotative function. When trying to elicitate the meaning of *ti* out of context, it might well be possible to receive as a first response something like 'say'. This, however, only indicates that the speech verb reading of *ti* has gained in salience. The previous lexical accounts of *ti* are inadequate in the sense that such meanings as 'say/think' or 'do/act' appear to be translation equivalents in a specific context rather than inherent semantic features of this verb. The feature of utterance, for example, should be viewed as triggered first of all by the use of *ti* in a quotative construction. This explains why a meaning 'say' is only there evident in any straightforward way.

4.2 Comparative evidence in a wider genetic context

The stem *ti* is so widespread in the family that it was reconstructed by Guthrie (1967–71) for Common Bantu. Here is his complete entry except for his list of reflexes in individual test languages:

> C.S.1727 *-tì that, namely; say . . .
>
> Most of these entries form verbal bases with a limited number of tenses, and from the evidence of their distribution it seems possible that *-TÈ occurred in P[roto]B[antu]-X, probably with the meaning 'that, namely'. The extension of this to provide an all purpose radical, the meaning of which can perhaps be best expressed in English as 'saying', may have taken place later.

Although Guthrie's semantic characterization is vague, too, it is remarkable in three respects vis-à-vis the meaning proposed here: First, he views the more grammaticalized function of *ti* as a complementizer to be original. This reconstruction is apparently motivated by the fact that in a great number of individual Bantu languages the stage of grammaticalization of *ti* is today fairly advanced and the complementizer function is central. However, it is important to bear in mind that a *synchronic* frequency and distribution of a particular meaning or function in a group of languages often does not illuminate a diachronically earlier situation. A second point is that, with his second meaning 'namely', he explicitly refers to *ti*'s function of identifying nominal entities or more abstract propositional content (compare 3.1/2.4). Finally, the semantic feature of utterance is parallel to the present discussion considered to be a *secondary* characteristic so that *ti* would not have been a speech verb originally. All in all, Guthrie's cross-family account agrees to a certain extent with my reconstructed meaning 'thus'.

Much more space would be needed to describe the behavior of *ti* across the Bantu family in a representative way. Suffice it to say that many of the functions given above are widespread in other Bantu languages. There also exist additional functions which are mostly later stages of grammaticalization of individual uses encountered in Shona. I will confine myself to presenting only comparative data directly relating to my semantic analysis of *ti* as 'thus'.

Evidence to this effect comes from the geographically near Nguni group. First, these closely related varieties add another type of expression that can be introduced by **ti*, that is, bodily gestures and other non-verbal means of performance. For example, a clause with the cognate stem *thi* is regularly used when counting by way of hand gestures. Compare also the two following examples from Xhosa:

(60) iim-pondo zen-kunzi ya-kowethu zi-*the:*
 10-horn 10:ASS:9-bull 9:ASS-our.place 10-like.this:PFV
 'The horns of our bull are shaped like this.' (As indicated by the hands, arms or body)

(61) u-cula ngelizwi eli-krasa-yo eli-*thi*
 3-sing:PRS INSTR:5:voice 5:REL-shrill-REL 5:REL-like.this
 'She sings in a shrill voice, like this.' (The speaker imitates her singing)
 (Pahl, Pienaar and Ndungane (eds.) 1989: 295)

Such a representation of a state of affairs is from a stylistic viewpoint clearly reminiscent of reported discourse and ideophonic constructions and, as will be discussed in 4.3 below, can be aligned functionally with these contexts.

Another interesting detail is the focus behavior of *thi* in Nguni: According to Doke (1992: §808, footnote), it cannot be used in Zulu in the so-called long forms which mark focus on the predicate. This characteristic can be explained by the plausible principle that an introducing demonstrative like 'thus', which has itself focussing force, cannot be in the scope of predication focus.

Nguni *thi* also demonstrates a clear *cataphoric* deictic component because it has an *anaphoric* counterpart (*t*)*sho* derived from it by a suffix *o* widely known in Bantu to mark a referent that was previously mentioned in discourse. Both *thi* and (*t*)*sho* are exploited in Nguni as quotative markers, the former in a preposed cataphoric and the latter in a postposed anaphoric construction. The following examples are from Zulu:

(62) ba-*thi* ni-fanele uku-lima
 2:REM.PST-QUOT 2P-must:STAT INF-plough
 'They said, "You must plough!"' [They (said) like *this*, . . .]

(63) izi-nkabi zi-lahlekile se-ku-*sho* aba-fana
 10-cattle 10-be.lost:STAT INIT-IP-QUOT:ANA 2-child
 '"The cattle are lost," now say the boys.' [. . . *that* is what the boys say now] (Doke 1992: §819/20)

Finally, the conjugational properties of the above stem pair in Nguni offer an interesting perspective on the possible historical dynamics of Bantu *ti. Recall that Shona *ti* cannot be inflected by stem-final morphology and this is the original and synchronically still normal situation in Bantu. This kind of verbal inflection is, however, available in Nguni. Doke (1992: §482–5), for example, gives for Zulu *thi* a negative past form *thanga*, a perfective *thé:*, and a relative perfective *thile*. Stem-final changes are even more prominent with the derived stem *sho*, which already contains a deictic suffix *o*: there are a negative past form *shongo*, a perfective *shilo*, an applicative *sholo*, a neuter passive *shoko*, a causative *shwisa*, and a passive *shiwo*. These are all Nguni innovations and indicate a clear tendency of *thi* and (*t*)*sho* to become morphologically more canonical verb stems. The stem (*t*)*sho* is also from a semantic viewpoint strongly associated with secondarily acquired features. It is almost always used in contexts referring to speech and mental processes (compare Doke et al. 1990, Part 2: 743) so that the meaning 'say/think' is more tenable here.

Some Bantu languages of zone J provide even more direct evidence for the above semantic account and this conforms closely with the Nguni data. Inter alia in Nkore-Kiga, *ti* explicitly means 'like this' (alias 'thus') being part of a series of manner deictics corresponding etymologically to the stem pair *thi*/(*t*)*sho* in Nguni. This is illustrated below:

(64)   n-ki-kore   n-*ta*
       1s.SBJ-7IA.OBJ-do:SUBJ   1s:DEP-how
       'How shall I do it?'
       n-ki-kore   n-*ti*   ... n-*tyo*
       1s.SBJ-7IA.OBJ-do:SUBJ   1s:DEP-like.this   1s:DEP-like.that
       'I'll do it like this   ... like that.' (Taylor 1985: 186)

In summary, comparative data give strong support for reconstructing *ti* with a meaning 'thus/like this' — and this not only for some earlier Shona stage but instead for a relatively old chronolect of Bantu.[3]

Another relevant fact is that Piron (1998: 155 ff.) in her comparative study of Bantoid — the higher-order genetic unit above Bantu — does not relate a single verb 'say' etymologically to Bantu *ti from her long list of test languages, let alone reconstruct a comparable form for the entire genetic group. The regular sound correspondences between non-Bantu languages and Bantu do not become sufficiently clear from the study. If there were one between Bantu [t] and the sonorants [r] and [l] in some non-Bantu languages, there would exist a few comparable items. What this would mean for the semantic account of Bantu *ti cannot be discussed in detail. Piron (1998: 156) remarks that 'Le verbe "dire" de cette série est celui qui introduit le discours direct ... ou le discours rapporté ... .' This means that her list rather contains verbs used as the nucleus of a quotative construction. From the fact that such items are not necessarily true speech verbs, it becomes clear that her data cannot really falsify the claim made here.[4] In general, this comparative evidence, too, does not contradict my claim that *ti is not a speech verb.

On the contrary, individual non-Bantu languages of the Bantoid group possess elements with a behavior very similar to Bantu *ti 'thus'. Tikar, for example, has a triplet of stems encoding manner deixis with the same semantic structure of *ti in Bantu languages of zone J and Nguni:

(65) lɛ   li   lɛ-ɛ
     ainsi   ainsi   comment
     [cataphoric: like this] [anaphoric: like that]   (Stanley 1991:297f., 316)

The difference in the vowel quality between the first two items above is a property of all deictics in Tikar. This is a structural match of the alternation in Bantu between elements without and with the *o* of anaphoric reference in general and the pair *ti 'like this' and *ti+o 'like that' in particular. As a significant parallel to Bantu *ti*, the cataphoric member of this series of manner deictics lɛ is regularly used in a preposed quotative construction:

(66) ci-njinɔ' shè   lè   lwikwǎn lɛ   . . .
     DET-hare say:PFV COM other   like.this
     'Le lépreux a dit à l'autre: ". . ."' (Stanley 1991:516–7)

Tiv, another Bantoid language, has an extremely versatile element *er* that can also be compared fruitfully with Bantu *ti, because it has a very similar functional range (compare Abraham 1940:222–4). Beside many uses in clause linkage and such verbal meanings as 'do', 'act', 'happen', 'behave towards', 'affect' it serves as a similative and manner marker. Compare the following:

(67) `Akèr táv èr   ´Afá nàhán`
     PROP tall like PROP thus
     'Aker is as tall as Afa.' (Jockers 1991:87)

This meaning is clearly related to a manner deictic 'thus'. This similative *èr* can be compared in shape with the quotative marker of Tiv given in (68):

(68) né   kàà (né) ér` yèm´
     you:P say you:P QUOT go:IMP
     'You (pl) said: "Go!"' (Jockers 1991:148)

It is reasonable to assume for Tiv that the quotative marker developed from the element 'like/as' marking similarity and manner. This would only be one of many cross-linguistically attested similar cases (compare Section 5). Moreover, the comprehensible development of Bislama *olsem* (Meyerhoff, this volume) shows that a stem with a synchronic use of 'thus/like this' can have acquired its deictic component secondarily within a complex grammaticalization process starting from a plain similative marker 'like'. Such precedents suggest that even Bantu *ti 'thus' might have emerged ultimately from a meaning 'like'.

It should also be noted that Tikar *lɛ* and Tiv *er* are not canonical verbs. In a number of languages in this geographical area, very similar elements have become grammaticalized quotative markers that can be used on their own, that is, a speech verb is omitted (compare inter alia Frajzyngier (1996:125–41) for Chadic languages). This observation throws light on the morphological property of Bantu *ti of having a restricted conjugational paradigmaticity as a verb stem. It is conceivable that this behavior is a relic of its earlier status as a similar non-verbal particle that was capable of occurring in a quotative construction of the simple form *subject+ti*. Predicative force and obligatory subject cross-reference by means of a specific series of bound pronominal prefixes is the most basic criterion in the majority of modern Bantu languages to assign a stem to the lexical category of verbs. However, the structure in the pre- or proto-Bantu stage out of which subject agreement developed was most likely identical with the pattern *subject pronoun+verb* found to this date in most Bantoid languages. It was only subsequent to this stage that *ti* could have acquired prefixed subject cross-reference as the minimal requirement to be viewed as verb-like. There still exist Bantu languages where the inflection of *ti* is restricted to precisely this feature. Significantly, the languages of zone J which still show also its assumed original meaning 'thus' are among them. The next stage in the process of increasing 'verbification' of *ti* would have been its possible cooccurrence with other verbal *prefixes* like object concords and various tense–aspect markers. This situation — inter alia achieved in Shona — still represents a fairly incomplete acquisition of the category features of canonical Bantu verbs. The historically older *suffix* morphology is only evident in a few languages like Nguni where *ti* and derived stems have apparently been subject to strong analogical leveling.

4.3 A scenario for the development of the polyfunctionality of *ti* in Shona

Starting from the original meaning 'thus/like this' for Shona *ti*, I will now try to give a plausible and transparent scenario of how the multiplicity of its synchronic functions developed. Two basic meaning components of 'thus' are identified for this purpose: On the one hand, it has a connotation of *similarity* and *manner*; on the other hand it has a *demonstrative* force for propositional contents. This characterization is conveniently captured in the term *manner deictic*. It remains unresolved here whether the deictic component of *ti* is secondary, and if so, when the development from 'like' to 'like this' occurred. In any case, although a similarity/manner connotation still transpires in Shona in individual uses of *ti*, it is largely bleached out synchronically. Shona today possesses other expressions for this meaning. Its introductory and demonstrative function is most salient today. As mentioned above, *ti* can often be translated by such expressions as 'be as follows', 'be this', 'that is to say', 'namely,' etc. The major precondition for *ti* to develop into a grammatically versatile element was the change of its cooccurrence restrictions. However, given the fact that a very general introductory function is inherent in its original meaning, it is probable that extending the range of constituent types possibly following it was not a too dramatic process.

The half a dozen domains of *ti*-uses identified in Section 3 will now be reduced further to only three. Two grammatical functions and one specialized meaning can be derived directly from its proposed original meaning 'thus'. The grammatical functions are in turn the source for other uses. Thus, *ti* has:

1. the function of embedding mimetic expressions in linguistic discourse,
2. a demonstrative-introductory function above the sentence level,
3. the meaning 'such and such', 'particular', 'some'.

1. Regarding the first functional domain of *mimesis* a few explanations are in place, because it does not refer to a well-established linguistic concept. The term *mimesis* is a convenient label for a formally and functionally fairly homogeneous domain that has been identified by the author in research on African languages (*Güldemann* 2001). A short and still preliminary characterization can be given as follows: A *mimetic expression* is a self-sufficient representation of a state of affairs by means of enacting/performing rather than with the help of canonical linguistic signs. The following types of mimetic expressions within normal linguistic communication can be distinguished so far. First, properties and behavior of an entity can be expressed via *non-verbal gestures*. Second, a situation or event can be represented symbolically by such *non-canonical linguistic signs* as onomatopoetics, ideophones, etc. The *imitation of sound* is a third expression pertaining to the domain of mimesis. Finally, the secondary performance of an instantiation of human language, that is, *directly reported discourse* in the narrow sense, belongs here. Since the above expressions are not canonical linguistic signs, the mimesis domain can be said to stand in a kind of opposition vis-à-vis the conventional *linguistic* type of event representation. This formal property is associated by an important functional aspect: mimetic expressions have a special stylistic role in that they tend to be employed when states of affairs are represented in stretches of dramatic, vivid language — typical discourse contexts being, for example, story peaks of a narrative. Mimesis can thus be viewed as a functionally and formally distinct style of communicating information embedded within 'normal' speech.

Such a concept of two separate modes of speech is even entertained by Fortune (1971:237) for Shona: he distinguishes between a 'narrative predicative style' using verbal clauses and another formally coherent 'dramatic predicative style' using such expressive means as ideophones and quotations. Here, we come back to the discussion of *ti* in Shona: it serves to introduce at least three of the above mimesis types, that is, quotations (see 3.1/2.1), ideophonic constructions (see 3.1/2.3), and sound imitations. Moreover, the fourth type of non-verbal gestures is attested for the cognate *thi* in Nguni. That **ti* 'thus' has become the most important marking device of mimesis in Shona and other Bantu languages can certainly be motivated by its meaning components. First, a mimetically represented event can pretend to be close to a real experience whereby the degree of closeness depends first of all on the nature of the represented event and the abilities of the performer. However, it can never be authentic; it will always be nothing but an approximation of reality. The similarity/manner connotation of *ti* is a token of this fact. The second function of *ti* as a deictic on the level of discourse organization can also be related functionally to possible exigencies of mimesis embedding. Beside the simple effect of marking the initial boundary of a mimetic expression, the *ti*-clause can serve as an important signal for the hearer that (s)he will be confronted with a switch from the normal linguistic mode to the mimetic mode of speech. A specialized mimesis marker is appropriate as a reorientation signal because such a switch is often associated with serious changes in the deictic and pragmatic setting, for example, a change in the reference of shifter categories or a role change of the narrator.

My classification of direct reported discourse as a subdomain of mimesis requires some additional remarks. Although explaining reported speech in terms of an invoked original utterance can prevail even in some recent discussions, it has been demonstrated repeatedly that this is a very simplifying approach. The report of an utterance does not necessarily refer to a real event of communication, let alone repeat the exact words of such a speech event. In principle, it does not even need to convey meaning which is evident when the quote is an imitation of a foreign language. All these characteristics can be explained if direct reported discourse is viewed as a mimetic expression that can be triggered merely by stylistic considerations. Having said this it must be noted, however, that direct speech is special vis-à-vis all other mimesis types in having a double nature. On the one hand, it is a mimetic sign. On the other hand, it is per se also a string of canonical *linguistic* signs conveying propositional meaning in the majority of cases. This second aspect provides the possibility of slipping within reported discourse gradually from the mimetic into the normal, linguistic mode of event representation. This is evident at the scalar organization of the different categories of reported discourse. These can be defined by the degree to which the reporter manipulates the representation of a non-immediate speech event for his purpose and thereby makes it more or less mimetic. The highest degree of mimesis is found in direct reported discourse while indirect reported discourse can be identified as the least mimetic type. Such reported-discourse types as semi-indirect, free indirect, etc. are categories in-between these two extreme poles.

The least mimetic indirect discourse was shown to be the source of other grammatical functions. This cross-linguistically widely attested phenomenon called above the quotation complex of grammaticalization will not be discussed here again. It is sufficient to repeat with regard to the historical development of Shona *ti* that its role in sentential complementation and related clause linkage (see 3.1/2.2) can be explained within this account. While the ultimate source of these functions is direct reported discourse as a subdomain of mimesis, they pertain themselves to the non-mimetic linguistic mode of speech.

2. The demonstrative-introductory function of *ti* 'thus' is the second major source for its wide range of uses. The discourse constituent it refers to and which is attributed to the entity cross-referenced as its subject can also be regarded as a 'referent'. It is a propositional referent within the text. This function of discourse deixis motivates that *ti* identifies and lists nominal entities (see 3.1/2.4) and introduces expressions of quality (see 3.1/2.5). The function of *ti* to orient the hearer toward a particular piece of following information correlates with its foregrounding and focussing characteristic.[5] This makes it a suitable device to emphasize states of affairs in discourse (see 3.1.6) which in turn is the source for the expression of pragmatically marked verbal categories (see 3.1.6) and clause linkage (see 3.1.6).

3. The third and last use of *ti* directly related to its original semantics 'thus' should be viewed as a derived lexical meaning triggered in a specific context. The sense of 'such and such', 'some', 'particular' (see 3.2.6) is only evident when the stem is used as a modifier of a noun *without* a following constituent. The above translations can be generalized in the meaning *specific quality left unspecified* implying a similative component. What this expression transpires pragmatically is something like 'X is of a certain quality which I need not specify now'. The 'lacking' information is for some reason not necessary in the given communicative situation. The reasons can be that (1) the information is otherwise available, for example, it belongs to universal knowledge, (2) it has been referred to in the previous discourse, or (3) — the data are insufficient to state this more firmly — it is instantiated by non-verbal means whereby the original meaning as a manner deictic would still be evident. All this explains the aberrant syntax of this *ti*-construction: as the information about the modified entity is left unexpressed, *ti* does not introduce a constituent.[6]

The scenario of how the different meanings and functional domains of *ti* relate to each other is illustrated in a schematic way in Figure 1. It must be repeated, though, that the semantic-functional core of demonstration and introduction is quasi omnipresent in the early grammatical functions of *ti*. A strict separation of different domains of uses and a derivation of an individual function from only one source is therefore partly arbitrary. This is evident at the fact that formally identical constructions sometimes express two functions which pertain to different domains according to the schema (compare, e.g., the *expression of internal conflict* vs. the clause linkage 'both ... and ...' or the *introduction of quality expressions* vs. the clause linkage 'whenever'). Instead of the unilinear branching model presented in Figure 1, the concept of a network of related meanings and functions is certainly more appropriate. Due to the large number of individual *ti*-functions and the complexity of their interrelation such a representation will not be attempted here.

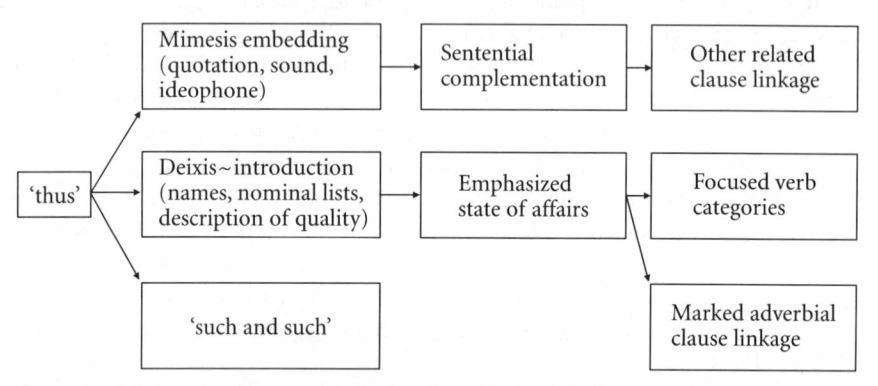

```
                    ┌─────────────────┐     ┌─────────────────┐     ┌─────────────────┐
                    │ Mimesis embedding│     │   Sentential    │     │  Other related  │
                  ┌→│ (quotation, sound,│────→│ complementation │────→│  clause linkage │
                  │ │    ideophone)   │     │                 │     │                 │
                  │ └─────────────────┘     └─────────────────┘     └─────────────────┘
                  │ ┌─────────────────┐     ┌─────────────────┐     ┌─────────────────┐
        ┌──────┐  │ │Deixis~introduction│     │   Emphasized    │     │  Focused verb   │
        │'thus'│──┼→│(names, nominal lists,│──→│ state of affairs│────→│   categories    │
        └──────┘  │ │description of quality)│   │                 │     │                 │
                  │ └─────────────────┘     └─────────────────┘     └─────────────────┘
                  │                                 │
                  │ ┌─────────────────┐             │              ┌─────────────────┐
                  │ │                 │             │              │Marked adverbial │
                  └→│ 'such and such' │             └─────────────→│  clause linkage │
                    │                 │                            │                 │
                    └─────────────────┘                            └─────────────────┘
```

Figure 1. Schema for the grammaticalization relationship between the major functional domains of Shona *ti*

5. Conclusions for a general account of the quotation complex

The development of an element meaning 'thus' to a quotative marker as such is not new in grammaticalization research. In fact, one of the first cross-linguistic studies of the quotation complex carried out by Saxena in the late 1980s had already treated this source. However, *Saxena* (1995:360) still remarks in the published version of that paper that

> With few exceptions, very little attention has been paid to this topic in the literature with the result that a cross-linguistic study such as the present one, can only be suggestive of the direction of its grammaticalization.

This situation is first of all due to a too strong orientation toward the speech-verb account. So the present findings, which are summarized in the following, are highly relevant for the analysis in other languages with similar complexity in this domain and a possible cross-linguistic comparison.

Quotative markers do not necessarily originate in lexemes with utterance meaning. They all undergo subsequent processes of grammaticalization out of a quotative construction irrespective of their origin. The crucial position for the emergence of complementizers and derived conjunctions along this path is the quotative function — an observation made also by *Saxena* (1995:368). *Quotation complex* is a convenient label for this subdomain of grammaticalization. On the other hand, additional functions of an element used as a quotative marker need not be derived from the quotation complex and/or the meaning components of a speech verb.[7] Thus, the prevailing model of a basic, unilinear grammaticalization chain *speech verb* > *quotative marker* > *complementizer* > *other* should be supplemented. In neglecting closely related processes it tends to simplify a potentially complex situation and can result in an analysis where the origin of a particular function of a versatile element is looked for in the wrong source. Grammaticalization takes place in the context of a possibly intricate network of related functions through which individual linguistic items move in a motivated and thus partly predictable way. One functional context — as a node in such a network — can draw its formal expression from different sources and can in turn be the source of different targets. The model in Figure 2 is more appropriate theoretical input when trying to make plausible hypotheses about the historical dynamics of a versatile language-specific element inter alia prominent in quotative constructions:

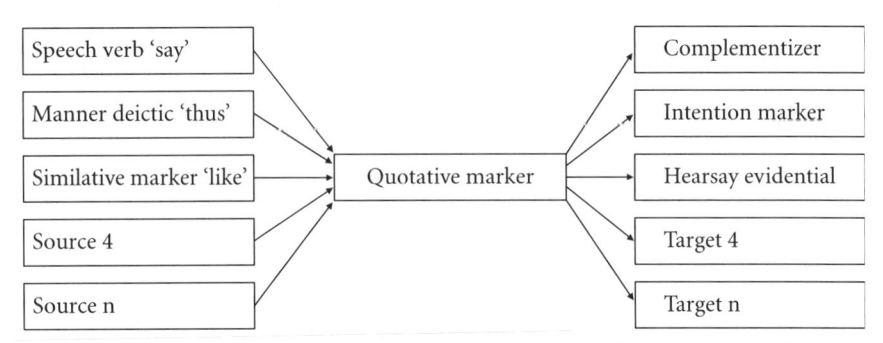

Speech verb 'say'	→	Quotative marker	→	Complementizer
Manner deictic 'thus'	→		→	Intention marker
Similative marker 'like'	→		→	Hearsay evidential
Source 4	→		→	Target 4
Source n	→		→	Target n

Figure 2. Schema for the grammaticalization relationship of a quotative marker

The available data make it clear that it is wise to distinguish between a verb with a lexical feature of locution alias *speech verb* and an element used as the predicative nucleus of a quotative construction. A cross-linguistic study of African languages by *Güldemann* (2001) reveals that the second, more general category, conveniently called *quotative verb/predicator*, often has many other functions that are not captured by the previous explanatory framework of the quotation complex. However, it can be observed in individual languages that such an item is characterized synchronically or reconstructed diachronically as a speech verb 'say' despite its variable meanings. The primary basis for this interpretation is its occurrence in a quotative construction. The above data suggest that a revision of the philological treatment of such elements may be appropriate in certain cases.

Versatile lexemes having a functional range similar to Bantu *ti* might well turn out to be derived from a comparable element with a semantic make-up similar to that reconstructed here, i.e., expressing similarity, manner and related meanings. On the African continent, this appears to be a fairly frequent pattern according to my findings. It is also widely attested outside this area. To mention just a few examples, similar cases are found in Europe, South Asia, the Pacific and South America in such different language groups as Indo-European: American English (see inter alia *Blyth, Recktenwald and Wang* 1990), German (*Golato* 2000), and Sanskrit (*Hock* 1982); Austronesian: inter alia Kwaio (Keesing 1985:72) and Tongan (J. Broschart p.c.); Neo-Melanesian: Bislama (Meyerhoff, this volume); and Choco:[8] inter alia Epena Pedee (Harms 1994:174).

Given this evidence, at least *Saxena*'s (1995:360-3) stage model regarding 'thus' needs revision in a more comprehensive study. This will be illustrated by one example: she assigns the similative and manner function of the element *qhe* in Lahu (Tibeto-Burman) to her last grammaticalization stage IV 'Links nominals to the rest of the clause'. Her motivation appears to be the observation that one stage-IV endpoint in her speech-verb channel is a comparative marker. In analogy to this, she views also the similative function to be a late stage of grammaticalization. However, comparative 'than', even if valid for the speech-verb channel, must not be confounded with similative 'like'. Although both are syntactically and semantically akin, they cannot be associated promptly with one and the same node in a grammaticalization network.[9] In view of the above discussion, the similative and manner function of *qhe* is, pace Saxena, unlikely its latest development, but rather the source for its functions in the quotation complex. Thus, Lahu is instead a likely candidate for the development *'like'/'thus'* > *quotative marker* > *other*.

A final remark concerns a more general problem of grammaticalization research. Even if it remains unclear whether Bantu *ti* originated in a completely non-verbal lexeme, it can still be observed that it has been subject to a process of increasing 'verbification'. One can speak of a scale from a more to a less defective verb stem across Bantu. According to the languages discussed here, the parameter of verbhood even seems to correspond to a geographical North-South cline: Nkore-Kiga > Shona > Nguni. If this picture was confirmed by wider comparative data, this could be a significant detail in the sense that languages farthest removed from the Bantu homeland in West Africa would also be the most innovative vis-à-vis a conservative stage regarding the verbhood of *ti*.[10] A similar picture emerges from the semantic properties of *ti* across Bantu: the originally secondary meaning component of utterance has become more strongly entrenched in languages of the southern realm of the family. Compare in this regard just the extreme poles on a scale of central meanings: *ti* 'thus'/?'like' in some early stage of Bantu and still today in languages like Nkore-Kiga vs. cognate *(t)sho* 'say/think' in Nguni. Admittedly, even *(t)sho* is still far from being a canonical speech verb. In principle, however, an important question arises: Is it possible that a fairly grammaticalized stem used as the predicative nucleus of a quotative construction develops into a canonical verb 'say/think'? In other words, can a linguistic sign acquire *lexical* properties out of the use in a *grammatical* construction? If more evidence could be accumulated for answering these questions positively, this would certainly be relevant for the continuing controversy around unidirectionality in grammaticalization. Given the limited data presented in this chapter, the idea will still appear speculative. It merits, however, further consideration in future research on this topic.

Notes

* I thank first of all Samson Huni, who offered his native-speaker competence in Shona for discussing this versatile element. Thanks for valuable comments and discussions on this chapter are due to M. Klamer, S. H. Levinsohn, M. Meyerhoff and the audiences at previous presentations at the Department of African Languages/ University of Pretoria, at the 20th Annual Meeting of the 'Deutsche Gesellschaft für Sprachwissenschaft' at Halle, and at the Institut für Afrikanistik/ Universität Leipzig. Last but not least, I am grateful to the 'Volkswagen-Stiftung' for having sponsored this research.

1. The interlinearization of examples is mine. The morpheme *ti* will be glossed with X as its meaning is under dispute. Arabic numbers indicate noun classes. They refer to personal categories only when immediately followed by the glosses S or P. A source is usually given in the translation line. Examples from a narrative text in Chifamba (1982) have the line number after the page number. Examples without a reference are taken from own text recordings or elicitation with Shona speakers. My comments are given in square brackets.

2. See, however, Botne (1993: 23–6) who hypothesizes that the functions of *ti* in a related language Tumbuka derive from two different verbs meaning 'say' and 'do/act' respectively.

3. Given that a reflex of *ti 'thus' may have an interrogative counterpart 'how' as in languages of zone J (see example (64) of Nkore-Kiga), a more exhaustive comparative analysis in Bantu should incorporate the interrogative reconstructed by Guthrie (1967–71) as his adnominal stem C.S.1728 *-*ti* 'which?', alias 'being of what kind/how?' (see also Meyer 1949/50).

4. An observation which, if at all relevant, could be support for my claim is that a number of items in Piron's list of quotative verbs have a final syllable that might turn out to be comparable in sound to Bantu *ti. If these elements were indeed cognates, these could represent cases of possible incorporation of a quotative marker into a verb used as the nucleus of a quotative construction.

5. Underhill (1988) observes a focussing function also for *like* in American English — an element that does not have an original deictic component, but has a similar functional behavior to Shona *ti* 'thus'. It is inter alia a quotative marker (see below).

6. This meaning of *ti* also turns out to be identical with a use of Bislama *olsem*, that is, when the latter occurs after a noun on its own (see Meyerhoff 1998, this volume).

7. This can even be a complementizer function as suggested by Meyerhoff (this volume) for Bislama *olsem*.
8. I owe this information to S. H. Levinsohn.
9. Moreover, the grammaticalization of comparative structures is fairly intricate. Beside a number of functions that are not related to the quotation complex, at least two functional nodes of the truncated grammaticalization network in Figure 2 above seem to be direct sources for a standard marker in a comparative construction, that is, a complementizer (compare *que* in some Romance languages) and a similative marker itself (compare *wie* in sub-standard German).
10. Compare the quotative element *wa* in Kambera (Klamer, this volume) which can also be shown to undergo a process of reanalysis whereby its formal properties as a verb are increased via reinterpreting the most frequent pronominal subject marker as an integral part of its phonetic substance.

References

Abraham, Roy C. 1940. *A dictionary of the Tiv language*. Hertford: Stephen Austin and Sons.
Botne, Robert. 1993. "Differentiating the auxiliaries *-TI* and *-VA* in Tumbuka (N.21)". *Linguistique Africaine* 10: 7–28.
Chifamba, Jane. 1982 [1964]. *Ngano dzepasichigare*. Gwelo, Zimbabwe: Mambo Press.
Dale, Desmond. 1972. *Shona companion*. Gwelo, Rhodesia: Mambo Press.
Doke, Clement M. 1992 [1927]. *Textbook of Zulu grammar*. Cape Town: Maskew Miller Longman.
Doke, Clement M. et al. 1990. *English-Zulu/ Zulu-English dictionary*. Johannesburg: Witwatersrand University Press.
Foley, William A. 1986. *The Papuan languages of New Guinea*. Cambridge: Cambridge University Press.
Fortune, George. 1955. *An analytical grammar of Shona*. London: Longmans and Green.
Fortune, George. 1962. *Ideophones in Shona*. Oxford: Oxford University Press.
Fortune, George. 1971. "Some notes on ideophones and ideophonic constructions in Shona". *African Studies* 30,3/4: 237–57.
Frajzyngier, Zygmunt. 1996. *Grammaticalization of the complex sentence: a case study in Chadic* (=Studies in Language Companion Series 32). Amsterdam: John Benjamins.
Jockers, Heinz. 1991. *Studien zur Sprache der Tiv in Nigeria* (=Europäische Hochschulschriften, Reihe 21: Linguistik 94). Bern/ Frankfurt/Main/ München: Peter Lang.
Güldemann, Tom. 1997a. *Prosodische Markierung als sprachliche Strategie zur Hierarchisierung verknüpfter Prädikationen am Beispiel des Shona* (=University of Leipzig Papers on Africa 2). Leipzig: Institut für Afrikanistik, Universität Leipzig.
Güldemann, Tom. 1997b. "Prosodic subordination as a strategy for complex sentence construction in Shona: Bantu moods revisited". In Herbert, Robert K. (ed.), *African linguistics at the crossroads: papers from Kwaluseni (1st World Congress of African Linguistics, Swaziland, 18–22, July, 1994)*. Köln: Rüdiger Köppe, 75–98.

Guthrie, Malcolm. 1967–71. *Comparative Bantu*, 4 vols. Farnborough: Gregg Press.
Hannan, Michael. 1984. *Standard Shona dictionary*. Harare/ Bulawayo: The Literature Bureau.
Harms, Phillip L. 1994. *Epena Pedee syntax* (=Studies in the languages of Colombia 4, Publications in Linguistics 118). Summer Institute of Linguistics and The University of Texas at Arlington.
Heine, Bernd and Mechthild Reh. 1984. *Grammaticalization and reanalysis in African languages*. Hamburg: Helmut Buske.
Heine, Bernd, Ulrike Claudi and Friederike Hünnemeyer. 1991. *Grammaticalization: a conceptual framework*. Chicago: Chicago University Press.
Heine, Bernd et al. 1993. *Conceptual shift: a lexicon of grammaticalization processes in African languages* (=Afrikanistische Arbeitspapiere 34/5).
Hyman, Larry M. and John R. Watters. 1984. "Auxiliary focus". *Studies in African Linguistics* 15,3: 233–73.
Keesing, Roger M. 1985. *Kwaio grammar* (=Pacific Linguistics B88). Canberra: Australian National University.
Lord, Carol. 1993. *Historical change in serial verb constructions* (=Typological Studies in Language 26). Amsterdam: John Benjamins.
Meyer, Emmi. 1949/50. "Das Fragewort in den Bantusprachen". *Zeitschrift für Eingeborenensprachen* 35: 81–106.
Meyerhoff, Miriam. 1998. "Comparing old and new information in Bislama: nominal deletion with *olsem*". In Tent, Jan and France Mugler (eds.), *Proceedings of the Second International Conference on Oceanic Linguistics, Vol. 1: Language Contact* (=Pacific Linguistics C141). Canberra: Australian National University, 85–93.
Pahl, Herbert W., A.M. Pienaar and T.A. Ndungane (eds.). 1989. *The greater dictionary of Xhosa*, 3 vols. Alice: University of Fort Hare.
Piron, Pascale. 1998. *Classification interne du groupe bantoïde*, 2 vols. (=Lincom Studies in African Linguistics 11/2). München/ Newcastle: Lincom Europa.
Stanley, Carol. 1991. *Description morpho-syntaxique de la langue tikar (parlée au Cameroun)*. Epinay: Summer Institute of Linguistics.
Taylor, Charles. 1985. *Nkore-Kiga*. London/ Sydney/ Dover, New Hampshire: Croom Helm.
Underhill, Robert. 1988. "Like is, like, focus". *American Speech* 63,3: 234–46.

CHAPTER 13

Reported speech in Egyptian
Forms, types and history*

Frank Kammerzell and Carsten Peust
Georg-August-Universität Göttingen

1. Introduction

Egyptian is considered to be genetically related to Berber, Chadic, Cushitic, Omotic, and Semitic languages and thus classified as an independent branch of the Afroasiatic group.[1] It comprises several varieties that span diachronically from pre-Old Egyptian (c.3000 BCE) to Coptic which ceased to be used as a medium of everyday communication in rural areas of southern Egypt not before the middle of our millennium.

On typological grounds, the Egyptian language history is divided into two major stages: Earlier Egyptian includes Old Egyptian (c.27th–21st centuries BCE) and Middle Egyptian (c.23rd cent. BCE to 4th cent. CE), while Late Egyptian (c.15th–7th cent. BCE), Demotic (c.8th cent. BCE to 5th cent. CE) and Coptic (c.3rd–16th cent. CE) are labeled as Later Egyptian.

The overwhelming majority of Egyptian texts are recorded either in hieroglyphic, hieratic or demotic script — the last two being cursive forms of the autochthonous Egyptian writing system — or are written by means of the Coptic alphabet, which consists of the letters of a Greek uncial alphabet and a few additional signs derived from demotic prototypes.

The usual manner of transcribing Egyptian language elements is conventionalized to a high degree and must not be interpreted as a direct indicator of historical sound values. As the keys for deciphering the Egyptian writing system in modern times had been — besides the knowledge of Coptic — primarily bilingual texts from the Hellenistic period and cuneiform transcriptions of Egyptian words and proper names originating from the late second millennium BCE, the traditional Egyptological transcription alphabet, which is used indiscriminately in dealing with hieroglyphic sources of all periods, at best represents the phonological inventory of Later Egyptian. Information about the sound shape of Earlier Egyptian is given in Figure 1.

(Groups of) signs corresponding to single cons.		Conventional Egyptological transcription	Corresponding sounds		
Older	Later		Old Egyptian	Middle Egyptian	Late Egyptian
🦅		ꜣ	r	ʀ, ʔ	j, Ø
𓇋	𓇋🦅	j	j, ɟ, ɉ	j	j, Ø
—	—	ꜥ	d	d, ʕ, j	ʕ, d, j, Ø
𓊃	𓆑🦅	w	w	w	w, Ø
𓃀	𓃀🦅	b	b	b	b, ß
𓊪	𓊪🦅	p	p	p	pʰ
𓆑		f	f, ɸ (<*ʃ)	f	f
𓅓	𓅓🦅	m	m	m	m
𓈖	🦅	n	n, ŋ, ŋʷ	n	n
𓂋		r	l, ʎ	l, ʎ, Ø	r, l, ʎ, Ø
𓉔	𓉔🦅	h	h (<*ʃ)	h	h
𓎛		ḥ	ħ	ħ	ħ
𓐍	𓐍🦅	ḫ	ɣ, ɣʲ	ɣ, ɣʲ	ɣ, ɣʲ
𓄡		ẖ	x	x	x
𓊃		z	t͡s, s (<*t)	s	s
𓋴		s	ʃ	s	s
𓈙	𓈙🦅	š	ç (<*x)	ʃ	ʃ
𓈎	𓈎🦅	q	kʼ	kʼ	kʼ, kʷ
𓎡	𓎡🦅	k	k	k	kʰ
𓎼	𓎼🦅	g	g, gʲ	g, gʲ	g, gʲ
𓏏		g	gʷ, g	gʷ, g	g
𓏌	𓏏🦅	t	t	t, ʔ, Ø	tʰ, Ø
𓍿	𓍿🦅	ṯ	c (<*k)	c, t, ʔ, Ø	cʰ, tʰ, Ø
𓂧	𓂧🦅	d	tʼ	tʼ	t, d
𓆓	𓆓🦅	ḏ	cʼ (<*kʼ)	cʼ, tʼ	c, t

Figure 1. Elementary hieroglyphic graphemes and corresponding phonemes

2. Reported speech and its subtypes

A comprehensive discussion of different approaches to defining reported speech (e.g., *Plank* 1986, *Roncador* 1988), particularly with respect to the specific conditions of Later Egyptian, can be found in *Peust* (1996: 15–37). In this section we will present only a concise outline of what was dealt with then in greater length.

A speaker can insert a text or a segment of a text which he purports to derive from another speaker's utterance into his/her speech. His/her actual speech shall be called *embedding context*, quoted speech *embedded context* — even though it is not necessarily embedded syntactically — or, to use a more familiar term, *reported speech*. Reported speech can be further subcategorized into several subtypes, the most prevailing of which are *direct speech* and *indirect speech*. Among the various attempts to define the difference between direct speech and indirect speech, most include the idea that indirect speech is somehow more integrated into the embedding context than direct speech. In 19th-century grammar books, the contrast between direct and indirect speech was frequently understood in terms of syntactic dependence, i.e. direct speech was considered to be reported speech in the form of an independent clause, whereas indirect speech was identified with subordinate clauses.

While this possibly makes sense in the case of Latin and certain other languages, it has now become apparent that syntactic constituency is not a very useful concept for defining direct and indirect speech in a universal frame; it is certainly not so for Egyptian, where reported speech is invariably expressed in the form of a syntactically independent clause. Let us now turn our attention to another well-known definition of indirect speech. Direct speech can be understood as a mode of reporting in which an original utterance is reproduced without changes, whereas indirect speech allows for several adaptations to be made under the influence of the embedding context, most typically of deictic elements. A definition of this kind was proposed by Otto Jespersen long ago:

> When one wishes to report what someone else says or has said (thinks or has thought) — or what one has said or thought oneself on some previous occasion — two ways are open to one. Either one gives, or purports to give, the exact words of the speaker (or writer): *direct speech*. Or else one adapts the words according to the circumstances in which they are now quoted: *indirect speech* (oratio obliqua). (Jespersen 1924:290)

When mentioning the possibility of *purporting* to give the exact words of the speaker, Jespersen already had in mind a problem which is one of the more serious challenges to his own definition: reported speech is frequently not exactly a report of something that was spoken previously, but the utterance "that someone else says or has said" can be of an entirely fictional nature. Deborah Tannen put this fact into the following words:

> The term 'reported speech' is a misnomer. Examinations of the lines of dialogue represented in storytelling or conversation, and consideration of the powers of human memory, indicate that most of those lines were probably not actually spoken. What is commonly referred to as reported speech or direct quotation in conversation is constructed dialogue, just as surely as is the dialogue created by fiction writers and playwrights. (*Tannen* 1986:311)

So we cannot define the contrast between direct and indirect speech by means of whether or not changes were made in reported speech with respect to an original utterance. We rather have to consider whether or not a reported speech is expressed in a way it *could have* been spoken in the purported speech situation as defined in the embedding context. Both, the embedding context and the embedded context constitute two distinct speech situations, each having their own speaker and addressee and their own deictic point of origin. Each speech situation also has its own *universe of discourse* which continually changes in the course of the communication. The universe of discourse determines, e.g., which noun phrases are to be considered definite and which to be indefinite, which noun phrases are currently so salient that they may be pronominalized and which are not, etc.

If we turn to the problem of which speech situation a given reported speech is based on, there will be several parameters to be scrutinized. It is clear from the beginning that not all parameters necessarily point in the same direction. Let us take a basic example from German and assume that a person A said to B in the past:

(1) Er begann mit ihr zu streiten und sagte: "Morgen werde ich fahren!"
(He began quarreling with her and said: "I am leaving tomorrow.")

This being transformed into "free indirect style" (a subtype of indirect speech frequently found in modern literature), something like the following may result:

(2) Er begann mit ihr zu streiten. Morgen würde er fahren!
(He began quarreling with her. He would leave tomorrow.)

We can see that in this mode of reported speech both personal deixis and verbal tense are influenced by the embedding context. The future tense which is appropriate in the speech situation of the (purported or real) "original" context coalesces with the past tense appropriate to the speech situation of the actual narrator into a conditional tense (the same holds true in English). On the other hand, the time adverbial *morgen* ('tomorrow') is expressed with respect to the speech situation of the "original" utterance, disregarding the fact that from the narrator's perspective the event took place in the past.

In (3) the same utterance is transformed into what would be "ordinary" indirect speech:

(3) Er begann mit ihr zu streiten und sagte, daß er am nächsten Tag fahren werde. (He began quarreling with her and said that he would — literally: will — leave the next day.)

In this case, the time adverbial must not be chosen from the point of view of the "original" speech situation. It is rather changed in a way that it becomes interpretable from the speech situation of the actual speaker. On the other hand, in German literary language the verb — while shifted in mood — may remain in the future tense and is not indispensably affected by the fact that it has now been put into a past context and refers to an event that took place in the past. We can generally state for German that, in "ordinary" indirect speech, time adverbials are adapted to the speech situation of the embedding context whereas verbal tense is not (or at least need not be), and in free indirect discourse verbal tense is adapted to the speech situation of the embedding context whereas time adverbials are not changed. The chart in Figure 2 summarizes which linguistic elements are adapted to the embedding speech situation (+) and which are not (−) in a particular type of reported speech.

	Adaptation of grammatical person	Adaptation of verbal tense	Adaptation of time adverbials	Modally marked
Direct speech	−	−	−	−
Indirect speech proper	+	(−)	+	+
Free indirect discourse	+	+	−	−

Figure 2.

Figure 2 also shows that not all modes of reported speech can be arranged on a single linear scale stretching from "prototypical direct speech" to "prototypical indirect speech", as some scholars have assumed (e.g., *Plank* 1986), but that the subtypes of reported speech possibly must be arranged into a more complex system, even within an individual language. Keeping this in mind, we propose to define direct and indirect speech as two distinct categories one of which (indirect speech) shows (any) adaptations of deictic and pragmatic elements to the embedding context, whereas the other (direct speech) does not. It is necessary to emphasize that not any alterations which occur in the process of quotation are sufficient for labelling it as indirect speech. If, for instance, the reporting speaker is unable or unwilling to imitate idiosyncratic articulatory properties of the quoted speaker, s/he does not necessarily produce indirect speech. Only those systematic alterations are relevant that are due to the specific conditions of the given embedding context. So we define:

> Direct speech is a mode of reporting in which all deictic and pragmatic elements are based on the speech situation which is purportedly that of the "original" speech situation as defined in the embedding context.
> Indirect speech is a mode of reporting which shows adaptations from this pragmatic setting to the speech situation of the embedding context in at least one item, provided that these deviations are explainable as specific interferences of the new context into which the reported speech is embedded (for details and further discussion, cf. *Peust* 1996: 15–37).

It is obvious that — depending on the specific grammatical categories of an individual language which are affected by adaptations to the speech situation of the embedding context — more than one subtype of indirect speech may coexist in that language. This is actual the case in Egyptian, as will be shown in the next paragraphs.

3. The very beginnings of speech recording

The most ancient example of reported speech is not found in a text *strictu sensu* but in a document combining pictorial representations with short annotations. Figure 3 shows the obverse of a sandal tag belonging to the burial inventory of King T'en, a ruler of the First Dynasty (*c.*2900 BCE) and also known as Den, Dewen, Niudi, Udimu or Usaphais. The monarch Horus T'en (4a) is depicted striking a person that represents the defeated enemies. The scene is accompanied by the standard of the god ⚘ W*p-wꜣ.wt* 'Opener of the ways' and labeled 'The first time of defeating the East' (4b) — the usual way of naming a year in the Early Dynastic Period. The group of three hieroglyphs in the space between the victorious king and the smitten foe displays an utterance of the king and reads 'May they be finished!' (4c). The three hieroglyphic signs to the left of the ruler (4d) do not belong to the pictorial scene but seem to indicate the name of the official who was in charge of producing, delivering or controlling the goods that are specified on the other side of the tag.

The document shown in Figure 3 is not only the first case of a recorded speech report in Ancient Egypt — and probably in human history as well — but also marks the onset of a long tradition in Egypt of associating written texts rendering the contents of a speech with depictions representing the respective speaker. Its typological similarity to modern comic strips is astonishing.

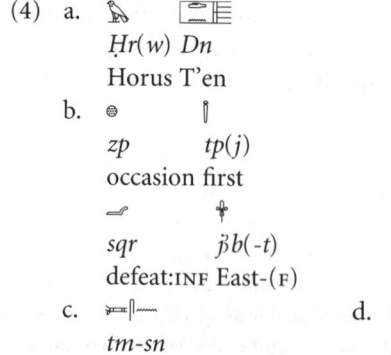

(4) a. *Ḥr(w) Dn*
       Horus T'en
    b. *zp   tp(j)*
       occasion first
       sqr   jb(-t)
       defeat:INF East-(F)
    c. *tm-sn*
       be.finished:SUBJ-3P
    d. *Kꜣ.j.jn*
       Karijanu

Figure 3. From Spencer 1980: pl. 53, no. 460F

A more elaborate form of this practice is shown on the fragments of a temple inscription from Heliopolis (Third Dynasty, *c.*2620–2600 BCE) in Figure 4. One part of the speech of the anthropomorphic deity is rendered in front of his image within the same compartment (5).

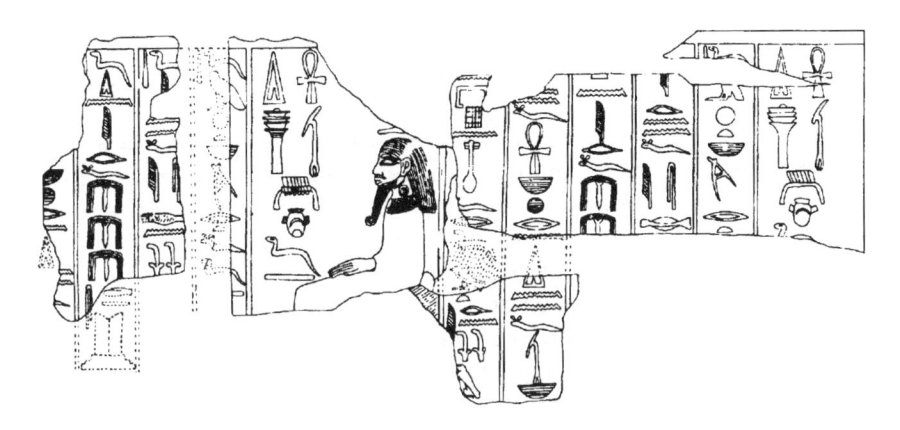

Figure 4. From Kahl, Kloth and Zimmermann 1995: 116–18, no. Ne/He/4

(5) ḏ(-j) ꜥnḫ ḏd wꜣs
give:SUBJ-1s life permanence dominion
ꜣw(-t)-jb ḏ-t
length-(F)-heart eternity-F
'I will bestow life, stability, dominion, and exultation for ever.'

Another utterance was recorded in five now partially destroyed columns to the left, which can be reconstructed by comparing them with the almost identical sections in the right half of the monument which belonged to another deity. Each column started with ⟨md-ḏ⟩. This sequence is usually transcribed as ḏd-mdw(j).(w) 'saying words' and was apparently interpreted as such also by the speakers of Egyptian during later periods, so that it was written ⟨ḏ-d md-1-1-PLURAL⟩ ḏd-mdw(j).(w) sporadically. As, however, the younger form or ⟨ḏ-md⟩ slightly differs from Old Egyptian ⟨md-ḏ⟩, we prefer to analyze the latter merely as mdw(j), this being the original form of the lexeme mdw(j) 'word, spell, utterance'. In Figure 4, is repeated at the beginning of every column in spite of the fact that sentence boundaries do not necessarily coincide with the end of a column. For that reason, instead of corresponding with an element of the spoken language, mdw(j) had the function of a quotation mark. This method of labeling reported speech in monumental inscriptions by means of was utilized with scarcely any alteration until the end of glyphographic data processing in the 4th century CE, but it should be noted that there are also many texts that did without repeating 𓉻 in every column.

A final example of the intertwining of recorded speech and pictorial scenes which might be described as corresponding with the embedding context is presented in Figure 5. What we see is two sculptors at work, the one on the left side putting the finishing touches to a wooden statue, the other polishing a seated figure of stone. The text is a short dialogue consisting of two utterances, each of which starts as a horizontal line facing the head of the respective craftsman, running to the right and closing in a column behind their pieces of work. The wood-carver complains about the hardship of his labour (6a), and this somewhat insensitive lament is put in the right light by his comrade. The stone-mason's response (6b) not only contains an example of direct speech, but also verifies the fact that reported speech is not necessarily a quotation of an utterance that was actually spoken before (cf. Section 2).

(6) a.
3bd   wʿ(-w)   r-   nn   n(j)-   h(rw)-(w)   dr-
month one-NUM until- DEM DETER- day-P since-
dw(-j)   ʿ(-j)   m-   twt   pn   nt(j)   m-   ʿ(-j)
put:INF 1s hand-1s in- figure DEM REL.PRO in- hand-1s
'It is one month in these days since I began working with this statue which is in my charge.'

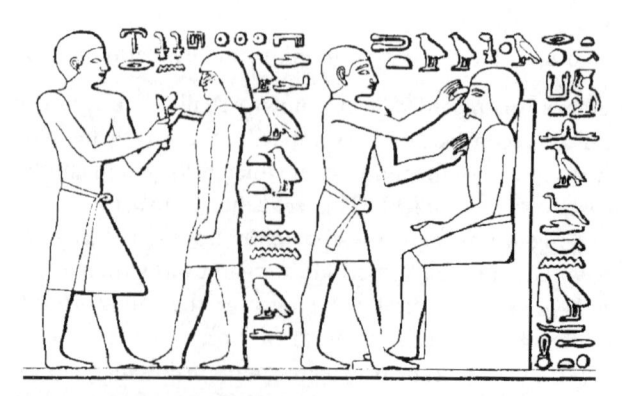

Figure 5. From Hassan 1936: 194, fig. 219 [segment]

b. 𓂋𓂧𓅨𓏤 𓂋𓏤𓏏𓎡 𓂓𓏏𓂋 𓂜 𓇋
   twt wḫꜣ   rḫ-t-k   kꜣ-t(-j) n- ꜣ-
   2M.S stupid:PAP know:REL-F-2M.S work-1S NEG- indeed-
   𓆓𓂧𓎡 𓈖 𓂓𓏏 𓅓 𓇋𓈖𓂋
   ḏd-k   n(-j) jw ḫt(-j) mj- ꜣ-t
   say:PRS-2M.S for-1S TOP wood-1S like- stone-F
   'You are stupid. What do you know! It's my work, and you are not going to tell me "My wood is like stone."'

The discourse under (6) is a typical member of a class of more informal utterances that are attested from the second half of the third millennium (the so-called *Reden und Rufe*, cf. Erman 1919) and constitute the earliest cases of a linguistic norm close to everyday language ("written as if spoken").

4. Embedding reported speech in Old Egyptian (direct speech and indirect speech, type 1)

Let us now turn to examples of reported speech within the framework of written communication. With very few exceptions, the examples discussed in this section are taken from the Pyramid Texts (abbreviation: Pyr., principal editions: Sethe 1908–1922 and Jéquier 1933, translation: Faulkner 1969), a corpus of funerary texts carved on the inner walls of subterranean chambers in the monumental tombs of six kings and three queens who lived in the period from the late Fifth to the Eighth Dynasty (*c.*2300–2100 BCE).

Within our corpus, there are various syntactic possibilities of implanting reported speech in the embedding context. The embedding context usually contains some kind of quotation index which may precede and/or follow the reported speech or may be inserted into it.

The most frequently employed type of reported speech in Egyptian is built by a form of the verb 𓆓 *ḏd*- 'say' (which acts as a quotation index) and the utterance following without any overt mark of embedding and without any adaptation of person, tense or deictic adverbs. Although this sort of reported speech is extant in the Pyramid Texts (cf. 7), it does not yet — or: does not within the linguistic norm of religious texts — represent the standard type as in later periods, when a larger variety of text sorts is attested, all of which show a clear preference for the quotation index 𓆓 *ḏd*-.

(7) 𓂋𓂧𓂧𓏥 — 𓈖 𓊨 𓂻𓈖𓎡 𓂻𓈖𓎡
j.dd-sn n- Wsjr śm-n-k jw-n-k
say:PRS-3P for- Osiris go-PRET-2M.S come-PRET-2M.S

𓂋𓋴𓈖𓎡 𓋴𓂧𓂋𓈖𓎡 𓏠𓈖𓏏
rs-n-k sḏr-n-k mn-tj
wake.up-PRET-2M.S sleep-PRET-2M.S remain:STAT-2M.S

𓅓 𓋹 𓊤 𓌳𓎡 𓇋𓇋 𓊤
m- ꜥnḫ ꜥḥꜥ mꜣ-k nn ꜥḥꜥ
in- life stand.up:IMP see:SUBJ-2M.S DEM stand.up:IMP

𓁹𓎡 𓇋𓇋 𓐍𓂋𓈖 𓈖𓎡 𓅆𓎡
sḏm-k nn j.jr-n n-k ẓꜣ-k
hear:SUBJ-2M.S DEM do:REL-PRET for-2M.S son-2M.S

𓐍𓂋𓈖 𓈖𓎡 𓅃
j.jr-n n-k Or(w)
do:REL-PRET for-2M.S Horus

'... and they say to Osiris: "You went and came back, you woke up and fell asleep, while you endured in life. Stand up so that you see this, stand up so that you hear this, what your son has done for you, what Horus has done for you."' (Pyr. 1005d–1007b^N)

In Old Egyptian, examples of reported speech with adaptations from the pragmatic setting to the reported utterance are not abundant, and the few cases of indirect speech often seem to require the usage of an overt signal of embedding. This can be the complementizer 𓃹 *wnt* 'that' (cf. 8), which is a grammaticalization of 𓃹 *wn.t*, the feminine form of a neutral — or "perfective" (as opposed to distributive or "imperfective") — active participle of the verbal root 𓃹 *wnn-* 'exist'.

(8) 𓂋𓂧𓂧𓏏𓈖 — 𓇋𓏏𓈖 𓃹𓏏 𓂋𓂧𓈖 𓈖𓏏𓈖
j.dd-tn n- jt(j)-tn wnt rd-n n-tn
say:FUT-2P for- father-2P COMP give-PRET for-2P

𓃹𓈖𓋴 𓊪𓄿𓃹𓏏𓈖 𓅓𓊵𓈖 𓏏𓈖
Wnjs pꜣw-(w)t-tn s-ḥtp-n tn
Wanjash offering.bread-F.P-2P CAUS-satisfy-PRET 2P

𓃹𓈖𓋴 𓅓 𓏏𓅱𓏏𓈖
Wnjs m- twt-tn
Wanjash with- 2P:POSS-2P

'You shall say to your father that Wanjash has presented to you your offering breads, so that Wanjash has satisfied you with your very belongings.' (Pyr. 448a–b^W)

An earlier version of this utterance, which was reformulated only after it had already been carved on the wall, is still visible beneath the modified text (cf. 8' for the relevant section). The fact that in (8′) the prepositional phrase *n-ṯn* 'to you' does not appear clitically between verb and nominal subject — as is the rule in the case of a pronominal "indirect object" of that kind — indisputably verifies that even the reading intended to be out of sight had not been the original composition, but the transformation of an unattested phrase with the first person suffix pronoun serving as the subject (cf. 8″).[2] In this sentence, three personal pronouns would have been changed as compared to the purported primary speech situation. So an "original" direct speech to be uttered by the group of addressees as 'he has presented to us our offering breads' became 'that I have presented to you your offering breads.'

(8′) ... *wnt*   *rḏ-n-*   *Wnjs*   *n-ṯn* ...   (Pyr. 448a^(W′))
   ... COMP give-PRET- Wanjash for-2P ...

(8″) ... *wnt*   *rḏ-n(-j)*   *n-ṯn* ...   (reconstructed prototype of 8′)
   ... COMP give-PRET-1S for-2P ...

An authentic example of indirect speech with the adaptation of a personal pronoun to the speech situation of the embedding context is given in (9). For further cases of this type see Edel (1955/64: §§ 1015, 1022, and 1026).

(9) *sk*   *ṯw*   *ḏd-k*   *ḥr-*   *ḥm(-j)*   *wnt*
   PTCL 2M.S say:PRS-2M.S to- majesty-1S COMP
   jr-n-k   *sw*
   do-PRET-2M.S 3M.S
   'Now you say to My Majesty that you made him.' (Urk. I 63,2)

Likewise, the feminine form of the relative pronoun *nt(j)* 'that' was used grammaticalized as complementizer *ntt* (cf. 10).

(10) *ḏd*   *n-k*   *n-*   *Rˁ(w)*   *ntt*   *N-t*   *jw-s*
   say:IMP for-2M.S to- Re COMP Neith-F come:FUT-3F.S
   'Tell Re that Neith will come.' (Pyr. *2243 = Jéquier 1933: pl. VII, col. 40–41)

If there was any difference in meaning between *wn.t* and *ntt* it is not apparent. All we can state is that *wn.t* was first attested and became more or less superseded by *ntt* in Middle Egyptian.

As a different sort of complementizer, the enclitic element *-js* is utilized in (11) to indicate that the sentence *j.n-k Pjpj -pn ʒ- Gb(b) -js* 'You have come, o Pijaapij, as the son of Geb.' is embedded as an object of the quotation index 𝒹𝒹-sn 'that they can say'.³ It seems that — in contrast to *wnt* and *ntt* — *-js* does not mark its complement clause as factive or putative, but rather as questionable.

(11) z   jn-(w)-k   sjn   sjn-(w)-k   nqrqr
      hasten:PRS porter-P-2M.S run:PRS   runner-P-2M.S hurry:PRS
      ḥw(w)t-w-k   ḏd-sn   n-   R'(w)   j-n-k
      messenger-P-2P   say:SUBJ-2P   for- Re   come-PRET-2M.S
      js   Pjpj   pn   ẑ-   Gb(b)   js
      COMP   Pijaapij DEM   son-   Geb   as

      'Your bearers bustle, your runners rush, and your messengers hurry so that they can tell Re whether you have come, o Pijaapij, as the son of Geb.' (Pyr. 1539c–1540b^P)

Cases of indirect speech without introductory complementizer are extremely rare in Old Egyptian. We know of no more than five instances, all of which represent only two utterances attested in slightly different versions. In (12) the suffix pronoun of the final prepositional phrase is the third person — in contrast to the alleged first person of the respective direct speech. Example (13) attests to the adaptation of two pronouns to the embedding context, an "original" utterance 'I will kill him' was reported in indirect speech as 'that he would kill you.'

(12) jn   smȝ-n-f   tw   ḏd-n   jb-f   m(w)t-k   n-f
      PQ   kill-PRET-3M.S 2M.S   say-PRET   heart-3M.S   die:SUBJ-2M.S   for-3M.S
      'Has he killed you or has his heart said that you shall die for him?' (Pyr. 481a^W)

(13) j-n-f   jr-k   ḏd-n-f   smȝ-f   tw
      come-PRET-3M.S   to-2M.S   say-PRET-3M.S   kill:SUBJ-3M.S   2M.S
      'He came against you and said that he would kill you.' (Pyr. 944a^N)

As one should expect in the case of a language which exhibits VO structure, the quotation index ḏd- regularly precedes the reported speech. Nevertheless, there are rare cases of this matrix verb following the reported utterance (cf. 14).

(14) nfr(-j)   ḏd-n   mʾw-t-f   jwʿ(-j)
      be.beautiful:PAP-1S say-PRET   mother-F-3M.S   heir-1S

ḏd-n   jt(j)-f
say-PRET father-3M.S
'"My beautiful one!" said his mother, "My heir!" said his father.' (Pyr. 820b^P)

Other quotation indexes do not precede but either follow a direct speech or are inserted into the quotation. The matrix verb most frequently used in the Pyramid Texts is defective *j-* 'say', a root that solely appears in preterite , , or *j.n-* 'said', in stative *j-* (plus personal ending), and perhaps also as a verbal noun , or *j(y)* 'utterance' (cf. Allen 1984: §§ 206–210). As a rule, *j-* with a pronominal subject in the singular appears in the stative only (cf. 15c–d), while plural (cf. 16) and noun subjects (cf. 15a–b) seemingly require the usage of preterite tense (see Allen 1984: § 209). This complementary distribution of verbal TAM-features according to the number of the subject (in clauses with pronominal subject) is to some extent astonishing but not entirely without counterparts in other constructions of Earlier Egyptian (cf. Jansen-Winkeln 1997 on "verbal plurality").

(15) a. *mʾw-t(-j)   jy-n   Pjpj   Nfr.k̠.Rᶜ(w)*
mother-F-1s say-PRET Pijaapij Nafirkarliiduw

b. *jm   n(-j)   mnḏ-t   snq(-j)   sw   jy-n*
give:IMP for-1s breast-2F.S suck:SUBJ-1s 3M.S say-PRET
Pjpj   Nfr.k̠.Rᶜ(w)
Pijaapij Nafirkarliiduw

c. *z(-j)   j-t   jr   Pjpj   Nfr.k̠.Rᶜ(w)*
son-1s say.STAT-2F.S to Pijaapij Nafirkarliiduw

d. *m   n-k   mnḏ(-j)   snq   sw   j-t*
take:IMP for-2M.S breast-1s suck:IMP 3M.S say.STAT-2F.S
'"My mother" said Pijaapij Nafirkarliiduw, "give me your breast that I may suck it" said Pijaapij Nafirkarliiduw. "My son" said she to Pijaapij Nafirkarliiduw, "take my breast and suck it," said she.' (Pyr. 911b-912a^N)

(16) 𓃭 𓏏𓅱𓏏 𓈖𓆑 𓇋𓈖
    m   twt   n-f   j-n
    who resemble:PAP for-3M.S say-PRET
    𓐠𓐠𓐠𓐠𓐠𓐠𓐠𓐠𓐠   𓅨𓏏   𓊃𓏏
    psd-(tj)   wr-t   ꜥꜣ-t
    Two.Enneads.of.gods-F.D be.great:PAP-F be.great:PAP-F
    '"Who is like him?" said the Two Great and Powerful Enneads.' (Pyr. 1689c^M)

Sporadically, an inflected form of 𓇋 j- 'say' is inserted into direct speech, which is preceded by 𓆓 dd-. Whether this fairly tautological aggregation of quotation signals reflects actual usage of spoken Old Egyptian or should rather be considered a specific device of certain religious texts, cannot be decided. Be that as it may, example (17) as well as similar cases of double quotation index (e.g. Pyr. 1696a-d^M) display a diction that is repetitive to some extent not only in respect of embedding marks.

(17) 𓅱𓇋𓇋 Rꜥ(w) 𓏌𓏌 𓂋𓆑 𓆓𓈖𓎡   Rꜥ(w) 𓎛𓏌𓏲𓇋
     wjj   Rꜥ(w)   nw   rf   dd-n-k   Rꜥ(w) hwj
     INTJ Re   DEM   PTCL say:REL-PRET-2M.S Re PTCL
     𓅬   𓇋𓏏   𓏏𓅱   Rꜥ(w) 𓃀𓇋
     ꜣ(-j) j-t   tw   Rꜥ(w) bꜣ-j
     son-1S say:STAT-2M.S 2M.S Re be.besouled:STAT-3M.S
     𓋴𓎛𓅓𓇋   𓅱𓌞𓇋
     shm-j   wꜣš-j
     be.mighty:STAT-3M.S be.strong:STAT-3M.S
     'O Re, this is just what you have said, Re: "Be it that my son ...." — so you said, you, Re — "... is besouled, is mighty and is strong!"' (Pyr. 886a–b^P)

In addition, there are two other elements customarily described by Egyptologists as defective verbs. Their syntactic usage is quite similar to that of 𓇋 j- described above. Combinations of 𓁷 (variants 𓁷𓏤, 𓁷𓂋𓏤) hr(w) 'say' or 𓎡ꜣ kꜣ 'say' and a subject noun or pronoun follow the reported speech. Unlike 𓇋 j-, they do not occur in preterite and stative, but in utterances of present and/or future tense (cf. 18).

(18) 𓇋𓂧𓂋𓆑   𓅭𓏏   𓇋𓂋𓏏𓎡
     j.dr-f   dw-t   jr-t-k
     remove:SUBJ-3M.S evil:PAP-F against-ADJR:F–2M.S
     𓊪𓏭𓊪𓏭   𓊪𓅱   𓁷   (J)tm(w)
     Pjpj   pw   hr   (J)tm(w)
     Pijaapij DEM say:PRS Atum
     '"He shall remove the evil which is against you, o Pijaapij", says Atum.' (Pyr. 840c^P)

It is worth noting that three morphemes which are formally identical with the quotation indexes *jn*, *ḥr*, and *kȝ* are used in Earlier Egyptian as inflectional suffixes of particular verbal forms. Usually these are analyzed as different tense markers of the so-called contingent tenses *sḏm.jn-f* (i.e. STEM-*jn*-SBJ) *sḏm.ḥr-f* (STEM-*ḥr*-SBJ), and *sḏm.kȝ-f* (STEM-*kȝ*-SBJ). As, however, each of these affixes can be linked to various tense stems — a fact that till now has never been taken into consideration — the explanation suggested by Depuydt (1989) cannot be considered entirely satisfactory. They should rather be characterized as manifestations of distinct moods, and possibly *sḏm.jn-f* is to be identified as *consecutive*, *sḏm.ḥr-f* as *obligative*, and *sḏm.kȝ-f* as *potential* mood. Whether or not the assumed modality marker might be connected functionally and/or etymologically with the quotation indexes, is debatable (see *Chetveruchin* 1988 for a discussion of the existing opinions and a new — in some of its far reaching conclusions not utterly convincing — hypothesis on the origin of *jn*-). Yet, it seems not beyond feasibility to interpret the few instances of reported speech embedded by means of *kȝ*-, which are attested from the third millennium, as utterances of a potential mood (cf. 19 and 20).

(19) hȝ   N-t   pw   nḏ-sn   rn(-j)
     INTJ   Neith-F   DEM.M   ask:PRS-3P   name-1S

     m.ʿ-k   jm-k   ḏd   n-sn
     from-2M.S   not.do:SUBJ-2M.S say:NEG.CPL   for-3P

     rn(-j)   jn-   m   j.jr   n-k   kȝ-sn
     name-1S   FOC-   who   act:PAP   for-2M.S say:POT-3P

     jn-   s-t-j   j.jr   n(-j)   kȝ-k
     FOC-   place-F-1S   act:PAP   for-1S   say:POT-2M.S

'Ho, Neith! Should they inquire as to my name from you, you shall not tell them my name. "Who is the one who acts for you?", they may ask. "It is my substitute who acts for me", you can say.' (Pyr. *1942a-c^{Ntb} = Jéquier 1933: pl. XXX, col. 771–2)

(20) jr-   nfr.n wnn   m.ḫt-tn   ḏd-kȝ-tn   m-
     COMP-   NEG   exist:PRS   after:PREP.ADJ-2P   say-POT-2P.S   in-

     r'-tn   wdn   m- ʿ-tn   hȝ   m- sntr
     mouth-2P   offer:CONV   in- arm-2P   thousand in- incense

ḫ3   m- śś   mnḫ-t   3pd(-w)   k3(-w)   m3(-w)   k3-tn
thousand in- alabaster garment-F bird-P ox-P antelope-P say:POT-2P
'If you have nothing, you may speak with your mouth and consecrate with your hand. "A thousand portions of incense, a thousand pieces of alabaster, garments, birds, oxen, and antelopes", so you can say.' (Drioton 1943: 503)

Finally, utterances sometimes were embedded as direct speech by means of adding the expression *m-r'-X / m-r'-n(j)-X* 'is in the mouth of a person' (cf. 21), and dialogues without quotation index occurred, too (cf. 22).

(21)   ʿb3   Stš   m3ʿ-w   Wsir   m- r'-   nṯr-(w)   jr-
        offer:PPP Seth justify-PPP Osiris in- mouth- god-P to-
        hrw(w) pw   nfr   —   n(j)-   pr-t   tp-   ḏw
        day   DEM be.beautiful:PAP DETER- go.up-INF upon- hill
'"Seth is sacrificed, Osiris is justified!" is in the mouth of the gods on this auspicious day of going up to the top of the hill.' (Pyr. 1556ᴾ)

(22) a.   ỉwt   j3b t j   wʿb
           2M.S   west-F-ADJR be.pure:PAP
'"You are a pure westerner?"'

     b.   prr(-j)   m- bjk-t
           come.forth:PRS-1s in- Falcon.City-F
'"I come forth from the Falcon City."' (Pyr. 471aᴺ)

Summarizing the situation in Old Egyptian, we can state that there are various types of embedding reported speech (see Figure 6), particularly in the Pyramid Texts. Statistically, this corpus shows a certain preference for the usage of the quotation index *j-* inserted after or within the reported text, while the matrix verb *ḏd* 'say' does not occur as often as one might expect, considering that this was by far the most frequent quotation index of Egyptian as a whole. To what extent the different means of embedding reported speech expressed distinct semantic and/or stylistic functions is difficult to determine. We can only assume that some of them were typical phenomena of religious language.

Indirect speech was used but sporadically in Old Egyptian texts. It always followed a form of the matrix verb *ḏd* 'say' and was usually syntactically embedded by means of a complementizer. Instances without overt complementizer are uncommon. The complementizers of indirect speech (*wnt*, *ntt*, *-js*) are identical

Type of quotation index		Complementizer	Direct speech (ex.)	Indirect speech (ex.)
ḏd- S	Speech	wnt	–	+ (8.8′.8″.9)
ḏd- S	Speech	ntt	–	10
ḏd- S	Speech	–js	–	11
ḏd- S	Speech	–	+ 6.7	(+) (12.13)
ḏd- S	Speech ḏd- S	–	+ 14	–
	Speech j- S	–	+ 15.16	–
	Speech j- S	–	+ 17	–
	Speech ḥr- S	–	+ 18	–
	Speech kȝ- S	–	+ 19.20	–
	Speech m- rʾ (nj-) S	–	+ 21	–
without quotation index		–	(+) (4.5.22)	–

Figure 6. Types of reported speech embedding in Old Egyptian (S = speaker)

with those of object clauses dependent on non-communicative verbs (e.g. gmj- 'discover', rḫ- 'know') and were never used to govern direct speech. Notwithstanding the scarcity of indirect speech in texts of the third millennium, there are some hints substantiating the fact that indirect speech with the adaptation of more than one grammatical person to the embedding context existed in Old Egyptian (*indirect speech type 1*, as in the exx. 8″ and 13). We are not aware of any example of indirect speech with restricted adaptation of only one personal role in Old Egyptian, which one could have expected facing a radically different situation in Late Egyptian (cf. Section 5).

5. Adaptation of one grammatical personal role (indirect speech, type 2) in Late Egyptian reported speech

Certain instances of reported speech in Egyptian exhibit indicators that allow for identifying them specifically as indirect speech. About half a dozen examples of indirect speech in Old Egyptian, which are obvious as such by their adaptations of personal deixis have been cited above (cf. 8–9, 11–13). Clearly identifiable cases of indirect speech can be found much more frequently in texts of the Late Egyptian period. Hence, the mechanics of indirect speech in Late Egyptian will be discussed in the following two sections (for more details, see *Peust* 1996: 41–86).

Looking for specimens of reported speech in texts of the late second millennium, we find that grammatical person is frequently chosen with respect to the embedding context. Example (23) is an excerpt from a letter which was written at some date during the 11th century BCE by a certain Pentahures to the scribe Butehamun.

(23) dj py-k- jt jn-t n-j
cause:PST DEM-2M.S- father send:SUBJ-PASS for-1S
t- š-t r-dd jm- ḏy-w
ART.F- letter-F in.order.to.say cause:IMP- bring:SUBJ-3P
st n-k
F.S for-2M.S

'Your father sent me the letter telling me to have it delivered to you (=Butehamun).' (Černý 1939: 52,5–6 = pBibl. Nat. 196/III, vs. 2–3)

There are three individuals and two distinct speech situations involved. In what we will call henceforward *primary speech situation* — i.e. the speech situation of the assumed communication of Butehamun's father with Pentahures — Butehamun's father would be the speaker (grammatically first person) and Pentahures the recipient (second person). Butehamun could only be referred to in the third person. This situation can be symbolized as follows:

(23')		Primary speech situation
	Butehamun's father	1
	Pentahures	2
	Butehamun	3

In what we will call secondary speech situation — namely the speech situation of the actual communication (the embedding context) —, Pentahures is addressing Butehamun, so that Pentahures is referred to as a first person and Butehamun as a second person:

(23")		Secondary speech situation
	Butehamun's father	3
	Pentahures	1
	Butehamun	2

If we now consider which grammatical persons are chosen in the actual reported speech, we find that Butehamun is referred to as a second person, while the two other individuals are not mentioned explicitly at all within the reported speech (23‴). Butehamun is referred to from the vantage point of the secondary speech situation; thus, according to our definition, we have an example of indirect speech.

(23‴)

	Primary sp. sit.	Second. sp. sit.	Reported sp.
Butehamun's father	1	3	–
Pentahures	2	1	–
Butehamun	3	2	2

Let us now consider an instance of reported speech in which more than one of the grammatical personal roles involved are referred to explicitly. (24) is taken from a literary composition, the narrative of Wenamun that is more or less contemporary with (23). Wenamun is telling the King of Byblos why Pharaoh Herihor sent him abroad:

(24) ... (j)n- Jmn-R^c nsw- nṯr-(w) ḏd   n-
    FOC- Amun-Re king- god-P   say:PAP for-

Ḥr(j).Ḥr   py-j-nh   j.wḏ   (w)j
Herihor   DEM-1s-lord send:IMP 1s

'It was Amunrasonther who told my lord Herihor to send me.'
(Gardiner 1932: 69,9–10 = Wenamun 2,25–26)

The primary communication took place between the god Amunrasonther ('Amun-Re, king of the gods') and Herihor, whereas in this part of the narrative Wenamun is speaking to the King of Byblos. Within the reported speech, Wenamun is referred to as first person. Herihor is the subject of an imperative and thus acts as second person.

(24′)

	Primary sp. sit.	Second. sp. sit.	Reported speech
Amunrasonther	1	3	–
Herihor	2	3	2
Wenamun	3	1	1
King of Byblos	3	2	–

The phrase j.wḏ -(w)j, literally 'send me', is as such neither acceptable from the vantage point of the primary nor of the secondary speech situation on their own.

Instead, we find that in reported speech one grammatical person is chosen with respect to each of the two speech situations, thus resulting in a "mixture" of both pragmatic settings.

This type of reported speech is very common in written Egyptian of the Ramesside Period (19th–20th Dynasties, c.1300–1070 BCE), and we can actually formulate the following rule based on the evidence of the material collected by *Peust* (1996:87–124):

> In Late Egyptian reported speech, one of the grammatical personal roles within the utterance may be chosen with respect to the deictic setting of the embedding context, but never more than one.

An adaptation of all grammatical personal roles to the embedding context, as well-known from English and many other languages (and extant in Old Egyptian), is not attested at all for indirect speech in Late Egyptian. This chronolect exhibits exclusively what we will refer to as *indirect speech, type 2*. Therefore, it is possible that, within a single reported speech, pronouns of (formally) identical grammatical person have different referents — even in the case of the first and second person. The utterance under (25) is an example from a juridical text. A certain Nakhtmutef has behaved improperly towards the daughter of Talmonth. Now, Talmonth demands in court that Nakhtmutef swear not to repeat his action:[4]

(25) *jm   jr-y   Nḫt.mw.t.f   ʿnḫ   n-   nb*
AUX.IMP make-SUBJ Nakhtmutef oath for- lord

r-ḏd   bn   jw.j.r-   nt͗   m-   ty-j-   šr(t)
COMP NEG FUT:1s- divorce:INF from- DEM.F-1s- daughter

'Nahktmutef should take an oath by the Lord (i.e. Pharaoh) that *he*₁ will not divorce my daughter.' (Gardiner and Černý 1957:pl. LXIV, 2 rto. 3–4)

(25′)

	Primary sp. sit.	Second. sp. sit.	Reported speech
Nakhtmutef	1	3	1
Court members	2	2	—
Talmonth	3	1	1

In this example, the pronoun of the first person singular occurs twice and refers to different individuals in each case.

All the examples cited in this section up to now would also allow for an alternative explanation. Instead of assuming a specific Egyptian type of indirect speech with only a single grammatical person being adapted to the embedding context (*indirect speech, type 2*), it could be claimed that the quotation is only partially coined as indirect speech, while another part of it is formed as ordinary direct speech. The following example clarifies that such an explanation would be inconclusive. Amenhotpe writes a letter to Thutmose, assuring him that he regularly prays for the sake of Thutmose to the deified late king Amenophis I and describing the response of that god:

(26) jw.j-   ꜣw-k   jw.j-   jn-t-k
      FUT:1S- protect:INF-2M.S   FUT:1S- bring-INF-2M.S
      jw-k-   wḏꜣ-tj   jw-k-   mḥ
      COMP-2M.S- be.save:STAT-2S COMP-2M.S- fill:INF
      jr-t-k   m-   p-   wbꜣ   ḥr-f
      eye-F-2M.S with- ART- courtyard say:PRS-3M.S

'He₁ would protect you, he₁ would bring you back safe, and you would be able to see the court (of the temple) again, he always says.' (Černý 1939: 28,5–6 = pBM 10417, vso. 4–5)

(26')		Primary sp. sit.	Second. sp. sit.	Reported speech
	Deified Amenophis	1	3	1
	Thutmose	3	2	2
	Amenhotpe	–	1	–

Here, it is significant that within one and the same reported speech, Thutmose is referred to several times by means of a second person pronoun, with the first person pronoun referring to the deified king intervening. It would be very peculiar to assume that this reported speech is composed of no less than four distinct fragments of direct and indirect speech alternating with each other — and, in addition, changing from one type to the other within a single phonological word (*jw-j- jn.t-k* > Coptic ⲉⲓⲉⲛⲧⲕ, see *Peust* (1996: 55), for more evidence of this kind).

So as not to make things too easy, however, we must state that there is indeed a "composite type" of reported speech in Late Egyptian. Sometimes in a reported speech, all grammatical persons are initially expressed with respect to the primary speech situation (i.e. as direct speech), but at some point within the quotation one of the grammatical persons is shifted resulting in the type of indirect speech with adaptation of a single personal role as outlined above. Example (27) is taken from the Tale of the Two Brothers, the only extant copy of which was written c.1200 BCE. The wife of one of the two protagonists attempts to seduce her brother-in-law Bata.

(27) jw-s- ḏd n-f mj jr-y-n
COMP-3F.S- say:INF for-3M.S come:IMP make-SUBJ-1P
n-n wnw-t sḏr-w
for-1P hour-F sleep:STAT-3P

'... and she said to him: "Come and let us spend some time *making*₃ₚ love."' (Gardiner 1932: 12,10–11 = Two Brothers 3,7)

While the narrator let the woman's speech begin in the first person plural as she would have expressed the utterance herself, he shifted to the third person ending of the final verb form (literally: 'while *they* sleep'). In translating this utterance into English we must not render the personal pronouns mechanically but have to decide either for direct speech as above or for an alternative version in indirect speech which would run: '... and she said to him that *he*₂ should come so that *they*₁ would spend some time making love.'

(27')		Primary sp. sit.	Second. sp. sit.	Reported speech
	Woman	1	3	–
	Bata	2	3	2
	Woman and Bata	1 (pl.)	3 (pl.)	1 (pl.) > 3 (pl.)
	Narrator	3	1	–
	Readers	3	1	–

The subsequent passage (28) is even more complex. It is required to assume the existence of a third speech situation since the reported speech in question is doubly embedded. The example is extracted from the narration of Merire in the Netherworld which is attested on a manuscript of Late Period origin and narrated in the third person. The young priest Merire is about to sacrifice his life on behalf of the Pharaoh and desires that after his early death, the king should protect the departed's family. Merire's urgent request (secondary speech situation) is expressed in direct speech but contains another utterance ascribed to the Pharaoh (primary speech situation). This speech within the speech exhibits a delayed adaptation of the personal role to the basic level of the narrative (tertiary speech situation).

(28) 𓏞 𓏭 𓅓𓂋𓇳 𓂋𓈎 𓈖𓂝 𓅓𓂦𓎛
    ḏd   n-f   Mr.Rʿ ʿrq   n-j   m.bȝḥ
    said:PST for-3M.S Merire swear:IMP for-1S before

𓊪𓏏𓎛 𓏞 𓂜𓈖 𓇋𓅱𓂝𓀜 𓂞𓏏 𓇋𓅱
Ptḥ   ḏd   bn-   jw.j-   dj-t-   jw
Ptah COMP NEG- FUT:1S- cause-INF- go:SUBJ

𓊵𓏏𓏐𓈖𓀗𓏪 𓏏𓏭𓎡   𓈔𓏏   𓂋𓏤𓃀𓃭   𓈖   𓉐𓉻𓎡
Ḥnw.t.Nfr.t ty-k-   ḥm-t   r.bl   n-   py-k-
Henutnofret DEM.F–2M.S- wife–F out of- DEM-2M.S-

𓉐 (...) 𓂜 𓇋𓅱𓂝𓀜 𓂸𓃀𓀁 𓂋𓋴 𓎛𓂝𓏤𓀀
prw   bn-   jw:j-   nw   r-s   ḥʿ-j
house   NEG- FUT:1S- look:INF to-3F.S REFL-1S

𓅓𓏏𓆑 𓃀𓏤𓎛𓀜 𓊪 𓋹𓈖𓐍 𓂋𓏤𓀁
mt-f-   lwḥ   p-   ʿnḫ   j:jr
DEP-3M.S- break:INF ART- oath do:PPP

𓂋𓆓𓃀𓀁 𓉐𓋴𓏥 𓂝𓈖𓅱
r.ḏbȝ-   py-s-   ʿnw
because.of- DEM-3F.S- beauty

'Merire asked him to swear to him₁ before Ptah that he₁ would not drive his₂ wife Henutnofret out of his₂ house [...], that he₁ would not ogle at her himself₁ [...] and break the agreed oath because of her beauty.'
(Posener 1985:51 = pVandier 2,6 and 2,8–9 [with omissions], c.500 BCE)

(28′)

	Prim. sp. sit.	Sec. sp. sit.	Tert. sp. sit.	Reported speech
Pharaoh	1	2	3	1 > 3
Merire	2	1	3	2
Merire's wife	3	3	3	3
Narrator	–	–	1	–

Again, it is impractical to render the personal pronouns quite mechanically. We are free to choose between a variety of possible translations into English, but in any case have to shift at least one personal pronoun (cf. 28″ and 28‴).

(28″) Merire asked him: "Swear to me before Ptah that *you*₁ will not drive *my*₂ wife Henutnofret out of *my*₂ house [...], that *you*₁ will not ogle at her *yourself*₁ [...] and that *you*₃ (will not) break the agreed oath because of her beauty."

(28''') Merire asked him: "Swear to me before Ptah, saying: 'I will not drive your wife Henutnofret out of your house [. . .], I will not ogle at her myself [. . .] and I₃ (will not) break the agreed oath because of her beauty."

Indirect speech of type 2 as discussed in this section is still to be found in Coptic. The following literary text recounts how the sick daughter of the Byzantine Emperor was sent to a monastery in Egypt to be healed. After she returned home healthy, her father inquired how she had been cured. She told him that the monk in whose cell she lived used to kiss her and to sleep with her in one bed. The Emperor arranges a meeting with the monk and speaks to him:

(29) ⲁ-ⲥ-ϫⲟⲟ-ⲥ ⲅⲁⲣ ⲛⲁ-ⲓ ⲛϭⲓ ⲧⲁ-ϣⲉⲉⲣⲉ
a-s-'jɔː-s gar na-j nkʲi ta-'ʃeːrə
PST-3F.S-say:INF-3F.S PTCL for-1S PTCL POSS:1s-daughter

ϫⲉ ϩⲁϩ ⲛ-ⲥⲟⲡ ϣⲁ-ⲕ-ⲁⲥⲡⲁϫⲉ
jə 'hah n-'sɔp ʃa-k-as'padʒə
COMP many of-occasion HAB-2M.S-kiss:INF

ⲛ-ⲧⲁ-ⲧⲁⲡⲣⲟ ⲁⲩⲱ ϫⲉ ϣⲁ-ⲕ-ⲉⲛⲕⲟⲧⲕ
n-ta-tap'rə awo jə ʃa-k-ən'kɔtk
PREP-POSS:1s-mouth CNJ COMP HAB-2M.S-sleep:INF

ϩⲓϫⲛ ⲟⲩ-ⲡⲟⲓ ⲛ-ⲟⲩⲱⲧ ⲛⲙⲙⲁ-ⲓ ⲛ-ⲧⲉ-ⲟⲩϣⲏ ⲧⲏⲣ-ⲥ
hijn- u-'pɔj n-'wot nmma-j n-tə-w'ʃi 'tir-s
on- IDEF-bed ATTR-single with-1s in-ART.F-night all-3F.S

'My daughter has told me that you frequently kissed her on the mouth and that you used to sleep with her₁ in a single bed all night.' (Drescher 1947: 11, lines 16–18)

The communicative roles of (29) are represented in the following chart:

(29')		Primary sp. sit.	Second. sp. sit.	Reported speech
	Emperor's daughter	1	3	1
	Emperor	2	1	–
	Monk	3	2	2

6. Interference on the universe of discourse (indirect speech, type 3) in Late Egyptian reported speech

Having focused on the adaptation of personal roles in Late Egyptian indirect speech, we will now turn our attention to another type of reported speech. Here, all pronominal elements are selected with respect to the primary speech situation, in the manner of direct speech. Nevertheless, there is some influence of the embedding context on the quotation with respect to the usage of articles and the possibilities of pronominalization. This is a second type of indirect speech in Egyptian, which has to be distinguished from type 2, discussed in Section 5.

Let us first consider the following citation from a letter written by Butehamun, whom we have already encountered above (cf. example 23), to his father Thutmose:

(30) jr- py-k- ḏd t- md-t n-
TOP- DEM-2M.S- saying:INF ART.F- matter-F of-
py- šrj n- Jw.Nfr(.t) r.ḏd bp-k-
DEM- son of- Iunofre COMP NEG-2M.S-
ḥꜣb n-j ꜥ-f
report:INF for-1s state-3M.S
'When you talked about this son of Iunofre, saying that I had not informed you about his state . . .' (Černý 1939: 32,14–15 = pTurin 1971, vs. 6–7)

The quotation *bp-k- ḥꜣb -n-j ꜥ-f*— literally 'you did not inform me about his state' — is composed like a direct speech in that none of the grammatical personal roles has been adapted to the embedding context. On the other hand, an utterance 'you did not inform me about his state' is not likely to be expected as a direct speech — at least not as isolated as it occurs in example (30), when the referent of the third person pronoun is not included in the quotation. We might surmise that the "original" wording of Thutmose would have contained the full name of the person referred to instead of a mere pronoun. The use of the pronoun has only become possible in the reported speech because the referent has already been identified in the preceding embedding context. Luckily, Thutmose's original letter to which Butehamun is referring in the passage cited above has also been preserved and is thus known to us. In this memorandum addressed to Butehamun (Papyrus British Museum 10326), the situation was stated by his father as follows:

(31) ḥr   mdj-   p-   tm-   ḥ3b   j.jr-k-
     CNJ with- ART- abstain:INF report:INF do:REL-2.M.S-

     n-j   p-   jr-y-k   n-   p-   śrj   n-   Jw.nfr.t
     for-1S ART- do-PPP–2M.S for- ART- son   of- Iunofre

'And as to the fact that you did not inform me about what you did with the son of Iunofre . . .' (Černý 1939:19,6–7 = pBM 10326, vs. 4)

The reader will recognize that in Butehamun's quoting this text (cf. 30), the passage has been basically reworded, including a pronominalization of the noun phrase 'the son of Iunofre' which has become possible only due to the preceding embedding context. A reported speech of this type may also be viewed as being pragmatically adapted to the embedding context and thus fits the definition of indirect rather than that of direct speech.

In example (32), the female official Henuttawi informs her male colleague Nesamenope that, collecting taxes from a fisherman, she received less than the 80 sacks of barley which Nesamenope had ordered her to obtain.

(32)   jw-j-   dd   n-f   jḫ   p-   ḫ3r   72½
       COMP-1F.S- say:INF for-3M.S what ART- sack   72½

       ḫ3r   n-   jt   j-n-j   n-f   ḥr.jw ḫ3r   80
       sack of- barley say-PRET-1F.S for-3M.S CNJ   sack   80

       ḥr-s   m-   ty-f-   šꜥ-t
       say:PRS-3F.S namely- DEM.F-3M.S- letter-F

'And I asked him (i.e. the fisherman): "How come the 72½ sacks of barley?" that's what I said to him, "whereas *his* letter says 80 sacks?"' (Černý 1939:58,4–5 = pGeneva D191, 14–15)

The address of Henuttawi to the fisherman exhibits the grammatical personal roles of the primary context and thus, at first glance, seems to be direct speech. When speaking to the fisherman however, Henuttawi could not simply have referred to 'his letter' but would have had to mention Nesamenope by name or title to make her message understandable. What happened in (32) is that Henuttawi pronominalized the noun phrase referring to Nesamenope because Nesamenope was one of the comunication partners of the embedding context. On the other hand, Henuttawi referred to Nesamenope by means of a third person pronoun, as it was required from the vantage point of the primary speech situation. We may state that personal pronouns are selected as appropriate for direct speech, while the possibilities of pronominalization depend on the speech situation of the embedding context. This is actually an example of indirect speech labeled here *type 3*.

Closely related is another phenomenon. The usage of the definite article sometimes gives evidence for the embedding context influencing a reported speech although no adaptation in the domain of personal deixis takes place. The two final examples of this section are taken from administrative protocols written down during investigations into the robberies of royal sepulchres (c.1110 BCE). To begin with (33), Peikhal admitted that he had broken into the tomb of a queen and confessed:

(33) jn-j   nhy-n-   ꜣḫ-t   jm
     fetch:PST-1S IDEF.P-of-   property-F.P   there
     'I took some property from there.' (Peet 1930: pl. 2 = pAbbot 4,16–17)

Subsequently, Peikhal was taken close to the place in question and asked by the investigator:

(34) j.śm   r.ḫꜣ.t-n   r-   p-   ḥr   j.ḏd-k
     go:IMP   before-1P   to-   ART-   tomb   say:REL-2M.S
     jn-j   n   ꜣḫ-t   jm-f
     fetch:PST-1S   ART.P-   property-F.P in–3M.S
     'Go ahead of us to the tomb about which you said "I stole *the* property from it."' (Peet 1930: pl. 3 = pAbbot 5,2)

In (33) the thief referred to the stolen properties by means of an indefinite article since he was mentioning them for the first time. Later his confession is quoted virtually unchanged, except for the fact that the indefinite article is replaced by a definite one (cf. 34), as the properties have now become known to all communication partners. The wording of the reported speech may thus indeed be said to have been influenced by the speech situation of the actual embedding context.

We can generalize that indirect speech in Late Egyptian does not necessarily imply the adaptation of one personal role (*indirect speech, type 2*), but may also be obvious from more subtle grammatical criteria which indicate that knowledge of the embedding context is accessible within the quotation (*indirect speech, type 3*).

7. A few remarks on diachrony

Due to the lack of studies on reported speech in different chronolects over more than four millennia of Egyptian language history[5] (and in particular because of the fact that the classical literary norm of Middle Egyptian is still awaiting a thorough investigation), it is not possible now to reconstruct the diachronic development in detail. So we shall only present a few isolated observations which nevertheless may shed light on some remarkable processes of linguistic change.

The grammaticalization of a verb of utterance like Egyptian ḏd 'say' into a quotative marker is a semantic shift not uncommon in human languages (*Roncador* 1988: 110–113, Heine et al. 1993: 190–191), and such a development took place in Egyptian, too. Two of the examples cited above show the use of the expression r-ḏd — originally: 'in order to say' — or its younger successor ḏd serving as a quotative mark which follows another lexical item referring to a communicative action (cf. ꜥnḫ r-ḏd 'an oath that' in 25, ꜥrq ḏd 'swear that' in 28). We may conjecture that the process of grammaticalization of ḏd began because communicative verbs presupposing information about the semantic content of the reported utterance (e.g. 'ask', 'swear', 'foretell', 'deny', 'assure', 'praise') apparently were not capable to govern quotations in Old Egyptian. Thus, under such circumstances the speaker could refer to the respective utterance only by means of descriptive expressions (e.g. 'what you said', 'oath'). If it seemed necessary to quote the wording, an additional quotation index r-ḏd or m-ḏd — originally: 'in saying' — was used. Not later than when r-ḏd / m-ḏd was employed after the verb ḏd 'say' also, had the former lost its lexical meaning and become a grammatical morpheme. Whether (35), taken from a text of the late third millennium, already exhibits such a pleonastic use of m-ḏd is questionable, as transitive ḏd 'say' and ḏd ḥr- 'call' (with obligatory prepositional complement) might be analyzed as two different verbs. A less ambiguous example of r-ḏd, attested in a tomb inscription of the Twelfth Dynasty (c.1991–1785 BCE), is quoted in (36).

(35) j-w   ḏd(-j)   ḥr-k   ḥḥ   n(j)-   zp   m-
     TOP-1s say:PRS-1s near-2M.S million   DETER-   case   in-
     ḏd   mrr-w-   nbw-f
     say:INF   love-IPP-   lord-3M.S
     'I have been calling you ceaselessly a favourite of his lord.' (Edel 1955/64: §713 = Urk. I 180,2–3)

(36) ꜥḥꜥ-n   ḏd-n-f   n-sn   r.ḏd   m-tn   rḏ-n-j   n-tn
     stand:DEP-PRET   say-PRET-3M.S for-3P   COMP   PTCL-2P   give-PRET-1s   for-2P
     'And then he said to them: "I have given to you (...)"' (Gardiner 1957: §224 = Siut I 275)

The process of grammaticalization going on further, (r-)ḏd could be used as complementizer to mark clauses governed by non-communicative verbs by the middle of the second millennium (cf. Gardiner 1957: § 224, Junge 1996: 84–5) and occurred in the function of a purpose and result clause marker no later than the Demotic period and perhaps already in Late Egyptian (cf. 37 and see Junge 1996: 151).

(37) jw-s-   ḥr-   ḏd   n-f   j.jr-j-   jy   n-k
COMP-3F.S- on- say:INF for-3M.S AUX-1F.S- come:INF for-2M.S

r-ḏd   ḏꜣ-y-k   r-   p-   jw-ḥrj-jb
COMP ferry.over–SUBJ–2M.S to- ART- Island-in-the.Midst

'And she said to him: "I have come to you that you ferry over to the Island-in-the-Midst."' (Gardiner 1932: 43,9–10 = Horus and Seth 5,8–9, c.1140 BCE)

The complementizer (r-)ḏd developed into Coptic ϫⲉ /je/, which had an even wider range of usage (cf. Steindorff 1951: §§ 144, 207, 438, 440).

The final issue to be touched on is whether or not the constraints of adapting no more than one grammatical person from within the reported utterance to the embedding context in Late Egyptian indirect speech were valid already in earlier chronolects. Even though a detailed inquiry about the mechanics of indirect speech in Middle Egyptian is still a desideratum, it is by no means impossible to present a few preparatory assumptions.

On the one hand, we could see above in Section 4 that there were cases of indirect speech with total shift of personal roles in Old Egyptian. Instances akin to these are not attested in Late Egyptian. On the other hand, we do not know of any old example of indirect speech of type 2 (adapting no more than one of several grammatical persons to the embedding context), as is the rule in Late Egyptian. *Kammerzell* (1997) has discussed one Middle Egyptian instance of indirect speech with pronoun shift according to the principles as described by *Peust* (1996) and in Section 5 above. However, that very example was taken from a classical literary text the extant copy of which was written down no earlier than the late 15th century BCE. So it cannot be excluded that the wording of the respective quotation had already been influenced by Late Egyptian. That remodeling of Middle Egyptian literary compositions not infrequently happened during the New Kingdom (c.1550–1070) is indisputable. A pertinent example is cited under (38) and (39). In the first instance we see a section from the narrative of Sinuhe as it was passed on in a manuscript written shortly after the original composition of the literary work in the Twelfth Dynasty (c.1800 BCE). The setting is as follows: Sinuhe, the protagonist and narrator of the story, reports that he has been challenged to a duel by an anonymous 'hero from (the country) Retjenu' and contemplates about the warrior's objectives:

(38) 𓂋𓏤 𓉔𓀜 𓎛𓀁 𓐍𓏏𓀜
    ḏd-n-f ꜥḥ3-f ḥnꜥ-j ḥmt-n-f
    say-PRET-3M.S fight:SUBJ-3M.S with-1S intend-PRET-3M.S
    𓉔𓀜 𓎡𓏏𓀁 𓐍𓏤 𓄟𓈖𓀜
    ḥwt(f)-f w k3-n-f ḥ3q mnmn-t-j
    kill:SUBJ-3M.S 1S plan-PRET-3M.S pillage:INF cattle-F-1S
    'He said that he would fight with me, intended to kill me and planned to pillage my cattle.' (Koch 1990: 46,6 and 46,10 = Sinuhe B 111–112, c.1800 BCE)

The clause ꜥḥ3-f ḥnꜥ-j 'that he would fight with me' is embedded as an indirect speech of the same type that we came across in Old Egyptian examples (*type 1*, cf. 12 and 13). Both personal pronouns are adapted to the respective communicative roles of the embedding context and differ from the "original" utterance of Sinuhe's enemy which must have run either 'I will fight with you' or 'I will fight with him' (cf. 38').

(38')		Primary sp. sit.	Second. sp. sit.	Reported speech
	Sinuhe (= narrator)	2 or 3	1	1
	Hero from Retjenu	1	3	3

About half a millennium later, the passage had been considerably altered. First, the reported speech dependent on the initial verb 'say' is ascribed to Sinuhe, and further on several verb forms and pronouns are changed. It is only in this version that k3j 'plan' is treated as a communicative verb governing a reported speech ḥ3q-f mnmn.t-f, which is another example of indirect speech, type 2 (literally: 'that he would pillage his cattle').

(39) 𓂋𓏤 𓈖𓀜 𓉔𓀜 𓎛𓀁
    ḏd-n-j n-f ꜥḥ3-f ḥnꜥ-j
    say-PRET-1S for-3M.S fight:SUBJ-3M.S with-1S
    𓐍𓏏𓀜 𓉔𓀜 𓈖𓀜 𓎡𓏏𓀁
    ḥmt-n-f ḥwtf n-f k3-n-f
    intend-PRET-3M.S kill:INF for-3M.S plan-PRET-3M.S
    𓐍𓏤 𓄟𓈖𓀜
    ḥ3q-f mnmn-t-f
    pillage:SUBJ-3M.S cattle-F-3M.S
    'I told him that he should fight with me. He intended killing for me_3, as he planned that he would pillage my_3 cattle.' (Koch 1990: 46,8 and 46,12 = Sinuhe AOS 44, c.1200 BCE)

The change from $\underline{d}d.n$-f 'he said' into $\underline{d}d.n$-j -n-f 'I said to him' (or any other significant modification of the wording) was inevitable within the frame of rules of a chronolect that allowed adapting no more than one personal role to the embedding context. The situation is shown in the tables below: assuming that in the Ramesside Period only one pronoun could refer to the secondary speech situation, while the other had to be identified with a communicative role of the primary speech situation, the initial clause of (38) at that time would have meant nothing else but either 'The hero of Retjenu said that he (himself) would fight with $himself_1$.' (cf. 39′) or 'The hero of Retjenu said that Sinuhe would fight with $himself_1$.' (cf. 39″).

(39′)

	Primary sp. sit.	Second. sp. sit.	Reported speech
Sinuhe (= narrator)	2 or 3	1	—
Hero from Retjenu	1	3	1 and 3

(39″)

	Primary sp. sit.	Second. sp. sit.	Reported speech
Sinuhe (= narrator)	3	1	3 and 1
Hero from Retjenu	1	3	—

As, however, neither of the alternatives makes sense, the scribe of the Ashmolean Ostracon living six hundred years after the original composition (or already one of his predecessors) evidently decided to modify the text. Why the reported speech was left untouched — as opposed to the subsequent clauses — and the embedding context was modified, we do not know.

Be that as it may, examples (38) and (39) give ample reason for inferring that the rules of Late Egyptian indirect speech of type 2 came into being but after the period of Classical Middle Egyptian — even though the evidence stands quite isolated for the time being. That the specific appearance of indirect speech in Late Egyptian should reflect a primitive state of language development or even mirror cognitive deficiencies of the respective speakers — as has repeatedly been suggested in Egyptological studies (see *Peust* 1996: 41–8 for a review of older opinions) — can at any rate be dismissed.

8. Conclusions

We defined indirect speech as a mode of reporting which shows deviations from the pragmatic setting to be reconstructed for the primary speech situation in at least one point, provided that these deviations are explainable by specific interferences of the secondary context into which the reported speech is embedded. Egyptian quotations can be formulated in direct speech as well as in indirect speech. There are several subtypes of indirect speech depending on which grammatical category is adapted to the embedding context. If personal deictic elements are adapted, this could affect all personal roles in Earlier Egyptian (*indirect speech, type 1*). In Late Egyptian, however, only one personal role can be affected, whereas the others have to be expressed as would be appropriate for direct speech (*type 2*). Furthermore, the adaptation of one personal role need not be applied from the very beginning of the citation but may start in a later part of it. In addition to these, there is another type of indirect speech which shows no shifting of personal pronouns at all but rather an influence of the universe of discourse connected with the speech situation of the embedding context (*type 3*). This can manifest itself in the use of a definite article or in a pronominalization indicating that particular items of knowledge present in the situation of the embedding context are accessible within the reported speech. There is no shifting of verbal tense in any type of Egyptian indirect speech.

Notes

* We are obliged to the editors for their invitation to contribute to this volume and in particular thank Tom Güldemann for valuable comments on an earlier draft of this chapter. Gordon Whittaker was so kind to correct the English. Sections 2, 5, 6, and 8 were written by Carsten Peust. Frank Kammerzell is the author of Sections 1, 3, 4, and 7.

1. There is, however, some evidence (e.g. two different lexical strata discernible already in the earliest period) that the formation process of the Egyptian language took place during a situation of intense language contact in a not to distant past from the historical period, and that two distinct linguistic communities contributed to the emergence of what we know as the Egyptian language.

2. It is a well-known fact that particular utterances of the Pyramid Texts had originally been composed as if they were spoken by the dead king. At some time during the process of copying them on the walls, many first person pronouns were substituted by pronouns of the third person or by the name of the pyramid owner. The reader should not be bewildered by the fact that the pronominal suffix of the first person did not leave any trace in the hieroglyphic form of (8″). Its phonological shape can be reconstructed as a long vowel /iː/, which according to the rules of the Egyptian writing system was frequently not represented in texts of the third millennium.

3. Since a development 'as, like' > COMP is a common path of semantic change, there is good reason to assume that both -*js* are etymologically related.
4. Personal pronouns that had to be shifted in the translation are given in italics. The index informs about which grammatical person appears instead in the Egyptian text.
5. To date, only one exhaustive, corpus-based study has been conducted (*Peust* 1996). Its thematic frame is the period of Late Egyptian (14th–7th centuries BCE).

References

Allen, James P. 1984. *The inflection of the verb in the Pyramid Texts* (=Bibliotheca Aegyptia 2). Malibu: Undena Publications.
Černý, Jaroslav. 1939. *Late Ramesside letters* (=Bibliotheca Aegyptiaca 9). Bruxelles: Fondation Égyptologique Reine Élisabeth.
Černý, Jaroslav and Alan H. Gardiner. 1957. *Hieratic ostraca, Volume 1*. Oxford: Griffith Institute.
Depuydt, Leo. 1989. "The contingent tenses of Egyptian". *Orientalia* 58: 1–27.
Drescher, James. 1947. *Three Coptic legends: Hilaria, Archellites, The Seven Sleepers, edited with translation and commentary* (=Annales du Service des Antiquités de l'Égypte, supplement 4). Cairo: Institut Français d'Archéologie Orientale.
Drioton, Étienne. 1943. "Description sommaire des chapelles funéraires de la VIe dynastie récemment découvertes derrière le mastaba de Mérérouka à Sakkarah". *Annales du Service des Antiquités de l'Égypte* 43: 487–514.
Edel, Elmar. 1955/64. *Altägyptische Grammatik*, 2 vols. (=Annalecta Orientalia 34 and 39). Roma: Pontificium Institutum Biblicum.
Erman, Adolf. 1919. *Reden, Rufe und Lieder auf Gräberbildern des Alten Reiches* (=Abhandlungen der Preußischen Akademie der Wissenschaften, Jahrgang 1918, Phil.-Hist. Klasse 15). Berlin: Verlag der Akademie der Wissenschaften.
Faulkner, Raymond O. 1969. *The Ancient Egyptian Pyramid Texts translated into English*. Oxford: Oxford University Press.
Gardiner, Alan H. 1932. *Late-Egyptian stories* (=Bibliotheca Aegyptiaca 1). Bruxelles: Fondation Égyptologique Reine Élisabeth.
Gardiner, Alan H. 1957. *Egyptian grammar. Being an introduction to the study of hieroglyphs*. 3rd edition. Oxford: Griffith Institute, Ashmolean Museum
Hassan, Selim (with the collaboration of Abdelsalam Abdelsalam). 1936. *Excavations at Gîza 1930–1931* (=Gîza 2). Cairo: Faculty of Arts of the Egyptian University.
Heine, Bernd, Tom Güldemann, Christa Kilian-Hatz, Donald A. Lessau, Heinz Roberg, Mathias Schladt and Thomas Stolz. 1993. *Conceptual shift. A lexicon of grammaticalization processes in African languages* (=Afrikanistische Arbeitspapiere 34/5).
Jansen-Winkeln, Karl. 1997. "Intensivformen und 'verbale Pluralität' im Ägyptischen". *Lingua Aegyptia* 5: 123–136.
Jéquier, Gustave. 1933. *Les pyramides des reines Neit et Apouit*. Cairo: Service des Antiquités de l'Égypte.

Jespersen, Otto. 1924. *The philosophy of grammar*, London: Allen and Unwin.
Junge, Friedrich. 1996. *Einführung in die Grammatik des Neuägyptischen*, Wiesbaden: Harrassowitz.
Kahl, Jochem, Nicole Kloth and Ursula Zimmermann. 1995. *Die Inschriften der 3. Dynastie. Eine Bestandsaufnahme* (=Ägyptologische Abhandlungen 56). Wiesbaden: Harrassowitz.
Koch, Roland. 1990. *Die Erzählung des Sinuhe* (=Bibliotheca Aegyptiaca 17). Bruxelles: Éditions de la Fondation Égyptologique Reine Élisabeth.
Lange, Hans O. 1925. *Das Weisheitsbuch des Amenemope aus dem Papyrus 10.474 des British Museum*, Copenhagen: A.S. Host.
Peet, Thomas E. 1930. *The great tomb-robberies of the Twentieth Egyptian Dynasty*, Oxford: Clarendon Press.
Posener, Georges. 1985. *Le Papyrus Vandier* (=Bibliothèque Générale 7). Cairo: Institut Français d'Archéologie Orientale.
Sethe, Kurt. 1908–1922. *Die altägyptischen Pyramidentexte nach den Papierabdrücken und Photographien des Berliner Museums neu herausgegeben und erläutert*, 4 vols., Leipzig: Hinrichs.
Spencer, A. Jeffrey. 1980. *Catalogue of Egyptian antiquities in the British Museum, Vol. V: Early dynastic objects*, London: British Museum.
Steindorff, Georg. 1951. *Lehrbuch der koptischen Grammatik*, Chicago: University of Chicago Press.

CHAPTER 14

'Report' constructions in Kambera (Austronesian)*

Marian Klamer
Universiteit Leiden

1. Introduction

Despite the typological data presented by *Munro* (1982), *Roeck* (1994) and others, three major assumptions about quotative constructions seem to persist in both functional and generative linguistic models: (1) that the quote is a complement of the main predicate, (2) that there is a strict dichotomy between direct and indirect speech, and (3) that quotative verbs are speech verbs, or historically derived thereof.[1]

In this chapter I present a brief analysis of quotative constructions in Kambera and demonstrate that these assumptions do not tally with the facts of this language. Kambera belongs to the Central Malayo-Polynesian subgroup of Austronesian languages, is spoken on the island of Sumba in eastern Indonesia by approximately 150,000 speakers, and described in Klamer (1998).

In Section 1, I consider the structural properties of the Kambera quotative construction and contrast them with the morphosyntax of common Kambera verbs and arguments. In Section 2, we will see that Kambera quotative constructions do not make a syntactic distinction between direct and indirect speech. More particularly, the quotative construction is not only used for speech reports, but also to report thoughts, intentions, and physical perceptions. The latter is done by employing ideophonic roots in a quotative construction. In Section 3, I discuss the use of *wà* as a discourse particle in two distinct types of contexts. In Section 4, the consequences our findings have for a semantic analysis of *wà* are discussed. I propose that, rather than a speech verb, *wà* is a verb with the semantics of a [REPORT]. In other words, it does not derive from a speech verb, but is much more generic in nature (see also *Klamer* 2000).

2. The syntactic status of the Kambera 'quote'

Kambera is a head-marking language; verbal arguments are commonly marked on the verb by pronominal clitics. The agent argument of a simple declarative sentence and the single argument of an intransitive predicate are canonically marked with a nominative proclitic, a patient object is canonically marked with an accusative enclitic. The coreferential noun phrases are optional.

(1) Na tau wútu na-palu-ka nyungga
    ART person be.fat 3s.NOM-hit-1s.ACC I
    'The big man hit me.'

(2) Na ài na-tambuta dàngu amung
    ART wood 3s.NOM-drop.out with root
    'That tree is uprooted.'

Despite the fact that a nominative proclitic is their unmarked expression, we also find subjects expressed as genitive enclitics. The core function of a genitive clitic is to mark nominal possessors, as in (3).

(3) Na ama-mu
    ART father-2s.GEN
    'your father'

As a subject marker, the genitive is commonly used in syntactically embedded clauses: the relative clauses in (21)–(22) and the complement clause in the next example have genitive subjects:

(4) Nda ku-pí-a-nya na ngàndi-*mu* kuta
    NEG 1s.NOM-know-MOD-3s.DAT ART take-2s.GEN plant
    'I didn't know that you would bring kuta.'

But we also find genitive subjects in syntactically non-embedded clauses:

(5) Ba meu-meu-*na*, ba na-imbu-ya
    while RDP-roar-3s.GEN as 3s.NOM-search-3s.ACC
    'And it roared while it went after him'

This type of 'nominal clause' functions to provide the background information for the clauses that carry the main narrative. They express irrealis mood, which explains why they are often used in questions or in expressions of concession, amazement, exaggeration, or unexpectedness, for example:

(6) Hangu butang-butang-ma-a-*na* bai manila,
    straight.away RDP-pull.out-EMPH-just-3s.GEN real peanut
    nda na-hili karai
    NEG 3s.NOM-again ask
    'He just began to pull out peanuts straight away, he didn't even ask'

Though syntactically not embedded, nominal clauses are functionally dependent. This is also reflected in the fact that adverbials expressing tense, aspect, mood and degree have scope over them, as illustrated by *hangu* 'straight away' in (6) and *lundu* 'until' in (7), which are both obligatorily followed by nominal clauses.

(7) Lundu njili-nggu   ba ku-yaulu-ya   na wei
     until   be.tired-1s.GEN as   1s.NOM-chase-3s.ACC ART pig
     'Till I got tired I chased the pig.'

In sum, genitive subjects are marked because they feature in clauses that are syntactically and/or discourse dependent, while the unmarked expression of subjects in main declarative clauses is by a nominative proclitic (for more discussion, see Klamer 1998, Section 4.2).

Kambera complements (including clausal ones) are crossreferenced on the verb with a pronominal object clitic. The regular form for patients/ themes is an accusative clitic, as illustrated in (1) and (8), and for benefactives/ addressees/ recipients a dative one, as in (9). However, the dative is always selected (both for patients/ themes *and* benefactives/ addressees/ recipients) when the citation form of the verb ends in a nasal. Illustrations are *paàrang* 'ask someone' in (10), where the dative object clitic *-nya* marks the addressee, and *píng* 'know something' in (4) where *-nya* marks the theme.

(8) Da-ngàndi-*ya*   na uhu
     3P.NOM-take-3s.ACC ART rice
     'They take the rice'

(9) Da-ngàndi-*nya*   na uhu i   Ama
     3P.NOM-take-3s.DAT ART rice ART father
     'They bring father the rice'

(10) Jàka na-paàra-*nya*-ka   nggi-ya-ka   i   Umbu, . . .
     if   3s.NOM-ask-3s.DAT-PFV where-3s.ACC-PFV ART Lord
     'If he asks him where the Master is, if he asks that . . .'

With this background information we are equipped to analyze the structure of quotative constructions in Kambera. The default marker in these constructions is the quotative verb *wà*: more than 90% of the cases of reported speech in my database (12 hours of spontaneous texts) are accompanied by this element. It has always at least one pronominal clitic attached to it: a genitive enclitic that marks the speaker. The quote itself does not differ from any other declarative clause in Kambera (neither in the morphological form of the verb, or in its mood, aspect or pronominal marking). Usually, there is no intonation break between the quote and the quotative verb. The following sentences are some illustrations. The quotative verb *wà* is glossed as 'report' in the examples for reasons to be discussed below.

(11) "Ku-ngangu-ma duku" wà-na-ma
1s.NOM-eat-EMPH 1s.EMPH report-3s.GEN-EMPH
'"I have eaten (it)", she said'

(12) "Bidi mini-a nú" àmbu wà-nda-i!
new male-MOD DEI NEG.IRR report-1P.GEN-ASP
'Don't say it's just the young guys!'

(13) Njadi u u nda wà-na, ndia nda wà-na,
so yes NEG report-3s.GEN NEG.EMPH NEG report-3s.GEN
hí-hí-bia-nanya-ka duna
RED-cry-just-3s-PFV 3s.EMPH
'So he neither consents nor protests, he just keeps on crying'

The verb wà is an intransitive root verb, and is mostly used in quotative constructions, though it can also function as a main speech verb:

(14) Wà-nggu ba wà-na hama tu-na-i nú
report-1s.GEN while report-3s.GEN be.same put-3s.GEN-ASP DEI
'I tell (it) as it was told'

Wà's argument-marking properties are limited: its subject must always be a clitic from the genitive paradigm (-nggu 1s.GEN, -mu 2s.GEN, -na 3s.GEN, -ma 1P.E.GEN, -nda 1P.I.GEN, -da 3P.GEN). In other words, wà is always part of a nominal clause, and as such constitutes a dependent clause (see above).

Wà is morphologically regular in that it can be derived with an applicative suffix -ng. This suffix licenses an additional addressee argument: wà 'report' > wà-ng 'report, say to X'. However, the other major Kambera word formation process, causativization, is resisted by wà, so we may say its morphological properties are reduced.[2]

The applicative suffix -ng is not visible when the verb is inflected, but is part of its citation form. The addressee is commonly expressed by a dative object clitic. Illustrations with the applicative form wà-ng are:

(15) E, wà-nggu-nya na ama-mu!
EXCL report-1s.GEN-3s.DAT ART father-2s.GEN
'Hey, I was talking to your father!'

(16) "Mài-kai-wa" wà-na-nggai
come-2P.ACC-HORT report-3s.GEN-2P.GEN
'He says that you must come' (lit. '"You come", he tells you')

Unlike ordinary complement clauses as the one in (4), quotes are not cross-referenced with clitics on the quotative verb, but are simply juxtaposed to the quotative clause. This is another indication that a quote is not a syntactic complement of the quotative verb. Sentence (17a) contains two quotes: "Kill the foal" and "Kill the foal, I said". Neither can be crossreferenced on the quotative verb, as shown in (17b) and (17c).

(17) a. Tobu-nya   na ana njara wà-nggu
       slaughter-3s.DAT ART child horse report-1s.GEN
       ba wà-mi   nú
       as report-2P.GEN DEI
       '"We'll kill the foal", you (pl.) said'
   b. [Tobu-nya   na ana njara]ᵢ wà-*nggu-*nyaᵢ* ...
       slaughter-3s.DAT ART child horse report-1s.GEN-3s.DAT
   c. [Tobu-nya   na ana njara wà-nggu]ᵢ
       slaughter-3s.DAT ART child horse report-1s.GEN
       ba wà-*mi-*nyaᵢ* ...
       as report-2P.GEN-3s.DAT

In fact, coordinating conjunctions such as *hi* 'and, so', *ka* 'so that', *ba* 'and, as, while, because' and *jàka* 'if, when' may always appear optionally between the quote and the quotative clause, also suggesting that they are two independent, coordinated clauses. In (18) the conjunction in the quotative clause is *hi*, in (19) *ka* and in (20) *jàka*. Note that the quotes themselves also contain initial conjunctions: *ka, hi* and *hi*, respectively.

(18) "Ai Umbu, ka   nda u-mila-ngga   nú eti"
     EXCL Lord so.that NEG 2s.NOM-be.poor-1s.DAT DEI liver
     hi wà-na-nya
     and report-3s.GEN-3s.DAT
     '"Oh sir, if you would take pity on me," he said to him.'
     (Lit. '"Wouldn't you have a poor liver for me," he said to him.')

(19) "... hi na-ana   hàmu na wài ngera-mu"
          and 3s.NOM-DIM be.good ART water spirit-2s.GEN
     ka   wà-da-du-nya-ka   nú
     so.that report-3P.GEN-MOD-3s.DAT-PFV DEI
     '"... so that you will fare well" (lit. so that your fate will be a little better), they said to him.'

(20) "... hi nda rongu hàmu-bia-da-nya-ika   uda"
          and NEG hear be.good-MOD-3P.GEN-3s.DAT-ASP 3P.EMPH
     '"... and they won't hear it clearly once again",
     jàka wà-na-ka   i Umbu Mbara, ...
     when report-3s.GEN-PFV ART Lord Mbara
     "when Lord Mbara said that..."

Another important difference between Kambera quotes and true verbal complements is the fact that though the unmarked constituent order in Kambera is verb-object, without exception quotes *precede* the quotative verb (i.e. represent object-verb word order).

In addition, the fact that Kambera quotes may appear *without* the quote verb *wà* also suggests that they are not verbal complements but embedded at the discourse level.

Evidence for the non-transitive status of *wà* is that this verb, unlike normal transitive verbs, cannot appear in object relativizations. Object relativizations in Kambera are marked by the morpheme *pa-*. Patients/ themes and beneficiaries/ addressees/ recipients undergo the same relativization. Below this is illustrated for the theme of *ngàndi* 'take something' and the recipient of *ngàndi-ng* 'take something to someone':

(21) Na nggula na *pa*-ngàndi-nggu
 ART sugar ART OBJ.REL-take-1S.GEN
 'The sugar that I took (along)'

(22) Da makaweda da *pa*-ngàndi-nggu nggula
 ART old.woman ART OBJ.REL-take.to-1S.GEN sugar
 'The old ladies whom I brought the sugar'

Relativizations are standardly used in questions, as in (23), and may function like passives, as in (24) and (25). (Kambera does not have a separate passive construction, as argued in Klamer 1996; 1998, Section 8.1.5).

(23) Nggàra *pa-ngàndi*-mu, Rambu?
 what OBJ.REL-take-2P.GEN Lady
 'What did you bring, ma'am?'

(24) a. [Nggula [pa-ngàndi-na$_j$]]-nya$_k$
 sugar OBJ.REL-take-3S.GEN-3S.DAT
 'It$_k$ (is) sugar that (is) brought by her$_j$'
 b. [Pa-ngàndi(-na$_j$)]-ya$_k$
 OBJ.REL-take(-3S.GEN)-3S.ACC
 'It$_k$ is brought (by her$_j$)'

If we now consider the quotative verb *wà*, we find that this verb never appears in object relativizations, or in such passive-like structures:

(25) *[Pa-wà-mu]-nya
 OBJ.REL-report-2S.GEN-3S.DAT
 'It is said (by her)'

Does this mean that a Kambera speaker cannot question what is being said? The answer is negative: in questions about the content of a quote, a bare form of *wà* is used — the object relative marker *pa-* is absent:

(26) Nggàra *wà*-mu, Rambu?
 what report-2P.GEN Lady
 'What did you say/think, ma'am?'

Interestingly, the same construction is used to question adjuncts of *wà*, such as *pira* 'how much', and *nggiki* 'how, in what way':

(27) "Pira wà-mu-nja nú?" "Ana hau ndui"
 how.much report-2S.GEN-3P.DAT DEI DIM one money
 wà-na
 report-3S.GEN
 '"How much did you ask from them?" '"Just one coin", he said'

(28) Nggiki *wà*-nggu ba ku-karai-nya?
 how report-1S.GEN while 1S.NOM-ask-3S.DAT
 'How should I ask him?'

(29) Nggiki *wà*-mu?
 how report-2S.GEN
 'How do you think about it?'

The absence of the relative marker in these questions is explained when we assume that the questioned elements are all adjuncts: like *pira* 'how much', and *nggiki* 'how', *nggàra* 'what' does not question an argument but an adjunct of *wà*. This confirms our analysis that Kambera quotes are not syntactic complements of the quotative verb.

In sum, we analyze the Kambera quote verb *wà* as an intransitive verb. This converges with the crosslinguistic observations about 'say' verbs of *Munro* (1982) and the typological findings reported by *de Roeck* (1994). Indeed, intransitive quote verbs are very common crosslinguistically: 37,5 % of the verbs of Roeck's sample behave intransitively, and 10 % behave transitively only with an addressee argument (like Kambera *wà-ng*). Only 47,5 % allow for the quote to be treated as the verbal complement. In other words, Kambera is very common in this respect.

Interestingly, there are indications that *wà* with a third person singular genitive marker may become reanalyzed as a monomorphemic verbal root. The motivation for this reanalysis comes from the prosodic structure of the verbal root *wà*. Phonologically, this root does not comply with the minimal word requirements of Kambera, which state that the roots of content words must be bimoraic feet. The sequence *wà-na*, however, is a bimoraic foot, and is therefore a good candidate to become analyzed as a verbal root. In this reanalysis, the genitive clitic loses its referential function, so the subject must be marked otherwise. What we find is that the nominative may take over the job:

(30) Ba   *na*-wà*na*-nya   i   Zacharia ama-na   ...
when 3s.NOM-report-3s.DAT ART Zacharias father-3s.GEN
'When he told his father Zacharias . . .'

Evidence that *wà-na* is treated as a morphological unit comes from the relative position of emphatic clitics and adverbs. Normally, emphatic clitics such as -*ma* and -*du* must precede the genitive clitic, see (31) (and (19)–(20)). With *wà*, however, the order is obligatorily reversed, as the grammaticality contrast in (32) shows:

(31) E,   ba namu-*ma-na*-nya   na ana njara
EXCL as remember-MOD-3s.GEN-3s.DAT ART child horse
'Hey, he loves the foal'

(32) "Na-palu-ka   i   Ina"
3s.NOM-hit-PFV ART mother
nda wà-*na-ma*-nya-i   (*wà-*ma-na*-nya-i)
NEG report-3s.GEN-MOD-3s.DAT-ASP
'He never tells him that his mum hit him again'

Normally, adverbs appear directly adjacent to the verb, interfering between the verb and the clitic cluster, see the position of *mema* 'immediately' in (33). With *wà*, however, the adverb must appear to the right of the clitic, as in (34):

(33) Ngandi *mema-na*-nggai
take   immediately-3s.GEN-2s.DAT
'He brought it to you (pl) immediately'

(34) "U" wà-*na*   *mema*-nggai
yes report-3s.GEN immediately-2P.DAT
'He agreed with you (pl) immediately'

Other evidence comes from speech errors. Strictly speaking, sentence (35) is ungrammatical because it contains two subject markers, one genitive and one nominative. Similarly, sentences may contain two genitive markers:[3]

(35) "Ndia   ná" wà-*na*-ma-du-*na*-nya-ka   nú
NEG.EMPH DEI report-3s.GEN-MOD-MOD-3s.GEN-3s.DAT-PFV EMPH
'"No way!", he said to him'

These are all indications that the quotative verb *wà* plus the subject marking -*na* may be developing into a monomorphemic verb *wàna*. Note however that the reanalysis only concerns forms with a third person singular subject. In general, then, *wà* is still seen as the root form.

3. The variable nature of the Kambera 'quote'

In this section I discuss the various functions of the Kambera quote. We will see that there is no syntactic distinction between direct and indirect speech, and that the quotative construction is also used to report thoughts, intentions, and even physical perceptions. The latter is done by quotative constructions with ideophonic roots.

Let us first consider the direct-indirect speech distinction. In Kambera this distinction is not expressed syntactically. Instead, the language uses pronominal reference strategies and the semantic embedding of quotes to indicate distinct speaker perspectives. A simple illustration is (36). Example (36a) is a direct quote, because the speaker is expressed in the quote by the first person singular *ku-*. In (36b) the subject pronominal in the quote is third person singular *na-*, and this makes it an indirect speech report.

(36) a. *Ku$_j$-lua   haromu   wà-na$_j$-ngga$_k$*
   1s.NOM-go tomorrow report-3s.GEN-1s.DAT
   '"I am leaving tomorrow", she told me'

   b. *Na$_j$-lua   haromu   wà-na$_j$-ngga$_k$*
   3s.NOM-go tomorrow report-3s.GEN-1s.DAT
   'She$_j$ told me$_k$ that she$_j$ is leaving tomorrow'

The following example illustrates how indirect quotations may be embedded into another quote:

(37) *Kambí wà-da   wà-mu-nya*
   bean   report-3P.GEN report-2s.GEN-3s.DAT
   'Tell her that they want beans.' (Lit. '"They said "beans"", you tell her')

Embedding is often used in combination with pronominal reference strategies. This is illustrated in the following sentence, where a man instructs someone else to tell his future father-in-law about his ability to pay a dowry:

(38) "*Na tanda-na   na mila-nggu$_j$,"   ka*
   ART sign-3s.GEN ART be.poor-1s.GEN so
   wà-mu$_k$-nya$_i$ i   Ama$_i$, wà-nggu$_j$-nggau$_k$-ka
   report-2s.GEN-3s.DAT ART father report-1s.GEN-2s.GEN-PFV
   nú, wà-na$_j$-nya$_k$
   DEI report-3s.GEN-3s.DAT
   'I$_j$ ask you$_k$ to inform Father$_i$ about my poverty,[4] he$_j$ said to him$_k$.'
   (Lit. "The evidence of my poverty", you tell Father, I say to you, he said to him')

The embedding of quotes may become rather complex. The following piece of narrative is itself a quote: the narrator quotes someone who is warning the main character of the story, Prince Ndilu, to be aware that he'll need to pay a dowry to get a bride. This is done by quoting a future bride's reaction to his proposal: "If you want it, I'll be your wife — but first get me some dowry":

(39) a. Napa na-paàra-nya-ka   nyuna lai nú:
later 3s.NOM-ask-3s.DAT-PFV her   LOC DEI
'When he'll propose over there, (she'll say:)
b. " "tunú" wà-nggu"   ba wà-mu
like.this report-1s.GEN as report-2s.GEN
"if you want it,
c. kalembi-ya   wà-nggu-ma-nggau-ka   úna nú
family-3s.ACC report-1s.EMPH-DEI-2s.DAT-PFV 3s.DEI DEI
I'll be your wife (Lit. "He's family", I'll say to you)
d. nanyuna, ngàndi-ngga bùdi banda",
but   take.to-1s.GEN firstly cattle
but first get me some dowry",
e. wà-na-nya-ka   nú i Umbu Ndilu.
report-3s.GEN-3s.DAT-PFV DEI ART Lord Ndilu
she'll say to Prince Ndilu.'

The fact that it is the future bride who says the words in (39b-d) is evident from (39e), where Prince Ndilu is the addressee. The woman's quote contains two more embedded quotes. The first of those is in (39b), where she expresses Ndilu's intentions by entering him verbally ("'like this' I want", you say). The second is in (39c), where she expresses her own intentions by quoting the words she would use to him in the future ("'He's family' I'll say to you", i.e., "I'll be your wife").

Note that the latter quotation expresses an intention, but is also a naming strategy. In general, Kambera quotative constructions are regularly used for both of these purposes. The following sentences are additional illustrations of naming constructions:

(40) Laku pa-peknik ba wà-da
go   CTR-picnic as report-3P.GEN
'"Go for a picnic", as they call it'

(41) a. Nyumu Peteru-kau, Peteru wà-nggu-ka   nàhu,
you   Peter-2s.ACC Peter report-1s.GEN-PFV now
"You (are) Peter, I'll say Peter now,
b. nyumu nàhu Peteru wà-nggu-nggau,
you   now Peter report-1s.GEN-2s.DAT
I call you Peter now,

c. Peteru ba *wà*-na, watu *wà*-na.
Peter as report-3s.GEN rock report-3s.GEN
'Peter' means 'rock' (Lit. when one says 'Peter' one says 'rock')"

And the following quotative constructions express intentions and thoughts:

(42) Tobu-nya na ana njara *wà*-nggu
slaughter-3s.DAT ART child horse report-1s.GEN
ba *wà*-mi nú
as report-2P.GEN DEI
'You wanted to kill the foal'

(43) Nggiki *wà*-nggu ba ku-wua-nggau?
how report-1s.GEN as 1s.NOM-give-2s.DAT
'How should I give it to you?'

(44) Nda na-tanda-a-ya una na bai tau . . .
NEG 3s.NOM-know-MOD-3s.ACC 3s.DEI ART real man
'She didn't recognize him, that man . . .
jia na lei-nggu amang nda *wà*-na mbu-pa
exist ART husband-1s.GEN earlier NEG report-3s.GEN also-IPFV
(that) he was her former husband she didn't even realize'

(45) "Banda-nggu nda ningu-a"
cattle-1s.GEN NEG be-MOD
wà-na-ka nú dá la eti-na i Ndilu
report-3s.GEN-PFV DEI inside LOC liver-3s.GEN ART Ndilu
'I don't have property, thought Ndilu'

Finally, to express physical perceptions of motions, sounds and visions, quotative constructions are used in combination with ideophones exemplified in (46). Unlike what the English glosses suggest, these are not verbs but sound-symbolic roots. (To be used as verbs they must undergo circumfixation). These items constitute a separate lexical category with its own formal features: they use special, low vowels (*ò, è, à, ù*) and are the only Kambera roots undergoing circumfixation with *ka-k* (e.g., *mbùtu* 'thud' > *ka-mbùtu-k* 'fall with a thud'.[5]

(46) pòk 'grunt' yidi 'shiver'(dislike)
ngùru 'murmur' wàdi 'blink'
hèri 'tearing noise' ngàdu 'nod'
tòru 'rattle' linji 'jump'
mbùtu 'thud' nggidi 'shiver'(cold)
pàka 'smack' jila 'glimmer, flash'
mbùku 'snap/tap' bila 'light, brightness'

In quotative constructions they occur as they are, but in order to be used verbally, they must be morphologically derived, circumfixed or reduplicated:

(47) a. *Mbùtu* wà-na tu-na nú
    thud report-3s.GEN put-3s DEI
    'Thud!, it did'
  b. Hili odah-ya na hapapa *ka-mbùtu-k*-danya da marara
    again stroke-3s.ACC ART side fall.thudding-3P ART gold
    'Again (he) stroke the (horse's) side, thudding the gold fell out'
  c. Waring... nggiki-na wà-mu,[6] *mbùtu-mbùtu* da njara
    rub how-3s.GEN report-3s.GEN RDP-thud ART horse
    '(He) rubbed... amazing!, 'thud!' fell the horses'

Additional illustrations of ideophonic roots in quotative constructions are (48) and (49). The subject of the sentence is marked by the genitive clitic attached to *wà*. The ideophonic root itself expresses the perceived state of affairs and is found in the position that would otherwise be occupied by a quote. In this way, the perception of states of affairs is given a vivid, lively and direct sense.

(48) Pòk wà-da-ka da wei lua
    grunt report-3P.GEN-PFV ART pig over.there
    '"Grunt", did the pigs over there'

(49) Mbùku wà-na-bia-ka na tau metl yena
    snap report-3s.GEN-MOD-PFV ART person die this.one
    '"Snap", did the dead body'

There is one other class of roots that appear in quotative constructions: roots derived with the prefix *ha*-:[7]

(50)
Root	Meaning without ha-	Meaning with ha-
ngàtar	'be amazed'	'be amazed'
lutur	'be sad'	'be sad'
nduka	'be stuck/hidden'	'be in trouble'
likir	'tilt head'	'tilt/lean over'
lata	'base/foundation'	'be stiff'
mbàda	'extinguished' (fire)	'be gone/have left'
lela	'cut thongs/slivers'	'be light'(not heavy)
mbila	'clear/clean'	'be clear/shiny'
ngganggar	'sway'	'fall backwards'
ngànja	'snobbish/arrogant'	'watch with surprise'
dànggit	'brief/short'	'be brief/short'
ngijir	'pull a face' (with lips)	'pull a face' (with lips)
wanjir	'sway with arms'	'prepare X'

mata	(1) 'raw' (2) 'face/eye'	'keep eye on X'
kuku	'cock-a-doodle-doo'	'to crow' (rooster)

The derived forms with *ha-* and their roots have distinct functional and distributional characteristics. This is illustrated for the verb *ha-likir* 'tilt, lean away' in (51). The verb can be used as a normal predicate, but the root *likir* can only appear in a quotative construction. A full verb cannot appear in such a context.

(51) a. *Halikir*-ki-nya!
 lean.away-MOD-3S.DAT
 'Lean away from it a bit!'
 b. *Likir* wà-na-bia-ka
 tilted.(of.head) report-3S.GEN-MOD-PFV
 'He just tilted his head'

In other words, quotative constructions appear with roots from two different categories. The roots of the derivations with *ka-, pa-, la-, ma-, ta-* never appear in quotative constructions, but *ha-*roots do. In this respect, they behave like ideophones, although they do not share their other structural characteristics. The explanation for the partly similar behavior of ideophones and *ha-*roots is found in their similar semantics: both describe physically and mentally perceived states or actions. And the quotative construction is used to report on these perceptions.

We conclude that the quotative construction is used to report perceived events that can be mentally or physically perceived. Speech acts belong to the physically perceived events; thoughts and intentions are mentally perceived. The naming function of the quotative construction is clearly related to its function to report speech acts. This is to say that, though *wà* may be *used* as a speech verb, its semantics does not necessarily include the notion of a speech act. Rather, the common denominator of the various uses of *wà* seems to be that it always reports something — words, thoughts or perceptions. Therefore, the semantics of *wà* must be [REPORT] rather than, for example, [SAY]. In such an analysis, 'real' quotes are a subclass of the set of physically perceived events that speakers may report on using the verb *wà*.[8] I will return to this in Section 4, after discussing some derived functions of the quotative construction.[9]

4. Derived functions of the Kambera report construction

The Kambera quotative verb has developed a secondary function as a discourse particle with two related, but distinct functions. Firstly, it is commonly used in questions concerning a wish, an intention or a guess; i.e. something that has not (yet) taken place. In this sense, it is a type of irrealis marker. Of course, this function of *wà* is derived from its function to express intentions or wishes, discussed in the previous section. Illustrations are (52)–(55).

As such, the clause *kama-nya* 'try it' in (52a,b) could also be used as an imperative, as could *karia-ngga* 'accompany me' in (54). However, (52b) does not have an imperative reading, and the use of *unung* 'drink' in (53), an uninflected verb form with an implied object, shows that imperative constructions are not obligatory when *wà* is used in a question context. Sentence (54) shows that *kama-nya*, *karia-ngga* and *unung* are not actual quotes either: to be a 'real' quote, *karia-ngga* '(you) come with me' should have been *karia-nggau* '(I) come with you'. Given the question contexts, it is not surprising that the subject of *wà* is mostly a second person singular, but (55) shows that this is not obligatory.

(52) a. Kama-nya *wà-mu*?
    try-3S.DAT report-2S.GEN
    'Wanna try it?'
  b. M, kama-nya *wà-nggu*-dú   làti
    yes try-3S.DAT report-1S.GEN-MOD in.fact
    'OK, let me try it'

(53) Unung *wà-mu*?
    drink   report-2S.GEN
    'Do you want a drink?'

(54) Karia-ngga   *wà-mu*?
    accompany-1S.DAT report-2S.GEN
    'Are you coming with me?'/'Want to come with me?'

(55) Màla la   Umalulu na-mbana   *wà-nggu*?[10]
    well LOC Melolo 3S.NOM-be.hot report-1S.GEN
    'Well, I guess it's hot in Melolo?'

In contrast to the analysis I proposed in Klamer (1998:351), *wà-mu* does not seem to be a question tag: it is not literally a tag because it is not preceded by an intonation break, and it occurs in contexts other than questions — in (52b) it expresses an intention.

The other discourse function of the element *wà* is as an interjection that adds vividness to the discourse. Though its exact function is still unclear, it seems to draw the attention of the listener, especially in contexts where something unexpected happens.[11] The following piece of discourse comes from a conversation between three women about pictures that they considered hilarious.[12] One woman tells about a picture taken of M., while she was preparing food on an open fire in the field, for the workers who were harvesting there. She uses *wà-mu* three times:

(56) Hàla-i-ka   úna   i   M.   úna   wà-mu,
    finish-again-PFV 3S.DEI ART PROP 3S.DEI report-2S.GEN
    'And then that M., oh no!
    ba   padukul-na-nya   na bai tulur,
    when lighten-3S.GEN-3S.DAT ART real stone
    when she was lighting the fire,
    bai wuru bàhi úna   wà-mu,
    real pot iron 3S.DEI report-2S.GEN
    (handling) that iron pot, you know,
    ka tiri   mànu-ma-nanya-ka úna   nàhu wà-mu,
    so capsize always-EMPH-3S-PFV 3S.DEI now report-2S.GEN
    and she was capsizing there (crouching, turned away from photographer),
    ba   na-yutu-ya   na wuru bàhi!
    when 3S.NOM-hold-3S.ACC ART pot iron
    when she held the iron pot!'

The following examples come from different narratives, where *wà-mu* signals a peak in the narrative. This function of *wà-mu* as an interjection calling for the listener's involvement in the story would be comparable to the form and function of English interjections like *you know!* and *what d'you say!*

(57) Ka da-puru-ka   uda   nú wà-mu,
    CNJ 3P.NOM-descend-PFV 3P.EMPH DEI report-2S.GEN
    'So they got down, man!
    ngandi-danya bi kabela   bi nímbu du-ka   nú
    take-3P   real machete real spear-EMPH-PFV DEI
    wà-mu   . . .
    report-2S.GEN
    they (were) all bringing along machetes and spears, you know!'
(58) Njadi na-pàda-nya-ka   una   nú wà-mu,
    so   3S.NOM-feel-3S.DAT-PFV 3S.EMPH DEI report-2S.GEN,
    'She knew it was him, you know!,
    na ma-kaliti njara miting!
    ART SBJ.REL-ride horse be.black
    the one riding the black horse!'

5. The grammaticalization of the Kambera report construction

In the preceding sections we have seen the following evidence for the idea that *wà* is not a canonical Kambera verbal root: (1) it is smaller than the minimal prosodic word, (2) it has limited argument-marking possibilities (subjects are always genitive), (3) it has limited morphological possibilities (it allows no causative derivation), (4) it cannot occur in an object-relative clause (a passive-like structure), (5) it has a very general semantics: [REPORT], and (6) it has two distinct non-verbal discourse functions. The reduced structural properties and multifunctionality of *wà* suggest that it is grammaticalized to a certain extent.

The grammaticalization of *wà* involves a network of related functions that is represented in Figure 1 (see Güldemann (this volume) for another proposal in which the grammaticalization of an item involves a network of functions).[13] The element that lies at the heart of the *wà* network is a [REPORT] verb, which reports about events perceived by the speaker, either physically or mentally. The shaded circle in the center of Figure 1 indicates this central meaning. The figure also indicates that there are three types of reports: of audibly, visibly and mentally perceived events. The audibly perceived events include perceptions of all sounds: sounds expressed by ideophonic roots, but also speech sounds. In Kambera, quotes are thus treated as a subtype of perceived events. In this function, *wà* developed secondary functions as the predicate of a naming construction ('we report on it as X' = 'we call it X') and as a discourse particle calling for the listeners involvement ('you report!' = 'you know!'). The visible events reported on

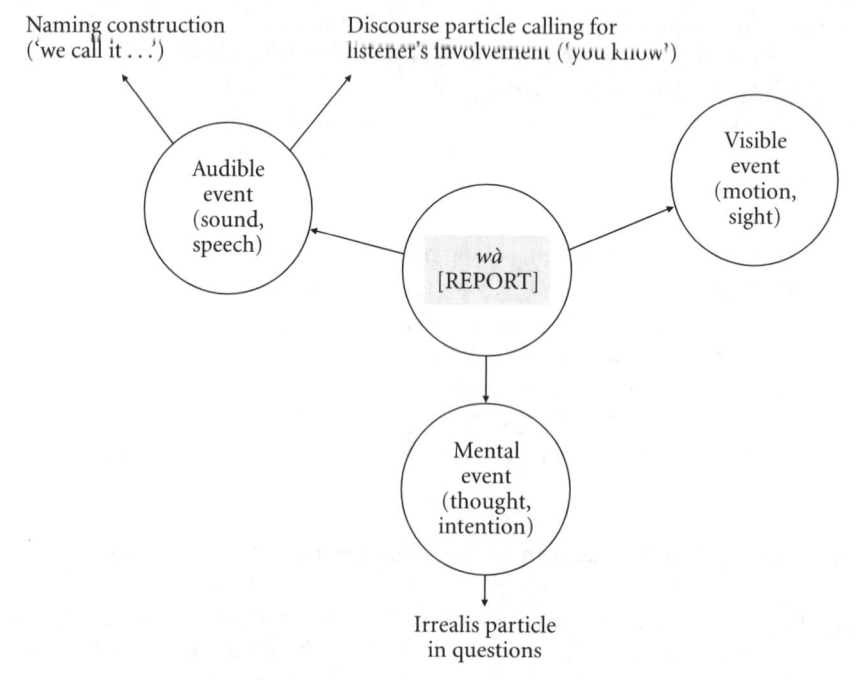

Figure 1. Network of meanings and functions of *wà*

by *wà* include the visible characteristics as they are expressed by ideophonic roots and roots of *ha*-verbs. The mentally perceived events are thoughts, intentions and wishes. In this function, *wà* developed a secondary use as a discourse particle expressing irrealis modality, to be used in questions.

Notes

* This chapter is based on primary language data gathered by the author during fieldwork on Sumba in 1990–1994. The example sentences come from a corpus of 12 hours spontaneous texts, provided by a number of native Kambera speakers. The texts were transcribed with the help of Umbu Musa Maramba Hau, whom I owe many thanks. Thanks also to the editors of this volume for their help in shaping the chapter in its present form. The research for this chapter was supported by a fellowship of the Royal Netherlands Academy of Arts and Sciences (KNAW) at the Vrije Universiteit in Amsterdam.

1. For a recent overview, see de Roeck (1994), who discusses some of the origins of the first two assumptions, and tests them against the data from a representative sample of 40 languages. It appears that the assumptions are valid for at most half of the languages investigated.

2. This raises the question of whether the language employs other causativized speech verbs. After *wà*, the most general speech verb is *paní* 'tell', but as this is a lexicalized causative form (*pa-ní* 'cause-be'), causativization of this verb is blocked. Other, more specialized verbs such as *peka* 'confess, inform' may undergo both applicative and causative derivation: *pa-peka-ng* 'teach, proclaim'.

3. When we came across such sentences during text transcription, my consultant initially did not consider them ill-formed, but after thinking about them for a while he explained that the first *-na* should better not be there.

4. *Na mila-nggu* 'my poverty' is idiomatic for 'my wealth'.

5. Common roots may be prefixed, suffixed, reduplicated, but not circumfixed.

6. This is the same quotative construction as (29); here it is idiomatic for 'Wow! Gee! Amazing!'

7. Not all the roots of *ha*-verbs can occur in the quotative construction. The following classes are the major exceptions: (1) the roots of fully lexicalized *ha*-derivations that do no longer function as independent words, (2) 'roots' with a foreign origin, for instance in phonotactically adapted loans from Indonesian (*se-* > *ha-*).

8. In their contributions to this volume, Güldemann and Meyerhoff discuss other cases where quotative verbs/markers do not derive from a speech verb: *olsem* in Bislama (a Southwest Pacific creole) and the element *ti* in Shona (a Bantu language) are both originally deictic elements meaning something like 'thus, like'.

9. See also *Klamer* (2000), where the Kambera quotative construction is compared to similar constructions in two other Austronesian languages (Buru and Tukang Besi), and

which contains a proposal for the lexical representation and grammaticalization of [REPORT] verbs.

10. Alternatively, the emphatic negation *ndia* can be used:

(i) Màla la Umalulu na-mbana ndia?
well LOC Melolo 3s.NOM-be.hot NEG.EMPH
'Well, it's hot in Melolo, isn't it?'

11. The notion of unexpectedness is also found in the Dutch translations of *wà-mu*: it would often translate as *man!*, but also as *toch* 'yet, still, nevertheless' or *immers* 'after all', adverbials expressing contrast to expectation:

(1) Kwam hij (**toch**) ineens naar beneden met een mes, **man**!
came he yet suddenly to downstairs with a knife man
'Man! He came down carrying a knife!'

(2) Hij zat **toch** te liegen!
he sat yet to lie
'Boy, was he lying!'

(3) Waarom deed ze het, ze kénde **immers** de gevaren?
why did she it she knew after.all the dangers
'Why did she do it, while she knew about the dangers?'

12. Pictures of Sumbanese people in working clothes, engaged in every-day activities are a source of fun because the costs involved in picture-taking make it a serious event for which many Sumbanese dress up and adopt a solemn posture.

13. The advantage of a network representation is that items are allowed more interconnections than when the relation between them is assumed to be linear (a>b>c).

References

Klamer, Marian. 1996. "Kambera has no passive". In Klamer, Marian (ed.), *Voice in Austronesian* (=NUSA 39). Jakarta: Universitas Atma Jaya, 12–30.

Klamer, Marian. 1998. *A grammar of Kambera* (=Mouton Grammar Library 18). Berlin: Mouton de Gruyter.

CHAPTER 15

All the same?
The emergence of complementizers in Bislama*

Miriam Meyerhoff
University of Edinburgh

1. Introduction

Over the last century, Bislama, the English-lexified creole spoken in Vanuatu (SW Pacific), has expanded from a Pacific maritime pidgin to the more syntactically elaborated language currently used by c.190,000 people in Vanuatu (estimated Vanuatu population, July 2000 CIA Factbook). This history of innovation and expansion has resulted in a grammatical system in which four complementizers are now used productively as a means of introducing subordinate, or dependent, clauses. This chapter will focus on the most recent of these forms to emerge, *olsem* originally from the English *all (the) same*. *Olsem* provides an interesting case study in the typology of complementizers for two reasons.

First, as has often been noted, creoles provide excellent 'laboratory' settings for examining grammaticization paths in natural languages. The synchronic variation and continued multifunctionality of *olsem* in Bislama clearly shows that people tolerate structural ambiguity, but it is also highly suggestive of how the ambiguity resulting from semantic shift is constrained. Poser (1985) argues that the reanalysis of deictics and prepositions in creoles based on Romance languages is constrained both by factors inherited from (non-standard varieties of) the lexifier and creole speakers' substrate grammars. Similarly, this chapter takes the position that a lexical item enters the process of reanalysis and change with certain properties that perdure throughout the reanalysis (cf. Hopper's (1991) notion of 'persistence'). In other words, it is not just that every word has its own history; the way a word is now is constrained by its history.

However, it will not be argued that lexifier and substrate alone account for grammaticization patterns. Like *Plag*'s (1992) account of the development of the complementizer *taki* in Sranan, this chapter will suggest that universal factors play a role in constraining the innovation of complementizers in Bislama.

The second reason *olsem* provides an interesting case study is that its development poses questions about the necessary grammaticization path for complementizers. Specifically, the history of *olsem* raises questions about what exactly is meant by a hypothesis of 'unidirectionality' in grammaticization paths.

This chapter is structured as follows. Section 2 provides a brief discussion of the development of *se* 'say' as a complementizer. *Se* follows a well-attested grammaticization path for complementizers and provides an interesting internal contrast with the development of *olsem*. Section 3 describes the derivation of *olsem*, from two English lexemes to a range of functions in current Bislama. The data on *olsem* illustrates another possible path along which complementizers may emerge; one that has received much less attention than the more canonical development from locutionary verbs. It is, nonetheless, consistent with data from other languages and merits our attention. The final section of the chapter considers the implications of the apparent grammaticization paths associated with *olsem* for our understanding of the structure of Bislama, in particular, and linguistics in general.

The chapter uses tools and methods from a number of different schools of linguistic thought. In addition to examining the data in terms familiar to typological and functional syntax, it seeks to unify this analysis of language change with quantitative data (as used in sociolinguistics) and principles of formal syntax (e.g. Chomsky 1995). This kind of synthetic approach to the analysis of synchronic variation and change in progress is particularly illuminating in the study of creoles, such as Bislama.

2. The genesis of complement clause markers in Bislama

There are four subordinating conjunctions in use in current Bislama: *blong* (from English *belong*) introduces purpose or manner clauses; *we* (from English *where*) introduces relative clauses; *se* (from English *say*, but more on the origins of this in §2.1) and *olsem* (from English *all [the] same*) which introduce complement clauses following perception verbs and locutionary verbs. Complement and relative clauses may also lack an overt complementizer.[1] This chapter will focus only on the complementizers *se* and *olsem*.

In Bislama's very early stages, there were no overt strategies for signaling clause subordination. This might be consistent with the bioprogram grammar proposed by Bickerton (1984). Bickerton hypothesized that the innate grammar generated by the bioprogram has a complementizer position, but that the default for a creole is for the complementizer to be phonetically null. On the other hand, Woolford's (1981) analysis of Tok Pisin took the position that the development of a complementizer was a syntactic innovation. In essence, her argument amounted to a claim that what grammaticization means in a generative framework is that

Tok Pisin developed a structural position that could be filled by a complementizer. Once this innovation was complete, Tok Pisin was able to form two types of clauses, main tensed clauses (an IP, or 'inflectional phrase', in current generative terms) and subordinate clauses (CPs, or 'complementizer phrases'). The Bickerton and Woolford analyses differ, therefore, in whether the early absence of complementizers in Bislama is characterized as a gap in the lexical or structural system.[2]

2.1 Complementizer *se*: lexifier, universal and substrate influences

Crowley (1989) discusses the emergence of *se* as a complementizer in modern Bislama. *Se* is a particularly interesting case study in creole grammaticization because it seems to have dual lexifier sources. During the colonial period, Vanuatu was jointly administered by Britain and France and both anglophone and francophone interests continue to be represented in the country today. While the principal lexifier language for Bislama has been English, between 6–12% of the vocabulary in modern Bislama is derived from French (Crowley 1991:110).[3] Crowley suggests that the current distribution of *se* in Bislama and the varied functions it serves indicate that speakers have reanalyzed the word as deriving both from English *say* and French *c'est* (he suggests the latter derivation licenses use of *se* as a copula). It is the use of *se* derived from English *say* which is of concern to us here.

Originally, the functions of *se* were those of English *say*, introducing direct and indirect speech in discourse. Crowley (1989) shows that it increasingly began to be used to reinforce other verbs that introduce reported speech. This left it open to reanalysis as a complementizer rather than a verb. In this respect, the behavior of *se* is similar to the well-documented route taken by many other locutionary verbs which, through a similar process of association and lexical redundancy, are reanalyzed as functional rather than lexical items.

Crowley claims that *se* is "almost defunct" (1989:187) as a verb of speaking, although my own data shows that this overstates the case. *Se* continues to be productively used as a verb of speaking in conversational Bislama recorded in northern Vanuatu in 1994–95.[4] Forty-eight percent of all tokens of *se* in the conversation corpus occurred as the main verb (N=244 out of total 504 tokens of *se*).[5] However, it is clear that *se* is well-established as a complementizer. While use of *se* as a complementizer is optional, it is now the preferred strategy when reporting discourse. In the historical example in (1), the main verb *tell-im out* (modern Bislama *talemaot*) occurs without a complementizer following.[6] This sentence is technically grammatical in modern Bislama, however, a straw-poll of eight adult speakers in the town of Santo in 1998 elicited the unanimous judgement that (1'), with the complementizer, is preferred.[7]

(1) What name! you been tell-im out along Court you savvy spik pidgin-English! (Jacomb 1929: 46)
'What! You told the court you can speak pidgin English!'

(1') Yu talemaot long Kot se   yu save toktok Inglis.
     2s tell   to   court COMP 2s can talk   English
     'You told the court *that* you can speak English.'

In the conversational corpus, there were only 7 clausal complements of verbs of speaking that were not introduced with *se*. One of these, (2), merits closer inspection since it provides telling evidence for the probable origin of *se* as a complementizer.

(2) Hem i talem hem i se from   kastom blong ples   ya   i
    3s AGR tell 3s AGR say because custom of   place SPEC AGR
    nogud.
    bad
    'He told (my father) *he said* because according to our customs it's wrong.'

In (2), the speaker follows a clause with the main verb *talem* 'tell' with another clause in which *se* 'say' is the main verb. It is relevant at this point to note that Bislama allows phonetically null subjects, especially when the subject is third person and especially when there is referential continuity between the subjects of adjacent clauses (Meyerhoff 2000). Obviously, it is a short step from *hem i talem hem i se* to *hem i talem Ø i se*, and a short step from there to a reanalysis of the second verb as a functional element, i.e. a complementizer.

(3) hem i talem, hem i se ...   [two finite clauses]
    ?hem i talem Ø i se ...   [two finite clauses, 2nd subject null]
    ?hem i talem Ø Ø se ...   [reanalysis: finite clause + complementizer]

The abundant cross-linguistic evidence of similar processes (*Lord* 1976, *Saxena* 1995, *Bashir* 1996) suggests that this reanalysis may have been motivated by universal similarities in the way these lexical items are perceived and related to other lexemes. However, we must also assume that the influence of any universal tendency would have been amplified by analogous substrate patterns.

In many of the Melanesian languages spoken in Vanuatu, a verb meaning 'say' also functions as a complementizer introducing clausal complements of verbs of reported discourse, propositional attitudes ('know', 'believe'), and in some cases also propositional predicates ('seem', 'be clear/obvious'). Codrington noted this for *wa* (*si*) in Mota (northern Vanuatu) (1885: 300–1) and *wa(r)* in Maewo (north-east Vanuatu) (1885: 418). Ray observed similar multifunctionality of *cha* 'say' in Ambrym (central Vanuatu) (1926: 346) and Nogugu (West Santo) *vetiwa*, which appears to be a participial form of 'say' (1926: 400). The languages of southern Tanna likewise introduce reported discourse with a functional element derived from a verb of speaking, *mima* in South-West Tanna (Lynch 1982a: 57) and *mua* in Kwamera (Lindstrom 1986: 107). *Mua* functions as a complementizer with verbs of numerous semantic types (speech, perception, propositional attitudes and even propositional predicates like 'be possible'). This seems to also be true of Anejom *mika* (Lynch 1982b: 142), though the Anejom data on propositional predicates is lacking.

At present there is no way of resolving whether the emergence of *se* as a complementizer in Bislama is due principally to transfer from these indigenous language patterns, or universal linguistic principles. We cannot tell whether the same patterns appear in the substrate languages because of their genetic relatedness or because they too are the product of universals. It is probably more important to note that there are multiple sources for the grammaticization of *se* as a complementizer, and to take from this that where two sources for a particular pattern of grammaticization exist, it is all the more likely to crystallize.

The synchronic distribution of *se* suggests that it followed a typical path in becoming complementizer. As Table 1 shows, in modern Bislama it is used most frequently with the verbs *talem* or *talemaot* 'tell', and also with other speech act verbs (in which are included internal speech acts or discourse verbs such as *ting(ting)* 'think' or verbs that presuppose a speech event, such as *agri* 'agree'). It occurs next most frequently introducing complements of verbs of perception and understanding *luk* 'see, understand', *harem* 'hear, feel', *save* 'know', *haremsave* 'understand'. Then with propositional predicates, such as *posibol* 'be possible', *min(im)* 'mean' and causatives, principally *mekem* 'make'.

Table 1. Frequency of *se* complementizer in spoken and written Bislama

	Conversational corpus		Written corpus	
	N of V = *se*	% of corpus	N of V = *se*	% of corpus
Speech act: *talem* -type	147	56.5*	160	65
Perception: *luk*-type	74	28.5	36	14.5
Propositional: *minim*-type	26	10	31	12.5
Causative: *mekem*	13	5	20	8
Total	260	100	247	100

*The spoken corpus also included 244 tokens of *se* as main verb 'say')

Table 1 shows that the frequency with which *se* complementation occurs in each verb class decreases from top to bottom. This is not simply an artifact of the overall frequency of these verb types in the corpus, as frequency of *se* complementation decreases within each verb class as well. It was noted earlier that only 7 tokens of *talem* 'tell' occurred without the complementizer in the spoken corpus, i.e. 7 out of 154 of this type of verb. In the perception class (e.g. *save* 'know' and *luk* 'see, understand'), this increases to 16 tokens, i.e. 16 out of 90 total tokens of this verb class occurred without *se*. So far, then, the data on *se* shows Bislama complementation marching along the grammaticization path Saxena (1995) proposed as a universal for *verba dicendi*. However, the next section will show that this trajectory is by no means the cognitive and cross-linguistic universal that previous work on the grammaticization of complementizers might suggest.

3. Emergence of *olsem*: a view of grammaticization in progress

Let us now turn to the most recent lexical item to emerge with complementizer functions. A close examination of the current distribution of *olsem* is particularly interesting since the picture it provides is of a dynamic system of on-going grammaticization. However, since the process is far from complete it must be made clear at the outset that there is also a good deal of internal variation among Bislama speakers and frequent ambiguities in the use of *olsem*.

In this section, patterns and generalizations that seem to be emerging are reviewed. In each case, historical data is introduced and in this way uses of *olsem* in modern spoken Bislama can be seen in a diachronic perspective.[8] In each section, an attempt will be made to balance the possible effects of universals (structural or functional), and influences of the substrate and the lexifier. The data provides an interesting counter-point to the data on *se* discussed in §2, and deep and striking parallels with the data on Shona *ti* (Güldemann, this volume).

3.1 Similative preposition or predicate

As noted earlier, *olsem* derives from the English *all (the) same*. Its first appearance in the historical record is as a preposition expressing similative relations, where it can be glossed 'like, as'. It also appears early as a predicate, which can be glossed 'be like'. The semantics of the core constituents inherited from the lexifier have altered somewhat over the years. Initially, the universal quantification introduced by *ol* 'all' seems to have forced an exhaustive reading. That is, *sem* indexed a 'sameness' of identity. This is shown in examples (4) and (5) from early Bislama. These favor an exhaustive reading, where *olsem* predicates strict identity. Obviously, 'identity' should not be taken to mean referential identity, rather it indicates identity of qualities in two referents.

(4) *Olsem* as similative preposition: 'like, as'.
He [God] love Black Man *all same* White Man.
'He loves black people *(just) like* white people.' (Paton 1895:7)

(5) *Olsem* as similative predicate: 'be the same as, be like'.
You plenty lie! You *all same* Tiapolo!
'You lie all the time! You're *(just) like* the Devil!' (Paton 1895:39)

In modern Bislama, the exhaustiveness of the morpheme *ol* 'all' has bleached somewhat, thus *olsem* no longer only signifies exact identity between the qualities of two referents or propositions. A weaker relation of similarity or resemblance may be indicated, or a token-type relation. In fact, when *olsem* is the main predicate, as in (6), the weaker interpretation is now required. Strict denotation cannot be expressed in this way — the semantic information originally contributed by 'all' has been bleached so much.

(6) Brata   blong mi *i*   *olsem* man ya   i   stap wok long ba.
    brother of   1s AGR olsem man SPEC AGR CONT work in   bar
    'My brother *is like* the man working at the bar.'
    *'My brother *is* the man working at the bar.'

We note, too, that when *olsem* is used as a preposition now, it no longer generates the stricter reading of identity that it did originally, as seen in (4). Rather the sameness evoked in (7) and (8) is that of a type-token relationship:

(7) Ol wokman ya   *olsem* Pakoa i   gat raet blong...
    P worker   SPEC olsem P.   AGR have right to
    'All workers *like* Pakoa have the right to...' (VWH, 13/6/98, p.7).

(8) Controller ya   i   stap *olsem* wan temporeri wokman nomo
    controller SPEC AGR stay olsem a   temporary worker   only
    'The controller was only there *as* a temporary worker.' (ibid.)

In sum, since the use of *olsem* to index similarity emerged earliest, it can be considered the core meaning of the lexeme. It also occurs frequently in texts from all periods. Today, there is still a transparent link between the semantics of the lexifier components and the core meaning of *olsem*, even if the link is attenuated. We can also identify a core structural property of *olsem*, whether verb or preposition, i.e. it takes a noun as its complement.

However, occurrences of *olsem* without a following noun phrase also begin to appear in the early records, as in (9):

(9) You savey catch big fellow yam stop garden belong you
    Very good, you bring plenty fellow yam *all same*.
    'Can you get some big yams from your garden? Excellent, [then] bring plenty of yams *like [that]*.' (Anderson 1880:157)

Examples (10) and (11) show that tokens of *olsem* on its own continue to be found in written and spoken Bislama today.

(10) Presiden i   talem se   hem i   sore blong hem i
     President AGR tell that 3s   AGR sorry that   3s   AGR
     tekem disisen   olsem.
     take   decision olsem
     'The President said that he was sorry to make a decision (*like* [*that decision*]/*thus*).' (VWH, 29/11/97)

(11) Mifala i   mas kasem smolsmol wok *olsem* nao.
     1P.E   AGR must catch small   work olsem now
     'We have to get part-time work *like* ([*that*/*I just said*]).'

Dictionary entries for *olsem* include an adverbial, glossed 'thus' (Crowley 1995: 176, gives this as the principal entry). But Meyerhoff (1998) suggests that this categorization is too strongly influenced by the English translation. Instead, it is shown that such cases of bare *olsem* can be analyzed as a preposition with a deleted (or understood) complement. The constraints on the deletion of objects of *olsem* are located in the discourse grammar,[9] such that discourse-old arguments (Walker and Prince 1996) are most likely to be omitted.

This is especially clear when only the head noun in a complex noun phrase is the old information. In these cases, *olsem* is immediately followed by a modifying PP or relative clause. In example (12), the head of the relative clause, 'help' is null because it is discourse-old information; all that surfaces is the new information modifying the head noun in the relative clause starting *we*.

(12) Hem ya   i   bin longtaem blong wet long sam
     3s SPEC AGR ANT long.time COMP wait for some
     help *olsem* we bae i   kam long gavman.
     help olsem REL IRR AGR come from government
     'It's been a long wait for some help *like* [this help] that's coming from the government.'

(12') ... sam help olsem help we bae i kam long gavman [understood]

Meyerhoff's (1998) analysis means that when the complement of *olsem* is phonetically null because it refers anaphorically to a discourse-old proposition (or clause), it gives the appearance (to an English eye) of a sentence-final adverb. For the early stages of Bislama, it seems more parsimonious to analyze bare *olsem* as being the preposition with a null argument, than it does to posit a homophonous preposition and adverb. In addition, the analysis of preposition with a null argument is consistent with synchronic constraints on null arguments elsewhere in the grammar. When native speakers are asked to paraphrase utterances like (10) to (12), they tend to insert a noun coreferential with the preceding noun, or (if comparison is being made between clauses) will use a dummy noun like 'something' or 'situation'.

This is not to say that at some point, speakers will not reanalyze bare *olsem* as an adverb. What it does do is (i) explain how a novel adverb might develop from a preposition and (ii) point out that even today, speakers are more or less aware of the link with *olsem* as a similative predicate. This means that in the context of on-going grammaticization, the constraints imposed by its core syntax are still relevant (Klamer, this volume, discusses how syntactic factors have similarly constrained the grammaticization of the REPORT lexeme in Kambera).

The fact that *olsem* may be understood or analyzed as a preposition with a null complement is significant. This syntactic fact, in addition to the core meaning which asserts close similarity or identity, seems to play a role in further reanalysis, including the reanalysis of *olsem* as a complementizer.

In the next sections, it will be seen that in recent spoken and written Bislama, *olsem* may now function as a demonstrative (including uses when gesturing deictically, i.e. what Kaplan (1989) calls a "true demonstrative"). It is also used sometimes to introduce reported speech, or reports of perceptions.

3.2 Deictic and demonstrative

Based on the historical record and the synchronic frequency of the newer functions, it might be tempting to propose a grammaticization path from preposition and predicate, to demonstrative, and then to complementizer. However, Kroch (1989) cautions us that environments in which a variable is historically most frequent are not necessarily the environments in which the variant was most favored. For instance, it may simply be that demonstrations and discourse deixis are more common than reports of propositions, attitudes or discourse. Consequently, the path for the development of *olsem* proposed in this chapter is tentative only. Future, more subtle distributional analyses will be needed to resolve it conclusively.

Let us turn first to the apparent cases of *olsem* as a demonstrative. Cases of *olsem* occurring at the same time as a demonstration abound, as in (13). In (14) the utterance is accompanied by gestures marking out places on the speaker's arm.

(13) Mifala foltem han   *olsem*.
 1P.E   fold   hand olsem
 'We cross our arms (*so/like* [*this*]).' (speaker crosses arms)

(14) Oli go antap   *olsem*.
 AGR go on.top olsem
 '[They] go up (*here/like* [*this*]).'

It is a short step from these kinds of deictic uses to its use as a pure demonstrative. Indeed, it is possible today for a speaker to ask for something behind the counter at a store, picking out the item by pointing and saying (15):

(15) No, *olsem* ya.
No, olsem SPEC
'No, (*that one/one of those*).' [pointing]

The semantics of likeness are retained, though in this case it is likeness between linguistic and non-linguistic domains. The speaker implies identity between a word and a gesture.

A search for possible substrate models here found some limited evidence that this development in Bislama also reflects patterns in vernacular languages. Codrington (1885) records that in Efate (central Vanuatu) *netu* means both 'like this' (p. 475) and is a demonstrative pronoun (p.473). It seems (Crowley 1991: 165 ff.) that, of all the vernaculars, the languages of central Vanuatu contributed the most vocabulary to Bislama. The parallelism between Bislama and Codrington's Efate data suggests that perhaps the languages of the central region have exerted an even greater influence, also shaping the syntax of modern Bislama. Clearly, this is an area that will reward much further study.

3.3 Demonstrative to complementizer

Now having seen the development of deictic or demonstrative functions for *olsem*, it is not surprising to subsequently find assorted tokens that appear in complementizer-like positions. Parallel cases in which some form of demonstrative has gradually been reanalyzed as a sentential complementizer can be found in other languages. Hopper and Traugott (1993:183–9) outline the process by which English *that* underwent precisely this reanalysis from demonstrative to complementizer, and Romance complementizers likewise developed from Latin *quod* or *quam* (*Eilfort* 1986:65, Poser 1985).

In Bislama we see uses of *olsem* in ways that are reminiscent of the stages Hopper and Traugott document for English *that*. For example, in (16) we see it being used cataphorically.

(16) Hem ya i keis blong ol tim *olsem* Spain, Morocco,
3s SPEC AGR case of P team olsem S., M.,
Cameroun o Belgium.
C., or B.
'This is the case of *these* teams: S., M., C., or B.' (VWH, 27/6/98)

Note that in (16) the context (surprise dismissals after the first round of the 1998 World Cup) makes clear that Spain etc. are not considered exemplars. They are, in fact, the very teams ('the case') being talked about.

In addition, we find tokens of *olsem* as in (17). If it is assumed that in cases like (17) the reported speech is actually the fronted complement of *talem* 'tell',[10] then *olsem* could either be interpreted analogously with (16) or it could be interpreted as a complementizer.

(17) "Mama blong yu i stap long nambangga?" hem i talem olsem.
    M. of 2s AGR stay in nambangga, 3s AGR tell olsem
    '"Is that your mother in the banyan tree?" she says [like] this.'

In modern Tok Pisin (closely-related to Bislama), the cognate *olosem* has clearly grammaticized as a complementizer introducing direct and indirect discourse (Verhaar 1995). In unpublished research, G. Sankoff has undertaken a comparison of the distribution and functions of Bislama *olsem* and Tok Pisin *olosem* and reports (p.c.) that the latter is overwhelmingly used in her spoken corpus to introduce reported speech or refer anaphorically to speech events.

In the written and spoken corpora of Bislama there are rather more tokens where *olsem* fills the complementizer slot when the main verb is a verb of perception as in (18) to (20), than when it is a verb of speaking as in (21).

(18) Long tingting blong mi, mi luk olsem man we i raetem
    in opinion of 1s 1s look olsem man REL AGR write
    leta ya i ting se ...
    letter SPEC AGR think COMP
    'In my opinion, it seems to me *that* the man who wrote this letter thinks that ...' (VWH, 1/7/95). (lit. 'I see like the man ...')

(19) Mi luk olsem bubu ya i kakae fulap tumas.
    1s look olsem bubu SPEC AGR eat a.lot very
    'It seems to me *that* this bubu [= grandmother] eats too much' (lit. 'I see like this grandmother ...')

(20) Mi harem olsem mi sore long pikinini ya.
    1s hear olsem 1s sorry for child SPEC
    'I felt sorry for the baby.'

(21) Lili i tok olsem "E, yu!"
    L. AGR talk olsem hey 2s
    'Lily says, "Hey you!"'

The corpus provides no examples of indirect speech. However, many speakers find utterances like (22) perfectly acceptable, where the subject of the second clause refers not to Sale, but to the person uttering the entire sentence.

(22) Sale$_i$ i talem olsem mi$_j$ sik.
    S. AGR tell olsem 1s sick.
    'Sale said *that* I was sick.'

The preferred use of *olsem* with perception verbs rather than speech verbs is atypical for the grammaticization of complementizers. This data shows that the grammaticization of a complementizer need not start with reported speech, only subsequently spreading to use with verbs of perception and possibility.

Again, it must be assumed that the core semantics of *olsem* has been an important factor in this. Reports of perception are inherently more similative than reports of speech (Cohen *et al.*, this volume, analogize 'say' with 'be'). Therefore, a complementizer derived from 'like' might seem to concatenate more appropriately with verbs such as 'hear', 'appear', and 'seem'.[11] This is rather different to *Saxena*'s (1995) grammaticization path for complementizers emerging from verbs of speech. Clearly, there is no single path along which all complementizers grammaticize. The paths appear to be constrained by the semantics of the lexical item's core meaning. The implications of this for Bislama are that the reanalysis required of *olsem* is principally syntactic, and does not concern the core semantics.

Though one should not be tempted to overstate the degree of syntactic reanalysis required. Historically, *olsem* selected a noun or a tensed clause as its second argument. If it is reanalyzed as a complementizer, its argument is still a tensed clause. Moreover, there is evidence to suggest that it is a clause with nominal qualities. A comparison with some English data is useful here.

Kiparsky and Kiparsky (1970) note some important syntactic asymmetries between factive and non-factive sentences in English, which they attribute to differences in the assertions or presuppositions underlying the two classes of verbs. Of relevance here is their observation that non-factive verbs can be referred to in English by the pro-form *so*.[12]

(23) John supposed that Bill had done it, and Mary supposed so, too. [non-factive]
*John regretted that Bill had done it, and Mary regretted so, too. [factive]
(Kiparksy and Kiparsky 1970: 166)

They attribute the contrast in (23) to a difference in the underlying structure of factives and non-factives. They propose that the complement clause of non-factives is a sentence dominated by a noun (in non-hierarchical terms, this amounts to a claim that the complement is functionally a noun, but has the form of a clause).

There are interesting parallels to be drawn between Bislama *olsem* and English non-factives. Like the pro-form *so*, *olsem* also has anaphoric readings (this, of course, is what the translation of bare *olsem* as 'thus' is an attempt to capture). Also like *so*, *olsem* is strongly favored with complements of non-factive verbs.[13] If Kiparsky and Kiparsky's analysis of non-factive complements holds cross-linguistically, then the reanalysis of *olsem* as a complementizer requires no significant change in the kind of complement it selects. Both in its core sense as a preposition and as a non-factive complementizer, it would select a nominal complement. In other words, it is not simply that it is possible for a complementizer to emerge first with perception verbs, spreading later to speech verbs, but in some cases, the argument selecting properties of the word being reanalyzed may require that this be the initial stage of grammaticization.

Finally, it should be noted for the sake of completeness that this shift from preposition (or predicate) meaning 'like' to a complementizer may have been facilitated by parallels within some of the substrate languages. Lexemes meaning 'like' also serve as complementizers in South-West Tanna (southern Vanuatu), Baki (central Vanuatu), and Tamambo (north west Vanuatu).

Lynch (1982a) records that the root *-ima* in South-West Tanna functions both to introduce complements of verbs of speaking and to express predications of 'like, as'. For Baki (central Vanuatu), Ray (1926) gives *ka* introducing complements of 'know', 'fear' and 'order', and in comparisons of, e.g., greater or less than relations. The data on comparisons is not sufficient to draw a conclusive parallel with Bislama, however it is suggestive.

Jauncey's (1997) especially rich grammar of Tamambo shows that *sohen* functions both as a predication meaning 'be (just) like', and is also productive as a complementizer following verbs of speaking ('say', 'promise', 'explain'), perception ('understand', 'appear/seem') and propositional attitudes ('believe'). It should be noted that Tamambo is the substrate language of many of the speakers in the corpus of spoken Bislama that has been used here.

However, the exact parallelisms that Jauncey draws between Tamambo and the only distantly related Manam (Lichtenberk 1983) remind us how difficult it is to ever definitely ascribe a particular pattern to substrate influences in a contact language. We cannot rule out the possibility that just as Manam and Tamambo independently developed similar syntactic structures for the same lexical item, Bislama independently developed them as well. If an abstract sense of identity or likeness is one of the factors that has supported the reanalysis of *olsem* in Bislama, then we would expect this factor to be equally likely to support the development of similar patterns elsewhere.[14]

Indeed, *Manessy* (1989) discusses a similar situation in Kriyol, where *kuma*, derived from 16th-century Portuguese *coma* 'like', introduces citations and complements of verbs of perception.[15] Poser (1985) also notes that the complementizer *kom* in Louisiana French Creole must be derived from either French *comme* or Portuguese *coma/como*. Michael Ewing has observed that the root of the complementizer and the equative predicate and the demonstrative are all the same in Cirebon Javanese (Indonesia: complementizer *ka, konon*; equative *kaya*; demonstrative *ika*, see Meyerhoff and Niedzielski 1998). Güldemann (this volume) presents data from Shona which also supports the notion that there are deep, cross-linguistic generalizations to be made about this grammaticization network. In short, the parallels extend beyond the immediate region in which Bislama is spoken; a possibility exists that the semantic links between these functions are of universal significance.

4. Conclusion: underlying structures and grammaticization paths

What, then, are we to conclude from this discussion about Bislama in particular, and about grammaticization processes in general? We have seen that relatively recently Bislama has reanalyzed two lexical items which now serve as complementizers. One of these, *se*, is typologically unremarkable both in its provenance (a verb of locution) and in its apparently orderly, unidirectional grammaticization path. The other, *olsem*, presents a picture that, until the publication of this collection, has been less familiar in the field. The picture of *olsem* outlined here has highlighted structural facts that are particularly relevant to the analysis of language change in contact languages, i.e. the effects of substrate and lexifier, and at the same time highlighted structural and semantic facts shared with unrelated languages. In other words, the synchronic distribution of *olsem* (as is often the case with creole variables) represents a rich and heterogeneous combination of universals, substrate(s) and lexifier.

It was argued that in Bislama *olsem* (originally a verb or preposition) lost its reading of exhaustiveness, with 'all the same' essentially coming to mean 'as good as the same'. Notions of qualitative or salient similarity came to the fore and the persistence of this core meaning has been the vector for, and a constraint on, the grammatical reanalysis of *olsem*. Evidence from its functions in discourse and restrictions on its interpretation and use suggest that speakers are beginning a process of reanalysis such that *olsem* may function as a demonstrative, a manner pro-form (with interesting parallels to the English pro-form *so*), and also as a complementizer. In all cases, it was suggested that *olsem* retains a sense of implied or asserted identity, either identity of reference or identity between the main verb event and the content of the complement. Cross-linguistic evidence showing that these reanalysis patterns are attested elsewhere was also reviewed. It must be concluded that such innovations with 'like'-lexemes are highly functional in a very deep sense of the word.

What we are to draw from this in the way of implications for grammaticization theory is somewhat unclear. Peculiarities in the apparent history of *olsem* raise questions about claims (e.g. Saxena 1995) regarding the universality of complementizer grammaticization paths. Certainly, by starting out as a means of expressing (equative) comparisons, a function occurring late in the grammaticization path Saxena outlines, *olsem* is peculiar.[16]

Perhaps more intriguingly, though, data was presented suggesting that as a complementizer *olsem* emerged first with non-factive verbs, and not with verbs of locution as is generally seen in the development of complementizers. It was suggested that two factors account for this. First, the persistence of the similative meaning of *olsem*, and second, a congruence between the underlying (nominal) form of non-factive complements and *olsem*'s inherited preference for a nominal argument might account for this peculiarity.

However, whether this constitutes evidence *against* Saxena's proposal is not clear. Her work outlines a simple, monovalent, and unidirectional grammaticization path, of the kind that has been a cornerstone of the grammaticization literature (Heine *et al.* 1991, Hopper and Traugott 1993). But the data from Bislama looks considerably messier. It might be the case that the generalization Saxena argued for simply is not relevant in a case like *olsem*. On the one hand, *olsem* does not start out as a verb of locution (the initial point in Saxena's account). On the other hand, the lack of any clear, single trajectory for the development of *olsem* suggests that we are dealing with a grammaticization network, not a grammaticization path. It seems quite plausible that the constraints on development via networks might be rather different to the constraints operating on development via paths. For instance, networks might favor and actually sustain continued ambiguity of function, while paths might be constrained by unidirectionality.

Finally, the data on *olsem* raises questions about another aspect of directionality in grammaticization theory. Hopper and Traugott (1993) also proposed that grammaticization involves concrete meanings becoming more abstract. I would argue that both the starting point of *olsem* (as a preposition) and stages in its ontogeny (apparently occurring as a complementizer with perception verbs before locution verbs) suggest that a highly abstract meaning is basic. Its subsequent development as a true demonstrative suggests that, *contra* the theory's prediction, *olsem* has acquired more concrete meanings.

Again, it is not clear precisely what this means for grammaticization theory. I would argue that it suggests that some proposed universals need to be critically re-evaluated. However, I can also see that one might argue that the theory (as stated) makes no explicit claims about the trajectory of lexical items that start out with highly abstract meanings. Indeed, one might argue that there has been no palpable shift at all along this dimension: preposition, complementizer, demonstrative all behave (in some languages) as functional, rather than lexical items.

In conclusion, I want to make a strong plea against being too quick to put the data from *olsem* into the "not applicable" category, somewhere beyond the concern of grammaticization theory. If a collection such as this is to have merit to typologists, functional and formal syntacticians, and students of language variation and change, it will only do so if we treat the data presented seriously, and if we engage with it in ways that challenge our assumptions and theories.

In this chapter, I have tried to approach the analysis of *olsem* from a number of different perspectives. At times I have tested the data within the framework of generative syntax, and at times within the framework of functional syntax and grammaticization theory. In the analysis of *se*, I employed quantitative methods in order that variation in the present might shed light on the past (Labov 1994). Where, with *olsem*, the quantitative evidence is still sparse, methods of discourse analysis and straight-forward grammaticality judgments were brought to play.

I chose to present the data in this way, not for lack of conviction in any one method or theoretical framework, but rather out of a strong conviction that the full picture of language change, not just in creoles but perhaps especially in contact languages, requires explanations that eschew existing orthodoxy and assumptions of excessive modularity in the grammar. Only research that is maximally inclusive, in the spirit of the collected works of this volume, will result in theories that are maximally constrained. This may seem a paradox, but let us make full use of all the data collected here to both test the orthodox, and to position ourselves as exponents of the paradox.

Notes

* My thanks go to the Wenner-Gren Foundation for their support of my fieldwork (grant no. 5742), and Sharon Tabi whose help enabled me to understand the meanings of *olsem*, even though it meant she started hearing it everywhere. Thanks also to the numerous people who have taken time to discuss this one word with me over the years. Comments from Tom Güldemann, Chris Collins, Susanna Cummings and Gillian Sankoff have been especially helpful. None of the above necessarily agree with the analysis here. I am also grateful to Terry Crowley for sharing his historical corpus of Pacific pidgin spoken in Vanuatu.

1. This seems to be more frequent than the null option in English, however this variant will be glossed over here. A number of the substrate languages of Vanuatu do not overtly mark relative or complement clauses, so it is possible that this option has developed under the influence of the Oceanic vernaculars. However the constraints on, and the significance of, the variation between zero and overt relative and complement clause markers in the substrate languages remains unexamined, as does the variation between these strategies in Bislama. Consequently, the extent to which the Bislama variation is shaped by the substrate remains an open question.

2. In fact, Bickerton would characterize Bislama as irrelevant to the bioprogram hypothesis, given its stability as a pidgin, and its substrate contact.

3. The range is due to the fact that the derivation of some Bislama words is ambiguous, they could equally come from French or English.

4. The spoken corpus consists of more than 30,000 words of spoken Bislama recorded in 1994–95 in my own and other speakers' homes in northern Vanuatu (42 speakers, ages 8–*c*.65 years). Two written corpora have been used, historical examples (sources cited), and

a 1998 corpus of more than 15,000 words of newspaper texts, letters to the editor, and signage. Examples from the newspaper *Vanuatu Weekly Hedomadaire* (VWH) sourced dd/mm/yy.

5. Written tokens of *se* also occur, e.g. VWH, 6/6/98, p.8. Crowley's claim that *se* no longer means 'say' may reflect a regional difference in the Bislama spoken in central Vanuatu (where he worked), and the north. For instance, *se* as a copula is frequently heard on radio broadcasts from the central capital, Port Vila, but I have few tokens of this in my conversational Bislama from the northern region (despite the fact that some speakers originally came from central islands or Port Vila).

6. For historical examples, I have retained original spellings. For modern written examples, I have standardized spellings after the norms drawn up by the Vanuatu Literacy Council.

7. In the absence of a clear standard for Bislama, I have found that judgements cannot be elicited by asking which of the two variants sounds 'better', instead I ask which one sounds '(a little bit) different'.

8. The full range of functions is outlined in Meyerhoff and Niedzielski (1998).

9. This seems to be the case with the deletion of objects of verbs as well, however this remains to be studied in detail. Subject deletion is principally constrained by syntactic factors; more weakly constrained by discourse factors (Meyerhoff 2000, Chapter 6).

10. *Pace* Klamer's (this volume) arguments against this for Kambera, I will do so here. Both *talem* and *olsem* have (or appear to have) the transitive suffix *-em*.

11. Robert Early kindly confirmed this data and completed the enquiry with speakers in Port Vila. He agrees that with verbs of perception, *olsem* is very common, with verbs of speaking less so, and with propositional attitude verbs even less so: "Finding people [who] like *olsem* as a complementiser with *laekem* ['like'] is hard, and impossible for *hetem* ['hate']".

12. Thanks to Chris Collins for drawing my attention to this.

13. *Se* can introduce the complement of factives and non-factives.

14. Again, see Güldemann and Cohen *et al.* (this volume) for similar conclusions.

15. Note that the analysis of Kriyol *kuma* is disputed. Kihm (1990) argues that it is a verb, not a complementizer.

16. I am inclined to reject Tom Güldemann's suggestion that *olsem* fits Saxena's path 'thus' > quotative, since as I argued earlier translations of *olsem* as 'thus' reflect an anglocentric (more than a bislamic) analysis of bare *olsem*.

References

Anderson, J.W. 1880. *Notes of travel in Fiji and New Caledonia with some remarks on South Sea islanders and their languages*. London: Ellissen.

Bickerton, Derek. 1984. "The language bioprogram hypothesis". *The Brain and Behavioral Sciences* 7,2: 173–88.

Chomsky, Noam. 1995. *The minimalist program.* Cambridge, MA: MIT Press.
Codrington, R. H. 1885. *The Melanesian languages.* London: Henry Frowde.
Crowley, Terry. 1991. *From Beach-la-Mar to Bislama: the emergence of a national language.* Oxford: Oxford University Press.
Crowley, Terry. 1995. *A new Bislama dictionary.* Suva, Fiji: The University of the South Pacific
Heine, Bernd, Ulrike Claudi and Friederike Hünnemeyer. 1991. *Grammaticalization: a conceptual framework.* Chicago: The University of Chicago Press.
Hopper, Paul J. 1991. "On some principles of grammaticization". In Traugott, Elizabeth Closs and Bernd Heine (eds.), *Approaches to grammaticalization,* 2 Vols. (=Typological Studies in Language 19). Amsterdam: John Benjamins, Vol.1, 17–35.
Hopper, Paul J. and Elizabeth Closs Traugott. 1993. *Grammaticalization.* Cambridge: Cambridge University Press.
Jacomb, Edward. 1929. *The joy court.* London: Braybrook and Dobson.
Jauncey, Dorothy. 1997. *A grammar of Tamambo: the language of Western Malo, Vanuatu.* Ph.D. thesis: Australian National University.
Kaplan, David. 1989. "Demonstratives: an essay on the semantics, logic, metaphysics, and epistemology of demonstratives and other indexicals". In Almog, Joseph, John Perry and Howard Wettstein (eds.), *Themes from Kaplan.* New York: Oxford University Press, 481–563.
Kiparsky, Paul and Carol Kiparsky. 1970. "Fact". In Bierwisch, Manfred and Karl E. Heidolph (eds.), *Progress in linguistics: a collection of papers.* The Hague: Mouton, 143–73.
Kroch, Anthony S. 1989. "Reflexes of grammar in patterns of language change". *Language Variation and Change* 1: 199–244.
Labov, William. 1994. *Principles of language change: internal factors.* Oxford: Blackwell.
Lichtenberk, Frantisek. 1983. *A grammar of Manam.* Honolulu: University of Hawai'i Press.
Lindstrom, Lamont. 1986. *Kwamera dictionary* (=Pacific Linguistics C95). Canberra: Australian National University.
Lynch, John. 1982a. "South-West Tanna grammar outline and vocabulary". In Lynch, John (ed.), 1–91.
Lynch, John. 1982b. "Anejom grammar sketch". In Lynch, John (ed.), 93–154.
Lynch, John (ed.). 1982. *Papers in linguistics of Melanesia 4* (=Pacific Linguistics A64). Canberra: Australian National University.
Meyerhoff, Miriam. 1998. "Comparing old and new information in Bislama: nominal deletion with *olsem*". In Tent, Jan and France Mugler (eds.) *Proceedings of the Second International Conference on Oceanic Linguistics, Vol. 1: language contact* (=Pacific Linguistics C141). Canberra: Australian National University, 85–93.
Meyerhoff, Miriam. 2000. *Constraints on null subjects in Bislama (Vanuatu): social and linguistic factors* (=Pacific Linguistics 506). Canberra: Australian National University.
Meyerhoff, Miriam and Nancy Niedzielski. 1998. "The syntax and semantics of *olsem* in Bislama". In Pearson, Matthew (ed.), *Recent papers in Austronesian linguistics* (=UCLA Occasional Papers in Linguistics 20), 235–43.
Paton, Maggie W. 1895. *Letters and sketches from the New Hebrides.* London: Hodder and Stoughton.

Poser, Rebecca. 1985. "Creolization as typological change: some examples from Romance syntax". *Diachronica* 2,2: 167–88.

Ray, Sidney H. 1978 [1926]. *A comparative study of the Melanesian Island languages*. Cambridge: Cambridge University Press.

Verhaar, John W.M. 1995. *Toward a reference grammar of Tok Pisin: an experiment in corpus linguistics*. Honolulu: University of Hawai'i Press.

Walker, Marilyn and Ellen Prince. 1996. "A bilateral approach to givenness: a hearer-status algorithm and a centering algorithm". In Fretheim, Thorstein and Jeanette Gundel (eds.), *Reference and referent accessibility*. Amsterdam: Benjamins, 291–306.

Woolford, Ellen. 1981. "The developing complementizer system of Tok Pisin: syntactic change in progress". In Muysken, Pieter (ed.), *Generative studies on creole languages* (=Studies in Generative Grammar 6). Dordrecht: Foris, 125–39.

PART 5

A comprehensive bibliography of reported discourse

A comprehensive bibliography of reported discourse

Tom Güldemann, Manfred von Roncador
and Wim van der Wurff
Universität Leipzig, Universität Bayreuth, Universiteit Leiden

This bibliography concentrates on linguistic contributions to reported speech treating topics such as logophoricity, reported discourse constructions in relation to description, language change and grammaticalization, speech act verbs and related lexemes. It also contains contributions to the discussion on reported speech within the philosophy of language and logic, while excluding the general philosophical debate on opaque and transparent contexts as well as intension and extension. The bibliography further includes items relating to the discussion on free indirect discourse within literary criticism, although no heed is paid to the treatment of more general issues concerning the 'merging' of the narrator's and the character's voices or the representation of the character's perspectives and his speech. Inaccessible academic studies, e.g. master theses, and unpublished papers were left out. We have tried to be as comprehensive as possible, though of course such a collection cannot be exhaustive. A major problem is that the borderline between linguistic approaches on the one hand and philosphical or literary approaches on the other is not clear-cut. Further, there is a certain bias towards English, French, Spanish and German as languages of discription, though a considerable number of works written in other European languages are included. It has not been possible to cover the discussion on reported speech in other languages, as for example Japanese or Chinese; a bibliography of some aspects of reported speech in Japanese, mostly on free indirect discourse, is contained in Suzuki (in this volume) or can be found in Hosaka and Suzuki (1993). The majority of the entries are taken from the earlier collections by Roncador (1988),

---

After completion of the ms. of our bibliography, we discovered the existence of a French–Belgian–Spanish working group on the subject of reported speech (directed by Laurence Rosier, Sophie Marnette and Juan Manuel López), who have also compiled a bibliography, see: <http://www.ulb.ac.be/philo/serlifra/ci-dit/>.

Wurff (ms., cf. Jansen and Wurff (eds.) 1996) and Güldemann (2001). Most of the supplementary entries found in the literature have been cross-checked by the authors. Needless to say, the authors take all responsibility for wrong quotes and other shortcomings.

Aaron, Uche E. 1992. "Reported speech in Obolo narrative discourse". In Hwang and Merrifield (eds.), 227–40.
Aaron, Uche E. 1996/7. "Grammaticalization of the verb 'say' to future tense in Obolo". *Journal of West African Languages* 26,2: 87–93.
Abbott, Barbara. 1979. "Remarks on 'Belief Contexts'". *Linguistic Inquiry* 10: 143–9.
Abraham, Werner. 1969. "Verbklassifikation und das Komplement 'Indirekter Fragesatz'". *Die Sprache* 15,2: 113–34.
Abraham, Werner and Theo A. J. M. Janssen (eds.). 1989. *Tempus — Aspekt — Modus: die lexikalischen und grammatischen Formen in den germanischen Sprachen.* Tübingen: Niemeyer.
Abusch, Dorit. 1988. "Sequence of tense, intensionality and scope". In Borer, Hagit (ed.), *Proceedings of the 7th West Coast Conference on Formal Linguistics, Irvine, Calif., 1988.* Stanford: Center for the Study of Language and Information, 1–14.
Abusch, Dorit. 1992. "The present under past as *de re* interpretation". In Bates, Dawn (ed.), *The Proceedings of the Tenth West Coast Conference on Formal Linguistics, Tempe, Arizona, 1991.* Stanford: Center for the Study of Language and Information, 1–12.
Abusch, Dorit. 1997. "Sequence of tense and temporal *de re*". *Linguistics and Philosophy* 20: 1–50.
Adamson, Sylvia. 1994. "From empathetic deixis to empathetic narrative: stylisation and (de-)subjectivisation as processes of language change". *Transactions of the Philological Society* 92: 55–88. (also in Stein and Wright (eds.), 195–224)
Adamson, Sylvia. 1995. "Empathetic narrative — a literary and linguistic problem". In Ayres-Bennett, Wendy and P. O'Donovan (eds.), *Syntax and the literary system: new approaches to the interface between literature and linguistics.* Cambridge: Cambridge French Colloquia, 17–42.
Adelaar, Willem F. H. 1990. "The role of quotations in Andean discourse". In Pinkster and Genee (eds.), 1–12.
Agesthialingom, Shunmugom and S. V. Shanmugam (eds.). 1972. *Third Seminar on Dravidian Linguistics, Annamalainagar, 1971* (=Department of Linguistics Publication 27). Annamalainagar: Annamalai University.
Akoha, A. Bienvenu. 1983. "Les logophoriques dans la langue fon". *Cahier d'Études Linguistiques* 1: 13–18.
Aksedal, John O. 1996. "Zur Regrammatikaliserung des Konjunktivs in der indirekten Rede im Deutschen". *Deutsche Sprache* 24: 289–304.
Alekseeva, A. B. 1937. "Prjamaja i kosvennaja reč' v sovremennom russkom literaturnom jazyke". *Russkij Jazyk v Škole* 2: 30–4.
Alexandrescu, Sorin. 1976. "Sur les modalités *croire* et *savoir*". *Langages* 43: 19–27.
Allen, Bernard M. 1922. "Indirect discourse and the subjunctive of attraction". *The Classical Weekly* 15,24: 185–7.

Álvarez-Cáccamo, Celso. 1996. "The power of reflexive language(s): code displacement in reported speech". *Journal of Pragmatics* 25,1:33–59.
Andersen, Torben and Didier L. Goyvaerts 1986. "Reflexivity and logophoricity in Moru-Madi". *Folia Linguistica* 20,3/4:297–318.
Anderson, John R. 1974. "Verbatim and propositional representation of sentences in immediate and long-term memory". *Journal of Verbal Learning and Verbal Behavior* 13:149–62.
Anderson, Stephen R. and Paul Kiparsky (eds.). 1973. *A Festschrift for Morris Halle*. New York: Holt, Rinehart and Winston.
Andersson, G. 1846. *De oratione obliqua latinorum commentatio*. Lund: typis Berlingianis.
Andersson, Sven-Gunnar. 1994. "Zum Indikativ in eingeleiteten Nebensätzen der indirekten Rede nach präteritalem Anführungsausdruck". *Nordlyd* 22:38–52.
Andrieu, Jean. 1948. "Procédé de citation et de raccord". *Revue des Études Latines* 26:268–93.
Andrievskaja, A.A. 1967. *Nesobstvenno-prjamaja reč' v xudožestvennoj proze Lui Aragona*. Kiew: Izdatelstvo Kievskogo Universiteta.
Antoine, F. 1904. "Le style indirect partiel". *Le Musée Belge* 8:177–93.
Arnold, Paula. 1992. "The persuasive style of debates in direct speech in Thucydides". *Hermes* 120:44–57.
Authier, Jacqueline. 1978. "Les formes du discours rapporté: remarques syntaxiques et sémantiques à partir des traitements proposés". *Documentation et Recherche en Linguistique Allemande Contemporaine — Vincennes* 17:1–87.
Authier, Jacqueline. 1979. "Problèmes posés par le traitement du discours rapporté dans une grammaire de phrases". *Linguisticae Investigationes* 3:211–28.
Authier Revuz, Jacqueline. 1982. "Hétérogénité montrée et hétérogénité constitutive: éléments pour une approche de l'autre dans le discours". *Documentation et Recherche en Linguistique Allemande Contemporaine — Vincennes* 26:91–151.
Authier-Revuz, Jacqueline. 1992/93. "Repères dans le champ du discours rapporté I, II". *L'Information Grammaticale* 55:38–42; 56:10–15
Authier-Revuz, Jacqueline. 1995a. *Ces mots qui ne vont pas de soi: boucles réflexives et non-coïncidences du dire*. Paris: Larousse.
Authier-Revuz, Jacqueline. 1995b. "De quelques idées reçues au sujet du *discours rapporté*". *Perspectives* 4:15–21.
Authier-Revuz, Jacqueline. 1996. "Remarques sur la catégorie de 'l'îlot textuel'". In Claquin and Mochet (eds.), 91–115.
Authier-Revuz, Jacqueline. 1997. "Modalisation autonymique et discours autre: quelques remarques". *Modèles Linguistiques* 18,1:33–51.
Authier, Jacqueline and André Meunier. 1977. "Exercises de grammaire et discours rapporté". *Langue Française* 33:41–67.
Avery, Mary M. 1937. *The use of direct speech in Ovid's 'Metamorphoses'*. Chicago: University Library.
Bacon, John. 1979. "The logical form of perception sentences". *Synthese* 41:271–308.
Bakhtin, M., see Baxtin.
Bakker, Egbert J. 1991. "Foregrounding and indirect discourse: temporal subclauses in a Herodotean short story". *Journal of Pragmatics* 16:225–47.

Baldwin, Thomas. 1975. "Quantification, modality, and indirect speech". In Blackburn, Simon (ed.), *Meaning, reference and necessity: new studies in semantics*. Cambridge: Cambridge University Press, 56–108.

Ballard, L. 1974. "Telling it like it was, Part 1:4, 'hearsay particle' of the Philippine languages". *Notes on Translation* 51:28.

Bally, Charles. 1912. "Le style indirect libre en français moderne". *Germanisch-Romanische Monatsschrift* 4:549–56, 597–606.

Bally, Charles. 1914. "Figures de pensée et formes linguistiques". *Germanisch-Romanische Monatsschrift* 6:405–22, 456–70.

Bally, Charles. 1930. "Antiphrase et style indirect libre". In Bøgholm, Niels et al. (eds.), *A grammatical miscellany offered to Otto Jespersen on his seventieth birthday*. London: George Allen and Unwin, 331–40.

Bamgboṣe, Ajọ. 1986. "Reported speech in Yoruba". In Coulmas (ed.), 77–97.

Banfield, Ann. 1973. "Narrative style and the grammar of direct and indirect speech". *Foundations of Language* 10:1–39.

Banfield, Ann. 1978a. "The formal coherence of represented speech and thought". *PTL: A Journal for Descriptive Poetics and Theory of Literature* 3:289–314.

Banfield, Ann. 1978b. "Where epistemology, style, and grammar meet literary history: the development of represented speech and thought". *New Literary History* 9,3:415–54. (also in Lucy (ed.), 339–64)

Banfield, Ann. 1979. "La syntaxe de l'incise narrative et l'attribution de point de vue de phrase en phrase". *Linguisticae Investigationes* 3:229–43.

Banfield, Ann. 1981. "Reflective and non-reflective consciousness in the language of fiction". *Poetics Today* 2,2:61–76.

Banfield, Ann. 1982. *Unspeakable sentences: narration and representation in the language of fiction*. London: Routledge and Kegan Paul.

Banfield, Ann. 1995. *Phrases sans paroles: théorie du récit et du style indirect libre*. Paris: Seuil (=Banfield 1982)

Barat, Jean-Claude. 1985. "Le 'style indirect libre': défence et illustration". In Barat, Jean-Claude, *Sur l'énonciation* (=Fabula 5). Lille: Presses Universitaires de Lille, 141–7.

Barentsen, Adrian A. 1996. "Shifting points of orientation in Modern Russian: tense selection in 'reported perception'". In Janssen and Wurff (eds.), 15–55.

Bart, Benjamin F. 1989. "Le style indirect libre chez Flaubert: *Madame Bovary* et les richesses de l'indéterminé". In Lecercle, François and Simone Messina (eds.), *Flaubert, l'autre: pour Jean Bruneau*. Lyon: Presses Universitaires, 138–44.

Bashir, Elena. 1996. "Mosaic of tongues: quotatives and complementizers in NW Indo-Aryan, Burushaski, and Balti". In Hanaway, William L. and Wilma Heston (eds.), *Studies in Pakistani popular culture*. Lahore: Sang-e-Meel, 187–286.

Basset, Louis. 1986. "La représentation subjective d'un point de vue passé: l'optatif oblique dans les complétives déclaratives chez Thucydide". In Remi-Giraud, Sylvianne and Michel Le Guern (eds.), *Sur le verbe*. Lyon: Presses Universitaires de Lyon, 91–114.

Basso, Ellen. 1986. "Quoted dialogues in Kalapalo narrative discourse". In Sherzer, Joel and Greg Urban (eds.), *Native South American discourse*. Berlin: Mouton de Gruyter, 119–68.

Bauer, Brigitte L. M. 1996. "The verb in indirect speech in Old French: system in change". In Janssen and Wurff (eds.), 75–96.
Bausch, Karl-Heinz. 1975. "Die situationsspezifische Variation der Modi in der indirekten Rede". *Deutsche Sprache* 1975:332–45.
Baxtin, Mixail M. 1971. "Discourse typology in prose". In Matejka and Pomorska (eds.), 176–96 (="Tipy prozaičeskogo slova", in Baxtin, Mixail. 1929, *Problemy tvorčestva Dostoevskogo.* Leningrad, 105–35).
Baxtin, Mixail M. 1981. "Discourse in the novel". In Baxtin, Mixail M. (ed. and translated by Emerson, Caryl and Michael Holquist), *The dialogic imagination* (=University of Texas Slavic Series 1). Austin: University of Texas Press, 259–422.
Bayet, Jean. 1931/32. "Le style indirect libre en latin". *Revue de Philologie, de Littérature et de l'Histoire Anciennes* 57:327–42; 58:5–23.
Baynham, Mike. 1991. "Speech reporting as a discourse strategy: some issues of acquisition and use". *Australian Review of Applied Linguistics* 14,2:87–114.
Baynham, Mike. 1996. "Direct speech: what's it doing in non-narrative discourse". *Journal of Pragmatics* 25,1:61–81.
Becher, Marlis. 1989. *Der Konjunktiv der indirekten Redewiedergabe: eine linguistische Analyse der "Skizze eines Verunglückten" von Uwe Johnson* (=Germanistische Texte und Studien 30). Hildesheim: Olms.
Becher, Marlis and Henning Bergenholtz. 1985. "Sei oder nicht sei: Probleme des Modusgebrauchs in der indirekten Rede". *Nouveaux Cahiers d'Allemand* 3:443–57.
Behaghel, Otto. 1877. *Über die Entstehung der abhängigen Rede und die Ausbildung der Zeitformen im Altdeutschen.* 'Habilitation' thesis, Universität Heidelberg. (also in Behaghel, Otto. 1878. *Die Zeitfolge der abhängigen Rede im Deutschen.* Paderborn: Schöningh, 1–37)
Behaghel, Otto. 1899. *Der Gebrauch der Zeitformen im konjunktivischen Nebensatz des Deutschen — Mit Bemerkungen zur lateinischen Zeitfolge und zur griechischen Modusverschiebung.* Paderborn: Schöningh.
Benigny, Julius. 1929. "Zur einleitenden Konjunktion vor direkter Rede". *Indogermanische Forschungen* 47:105–23.
Benveniste, Emile. 1958. "Les verbes délocutifs". In Hatcher, Anna G. and K. L. Selig (eds.), *Studia philologica et litteraria in honorem L. Spitzer.* Bern: Francke, 57–63. (also in Benveniste, Emile. 1966. *Problèmes de linguistique générale.* Paris: Gallimard, 277–85)
Bergen, Robert D. (ed.). 1994. *Biblical Hebrew and discourse linguistics.* Dallas: Summer Institute of Linguistics.
Bers, Victor. 1997. *Speech in speech: studies in incorporated "Oratio recta" in Attic drama and oratory.* Lanham: Rowman & Littlefield.
Berthonneau, Anne-Marie and Georges Kleiber. 1996. "Subordination et temps grammaticaux: pour une conception non concordancielle de l'imparfait en discours indirect". In Muller, Claude (ed.), *Dépendance et intégration syntaxique: subordination, coordination, connexion* (=Linguistische Arbeiten 351). Tübingen: Niemeyer, 115–26.
Berthonneau, Anne-Marie and Georges Kleiber. 1997. "Subordination et temps grammaticaux: l'imparfait en discours indirect". *Le Français Moderne* 65,2:113–41.
Bertinetto, Pier M. et al. (eds.), 1995. *Temporal reference, aspect and actionality, Vol. 1: Semantic and syntactic perspectives.* Torino: Rosenberg and Sellier.

Bertolet, Rod. 1990. *What is said: a theory of indirect speech reports* (=Philosophical Studies 49). Dordrecht: Kluwer.

Bertoncini, Elena Zúbková. 1991. "Reported speech in Swahili literature". In Blommaert, Jan (ed.), *Swahili studies: essays in honour of Marcel van Spaandonck*. Ghent: Academia Press, 175–97.

Besnier, Niko. 1993. "Reported speech and affect on Nukulaelae Atoll". In Hill and Irvine (eds.), 161–81.

Beyerle, Dieter. 1972. "Ein vernachlässigter Aspekt der erlebten Rede". *Archiv für das Studium der neueren Sprachen und Literaturen* 208:350–66.

Bezold, Carl. 1900. "Anführendes [–'a] im Aethiopischen". *Zeitschrift für Assyriologie und verwandte Gebiete* 15:398.

Bickerton, Derek. 1967. "Modes of interior monologue: a formal definition". *Modern Language Quarterly* 28:229–39.

Bickerton, Derek. 1968. "James Joyce and the development of interior monologue". *Essays in Criticism* 18:32–46.

Bigelow, John C. 1975. "Contexts and quotation I, II". *Linguistische Berichte* 38:1–21; 39:1–21.

Bigelow, John C. 1978. "Semantics of thinking, speaking and translation". In Guenthner, Franz and M. Guenthner-Reutter (eds.), *Meaning and translation: philosophical and linguistic approaches*. London: Duckworth, 109–35.

Biraud, Michèle and Sylvie Mellet. 2000. "Les faits d'hétérogénéité énonciative dans les textes grecs et latins de l'Antiquité". In Mellet and Vuillaume (eds.), 9–48.

Bissinger, Helene. 1953. *Die "erlebte Rede", der "erlebte innere Monolog" und der "innere Monolog" in den Werken von Hermann Bahr, Richard Beer-Hofmann und Arthur Schnitzler*. Doctoral thesis, Universität zu Köln.

Bjork, Robert E. 1992. *The Old English verse saints' lives: a study in direct discourse and the iconography of style*. Toronto: University of Toronto Press.

Bjørndalen, Anders Jorgen. 1974. "Zu den Zeitstufen der Zitatformel ...KH 'MR im Botenverkehr". *Zeitschrift für die Alttestamentliche Wissenschaft* 86:393–403.

Blackstone, B. 1962. *Indirect speech: its principles and practice*. London: Longmans.

Blaß, Curt. 1924/5. "'Erlebte' Rede — Mittelbare Dacht". *Die Literatur* 27:572–3.

Blyth, Carl Jr., Sigrid Recktenwald and Jenny Wang. 1990. "I'm like, 'Say what?!': a new quotative in American oral narrative". *American Speech* 65,3:215–27.

Bodelot, Colette. 1987. *L'interrogation indirecte en latin: syntaxe, valeur illocutoire, formes*. Louvain: Peeters.

Boeck, W. 1957. "Zur Tempusgebrauch des Russischen in Objekt- und Subjektsätzen". *Zeitschrift für Slawistik* 2:206–18.

Boeck, W. 1958. "Der Tempusgebrauch in den russischen Objekt- und Subjektsätzen, seine historische Entwicklung und sein stilistischer Wert". *Zeitschrift für Slawistik* 3:209–34.

Boeder, Winfried. 2000. "Evidentiality in Georgian". In Johanson, Lars and Bo Utas (eds.), *Evidentials. Turkic, Iranian and neighbouring languages* (=Empirical Approaches to Language Typology 24). Berlin, New York: de Gruyter, 275–328.

Bögholm, Niels. 1911/2. "Oratio recta und oratio obliqua". *Englische Studien* 44:80–96.

Bolkestein, A. Machtelt. 1990. "Unreportable linguistic entities in functional grammar". In Pinkster and Genee (eds.), 13–26.
Bolkestein, A. Machtelt. 1996. "Reported speech in Latin". In Janssen and Wurff (eds.), 121–40.
Boogaart, Ronny. 1996. "Tense and temporal ordering in English and Dutch indirect speech". In Janssen and Wurff (eds.), 213–35.
Booker, John T. 1985. "Style indirect libre: the case of Stendhal". *Stanford French Review* 9,2:137–51.
Boon, Pieter. 1978. "Obliquitätskonjunktiv oder Konjunktiv der indirekten Rede". *Indogermanische Forschungen* 83:324–44.
Borgeaud, Willy. 1941. "La fonction du subjonctif dans l'interrogation indirecte en latin et en allemand". *Cahiers Ferdinand de Saussure* 1:18–19.
Bosch, Tineke. 1978. "Márgenes de citas en el dialecto hindostan de Surinam". In Levinsohn (ed.), 65–76.
Bosque, Ignacio. 1981. "Sobre la interrogación indirecta". *Dicenda* 1:13–34.
Botne, Robert. 1993. "Differentiating the auxiliaries -*TI* and -*VA* in Tumbuka (N.21)". *Linguistique Africaine* 10:7–28.
Botne, Robert. 1998. "The evolution of future tenses from serial 'say' constructions in central eastern Bantu". *Diachronica* 15,2:207–30.
Bračič, Stojan. 1988. "Figurenbeeinflußte Erzählerrede: zu einigen Aspekten des Verhältnisses von Erzähler- und Figurenperspektive im Text". *Grazer Linguistische Studien* 30:5–18.
Brandsma, Frank. 1998. "Knights' talk: direct discourse in Arthurian romance". *Neophilologus* 82:513–26.
Branigan, Phil and Chris Collins. 1993. "Verb movement and the quotative construction in English". *Massachusetts Institute of Technology Working Papers in Linguistics* 18:1–13
Brăteanu, Elena. 1984. "Flaubert et l'emploi métaphorique du discours indirect libre". *Analele Universități București: Limbi și Literaturi Straine* 33:39–42.
Bréal, M. 1901. "Les verbes signifiant 'parler'". *Revue des Études Grecques* 14:113–21.
Brecht, Richard D. 1974. "Deixis in embedded structures". *Foundations of Language* 11:489–518.
Brecht, Richard D. 1975. "Relative vs. absolute reference in embedded tense forms". *Slavic and East European Journal* 19:145–54.
Bres, Jacques. 1997. "Aspects de l'interaction rapportée dans le récit oral". *Modèles Linguistiques* 18,1:129–40.
Brinkmann, Hennig. 1969. "Die Einbettung von Figurensprache in Autorensprache: zur Grammatik der Rededarstellung". In Valentin, Paul and G. Zink (eds.), *Mélanges pour Jean Fourquet: 37 essais de linguistique germanique et de littérature du moyen âge français et allemand*. München: Hueber, 21–41.
Brinton, Laurel J. 1980. "Represented perception: a study in narrative style". *Poetics* 9,4:363–81.
Brinton, Laurel J. 1995. "Non-anaphoric reflexives in free indirect style: expressing the subjectivity of the non-speaker". In Stein and Wright (eds.), 173–94.

Broadwell, George A. 1991. "Speaker and self in Choctaw". *International Journal of American Linguistics* 57,4: 411–25.
Brondeel, H. 1977. "The non-application of the sequence of tenses after past embedding verbs in English and Dutch 'that'-clauses in terms of the speaker's commitment to the truth of the statement". In Putseys, Yvan (ed.), *Aspects of English and Netherlandic grammar* (=Contrastive Analysis Series 3). Leuven: Acco, 70–86.
Brøndum-Nielsen, Johannes. 1953. *Dækning — Oratio tecta i dansk litteratur før 1870: Festskrift udgivet af Københavns Universitet i anledning af Universitetets årsfest, november 1953*. Copenhagen: B. Lunos.
Bruña-Cuevas, Manuel. 1988. "Le style indirect libre chez Marie de France". *Revue de Linguistique Romane* 52: 421–46.
Bruña-Cuevas, Manuel. 1989. "Changer l'appellation 'style indirect libre'?" *Romania* 110: 1–39.
Bruña-Cuevas, Manuel. 1996. "Le discours direct introduit par *que*". *Le Français Moderne* 64,1: 28–50.
Brünner, Gisela. 1991. "Redewiedergabe in Gesprächen". *Deutsche Sprache* 19: 1–15.
Buck, Carl D. 1915. "Words of speaking and saying in the Indo-European languages". *American Journal of Philology* 36,1: 1–18; 36,2: 125–54.
Bühler, Willi. 1937. *Die "Erlebte Rede" im englischen Roman: ihre Vorstufen und ihre Ausbildung im Werke Jane Austen's* (=Schweizer anglistische Arbeiten 4). Zürich, Leipzig: Niehans.
Burge, Tyler. 1977. "Belief *de re*". *Jounal of Philosophy* 74: 338–62.
Bürling, Coletta. 1983. *Die direkte Rede als Mittel der Personengestaltung in den Íslendingasögur* (=Texte und Untersuchungen zur Germanistik und Skandinavistik 7). Frankfurt/Main: Lang.
Butler, R. 1981. "Flaubert's exploitation of the 'style indirect libre': ambiguities and perspectives in *Madame Bovary*". *Modern Languages* 62,4: 190–6.
Butters, Ronald R. 1980. "Narrative *go* 'say' ". *American Speech* 55,4: 304–7.
Buttny, Richard. 1997. "Reported speech in talking race on campus". *Human Communication Research* 23: 477–506.
Caldas-Coulthard, Carmen R. 1987. "Reported speech in written narrative texts". In Coulthard, Malcolm (ed.), *Discussing discourse*. Birmingham: University of Birmingham, 149–67.
Caldas-Coulthard, Carmen R. 1994. "On reporting: the representation of speech in factual and factional narratives". In Coulthard, Malcolm (ed.), *Advances in written text analysis*. London: Routledge, 295–308.
Cameron, Richard. 1998. "A variable syntax of speech, gesture, and sound effect: direct quotations in Spanish". *Linguistic Change and Variation* 10: 43–83.
Campbell, Bob and Barbara Campbell. 1981. "Preliminary observations concerning the rarity of exact repetition in Jamamadi". *Notes on Linguistics* 19: 10–20.
Cane, Eleonora. 1969. *Il discorso indiretto libero nella narrativa italiana del Novecento*. Roma: Silva.
Cappelen, Herman and Ernie Lepore. 1997. "On an alleged connection between indirect speech and the theory of meaning". *Mind and Language* 12: 278–96.

Carls, Uwe and Peter Lucho (eds.). 1999. *Form, function and variation in English: studies in honour of Klaus Hansen*. Frankfurt/Main: Lang.

Casad, Eugene H. 1989. *The grammaticalization of the Cora quotative 'yee'* (=LAUD A274). Duisburg: Linguistic Agency University of Duisburg.

Castelnovo, Walter and Roos Vogel. 1995. "Reported speech". In Bertinetto et al. (eds.), 255–72.

Cate, Abraham P. ten. 1995. "Zeitenfolge im komplexen Satz". In Bærentzen, Per (ed.), *Aspekte der Sprachbeschreibung: Akten des 29. Linguistischen Kolloquiums, Aarhus 1994* (=Linguistische Arbeiten 342). Tübingen: Niemeyer, 27–31.

Cate, Abraham P. ten. 1996. "Modality of verb forms in German reported speech". In Janssen and Wurff (eds.), 189–211.

Cattani, Mary S. 1982. *Quoted direct discourse in Michel Butor's "La modification"*. Ph.D. thesis, University of Massachusetts, Amherst.

Cerquiglini, Bernard. 1984. "Le style indirect libre et la modernité". *Langages* 73:7–16.

Chamberlain, Lori. 1983. "'A sentence in inquiry?': Banfield's *Unspeakable sentences*". In Palmer, Michael (ed.), *Code of signals: recent writings in poetics*. Berkeley: North Atlantic, 280–8.

Champaud, Christian, Dominique Bassano and Maya Hickmann. 1993. "Modalité épistemique et discours rapporté chez l'enfant français". In Dittmar, Norbert and Astrid Reich (eds.), *Modality in language acquisition* (=Soziolinguistik und Sprachkontakt 6). Berlin: Mouton de Gruyter, 185–209.

Chang, In-Bong. 1997. "Discours rapporté et verbes déictiques de déplacement en français et en coréen". *Modèles Linguistiques* 18,1:93–109.

Charolles, Michel. 1976. "Exercice sur les verbes de communication". *Pratiques: théorie, pratique, pédagogie* 9:83–107.

Chatton, René. 1953. *Zur Geschichte der romanischen Verben für 'sprechen', 'sagen' und 'reden'* (=Romanica Helvetica 44). Bern: Francke.

Chetveruchin, Alexander S. 1988. "Unexpected linguistic interpretation of *jn* 'say(s), said'". *Göttinger Miszellen: Beiträge zur ägyptologischen Diskussion* 104:75–88.

Chia, Emmanuel N. 1986. "Indirect quote as the dominant style of reporting in Kom". In Elson, Benjamin F. (ed.), *Language in global perspective: papers in honor of the 50th anniversary of the Summer Institute of Linguistics, 1935–1985*. Dallas: Summer Institute of Linguistics, 149–61.

Christ, Ingeborg. 1981. *Redeerwähnung als didaktisches Problem: Kommunikation über Kommunikation im Französischunterricht*. Tübingen: Narr.

Christian, Viktor. 1915. "Über einige Verba des Sprechens". *Wiener Zeitschrift für die Kunde des Morgenlandes* 29:438–44.

Church, Alonzo. 1954. "Intensional isomorphism and identity of belief". *Philosophical Studies* 5,5:65–73.

Claquin, Françoise and Marie-Anne Mochet (eds.). 1996. *Hétérogénéités en discours* (=Cahiers du Français Contemporain 3). Paris: Didier.

Clark, David J. 1972. "A four-term person system and its ramifications". *Studies in African Linguistics* 3:97–105.

Clark, Douglas Ralph. 1984. *The citations in in the Book of Ezekiel: an investigation into method, audience, and message*. Ph.D. thesis, Vanderbildt University.

Clark, Herbert H. and Richard J. Gerrig. 1990. "Quotations as demonstrations". *Language* 66,4:764–805.

Clements, George N. 1975. "The logophoric pronoun in Ewe: its role in discourse". *Journal of West African Languages* 10,2:141–77.

Cloarec-Heiss, France. 1969. "Les modalités personnelles dans quelques langues oubanguiennes (discours direct — discours indirect)". In Cloarec-Heiss, France, *I. Banda-linda de Ippy: phonologie — dérivation et composition; II. Les modalités presonelles dans quelques langues oubanguiennes (discours direct — discours indirect)* (=Bibliothèque de la SELAF 14). Paris: Société d'Études Linguistiques et Anthropologiques de France, 59–71.

Coelho, Jacinto do Prado. 1949. "O discurso semi-directo no romanceiro popular". *Revista de Portugal, Série A: Língua portuguesa* 14:18–20.

Cogen, Cathy and Herrmann, Leora. 1975. "Interaction of the expression 'let's just say' with the Gricean maxims of conversation". *Berkeley Linguistics Society* 1:60–8.

Cohen, Marcel. 1952. "Le style indirect libre et l'imparfait en français après 1850". *Europe* 30,77:62–9 (also in Cohen, Marcel. 1954. *Grammaire et style 1450–1950: Cinq cent ans de phrase française*. Paris: Éditions sociales, 97–107).

Cohn, Dorrit. 1966. "Narrated monologue: definition of a fictional style". *Comparative Literature* 18:97–112.

Cohn, Dorrit. 1969. "Erlebte Rede im Ich-Roman". *Germanisch-Romanische Monatsschrift* 19:305–13.

Cohn, Dorrit. 1978. *Transparent minds: narrative modes for presenting consciousness in fiction*. Princeton: Princeton University Press.

Collins, Carrel. 1954. "The interior monologues of *The Sound and the Fury*". In Downer, Alan S. (ed.), *English Institute essays 1952*. New York: Columbia University, 29–56.

Collins, Chris and Phil Branigan. 1997. "Quotative inversion". *Natural Language and Linguistic Theory* 15,1:1–41.

Collins, Daniel E. 1996. "The pragmatics of indirect speech in Old Church Slavonic and other Early Slavic writings". In Barentsen, Adrian A. et al. (eds.), *Studies in South Slavic and Balkan linguistics* (=Studies in Slavic and General Linguistics 23). Amsterdam: Rodopi, 21–86.

Collins, Daniel E. 2001. *Reanimated voices: speech reporting in a historical-pragmatic perspective* (=Pragmatics and Beyond, New Series 85). Amsterdam: Benjamins.

Collins, James. 1987. "Reported speech in Navajo myth-narratives". In Verschueren, Jef (ed.), *Linguistic action: some empirical-conceptual studies* (=Advances in Discourse Processes 23). Norwood: Ablex, 69–84.

Combettes, Bernard. 1989. "Discours rapporté et énonciation: trois approches différentes". *Pratiques: théorie, pratique, pédagogie* 64:111–25.

Combettes, Bernard. 1990. "Énoncé, énonciation et discours rapporté". *Pratiques: théorie, pratique, pédagogie* 65:97–111.

Comrie, Bernard. 1986. "Tense in indirect speech". *Folia Linguistica* 20:265–96.

Cooper, Guy L. 1971. *Zur syntaktischen Theorie und Textkritik der attischen Autoren*. 1. Teil: Über *Oratio Obliqua* und *Oratio Recta*. Zürich: Juris.
Cornulier, Benoît de. 1978. "L'incise, la classe des verbes parenthétiques et le signe mimique". *Cahiers de Linguistique* (Montréal) 8:53–95.
Costa, Rachel. 1972. "Sequence of tenses in that-clauses". *Chicago Linguistic Society* 8,1:41–51.
Costello, D.P. 1960/1. "Tenses in indirect speech in Russian". *The Slavonic and East European Review* 39:489–96.
Cotticelli-Kurras, Paola. 1995. "Hethitische Konstruktionen mit verba dicendi und sentiendi". In Carruba, Onofrio, Mauro Giorgieri and Clelia Mora (eds.), *Atti del secondo Congresso Internazionale di Hittitologia*. Pavia: Iuculano, 87–100.
Coulmas, Florian. 1985. "Direct and indirect speech: general problems and problems of Japanese". *Journal of Pragmatics* 9:41–63.
Coulmas, Florian. 1986a. "Direct and indirect speech in Japanese". In Coulmas (ed.), 161–78.
Coulmas, Florian. 1986b. "Nobody dies in Shangri-La: direct and indirect speech across languages". In Tannen and Alatis (eds.), 140–53.
Coulmas, Florian. 1986c. "Reported speech: some general issues". In Coulmas (ed.), 1–28.
Coulmas, Florian (ed.). 1986. *Direct and indirect speech* (=Trends in Linguistics, Studies and Monographs 31). Berlin: Mouton de Gruyter.
Couper-Kuhlen, Elizabeth. 1996. "The prosody of repetition: on quoting and mimicry". In Couper-Kuhlen, Elizabeth and Margret Selting (eds.), *Prosody in conversation: interactional studies*. Cambridge: Cambridge University Press, 366–405.
Couper-Kuhlen, Elizabeth. 1998. *Coherent voicing: on prosody in conversational reported speech* (=Interaction and Linguistic Structures 1). Konstanz: Universität Konstanz, Fachgruppe Sprachwissenschaft.
Craig, Kenneth M. 1998. "Bargaining in Tov (Judges 11, 4–11): the many directions of so-called direct speech". *Biblica: Commentarii* 79:76–85.
Cram, Fred D. 1978. "The syntax of direct quotation". *Cahiers de Lexicologie* 33,2:41–52.
Crass, Joachim et al. 2001. "Von 'sagen' zum Verbbildungsmorphem: die Grammatikalisierung von 'sagen' einmal anders". *Afrikanistische Arbeitspapiere* 65:129–41.
Creissels, Denis. 1997. "The auxiliarization of *re* 'say' in Setswana". *Berkeley Linguistics Society* 23S:59–70.
Crim, Keith R. 1973. "Hebrew direct discourse as a translation problem". *The Bible Translator* 24,3:311–16.
Cristofaro, Sonia. 1998. "Grammaticalization and clause linkage strategies: a typological approach with particular reference to Ancient Greek". In Giacalone Ramat, Anna and Paul J. Hopper (eds.), *The limits of grammaticalization* (=Typological Studies in Language 37). Amsterdam: Benjamins, 59–88.
Crofts, Marjorie. 1986. "Direct or indirect quotes?" *Notes on Translation* 113:20–5
Cromack, R. 1962. "Discourse, direct and indirect". In *The interpreter's dictionary of the Bible — Supplementary volume*. Nashville: Abingdon, 236–7.
Crowley, Terry. 1989. "*Say, c'est*, and subordinate constructions in Melanesian Pidgin". *Journal of Pidgin and Creole Linguistics* 4,2:185–210.

Cullen, Richard. 1997. "Providing realistic practice in reported speech". *Modern English Teacher* 6,3: 27–31.
Culy, Christopher. 1994a. "A note on logophoricity in Dogon". *Journal of African Languages and Linguistics* 15,2: 113–25.
Culy, Christopher. 1994b. "Aspects of logophoric marking". *Linguistics* 32,6: 1055–94.
Culy, Christopher. 1997. "Logophoric pronouns and point of view". *Linguistics* 35: 845–59.
Cunha, Doris de Arruda Carneiro da. 1992. *Discours rapporté et circulation de la parole: contribution à une approche dialogique du discours d'autrui: étude de six commentaires oraux induits par la lecture d'un article de presse* (=Bibliothèque des Cahiers de l'Institut de Linguistique de Louvain 62). Leuven: Peeters.
Curilina, Ljubov' N. 1994. *Leksičeskaja struktura tekstovyx fragmentov prjamoj reč'ju na materiale romana F.M. Dostoeveskogo "Brat'ja Karamazovy"*. Sankt-Petersburg: Rossijskij Gosudarstvennyj Pedagogičeskij Universitet Imeni A.I. Gercena.
Czennia, Bärbel. 1992. *Figurenrede als Übersetzungsproblem: untersucht am Romanwerk von Charles Dickens und ausgewählten deutschen Übersetzungen* (=Neue Studien zur Anglistik und Amerikanistik 58). Frankfurt/Main: Lang.
Dahl, Liisa. 1967. "The attributive sentences structure in the stream-of-consciousness technique, with special reference to the interior monologue used by Virginia Woolf, James Joyce and Eugene O'Neill". *Neuphilologische Mitteilungen* 66: 440–54.
Dąmbska-Prokop, Urszula. 1958. "Stan badań nad mową pozornie zależną" (The state of the art of represented speech and thought). *Kwartalnik Neofilologiczny* 5: 227–33.
Dąmbska-Prokop, Urszula. 1960. *Le style indirect libre dans la prose d'Alphonse Daudet* (=Universytet Jagielloński Rozprawy i Studia 17). Kraków: Universytet Jagielloński.
Darden, Bill J. 1973. "Indirect speech and reported speech in Lithuanian and Bulgarian". *Chicago Linguistic Society* 9,2: *You take the high node, I'll take the low node*: 326–32.
Daube, David. 1977. "The Rabbinic treatment of 'and he said, saying'". In Rössler, Otto (ed.), *Hebraica* (=Marburger Studien zur Afrika- und Asienkunde, Serie B: Asien 4). Berlin: Reimer, 3–14.
Davidson, Donald. 1968/9. "On saying 'that'". *Synthese* 19: 130–46.
Davidson, Donald. 1975. "Thought and talk". In Guttenplan, Samuel (ed.), *Mind and language: Wolfson College lectures 1974*. Oxford: Oxford University Press, 7–23.
Davidson, Donald. 1984. "Quotation". In Davidson, Donald (ed.), *Inquiries into truth and interpretation*. Oxford: Clarendon Press, 79–92.
Davis, Edward P. 1923. *The semasiology of verbs of talking and saying in the High German dialects*. Leipzig: Teubner.
Davoine, Jean-Pierre. 1970. "Le pronom, sujet disjoint dans le style indirect libre de Zola". *Le Français Moderne* 38: 447–51.
Debrunner, Albert. 1948. "Indirekte Rede im Altindischen". *Acta Orientalia* 20: 120–32.
Decker, Heinz. "Der innere Monolog: zur Analyse des 'Ulysses'". *Akzente* 8: 99–125.
Declerck, Renaat. 1990. "Sequence of tenses in English". *Folia Linguistica* 24: 513–44.
Declerck, Renaat. 1995. "Is there a relative past tense in English?" *Lingua* 97: 1–36.

Declerck, Renaat and Ilse Depraetere. 1995. "The double system of tense forms referring to future time". *Journal of Semantics* 12: 269–310.
Declerck, Renaat and Kazuhiko Tanaka. 1996. "Constraints on tense choice in reported speech". *Studia Linguistica* 50: 283–301.
Deibler, Ellis. 1971. "Uses of the verb 'to say' in Gahuku". *Kivung* 4,2: 101–10.
Delavau, Annie. 1988. "La voix et les bruits: notes sur les verbes introducteurs du discours rapporté". *LINX: revue des linguistes de l'Université Paris X Nanterre* 18: 125–35.
Delhez-Sarlet, Claudette. 1964. "Style indirect libre et 'point de vue' dans *La Princesse de Clèves*". *Cahiers d'Analyse Textuelle* 6: 70–80.
Dendle, Peter. 1997. "Direct discourse and gender in the *Ágrip af Nóregs konunga Sögum*". *Neophilologus* 81,3: 403–8.
Denison, David. 1992. "The information present: present tense for communication in the past". In Rissanen et al. (eds.), 262–86.
Deutscher, Guy. 2000. *Syntactic change in Akkadian: the evolution of sentential complementation*. Oxford: Oxford University Press.
Dieling, Klaus. 1986. "Zeitrelationen und Sprechereinstellung in indirekter Rede". *Wissenschaftliche Zeitschrift der Karl-Marx-Universität Leipzig, Gesellschafts- und Sprachwissenschaftliche Reihe* 35,1: 33–9.
Diels, Paul. 1907. "Zur Entstehung der indirekten Rede im Deutschen". *Zeitschrift für vergleichende Sprachforschung* 41: 194–8.
Dillon, George L. and Frederick Kirchhoff. 1976. "On the form and function of free indirect style". *PTL: A Journal for Descriptive Poetics and Theory of Literature* 1: 431–40.
Dimmendaal, Gerrit J. 2001. "Logophoric marking and represented speech in African languages as evidential hedging strategies". *Australian Journal of Linguistics* 21,1: 131–57.
Dirven, René, Louis Goossens, Yvan Putseys and Emma Vorlat. 1982. *The scene of linguistic action and its perspectivization by SPEAK, TALK, SAY and TELL* (=Pragmatics and Beyond III, 6). Amsterdam: Benjamins.
Dobre, Dan. 1989. "Discours direct versus discours rapporté". *Revue Roumaine de Linguistique* 34: 29–40.
Doležel, Lubomir. 1973. "Represented discourse in Modern Czech literature". In Doležel, Lubomir, *Narrative modes in Czech literature*. Toronto: Toronto University Press, 15–55.
Dooley, Robert A. 1989. "Suggestions for the field linguist regarding quotations". *Notes on Linguistics* 44: 34–50.
Drew, Paul. 1984. "Speakers' reporting in invitation sequences". In Atkinson, J. Maxwell and John Heritage (eds.), *Structures of social action: studies in conversational analysis*. Cambridge: Cambridge University Press, 129–51.
Drimba, Vladimir. 1976. "Le style indirect libre en turc de Turquie". *Turcica* 8: 7–20.
Druce, Robert. 1998. "'I gotta use words when I talk to you'". In Barfoot, Cedric C. and Wim van der Wurff (eds.), *Varieties of English*. Leiden: University of Leiden, Department of English, 47–66.
Dry, Helen Aristar. 1990. "Language change and 'naturalization' in free indirect speech". *Journal of Literary Semantics* 19,3: 135–49.

DuBois, Betty L. 1989. "Pseudoquotation in current English communication: 'Hey, she didn't really say it'". *Language in Society* 18,3: 343–59.
Dubois, Jacques. 1964. "Avatars du monologue intérieur dans le nouveau roman". *La Revue des Lettres Modernes* 94–9: 17–29.
Ducrot, Oswald. 1980. "Pragmatique linguistique: II. Essai d'application: *Mais* — les allusions à l'énonciation — délocutifs, performatifs, discours indirect". In Parret, Herman et al. (eds.), *Le langage en contexte: études philosophiques et linguistiques de pragmatique* (=Linguisticae Investigationes, Supplementa 3). Amsterdam: Benjamins, 487–575.
Ducrot, Oswald. 1984. "Esquisse d'une théorie polyphonique de l'énonciation". In Ducrot, Oswald, *Le dire et le dit*. Paris: Éditions de Minuit, 171–233 (= Chapitre VIII).
Dujardin, Édouard. 1931. *Le monologue intérieur: son apparition, ses origines, sa place dans l'œuvre de James Joyce*. Paris: Messein.
Durry, Marie-Jeanne. 1961. "Le monologue intérieur dans *La Princesse de Clèves*". In Centre de Philologie Romane et de Langue et Littérature Françaises Contemporaines, *La littérature narrative de l'imagination: des genres littéraires aux techniques d'expression, Colloque de Strasbourg, 23–5 avril 1959*. Paris: Presses Universitaires de France, 87–96.
Dutta Baruah, P.N. 1994. "On generating indirect speech in Assamese and Bengali". *International Journal of Dravidian Linguistics* 23,1: 103–13.
Ebert, Karen H. 1986. "Reported speech in some languages of Nepal". In Coulmas (ed.), 145–59.
Ebert, Karen H. 1991. "Vom Verbum dicendi zur Konjunktion — ein Kapitel universaler Grammatikentwicklung". In Bisang, Walter and Peter Rinderknecht (eds.), *Von Europa bis Ozeanien — von der Antonymie zum Relativsatz, Gedenkschrift für Meinrad Scheller* (=Arbeiten des Seminars für Allgemeine Sprachwissenschaft 11). Zürich: Universität Zürich, 77–95.
Edgerton, Faye. 1965. "Relative frequency of direct and indirect discourse in Sierra Chontal and Navajo Mark". Beekman, John (ed.), *Notes on translation with drills*. Santa Ana: Summer Institute of Linguistics, 228–31.
Edzard, Dietz Otto. 1990. "Selbstgespräch und Monolog in der akkadischen Literatur". In Abusch, Tzvi, John Huehnergard and Pjotr Steinkeller (eds.), *Lingering over words: studies in ancient Near Eastern literature in honor of William R. Moran* (=Harvard Semitic Studies 37). Atlanta: Scholars, 149–62.
Ehrman, Albert. 1962. "What did Kain say to Abel?" *Jewish Quarterly Review* 53: 164–7.
Ehrman, Albert. 1964. "A note on the verb אמר;". *Jewish Quarterly Review* 55: 166–7.
Eilfort, William H. 1986. "Complementizers from introducers of reported speech". In Choi, Soonja et al. (eds.), *Proceedings of the 2nd Eastern States Conference on Linguistics*. Columbus: Ohio State University, 57–66.
Eliseev, K.A. 1956. "K voprosy izučenie temy: prjamaja i kosvennaja reč'". *Russkij Jazyk v Škole* 17,2: 69–72.
Ely, Richard and Allyssa McCabe. 1993. "Remembered voices". *Journal of Child Language* 20,3: 671–96.
Emberson, Jane. 1981. *Speech in the Eneide of Heinrich von Veldeke* (=Göppinger Arbeiten zur Germanistik 319). Göppingen: Kümmerle.

Emberson, Jane. 1986. "Reported speech in medieval German narratives". *Parergon: Bulletin of the Australian and New Zealand Association for Medieval and Renaissance Studies* 4:103–16.

Engelen, Bernhard. 1973. "Überlegungen zu Syntax, Semantik und Pragmatik der Redewiedergabe". In Moser, Hugo (ed.), *Linguistische Studien IV: Festgabe für Paul Grebe zum 65. Geburtstag, Teil II* (=Sprache der Gegenwart 24). Düsseldorf: Schwann, 46–60.

Engelen, Bernard. 1974. "Zur unterrichtlichen Behandlung der indirekten Rede". *Der Deutschunterricht* 26,2:17–28.

Ensink, Titus. 1994. "De juridische verantwoordelijkheid voor tekst: de mogelijke verantwoordelijkheidsdistantiëring door citaat". In Maes, Alfons A., P. van Hauwermeiren and L. van Waes (eds.), *Perspectieven in taalbeheersingsonderzoek*. Dordrecht: ICG, 362–74.

Eriksson, Mats. 1995. "A case of grammaticalization in Modern Swedish: the use of *ba* in adolescent speech". *Language Sciences* 17,1:19–48.

Ernst, Gerhard. 1985. *Gesprochenes Französisch zu Beginn des 17. Jahrhunderts: direkte Rede in Jean Héroards "Histoire particulière de Louis XII" (1605–1610)* (=Beihefte zur Zeitschrift für Romanische Philologie 204). Tübingen: Niemeyer.

Espinola, Judith C. 1974. "The nature, function, and performance of indirect discourse in prose fiction". *Speech Monographs* 41:193–204.

Essien, Okon. 1975. "Personal pronouns in indirect discourse in Efik". *Work in Progress, Edinburgh University* 8:133–44.

Fabricius-Hansen, Cathrine. 1989. "Tempus im indirekten Referat". In Abraham and Janssen (eds.), 155–82.

Fairclough, Norman. 1988. "Discourse representation in media discourse". *Sociolinguistics* 17,2:125–39.

Falk, Lilian. 1991. "Quoting and self-quoting". *Journal of the Atlantic Provinces Linguistic Association* (special issue) 15:1–11.

Fambrough, Preston. 1987. "The ironies of Flaubert's free indirect discourse". *West Virginia University Philological Papers* 33:10–15.

Farley, Rodger A. 1965. "Sequence of tenses: a useful principle?" *Hispania* 48:549–53.

Faucher, Eugène. 1978a. *Définition du discours indirect* (=Linguistica Palatina 24). Paris: Centre Universitaire du Grand Palais.

Faucher, Eugène. 1978b. "Sémantique des discours rapportés". *Verbum* 1:69–85.

Faucher, Eugène. 1979. "Définition du discours indirect". *Cahiers d'Allemand* 15:69–80.

Faulkner, Raymond O. 1935. "The verb '*i* 'to say' and its developments". *Journal of Egyptian Archaeology* 21:177–90.

Faulseit, Dieter. 1967. "Methoden und Möglichkeiten der Redewiedergabe und der Redekennzeichnung". *Sprachpflege* 16:115–18.

Fay, Edwin W. 1897. "Partial obliquitiy in questions of retort". *The Classical Review* 11:344–5.

Fernandez-Bravo, Nicole. 1975. *Histoire du discours indirect allemand (1699–1966)*. Doctoral thesis, Sorbonne, Paris.

Fernandez-Bravo, Nicole. 1976. *Histoire du discours indirect allemand de Grimmelshausen à nos jours* (=Linguistica Palatina 16). Paris: Centre Universitaire du Grand Palais.

Fernandez-Bravo, Nicole. 1980. "Geschichte der indirekten Rede im Deutschen vom siebzehnten Jahrhundert bis zur Gegenwart". *Deutsche Sprache* 1980,2: 97–132.
Ferrara, Kathleen and Barbara Bell. 1995. "Sociolinguistic variation and discourse function of constructed dialogue introducers: the case of be + like". *American Speech* 70,3: 265–90.
Fingerle, Anton. 1939. *Typik der homerischen Reden*. Doctoral thesis, Universität München.
Firle, Marga. 1988. "Indirekte und erlebte Rede als textstilistische Phänomene". *Zeitschrift für Germanistik* 9,2: 176–81.
Fischer, August. 1899. *Die indirekte Rede im Altfranzösischen*. Berlin: Ebering.
Flavin, Louise. 1987. "*Mansfield Park*: free indirect discourse and the psychological novel". *Studies in the Novel* 19: 137–59.
Fludernik, Monika. 1993. *The fictions of language and the languages of fiction: the linguistic representation of speech and consciousness*. London: Routledge.
Fludernik, Monika. 1995. "The linguistic illusion of alterity: the free indirect as paradigm of discourse representation". *Diacritics* 25,4: 89–115.
Fludernik, Monika. 1996. "Linguistic signals and interpretative strategies: linguistic models in performance, with special reference to free indirect discourse". *Language and Literature* 5: 93–113.
Fónagy, Ivan. 1986. "Reported speech in French and Hungarian". In Coulmas (ed.), 255–309.
Forget, Danielle. 1983. "Considérations sémantiques et pragmatiques: la transparence dans le discours indirect". *Lingvisticae Investigationes* 7: 221–36.
Fornel, Michel de. 1980. "Attributivité, discours rapporté et espaces référentiels". *Semantikos* 4,2: 55–77.
Forster, Jannette. 1983. "Use of dialogue in a Dibabawon narrative discourse". *Philippine Journal of Linguistics* 14,1: 45–60.
Fournier, Henri. 1946. *Les verbes "dire" en grec ancien (exemple de conjugaison supplétive)* (=Collection Linguistique, Société de Linguistique de Paris 51). Paris: Klincksieck.
Fox, Michael V. 1980. "The identification of quotations in Biblical literature". *Zeitschrift für die alttestamentliche Wissenschaft* 92: 416–31.
Frajzyngier, Zygmunt. 1984. "On the origin of *say* and *se* as complementizers in Black English and English-based creoles". *American Speech* 59,3: 207–10.
Frajzyngier, Zygmunt. 1985a. "Borrowed logophoricity". In Schuh, Russell (ed.), *Précis from the 15th Conference on African Linguistics, UCLA, March 29–31, 1984* (=Studies in African Linguistics, Supplement 9), 114–18.
Frajzyngier, Zygmunt. 1985b. "Logophoric systems in Chadic". *Journal of African Languages and Linguistics* 7,1: 23–37.
Frajzyngier, Zygmunt. 1989. "Three kinds of anaphors". In Haïk, Isabelle and Laurice Tuller (eds.), *Current approaches to African linguistics 6* (=Publications in African Languages and Linguistics 9). Dordrecht: Foris, 194–216.
Frajzyngier, Zygmunt. 1991. "The *de dicto* domain in language". In Traugott, Elizabeth Closs and Bernd Heine (eds.), *Approaches to grammaticalization* (=Typological Studies in Language 19). Amsterdam: Benjamins, vol. 1, 219–51.

Frank, Tenney. 1907/8. "On constructions of indirect discourse in early Germanic dialects". *Journal of English and Germanic Philology* 7,1:64–80.
Franklin, Karl J. 1992. "Speech act verbs and the words of Jesus". In Hwang and Merrifield (eds.), 241–61.
Friedman, Melvin. 1958. "Le monologue intérieur dans *As I Lay Dying*". *La Revue des Lettres Modernes* 5:555–68.
Friedrich, Johannes. 1943. "Die Partikeln der zitierten Rede im Achämenidisch-Elamischen". *Orientalia*, Nova Series 12,1–2:23–30.
Frye, Marilyn. 1976. "On saying". *American Philosophical Quarterly* 13,2:123–7.
Funke, Otto. 1929. "Zur 'Erlebten Rede' bei Galsworthy". *Englische Studien* 64:450–74.
Gakinabay, Mayange and Ursula Wiesemann. 1986. "Les styles de discours en sar et leur mode d'emploi". *Journal of West African Languages* 16,2:39–48.
Gallagher, Mary. 1970. "Accounting for indirect discourse". *Papers in Linguistics* 2:83–9.
Gather, Andreas. 1994. *Formen referierter Rede: eine Beschreibung kognitiver, grammatischer, pragmatischer und äusserungslinguistischer Aspekte* (=Studia romanica et linguistica 26). Franfurt/Main: Lang.
Gaulmyn, Marie Madeleine de. 1983. *Les verbes de communication dans la structuration du discours: essai sur la reflexivité du langage: récits d'enfants et échanges entre enfants et adultes*. Doctoral thesis, Université de Paris VIII.
Gaulmyn, Marie Madeleine de. 1989. "Grammaire du français parlé: quelques questions autour du discours rapporté". In Jaussaud, Anne-Marie (ed.), *Grammaire et français langue étrangère: actes du colloque organisé par l'Association Nationale des Enseignants de Français Langue Étrangère, Grenoble, 17 et 18 novembre 1989*. Bron: ANEFLE, 22–33.
Gaulmyn, Marie Madeleine de. 1997. "La génèse des marques formelles du discours rapporté dans le texte écrit". *Modèles Linguistiques* 18,1:53–73.
Gauvenet, Hélène. 1976. "Du discours direct au discours rapporté ou les avatars d'un énoncé". In Gauvenet, Hélène et al. 1976b, 7–27.
Gauvenet, Hélène and Sophie-Colette Moirand. 1974. "Le discours rapporté". *Le Français dans le Monde* 102:34–40.
Gauvenet, Hélène et al. 1973. "Du discours direct au discours rapporté". *Zielsprache Französisch* 1973,4:1–9.
Gauvenet, Hélène et al. 1976a. "Extraits d'un ensemble pédagogique sur le discours rapporté: 'Qu'en dira-t-on?'". In Gauvenet, Hélène et al. 1976b, 73–124.
Gauvenet, Hélène et al. 1976b. *Pédagogie du discours rapporté*. Paris: Didier.
Gelhaus, Hermann. 1974. "Untersuchungen zur consecutio temporum im Deutschen". In Gelhaus, Hermann and Sigbert Latzel (eds.), *Studien zum Tempusgebrauch im Deutschen*. Tübingen: Narr, 1–127.
Gerardi, Pamela. 1989. "Thus, he spoke: direct speech in Esarhaddon's royal inscriptions". *Zeitschrift für Assyriologie und vorderasiatische Archäologie* 79,2:245–60.
Gerasimov, G. I. 1963. "Kosvenno-prjamaja reč': k voprosu o sposobax peredači čužoj reči". *Voprosy jazykoznanija* (=Učenye Zapiski — Leningradskij Gosudarstvennyj Pedagogičeskij Institut Imeni A. I. Gercena 248), 155–60.
Gerntz, Hans J. 1960. *Formen und Funktionen der direkten Reden und der Redeszenen in der deutschen epischen Dichtung von 1150–1200*. 'Habilitation' thesis, Universität Rostock.

Gersbach-Bäschlin, Annette. 1970. *Reflektorischer Stil und Erzählstruktur: Studie zu den Formen der Rede- und Gedankenwiedergabe in der erzählenden Prosa von Romain Rolland und André Gide*. Aarau: Buchdruckerei Keller.

Gibbon, Dafydd. 1983. "Intonation in contest: an essay on metalocutionary deixis". In Rauh, Gisa (ed.), *Essays on deixis* (=Tübinger Beiträge zur Linguistik 188). Tübingen: Gunter Narr, 195–218.

Ginsburg, Michael P. 1982. "Free indirect discourse: a reconsideration". *Language and Style* 15,2: 133–49.

Girón Alconchel, José Luis. 1988a. *Las oraciones interrogativas indirectas en español medieval*. Madrid: Gredos.

Girón Alconchel, José Luis. 1988b. "Sobre la lengua poética de Berceo (y II): el estilo indirecto libre en los *Milagres* y sus fuentes latinas". *Epos: Revista de filologia* 4: 145–62.

Gjerløw, Jens R. 1956. "Bemerkungen über einige Einleitungen zur direkten Rede in Vergils Aeneis". *Symbolae Osloenses* 32: 44–68

Glauser, Lisa. 1948. *Die erlebte Rede (The Interior Monologue) im englischen Roman des 19. Jahrhunderts: von Scott bis Meredith* (=Schweizer anglistische Arbeiten 20). Solothurn: Gassmann.

Glock, Naomi. 1986. "The use of reported speech in Saramaccan discourse". In Huttar and Gregerson (eds.), 35–61.

Glowinski, Michail. 1974. "Der Dialog im Roman". *Poetica* 6: 1–16.

Goebel, Gerhard. 1966. "'Style indirect libre' in La Fontaines *Amours de Psyché et de Cupidon* (1669)". *Romanistisches Jahrbuch* 17: 98–111.

Golato, Andrea. 2000. "An innovative German quotative for reporting on embodied actions: *Und ich so/und er so* 'and I'm like/and he's like'". *Journal of Pragmatics* 32: 29–54.

Goldenberg, Gideon. 1991. "On direct speech and the Hebrew Bible". In Jongeling, Karel, H.L. Murre-van den Berg and L. van Rompay (eds.), *Studies in Hebrew and Aramaic syntax presented to Professor J. Hoftijzer on the occasion of his sixty-fifth birthday* (=Studies in Semitic Languages and Linguistics 17). Leiden: Brill, 79–96.

Goodell, Elizabeth W. 1987. "Integrating theory with practice: an alternative approach to reported speech in English". *TESOL Quarterly* 21,2: 305–25.

Goodell, Elizabeth W. and Jacqueline Sachs. 1992. "Direct and indirect speech in English-speaking children's retold narratives". *Discourse Processes* 15,4: 395–422.

Goodman, Nelson. 1978. "Some questions concerning quotation". In Goodman, Nelson (ed.), *Ways of worldmaking*. Indianapolis: Hackett, 41–56.

Goodwin, Marjorie H. 1990. *He-said-she-said*. Bloomington: Indiana University Press.

Goossens, Louis. 1985. "Framing the linguistic action scene in Old and Present-day English: OE *cweþan, secgan, sp(r)ecan* and Present-day English *speak, talk, say* and *tell* compared". In Fisiak, Jacek (ed.), *Papers from the 6th International Conference on Historical Linguistics* (=Current Issues in Linguistic Theory 34). Amsterdam: Benjamins, 149–70.

Gordis, Robert. 1943/44. "Quotations in wisdom literature". *Jewish Quarterly Review* 30: 123–47.

Gordis, Robert. 1949. "Quotation as a literary usage in biblical, oriental and rabbinic literature". *Hebrew Union College Annual* 22: 157–219.

Gordis, Robert. 1981. "Virtual quotation in Job, Sumer and Qumran". *Vetus Testamentum* 31:410–27.
Gorrell, J. Hendren. 1895. "Indirect discourse in Anglo-Saxon". *Publications of the Modern Language Association of America* 10:342–485.
Gouffé, Claude. 1970/1. "Sur les emplois grammaticalisés du verbe 'dire' en haoussa". *Comptes Rendus du Groupe Linguistique d'Études Chamito-Semitiques* 15:77–88.
Gougenheim, G. 1938. "La présentation du discours direct dans *La Princesse de Clèves* et dans *Dominique*". *Le Français Moderne* 6:305–20.
Gougenheim, G. 1947. "Du discours solitaire au monologue intérieur". *Le Français Moderne* 15:242–8.
Grad, Anton. 1965. "Remarques sur le style indirect libre en ancien français". *Linguistica* 7,1:3–27.
Grad, Anton. 1970. "Sur l'origine du style indirect libre". In Graur, Alexandru et al. (eds.), *Actes du Xe Congrès international des linguistes, Bucarest 28 août — 2 septembre 1967, Vol. 3*. Bucarest: Académie de la République Socialiste de Roumanie, 465–73.
Graf, Rainer. 1980. "Übergänge in den Formen der Redewiedergabe". In König, Werner and Hugo Stopp (eds.), *Historische, geografische und soziale Übergänge im alemannischen Sprachraum* (=Schriften der Philosophischen Fakultäten der Universität Augsburg 16). München: Ernst Vögel, 121–30.
Gragg, Gene B. 1972. "Semi-indirect discourse and related nightmares". *Chicago Linguistic Society* 8.1:75–82.
Gramberg, Anne-Katrin and Karin U. Heinze 1993. "Die indirekte Rede als Diskursstrategie: innovative Lehrmethoden zum Konjunktiv I". *Die Unterrichtspraxis: Teaching German* 26:185–93.
Gregory, Michael. 1965. "Old Bailey speech in 'A Tale of Two Cities'". *A Review of English Literature* 6,2:42–55.
Greimas, A. Julien et al. (eds.), *Sign, language, culture* (=Janua Linguarum, Series Minor 1). The Hague/Paris: Mouton.
Gresillon, Almuth. 1978. "Un cas de discours rapporté: reproduction, transformation, déformation du discours biblique dans le discours politique de Heine". *Documentation et Recherche en Linguistique Allemande Contemporaine — Vincennes* 17:123–50.
Guhl, Bernd. 1972. "Einige Fälle des Berichtens und der Bewertung von illokutiven Akten". In Hyldgaard-Jensen, Karl (ed.), *Linguistik 1971: Referate des 6. Linguistischen Kolloquiums, 11.-14. Aug. 1971 in Kopenhagen*. Frankfurt/Main: Athenäum, 76–90.
Guhl, Bernd. 1974. "Esquisse d'un langage sémantique pour la description des verbes de parole". In Rohrer, Christian and Nicolas Ruwet (eds.), *Actes du colloque franco-allemand de grammaire transformationnelle, Tome 2: Études de sémantique et autres* (=Linguistische Arbeiten 14). Tübingen: Niemeyer, 103–12.
Guiraud, Pierre. 1971. "Modern linguistics looks at rhetoric: free indirect style". In Strelka, Joseph (ed.), *Patterns of literary style*. University Park: Pennsylvania State University, 77–89.
Güldemann, Tom. 2001. *Quotative constructions in African languages: a synchronic and diachronic survey*. 'Habilitation' thesis, Universität Leipzig.

Gülich, Elisabeth. 1978. "Redewiedergabe im Französischen: Beschreibungsmöglichkeiten im Rahmen einer Sprechakttheorie". In Meyer-Hermann, Reinhard (ed.), *Sprechen — Handeln — Interaktion*. Tübingen: Niemeyer, 49–101.

Gulyga, E. V. 1957. "Kosvennaja reč' v sovremennom nemeckom jazyke". *Ucenye zapiski — Moskovskij Gosudarstvennyj Pedagogičeskij Institut Inostrannyx Jazykov* 15: 157–86.

Gunn, Mary R. 1978. "Distribución de los márgenes de citas en el discurso bokotá". In Levinsohn (ed.), 1–27.

Günther, Werner. 1928. *Probleme der Rededarstellung: Untersuchungen zur direkten, indirekten und 'erlebten' Rede im Deutschen, Französischen und Italienischen* (=Die Neueren Sprachen, Beiheft 13). Marburg: Elwert'sche Verlagsbuchhandlung and G. Braun.

Günthner, Susanne. 1997a. "Direkte und indirekte Rede in Alltagsgesprächen: zur Interaktion von Syntax und Prosodie in der Redewiedergabe". In Schlobinski, Peter (ed.), *Syntax des gesprochenen Deutsch*. Opladen: Westdeutscher Verlag, 227–62.

Günthner, Susanne. 1997b "Stilisierungsverfahren in der Redewiedergabe: die 'Überlagerung von Stimmen' als Mittel der moralischen Verurteilung in Vorwurfskonstruktionen". In Sandig, Barbara and Margret Selting (eds.), *Sprech- und Gesprächsstile*. Berlin: Mouton de Gruyter, 94–122.

Günthner, Susanne. 1997c. "The contextualization of affect in reported dialogues". In Niemeier, Susanne and René Dirven (eds.), *The language of emotions: conceptualization, expression, and theoretical foundations*. Amsterdam: Benjamins, 247–76.

Günthner, Susanne. 1998. "Polyphony and the 'layering of voices' in reported dialogues: an analysis of the use of prosodic devices in everyday reported speech". *Journal of Pragmatics* 31: 685–708.

Günthner, Susanne. 2000. "Zwischen direkter und indirekter Rede: Formen der Redewiedergabe in Alltagsgesprächen". *Zeitschrift für Germanistische Linguistik* 28,1: 1–22.

Gutiérrez Ordoñez, Salvador. 1986. "Observaciones sobre el estilo directo en español". *Estudios Humanísticos, Filología* 8: 26–38.

Gvozdanovic, Jadranka. 1996. "Reported speech in South Slavic". In Janssen and Wurff (eds.), 57–71.

Haarmann, Harald. 1970. *Die indirekte Erlebnisform als grammatische Kategorie: eine eurasische Isoglosse* (=Veröffentlichungen der Societas Uralo-Altaica 2). Wiesbaden: Harrassowitz.

Haberland, Hartmut. 1986. "Reported speech in Danish". In Coulmas (ed.), 219–53.

Hagège, Claude. 1974. "Les pronoms logophoriques". *Bulletin de la Société de Linguistique de Paris* 69,1: 287–310.

Hagenaar, Elly. 1992. *Stream of consciousness and free indirect discourse in modern Chinese literature*. Leiden: Centre of Non-Western Studies.

Hagenaar, Elly. 1996. "Free indirect speech in Chinese". In Janssen and Wurff (eds.), 289–98.

Hahn, E. Adelaide. 1929. "On direct and indirect discourse". *The Classical Weekly* 22,17: 131–2.

Hahn, E. Adelaide. 1952. "The moods in indirect discourse in Latin". *Transactions of the Philological Association* 33: 242–66.

Hahn, E. Adelaide. 1963. "The supposed reflexive pronoun in Latin". *Transactions and Proceedings of the American Philological Society* 94: 86–112.
Haiman, John. 1989. "Alienation in grammar". *Studies in Language* 13,1: 129–70.
Hallig, Rudolf. 1957. "Über Form und Eingliederung der wörtlichen Rede in den 'Memoiren' des Duc de Saint-Simon". In Reichenkron (ed.), 191–213.
Hamilton, Heidi E. 1998. "Reported speech and survivor identity in on-line bone marrow transplantation narratives". *Journal of Sociolinguistics* 2: 53–67.
Hammarberg, Björn and Åke Viberg. 1976. "Reported speech in Swedish and ten immigrant languages". In Karlsson, Fred (ed.), *Papers from the Third Scandinavian Conference in Linguistics, Hanasaari, October 1–3, 1976.* Turku: Text Linguistics Research Group, Academy of Finland, 131–48.
Hanssen, Rebekka. 1933. "Zum Gebrauch der *oratio obliqua* in Tacitus' *Historiae* und *Annales*". In Kragemo, Helge Bergh (ed.), *Overbibliotekar Wilhelm Munthe på femtiårsdagen 20. oktober 1933 fra fagfeller og venner.* Oslo: Grøndahl, 348–61.
Harman, I.P. 1990. "Teaching indirect speech: deixis points the way". *ELT Journal* 44: 230–8.
Harweg, Roland. 1970. "Einige Besonderheiten von Zitaten in linguistischer Rede". *Zeitschrift für vergleichende Sprachforschung* 84: 288–98.
Harweg, Roland. 1972. "Reduzierte Rede". *Linguistics* 80: 44–55.
Harweg, Roland. 1989. "Formen der Einbettung von Dialogwiedergaben in Erzähltexten". In Weigand, Edda and Franz Hundsnurcher (eds.), *Dialoganalyse II: Referate der 2. Arbeitstagung, Bochum 1988, Band 1* (=Linguistische Arbeiten 229). Tübingen: Niemeyer, 43–58.
Harwell, Henry O. 1976. "The 'say' auxiliary in Maricopa: some notes and speculations". In Redden, James E. (ed.), *Proceedings of the 1st Yuman Languages Workshop* (=Southern Illinois University Museum Studies 7). Carbondale: Southern Illinois University, 63–70.
Haverkate, Henk. 1996. "Modal patterns of direct and indirect discourse in Peninsular Spanish: an analysis within the framework of speech act typology". In Janssen and Wurff (eds.), 97–119.
Hawkins, Robert E. 1962. "Wawai translations: the use of direct discourse". *Bible Translator* 13: 164–71.
Hayashi, Yutaka. 1979. "An argument against direct discourse analysis". *Descriptive and Applied Linguistics* 12: 59–67.
Healey, Phyllis M. 1964. "Teleéfoól quotative clauses". *Linguistic Circle of Canberra Occasional Papers* 3: 25–34. (also in Householder, Fred W. (ed.). 1972. *Syntactic theory I: structuralist.* Harmondsworth: Penguin, 215–22)
Hedinger, Robert. 1984. "Reported speech in Akɔɔse". *Journal of West African Languages* 14,1: 81–102.
Heemstra, Joh. 1932. "Grammatische und stilistische Bemerkungen zum Gedankenbericht". *De Drie Talen (Duits)* 48: 1–4, 17–20, 33–8, 49–52, 65–7, 81–4.
Heeschen, Volker. 1978. "The metalinguistic vocabulary of a speech community in the highlands of Irian Jaya (West New Guinea)". In Sinclair, Anne, Robert J. Jarvella and Willem J.M. Levelt (eds.), *The child's conception of language* (=Springer Series in Language and Communication 2). Berlin: Springer, 155–87.

Heinermann, Theodor. 1931. *Die Arten der reproduzierten Rede* (=Forschungen zur Romanischen Philologie 2). Münster: Aschendorff.
Heller, Jan. 1979. "Sagen und Sprechen". *Communio Viatorum* 22:173–9
Henning, Eberhard. 1969. "Möglichkeiten und Grenzen der Redeeinleitung". *Muttersprache* 79:107–19.
Herczeg, Giulio. 1950. "Il 'discorso diretto legato' in Renato Fucini" *Lingua Nostra* 11:39–42.
Herczeg, Giulio. 1963. *Lo stile indiretto libero in italiano* (=Biblioteca di Lingua Nostra 13). Firenze: Sansoni.
Herdin, Elis. 1905. *Studien über Bericht und indirekte Rede im modernen Deutsch.* Uppsala: Almqvist & Wiksells.
Herdin, Elis. 1919. "Le style indirect libre (imperfektsanföring)". *Moderna Språk* 13:2–9.
Herman, David. 1993. "Towards a pragmatics of represented discourse: narrative, speech and context in Woolf's *Between the Acts*". *Poetics* 21:377–409.
Herrmann, Michael. 1973. "Gibt es redeeinführende Verben in indirekter Rede?" *Zeitschrift für Romanische Philologie* 89:73–87.
Hermon, Gabriella. 1979. *On the discourse structure of direct quotation* (=Center for the Study of Reading, Technical report 143). Urbana-Champaign: University of Illinois.
Hernadi, Paul. 1972. "Dual perspective: free indirect discourse and related techniques". *Comparative Literature* 24:32–44.
Heusler, Andreas. 1901. "Der Dialog in der altgermanischen erzählenden Dichtung". *Zeitschrift für deutsches Altertum* 46:189–284.
Heuvel, Pierre van den. 1978. "Le discours rapporté". *Neophilologus* 62:19–38.
Hewitt, B. George. 1981. "Eine weitere Betrachtung der georgischen Redepartikel '-tko// -tkva'". *Georgica* 4:83–5.
Hewitt, B. George. 1982. "From direct to indirect speech: a South Caucasian anomaly". *Folia Slavica* 5:206–13.
Hewitt, B. George. 1984a. "Another look at the Georgian speech-particle '-tko//-tkva'". *Bedi Kartlisa* 42:354–60.
Hewitt, B. George. 1984b. "Parataxis revisited (via the Caucasus)". *General Linguistics* 24,1:1–20.
Hewitt, B. George and S.R. Crisp 1986. "Speech reporting in the Caucasus". In Coulmas (ed.), 121–43.
Hickmann, Maya. 1993. "The boundaries of reported speech in narrative discourse: some developmental aspects". In Lucy (ed.), 63–90.
Hickmann, Maya and D. Warden 1991. "Children's narrative strategies when reporting appropriate and inappropriate speech events". *Pragmatics* 1,1:27–70.
Hilka, Alfons. 1902. *Die direkte Rede als stilistisches Kunstmittel in den Romanen des Chrestien de Troyes.* Breslau: Schlesische Volkszeitung-Buchdruckerei.
Hill, Harriet. 1995. "Pronouns and reported speech in Adioukrou". *Journal of West African Languages* 25,1:87–106.
Hill, Jane H. and Judith T. Irvine (eds.). 1993. *Responsibility and evidence in oral discourse* (=Studies in the Social and Cultural Foundations of Language 15). Cambridge: Cambridge University Press.
Hilty, Gerold. 1966. "Oratio reflexa en català". *Estudis Romànics* 8:185–7.

Hilty, Gerold. 1973a. "Imaginatio reflexa: à propos du style réflecteur dans *La Modification* de Michel Butor". *Vox Romanica* 32: 40–59.
Hilty, Gerold. 1973b. "*Oratio reflexa* im Italienischen". In Barrera-Vidal, Albert, E. Ruhe and P. Schunck (eds.), *Lebendige Romania: Festschrift für Hans-Wilhelm Klein*. Göppingen: Kümmerle, 143–75.
Hirose, Yukio. 1995. "Direct and indirect speech as quotations of public and private expression". *Lingua* 95,4: 223–38.
Hirose, Yukio. 2000. "Public and private self as two aspects of the speaker: a contrastive study of Japanese and English". *Journal of Pragmatics* 32: 1623–56.
Hirsch, Michèle. 1980. "Le style indirect libre: linguistique ou histoire littéraire? — La question du style indirect libre". In Joly, André (ed.), *La psychomécanique et les théories de l'énonciation: actes de la table ronde tenue à Lille les 16 et 17 mars 1979*. Lille: Presses Universitaires de Lille, 79–89, 91–104.
Hjelmquist, Erland and Åke Gidlund. 1985. "Free recall of conversations". *Text* 5: 169–85.
Hock, Hans H. 1982. "The Sanskrit quotative: a historical and comparative study". *Studies in the Linguistic Sciences* 12,2: 39–85.
Hoegg, F. Xaver. 1854. "Ueber den Gebrauch der Zeiten in der indirecten Rede der deutschen Sprache". *Jahresbericht über das Königliche Laurentianum zu Arnsberg 1853-1854*, 1–20.
Hoffmann, Yair. 1988. "The technique of quotation and citation as an interpretive device". In Uffenheimer, Benjamin and Henning Graf Reventlow (eds.), *Creative biblical exegesis: Christian and Jewish hermeneutics through the centuries*. Sheffield: Sheffield Academic, 71–9.
Hoffmeister, Werner. 1965. *Studien zur erlebten Rede bei Thomas Mann und Robert Musil*. The Hague: Mouton.
Hofmann, Michael. 1995. "Reported speech (a poem)". *London Review of Books* 17/12.9 (22 June 1995).
Holthusen, Johannes. 1970. "Stilistik des 'uneigentlichen' Erzählens in der sowjetischen Gegenwartsliteratur". *Welt der Slaven* 15: 225–45.
Hosaka, Muneshige and Yasushi Suzuki. 1993. *Literaturverzeichnis zur Erlebten Rede, mit einer Forschungsgeschichte der ER in Japan*. Bunkyo: College of General Education, Ibaraki University.
Hosaka, Muneshige, Yasushi Suzuki and Monika Fludernik. 1999. "Die Erlebte Rede im Japanischen". *Klagenfurter Beiträge zur Sprachwissenschaft* 25: 31–47.
Houwen, Fleur van der. 1998. "Direct and indirect speech in Mexican Spanish". In Bezooijen, Renée van and René Kager (eds.), *Linguistics in the Netherlands 1998*. Amsterdam: Benjamins, 123–34.
Huddleston, Rodney. 1989. "The treatment of tense in indirect speech". *Folia Linguistica* 23: 335–40.
Hudson, Joyce. 1986. "An analysis of illocutionary verbs in Walmatjari". In Huttar and Gregerson (eds.), 63–83.
Hüllen, Werner. 1988. "Direkte und indirekte Rede im Englischen". In Bald, Wolf-Dietrich (ed.), *Kernprobleme der englischen Grammatik: sprachliche Fakten und ihre Vermittlung*. München: Langenscheidt-Longman, 123–51.

Hulstaert, Gustave. 1946. "Rechtstreeksche rede en chronologische orde in de Kongotalen". *Aequatoria* 9: 100–3.
Huttar, George and Kenneth Gregerson (eds.). 1986. *Pragmatics in non-Western perspective* (=Publications in Linguistics 73). Arlington: Summer Institute of Linguistics and University of Texas.
Hwang, Shin J.J. and William R. Merrifield (eds.). 1992. *Language in context: essays for Robert E. Longacre* (=Publications in Linguistics 107). Dallas / Arlington: Summer Institute of Linguistics and University of Texas.
Hyart, Charles. 1954. *Les origines du style indirect latin et son emploi jusqu'à l'époque de César* (=Académie Royal de Belgique, Classe des Lettres et des Sciences Morales et Politiques, Mémoires, série 2, 48,2). Bruxelles: Académie Royal.
Hyman, Larry M. and Bernard Comrie. 1981. "Logophoric reference in Gokana". *Journal of African Languages and Linguistics* 3: 19–37.
Ikola, Osmo. 1960. *Das Referat in der finnischen Sprache: syntaktisch-stilistische Untersuchungen* (=Suomalainen Tiedeakatemian Toimituksia — Annales Academiea Scientiarum Fennicae, series B, 121). Helsinki.
Infantova, G.G. 1953. "K voprosu o nesobstvenno-prjamaja reči". *Učenye zapiski Taganrogskogo Gosudarstvennogo Pedagogičeskogo Instituta* 6.
Jackendoff, Ray. 1975. "On belief-contexts". *Linguistic Inquiry* 6: 53–93.
Jackendoff, Ray. 1980. "Belief-contexts revisited". *Linguistic Inquiry* 11: 395–413.
Jackson, Ellen M. 1987. "Direct and indirect speech in Tikar". *Journal of West African Languages* 17,1: 98–109.
Jacob, Lise. 1987. "Discours rapporté et intonation: illusion ou réalité de la polyphonie?" Callamand, Monique (ed.), *Aspects prosodiques de la communication* (=Études de linguistique appliquée 66). Paris: Didier Érudition, 71–87.
Jacquier, Henri. 1944. "Discours direct lié". *Bulletin Linguistique* (Bucarest) 12: 7–13.
Jäger, Siegfried. 1968. "Die Einleitungen indirekter Rede in der Zeitungssprache und in anderen Texten der deutschen Gegenwartssprache: ein Diskussionsbeitrag". *Muttersprache* 78: 236–49.
Jäger, Siegfried. 1970a. "Die Pronominalverschiebung bei der Transformation direkter in indirekte Rede, mit besonderer Berücksichtigung der Referenzidentitäten". *Muttersprache* 80: 217–25.
Jäger, Siegfried. 1970b. "Indirekte Rede und Heischesatz: gleiche formale Strukturen in ungleichen semantischen Bereichen". In Moser, Hugo (ed.), *Studien zur Syntax des heutigen Deutsch: Paul Grebe zum 60. Geburtstag* (=Sprache der Gegenwart 6). Düsseldorf: Schwann, 103–17.
Jagt, Bouke B. 1971. "Funktie en punctuatie van de direkte rede". *Levende Talen* 1971: 259–63.
Jahn, Manfred. 1992. "Contextualizing represented speech and thought". *Journal of Pragmatics* 17,4: 347–67.
Jamison, Stephanie W. 1991. "The syntax of direct speech in Vedic". In Brereton, Joel P. and Stephanie W. Jamison (eds.), *Sense and syntax in Vedic*. Leiden: Brill, 40–57.

Janssen, Theo A. J. M. 1991. "Consecutio temporum in de *Ferguut*". In Noordegraaf, Jan and Roel Zemel (eds.), *Accidentia: taal- en letteroefeningen voor Jan Knol*. Amsterdam: Stichting Neerlandistiek VU, 135–51.
Janssen, Theo A. J. M. 1996. "Tense in reported speech and its frame of reference". In Janssen and Wurff (eds.), 237–59.
Janssen, Theo A. J. M. and Wim van der Wurff. 1996. "Introductory remarks on reported speech and thought". In Janssen and Wurff (eds.), 1–12.
Janssen, Theo A. J. M. and Wim van der Wurff (eds.). 1996. *Reported speech: forms and functions of the verb* (=Pragmatics and Beyond, New Series 43). Amsterdam: Benjamins.
Jaszczolt, Katarzyna M. 1996. "Reported speech, vehicles of thought, and the horizon". *Lingua e Stile* 31:113–33.
Jaszczolt, Katarzyna M. 1997. "The 'default *de re*' principle for the interpretation of belief utterances". *Journal of Pragmatics* 28:315–36.
Jaubert, Anna. 1997. "Labyrinthes énonciatifs, 'Nouveaux discours du discours rapporté'". *Modèles Linguistiques* 18,1:17–31.
Jaubert, Anna. 2000. "Le discours indirect libre: dire et montrer: approche pragmatique". In Mellet and Vuillaume (eds.), 49–69.
Jefferson, Ann. 1980. "The place of free indirect speech in the poetics of fiction: with examples from Joyce's 'Evelyne'". *Essays in Poetics* 5:36–47.
Johnstone, Barbara. 1987. "'He says ... so I said': verb tense alternation and narrative depictions of authority in American English". *Linguistics* 25,1:33–52.
Jones, Charles. 1968. "Varieties of speech presentation in Conrad's *The Secret Agent*". *Lingua* 20:162–76.
Jones, Larry B. 1992. "A note on the text structure of the Odyssey". In Hwang and Merrifield (eds.), 263–73.
Joseph, Brian D. 1981. "Hittite *iwar, wa(r)* and Sanskrit *iva*". *Zeitschrift für Vergleichende Sprachforschung* 95,1:93–8.
Joseph, Brian D. and Lawrence Schourup. 1982/3. "More on *(i)–wa(r)*". *Zeitschrift für Vergleichende Sprachforschung* 96,1:56–8.
Juillard, Michel. 2000. "Les Huns sont-ils entrés à cheval dans la bibliothèque? Ou les libertés du style indirect libre". In Mellet and Vuillaume (eds.), 71–90.
Juret, Abel. 1925. "Sur le style indirect libre en latin". In *Mélanges linguistiques offerts à M. J. Vendryes par ses amis et ses élèves* (= Collection linguistique 17). Paris: Société de Linguistique de Paris, 199–201.
Juret, Abel. 1938. "Réflexions sur le style indirect libre". *Revue de Philologie, de Littérature et d'Histoire Anciennes* 12:163–7.
Kac, Michael B. 1972. "Clauses of saying and the interpretation of *because*". *Language* 48:626–32.
Kachru, Yamuna. 1979. "The quotative in South Asian languages". *South Asian Languages Analysis* 1:63–77.
Kalepky, Theodor. 1899. "Zur französischen Syntax VII: Mischung indirekter und direkter Rede (T.[obler] II, 7) oder V.R. [Verschleierte Rede]?" *Zeitschrift für Romanische Philologie* 23:491–513.

Kalepky, Theodor. 1913. "Zum 'Style indirect libre' ('Verschleierte Rede')". *Germanisch-Romanische Monatsschrift* 5: 608–19.
Kalepky, Theodor. 1928. "Verkleidete Rede". *Neophilologus* 13: 1–4.
Kalik-Teljatnicova, A. 1965/6. "De l'origine du prétendu 'style indirect libre'". *Le Français Moderne* 33: 284–94, 34: 123–36.
Kalugina, E. I. 1950. "Nesobstvennaja prjamaja reč' v sovremennom anglijskom jazyke". *Inostrannye Jazyki v Škole* 1950,5: 26–35.
Kamberelis, George and Karla Danette Scott. 1992. "Other people's voices: the coarticulation of texts and subjectivities". *Linguistics and Education* 4: 359–403.
Kameyama, Megumi. 1984. "Subjective/logophoric bound anaphor *zibun*". *Chicago Linguistic Society* 20: 228–38.
Kammerzell, Frank. 1997. "Merikare E 30–1: ein Fall von indirekter Rede mit Einaktantenanpassung im Mittelägyptischen". *Göttinger Miszellen: Beiträge zur ägyptologischen Diskussion* 161: 97–101.
Karič, Lilija V. 1986. *Grammatičeskie, semantičeskie i funkcional'nye osobennosti konstrukcij s pereključajušej povestvovanie prjamoj reč'ju*. Rostov-na-Donu: Gosudarstvennyj Universitet.
Karpf, Fritz. 1928. "Die erlebte Rede im älteren Englischen und in volkstümlicher Redeweise". *Die Neueren Sprachen* 36: 571–81.
Karpf, Fritz. 1931. "Die klangliche Form der erlebten Rede". *Die Neueren Sprachen* 39: 180–6.
Karpf, Fritz. 1933. "Die erlebte Rede im Englischen". *Anglia* 57 (Neue Folge 45): 225–76.
Kaufmann, Gerhard. 1971. "Zur Frage der Personenreferenz in der indirekten Rede". *Zielsprache Deutsch* 4: 153–73.
Kaufmann, Gerhard. 1973. "Beschreibung der deutschen Gegenwartssprache und Didaktik des Faches 'Deutsch als Fremdsprache': Vorüberlegungen zur didaktischen Auswertung linguistischer Forschungen am Beispiel der sogenannten 'indirekten Rede'". In Nickel, Gerhard (ed.), *Angewandte Sprachwissenschaft und Deutschunterricht*, München: Hueber, 56–83.
Kaufmann, Gerhard. 1976. *Die indirekte Rede und mit ihr konkurrierende Formen der Redeerwähnung* (=Heutiges Deutsch, Reihe III, Band 1). München: Hueber.
Kerkhoff, Emmy L. 1944a. "Die erlebte Rede". *De Drie Talen (Duits)* 60: 65–8.
Kerkhoff, Emmy L. 1944b. "Gedankenreferat". *De Drie Talen (Duits)* 60: 49–53.
Kerkhoff, Emmy L. 1945/6. "Die indirekte Rede". *De Drie Talen (Duits)* 61: 17–20, 33–6; 62: 1–4, 17–23.
Kerling, Johan. 1982. "A case of 'slipping': direct and indirect speech in Old English prose". *Neophilologus* 66,2: 286–90.
Kerr, Isabel. 1976/7. "The centrality of dialogue in Cuiva discourse structure". In Longacre and Woods (eds.), vol. 3, 133–73.
Kesteman, Dominique. 1984. "Le discours rapporté". *Cahiers de l'Institut de Linguistique de Louvain* 10,4: 93–102.
Kidda Awak, Mairo. 2000. "Logophoric pronoun and binding in Tangale". *Afrikanistische Arbeitspapiere* 62: 113–28.

Kieckers, Ernst. 1912. "Die Stellung der Verba des Sagens in Schaltesätzen im Griechischen und in den verwandten Sprachen". *Indogermanische Forschungen* 30: 145–85.

Kieckers, Ernst. 1913. "Zu den Schaltesätzen im Lateinischen, Romanischen und Neuhochdeutschen". *Indogermanische Forschungen* 32: 7–23.

Kieckers, Ernst. 1915/6. "Zur oratio recta in den indogermanischen Sprachen". *Indogermanische Forschungen* 35: 1–93, 36: 1–70.

Kieckers, Ernst. 1919/20a. "Die directe rede im neuhochdeutschen als object". *Paul und Braunes Beiträge zur Geschichte der deutschen Sprache und Literatur* 44: 350–1.

Kieckers, Ernst. 1919/20b. "Zur directen rede im neuhochdeutschen". *Paul und Braunes Beiträge zur Geschichte der deutschen Sprache und Literatur* 44: 79–83.

Kieckers, Ernst. 1919/20c. "Zur direkten Rede im Neuenglischen". *Englische Studien* 53: 405–18.

Kieckers, Ernst. 1920a. "Zum 'pleonastischen' *inquit*". *Glotta* 10: 200–9.

Kieckers, Ernst. 1920b. "Zur direkten Rede bei Plautus und Terenz". *Glotta* 10: 210–11.

Kieckers, Ernst. 1921a. "Zu *inquit, φησίν* 'heißt es'". *Glotta* 11: 184–5.

Kieckers, Ernst. 1921b. "Zum 'ὅτι 'recitativum'". *Glotta* 11: 183.

Kieckers, Ernst. 1921c. "Zum Schaltesatz im späteren Griechisch". *Glotta* 11: 179–83.

Kiefer, Ferenc. 1986. "Some semantic aspects of indirect speech in Hungarian". In Coulmas (ed.), 201–17.

Kihm, Alain. 1990. "Complementizer, verb, or both? Kriyol *kuma*". *Journal of Pidgin and Creole Languages* 5,1: 53–70.

Klamer, Marian. 2000. "How report verbs become quote markers and complementisers". *Lingua* 110: 69–98.

Klammer, Thomas P. 1971. *The structure of dialogue paragraphs in written dramatic and narrative discourse*. Ph.D. thesis, University of Michigan at Ann Arbor.

Knoke, Friedrich. 1881. "Ueber *hic* und *nunc* in der *oratio obliqua*". In *Einladungsschrift des Herzoglichen Karls-Gymnasiums in Bernburg, 8. April 1881*. Bernburg: Dornblüth, 1–11.

Koduxov, Vitalij I. 1955. "Sposoby peredači čužoj reči v russkom jazyke". *Učenye Zapiski — Leningradskij Gosudarstvennyj Pedagogičeskij Institut Imeni A.I. Gercena* 104: 107–72.

Koduxov, Vitalij I. 1957. *Prjamaja i kosvennaja reč' v sovremennom russkom jazyke*. Leningrad: Gosudarstvennoe Učebno-pedagogičeskoe izdatjel'stvo.

Koller, Werner. 1975. "Linguistik der Anführungszeichen". In Müssener, Helmut and Hans Rossipal (eds.), *Impulse: Dank an Gustav Korlén zu seinem 60. Geburtstag*. Stockholm: Deutsches Institut der Universität Stockholm, 115–61.

Koontz, Carol. 1976/7. "Features of dialogue within narrative discourse in Teribe". In Longacre and Woods (eds.), vol. 3, 111–32.

Koontz, Carol. 1978. "Características del diálogo en el discurso narrativo teribe". In Levinsohn (ed.), 29–61. (= Koontz 1976/7)

Koopman, Hilda and Dominique Sportiche. 1989. "Pronouns, logical variables, and logophoricity in Abe". *Linguistic Inquiry* 20,4: 555–88.

König, Ekkehard and Peter Siemund. 1999. "Reflexivity, logophoricity and intensification in English". In Carls and Lucho (eds.), 283–304.

Körner, Karl-Hermann. 1974. "Überlegungen zum *verbum dicendi* und zur Sprachkunst von Vargas Llosa in *Pantaleón y las visitadoras*". In *Filología y Didáctica Hispánica: Homenaje al Professor Hans-Karl Schneider*. Hamburg: Buske, 141–54.
Kovtunova, Irina I. 1953. "Nesobstvenno-prjamaja reč' v sovremennom russkom literaturnom jazyke". *Russkij Jazyk v Škole* 14,2:18–27.
Kovtunova, Irina I. 1956. *'Nesobstvenno-prjamaja reč' v jazyke russkoj literatury konca XVIII — pervoj poloviny XIX veka*. Doctoral thesis, Moskva.
Kozlovskij, P. S. 1890. "O sočetanii predloženij prjamoj i kosvennoj reči v russkom jazyke". *Filolog. Zapiski* 4–5:1–7.
Kranz, Dieter. 1970. "Ambivalente Formen des 'style indirect libre' in den Fabeln La Fontaines". *Archiv für das Studium der Neueren Sprachen* 122,207:36–42.
Küffner, Rolf. 1978. "Schwierigkeiten mit der indirekten Rede". *Muttersprache* 88:145–73.
Kühn, Ingrid. 1988. "Beziehungen zwischen der Struktur der 'erlebten Rede' und ihrer kommunikativen Funktionalität". *Zeitschrift für Germanistik* 9:182–209.
Kuipers, Joel C. 1992. "Obligations to the word: ritual speech, performance, and responsibility among the Weyewa". In Hill and Irvine (eds.), 88–104.
Kullmann, Dorothea. 1992a. "Systematische und historische Bemerkungen zum Style indirect libre". *Romanistische Zeitschrift für Literaturgeschichte* 16:113–40.
Kullmann, Dorothea. 1992b. "Zur Wiedergabe des *style indirect libre* durch die deutschen Übersetzer von *Madame Bovary*". In Knittel, Harald (ed.), *Geschichte, System, literarische Übersetzung — Histories, systems, literary translations*. Berlin: Schmidt, 323–33.
Kullmann, Dorothea. 1995a. "Beobachtungen zum Style indirect libre in den Romanen *Madame Bovary* und *L'Assommoir* sowie zu seiner Wiedergabe im Deutschen". In Kullmann, Dorothea (ed.), 89–135.
Kullmann, Dorothea. 1995b. "Versuch einer Systematik des Style indirect libre (mit französischen, italienischen und deutschen Beispielen)". In Kullmann, Dorothea (ed.), 309–23.
Kullmann, Dorothea. 2000. "Quelques observations sur l'emploi du style indirect libre dans les chansons de geste". In Englebert, Anninck et al. (eds.), *Actes du XXIe Congrès International de Linguistique et de Philologie Romane, Vol 8: Les effets du sens: travaux de la section "Rhétorique, sémiotique et stylistique; table ronde "La linguistique textuelle est-elle une linguistique?"* Tübingen: Niemeyer, 75–84.
Kullmann, Dorothea (ed.). 1995. *Erlebte Rede und impressionistischer Stil: europäische Erzählprosa im Vergleich mit ihren deutschen Übersetzungen*. Göttingen: Wallstein.
Kuno, Susumu. 1972. "Pronominalization, reflexivization, and direct discourse". *Linguistic Inquiry* 3:161–95.
Küper, Christoph. 1979. "Textlinguistik und Schulunterricht: am Beispiel der Behandlung der indirekten Rede im Englischen". *Linguistik und Didaktik* 37:51–68.
Kuroda, Sige-Yuki. 1973a. "On Kuno's direct discourse analysis of the Japanese reflexive *zibun*". *Papers in Japanese Linguistics* 2,1:136–47.
Kuroda, Sige-Yuki. 1973b. "Where epistemology, style and grammar meet: a case study from Japanese". In Anderson and Kiparsky (eds.), 377–91.
Kurt, Sibylle. 1999. *Erlebte Rede aus linguistischer Sicht: der Ausdruck von Temporalität im Französischen und Russischen: ein Übersetzungsvergleich* (=Slavica Helvetica 64). Bern: Lang.

Kurz, Josef. 1966. *Die Redewiedergabe: Methoden und Möglichkeiten*. Leipzig: Karl-Marx-Universität.
Kurz, Josef. 1984. *Möglichkeiten der Redewiedergabe*. Leipzig: Karl-Marx-Universität.
Kvavik, Karen H. 1986. "Characteristics of direct and reported speech prosody: evidence from Spanish". In Coulmas (ed.), 333–60.
Låftman, Emil. 1918. "Är 'le style indirect libre' ett indirekt framställninsätt?" *Moderna Språk* 12:171–4.
Låftman, Emil. 1919. "'Le style indirect libre' ännu en gäng". *Moderna Språk* 13:30–2.
Låftman, Emil. 1929. "Stellvertretende Darstellung". *Neophilologus* 14:161–8.
Låftman, Emil. 1930. "Referat: en studie i nusvensk syntax". *Nysvenska Studier* 10:91–118.
Lahiri, Utpal. 1991. *On embedded interrogatives and predicates that embed them*. Ph.D. thesis, Massachusetts Institute of Technology.
Lamarque, Peter. 1982. "Metaphor and reported speech: in defense of a pragmatic theory". *Journal of Literary Semantics* 11:14–18.
Lambert, André. 1946. *Die indirekte Rede als künstlerisches Stilmittel des Livius*. Doctoral thesis, Universität Zürich.
Lambert, Mark. 1981. *Dickens and the suspended quotation*. New Haven: Yale University Press.
Lancy, David F. 1980. "Speech events in a West African court". *Communication and Cognition* 13,4:397–412.
Landén, Barbro. 1985. *Form und Funktion der Redewiedergabe in einigen ausgewählten historischen Darstellungen* (=Lunder germanistische Forschungen 54). Stockholm: Almqvist and Wiksell.
Landeweerd, Rita and Co Vet. 1996. "Tense in (free) indirect discourse in French". In Janssen and Wurff (eds.), 141–62.
Landry, Anne G. 1953. *Represented discourse in the novels of François Mauriac* (=Studies in Romance Languages and Literatures 44). Washington, D.C.: Catholic University of America.
Langdon, Margaret. 1977. "Semantics and syntax of expressive 'say' constructions in Yuman". *Berkeley Linguistics Society* 3:1–11.
Larkin, D. 1972. "'Enru' and 'enpatu' as complement markers in Tamil". In Agesthialingom and Shanmugam (eds.), 37–73.
Larson, Mildred L. 1978. *The functions of reported speech in discourse* (=Publications in Linguistics and Related Fields 59). Dallas / Arlington: Summer Institute of Linguistics and University of Texas.
Larson, Mildred L. 1981. "Quotations, a translation problem". *Notes on Translation* 82:2–15.
Laufer, Roger. 1979. "Guillemets et marques du discours direct". In Catach, Nina (ed.), *La ponctuation: recherches historiques et actuelles*, vol. 2. Paris: Centre National de la Recherche Scientifique, 235–251.
Lawson, Marjorie F. 1940. "Enter author: Erlebte Rede in the work of Karl Heinrich Waggerl". *Monatshefte für deutschen Unterricht* 32,6:279–88.
Lebsanft, Franz. 1981a. "Adverbes de temps, style indirect et 'point de vue' dans la *Queste del Saint Graal*". *Travaux de Linguistique et de Littérature* 19,1:53–61.

Lebsanft, Franz. 1981b. "Perspektivische Rededarstellung (Erlebte Rede) in Texten des französischen und spanischen Mittelalters". *Zeitschrift für Romanische Philologie* 97:65–85.
Lee, Benjamin. 1993. "Metalanguages and subjectivities". In Lucy (ed.), 365–91.
Lee, Cheong-Hie. 1994. *Die Wiedergabe gesprochener und gedachter Rede in Thomas Manns Roman "Buddenbrooks": eine Untersuchung grammatischer Formen und narrativer Funktionen*. Doctoral thesis, Philipps-Universität Marburg.
Lee, P. Gregory. 1970. "The deep structure of indirect discourse". *Ohio State University Working Papers in Linguistics* 4:64–73.
Leger, Simone. 1979. "Présupposition et discours oblique". *Documentation et Recherche en Linguistique Allemande Contemporaine — Vincennes* 21:146–55.
Lehmann, Dorothea. 1976. *Untersuchungen zur Bezeichnung der Sprechaktreferenz im Englischen* (=Forum Linguisticum 8). Bern: Lang.
Lehmann, Dorothea. 1977. "A confrontation of *say, speak, talk, tell* with possible German counterparts". *Papers and Studies in Contrastive Linguistics* 6:99–109.
Lehrer, Adrienne. 1989. "Remembering and representing prose: quoted speech as a data source". *Discourse Processes* 12:105–25.
Lekomcev, Jurij K. 1962. "K voprosu o sistemnosti glagolov reči v anglijskom jazyke". Akademija Nauk SSSR, Institut Russkogo Jazyka, *Problemy strukturnoj lingvistiki,* Moskva: Nauka, 190–7.
Léon, Jacqueline. 1988. "Formes de discours direct dans des récits oraux". *LINX: revue des linguistes de l'Université Paris X Nanterre* 18:107–24.
Lerch, Eugen. 1914. "Die stilistische Bedeutung des Imperfektums der Rede ('style indirect libre')". *Germanisch-Romanische Monatsschrift* 6:470–89.
Lerch, Eugen. 1922. "Das Imperfektum als Ausdruck der lebhaften Vorstellung". *Zeitschrift für Romanische Philologie* 42:311–31, 385–425.
Lerch, Eugen. 1928. "Ursprung und Bedeutung der sog. 'Erlebten Rede' (Rede als Tatsache)". *Germanisch-Romanische Monatsschrift* 16:459–78.
Lerch, Gertraud. 1922. "Die uneigentliche direkte Rede". In Klemperer, Viktor and Eugen Lerch (eds.), *Idealistische Neuphilologie: Festschrift für Karl Vossler zum 6. September 1922* (=Sammlung romanischer Elementar- und Handbücher V,5). Heidelberg: Winter, 107–19.
Lethcoe, Ronald J. 1969. *Narrated speech and consciousness.* Ph.D. thesis, University of Wisconsin.
Leuschner, Burkhard. 1972. "Die indirekte Rede im Englischen: zur sogenannten 'Zeitenfolge'". *Die Neueren Sprachen* 71:82–90.
Levine, Robert. 1963. *Direct discourse in "Beowulf": its meaning and function.* Ph.D. thesis, University of California, Berkeley.
Levinsohn, Stephen H. 1992. "The historic present and speech margins in Matthew". In Hwang and Merrifield (eds.), 451–73.
Levinsohn, Stephen H. (ed.). 1978. *La estructura del diálogo en el discurso narrativo* (=Lenguas de Panama 5). Ciudad de Panamá: Instituto Nacional de Cultura.
Leys, Odo. 1980. "Vergleichssätze als Indirekte-Rede-Sätze". *Deutsche Sprache* 1980,3:193–9.

Li, Charles N. 1986. "Direct and indirect speech: a functional study". In Coulmas (ed.), 29–45.
Lips, Marguerite. 1921. "Le style indirect libre chez Flaubert". *Journal de Psychologie* 18:644–53.
Lips, Marguerite. 1926. *Le style indirect libre*. Paris: Payot.
Locht, Johannes van de. 1995. *Der style indirect libre in den Romanen Edmond Durantys* (=Bonner romanistische Arbeiten 52). Frankfurt/Main: Lang.
Loesch, W. Max. 1927. *Die Einführung der direkten Rede bei den epischen Dichtern der Römer bis zur domitianischen Zeit*. Doctoral thesis, Universität Erlangen.
Lombard, Lawrence B. 1974. *Quotation and quotation marks: semantic considerations*. Ph.D. thesis, Stanford University.
Longacre, Robert E. 1994. "The dynamics of reported dialogue in narrative". *Word* 45,2:125–43.
Longacre, Robert E. and Frances Woods (eds.). 1976/7. *Discourse grammar: studies in indigenous languages of Colombia, Panama, and Ecuador*, 3 vols. (=Publications in Linguistics and Related Fields 52). Dallas: Summer Institute of Linguistics.
Lopez-Blanquet, Marina. 1968. *El estilo indirecto libre en Español*. Montevideo: Talleres Don Bosco.
Lorck, Etienne. 1921. *Die 'erlebte Rede': eine sprachliche Untersuchung*. Heidelberg: Winter.
Lorck, Etienne. 1927. "Noch einiges zur Frage der 'Erlebten Rede'". *Die Neueren Sprachen* 35:456–64.
Lorenz, Johann. 1910. "Kunst in der Einführung der direkten Rede bei den Epikern Hartmann von Aue und Gottfried von Straßburg". *III. Programm der K.K. Staats-Realschule in Kufstein für des Studienjahr 1909/10*. Kufstein: Staats-Realschule, 3–91.
Lord, Carol. 1976. "Evidence for syntactic reanalysis: from verb to complementizer in Kwa". *Chicago Linguistic Society* 12: *Papers from the parasession on diachronic syntax*: 179–91.
Lorrot, Danielle. 1993. "Pratique spontanée du discours rapporté et apprentissages narratifs au cours moyen". In Peytard, Jean (ed.), 151–68.
Loss, Nicolò M. 1970. "Il discorso indiretto nell'Ebraico Biblico". *Rivista Biblica* 18:195–202.
Lowe, Ivan. 1969. "An algebraic theory of English pronominal reference (part I)". *Semiotica* 1:397–421.
Lucy, John A. 1993a. "Metapragmatic presentationals: reporting speech with quotatives in Yucatec Maya". In Lucy (ed.), 91–125.
Lucy, John A. 1993b. "Reflexive language and the human disciplines". In Lucy (ed.), 9–32.
Lucy, John A. (ed.). 1993. *Reflexive language: reported speech and metapragmatics*. Cambridge: Cambridge University Press.
Lüdi, Georges, Hans Stricker and Jakob Wüst (eds.). 1987. *Romania Ingeniosa: Festschrift für Prof. Dr. Gerold Hilty zum 60. Geburtstag*. Bern: Lang.
Lugli, Vittorio. 1952. "Lo stilo indiretto libero in Flaubert e in Verga". In Lugli, Vittorio, *Dante e Balzac, con altri italiani e francesi*. Napoli: Edizioni scientifiche italiane, 221–39.
Lustoza Leão, Maria M. Sampaio. 1973. "Alguns verbos dicendi en português: uma tentativa de análise componencial". *Littera* (Rio de Janeiro) 3,9:96–107.

Macaulay, Ronald K.S. 1987. "Polyphonic monologues: quoted direct speech in oral narratives". *International Pragmatics Association, Papers in Pragmatics* 1,2:1–34.

Madini, Mongi. 1993. "Une parole au pluriel". In Peytard, Jean (ed.), 169–202.

Maingueneau, Dominique. 1981. *Approche de l'énonciation en lingustique française: embrayeurs, "temps", discours rapporté.* Paris: Hachette.

Maldonado, Concepción. 1990. *El discurso directo y el discurso indirecto en español.* Doctoral thesis, Universidad Complutense de Madrid.

Maldonado, Concepción. 1991. *Discurso directo y discurso indirecto* (=Gramática del español 3). Madrid: Taurus Universitaria.

Mancaş, Michaela. 1972. *Stilul indirect liber în româna literară,* Bucarest: Editura Didactică şi Pedagogică.

Manessy, Gabriel. 1989. "Dire que... (de l'origine des créoles atlantiques)". *La Linguistique* 25,2:19–43.

Marinova, Jordanka. 1975. *Prjakata rec kato strukturno oformena sintakticna edinica.* Sofija: Tarnovkija Universitet.

Marinova, Jordanka. 1983. *Prjakata rec v balgarskija knizoven ezik.* Sofija: Darzavno Izdat. Narodna Prosveta.

Markus, Manfred. 1999. "Word order in English reporting clauses of direct speech (corpus-based)". In Carls and Lucho (eds.), 319–32.

Marnette, Sophie. 1996. "Réflexions sur le discours indirect libre en fançais médiéval". *Romania* 114:1–49.

Martin, Jean-Maurice. 1987. *Untersuchungen zum Problem der Erlebten Rede: der ursächliche Kontext der Erlebten Rede, dargestellt an Romanen Robert Walsers.* Frankfurt/Main: Lang

Martins-Baltar, Michel 1976. "Les verbes transcripteurs du discours rapporté". In Gauvenet, Hélène et al. 1976b, 63–72.

Massamba, David P.B. 1986. "Reported speech in Swahili". In Coulmas (ed.), 99–119.

Matejka, Ladislav and Krystyna Pomorska (eds.). 1971. *Readings in Russian poetics: formalist and structuralist views.* Cambridge, Mass.: MIT Press.

Mathis, Terrie. 1991. *The form and function of constructed dialogue in reported discourse.* Ph.D. thesis, Louisiana State University.

Mathis, Terrie and George Yule. 1994. "Zero quotatives". *Discourse Processes* 18,1:63–76.

Matthews, David. 1995. "Preterites in direct discourse in three Old East Slavonic chronicles". *Russian Linguistics* 19:299–318.

Maybin, Janet. 1996. "Story voices: the use of reported speech in 10–12 year olds' spontaneous narratives". *Current Issues in Language and Society* 3,1:36–48.

Mayenova, Maria R. 1970. "Expressions guillemetées: contribution à l'étude de la sémantique du texte poétique". In Greimas et al. (eds.), 645–57.

Mayes, Patricia. 1990. "Quotation in spoken English". *Studies in Language* 14,2:325–63.

Maynard, Senko K. 1984. "Functions of *to* and *koto-o* in speech and thought representation in Japanese written discourse". *Lingua* 64:1–24.

Maynard, Senko K. 1986. "The Particle *-o* and content-oriented indirect speech in Japanese written discourse". In Coulmas (ed.), 179–200.

Maynard, Senko K. 1996. "Multivoicedness in speech and thought representation: the case of self-quotation in Japanese". *Journal of Pragmatics* 25:207–26.

McCarthy, Michael. 1998. "'So Mary was saying': speech reporting in everyday conversation". In McCarthy, Michael, *Spoken language and applied linguistics*. Cambridge: Cambridge University Press, 150–75.

McCormick, John P. 1935. *A study of the nominal syntax and indirect discourse in Hegesippus* (= Patristic Studies 43). Washington, D.C.: Catholic University of America.

McDowell, Alfred. 1973. "Fielding's rendering of speech in *Joseph Andrews* and *Tom Jones*". *Language and Style* 6:83–96.

McGregor, William. 1994. "The grammar of reported speech and thought in Gooniyandi". *Australian Journal of Linguistics* 14,1:63–92.

McHale, Brian. 1978. "Free indirect discourse: a survey of recent accounts". *PTL: A Journal for Descriptive Poetics and Theory of Literature* 3:249–87.

McHale, Brian. 1981. "Islands in the stream of consciousness: Dorrit Cohn's *Transparent Minds*". *Poetics Today* 2,2:183–91.

McHale, Brian. 1983. "Unspeakable sentences, unnatural acts: linguistics and poetics revisited". *Poetics Today* 4,1:17–45.

McKenzie, Malcolm. 1987. "Free indirect speech in a fettered insecure society". *Language and Communication* 7:153–9.

McKercher, David. 2000. "Switch-reference and direct quotation in Zuni". In *Proceedings from the 3rd Workshop on American Indigenous Languages* (=Santa Barbara Papers in Linguistics 10). Santa Barbara: Department of Linguistics, University of California, 65–79.

Meehan, Teresa. 1991. "It's like, 'What's happening in the evolution of *like*?' A theory of grammaticalization". *Kansas Working Papers in Linguistics* 16:37–51.

Meenakshi, K. 1986. "The quotative in Indo-Aryan". In Krishnamurti, Bhadriraju (ed.), *South Asian languages: structure, convergence and diglossia* (=MLBD Series in Linguistics 3). Delhi: Motilal Banarsidass, 209–18.

Meer, Geart van der. 1988. "Reported speech and the position of the finite verb (some facts from West Frisian)". *Leuvense Bijdragen* 77:301–24.

Meier, Samuel A. 1992. *Speaking of speaking: marking direct discourse in the Hebrew Bible* (=Supplements to Vetus Testamentum 46). Leiden: Brill.

Meiller, Albert. 1966. "Le problème du style direct introduit par *que* en ancien français". *Revue de Linguistique Romane* 30:353–73.

Meillet, Antoine. 1916. "Les verbes signifiant 'dire'". *Bulletin de la Société de Linguistique de Paris* 20:28–31.

Mellet Sylvie. 1998. "Imparfait et discours rapporté". *Études Luxembourgeoises* 1:116–25.

Mellet Sylvie. 2000. "A propos de deux marqueurs de 'bivocalité'". In Mellet and Vuillaume (eds.), 91–106.

Mellet, Sylvie and Marcel Vuillaume. 2000. "Introduction: le style indirect libre et ses contextes". In Mellet and Vuillaume (eds.), I-III.

Mellet, Sylvie and Marcel Vuillaume (eds.). 2000. *Le style indirect libre et ses contextes* (=Cahiers Chronos 5). Amsterdam: Rodopi.

Mennicken, Franz. 1919. "Eine eigentümliche Gestaltung des abhängigen Fragesatzes im Englischen, zugleich eine Bemerkung zur 'freien indirekten Rede'". *Die Neueren Sprachen* 27:263–5.

Metzger, Bruce M. 1951. "The formulas introducing quotations of scripture in the NT and the Mishnah". *Journal of Biblical Literature* 70: 297–307.
Meyer, Herman. 1961. *Das Zitat in der Erzählkunst: zur Geschichte und Poetik des europäischen Romans*. Stuttgart: Metzler.
Meyer, Kurt R. 1957. *Zur erlebten Rede (the interior monologue) im englischen Roman des zwanzigsten Jahrhunderts* (=Schweizer anglistische Arbeiten 43). Winterthur: Keller.
Meyer-Hermann, Reinhard. 1978. "Aspekte der Analyse metakommunikativer Interaktion". In Meyer-Hermann, Reinhard (ed.), *Sprechen — Handeln — Interaktion: Ergebnisse aus Bielefelder Forschungsprojekten zu Texttheorie, Sprechakttheorie und Konversationsanalyse*. Tübingen: Niemeyer, 103–42.
Meyer-Hermann, Reinhard. 1979. "'Attention à la métacommunication!' (Zur Bedeutung interaktionsbenennender Ausdrücke in metakommunikativen Sprachen für eine empirisch fundierte Beschreibung kommunikativer Interaktionstypen)". In Kloepfer, Rolf et al. (eds.), *Bildung und Ausbildung in der Romania, Band II: Sprachwissenschaft und Landeskunde, Akten des Romanistentages in Gießen 1977*. München: Fink, 161–76.
Michel, Georg. 1966. "Sprachliche Bedingungen der Wortwahl: eine Untersuchung an Verben der Redeeinführung". *Zeitschrift für Phonetik, Sprachwissenschaft und Kommunikationsforschung* 19: 103–29, 213–40, 339–64, 512–32.
Miller, Cynthia L. 1994. "Introducing direct discourse in Biblical Hebrew narrative". In Bergen (ed.), 199–241.
Miller, Cynthia L. 1995. "Discourse functions of the quotative frames in Biblical Hebrew narrative". In Bodine, Walter R. (ed.), *Discourse analysis of biblical literature: what it is, and what it offers*. Atlanta: Scholars Press, 155–82.
Miller, Cynthia L. 1996. *The representation of speech in Biblical Hebrew narrative: a linguistic analysis* (=Harvard Semitic Museum Monographs 55). Atlanta: Scholars Press.
Miller, Norbert. 1958. "Erlebte und verschleierte Rede". *Akzente* 5: 213–26.
Milyx, Marija K. 1958. *Prjamaja reč' v xudožestvennoj proze*. Rostov-na-Donu: Izdatel'stvo Rostovskogo Universiteta.
Milyx, Marija K. 1975. *Konstrukcii s kosvennoj reč'ju v sovremennom russkom jazyke*. Rostov-na-Donu: Izdatel'stvo Rostovskogo Universiteta.
Mishler, Craig. 1981. "'He said, they say': the uses of reporting speech in native American folk narrative". *Fabula* 22,3/4: 239–49.
Mittwoch, Anita. 1977. "How to refer to one's own words: speech act modifying adverbials and the performative analysis". *Journal of Linguistics* 13: 177–89.
Mochet, Marie-Anne. 1993. "Place du discours narrativisé dans la mise en scène des situations de parole". In Peytard, Jean (ed.), 93–149.
Mochet, Marie-Anne. 1996. "De la non-littéralité à l'exemplification: discours direct en situation d'entretien". In Claquin, Françoise and Marie-Anne Mochet (eds.), *Hétérogénéités en discours* (=Cahiers du Français Contemporain 3). Paris: Didier, 61–76.
Moirand, S. 1976. "Propositions pour une didactique du discours rapporté". In Gauvenet, Hélène et al. 1976b, 29–45.
Monville-Burston, Monique. 1993. "Les *verba dicendi* dans la presse d'information". *Langue Française* 98: 48–66.

Moolman, M. M. K. 1984. "The defective verbs -*thi* and -*sho* in Zulu". In *South African Journal of African Languages*, Supplement 1, 135–44.

Moore, Robert E. 1993. "Performance form and the voices of characters in five versions of the Wasco Coyote Cycle". In Lucy (ed.), 213–40.

Morawski, Stefan. 1970. "The basic function of quotations". In Greimas et al. (eds.), 690–705.

Morel, Marie Annick. 1996. "Le discours rapporté direct dans l'oral spontané". In Claquin and Mochet (eds.), 77–90.

Mortara Garavelli, Bice. 1985. *La parola d'altri : prospettive di analisi del discorso*. Palermo: Sellerio.

Motyljowa, T. 1965. "Innerer Monolog und 'Bewußtseinsstrom'". *Kunst und Literatur* 13:603–17.

Müller, Andreas. 1981. *Figurenrede: Grundzüge der Rededarstellung im Roman*. Doctoral thesis, Universität Göttingen.

Müller, P. 1869. *Gebrauch der Modus-Zeitformen der deutschen abhängigen Rede*. Beilage zum Programm des Grossh. Gymnasiums in Bruchsal für das Schuljahr 1868/69. Bruchsal: Buchdruckerei Rodrian.

Müller, Wolfgang G. 1985. "Der freie indirekte Stil bei Jane Austen als Mittel der Rede- und Gedankenwiedergabe". *Poetica* 1,7:206–36.

Munro, Pamela. 1978. "Chemehuevi 'say' and the Uto-Aztecan quotative pattern". In Tuohy, Donald R. (ed.), *Selected papers from the 14th Great Basin Anthropological Conference, Carson City, Nevada, 1974* (=Publications in Archaeology, Ethnology, and History 11). Socorro: Ballena Press, 149–71.

Munro, Pamela. 1981. "Two notes on Yuman 'say'". In Redden, James E. (ed.), *Proceedings of the 1980 Hokan Languages Workshop, held at the University of California, Berkeley, June 30–July 2, 1980* (=Occasional Papers on Linguistics 9). Carbondale: Department of Linguistics, Southern Illinois University, 70–7.

Munro, Pamela. 1982. "On the transitivity of 'say' verbs". In Hopper, Paul J. and Sandra A. Thompson (eds.), *Studies in transitivity* (=Syntax and Semantics 15). New York: Academic Press, 301–18.

Mushin, Ilana. 1997. "Maintaining epistemological stance: direct speech and evidentiality in Macedonian". *Chicago Linguistic Society* 33,1:287–300.

Nef, Frédéric. 1976. "*De dicto, de re*, formule de Barcan et sémantique des mondes possibles". *Langages* 43:28–38.

Netter, Irmgard. 1935. *Die direkte Rede in den Isländersagas* (=Form und Geist 36). Leipzig: Eichblatt.

Neubert, Albrecht. 1957. *Die Stilform der 'Erlebten Rede' im neueren englischen Roman*. Halle: Niemeyer.

Neumann, Anne W. 1992. "Free indirect discourse in the Eighteenth-Century English novel: speakable or unspeakable? The example of *Sir Charles Grandison*". In Toolan, Michael J. (ed.), *Language, text and context: essays in stylistics*. London: Routledge, 113–35.

Neuse, Werner. 1934a. "'Erlebte Rede' und 'innerer Monolog' in den erzählenden Schriften Arthur Schnitzlers". *Publications of the Modern Language Association of America* 49:327–55.

Neuse, Werner. 1934b. "The importance of a form of speech for the interpretation of modern German texts". *The German Quarterly* 7:145–51.

Neuse, Werner. 1990. *Geschichte der erlebten Rede und des inneren Monologs in der deutschen Prosa*. Bern: Lang.

Nezvanov, A.A. 1949. "Izučenie temy: 'prjamaja i kosvennaja reč'". *Russkij Jazyk v Škole* 10,2:46–51

Nichols, Lynn. 1990. "Direct quotation and switch reference in Zuni". *Berkeley Linguistics Society* 16S:91–100.

Niess, Robert. 1975. "Remarks on the 'style indirect libre' in *L'Assomoir*". *Nineteenth Century French Studies* 3,1/2:124–35.

Noss, Philip A. 1988a. "Quotation, direct, indirect and otherwise in translation". In Stine, Philip C. (ed.), *Issues in Bible Translation* (=United Bible Societies Monograph Series 3). London: United Bible Societies, 129–45.

Noss, Philip A. 1988b. "Speech, structure and aesthetics in a Gbaya tale". *Journal of West African Languages* 18;1:97–115.

Nunes, Jairo and Ellen Thompson. 1995. "The discourse representation of temporal dependencies". In Bertinetto et al. (eds.), 365–79.

Obaid, Antonio H. 1967. "A sequence of tenses? — What sequence of tenses?" *Hispania* 50:112–19.

Ogura, Michiko. 1981. *The syntactic and semantic rivalry of quoth, say and tell in Medieval English*. Hirakata City: Kansai University of Foreign Studies.

Ogura, Michiko. 1991. "Is indirect discourse following OE *cwedan* always in the subjunctive mood?", *English Studies* 72:393–9.

Ogura, Michiko. 1992. "Why is the element order *to cwæð him* 'said to him' impossible?". In Rissanen et al. (eds.), 373–8.

O'Kelly, Dairine. 1997. "Discours rapporté et discours importé dans les échanges dialogiques". *Modèles Linguistiques* 18,1:111–27.

Oliveira, Ana Maria P. de, Beatriz N.O. Longo and Maria Celeste C. Dezotti. 1985. "Verbos introdutores de discurso direto". *Alfa* 29:91–6.

Oltean, Ştefan. 1976. "On Free Indirect Speech". *Revue Roumaine de Linguistique* 21,13:647–51.

Oltean, Ştefan. 1993. "A survey of the pragmatic and referential functions of free indirect discourse". *Poetics Today* 14:691–714.

Oltean, Ştefan. 1995. "Free indirect discourse: some referential aspects". *Journal of Literary Semantics* 24:21–41.

Osam, E. Kweku. 1996. "The history of Akan complementizers". *Journal of Asian and African Studies* 51:93–103.

Ouzounian, Agnès. 1992. *Discours rapporté en arménien classique* (=Bibliothèque des Cahiers de l'Institut de Linguistique de Louvain 63). Leuven: Peeters.

Ouzounian, Agnès. 1997. "Movses Xorenac'i ou le paradoxe de l'historien: à propos du discours rapporté dans l'*Histoire de l'Arménie*". *Modèles Linguistiques* 18,1:75–91.

Overbeke, Maurits van. 1978. "La pragmatique du discours rapporté". In Lerot, Jacques (ed.), *Mélanges de linguistique et de littérature offerts au professeur Henry Draye à l'occasion de son éméritat*. Louvain: Nauwelaerts, 141–53.

Pabst, Walter. 1957. "Patois als 'Erlebte Rede' bei Des Péries". In Reichenkron (ed.), 411–20.
Paccaud, Josiane. 1991. "La grammaire du discours indirect libre et le sujet". In *Structures lexicales et grammaticales : domaine anglais: communications présentées à l'Atelier de Linguistique du 28. Congrès de la SAES, tenu à Besançon du 29 avril au 1. mai 1988*. Saint Étienne: Université Jean Monnet, 107–23.
Page, Norman. 1973. *Speech in the English novel*. London: Longman.
Palacas, Arthur L. 1992. "Forms of speech: linguistic worlds and Goffman's embedded footings". In Hwang and Merrifield (eds.), 275–91.
Panagl, Oswald. 1972. "Zur Funktion der direkten Reden in den 'dithyrambischen Stasima' des Euripides". *Wiener Studien — Zeitschrift für klassische Philologie*, Neue Folge 6: 5–18.
Parmentier, Richard J. 1993. "The political function of reported speech: a Belauan example. In Lucy (ed.), 261–86.
Partee, Barbara Hall. 1970. "Opacity, coreference, and pronouns". *Synthese* 21: 359–85.
Partee, Barbara Hall. 1973a. "The semantics of belief-sentences". In Hintikka, K. J. Jaakko, Julius M. E. Moravcsik and Patrick Suppes (eds.), *Approaches to natural languages: proceedings of the 1970 Stanford Workshop on Grammar and Semantics* (=Synthese Library 49). Dordrecht: Reidel, 309–36.
Partee, Barbara Hall. 1973b. "The syntax and semantics of quotation". In Anderson and Kiparsky (eds.), 410–18.
Partee, Barbara Hall. 1974. "Opacity and scope". In Munitz, Milton K. and Peter K. Unger (eds.), *Semantics and philosophy*. New York: New York University Press, 81–101.
Parunak, H. Van Dyke. 1994. "Some discourse functions of prophetic quotation formulas in Jeremiah". In Bergen (ed.), 489–519.
Pascal, Roy. 1977. *The dual voice: free indirect speech and its functioning in the nineteenth century European novel*. Manchester: Manchester University Press.
Passias, Katherine. 1976. "Deep and surface structure of the narrative pronoun *vous* in Butor's *La Modification* and its relationship to free indirect style". *Language and Style* 9,3: 197–212.
Pecora, Laura. 1984. "La particella — *wa(r)*- e il discorso diretto in antico-eteo". *Indogermanische Forschungen* 89: 104–24.
Pérennec, Marie-Hélène. 1992. "Les techniques du discours rapporté dans la nouvelle d'I. Bachmann *Simultan*". In Gréciano, Gertrud and George Kleiber (eds.), *Systèmes interactifs: mélanges en honneur de Jean David*. Metz: Université de Metz, 323–33.
Perret, Michèle. "Le discours rapporté dans 'Le bel inconnu'". *L'Information Grammaticale* 72: 13–17.
Perridon, Harry. 1996. "Reported speech in Swedish". In Janssen and Wurff (eds.), 165–88.
Perrin, Laurent. 1989. "L'interprétation du discours rapporté". In Rubattel, Christian (ed.), *Modèles du discours: recherches actuelles en Suisse romande: Actes des rencontres de linguistique française, Crêt-Bérard, 1988*. Bern: Lang, 337–58.
Perrin, Mona. 1974. "Direct and indirect speech in Mambila". *Journal of Linguistics* 10: 27–37.
Perruchot, Claude. 1975. "Le style indirect libre et la question du sujet dans *Madame Bovary*". In Gothot-Mersch, Claudine et al. (eds.), *La production du sens chez Flaubert*. Paris: Union Générale d'Éditions, 253–85.

Petitjean, André. 1987. "Les fait divers: polyphonie énonciative et hétérogéneité textuelle". *Langue Française* 74:73–96.
Peust, Carsten. 1996. *Indirekte Rede im Neuägyptischen* (=Göttinger Orientforschungen, 4. Reihe: Ägypten 33). Wiesbaden: Harrassowitz.
Peytard, Jean. 1993. "Du 'discours rapporté' au 'discours relaté'". In Peytard, Jean (ed.), 9–33.
Peytard, Jean. 1996. "Discours intérieur vs. discours raporté chez Volochinov / Bakhtine". In Claquin and Mochet (eds.), 9–26.
Peytard, Jean (ed.). 1993. *Les manifestations du "discours relaté" (oral et écrit)* (=Les Cahiers du Centre de Recherche en Linguistique et Enseignement du Français 35). Besançon: Université de Franche-Comté.
Philips, Susan U. 1986. "Reported speech as evidence in an American trial". In Tannen and Alatis (eds.), 154–70.
Pietrzkiewicz-Kobosko, Ewa. 1979. "Il valore stilistico del discorso indiretto libero in italiano". *Kwartalnik Neofilologiczny* 26:55–62.
Pike, Kenneth L. 1968. "Indirect vs. direct discourse in Bariba". In Zale, Eric M. (ed.), *Proceedings of the Conference on Language and Language Behavior, Ann Arbor, Michigan, 17–18 Oct., 1966.* New York: Appleton-Century-Crofts, 165–73.
Pike, Kenneth L. and Lowe, Ivan. 1969. "Pronominal reference in English conversation and discourse — a group theoretical treatment". *Folia Linguistica* 3:68–106.
Pinkster, Harm and Inge Genee (eds.). 1990. *Unity in diversity: papers presented to Simon C. Dik on his 50th birthday.* Dordrecht: Foris.
Pioacano, Chiara and Walter Pecoraro. 1983–86. "Indirect speech in Italian". *Journal of Italian Linguistics* 8,2:67–106.
Plag, Ingo. 1992. "From speech act verb to conjunction: the grammaticalization of *taki* in Sranan". *Journal of Pidgin and Creole Language* 7,1:55–73.
Plank, Frans. 1986. "Über den Personenwechsel und den anderer deiktischer Kategorien in der wiedergegebenen Rede". *Zeitschrift für germanistische Linguistik* 14,3:284–308.
Plann, Susan. 1982. "Indirect questions in Spanish". *Linguistic Inquiry* 13,2:297–312.
Plann, Susan. 1985. "Questions in indirect discourse in Spanish". *Hispania* 68,2:267–72.
Plénat, Marc. 1979. "Sur la grammaire du style indirect libre". *Cahier de Grammaire* (Université de Toulouse-Le Mirail) 1:95–140.
Polzin, Robert. 1981. "Reporting speech in the book of Deuteronomy: toward a compositional analysis of deuteronomic history". In Halpern, Baruch and J. Levenson (eds.), *Traditions in transformation : turning points in biblical faith.* Winona Lake: Eisenbrauns, 192–211.
Prat, Marie-Hélène. 1986. "Quelques particularités du discours rapporté dans *La Parisienne*". *L'Information Grammaticale* 28:38–42.
Prince, Gerald. 1978. "Le discours attributif et le récit". *Poétique* 9:305–13.
Przyluski, Jean. 1934. "Sanskrit *iva*, hittite *iwar*". *Revue Hittite et Asianique* 3:225–6.
Pütz, Herbert. 1989. "Referat — vor allem berichtete Rede — im Deutschen und Norwegischen". In Abraham and Janssen (eds.), 183–223.
Pütz, Herbert. 1994. "Berichtete Rede und ihre Grenzen". *Nordlyd* 22:24–37.

Purkhosrow, Khosrow. 1980. *A contrastive analysis of Persian and English reported speech and the effects of interference in learning English as a foreign language*. Ph.D. thesis, University of Illinois at Urbana-Champaign.
Quincke, Ilse. 1937. *Das Auftreten der subjektiven indirekten Rede im englischen Roman*. Doctoral thesis, Universität zu Köln.
Rama Rao, C. 1972. "Causal use of the quotative morpheme in Dravidian". In Agesthialingom and Shanmugam (eds.), 135–53.
Ramazani, Vaheed K. 1988. *The free indirect mode: Flaubert and the poetics of irony*. Charlottesville: University Press of Virginia.
Rasmussen, Detlef. 1963. *Caesars Commentarii: Stil und Stilwandel am Beispiel der direkten Rede*. Göttingen: Vandenhoeck und Ruprecht.
Rau, Nalini. 1987. "SAY (Abs.) as a quotative marker: evidence for convergence in Kannada and Marathi". In Bashir, Elena, P.E. Hook, and M.M. Deshpande (eds.), *Select papers from SALA-7: South Asian Languages Analysis Roundtable Conference, held in Ann Arbor, Michigan, May 17–19, 1985*. Bloomington: Indiana University Linguistics Club, 269–82.
Ravotas, Doris and Carol Berkenkotter. 1998. "Voices in the text: the use of reported speech in a psychotherapist's notes and initial assessments". *Text* 18:211–40.
Rebera, Basil. 1981. *The Book of Ruth: dialogue and narrative — the function and integration of the two modes in an ancient Hebrew story*. Ph.D. thesis, Macquarie University.
Redeker, Gisela. 1991. "Quotation in discourse". In Hout, Roeland van and Erica Huls (eds.), *Artikelen van de Eerste Sociolinguïstische Conferentie*. Delft: Eburon, 341–355.
Redeker, Gisela. 1996. "Free indirect discourse in newspapers reports". In Cremers, Crit and Marcel den Dikken (eds.), *Linguistics in the Netherlands 1996*. Amsterdam: Benjamins, 221–32.
Reesink, Ger P. 1993. "'Inner speech' in Papuan languages". *Language and Linguistics in Melanesia* 24,2:217–25.
Reichenkron, Günter (ed.). 1957. *Syntactica und Stilistica: Festschrift für Ernst Gamillscheg zum 70. Geburtstag*. Tübingen: Niemeyer.
Reid, Aileen A. 1979. "The dynamics of reported speech in Totonac". In Jones, Linda K. (ed.), *Discourse studies in Mesoamerican languages, Vol. 1: Discussion* (=Publications in Linguistics 58). Dallas: Summer Institute of Linguistics, 293–328.
Reinhart, Tanya. 1975. "Whose main clauses? (Point of view in sentences with parentheticals)". *Harvard Studies in Syntax and Semantics* 1:127–71.
Reinhart, Tanya. 1979. "Reported consciousness and point of view: a comparison between Joyce's *Stephen Hero* and *A Portrait of the Artist as a Young Man*". *PTL: A Journal for Descriptive Poetics and Theory of Literature* 4:63–75.
Reinhart, Tanya. 1983. "Point of view in language: the use of parentheticals". In Rauh, Gisa (ed.), *Essays on deixis*. Tübingen: Narr, 169–94.
Ressel, Gerhard. 1977. "Redetechnik und Erzählstruktur in A.P. Čechovs *Višnevyj Sad*". *Die Welt der Slaven* 22:350–69.
Rey-Debove, Josette. 1967. "Autonymie et métalangage". *Cahiers de Lexicologie* 11,2:15–27.
Rey-Debove, Josette. 1975. "Benveniste et l'autonymie: les verbes délocutifs". *Travaux de Linguistique et de Littérature* 13,1:245–51.

Rey-Debove, Josette. 1971. "Notes sur une interprétation autonymique de la littérarité: le mode du 'comme je dis'". *Littérature* 4: 90–5.
Rey-Debove, Josette. 1978. *Le métalangage: étude linguistique du discours sur le langage.* Paris: Le Robert.
Reyes, Graciela. 1982. "El estilo indirecto en el texto periodístico". *Lingüística Española Actual* 4,1: 1–21
Reyes, Graciela. 1984. *Polifonía textual: la citación en el relato literario* (=Biblioteca Románica Hispánica 2, 340). Madrid: Gredos.
Reyes, Graciela. 1994. *Los procedimientos de cita: citas encubiertas y ecos.* Madrid: Arco.
Rhodes, Richard. 1986. "The semantics of the Ojibwa verbs of speaking". *International Journal of American Linguistics* 52,1: 1–19.
Rice, Keren D. 1986. "Some remarks on direct and indirect discourse in Slave (Northern Athapaskan)". In Coulmas (ed.), 47–76.
Richard, Mark. 1986. "Quotation, grammar, and opacity". *Linguistics and Philosophy* 9,3: 383–403.
Riddle, Elizabeth. 1975. "What they say about *say*". *Studies in the Linguistic Sciences* 5,1: 113–24.
Ridruejo, Emilio. 1987. "Sobre las oraciones interrogativas indirectas deliberativas en español medieval". In In Lüdi, Stricker and Wüst (eds), 365–83.
Rissanen, Matti et al. (eds.). 1992. *History of Englishes: new methods and interpretations in historical linguistics* (=Topics in English Linguistics 10). Berlin: Mouton de Gruyter.
Rivarola, José Luis and Susana Reisz de Rivarola. 1984. "Semiótica del discurso referido". In Schwartz Lerner, Lía and Isaias Lerner (eds.), *Homenaje a Ana María Barrenechea.* Madrid: Castalia, 151–74.
Rivero, María-Luisa. 1994. "On indirect questions, commands, and Spanish quotative *que*". *Linguistic Inquiry* 25,3: 547–54.
Roberts, Hilary. 1981. "Voice in fictional discourse". *Berkeley Linguistics Society* 7: 265–74.
Robertson, Duncan. 1985. "Epic direct discourse". *Pacific Coast Philology* 20,1/2: 70–4.
Rodin, E.L. 1955. *Raznovidnosti nesobstvennoj prjamoj reči v romane Černyševskogo 'Čto delat'* (=Kievskij Gosudarstvennyj Pedagogičeskij Institut imeni A.M. Gor'kogo 1, 1). Kiev: Radjans'ka Škola.
Rodriguez-Pasqués, Petrona Domínguez de. 1968. *El discurso indirecto libre en la novela argentina* (=Studies in Romance Languages and Literature 18). Washington, D.C.: The Catholic University of America.
Roeck, Marijke de. 1994. "A functional typology of speech reports". In Engberg-Pedersen, Elisabeth, Lisbeth Falster Jakobsen and Lone Schack Rasmussen (eds.), *Function and expression in functional grammar* (=Functional Grammar Series 16). Berlin: Mouton de Gruyter, 331–51.
Roeh, Itzhak and Raphael Nir. 1990. "Speech presentation in the Israel radio news: ideological constraints and rhetorical strategies". *Text* 10: 225–44.
Rohrer, Christian. 1976. "Die Vergangenheitstempora des Französischen in der indirekten Rede". *Linguistik und Didaktik* 28: 307–14.
Rohrer, Christian. 1986. "Indirect discourse and 'consecutio temporum'". In Lo Cascio, Vincenzo and Co Vet (eds.), *Temporal structure in sentence and discourse* (=Groningen-Amsterdam Studies in Semantics 5). Dordrecht: Foris, 79–97.

Rojas, Mario. 1980/1. "Tipologia del discurso del personaje en el texto narrativo". *Dispositio* 5/6: 15–16, 19–55.
Rojtman, Betty. 1980. "Désengagement du Je dans le discours indirect". *Poétique* 11: 90–107.
Romaine, Suzanne and Deborah Lange. 1991. "The use of *like* as a marker of reported speech and thought: a case of grammaticalization in progress". *American Speech* 66,3: 227–79.
Ron, Moshe. 1981. "Free indirect discourse, mimetic language games, and the subject of fiction". *Poetics Today* 2,2: 17–39.
Roncador, Manfred von. 1988. *Zwischen direkter und indirekter Rede: nichtwörtliche direkte Rede, erlebte Rede, logophorische Konstruktionen und Verwandtes* (=Linguistische Arbeiten 192). Tübingen: Niemeyer.
Roncador, Manfred von. 1992. "Types of logophoric marking in African languages". *Journal of African Languages and Linguistics* 13: 163–82.
Roncador, Manfred von. 2002. "Zur Bindung der Logophoren: Fallstudien aus Gursprachen". In Bublitz, Wolfram, Manfred von Roncador and Heinz Vater (eds.), *Philologie, Typologie und Sprachstruktur: Festschrift für Winfried Boeder zum 65. Geburtstag — Philology, typology and language structure: Festschrift for Winfried Boeder on the occasion of his 65th birthday*. Frankfurt/Main: Lang, 171–90.
Rosier, Laurence. 1993a. "Le discours direct libre: béquille théorique ou objet d'étude grammaticale?" *Revue de Linguistique Romane* 57: 361–71.
Rosier, Laurence. 1993b. "L'incise dit-elle ou l'attribution du dire en discours rapporté". *Actes du XXe Congrès International de Linguistique et de Philologie Romanes*, tome 1, 657–67.
Rosier, Laurence. 1993c. "Vers une extension de la notion de subordination: l'exemple du discours indirect" *Travaux de Linguistique* 27: 81–96.
Rosier, Laurence. 1997a. "Discours rapporté et psychomécanique du langage: mariage d'amour ou de raison?" In Carvalho, Paolo de (ed.), *Psychomécanique du langage: problèmes et perspectives: Actes du 7e Colloque International de Psychomécanique du Langage (Córdoba, 2–4 juin 1994)*. Paris: Champion, 277–87.
Rosier, Laurence. 1997b. "Entre binarité et continuum, une nouvelle approche théorique du discours rapporté?" *Modèles Linguistiques* 18,1: 7–16.
Rosier, Laurence. 1999. *Le discours rapporté: histoire, théories, pratiques*. Paris: Duculot.
Rosier, Laurence. 2000. "Le discours rapporté: histoire, théories, pratiques: présentation". In Mellet and Vuillaume (eds.), 1–8.
Ross, Claudia. 1976/7. "Reporting styles as discourse strategies: a study in Japanese and English". *Papers in Japanese Linguistics* 5: 243–59.
Rumsey, Alan. 1994. "On the transitivity of 'say' constructions in Bunuba". *Australian Journal of Linguistics* 14,2: 137–53.
Russel, Maria. 1989. "Eine Klassifikation redebewertender Adverbiale". In Reiter, Norbert (ed.), *Sprechen und Hören: Akten des 23. Linguistischen Kolloquiums, Berlin 1988* (=Linguistische Arbeiten 222). Tübingen: Niemeyer, 451–60.
Ryan, Marie-Laure. 1981. "When 'je' is 'un autre': fiction, quotation and the performative analysis". *Poetics Today* 2,2: 127–55.

Rychner, Jean. 1987. "Description subjective et discours indirect libre: observation sur leurs formes au XIIe siècle". In Lüdi, Stricker and Wüst (eds), 221–36
Rychner, Jean. 1988. "Messages et discours double". In North, Sally B. (ed.), *Studies in medieval french language and literature presented to Brian Woledge in honour of his 80th birthday* (=Publications Romanes et Françaises 180). Genève: Droz, 145–61.
Rychner, Jean. 1989a. "Le discours subjectif dans les *Lais* de Marie de France: à propos d'une étude récente". *Revue de Linguistique Romane* 53:57–83.
Rychner, Jean. 1989b. "Le monologue de discours indirect dans quelques récits français des XIIe et XIIIe siècles". In Antonelli, Roberto et al. (eds.), *Miscellanea di studi in onore di Aurelio Roncaglia a cinquant'anni dalla sua laurea*. Modena: Mucchi, vol. 4, 1187–97.
Rychner, Jean. 1990. *La narration des sentiments, des pensées et des discours*. Genève: Droz.
Sabban, Annette. 1978. "Verben der Redeeinleitung im Französichen und im Deutschen: ein Beitrag zum Problem der Redeerwähnung". *Zeitschrift für französische Sprache und Literatur* 88:28–63.
Sakita, Tomoko I. 1996. "Style choice of reporting discourse related to sentence length and complexities." *KLS: Kansai Linguistic Society* 16:89–99.
Sakita, Tomoko I. 1998. *Reporting discourse in English: discourse, cognition, and consciousness*. Ph.D. thesis, Kyoto University.
Salkie, Raphael and Susan Reed. 1997. "Time reference in reported speech". *English Language and Linguistics* 1,2:319–48.
Salmon, E.T. 1931. "A note on the subordinate clauses in oratio obliqua". *The Classical Review* 45,5:173.
Salverda de Grave, Jean Jacques. 1927. "Indirecte rede in onafhankelike zinnen". *Neophilologus* 12:161–6.
Sanders, José and Gisela Redeker. 1996. "Perspective and the representation of speech and thought in narrative discourse". In Fauconnier, Gilles and Eve Sweetser (eds.), *Spaces, worlds, and grammar*. Chicago: University of Chicago Press, 290–317.
Sangmeister, Ursula. 1978. *Die Ankündigung direkter Rede im 'nationalen' Epos der Römer* (=Beiträge zur klassischen Philologie 86). Meisenheim/Glahn: Hain.
Savova, Marta. 1983. "Tekst i poluprjakata reč". *Philologia* 12/13:83–90.
Savran, George W. 1988. *Telling and retelling: quotation in biblical narrative*. Bloomington: Indiana University.
Saxena, Anju. 1988. "On syntactic convergence: the case of the verb 'say' in Tibeto-Burman". *Berkeley Linguistics Society* 14:375–88.
Saxena, Anju. 1995. "Unidirectional grammaticalization: diachronic and cross-linguistic evidence". *Sprachtypologie und Universalienforschung* 48,4:350–72.
Schank, Gerd. 1989. *Redeerwähnung im Interview: strukturelle und konversationelle Analyse an vier Interviewtypen* (=Sprache der Gegenwart 78). Düsseldorf: Schwann.
Scheffler, Israel. 1954. "An inscriptional approach to indirect quotation". *Analysis* 14:83–90.
Scheffler, Israel. 1955. "On synonymy and indirect discourse". *Philosophy of Science* 22:39–44.
Scheidweiler, Gaston. 1980. "Das Verb 'sollen' in der indirekten Rede — ein Sonderfall". *Muttersprache* 90:36–42.

Scheidweiler, Gaston. 1991. "Die Einblendung der erlebten Rede in die indirekte Rede: zur Verwendung des Indikativs Präsens in präteritalem Kontext". *Muttersprache* 101: 338–47.

Scherer, Baptist. 1935. *Zur Einführung der direkten Rede in neuhochdeutscher Prosa.* Doctoral thesis, Universität Marburg.

Scherner, Maximilian. 1976. "Kommunikationsebenen und Texteinbettung: zur Textlinguistik der Rededarstellung und einiger textueller Rahmenangaben". In *Wirkendes Wort* 26:292–304.

Schlicher, John J. 1905. "The moods of indirect quotation". *American Journal of Philology* 26:60–88.

Schmid, Wolf. 1968. "Zur Erzähltechnik und Bewußtseinsdarstellung in Dostoevskijs 'Večnyj muž'". *Die Welt der Slaven* 13:294–306.

Schmitt, Andreas W. 1995. *Die direkten Reden der Massen in Lucans Pharsalia* (=Studien zur klassischen Philologie 95). Frankfurt/Main: Lang.

Schmitt-Ackermann, Sylvia. 1996. *Kohärenz in Redewiedergaben: eine empirische Untersuchung zur Verständlichkeit von Redewiedergaben auf textueller Ebene* (=Sammlung Groos 62). Heidelberg: Groos.

Schoeller, Willy. 1924. *Die erlebte Rede im Deutschen.* Doctoral thesis, Universität Köln.

Schourup, Lawrence. 1982. "Quoting with *go* 'say'". *American Speech* 57,2:148–9.

Schuelke, Gertrude L. 1958. "'Slipping' in indirect discourse". *American Speech* 33:90–8.

Schulte, W. 1970. *Epischer Dialog: Untersuchungen zur Gesprächstechnik in frühmittelhochdeutscher Epik.* Doctoral thesis, Universität Bonn.

Schwanitz, Dietrich. 1978. "Zwei Beispiele zur Erlebten Rede und ihrer Entstehungsgeschichte". *Germanisch-Romanische Monatsschrift* 59:349–53.

Schwartzkopff, Werner. 1909. *Rede und Redeszene in der deutschen Erzählung bis Wolfram von Eschenbach.* Berlin: Mayer und Müller.

Schwieder, Adolphe. 1890. *Le discours indirect dans Crestien de Troyes* (=Wissenschaftliche Beilage zum Programm des Andreas-Realgymnasiums zu Berlin 93). Berlin: Gaertner.

Scollon, Ron. 1998. *Mediated discourse as social interaction: a study of news discourse.* New York: Longman.

Scollon, Ron and Suzie Scollon. 1997. "Point of view and citation: fourteen Chinese and English versions of the 'same' news story". *Text* 17:83–125.

Scorza, Sylvio J. 1973. *Indirect discourse and related phenomena in Xenophon.* Ph.D. thesis, University of Michigan.

Segal, Naomi. 1990. "'Style indirect libre' to Stream-of-Consciousness: Flaubert, Joyce, Schnitzler, Woolf". In Collier, Peter and Judy Davies (eds.), *Modernism and the European unconscious.* Cambridge: Polity Press, 94–114.

Seiler, Hansjakob. 1966/7. "Zur Erforschung des lexikalischen Feldes". In *Sprachnorm, Sprachpflege, Sprachkritik* (=Jahrbuch des Instituts für Deutsche Sprache). Düsseldorf: Schwann, 268–86.

Seiler, Hansjakob. 1967. "Toward an exploration of the lexical field". In *To honor Roman Jakobson: essays on the occasion of his seventieth birthday.* The Hague: Mouton, 1783–98. (=Seiler 1966/7)

Sellars, Wilfried. 1969. "Some problems about belief". In Davidson, Donald and K.J. Jaakko Hintikka (eds.), *Words and objections: essays on the work of W. v. Quine*. Dordrecht: Reidel, 168–205.
Sells, Peter. 1987. "Aspects of logophoricity". *Linguistic Inquiry* 18,3:445–79.
Semino, Elena, Michael H. Short and Jonathan Culpeper. 1997. "Using a corpus to test a model of speech and thought presentation". *Poetics* 25:17–43.
Serzisko, Fritz. 1987. "The verb 'to say' in Ik (Kuliak)". *Afrikanistische Arbeitspapiere* 11:67–91.
Shapiro, Marianne. 1984. "How narrators report speech". *Language and Style* 17:67–78.
Shaw, Philip. 1992. "Reasons for the correlation of voice, tense and sentence function in reporting verbs". *Applied Linguistics* 13:302–19.
Shih-ch'ang, Wu. 1933. "A new interpretation of the word *yin* in Shih ching". *Yenching Journal of Chinese Studies* 13:153–70.
Shirt, David J. "Les 'verba cogitandi' dans les construction interrogatives en ancien français". *Revue de Linguistique Romaine* 39:351–80.
Short, Michael H. 1988. "Speech presentation, the novel and the press". In Peer, Willie van (ed.), *The taming of the text: explorations in language, literature and culture*. London: Routledge, 61–81.
Short, Michael H., Elena Semino and Jonathan Culpeper. 1996. "Using a corpus for stylistic research: speech and thought presentation". In Thomas, Jenny and Michael H. Short (eds.), *Using corpora for language research: studies in the honour of Geoffrey Leech*. London: Longman, 110–31.
Short, Michael H., Elena Semino and Martin Wynne. 1997. "A (free direct) reply to Paul Simpson's discourse". *Journal of Literary Semantics* 26:219–28.
Siefer, Claus. 1982. "Die indirekte Rede im Deutschunterricht der Sekundarstufe 1". *Der Deutschunterricht* 34,3:34–48.
Silverstein, Michael. 1985. "The culture of language in Chinookan narrative texts; or, on saying that ... in Chinook". In Nichols, Johanna and Anthony C. Woodbury (eds.), *Grammar inside and outside the clause*. Cambridge: Cambridge University Press, 132–71.
Simpson, Paul. 1997. "A quadrant model for the study of speech and thought presentation". *Journal of Literary Semantics* 26:211–18.
Slembrouck, Stefaan. 1986. "Towards a description of speech presentation and speech reportage in newspaper language". In Simon-Vandenbergen, Anne M. (ed.), *Aspects of style in British newspapers* (=Studia Germanica Gandensia 9). Gent: Seminarie voor Duitse Taalkunde, 44–115.
Slembrouck, Stefaan. 1992. "The Parliamentary Hansard 'verbatim' report: the written construction of spoken discourse". *Language and Literature* 1:101–19.
Smyth, Ron. 1995. "Conceptual perspective-taking and children's interpretation of pronouns in reported speech". *Journal of Child Language* 22:171–87.
Söderlind, Johannes. 1989. "The interior monologue: a linguistic approach". In Bessière, Jean (ed.), *Fiction, narratologie, texte, genre* (=Actes du symposium de l'Association Internationale de Littérature Comparée, XIème Congrès international, Vol. 2). New York: Lang, 23–31.

Sokolov, S. A. 1978. "Sintaktičeskie funkcii konstrukcij s prjamoj reč'u v tureckom jazyke". *Sovjetskaja Tjurkologija* 2:41–7.
Sokolova, Ljudmila A. 1957. "K voprosu o nesobstvenno-prjamoj reči". *Učenye Zapiski — Tomskij Gosudarstvennyj Pedagogičeskij Institut* 16.
Sokolova, Ljudmila A. 1961. "O stilističeskix vozmožnostjax nesobstvenno-prjamoj reči". *Učenye Zapiski — Tomskij Gosudarstvennyj Pedagogičeskij Institut* 19,2.
Sokolova, Ljudmila A. 1968. *Nesobstvenno-avtorskaja (nesobstvenno-prjamaja) reč' kak stilističeskaja kategorija*. Tomsk: Izdatel'stvo Tomskogo Universiteta.
Solfjeld, Kåre. 1983. "Indikativ in der indirekten Rede: ein Vergleich Deutsch-Norwegisch". *Zielsprache Deutsch* 1983,1:41–7.
Solfjeld, Kåre. 1989. *Indikativische Tempora in der indirekten Rede: Strukturvergleich deutsch–norwegisch*. Heidelberg: Groos.
Sommerfeldt, Karl-Ernst. 1972. "Zur Parteilichkeit bei der Wiedergabe vermittelter Äußerungen". *Zeitschrift für Phonetik, Sprachwissenschaft und Kommunikationsforschung* 25:366–95.
Sommerfeldt, Karl-Ernst. 1983. "Wie PAP meldet..." *Sprachpflege: Zeitschrift für gutes Deutsch* 32:177–9.
Sommerfeldt, Karl-Ernst. 1990. "Zum Modusgebrauch in der indirekten Rede — Regel und Realität". *Deutsch als Fremdsprache* 27,6:337–42.
Sonnek, Franz. 1940. "Die Einführung der direkten Rede in den epischen Texten". *Zeitschrift für Assyriologie und vorderasiatische Archäologie* 46:225–35.
Soutar, Jean and Kenneth L. Pike 1982. *Texts illustrating the analysis of direct versus indirect quotations in Bariba* (=Publications in the Language Data Africa Series 19). Dallas: Summer Institute of Linguistics.
Spencer, John. 1965. "A note on the steady monologue of the interior". *A Review of English Literature* 6,2:32–41.
Spieker, Edward H. 1884. "On direct speech introduced by a conjunction". *American Journal of Philology* 5:221–7.
Spitzer, Leo. 1921. "Zur stilistischen Bedeutung des Imperfekts der Rede". *Germanisch-Romanische Monatsschrift* 9:58–60.
Spitzer, Leo. 1924. "Romanisch *facit 'er sagt' (Zur Bewertung des 'Schöpferischen' in der Sprache)". *Archivum Romanicum* 8,4:349–85.
Spitzer, Leo. 1928. "Zur Entstehung der sog. 'erlebten Rede'". *Germanisch-Romanische Monatsschrift* 16:327–32.
Spitzer, Leo. 1939. "Verlebendigende direkte Rede als Mittel der Charakterisierung". *Vox Romanica* 4:65–86.
Spitzer, Leo. 1946. "Sur le discours direct lié (DDL)". *Bulletin Linguistique* (Bucarest) 14:17–45.
Stanley, Carol. 1982. "Direct and reported speech in Tikar narrative texts". *Studies in African Linguistics* 13,1:31–52.
Stanzel, Franz K. 1959. "Episches Präteritum, erlebte Rede, historisches Präsens". *Deutsche Vierteljahresschrift für Literaturwissenschaft und Geistesgeschichte* 33:1–12.

Stanzel, Franz K. 1991. "Zur Problemgeschichte der 'Erlebte Rede': eine Vorbemerkung zu Yasushi Suzukis Beitrag 'Erlebte Rede und der Fall Jenniger'". *Germanisch-Romanische Monatsschrift* 41,1:1–4.

Stanzel, Franz K. 1995. "Begegnungen mit Erlebter Rede 1950–1990". In Kullmann, Dorothea (ed.), 15–27.

Starke, Günter. 1985. "Zum Modusgebrauch bei der Redewiedergabe in der Presse". *Sprachpflege* 34:163–5.

Starovojtova, Ol'ga A. 1988. *Konstrukcii s prjamoj rec'ju v drevnerusskix pamjatikax povestvovatel'nogo zanra konca XIV — nacala XVI vekov.* Leningrad Universitet.

Stein, Dieter and Susan Wright (eds.). 1995. *Subjectivity and subjectivisation: linguistic perspectives.* Cambridge: Cambridge University Press.

Stein, Ellen. 1990. "*I'm sittin' there*: another new quotative?" *American Speech* 65,4:303.

Stein, Oswald. 1987. "Wie Gesagtes berichtet wird: zur indirekten Rede im Englischen". *Praxis des neusprachlichen Unterrichts* 34,2:159–67.

Steinberg, Günther. 1971. *Erlebte Rede: ihre Eigenart und ihre Formen in neuerer deutscher, französischer und englischer Erzählliteratur*, 2 vols. (=Göppinger Arbeiten zur Germanistik 50, 51). Göppingen: Kümmerle.

Steinberg, Günther. 1972. "Zur erlebten Rede in Michel Butors 'La Modification'". *Vox Romanica* 31:334–64.

Steinrück, Martin. 1992. *Rede und Kontext: zum Verhältnis von Person und Erzähler in frühgriechischen Texten.* Bonn: Habelt.

Stempel, Wolf-Dieter. 1972. "Perspektivische Rede in der französischen Literatur des Mittelalters". In Leube, Eberhard and Ludwig Schrader (eds.), *Interpretation und Vergleich: Festschrift für Walter Pabst.* Berlin: Schmidt, 310–30.

Stephens, Laurence. 1985. "Indirect questions in Old Latin: syntactic and pragmatic factors in conditioning modal shift". *Illinois Classical Studies* 10:195–214.

Sternberg, Meir. 1982a. "Point of view and the indirections of direct speech". *Language and Style* 15,2:67–117.

Sternberg, Meir. 1982b. "Proteus in quotation-land: mimesis and the forms of reported discourse". *Poetics Today* 3,2:107–56.

Sternberg, Meir. 1991. "How indirect discourse means: syntax, semantics, poetics, pragmatics". In Sell, Roger D. (ed.), *Literary pragmatics.* London: Routledge, 62–93.

Steube, Anita. 1983. "Indirekte Rede und Zeitverlauf". In Ruzicka, Rudolf and Wolfgang Motsch (eds.), *Untersuchungen zur Semantik* (=Studia Grammatica 22). Berlin: Akademieverlag, 121–68.

Steube, Anita. 1984. "Frage und Befehl in erlebter Rede". *Linguistische Arbeitsberichte* 44:40–6.

Steube, Anita. 1985. "Erlebte Rede aus linguistischer Sicht". *Zeitschrift für Germanistik* 6:389–406.

Steube, Anita. 1986. "Kontext und mögliche Welt: eine Untersuchung der indirekten Rede". In Mey, Jacob L. (ed.), *Language and discourse: test and protest.* Amsterdam: Benjamins, 327–72.

Strauch, Gérard. 1972. "Contribution à l'étude sémantique des verbes introducteurs du discours indirect". *Recherches Anglaises et Américaines* 5:226–42.

Strauch, Gérard. 1974. "De quelques interprétations récentes du style indirect libre". *Récherches Anglaises et Américaines* 7:40–73.
Strauch, Gérard. 1975. "Problèmes et méthodes de l'étude linguistique du style indirect libre". *Tradition et innovation: littérature et paralittérature: Actes du Congrés de Nancy 1972.* Paris: Didier, 409–28.
Strauch, Gérard. 1984. "De la 'littéralité' du discours rapporté". *Recherches Anglaises et Américaines* 17:159–82.
Strauss, Dieter. 1972. *Redegattungen und Redearten im Rolandslied.* Göppingen: Kümmerle.
Stross, Brian. 1972. "Speaking of speaking: Tenejapa Tzeltal metalinguistics". In Baumann, Richard and Joel Sherzer (eds.), *Explorations in the ethnography of speaking.* Cambridge: Cambridge University Press, 213–39.
Subbarao, Karumuri V. et al. 1983. "Verb *say* in South Asian languages". In Mukerjee, Aditi (ed.), *Language change and language variation.* Hyderabad: Osmania University Publications.
Suñer, Margarita. 1992. "Indirect questions and the structure of CP: some consequences". In Campos, Héctor and Fernando Martínez-Gil (eds.), *Current studies in Spanish linguistics.* Washington, D.C.: Georgetown University Press, 283–312.
Suñer, Margarita. 1993. "About indirect questions and semiquestions". *Linguistics and Philosophy* 16:45–77.
Suñer, Margarita. 2000. "The syntax of direct quotes with special reference to Spanish and English". *Natural Language and Linguistic Theory* 18,3:525–78
Suñer, Margarita and José Padilla-Rivera. 1987. "Sequence of tenses and the subjunctive again". *Hispania* 70:634–42.
Suzuki, Yasushi. 1988a. "Die erlebte Rede in der Nonfiktion". *Doitsu Bungaku* 80:80–91.
Suzuki, Yasushi. 1988b. "Erlebte Rede und Innerer Monolog im Ich-Roman: zu einer Darstellung dieses Problems in der Duden-Grammatik (3. und 4. Auflage)". *Tsukuba Daigaku Gengo-bunka Ronshu* 25:37–50.
Suzuki, Yasushi. 1991. "Erlebte Rede und der Fall Jenniger". *Germanisch-Romanische Monatsschrift* 41,1:5–12.
Suzuki, Yasushi. 1995. "Die erlebte Rede in pragmatischer Kommunikation — Im Vergleich mit 'Echoausdrücken'". *Energeia* 20:52–66.
Suzuki, Yasushi. 1999. "Die schwer erkennbare 'erlebte Rede' in *Buddenbrooks*". *Doitso Bungaku* 103:162–9.
Suzuki, Yasushi. 2000. "Erlebte Rede versus Indirekte Rede — Ignaz Bubis zitiert Jennigers umstrittene Passage". *Zeitschrift für Angewandte Linguistik* 33:91–100.
Swiggers, Pierre. 1982. "Frege on reference in quotation". *Linvisticae Investigationes* 6,1:201–4.
Tannen, Deborah. 1986. "Introducing constructed dialogue in Greek and American conversational and literary narrative". In Coulmas (ed.), 311–32.
Tannen, Deborah. 1989. *Talking voices: repetition, dialogue, and imagery in conversational discourse* (=Studies in Interactional Sociolinguistics 6). Cambridge: Cambridge University Press, 98–133.
Tannen, Deborah and James E. Alatis (eds.). 1986. *Language and linguistics: the interdependence of theory, data, and application* (=Georgetown University Round Table on Language and Linguistics 1985). Washington, D.C.: Georgetown University Press.

Tarrant, Dorothy. 1955. "Plato's use of extended *oratio obliqua*". *The Classical Quarterly* 5:222–4.

Temin, Marc. 1975. "The relational sense of indirect discourse". *Journal of Philosophy* 72,11:287–306.

Terrell, G. 1904. "The apodosis of the unreal condition in *oratio obliqua* in Latin". *American Journal of Philology* 25:59–73.

Thomason, Richmond H. 1977. "Indirect discourse is not quotational". *The Monist* 60:340–54.

Thompson, Geoff. 1994. *Reporting* (=Collins COBUILD English Guides 5). London: Harper and Collins.

Thompson, Geoff. 1996. "Voices in the text: discourse perspectives on language reports". *Applied Linguistics* 17,4:501–30.

Thompson, Geoff and Yiyun Ye 1991. "Evaluation in the reporting verbs used in academic papers". *Applied Linguistics* 12:365–82.

Tietze, Andreas. 1959. "Die Eingliederung der wörtlichen Rede im Türkischen". *Wiener Zeitschrift für die Kunde des Morgenlandes* 55:89–121.

Tietze, Andreas. 1962. "Erlebte Rede im Türkischen". *Oriens* 15:337–44.

Tixonov, Sergej E. 1987. *Prjamaja reč' i prjamoe vyskazyvanie v xudožestvennom stroe narodnoj liriki*. Voronež: Gosudarstvennyj Universitet.

Tobler, Adolf. 1886. "Direkte Rede durch *que* eingeleitet — Direkte Rede die indirekte Rede ablösend". In Tobler, Adolf, *Vermischte Beiträge zur französischen Grammatik I*, Leipzig: Hirzel, 216–21 (2nd edition 1902, 264–70).

Tobler, Adolf. 1900. "Mischung direkter und indirekter Rede in der Frage". *Zeitschrift für romanische Philologie* 24:130–2.

Todemann, Friedrich. 1930. "Die erlebte Rede im Spanischen". *Romanische Forschungen* 44:103–84.

Traugott, Elizabeth Closs. 1991. "English speech act verbs: a historical perspective". In Waugh, Linda R. and Stephen Rudy (eds.), *New vistas in grammar: invariance and variation* (=Current Issues in Linguistic Theory 49). Amsterdam: Benjamins, 387–406.

Turewicz, Kamila. 1997. "Cognitive grammar for contrastive linguistics: a case study of indirect speech in English and Polish". In Hickey, Raymond and Stanislaw Puppel (eds.), *Language history and linguistic modelling: a Festschrift for Jacek Fisiak on his 60th birthday*. Berlin: Mouton de Gruyter, 1859–86.

Uchida, Seji. 1997. "Immediate contexts and reported speech". *University College London Working Papers in Linguistics* 9:149–75.

Ullendorff, Edward. 1974. "Animistic expressions and some other aspects of direct speech in Amharic". In *IV Congresso Internazionale di Studi Etiopici, Roma 10–15 aprile 1972, Tomo II: Sezione Linguistica* (=Problemi Attuali di Scienzia e di Cultura, Quaderno 191). Roma: Academia Nazionale dei Lincei, 269–74.

Ullmann, Stephen. 1957. "Reported speech and internal monologue in Flaubert". In Ullmann, Stephen, *Style in the French novel*. Cambridge: Cambridge University Press, 94–120.

Ulvestad, Bjarne. 1955. "Object clauses without 'daß' dependent on negative governing clauses in modern German". *Monatshefte für deutschen Unterricht, deutsche Sprache und Literatur* 47:329–38.

Ulvestad, Bjarne. 1956a. "A note on object clauses without 'daß' after negative governing verbs". *Monatshefte für deutschen Unterricht, deutsche Sprache und Literatur* 48:273–6.
Ulvestad, Bjarne. 1956b. "Gliedsätze mit und ohne 'daß' im modernen Deutschen". *Revue des Langues Vivantes* 22:203–13.
Urban, Greg. 1984. "Speech about speech in speech about action". *Journal of American Folklore* 97:310–28.
Urban, Greg. 1993. "The represented functions of speech in Shokleng myth". In Lucy (ed.), 241–59.
Urtel, Friedrich. 1884. *Über den homerischen Gebrauch des Optativs der abhängigen Rede* (=Beilage zum Jahresbericht des Gymnasiums zu Weimar 616). Weimar: Hofdruckerei.
Ustrickij, I. B. 1949. "Prjamaja i kosvennaja reč'". In Barxudarov, Stepan G. (ed.), *Metodičeskie razrabotki po grammatike*. Moskva : Učpedgiz, 330–43.
Ustrickij, I. B. and G. R. Tukumcev. 1938. "Soderžanie i metodika temy: prjamaja i kosvennaja reč'". *Russkij Jazyk v Škole* 3,2:69–84.
Vasseur, Marie-Thérèse. 1977. "'Il dit qu'elle arrive / Il dit: 'Elle arrive': variation dans l'indication de la fonction". *Langue Française* 33:71–6.
Verdín Díaz, Guillermo. 1970. *Introducción al estilo indirecto libre en español* (=Revista de Filología Española, Anejo 91). Madrid: C. S. I. C.
Verschoor, Jan A. 1959. *Étude de grammaire historique et de style sur le style direct et les styles indirects en français*. Groningen: V. R. B. Kleine.
Verschueren, Jef. 1977. *The analysis of speech act verbs: theoretical preliminaries*. Bloomington: Indiana University Linguistics Club.
Verschueren, Jef. 1980. *On speech act verbs* (=Pragmatics and Beyond 4). Amsterdam: Benjamins. (=Verschueren 1977)
Verschueren, Jef. 1984. "Some methodological reflections of the comparative study of basic linguistic action verbs, illustrated with reference to the Polynesian languages". In Daems, Fr. and Louis Goossens (eds.), *Een Spyeghel voor G. Jo Steenbergen: Huldealbum aangeboden bij zijn emeritaat*. Leuven: Acco, 393–411.
Vetters, Carl. 1989. "Le style indirect libre". In Vetters, Carl, *Temps et discours*. Antwerpen: Universiteit Antwerpen, 30–70.
Vetters, Carl. 1994. "Free indirect speech in French". In Vet, Co and Carl Vetters (eds.), *Tense and aspect in discourse* (=Trends in Linguistics, Studies and Monographs 75). Berlin: Mouton de Gruyter, 179–225.
Vincent, Diane. 1989. "Les particules d'attaque d'énoncés de conversations rapportées en discours direct". Weydt, Harald (ed.), *Sprechen mit Partikeln*. Berlin: Mouton de Gruyter, 592–600.
Vincent, Diane and Sylvie Dubois. 1996. "A study of the use of reported speech in spoken language". In Arnold, Jennifer et al. (eds.), *Sociolinguistic variation: data, theory, and analysis*. Stanford: Center for the Study of Language and Information, 361–74.
Violi, Patrizia. 1986. "Unspeakable sentences and speakable text". *Semiotica* 60,3–4:361–78.
Viorel, Elena. 1986. "Der Modusgebrauch in der indirekten Rede — ein kontroverses Problem". In Polenz, Peter von, Johannes Erben and Jan Goossens (eds.), *Sprachnormen: lösbare und unlösbare Probleme. Kontroversen um die neuere deutsche Sprach-*

geschichte. Dialektologie und Soziolinguistik: Die Kontroverse um die Mundartforschung (=Kontroversen, alte und neue: Akten des VII. Internationalen Germanisten-Kongresses 1985, Vol 4). Tübingen: Niemeyer, 60–3.

Vita, Nicola. 1955. "Genesi del 'discorso rivissuto' e suo uso nella narrativa italiana". *Cultura Neolatina* 15,1–2: 5–34.

Vlatten, Andrea. 1997. *Quotatives, reported speech, and constructed dialogue in everyday German conversation — a conversation analytic perspective*. Ph.D. thesis, University of Texas at Austin.

Vogel, Roos. 1996. "From consecutio temporum to Aktionsart". *Lingua e Stile* 31: 27–48.

Vogelzang, Marianna E. 1990. "Patterns introducing direct speech in Akkadian literary texts". *Journal of Cuneiform Studies* 42: 50–70.

Vološinov, Valentin N. 1971. "Reported speech". In Matejka and Pomorska (eds.), 149–75 (="Ekspozicija problemy čužoj reč'" and "Kosvennaja reč', prjamaja reč' i ix modifikacii", in Vološinov 1972, 113–38).

Vološinov, Valentin N. 1972. *Marksizm i filosofija jazyka: osnovnye problemy sociologičeskogo metoda v nauke o jazyke* (=Janua Linguarum Series Anastatica 5) (Repr. of the 2nd edition Leningrad 1930). The Hague: Mouton

Vološinov, Valentin N. 1973. "Indirect discourse, direct discourse, and their modifications". In Vološinov, Valentin N. (translated by Matejka, Ladislav and I.R. Titanik), *Marxism and the philosophy of language* (=Vološinov 1972). New York: Seminar, 125–59.

Voorhoeve, Jan. 1979. "Het logoforisch pronomen in Ngwo". *Glot* 2: 5–14.

Voorhoeve, Jan. 1980. "Le pronom logophorique et son importance pour la reconstruction du proto-bantou". *Sprache und Geschichte in Afrika* 2: 173–87.

Voort, Cok van der. 1986. "Hoe vrij is de vrije indirecte rede?" *Forum der Letteren* 27,4: 241–55.

Vouk, Vera. 1967. "Comparison of speech forms used in utterances and references to utterances". *English Studies* 48: 156–63.

Vowles, Guy R. 1943. "Unreal conditions in 'Erlebte Rede' in German". *The German Quarterly* 16: 23–31.

Vries, Lourens J. de. 1990. "Some remarks on direct quotation in Kombai". In Pinkster and Genee (eds.), 291–309.

Vuillaume, Marcel. 1996. "Les variétés de discours indirect libre". *Travaux du Cercle de Linguistique de Nice* 18: 51–67.

Vuillaume, Marcel. 1998. "Le discours indirect libre et le passé simple". In Vogeleer, Svetlana et al. (eds.) *Temps et discours*. Leuven: Peeters, 191–201.

Vuillaume, Marcel. 2000. "La signalisation du style indirect libre". In Mellet and Vuillaume (eds.), 107–30.

Vykoupil, Susanna. 1995. "Erlebte Rede und verwandte Verfahren zur Bewußtseinsdarstellung in deutschen Übersetzungen von *Prestuplenie i nakazanie* nach 1924". In Kullmann, Dorothea (ed.), 179–220.

Wade, Elizabeth and Herbert H. Clark 1993. "Reproduction and demonstration in quotations". *Journal of Memory and Language* 32,6: 805–19.

Wagner, Burkhardt. 1972. *Innenbereich und Äußerung: Flaubertsche Typen indirekter Darstellung und Grundtypen der Erlebten Rede* (=Freiburger Schriften zur romanischen Philologie 18). München: Fink.
Waley, Arthur and Charles H. Armbruster 1934. "The verb 'to say' as an auxiliary in Africa and China". *Bulletin of the School of Oriental and African Studies* 7,3:573–6.
Walther, Helmut. 1992. "Unidirekte Rede". *Der Sprachdienst* 36:144.
Waltz, Carolyn H. 1976/7. "Some observations on Guanano dialogue". In Longacre and Woods (eds.), vol. 3, 67–109.
Walzel, Oskar. 1924. "Von 'erlebter Rede'". *Zeitschrift für Bücherfreunde* 16:17–28. (also in Walzel, Oskar. 1926. *Das wortkunstwerk, mittel seiner erforschung*. Leipzig: Quelle und Meyer, 207–30)
Ware, Jan. 1993. "Quote formulae in *The Final Diagnosis*". *Journal of Translation and Text Linguistics* 6,2:161–78.
Waugh, Linda R. 1995. "Reported speech in journalistic discourse: the relation of function and text". *Text* 15,1:129–73.
Weber, Hans. 1956. "Die indirekten Tempora des Deutschen und Französischen". *Vox Romanica* 15:1–38.
Wege, Heike. 1994. *Stilisierungen: nachgewiesen anhand von Figurenrede in kinder- und jugendliterarischen Texten zum Thema "Ausländische Arbeitsimmigranten"*. Doctoral thesis, Pädagogische Hochschule, Erfurt/Mühlhausen.
Weider, Eric. 1992. *Konjunktiv und indirekte Rede — mit einem Vorwort von M. Philipp* (=Göppinger Arbeiten zur Germanistik 569). Göppingen: Kümmerle.
Weinberg, Henry H. 1981. "Irony and 'style indirect libre' in *Madame Bovary*". *Canadian Review of Comparative Literature* 8,1:1–9.
Weisgerber, Jean. 1970. "The use of quotations in recent literature". *Comparative Literature* 22:36–45.
Wendell, Dag. 1986. "The use of reported speech and quote formula selection in Kagan Kalagan". *Studies in Philippine Linguistics* 6,1:1–79.
Whybray, R. N. "The identification and use of quotations in Ecclesiastes". In Emerton, John A. (ed.), *International Organization for the Study of the Old Testament, Congress Volume, Vienna 1980* (=Vetus Testamentum, Supplements 32). Leiden: Brill, 435–51.
Wiehl, Peter. 1974. *Die Redeszene als episches Strukturelement in den Erec und Iwein-Dichtungen Hartmanns von Aue und Chrestiens de Troyes* (=Bochumer Arbeiten zur Sprach- und Literaturwissenschaft 10). Müchen: Fink.
Wierzbicka, Anna. 1970. "Descriptions or quotations?" In Greimas et al. (eds.), 627–44.
Wierzbicka, Anna. 1974. "The semantics of direct and indirect discourse". *Papers in Linguistics* 7,3:267–307.
Wierzbicka, Anna. 1987. *English speech act verbs: a semantic dictionary*. Sydney / New York: Academic Press.
Wiesemann, Ursula. 1984. "How should Jesus be quoted?" *Notes on Translation* 101:27–39.
Wiesemann, Ursula. 1990a. "A model for the study of reported speech in African languages". *Journal of West African Languages* 20,2:75–80.
Wiesemann, Ursula. 1990b. "Researching quote styles". *Notes on Linguistics* 51:31–5.

Wiesthaler, Franz. 1956. *Die oratio obliqua als künstlerisches Stilmittel in den Reden Ciceros* (=Commentationes Aenipontanae 12). Innsbruck: Universitätsverlag Wagner.

Wigger, Arndt. 1997. "Aspekte der Redewiedergabe im gesprochenen Irischen". *Zeitschrift für celtische Philologie* 49/50: 965–99.

Wilkinson, Linda and Hilary Janks. 1998. "Teaching direct and reported speech from a critical language awareness (CLA) perspective". *Educational Review* 50: 181–90.

Woehr, Richard. 1977. "Syntactic atrophy and the indirect interrogative in Spanish". *Studia Neophilologica* 49: 311–26.

Wunderlich, Dieter. 1969. "Bemerkungen zu den verba dicendi". *Muttersprache* 79: 97–107.

Wunderlich, Dieter. 1972. "Redeerwähnung". In Maas, Utz and Dieter Wunderlich, *Pragmatik und sprachliches Handeln*. Frankfurt: Athenaion, 161–88.

Wurff, Wim van der. 1996. "Sequence of tenses in English and Bengali". In Janssen and van der Wurff (eds.), 261–86.

Wurff, Wim van der. 1999. "Speech reporting in retold narratives in Bengali". In Bezooijen, Renée van and René Kager (eds.), *Linguistics in the Netherlands 1999*. Amsterdam: Benjamins, 189–201.

Yamaguchi, Haruhiko. 1989. "On 'Unspeakable Sentences': a pragmatic review". *Journal of Pragmatics* 13: 577–96.

Yamaguchi, Haruhiko. 1994. "Unrepeatable sentences: contextual influence on speech and thought presentation". In Parret, Herman (ed.), *Pretending to communicate*. Berlin: Mouton de Gruyter, 239–52.

Yamaguchi, M. 1995. "A study of the speech and thought representation model proposed by Fludernik (1993)· with special reference to Japanese". *Kyôto furitsu daigaku gakujutsu hôkoku* 47: 33–64.

Yarmohammadi, Lotfollah. 1973. "Problems of Iranians in learning English reported speech". *IRAL : International Review of Applied Linguistics in Language Teaching* 11: 357–68.

Yimam, Baye. 1999. "The verb to say in Amharic". *Journal of Ethiopian Studies* 32,1: 1–50.

Yokoyama, Tsuneko O. 1975. "Personal or reflexive?: a functional approach". *Harvard Studies in Syntax and Semantics* 1: 75–111.

Yule, George. 1993a. "Reported discourse in contemporary English". *Revista Canaria de Estudios Ingleses* 26/7: 17–26.

Yule, George. 1993b. "Vera Hayden's dilemma, or the indirection in direct speech". In Eid, Mushira and Gregory Iverson (eds.), *Principles and prediction: the analysis of natural language* (=Current Issues in Linguistic Theory 98). Amsterdam: Benjamins, 233–42.

Yule, George. 1995. "The paralinguistics of reference: representation in reported discourse". In Cook, Guy and Barbara Seidlhofer (eds.), *Principle and practice in applied linguistics*. Oxford: Oxford University Press, 185–96.

Yule, George and Terrie Mathis. 1992. "The role of staging and constructed dialogue in establishing speaker's topic". *Linguistics* 30,1: 199–215.

Yule, George, Terrie Mathis and Mary F. Hopkins 1992. "On reporting what was said". *ELT Journal* 46: 245–51.

Yung, Vicki K.Y. 1995. "The presentation of voice in Chinese and English newspapers in Hong Kong". *Perspectives: Working Papers of the Department of English, City University of Hong Kong* 8,1: 64–96.

Ždanov, N.A. 1955. "Izučenie temy: prjamaja i kosvennaja reč'". *Russkij Jazyk v Škole* 16,2:65–72.

Zelizer, Barbie. 1989. "'Saying' as collective practice: quoting and differential address in the news". *Text* 9,4:369–88.

Ziegesar, Detlef von. 1976. "Pragma- und textlinguistische Untersuchungsmethoden zur indirekten Rede im Englischen (dargestellt am Referenzmittel *this*)". *Linguistik und Didaktik* 26:122–9.

Zorell, Franz. 1933. "Gibt es im Hebräischen ein *kî recitativum?*" *Biblica* 14:465–9.

Zribi-Hertz, Anne. 1989. "Anaphor binding and narrative point of view: English reflexive pronouns in sentence and discourse." *Language* 65,4:695–727.

Zutt, Herta. 1962. "Die Rede bei Hartmann von Aue". *Der Deutschunterricht* 14,6:67–79.

Zwicky, Arnold M. 1971. "On reported speech". In Fillmore, Charles J. and D. Terence Langendoen (eds.), *Studies in linguistic semantics*. New York: Holt, Rinehart and Winston, 72–7.

Zwicky, Arnold M. 1974. "Bibliography IV: direct and indirect discourse". *Ohio State University Working Papers in Linguistics* 17:198–205.

Index of names

Aaron, U.E. 71
Abesa3e, N. 29, 44
Abraham, R.C. 243, 248, 277, 286
Afevork, G.J. 228, 249
Aikhenvald, A.Y. 43, 45
Alarcos Llorach, E. 146, 170
Allen, J.P. 301, 321
Allen, R.L. 194, 197, 198
Anderson, J.W. 347, 357
Anderson, L.B. 157, 158, 170
Annamalai, E. 107, 108
Armbruster, Ch.H. 228, 240, 241, 245, 248, 249
Armstrong, R.G. 212, 224
Atkinson, J.M. 50, 68, 69
Auer, P. 54, 68

Baeteman, J. 228, 249
Bakhtin, M.M. (Bakhtine) 49, 59, 68, 148, 170
Bally, Ch. 143, 144, 146, 250
Bamgboṣe, A. 176
Banfield, A. 100, 147, 194
Barentsen, A.A. 176
Bargiela-Chiappini, F. 50, 68
Barnes J. 156, 158, 159, 170
Bashir, E. 344
Baynham, M. 138
Beckett, S. 196
Bendor-Samuel, J. 90
Beniak, E. 170, 171
Benveniste, É. 143, 148, 154, 170, 247, 249
Bernini, G. 67, 68
Bickerton, D. 342, 343, 356, 357
Bleichsteiner, R. 39, 45
Bliese, L.F. 229, 232, 249
Blyth, C.Jr. 284
Boeder, W. 3, 4, 6, 10, 11, 20, 31, 39, 40, 42, 43, 45, 107
Botne, R. 285, 286
Brecht, R.D. 194, 197
Brendemoen, B. 41
Brunot, F. 145, 170
Bryan, M.A. 89, 90
Bybee, J. 151, 156, 157, 170

Caldas-Coulthard, C.R. 137
Campbell, L. 7, 40, 41, 46, 157, 171
Canṭla3e, I. 23, 27, 28, 32, 43, 44, 45
Celce-Murcia, M. 194, 197

Černý, J. 306, 308, 309, 313, 314, 321
Cerulli, E. 241, 249
Chafe, W. 156, 170
Chappell, V.A. 50, 68
Chekhov, A. 112
Chetveruchin, A.S. 303
Chia, E.N. 71
Chifamba, J. 255, 257, 259, 260, 263, 267, 269, 270, 285, 286
Chomsky, N. 342, 358
Cikobava, A. 17, 41, 45
Činčarauli, A. 40, 45
Clark, H.H. 66, 121, 123, 136, 137, 138, 194
Claudi, U. 259, 287, 358
Clements, G. 201, 213
Codrington, R.H. 344, 350, 358
Cohen, D. 227, 228, 234, 239, 272, 352, 357
Cohen, M. 227, 228, 235, 236, 239, 249
Comrie, B. 31, 139, 170, 173, 174, 176, 178, 192, 194, 212, 213, 214, 223, 224
Condon, Sh.L. 50, 68
Coulmas, F. 61, 176, 194
Crisp, S.R. 7, 10, 11, 38, 39
Crowley, T. 259, 343, 348, 350, 356, 358
Culpeper, J. 121, 123
Culy, Chr. 201, 202, 203, 204, 205, 210, 214, 223
Cunha, D. 155
Cyffer, N. 242, 249

Dale, D. 46, 254, 257, 258, 259, 260, 261, 262, 263, 264, 265, 266, 267, 269, 270, 271, 272, 286
Davitiani, A. 20, 23, 24, 27, 28, 32, 41, 42, 45
Declerck, R. 173, 174, 175, 176, 177, 178, 180, 189, 192, 193, 194, 196, 197
Deeters, G. 26, 29, 36, 38, 45
Dendale, P. 152, 162, 163, 170, 171, 172
Denison, D. 130
Depuydt, L. 303, 321
Diakonoff, I.M. 239, 249
Dixon, R.M.W. 43, 45, 180, 197
Doke, C.M. 275, 276, 286
Doliʒe, G. 12, 45
Dostoevsky, F. 111, 112
Drescher, J. 312, 321
Drew, P. 68, 69
Drioton, É. 304, 321

Ducrot, O. 148, 171
Duranti, A. 68

Ʒiʒiguri, Š. 7, 9, 13, 14, 38, 39, 40, 41, 45, 46
Žikia, N. 10, 40, 41, 46

Ebert, K. 35, 40, 259
Edel, E. 299, 316, 321
Egbert, M. 67, 68
Eilfort, W. H. 350
Ely, R. 64
Endô, Sh. 114, 119
Erman, A. 297, 321
Ertelišvili, P. 40, 46

Falk, L. 64
Faulkner, R. O. 297, 321
Firle, M. 54
Flaubert, G. 109
Fleischmann, S. 54, 68, 151, 170, 171
Fludernik, M. 112
Fowley, W. A. 272, 286
Ford, C. 195
Fortune, G. 254, 255, 259, 260, 262, 264, 265, 267, 269, 272, 273, 279, 286
Frajzyngier, Z. 212, 259, 278, 286
Freeborn, D. 122, 139
Friedrich, J. 42, 46, 322
Futabatei, Sh. 110, 111, 119

Ɣlonți, A. 8, 11, 14, 39, 40, 42, 46

Gabliani, C. 38, 39
Gardiner, A. H. 239, 249, 307, 308, 310, 316, 317, 321
Gardner, R. J. 67, 68
Gerrig, R. J. 66, 121, 123, 136, 137, 138, 194
Gigineišvili, I. 13, 40
Goffman, E. 49, 59, 60, 66, 67, 68
Golato, A. 49, 63, 139, 284
Goodell, E. W. 176
Goodwin, Ch. 67, 68, 195
Goosse, A. 145, 171
Grevisse, M. 145, 171
Grice, P. 159, 194, 198, 211, 218, 220, 222, 223, 224
Gudjedjiani, Ch. 22, 35, 38, 39, 42, 44, 46
Guentchéva, Z. 152, 170, 171
Guillaume, G. 247, 249
Güldemann, T. 67, 136, 245, 248, 253, 263, 268, 279, 283, 286, 320, 321, 338, 339, 346, 353, 356, 357
Guthrie, M. 253, 274, 285, 287

Haarmann, H. 170
Hagège, Cl. 201, 213
Hahn, E. A. 39

Hai, M. A. 138, 139
Hale, K. 7, 46
Hannan, M. 254, 257, 258, 261, 262, 264, 265, 267, 271, 272, 287
Hannay, M. 125, 139
Harms, Ph. L. 284, 287
Harris, A. 7, 40, 41, 46, 157, 171
Harris, S. J. 50, 68
Hassan, S. 296, 321
Haßler, G. 152, 165, 171
Hatano, K. 119
Hayward, R. J. 228, 229, 230, 249, 250
Hedinger, R. 71
Heine, B. 247, 249, 259, 287, 316, 321, 355, 358
Henderson, L. S. 50, 68
Heny, F. 194, 198
Heritage, J. 50, 51, 68, 69
Hetzron, R. 236, 249
Hewitt, B. G. 7, 9, 10, 11, 12, 13, 15, 18, 23, 32, 33, 38, 39, 40, 42, 43, 44
Hill, J. H. ix
Hirose, Y. 119
Hock, H. H. 284
Hoff, B. 157, 171
Hopper, P. J. 350, 355, 358
Hornstein, N. 174, 198
Hosaka, M. 112, 119
Huang, Y. 103, 211, 212, 214, 220, 223, 224
Huddleston, R. 183, 194, 195, 198
Hünnemeyer, F. 259, 287, 358
Hurliman, R. 71, 90
Hutchison, J. P. 242, 249
Hyman, L. M. 212, 213, 214, 223, 262, 287

Ibuse, M. 111, 112, 119
Ikuta, Sh. 117, 118, 119
Imnaišvili, G. 39, 46
Imnaišvili, I. 9, 46
Irvine, J. T. ix
Isenberg, Ch. W. 228, 249
Ishikawa, T. 113, 114, 119

Jackson, H. 194, 198
Jacomb, E. 344, 358
Jakobson, R. 91, 96, 108, 156, 171
Jansen-Winkeln, K. 301, 321
Jauncey, D. 353, 358
Jefferson, G. 50, 51, 53, 60, 62, 63, 67, 68, 69
Jéquier, G. 297, 299, 303, 321
Jespersen, O. 96, 104, 108, 174, 194, 198, 291, 322
Jockers, H. 277, 286
Johnstone, B. 54, 182
Junge, F. 317, 322
Junod, H. A. 227, 250
Jurma, W. E. 50, 68

Ḳač̣arava, G. 12, 15, 40, 41, 46
Kahl, J. 295, 322
Kaldani, M. 39, 45, 47
Kammerzell, F. 289, 317, 320
Kaplan, D. 349, 358
Kato, K. 222, 224
Keesing, R. M. 284, 287
Khačikjan, M. 37, 46
Kieckers, E. 39
Kiefer, F. 176
Kihm, A. 357
Kim, S.-H. 216, 217, 221, 224
Kiparsky, C. 352, 358
Kiparsky, P. 352, 358
Kipšidze, I. 17, 41, 46
Kita, M. 114, 119
Klaiman, M. H. 122, 139
Klamer, M. 245, 247, 285, 286, 323, 325, 328, 336, 339, 340, 349
Kloth, N. 295, 322
Koch, R. 318, 322
Koderitsch, E. 126, 139
Kodio, K. 210
Kozinceva, N. A. 43, 46
Kristeva, J. 149, 171
Kroch, A. S. 349, 358
Kudo, M. 116, 119, 257
Kuno, S. 217, 224
Kutscher, S. 17, 46
Ḳvanṭaliani, L. 41, 46

La Fontaine, J. de 109
Labov, W. 356, 358
Lambrecht, K. 67, 68, 69
Lancy, D. F. 51
Lange, H. 322
Larsen-Freeman, D. 194, 197
Lee, J. R. E. 51, 69
Leech, G. N. 123, 138, 139, 174, 180, 181, 195, 198
Lefèbvre, G. 239, 250
Lehmann, Th. 107, 108
Lerner, G. H. 57, 69
Leslau, W. 235, 236, 237, 250
Levinson, St. C. 211, 218, 219, 221, 223, 224
Li, Ch. N. 8, 20, 26, 36, 37, 38, 194, 277
Liberman, K. 51, 69
Lichtenberk, F. 353, 358
Lindstrom, L. 345, 358
Longacre, R. E. 232, 250
Lord, C. 259, 287, 344
Lowe, I. 71, 118
Lynch, J. 345, 353, 358

Macaulay, R. K. S. 60
Maingueneau, D. 148, 171

Manessy, G. 89, 90, 353
Mann, Th. 109, 114, 115, 118
Manzo, J. F. 51, 69
Marr, N. 39, 47
Martinet, A. V. 174, 198
Mathis, T. 190, 198
Matthews, P. H. 197, 198
Mattissen, J. 46
Mayes, P. 194
Maynard, S. K. 59, 60, 64
McCabe, A. 64
McCawley, J. D. 94, 108
Mehan, H. 51, 69
Mensah, E. N. 90
Meyer, E. 285, 287
Meyerhoff, M. 277, 284, 285, 286, 287, 339, 341, 344, 348, 353, 357, 358
Mikame, H. 114, 119
Miller, J. 67, 69
Mochet, A.-M. 12, 34
Morin, D. 228, 231, 250
Mougeon, R. 170, 171
Mous, M. 245, 250
Mühlhäusler, P. 245, 250
Munro, P. 6, 170, 256, 323, 329

Naden, A. J. 90
Nakagawa, Y. 118, 120
Ndungane, T. A. 275, 287
Nichols, J. 156, 170
Niedzielski, N. 353, 357, 358
Nižaraʒe, I. 42
Noguchi, T. 111, 120
Nølke, H. 156, 171
Nougayrol, P. 242, 248, 250

O'Connor, M. C. 221, 224
Ochs, E. 58, 59, 63, 66, 69, 70
Oniani, A. 38, 44, 47

Pagliuca, W. 157, 170
Pahl, H. W. 275, 287
Palmaitis, M. L. 22, 35, 42, 44, 46
Palmer, F. R. 250
Parker, Elizabeth 213, 224
Parker, Enid M. 228, 229, 230, 250
Parmentier, R. J. 49
Paton, M. W. 346, 347, 358
Peet, Th. 315, 322
Pellat, J.-Ch. 145, 168, 171
Perkins, R. 157
Peust, C. 289, 290, 293, 305, 308, 309, 317, 319, 320, 321
Pienaar, A. M. 275, 287
Pike, K. L. 71
Piron, P. 276, 287
Plag, I. 259

Plank, F. 11, 33, 290, 293
Plungian, V. 210
Pomerantz, A. 54, 56, 69
Posener, G. 311, 322
Poser, R. 341, 350, 353, 359
Praetorius, F. 228, 234, 250
Prince, E. 348, 359

Quintilianus 40, 41
Quirk, R. 174, 188, 189, 196, 198

Rauh, G. 146, 171
Ravnholt, O. 51, 69
Ray, L. 138, 139
Ray, P.S. 138, 139
Ray, S.H. 344, 353
Raz, Sh. 235, 238, 250
Reah, D. 122, 139
Recktenwald, S. 284
Reeves, J. 195
Reh, M. 259, 287
Reinisch, L. 228, 247, 250
Reyes, G. 148, 152, 164, 165, 171
Riddle, E.M. 194, 198
Riegel, M. 145, 168, 171
Rioul, R. 145, 168, 171
Roeck, M.de 6, 323, 329, 339
Roncador, M.v. viii, 38, 43, 44, 67, 98, 109, 146, 155, 156, 170, 201, 213, 223, 248, 290, 316
Roper, E.M. 234, 250
Ross, J.R. 146, 171
Rudolph, D. 69

Sacks, H. 50, 69
Saha, P.K. 122, 139
Sakita, T.I. 173, 182, 183, 196, 198
Samarin, W.J. 245, 250
Sanctius Brocensis, Fr. 144, 171
Šaniӡe, A. 20, 39, 40, 41, 47
Šaraӡeniӡe, T. 26, 27, 42, 47
Sasse, H.-J. 67, 69
Saxena, A. 259, 282, 283, 284, 344, 346, 354, 355
Schegloff, E.A. 50, 63, 67, 69, 70, 195
Scheidweiler, G. 54
Schiffrin, D. 54, 70, 182, 198
Schuchardt, H. 39, 47
Sefi, S. 51, 68
Sells, P. 216, 223
Semino, E. 121, 123, 138
Sethe, K. 297, 322
Shibata, T. 120
Short, M.H. 121, 123, 125, 126, 131, 132, 135, 136, 137, 138, 139
Sigurðsson, H. 212, 224
Simeone-Senelle, M.-Cl. 227, 228, 249, 250, 272

Simpson, P. 123, 139
Smith, R. 69
Soden, W.v. 37, 47
Sornicola, R. 67, 70
Spencer, A.J. 294, 322
Sperber, D. 133, 139
Stanley, C. 277, 287
Stanzel, F. 109, 120
Steever, S. 91, 101, 102, 107, 108
Steinberg, G. 109, 119, 146
Steindorff, G. 317, 322
Stirling, L. 160, 161, 172, 214, 224
Stroomer, H. 233, 250
Sudermann, H. 112, 117, 119
Sumbatova, N. 38, 47
Suxišvili, M. 41, 47
Suzuki, Y. 109
Svartvik, J. 174, 198

Tanaka, K. 189, 197
Tannen, D. 54, 64, 70, 291
Tasmowski, L. 156, 170, 171, 172
Taylor, Carolyn, 69
Taylor, Charles 276, 287
Tchagbalé, Z. 90
Tembiné, I. 210
Tesnière, L. 247, 250
Thilault, P. 170, 172
Thompson, S.A. 63, 70
Thomson, A.J. 174, 198
Thorne, S. 122, 139
Tobler, A. 144
Togo, P. 210
Tokuzawa, T. 119, 120
Topuria, V. 13, 23, 32, 38, 40, 41, 42, 45, 47
Tuite, K. 22, 38, 42, 47

Uchida, S. 121, 123, 133, 134, 135, 137, 138
Uhmann, S. 54, 68
Underhill, R. 285, 287

Vanhove, M. 227, 228, 249, 250, 251, 272
Verhaar, J.W.M. 351, 359
Vernus, P. 239, 248, 251
Vet, C. 152, 172
Vincent, D. 170, 172
Vlatten, A. 54, 57, 60, 63
Voloshinov, V.N. 175, 198

Wackernagel, J. 23
Waley, A. 245
Walker, C.H. 228, 251
Walker, M. 348, 359
Wang, J. 284
Watters, J.R. 262, 287
Waugh, L.R. 137
Weinrich, H. 143, 148, 154, 172

Westermann, D. 37, 48, 89, 90
Wierzbicka, A. 146, 149
Wiesemann, U. 209, 210, 213, 224
Wigger, A. 11, 41
Wilhelm, G. 38
Willett, Th. 156, 157, 170, 172
Wilmet, M. 148, 172
Wilson, D. 133, 139
Wodarg, A. 46
Wolfson, N. 54, 70, 182, 186, 198
Woolford, E. 343, 359
Wurff, W.v.d. 121, 128, 135, 137

Wynne, M. 138

Xundaʒe, S. 39, 48

Yamada, Y. 113, 114, 119, 120, 222
Yamaguchi, M. 119
Yamanashi, M. 198
Yule, G. 190, 198

Zaborski, A. 234, 251
Zimmermann, U. 295, 322
Zribi-Hertz, A. 213, 223

Index of languages and language groups

Afar 228, 232–4, 242–50
Aghem 211
Aiki 228, 242, 243, 245, 246, 250
Akkadian 37, 38
Ambrym 344
Amharic 228, 235, 236, 238, 242–5, 247, 249, 251
Anejom 345, 358
Arabic:
  Maltese 248
  Yemeni 248
Argobba 236, 244, 245
Armenian 5, 39, 42
Aymellel 235, 245

Baki 353
Bambara 208
Bantoid 276–8
Bantu 245, 250, 253, 260, 272, 274–8, 280, 284–7, 339
Beja 234, 244, 245
Bengali 121–39
Berber 289
Bislama 277, 284–7, 339, 341–58
Bulgarian 157, 170
Buru 339

Čaha 244, 245
Canadian French 151
Caucasian (South) 3–44
Cerma 71–90
Chadic 228, 242–5, 278, 286, 289
Chinese 211, 215–18, 220–4, 245
Choco 284
Cirebon Javanese 353
Coptic 39, 228, 239, 240, 244, 289, 309, 312, 317, 321
Cushitic 227, 228, 233, 234, 239, 240, 244–6, 250, 251, 289

Demotic 289, 317
Dogon 201–10
Donno Sɔ 202
Dongolese 228, 240, 241, 244, 246, 248, 249
Dravidian 91, 93, 107, 108
Dutch 126, 138, 139, 340

Efate 350

Efik 211
Egyptian 227, 228, 238–40, 244, 246, 248, 249, 289–322
  Late 289, 244, 305–15
  Middle 238–9, 244, 289, 299, 316, 317, 319
  Old 227, 228, 238–9, 289, 295, 297–305
Elamite 37, 38, 46
English 8, 16, 33, 38, 41, 43, 50, 54, 65, 74, 83, 96, 103, 108–10, 112, 118, 119, 121–3, 126–8, 130–3, 135, 137–9, 147, 171, 173–97, 198, 250, 251, 256, 273, 274, 284–6, 292, 308, 310, 311, 320, 321, 333, 337, 341–4, 346, 348, 350, 352, 354, 356
Ennemor 237, 244, 245
Epena Pedee 284, 287
Ethio-Semitic 235, 237, 244, 245
Ewe 213, 232

French 144, 147, 148, 149–53, 161, 162–4, 168, 169, 171, 208, 210, 243, 248, 250, 343, 353, 356
Fula 210

Gafat 235, 245, 250
Georgian 3–25, 28, 30–4, 37–9, 41–4, 46, 157
German 33, 36, 49–68, 118, 139, 167, 168, 175, 284, 286, 292, 293
Gogot 235, 245
Gokana 212, 214
Gothic 39
Greek 4–6, 9, 39, 50, 64, 65, 67, 69, 70, 289
Gunnän-Gurage 236, 244, 245, 249
Gur 89

Harari 235, 245
Hausa 228, 242–5, 248
Hittite 42
Hungarian 67, 176

Icelandic 212, 224
Inuit 157
Iraqw 245, 250
Irish 41
Italian 67, 68, 155, 168

Japanese 109–20, 124, 125, 129, 134, 135, 176, 191, 192, 211, 215–18, 220–4

Index of languages and language groups 423

Kafa 241, 244, 245
Kambera 245, 286, 323–40, 349, 357
Kanuri 228, 242, 244, 246, 249
Kartvelian 3–44, 107
Korean 211, 215–18, 220, 221, 223
Kriyol 353, 357
Kwaio 284, 287
Kwamera 345, 358

Lahu 284
Latin 39, 144, 146, 291, 350
Laz 3, 17, 41
Lele 213
Lithuanian 39
Lobi 89
Louisiana French Creole 353

Maban 242, 245
Macedonian 157
Maewo 344
Manam 237, 353, 358
Mapun 212
Mingrelian 3, 4, 17, 18, 40, 41
Mota 344
Muher 237, 244, 245
Mundang 213
Mundani 213, 224

Newari 40
Nguni 275 8, 280, 284
Nkore-Kiga 276, 284, 285, 287
Nogugu 344
Nubian 228, 240, 241, 244, 246, 249

Old Church Slavonic 39
Old Georgian 3–11, 20, 39
Omotic 227, 241, 244, 245, 289
Oromo 233, 244, 245, 250

Papuan 272, 286
Persian 39
Portuguese 168, 353

Romance 39, 67, 98, 143–70, 286, 341, 350, 359

Russian 42, 67, 69, 108, 111, 171, 176, 194

Saharan 227, 228, 240, 242, 244
Saho 247, 248, 250
San 37
Sango 213, 260, 269
Sanskrit 284
Selti 237, 244, 245
Semitic 227, 228, 234, 235, 237, 244, 245, 289
Senufo 89
Shona 253–87, 339, 346, 353
Slavic 143
Soqotri 248
South-West Tanna 345, 353, 358
Spanish 67, 146–8, 153–5, 165–9
Svan 3, 4, 11, 17–37, 38, 41–4, 46, 47, 107

Tamambo 353, 358
Tamil 91–108
Tigre 235, 238, 244–6, 250
Tigrinya 235, 245
Tikar 277, 278, 287
Tiv 277, 278, 286
Tok Pisin 342, 343, 351, 359
Togo Kā 202
Tongan 284
Tuburi 211
Tucano 157
Tukang Besi 339
Tumbuka 285, 286
Turkic 3
Turkish 3, 17, 39, 41, 157
Tuyuca 156–60, 170

Udmurt 157

Wolan 237, 244, 245

Xhosa 275, 287

Yoruba 176, 212

Zulu 275, 276, 286
Zway 235, 244

In the series TYPOLOGICAL STUDIES IN LANGUAGE (TSL) the following titles have been published thus far:

1. HOPPER, Paul J. (ed.): *Tense-Aspect: Between semantics & pragmatics.* 1982.
2. HAIMAN, John & Pamela MUNRO (eds): *Switch Reference and Universal Grammar. Proceedings of a symposium on switch reference and universal grammar, Winnipeg, May 1981.* 1983.
3. GIVÓN, T.: *Topic Continuity in Discourse. A quantitative cross-language study.* 1983.
4. CHISHOLM, William, Louis T. MILIC & John A.C. GREPPIN (eds): *Interrogativity: A colloquium on the grammar, typology and pragmatics of questions in seven diverse languages, Cleveland, Ohio, October 5th 1981-May 3rd 1982.* 1984.
5. RUTHERFORD, William E. (ed.): *Language Universals and Second Language Acquisition.* 1984 (2nd ed. 1987).
6. HAIMAN, John (Ed.): *Iconicity in Syntax. Proceedings of a symposium on iconicity in syntax, Stanford, June 24-26, 1983.* 1985.
7. CRAIG, Colette (ed.): *Noun Classes and Categorization. Proceedings of a symposium on categorization and noun classification, Eugene, Oregon, October 1983.* 1986.
8. SLOBIN, Dan I. & Karl ZIMMER (eds): *Studies in Turkish Linguistics.* 1986.
9. BYBEE, Joan L.: *Morphology. A Study of the Relation between Meaning and Form.* 1985.
10. RANSOM, Evelyn: *Complementation: its Meaning and Forms.* 1986.
11. TOMLIN, Russel S.: *Coherence and Grounding in Discourse. Outcome of a Symposium, Eugene, Oregon, June 1984.* 1987.
12. NEDJALKOV, Vladimir (ed.): *Typology of Resultative Constructions. Translated from the original Russian edition (1983). English translation edited by Bernard Comrie.* 1988.
14. HINDS, John, Shoichi IWASAKI & Senko K. MAYNARD (eds): *Perspectives on Topicalization. The case of Japanese WA.* 1987.
15. AUSTIN, Peter (ed.): *Complex Sentence Constructions in Australian Languages.* 1988.
16. SHIBATANI, Masayoshi (ed.): *Passive and Voice.* 1988.
17. HAMMOND, Michael, Edith A. MORAVCSIK and Jessica WIRTH (eds): *Studies in Syntactic Typology.* 1988.
18. HAIMAN, John & Sandra A. THOMPSON (eds): *Clause Combining in Grammar and Discourse.* 1988.
19. TRAUGOTT, Elizabeth C. and Bernd HEINE (eds): *Approaches to Grammaticalization, 2 volumes (set)* 1991
20. CROFT, William, Suzanne KEMMER and Keith DENNING (eds): *Studies in Typology and Diachrony. Papers presented to Joseph H. Greenberg on his 75th birthday.* 1990.
21. DOWNING, Pamela, Susan D. LIMA and Michael NOONAN (eds): *The Linguistics of Literacy.* 1992.
22. PAYNE, Doris (ed.): *Pragmatics of Word Order Flexibility.* 1992.
23. KEMMER, Suzanne: *The Middle Voice.* 1993.
24. PERKINS, Revere D.: *Deixis, Grammar, and Culture.* 1992.
25. SVOROU, Soteria: *The Grammar of Space.* 1994.
26. LORD, Carol: *Historical Change in Serial Verb Constructions.* 1993.
27. FOX, Barbara and Paul J. Hopper (eds): *Voice: Form and Function.* 1994.
28. GIVÓN, T. (ed.) : *Voice and Inversion.* 1994.
29. KAHREL, Peter and René van den BERG (eds): *Typological Studies in Negation.* 1994.

30. DOWNING, Pamela and Michael NOONAN: *Word Order in Discourse*. 1995.
31. GERNSBACHER, M. A. and T. GIVÓN (eds): *Coherence in Spontaneous Text*. 1995.
32. BYBEE, Joan and Suzanne FLEISCHMAN (eds): *Modality in Grammar and Discourse*. 1995.
33. FOX, Barbara (ed.): *Studies in Anaphora*. 1996.
34. GIVÓN, T. (ed.): *Conversation. Cognitive, communicative and social perspectives*. 1997.
35. GIVÓN, T. (ed.): *Grammatical Relations. A functionalist perspective*. 1997.
36. NEWMAN, John (ed.): *The Linguistics of Giving*. 1998.
37. RAMAT, Anna Giacalone and Paul J. HOPPER (eds): *The Limits of Grammaticalization*. 1998.
38. SIEWIERSKA, Anna and Jae Jung SONG (eds): *Case, Typology and Grammar. In honor of Barry J. Blake*. 1998.
39. PAYNE, Doris L. and Immanuel BARSHI (eds.): *External Possession*. 1999.
40. FRAJZYNGIER, Zygmunt and Traci S. CURL (eds.): *Reflexives. Forms and functions*. 2000.
41. FRAJZYNGIER, Zygmunt and Traci S. CURL (eds): *Reciprocals. Forms and functions*. 2000.
42. DIESSEL, Holger: *Demonstratives. Form, function and grammaticalization*. 1999.
43. GILDEA, Spike (ed.): *Reconstructing Grammar. Comparative Linguistics and Grammaticalization*. 2000.
44. VOELTZ, F.K. Erhard and Christa KILIAN-HATZ (eds.): *Ideophones*. 2001.
45. BYBEE, Joan and Paul HOPPER (eds.): *Frequency and the Emergence of Linguistic Structure*. 2001.
46. AIKHENVALD, Alexandra Y., R.M.W. DIXON and Masayuki ONISHI (eds.): *Non-canonical Marking of Subjects and Objects*. 2001.
47. BARON, Irene, Michael HERSLUND and Finn SORENSEN (eds.): *Dimensions of Possession*. 2001.
48. SHIBATANI, Masayoshi (ed.): *The Grammar of Causation and Interpersonal Manipulation*. 2002.
49. WISCHER, Ilse and Gabriele DIEWALD (eds.): *New Reflections on Grammaticalization*. 2002.
50. FEIGENBAUM, Susanne and Dennis KURZON (eds.): *Prepositions in their Syntactic, Semantic and Pragmatic Context*. 2002.
51. NEWMAN, John (ed.): *The Linguistics of Sitting, Standing and Lying*. n.y.p.
52. GÜLDEMANN, Tom and Manfred von RONCADOR (eds.): *Reported Discourse. A meeting ground for different linguistic domains*. 2002.
53. GIVÓN, T. and Bertram MALLE (eds.): *The Evolution of Language from Pre-language*. n.y.p.